Also by David Shipman

THE STORY OF CINEMA
THE GREAT MOVIE STARS
MARLON BRANDO

Judy Garland

JUDY GARLAND

THE SECRET LIFE OF
AN AMERICAN LEGEND

❖❖❖❖❖❖❖❖❖❖❖❖❖❖❖❖❖❖❖❖❖❖❖❖❖❖❖❖❖❖❖❖❖❖❖❖❖

DAVID SHIPMAN

HYPERION

NEW YORK

The author gives grateful acknowledgment to the following for permission to quote from copyrighted material: "Judy" by Hoagy Carmichael & Sammy Lerner, © copyright 1934 by PSO Ltd., copyright renewed by PSO Ltd. and Samuel M. Lerner Publications, International copyright secured, all rights reserved, used by permission; "Dear Mr. Gable" lyric and music by Roger Edens, copyright © 1936 Roger Edens; "Too Marvelous for Words" (Richard Whiting, Johnny Mercer) © 1937 Warner Bros. Inc. (renewed). All rights reserved. Used by permission; "Over the Rainbow" by Harold Arlen and E. Y. Harburg copyright © 1938, 1939 (renewed 1966, 1967) Metro-Goldwyn-Mayer Inc. c/o EMI Feist Catalog Inc. World print rights controlled and administered by CPP/Belwin, Inc., P.O. Box 4340, Miami, FL 33014. All rights reserved; "Minstrel Girl Melody" lyric and music by Roger Edens, copyright © 1951 Roger Edens; "Smile" music by Saul Chaplin, lyrics by John Turner & Geoffrey Parsons, © copyright 1954 by Bourne Co., copyright renewed, all rights reserved, used by permission; "The Man That Got Away," music by Harold Arlen, lyric by Ira Gershwin, © copyright 1954 (renewed) Harwin Music Co. All rights reserved, used by permission; "Just in Time" (Betty Comden, Adolph Green, Jule Styne) © 1956 Chappell & Co. (renewed). All rights reserved. Used by permission; new verse to "San Francisco" by Roger Edens © copyright 1959 Roger Edens; "Call Me Irresponsible," music by James Van Heusen, lyrics by Sammy Cahn © copyright 1962 and 1963 by Paramount Music Corporation; "For Once In My Life" by Ronald Miller and Orlando Murden, © July 1965 Jobete Music Co., Inc.; "Make Someone Happy" (Betty Comden, Adolph Green, Jule Styne), © 1960 Chappell & Co. (renewed). All rights reserved, used by permission; "I Could Go On Singin' (Till the Cows Come Home)" from the motion picture "I Could Go On Singing," music by Harold Arlen, lyric by E. Y. Harburg © copyright 1962, 1963 (renewed) Harwin Music Co. All rights reserved, used by permission.

First United States Edition 1993

Copyright © 1992 David Shipman

Library of Congress Cataloging-in-Publication Data

Shipman, David.
    Judy Garland : the secret life of an American legend / David
Shipman. — 1st U.S. ed.
      p. cm.
    Includes bibliographical references and index.
    ISBN 1-56282-846-0
    1. Garland, Judy. 2. Singers—United States—Biography.
3. Motion picture actors and actresses—United States—Biography.
I. Title.
ML420.G253S5 1993
782.42164'092—dc20
[B]   92-43648
                                              CIP
                                             MN

First Edition
10 9 8 7 6 5 4 3 2 1

Design by Gloria Adelson

FOR FELIX

CONTENTS

Introduction

FROM THE VERY BEGINNING, almost every event in Judy Garland's life was beset by caprice, confusion, conjecture and contradiction. Those who knew her professionally are usually polarized: they either loved her or loathed her—and sometimes both. Two people who knew her well broke into tears as they talked to me about her, one of them after relating a large number of unflattering stories. There were those whom she drove to distraction, but who continued to love her despite everything. "Which Judy Garland are you writing about?" asked Joseph L. Mankiewicz, whom she once described as the only man she ever loved.

"How many were there?" I asked.

"You're on the right track," he replied.

Hers was a life lived publicly. From babyhood onwards, the name of Frances Gumm was frequently to be found in the local papers, and not long after Frances Gumm became Judy Garland she was, and continued to be, headline news.

* * *

I fell in love with her in a record shop in Oxford in 1955. Four of us, members of the University film society, asked to hear the soundtrack of *Seven Brides for Seven Brothers*, which we had all seen during the Christmas vacation. It hadn't yet come in, but the assistant suggested that we might like to listen to the soundtrack of *A Star Is Born*, which then had not yet opened in Britain. The important thing was that it was the new film directed by George Cukor. We knew that it starred Judy Garland, returning to films after a four-year absence, and we were glad to see her back but I don't think that any of us felt that she was far and away the best female singer in movies—as the record revealed to us. I had seen her on the stage and in some half-dozen of her movies, and I had liked her, but by the time I had listened to the first side of the album I had become her most devoted admirer. My chief qualification for writing this book is that I saw her on stage more than a dozen times. If I could live just one night of my life over again it would be a magical night at the London Palladium in 1960.

My second qualification turned out to be misguided, as my opening sentence above indicates. Shortly before my publisher approached me with the idea of a new biography of Judy Garland, I was redecorating my London flat, and happened upon a collection of press cuttings that I had collected, covering her life and career between *A Star Is Born* and her death. Realizing that these could provide a starting point for a comprehensive book, I had yet to learn that Garland was not addicted to the truth. She always preferred a good story to the facts.

I had, in fact, forgotten that I had kept this material—though I was reminded by a member of the Judy Garland fan club that thirty years ago (when she was still alive) I had been saying that I one day planned to write her life story. It was to the fan club that I turned when Garland's own interviews proved unreliable: and I want to list immediately Alan Boughton, Stephen Bourne, Brian Glanvill, Ken Sephton and Billy Tweedie, some of whom lent me scrapbooks and copies of the *Rainbow Review*. Some of them were able to share memories of Garland; all of them were unfailingly helpful. The *Rainbow Review* carried transcripts of many television and radio documentaries on Judy Garland; I was able to listen to or view another half a dozen myself thereby obtaining quotes on her as a personality and colleague by many people who are now dead.

The next step was to look at the previous books on Garland. It is a foolhardy biographer who criticizes his predecessors, but I found them all lacking. One in particular seems to be a work of fiction. It can't even get the films she made in the right order, but then, bingo, it is accurate on one important episode in Garland's life, left vague by the other books. So much goes unmentioned or unexplained in those books that I returned to work with a new eagerness.

Of those people who knew and worked with Garland, Deanna Durbin David was chronologically the first to agree to help. The second was another old friend, the late Joe Mankiewicz; and while researching the book I made a new one, Marcella Rabwin. Both knew Garland from the time she was twelve until she died. Both gave me time and attention to talk with me; both have read the manuscript at various stages.

I want to thank them, and also Michael Stapleton, Tony Sloman, Peter Parker and Richard Chatten, all of whom gave invaluable advice on the manuscript. My gratitude goes also to Christopher Potter, who initiated the project and brought it to a successful conclusion.

For the genealogical background of Garland's father I was helped by Virginia Wilkinson of Murfreesboro, who was able to answer my questions about the Gumm family when they lived there. Many people in Grand Rapids also talked about the Gumms, but they remembered Judy Garland only as a baby. John Kelsch of the Itasca Historical Society in Grand Rapids gave me access to every press cutting in the huge Garland collection there, as well as to every newspaper of the period which mentioned the Gumms. Perhaps this is the place to say that many of the Garland holdings in Grand Rapids do not include a source or a date; since this is also true of my own cuttings and of the scrapbooks it is not practicable for me to make a comprehensive list of sources, as do most modern biographers. The most contentious matters in most biographies are the sexual ones, and I can only say that of all the people I spoke to who knew Garland and Vincente Minnelli only one did not take it for granted that I already knew of Minnelli's homosexuality and of Garland's affair with one of the women who worked in the Freed unit.

More surprisingly, the Garland files in the Louis B. Mayer Memorial Library at the American Film Institute and the library of the American Motion Picture Academy in Los Angeles consist chiefly of unmarked cuttings. I should, incidentally, like to thank Ken Wlaschin and Sandra Archer, respectively, for their help.

Among those papers, I was able to see unpublished biographies of Garland by John Graham and Tom Green, and Joel E. Siegel allowed me to see the relevant portion of his unpublished biography of Vincente Minnelli. Robert Walsdorff, an expert on her radio work, was able to answer many of my questions. Randall Henderson presented me with a folio of his researches into Garland's career in records. Keith Bullington took me to meet Wayne Martin, whom other fans will know as the most ardent of them all. David Chierichetti is not only an expert on Hollywood costume but was also able to share memories of Garland as told him by the late Joe Pasternak. For my chapters on Garland's television work, I particularly wish to acknowledge my indebtedness to Coyne Steven Sanders's invaluable book on the subject, *Rainbow's End.*

Also in California, Mr. and Mrs. Carl Bergman of Lancaster and Mr. and Mrs. Glenn Settle in nearby Rosamond shared memories of the Gumm family and the young Garland.

Christopher Finch's *Rainbow*, Hugh Fordin's *The World of Entertainment*, Thomas Watson and Bill Chapman's *Judy, Portrait of an American Legend* were useful sources, and Ronald Haver's *A Star Is Born* and Mel Tormé's *The Other Side of the Rainbow* were most illuminating, respectively, on the making of the film and the "Judy Garland Television Show" and I am most thankful to all of them.*

Kind enough to share personal or professional memories of Garland were, in alphabetical order: Brian Baxter, Saul Chaplin, Leonard Gershe, the late Sheilah Graham, Clive Hirschhorn, Jean Howard, Dorris Johnson, Ronald Neame, Buddy Pepper, Harry Rigg, Harry Rubin, John Shirley, John Springer, Gloria Stuart, Jim Watters and Fred Zinnemann. I did not attempt to contact anyone who had written extensively about Garland in their own books—and many are, alas, now dead. Long before I had thought of writing a biography of Judy Garland I was lucky enough to meet the late James Mason and Rock Hudson, whose lengthy reminiscences of her have found their way into this book. The number of people who declined to cooperate or answer letters is quite large; they have to be nameless, except for David Begelman, whose secretary told me: "Mr. Begelman never speaks to the press, *especially* about Miss Garland."

I did not attempt to contact Sid Luft because he had told his side of the marriage to Gerold Frank—in a deal that *Variety* estimated gave him 33 percent and Frank 67 percent. I am most grateful to Mr. Frank for his, the first authorized, biography of Judy Garland, which is all-embracing. I wrote to both Liza Minnelli and Lorna Luft, admittedly in such terms which did not demand a reply. I feel that both

---

*Regrettably so many cuttings in archives and in my own collection are not identified, even though dated, that I am unable to cite them.

have been unfairly overshadowed by their mother; and I did not wish to remind Miss Minnelli that the contradictions of Judy Garland's life did not end with her death.

When a movie entitled *The Judy Garland Story* was first mooted in 1970, Liza Minnelli said that she would never consider playing her mother, and she has repeated this assertion since. In March 1973, however, when the film became a possibility, with Vincente Minnelli in charge, it was reported in *Photoplay* that she said:

Oh, I wanted to do the role all along, but it scared me. Desi [Arnaz, Jr., her boyfriend at the time] helped calm my fears and he convinced me that playing my mother on the screen would be a lasting tribute to her and not just an exploitation of her name and life. With Daddy handling it, I guess it couldn't be bad. I don't know why it still scares me. I guess it's because I don't think I'm even a fraction of the performer Mom was.

This is undoubtedly true. Yet Liza Minnelli and her half-sister, Lorna Luft, are light years ahead of almost all the other performers who have taken to the concert stage since Garland first made it her province. And when you see them now, Minnelli very famous and Luft undeservedly less so, you find them touched with the genius that was Judy Garland.

As Gene Kelly put it:

The finest all-round performer we ever had in America was Judy Garland. She was not trained as a dancer, like Cyd Charisse, but she always wanted to do well. There was no limit to her talent. Her brain was amazing. She would hear a song, or a page of dialogue, and immediately memorize it. She was the quickest, brightest person I ever worked with. Judy had a great sense of *joie de vivre* before her illness, and laughed a lot. She was superb!

I think that that makes up for the fact that Mr. Kelly was unable to see me, but I note his courtesy in telephoning me to explain why. To his tribute I would like to add one by Bing Crosby:

The most talented woman I ever knew was Judy Garland. She was a great, great comedienne and she could do more things than any girl I ever knew. Act, sing, dance, make you laugh. She was everything. I had a great affection for her. Such a tragedy. Too much work, too much pressure, the wrong kind of people as husbands.

Crosby also said: "There wasn't a thing that that gal couldn't do—except look after herself."

It is a tragic story, as I pointed out to Marcella Rabwin, who was responsible for Judy Garland becoming a Hollywood star in the first place. Was she sorry about that? "For having given the world that great talent? No."

1

❖❖❖❖❖❖❖

Born in a Trunk

"THE HISTORY OF MY LIFE is in my songs," Judy Garland declared in a lyric composed for her by her mentor, Roger Edens. One of her most famous songs announced that she had been "Born in a Trunk," and while this is not strictly accurate, she came from a theatrical background: her father managed a movie theater, where members of the family sometimes performed between screenings. Garland made her public debut on that stage when she was two and a half years old.

Although Garland often referred to her father's Irish charm, it is unlikely that much Irish blood flowed in Frank Gumm's veins. The name of Gumm is first recorded in England in the Middle Ages, and in America (in Sussex County, Delaware) in 1782. By way of Virginia, the Gumms arrived in Rutherford County, Tennessee, just after the beginning of the nineteenth century. Francis Avent Gumm was born in 1886 in Murfreesboro, a small town on the River Stones which had been settled at the time of the Industrial Revolution. It was a flourishing agricultural center, incorporated in 1817; two years later, it became the state capital for nine years. In 1862, it was the site of one of the most disastrous battles of the Civil War, which left the Union victorious but with losses almost as severe as those suffered by the Confederates. The establishment of the Stones River National Battlefield kept the event vivid while Frank was growing up.

Evidence that Frank's forebears had strong associations with this part of Tennessee is provided by the name of Gumm on the map—hardly even a hamlet, but boasting a cemetery largely occupied by members of the family. They were mostly brickmasons or farm laborers, and the eldest son was usually christened William. Though Frank's grandfather, John Alexander Gumm, was a second son, he followed the family tradition by calling his first son, who was born in 1859, William Tecumseh Gumm. In 1877, this William Gumm married into another old Tennessee family, the Baughs. In the 1880 census, his wife is listed as Elizabeth, but she was known throughout her life as Clemmie. Although the Baughs had bettered themselves materially earlier in the century, when Clemmie's mother, Mary, made her will in 1892, she was only able to sign it with an "X." She left her daughter a town lot on East Main Street, the prettiest thoroughfare in Murfreesboro, with instructions that it be sold and the proceeds used to build a dwelling for Clemmie's new family on the same property. The house in which Frank was born is antebellum, however, which suggests that William inherited rather than constructed it.

The same lot contained a butcher's shop, and as records vary as to whether William was a butcher-grocer or a "merchant," it is probable that, because he had married well, the clerics of Murfreesboro were somewhat at a loss as to how he should be classified. The Gumms were clearly well connected, since Frank was named after a prominent lawyer in the town, Frank Avent. He was the third of five children: the others were named Mary, Emmett, William and Alice. He was a happy, outgoing child, always singing. He later claimed that he had once run away to join a minstrel show. Brought back, he and one of his brothers sang on local trains, passing round the hat. He certainly possessed a photograph of himself, taken when he was about thirteen, in minstrel costume and blackface.

Another indication that the Gumms were highly thought of is the fact that Frank's godfather, George Darrow, was a prominent and wealthy Episcopalian who lived with his wife in Oakland Mansion, the house in which the Confederates had officially surrendered. Darrow was so struck by Frank's voice when he heard him sing at grade school, that he arranged for him to sing solos with the choir of St.

Paul's Church, where Darrow was the treasurer and the Gumms were communicants. William Gumm was widowed in 1895, and at fifteen, his elder daughter, Mary, was not really mature enough to help him look after the four younger children. Frank was nine; and by the time he was thirteen, William had agreed to consign him to the care of George Darrow.

Darrow was also patron of the Grammar School at Sewanee, a town some fifty miles south of Murfreesboro. He arranged for Frank to attend on a choral scholarship, and he accompanied him there himself in June 1899, after receiving a "kind letter" from its principal, Benjamin L. Wiggins. The school's records show that Frank was Mr. Darrow's "protégé."

Frank was soon being praised in the campus newspaper for his choral solos and, more significantly, for his role in the school play—suitably amorous, apparently, as the prince in *The Seven Little Dwarfs*.

After three years, he moved on to Sewanee College, later known as the University of the South, where his voice (now a baritone) was a leading feature in musical and dramatic entertainments. He left in 1907, after what he later called "six of the happiest, the most beautiful years of my life."

His father had died a year earlier, splitting the family and leaving Frank, at twenty-one, uncertain of his future. Many of his classmates went on to distinguished careers—one of his closest friends, Henry Gass, was one of the first Rhodes scholars, and eventually returned to Sewanee as professor of Greek—but Frank hesitated. He joined one of his brothers and a sister, who were living in Tullahoma, a small town on the railway line halfway between Murfreesboro and Sewanee, and drifted into a job as a bookkeeper and then office manager for Walter D. Fox. He took an active interest in the orphanage which Fox had founded, dabbled in journalism and again sang in the choir, as well as at the local vaudeville house, the Citizens Theater. Why he eventually left is not recorded.

His brother and sister quit Tullahoma at the same time, but he went north alone. He had loved the backstage atmosphere—and the applause—at the Citizens, and almost certainly decided that this latest family breakup offered him an opportunity to try to make a career in what was then called "the" show business. From boyhood, through college, and while working as a clerk in Tullahoma, he had been singing in public, both with friends round a piano and on the stage. He was young, without ties and fully aware of the popularity his sunny personality brought him.

He was also a dreamer, and dreams were provided cheaply by the new entertainment: motion pictures. Offices, main-street stores and barns were being converted the country over, as audiences flocked to the picture shows. The first film stars were anonymous, characterized only by the companies which made their pictures, as in the cases of "The Vitagraph Girl" and "The Biograph Girl": soon every picturegoer would know that "The Girl With the Curls" was Mary Pickford. Biograph and Vitagraph were two of the handful of companies recognized by the government as having the right to manufacture motion pictures—a right challenged by scores of maverick companies springing up at that time. Many of them fled to California, as far as possible from the authority of the U.S. Patents Office in Washington, D.C., and settled in a suburb of Los Angeles, close to the Mexican border, over which they could escape if the law did pursue them. In 1913, that suburb officially adopted the name by which it was known locally: Hollywood.

The new industry was struggling out of the nickelodeon era to achieve the respectability it had longed for since its infancy—and for which it would continue to hunger for many more years. Vaudeville theaters had been the first homes of motion pictures, but had dropped them after the novelty wore off. It was not long, however, before some of those same theaters were reducing the number of acts on the bill to find more time for movies. Some theaters were switching over to the new amusement entirely, while, more impressive yet, the first purpose-built cinemas were opening.

In 1912, Frank Gumm found work at the People's Amusement Company of Portland, Oregon, using his experience in Tullahoma to get a job managing a theater; but more importantly, he doubled as a singer. This not only gave the house cachet, as it was offering "live entertainment," but helped pass the time while the reels were changed. Someone of Frank's exceptional charm was needed to keep audiences from becoming impatient. He was a vigorous, roundly handsome man with a beaming smile and a pleasing voice, and for these performances appeared immaculately dressed in a gleaming, stiff white collar and a tailored three-piece suit.

In the summer of 1913, after almost two years in Portland, he moved to Superior, Wisconsin, a prosperous Great Lakes resort town with a resident population of 45,000, and then in the midst of its influx of holiday-makers. Superior boasted a large number of movie theaters, many of them owned by Ray Hadfield, who took on Frank as a singer in September. Frank's partner at Hadfield's Savoy Theater was Maude

Ayres, and the two vocalists were accompanied at the piano by Ethel Marian Milne, with whom Frank fell into an immediate accord. Like him, she came from a remote village, Michigamme, Michigan. She was of Irish stock on the side of her mother, Eva Fitzpatrick, and Scottish on the side of her father, John Milne. It was not a happy marriage, and indeed Eva was unlucky in this respect. She had already been married and divorced, at a time when divorce was virtually unknown except among the wealthy. John Milne was an engine driver, but drank so much that employment was hard to come by. Ethel was born in 1893, one of seven children, and grew up in Duluth, where the family had moved. Her father's improvidence had forced her to leave school while still quite young, but she had learned to play the piano sufficiently well to earn a living teaching others. For whatever reasons, Ethel had moved to Superior and, after a spell working at a Five and Ten, selling sheet music and playing for the "flickers" in the evening, she was taken on by Hadfield.

She was petite, vivacious, enthusiastic and splendidly in control of her life for someone so young. What she had above all was determination, a trait not uncommon in children from large families. Frank also came from a large family, and both he and Ethel were Episcopalians. Both were besotted with show business, and it seemed romantic to them to conduct their courtship in song before the unknowing audiences at the Savoy. She was captivated by his Southern accent and his Southern gentleman's manners, by his good humor and high spirits. She was twenty and he was twenty-seven.

He was also homosexual. Given the climate of the time, it may be that Frank thought that marriage could "cure" him. With the years he had already spent in show business, evidently he was not one of those men who discovered their sexual orientation only after marrying. It may be supposed that he intended to put temptation out of the way. He had already been engaged to a girl called Kathryn McGraw, but she became tired of waiting, and turned her attention to a minor vaudeville comic, Joe E. Brown, who later became a Hollywood star. Working before large audiences every night, Frank would have been justified in fearing public exposure and possible blackmail—indeed, these may have been the unexplained reasons why he left Portland.

The most likely reason for the marriage, however, was simply that Ethel had convinced them both that this was their destiny—and destiny was a concept then very appealing to the romantically minded. It would have been more usual for Frank to have formed an alliance with his singing partner, Maude, than the girl at the pit piano, but Ethel flattered him that together they could become a successful vaudeville act, with her accompanying him at the piano. From this there grew the idea of them as man and wife. With wedlock in view, Frank had a compulsive need to prove himself a worthy member of society. There would be no more roaming: he and Ethel would settle down and raise a family. They had recently made friends with Mr. and Mrs. C.E. Aikens, a middle-aged couple vacationing from Grand Rapids in the neighboring state of Minnesota, and from them they learned of a fine opportunity for Frank in that town. Frank's awareness of the severity of the Minnesota winters and his determination to live there indicates his wholehearted commitment to a new life. With the intervention of the Aikens, the job was confirmed, and Frank and Ethel were married on January 22, 1914, in Superior, an event celebrated with the customary banquet, but also with a dinner on stage at the Savoy for Maude and the bridal couple. They were not able to leave until the end of February, when his contract with Hadfield expired.

Grand Rapids was a somewhat cheerless, self-sufficient, immigrant community on the Mississippi River in the southeastern corner of the state. Not only were the winters brutally cold, but it was invaded by mosquitoes for two months in summer. The settlement had been named for the Pokegama Falls—which were later to be instrumental in the construction of the Itasca Paper Mill. Until 1891, when the town was incorporated, it was a lumberjack colony, and it was at this time that the production of paper succeeded logging as the chief industry. The manufacturing of paper brought with it the ever-present stench of bleach and the white smoke, blown crisply away by the winds from the plains. The village expanded rapidly in the 1890s, when the Central School (still standing) was built to tower over the wooden-cladded two- or three-story buildings.

It was a village barely distinguishable from many others in this part of the world, surrounded by pine and birch forests and deep blue lakes, which attracted huntsmen and fishermen. The settlement was built on the grid pattern with wide streets to take the logging wagons. The small railway station was at its very heart, and in 1914 most of the place, despite expansion, was still unpaved—but then, the population numbered under 2,500. An occasional gasoline pump stood in front of the wheelwrights' premises, and there were still blacksmiths. People shopped at the dry-goods stores and general stores for everything from a silk ribbon to a sack of corn. They were God-fearing folk, few of them going to the bars and fewer still to the brothels, a legacy of the lumber-camp days: but within memory the Gem movie house had assumed an unimagined importance, as a center for conviviality, vicarious excitement and as a focus of conversation.

On January 28, 1914, it was forced to acknowledge a custom-built rival, when the New Grand Theater opened, "to show 4,000 feet of fine film." The proprietors, Barlow and Bentz, had it constructed with a stage, enabling stock and vaudeville companies to appear there. The theater seated 450, and stood four-square on the main street of the town. On March 5, Mr. and Mrs. Gumm joined its staff, Frank as "singer and manager," while Ethel took charge of the musical arrangements. Fred Bentz operated the projector, happily leaving the bookings of the films and vaudeville acts to his enterprising new manager. Frank brought showmanship to this sleepy town, and the citizens of Grand Rapids took an instant liking to the young man and his wife, who were quickly recognized as model citizens: they attached themselves to the local Episcopalian church, where Ethel played the organ while Frank conducted the choir. They lived with the Aikens, whose large house could accommodate two more people with ease, and whose social prominence made their guests socially acceptable. Ethel ran a series of bridge parties, while Frank joined the local fire brigade. Sometimes Frank took his wife's place at the pit piano at the New Grand, and on occasion filled in when a touring act was late or failed to arrive altogether. As in most cinemas of that era, local would-be entertainers were encouraged to perform on "Amateur Night," and this was organized by the Gumms. The owners of the rival Gem responded by booking "a 15-installment spectacular," *Lucille Love*, and by ensuring that the press always referred to them as "two local lads," but business failed to quicken. In the summer, the New Grand announced itself as "the coolest place in town"; the Gem was shortly obliged to close.

In December Ethel's sister, Cevilla, replaced her as accompanist while the Gumms took a winter vacation, but Ethel became seriously ill and was taken to her parents' home to recuperate. On their return in February, the Grand Rapids *Herald-Review* noted: "that Mr. and Mrs. Gumm have lost none of their former popularity during their absence was evidenced by the large house that greeted their return and the enthusiastic reception of their songs and playing." In addition, Frank assured the paper that none of the towns he had seen on his trip "looked any better than Grand Rapids and that the chances are that he will hereafter be content to remain here."

He proved this by buying out Barlow's half-share in the New Grand two weeks later; and he and Ethel threw themselves into activities at the theater with renewed vigor. With the cooperation of local tradesmen, they organized a fashion show to publicize the latest styles for both men and women, and they appeared on stage in April in an act they had worked up themselves, "Jack and Virginia Lee, Sweet Southern Singers."

"Who are Jack and Virginia Lee?" teased the gossip column in the *Herald-Review*, which answered the question a few days later, after noting: "The entertainment given by Jack and Virginia Lee at the Grand Theater last Thursday and Friday evenings was one of the best and most highly appreciated singing acts ever witnessed here." Frank and Ethel had every reason to be content that they had chosen to live in Grand Rapids. They were an impressive couple. Frank, at 5 feet 11 inches, was a whole head taller than Ethel. He had a mane of dark hair, carefully brilliantined, while Ethel wore hers in small curls close to her head. The Gumms dazzled what passed there for the *beau monde*, which was delighted when it was announced that the young couple were to become parents.

Frank and Ethel moved from the Aikens' home into a rented house, and then into Hospital Apartments, which had the advantage of having a garden. In September 1915, a daughter was born, whom they christened Mary Jane. Two years later, on Independence Day, the family was increased by another daughter, Dorothy Virginia, always known as Virginia. In a short time, both little girls were conscripted into taking part in the various social and musical activities which their parents so much enjoyed.

The comings and goings of the Gumms are well recorded in the two local papers—especially the Itasca County *Independent*, which hired Frank to report on the social activities of Grand Rapids in March 1917. One of the first reports he filed, on March 24, reads as follows:

A surprise party was given at the home of Frank Gumm Tuesday evening, the occasion being the twenty (?) first birthday anniversary of Mr. Gumm. Mrs. Gumm had assembled some 16 young men friends of her husband and when Mr. Gumm came home from the show he found "some crowd" at the house. The evening was spent in cards and music, after which delicious "eats" were served.

In 1918, the family moved again; and in March 1919, Frank purchased the house on Hoffman Avenue which was to be Judy Garland's first home, and which she would remember as "a little white wooden house in a big garden." The house was moved in 1938, but in 1919 it stood on a corner site in the center of the town, a five-minute walk from the theater, three blocks west of the school and across the street from the railway station. Seen today, it is nondescript in an agreeable New England frame style, and much altered: the open porch with a balcony above, which the Gumms had, has since been incorporated into the parlor, a many-windowed, high-ceilinged room. Upstairs there are now three bedrooms, none of them large, and a small bathroom, which then made another bedroom. It is a house only just large enough for a family of four—plus Inga Mooren, a Swedish girl whose family lived on a farm twenty miles away, too far for her to travel back and forth daily to school. She lived with the Gumms, and in return for her board she looked after the house when Frank and Ethel went to the theater in the evening.

Inga almost certainly slept in the cottage, which has since joined the house on its present site. The arrangement was convenient for Ethel's family, who were almost continual visitors. Her parents and one or another of her several brothers and sisters were to be in Grand Rapids for periods of days or even weeks throughout the year—as often as Ethel herself, with or without the girls, was with her parents in Superior, or with her brother Jack's family in Duluth. It was extremely uncommon then to visit relatives so frequently when they lived some eighty or a hundred miles away. Ethel left Frank on his own so often, for short and long stretches, at least once a month, that it seems probable that the marriage was in difficulties almost from the beginning.

Although the Gumms continued to lead a normal social life, there was a tendency for Frank's evenings to be male-orientated, as he reported in the *Independent*:

Frank Gumm entertained on Saturday evening with a prettily appointed six o'clock stag dinner for the young men who were home for the Easter vacation from the university. Covers were laid for ten and Mrs. Gumm, assisted by Miss Katherine Gilbert, served a sumptuous three course dinner.

At the time Frank joined the *Independent*, he and Bentz opened a new theater and closed the New Grand. They retained the old name and decreased the seating to the more manageable 385. A seven-piece orchestra was installed in the pit for the opening attraction, *Poor Little Pepina* starring Mary Pickford. In 1918 they extended their activities to two nearby villages, taking on the leases of the Lyceum in Deer

Park and the Eclipse in Coleraine. Frank was often absent on business trips to Minneapolis, Duluth and, most significantly, Eveleth, a small town some miles to the north.

About the time Virginia was born in 1917, Frank made the acquaintance of someone who was to be a major figure in Judy Garland's life: Marc Rabwin. His original name, which he changed at this period, was Marcus Rabinowitz. His father, Frank, owned a cinema in Eveleth, which Marc, although only sixteen, helped to run. Frank Rabinowitz also held the local franchise for the W.W. Hodkinson Company, an agency for film distribution, and Marc had first met Frank Gumm on a business trip he made to Grand Rapids in order to persuade the New Grand to book some of the company's films. He had been warned by other film salesmen that the theater owner there was "nuts," constantly pacing the floor when they tried to talk to him, staring at them belligerently with his bulging eyes. Rabwin, who was planning a career in medicine, realized that Frank's manner suggested that he had a thyroid problem. Although the New Grand usually hired films from an exchange in Minneapolis, Rabwin managed to charm Frank sufficiently for him to book some Hodkinson movies.

Rabwin soon established a close friendship with both Frank and Ethel, and eventually sold the New Grand his entire portfolio of films. When, at their invitation, he came to stay with the Gumms, Rabwin explained to Frank that he needed medication and saw to it that he was put on some pills which eventually cleared up the thyroid problem.

The friendship continued when Rabwin went on to study medicine at the University of Minnesota in St. Paul, and in the winter of 1921, he was woken up in the middle of the night by Frank—a highly agitated Frank, pacing up and down and needing professional advice once more. Ethel was two months pregnant: she wanted an abortion, and Frank wanted his friend to sanction an operation which was then, while not uncommon, both illegal and dangerous. Frank maintained that the Gumms, with two growing girls, were a contented family with no desire for change; but a 200-mile drive across country suggests something darker, more desperate. He admitted that Ethel had even tried the accepted "home" methods of abortion. "She must have rolled down 19,000 flights of stairs, jumped off tables," was the way Garland put it. She claimed that never a day went by when Ethel did not take "great delight in telling rooms full of people" about her attempts to prevent the baby being born.

Rabwin came to believe that Ethel's unwillingness to have another child was that she thought that Frank was unfit to be a father because of his homosexuality. How long Ethel had known about her husband's proclivities is not known, but there had always been gossip. The figure he cut as a leading member of the community and the Episcopalians was at odds with the general concept of a homosexual, but Rabwin was certain that the matter was more than merely speculation and was an issue within the marriage.

Rabwin strongly counseled against abortion, and assured Frank that he would never regret having a third child. Despite considerable tension, the Gumms resigned themselves to the birth, and as they did so, they shared a conviction that the baby would be a boy. For all his bonhomie, Frank was a lonely man, and he looked forward to having a male companion in his female household. Ethel decided that she would raise a boy who would have all the considerable virtues of his father but none of his failings. Both husband and wife told everyone that the child would be a boy, and would be called after his father.

At 5:30 in the morning of June 10, 1922, in the local hospital, Ethel gave birth to another girl. The disappointment of her parents was perhaps the first element in that complex psychological pattern which was to contribute both to the greatness and the destruction of Judy Garland. The hoped-for "Frank" became Frances Ethel, and her baptism was noted in the *Herald-Review* of July 19.

Her activities, and those of the rest of the family, continued to be reported in both local newspapers, but nothing of significance appears until two years later, when Frances "Baby" Gumm made her public debut, singing at the annual style-show at the Itasca Dry Goods Store. Mary Jane and Virginia were wont to perform for their schoolfriends in the backyard or the garage, or at Ethel's bridge parties, and Frances was determined to follow in their footsteps. She seemed to know at that early age that she would become an entertainer, but there had been an evening in the late spring of 1924 when she positively craved it. Ethel had been sent to the hospital in Duluth for an operation to remove a goiter. It was the first time she had been separated from her children, so Frank brought them to the theater to take their minds off their mother's absence. He encouraged them to dress in their best to make these evenings special: and the first of these evenings proved a memorable one for them all.

A vaudeville act called the Blue Sisters had been engaged to support the picture. It consisted of three young girls—the eldest about twelve and the youngest five—and the Gumm girls were entranced. "Baby, especially, was all but uncontrollable," Virginia recalled. "She sat there, bouncing up and down, humming along." When the youngest

Blue Sister started to sing, alone, the Gumms "could all see how this was really going to send Frances into a fit. And it did. She sat transfixed. When it was all over, she turned to Daddy and—I'll never forget it—said, 'Can I do that, Daddy?' " Everyone laughed, but Virginia had no doubt that "even in her little two-year-old head, she already knew *exactly* what she wanted."

Her wishes were fulfilled in December, when it was announced that all three Gumm sisters would appear between shows at their father's cinema. The two older girls were accustomed to appearing at the Grand (as it was now generally called), but on this occasion they were to be an extra special Christmas attraction. The feature was *Through the Back Door*, a three-year-old Mary Pickford vehicle described in the Grand's advertisements, to disguise its age, as "One of the prettiest pictures she has ever appeared in"; supporting was *Motor Mad*, a two-reel comedy starring Lloyd Hamilton. When the Pickford film finished, Frank strode onto the stage to prolonged applause. When this died down, he said that it was always a pleasure to provide Grand Rapids with the finest entertainment on screen and stage, and concluded with his catch-phrase: "It pleases *us* to please *you*."

The curtains parted to reveal the three girls looking down at their mother in the pit. Ethel struck up, and Mary Jane and Virginia sang "When My Sugar Walks Down the Street," a song new to their repertoire. They did not sing with their accustomed élan, perhaps because they were uncertain whether or not little Frances would come in on key halfway through the first chorus, as planned. But Baby Gumm had no difficulty with the lyric, despite the fact that this was the first of the many songs she was to sing over the next dozen years which celebrated emotions she could not possibly comprehend. From the very first, she had a gift for putting across a song.

The two older girls did three more numbers quickly, in the midst of which they stood aside while Baby executed a nimble tap-dance. She reappeared after their exit to sing "Jingle Bells," accompanied by Ethel in the pit. She had a hand-bell, which she clanged once on every line of the song. The audience were delighted, and encouraged her to perform the song again, much to the surprise of her mother. Ethel started the song a third time, and the louder the audience laughed, the louder Baby sang and the more spirited grew her ringing of the bell. The audience was having a riotous time, roaring at the child so eagerly entertaining them; but it began to seem as if she would go on for ever. Frank eventually panicked, and ran down the aisle, signaling to Grandma Milne in the wings. She walked onstage, unceremoniously bundled Baby into her arms, and marched off to thunderous applause.

Backstage, Baby seemed uncertain whether or not to burst into tears, a scene Frank prevented by clasping her to his chest. He pushed Mary Jane and Virginia out to take their bows, and followed in their wake, carrying Baby. The house cheered and Baby rang her bell until the curtains closed.

On December 31, 1924, the debut of Judy Garland was reported in the *Herald-Review*:

> The three young daughters of Mr. and Mrs. Frank Gumm delighted a large audience at the New Grand Theater last Friday night with twenty minutes of singing and dancing. Mary Jane and Virginia, the two oldest girls, are becoming accomplished entertainers while the work of Frances, the two-year-old baby, was a genuine surprise. The little girl spoke and sang so as to be heard by everyone in the house and she joined in the dancing both alone and with her older sisters. The audience expressed their appreciation of all three girls by vigorous applause.

"The roar of the crowd—that wonderful, wonderful sound—is something I've been breathing in since I was two years old," Garland recalled. "I'll never forget the first time I heard it." She did, however, forget, or amend, details. Her own version of the evening was much like the official one later issued by M-G-M—that she was so enchanted by the spectacle of her sisters on stage that she rushed from the wings to sing the only song she knew, and she was so delighted by the response that she reprised "Jingle Bells" five times, until her father hauled her off. Whatever the truth of the matter, she learned a valuable lesson that night: "To this day whenever an enthusiastic audience gives me that 'wanting to sing all night' feeling, I hear the first notes of 'Jingle Bells' and make a quick exit." On other occasions, she likened that audience reaction to "taking nineteen hundred wake-up pills," and there is no doubt that later in her career she found it equally addictive.

The evening was the fulfillment of Baby Gumm's ambition, which was to be like her two older sisters: from then on, she became part of the family act. "She was always a very determined little girl," Virginia recalled, "and never had any trouble making up her mind about anything. Such a normal strong-willed little kid!" Her elder sisters had always indulged her, and they enjoyed the sheer glee she got from pleasing the audience. She was already, in Virginia's word, a "ham."

"If I had any talent in those days," Garland said later, "it was inherited. Nobody ever taught me what to do on stage. Like the words of the famous song, I just did 'what came naturally.' I still can't read music." Once again, the essence of this is true rather than the detail, for she clearly received some training from her parents. The first song she ever remembered learning was "America," which Frank taught her and a friend of the same age, accompanying them at the upright piano in the parlor. She was already quick to pick up a dance or a lyric. Ethel rehearsed her dance steps, and Frank coaxed her to sing the way he did—with enthusiasm, so that even if the audience disliked the song, it would warm to the singer.

She later claimed to "have worked since I was two," but in truth the girls were not subjected to an arduous schedule. Her childhood was not that different from that of other American children: swimming in Lake Pokegama, attending taffy-pulls, playing in the snow and then going indoors for a chocolate malt. "We were a normal, happy family, you know," she said. "Yes. Lots of fun, oh lots of fun in my family." At other times, she would claim that while her sisters had their own room, which they shared, she was forced to sleep wherever she could be fitted in, and this proved that she was unloved. She was, on the contrary, spoiled, but, like any other small infant, put to bed where most convenient. After the family moved, she had a room to herself. Her sisters didn't.

Shortly after her debut, during an Amateur Night in January 1925, Frances was watching from the wings with more interest than usual. As one contestant left the stage, she rushed on and began to sing "Jingle Bells" once more. A delighted audience applauded, encouraging her to continue, chorus after chorus, until Frank once again took the matter in hand and hauled his daughter off stage. The general opinion backstage was that he should take her on for the finale, in order to give the impression that her appearance had been planned. When he did so, the applause which greeted the little girl declared her the winner, but Frank decided he could not award first prize to his own daughter. He explained this to her, but the matter rankled. "That always stuck in my mind," Garland said in 1940, "and I thought to myself, 'Huh, I'll win prizes some day, prizes I can accept!' "

In March, Frances made her debut as a solo performer, supporting *Wanderer of the Wasteland*, a Zane Grey Western with Jack Holt, described by Frank as "a Paramount special done in natural colors throughout." It was announced that: "BABY FRANCES, the two-year-old daughter of Mr. and Mrs. Frank Gumm, will entertain between shows and there will be a vocal solo by Frank Gumm. The little girl will appear only Sunday evening." Later, all three girls appeared in blackface at the Grand in "The Kinky Kids Parade," during which Frances, not yet three, impersonated Al Jolson.

It was all useful experience for them and useful too for the theater. For example, when Frank engaged Miss Doris Small and Miss Pearl Trombley to demonstrate the tango and other popular dances, his daughters entertained while the two ladies changed costumes. For some years yet, the sisters were never a real trio: they might appear onstage at the same time, even perform to the same song, but Baby functioned chiefly as a solo act, while her sisters formed a duo, frequently imitating the much admired Duncan Sisters.

Since Frank wrote for the *Independent*, he almost certainly penned the report of Frances's third annual appearance at the Itasca Dry Goods Spring Style Show in March 1926:

> A hatbox, slightly larger than usual, was carried on the runway. In a few minutes it became active, the lid opened and out came little three-year-old Frances Ethel Gumm, who looked cautiously around and gave a lively performance of the Charleston. This was the hit of the evening and a round of applause greeted the little dancer as she went through her antics like a seasoned "Follie."

In June, the same newspaper reported that all five Gumms had appeared at the Grand Theater, Bemidji, and they had begun to travel to other nearby towns such as Virginia, Hibbing and Cohasset, as well as to other Bentz and Gumm theaters in Deer Park and Coleraine. Ethel was an organizer of some determination, and she decided that she could achieve something more than the plaudits of the citizens of Grand Rapids. A cheering audience of lumberjacks and their women was all very well, but this was still one of the world's more remote byways. Ethel's push was matched by Frank's optimism, and both Gumms decided that they could afford to venture further afield. They had been in the town twelve years, and it was time to test themselves in the great Out There. They wanted to see whether they could make it as vaudeville performers, not in vaudeville per se, since everyone knew that that was dying, but in movie houses more prestigious and discriminating than the Grand. This was not the only consideration, however.

It was certainly satisfying to be big fishes in a little pond. The Gumms enjoyed an enviable social life, since many of the visiting artists had become friends, to be shown off and shared with local friends in a reasonably "Open House" life-style. Frank, however, suffered from a recurring ear ailment (which had probably kept him from being conscripted in 1917), and this condition was not improved by the harsh Minnesota winters. Little Frances, too, was prone to earaches, and at the age of two had had to be rushed to the hospital to have her ears lanced—an operation she was to remember only too well, for it was done without anesthetic, with her mother holding her down. For the rest of her life she was terrified of physical pain. A year later, the family was thrown into panic when Frances was felled by a recurring high fever, a headache and vomiting. When she complained that she could not see properly, she was bundled off to a hospital in Duluth, where she was diagnosed as suffering from "acute acidosis" and was not expected to recover: she did, but it took a month and left her weak. As she grew, the Grand Rapids climate brought with it a variety of colds and chills, from which she took longer to recover than her sisters. Frank longed for the warmer, more gentle climate of his youth.

The Gumms were not, however, bound for the South, but the West. They had regularly kept in touch with Marc Rabwin, who had moved to California, after his parents had decided that they were wealthy enough to escape from the inclement Minnesota weather. He had been a student doctor in Los Angeles and was now a resident physician at Los Angeles General Hospital; his brother, Harry, was practicing law in the area. Rabwin had told Frank that Los Angeles was an ideal place for someone like him to be: it was the center of the movie industry, its population was completely movie-conscious and the hundreds of movie houses were well attended.

There was, however, a more pressing reason for Rabwin's suggestion that Frank should move on. Now approaching forty, Frank was no longer encumbered by guilt as he sought homosexual satisfaction. He had succeeded in persuading himself that show people were the "rogues and vagabonds" of tradition, not subject to the rules applying to ordinary mortals. Garland later recalled that, after moving from Grand Rapids, her family was not always accepted in the small towns in which it lived. She explained that "vaudeville people were considered sort of wicked," even though, on the surface, Frank was eminently respectable. He had none of the furtiveness traditionally associated with homosexuality at this period and was not in the least effeminate. He was enormously popular, and he used that popularity, and his respectability, to approach other men. There were, of course, rumors, and while the citizens of Grand Rapids refused to believe them, the inevitable speculation grew. Rabwin had no prejudice against homosexuality, but he feared that a small town would prove less tolerant. He wanted to save his friend from public disgrace. That this was a possibility may be judged from Rabwin's later assertion that Frank eventually left Grand Rapids because of a boy.

So far, the only hint that all was not well was when Frank was occasionally "cut" in the street. Ethel became conscious of pitying glances and was furious. In private, she treated her husband with contempt, not for his sexuality, which she ignored, but for anything else that came to mind. Virginia always maintained that she had never heard any rumors about her father's homosexuality, but, much later, Garland was to question Rabwin about it. It is quite possible that Garland first heard about her father's proclivities when she was comparatively young, and it may be that Ethel was her informant. At this stage, however, Ethel was keen to protect her children from any rumors that might reach them, and this made her keener than ever to move. Sunny California seemed as good a place as any to be.

In 1926, Los Angeles was still expanding. Just over fifty years earlier, its excellent harbor had meant that it was principally a seaport, exporting the citrus fruits grown in the hinterland. It remained basically a Spanish town until the coming of the railways, after which it had begun to grow. It had boomed in the 1890s with the discovery of oil, but although the newcomers seeking liquid gold soon overwhelmed the local community, it retained its rural character until the motion-picture industry mushroomed there. Since 1911, orange groves had disappeared under movie studios, sprawling residential estates and department stores; farms and shareholdings had given way to banks, bars and restaurants. The wide boulevards, lined with palms and oleanders, carried a spider's web of trolleys, which extended from the old harbor into the mountains.

As far as the world in general was concerned, Los Angeles meant Hollywood, home of the motion-picture industry, a place that spawned a million and one dreams. It poured forth a ceaseless torrent of glamour, action, excitement, romance and fun, all of which was avidly reported in the numerous magazines which had grown up with the colony. In their pages, the lives of the stars were reported at length: they were photographed and interviewed at work and play. Such magazines were a vital part of the industry and ranks of public-relations people were employed by the studios to feed the journalists with the latest news about the film colony and its enviable denizens. Like thousands of other American families, the Gumms were avid devourers of these magazines, which fed their readers' fantasies as enticingly as the movies themselves.

A perennial fantasy was that anybody could become a film star, and it struck Ethel that the Gumms might aim higher than vaudeville. The demand for child actors appeared to be growing all the time, and there seemed no reason why her daughters should not find employment with a studio. The public was enthralled by the bunch of ragamuffins who starred in the Our Gang comedies turned out by the Hal Roach studio, and had been following the fortunes of the diminutive Jackie Coogan ever since he appeared with Charlie Chaplin in *The Kid*. Frances already appeared to have the stamina and guts for a career in the business, and if she seemed young—well, Baby Peggy, the star of several silent films, was already growing up and was bound to be replaced. Frances always called her dolls, of which there were many, "Peggy," and this may have inspired Ethel.

The original plan was for Frank and Ethel to travel to California and take the lay of the land, while the children remained behind with Grandma Milne. At the last moment, however, just two days short of Frances's fourth birthday, the girls looked so disconsolate that their parents decided to flip a coin to decide whether or not to take them along. The outcome was that they eventually traveled *en famille*, paying for the trip, or some of it, by performing on the way, billing themselves as "Jack and Virginia Lee, and the Three Little Lees." The real Virginia recalled: "We'd stop in a town and my daddy would go to the newspaper, or to the theater owner, and offer to play a show that night. That's the way things were done then."

This momentous journey became part of the Judy Garland legend and consequently underwent some revision. The Gumms were sufficiently well-off to own an automobile, but bringing the girls along meant the extra expense of taking two rooms at any hotels they stayed in. Despite what Garland later claimed, they in fact traveled by rail. They left Grand Rapids on June 8, taking the Great Northern to Seattle, with several stops along the way. The towns in which they chose to stay—Devil's Lake, North Dakota; Havre, Shelby, Whitefish, Kalispell, Montana; Cashmere and Leavenworth, Washington—were those in which there were movie houses likely to hire live performers.

Working conditions were hardly ideal. First of all, Frank had to seek out the local movie-house manager and try to impress him with a sheaf of photographs and some posters; if it was possible to put a notice in the local paper, he would do that as well. He also undertook the time-consuming task of going around the town pasting up posters. The backstage facilities of the theaters were sometimes grim, often with lavatories serving as makeshift dressing-rooms.

Although she was grateful for the experience, Garland was scathing about what the Gumms offered to the public:

> It was a lousy act. My father had a wonderful voice, but my mother didn't sing well . . . and we kids were terrible, too. We appeared separately. First we'd sit out front and applaud Mother and Daddy, and then they'd do the same for us when we went on stage. After Mother and Father's act, she'd dash into the pit to play the piano, and he would dress us in our costumes backstage. I did those horrible Egyptian bellyrolls, in an Egyptian outfit with those big balloon pants and a lot of ankle bracelets and spangles.

Wearing Spanish costumes, "with those funny hats with little balls hanging all around the brims," her sisters would sing "In a Little Spanish Town"—sometimes up to fifteen times (or so Garland claimed), if her father was having difficulty dressing her. Neither Mary Jane nor Virginia, she maintained, had any talent for what Mama and Papa Gumm required them to do: "No wonder they hated show business." She did not rate her mother's playing much above her singing, but her song, "I've Been Saving for a Rainy Day" always made Frances cry. "She was a very lonely and determined woman, and I guess I'm the same way," Garland later observed. "I cried and applauded all the way to California."

The Gumms did not work after they left Leavenworth, since they wanted to enjoy what was supposed, in part, to be a vacation. They had earned some $300. After staying with friends in Seattle, they went by rail to Portland, where Frank looked up some old friends, and then by sea to San Francisco, where they saw the Golden Gate and visited Chinatown, before finishing the last stage of the journey by rail.

In Los Angeles, they stayed for ten days in a small hotel on Sunset Boulevard as guests of the Rabwins, who put one of their automobiles at their disposal. Frank filed several reports on their journey and its destination for the *Independent*. He felt compelled to admit to the paper's readers that by taking the bus tour of the stars' homes, the Gumms were merely another set of rubber-necking tourists, but he tried to turn it into a joke: "Gloria Swanson's palatial residence was advertised for sale and open for inspection. We thought of purchasing it, but found that it contained only 40 rooms so didn't bother. Gloria was in New York so couldn't invite us for dinner."

Meeting the cowboy star Fred Thomson was a high point of the visit, since he and his horse, Silver King, were great favorites of the family. In fact, Frank had stopped Thomson in the street. He knew that Thomson was married to Frances Marion, "the celebrated scenario writer" who worked at Metro-Goldwyn-Mayer, which was the studio above all others that the Gumms wanted to visit. Ordinarily, access was almost impossible, but Thomson offered to arrange a visit. At M-G-M's Culver City studio, they watched scenes being filmed for *The Red Mill, Tell It to the Marines, Annie Laurie* and other movies. They shook hands with Lon Chaney ("who isn't bad looking at all off the screen and is a regular fellow," Frank reported), and saw other stars such as William Haines, Carmel Myers, Buck Jones, Lillian Gish, Marion Davies, Conway Tearle and "Moana [*sic*] Loy." They also visited the studios of William Fox, Warner Bros. and the Film Booking Office. Old friends from Grand Rapids took them to the Hollywood Bowl, and they went in a spirit of skepticism to one of Aimee Semple McPherson's revival meetings—but were sufficiently impressed to return the following week.

Another high point was seeing the Duncan Sisters in *Topsy and Eva* at a Saturday matinee. The stars presented each child in the audience with a hand mirror with their photograph on the back as a souvenir. Frank reported:

> They took a special interest in our baby, had all three children sing and dance for them and took our name and address . . . as they might be able to give the baby, anyway, a chance next season. I hope this doesn't sound like bragging, the interest came unsolicited . . . They were not at all aware that we had anything to do with the show business until after they had made their statements regarding the baby's talents.

Despite the welcome $300 "pocket money" earned on the outward trip, the Gumms did not perform on the return journey. They reached home on July 17, "on the midnight train, two hours late, and pretty tired out . . . but glad to be home, which, after all, is the BEST place." In spite of this noble sentiment, Grand Rapids was to be home to the Gumms for only three more months. The song they had sung on the trip, "California, Here I Come," proved in the end to be prophetic.

2

The Gumm Sisters

IT TOOK SOME WEEKS for Frank to dispose of his interest in the Grand. Fred Bentz sold up at the same time in order to concentrate on the filling station he had recently purchased. Despite Marc Rabwin's earlier worries, it seems that the Gumms did not leave Grand Rapids under a cloud. Indeed, when they departed for southern California on October 27, 1926, the future looked very bright. The town bade them farewell with regret and a flurry of receptions and parties, including a gala at the theater.

The children had been sent on ahead to Ethel's parents in Superior, and their parents followed, in leisurely fashion, stopping off to visit Tennessee and Kansas City, and to stay with assorted relatives: Frank's brothers in Chicago and Birmingham, Alabama, and Ethel's brother and sister in Duluth. They picked up the girls from Superior at the beginning of December. Frank went on ahead to Los Angeles in search of somewhere to live. He rented a small, stucco, one-story residence in Atwater, near Glendale, and was shortly joined by his wife and children.

Frank, meanwhile, was looking for a theater to buy. There were few for sale in downtown Los Angeles, and those that were cost more than he could possibly afford. In the suburbs and outlying districts, the competition was fierce. He decided to make use of his other skills, and chose to found a newspaper. In Grand Rapids, the *Independent* received the first issue of the *West Hollywood Journal*, which had Frank's name proudly on the masthead as proprietor and editor. Doubtless taking its cue from the accompanying letter, the *Independent* described the *Journal* as "a public servant destined to further the interests of West Hollywood and its citizens, to encourage trading at home and to boost commerce for the district." No more was heard of the *Journal* after its first issue, however, probably because Frank simply did not have the capital needed to sustain this venture. Indeed, he had only started it in desperation, for he was lost now that he had finally left the security of Grand Rapids. Its quick demise left the family savings severely depleted.

Fortunately, Marc Rabwin heard of a theater for sale in Lancaster, which was in the Antelope Valley on the edge of the Mojave Desert, seventy miles northeast of Los Angeles. Rabwin knew of the town primarily because it was the most distant community to which he could send an ambulance in case of an emergency. It had only one movie house, the Antelope Valley Theater, which had opened the previous Christmas with *Cheerful Folly*, a brand-new Universal comedy starring the popular British actor Reginald Denny. The theater had been full that night, but seldom since. A community of 1,500 inhabitants was unlikely to fill 500 seats at every performance.

During its construction, the theater had been dubbed "Carter's Folly," after Whitford B. Carter, who owned it. Carter had leased it to former vaudevillian Sam Claman, who economized on wages by employing no cashier: he himself sat outside, while patrons dropped their quarters into his hat. Even so, he could not make the theater pay and was anxious to get rid of it.

Frank purchased the lease in April 1927 and moved with his family to Lancaster. He had little choice. The Gumms had found no pot of gold waiting for them in California, and their financial situation had become desperate.

Lancaster was another recent settlement, but—even at first sight—was so dreary that it made Grand Rapids seem a bustling metropolis in comparison. The past six months had been characterized by feelings of insecurity, impermanence and inadequacy, however, and the Gumms had no option but to resign themselves once again to being big fish in a little pond. At least the Antelope Valley Theater would return Frank to a milieu he knew and understood: but he would need every ounce of his flair for showmanship if he was going to persuade a smaller population to fill a house significantly larger than the New Grand.

The theater stood on the town's main thoroughfare, Antelope Avenue, and its chief virtue was that there was no competition within a fifty-mile radius. Like the Grand, it had a stage as well as a screen, and if the right attractions were put on, the farming folk from the surrounding countryside, who came to shop, might well want to take in a show as well. Marc Rabwin's brother, Harry, drew up the agreement and became Frank's lawyer.

Ethel was later to claim, in *Modern Screen*, that the family went to California "to get away from the coal bills, if you must know, and the storm windows . . . what Frank and I loved was the climate. Roses and balmy skies in the middle of winter. This was the place, we decided, this is it." In fact, Lancaster was unbearably cold in winter and uncomfortably hot in summer, and the move there meant that the girls had to be removed from the Meglin Studio. The family took a house on the corner of Cedar Avenue and Newgrove Street, just a few blocks from the theater—as was everything else in the town, including the train depot, around which, in desultory fashion, stood a few banks and offices. Apart from some farms to the south, the township simply stopped at the edge of the desert. The antelopes, after which the valley had been named, had long since departed, and the scrub was inhabited now only by rabbits, coyotes and snakes. The area had its picturesque qualities, it is true: Joshua trees grew there in the summer, desert flowers were plentiful and there was a mountain ridge on all sides—and the one to the north was the Tehachapi range, which looked particularly tranquil against pale, cloudless skies.

Skepticism in the town about the theater was tempered by the undoubted fact that its programs (changed twice-weekly) were essential viewing for most of its inhabitants. Consequently there was much curiosity about the Gumms, which they decided to satisfy as soon as possible. On May 20, less than a week after the family had settled in, a notice appeared in the local paper, the Lancaster *Ledger Gazette*, large enough to suggest future revenue from the same source and touchingly worded, under the heading "Extra Special":

Mr. and Mrs. Frank Gumm and Daughters will present a cycle of songs and dances between shows each evening [Sunday and Monday May 22–23] at 9 o'clock and also at the Sunday Matinee. Having purchased the theater, I am taking this method of introducing the family to the good people of Lancaster and Antelope Valley. It is my intention to continue presenting the high class picture program as given by Mr. Claman and I cordially ask the support of the public in keeping the entertainment up to the highest possible standard. Your cooperation will be appreciated.

Respectfully, FRANK A. GUMM.

The *Ledger Gazette* made the family front-page news the following week: "GUMM FAMILY WINS LANCASTER APPROVAL. Mr. and Mrs. Gumm are accomplished musicians and gave two very pleasing songs while the little daughters completely won the hearts of the audience with their songs and dances."

They continued to perform on that stage in various permutations throughout the year, and on December 17 Virginia played the title-role in *Little Snow White* at the grammar school, with Frances as one of the seven dwarfs. By the end of the year the *Ledger-Gazette* was describing the theater as "one of the finest assets of the community."

Although the Gumms were once again among the most prominent members of the community, Lancaster was much less impressed by them than Grand Rapids had been. As before, Frank and Ethel took charge of musical matters at the Episcopalian church, and the girls joined the choir. To supplement the family income, Ethel rented an old hall on the north side of the town to give dancing lessons, which soon became *de rigueur* for all the better-off daughters of the area. Every so often the pupils would be joined by the Gumm sisters, who demonstrated their own skills at the same steps. (This did nothing to enhance their popularity at school.) Each May, Ethel's class would perform at the theater—after the movie, so those in the audience who wanted to leave could do so. She designed the costumes for her pupils, which they then took home for their mothers to execute.

She also advertised for some musicians to form a quintet with her, to play for the Saturday evening dances at the Elks' Hall. Frank dutifully attended the luncheons for the Rotarians, the Masons and the Kiwanis, but the villagers were dour and reserved—and less than dazzled. They were close enough to Los Angeles to realize that the Gumms were operating only on the fringes of show business. Nor did many of them approve of the theatrical ambitions Ethel nurtured for the three girls.

A friend in Grand Rapids had given Ethel the address of a cousin in California, Laura Gilmore—who as it happened lived in Lancaster. She and her husband, Will, had three children, two boys and a girl, approximately the same ages as the Gumm girls, and the two women shared a passion for bridge. Frank liked Will Gilmore, a university-trained engineer working for one of the irrigation companies responsible for bringing water to the town and the nearby farmsteads from the Mojave River which flowed under the bedrock. The two families seemed inseparable and were in and out of each other's homes—until Laura suffered a stroke and was confined to the house, and, later, to a wheelchair. While Frank was busy with the affairs of the theater, it seemed natural that Will and Ethel should meet, and they did so with increasing frequency. As their friendship grew, so, gradually, did Frances's awareness of the reasons why. This was the first strand in the knot of hostility she felt toward her mother.

The adoration between herself and her father, on the other hand, was mutual, as if she were becoming the son and young companion for whom he had craved. Although they were both as crazy about performing as the other three Gumms, they stood apart while Ethel rehearsed Mary Jane and Virginia or when they were making costumes. Ethel and the older girls had no part in what was almost a sacred ritual, when Frank sang "Danny Boy" or "Nobody Knows the Trouble I've Seen" to Frances before going off to the theater for the evening. Father and daughter were often seen together at the Westcott and Plummer Drug Store (where he indulged her in her passion for chocolate ice cream), or at the Jazz Café and Candy Shop.

The latter was owned by Charlie Wakefield who, each Christmas, partnered Frank in putting on a free matinee, with free candy, for the local children—something Frank could ill afford, since the cinema only just paid its way. The weekend houses often made the difference between profit and loss, especially when it played host to the local troupes of strolling players.

Not long after their arrival in Lancaster, Frances suffered a recurrence of acidosis. The Gumms called Marc Rabwin, who had become the first ever surgical resident at the Los Angeles General Hospital. Rabwin was so concerned that he had Frances admitted to the hospital, where he supervised her treatment and saw to it that the finest doctors in Los Angeles were called in to see her. She was on the critical list, but the care she received saved her life. This brush with death so frightened Frances's parents that they began to spoil her more than ever. In character, she was like her father: normally happy, if pensive, but given to sudden, terrible fits of temper, particularly when crossed. In order to avoid these, Frank and Ethel indulged her to the extent that a neighbor, Peg DeVine, later told one of Garland's biographers that she had thought at the time: "This adorable child, without knowing that she is, is a tyrant."

The adorable child's health continued to be precarious, with bouts of hay fever brought on by the pollen of the exotic, night-blooming desert plants. When Frances was unable to sleep, Ethel would lie her down on the back seat of the car and drive to a pollen-free area. These excursions were occasionally taken for other reasons. Garland claimed that she spent many a summer night in the back of the car, not because Ethel wanted to help her to sleep, but because she was using her as a pawn in her increasingly frequent rows with Frank. These usually took place after the theater had closed for the night, when the Irish whiskey Frank loved to consume took effect. Ethel would announce that she was leaving him and taking Frances with her, cleverly choosing the one child on whom he really doted. These flights were intended to frighten Frank, and Ethel would return at dawn, having "forgiven" him.

In all Garland's accounts of her childhood, her mother is made out to be a villainess of gargantuan proportions, but many who knew Ethel at the time have reported that, although she was brusque of manner, and a disciplinarian, she was never deliberately inconsiderate or unkind. She was a driven being, who could not even buy groceries without showing an impatience which suggested that she had more important things to occupy her time. Ethel expected her children to work as hard as she did. Frances was far from lazy, but she liked having her own way. With her father, and to an extent her sisters, this was easy; but her mother was another matter. She was also quick-witted and perceptive, which led her to recognize the signs when things were about to go wrong. She learned to talk her way out of trouble when it became unavoidable, and discovered that singing was the best way in which to stay in her mother's good graces.

By this time, Ethel's mother, now widowed, had taken a house farther along Cedar Avenue and helped run the Gumm household. The local paper kept a fond eye on the family's social activities, and noted that Frances's sixth birthday, in June 1928, was celebrated with a party for thirty children. "Miss Gumm," it reported, "was the recipient of a large number of gifts of great variety and usefulness."

The people in Lancaster who remember the Gumms today recall an endless round of birthday parties given for, or attended by, the girls.

In August 1928, Ethel took the three girls on vacation to Santa Monica, where a local radio station, KFI, broadcast a freewheeling little program, *The Kiddies Hour*. The program was the brainchild of Kennard Hamilton, known as Big Brother Ken. His gimmick was to audition his guests on air, and whether or not Ethel was aware of the program in advance or learned about it when they were in Santa Monica, she knew that this was the opportunity for which she had been hoping. The girls' radio debut so impressed Hamilton that they became regular performers on his show, attracting the attention of William S. Hart, the famous star of Western movies, who requested them to sing "There's a Long, Long Trail."

Hamilton had provided Ethel with the turning point she needed, for it confirmed her view that what all her daughters needed was exposure: somewhere out there was a talent scout from the studios who would recognize their potential. Although Frances started attending the grammar school in September, Ethel wanted to get the girls out of Lancaster to anywhere that they might be "discovered." Their popularity on the show encouraged her to enroll them again that December at the Meglin Studio. It had been quite a haul from Lancaster to Santa Monica, and it was another to the Meglin Studio— an early three-hour drive in the Buick every weekend, through the San Gabriel mountains and the suburbs of the city. Fortunately, there were classes on both Saturday and Sunday, so the schedule did not conflict with school. Sandwiched wonderfully between dance classes were visits to the city's motion picture palaces.

Inconvenience, expense and perseverance paid off within a couple of weeks. The three Gumm girls were considered professional enough to perform in a holiday-season show, *The Meglin Kiddie Revue*. This played for one night, December 13, at a "Christmas All-Star Benefit"—or so it was described by its sponsor, the *Los Angeles Examiner*. Then, on December 20, it began a week-long run at Loew's State Theater, one of the movie houses in which Ethel and the children had spent excited Saturday evenings. The Meglin revues were always attended by talent scouts, and every "stage mother" hoped one would be there when her little darling was performing. Ethel Meglin believed that there was only one of her young pupils who could command the expected large audiences on her own: Baby Gumm.

This was not something Ethel Gumm was likely to dispute, and it was one reason the two women became so friendly, each recognizing in the other the same sort of strong, managing character. What Ethel did not like at all, however, was that the children were not individually named in the program; but she convinced herself that this was Hollywood, where dreams came true, and even a half-witted talent scout should be able to trace the identity and whereabouts of a Baby Gumm. Child stars continued to be in demand, and if—and, at this stage, it was a large if—the newfangled Talkies proved not to be a flash in the pan, what could be more appealing than a *singing* child star?

"The children perform like tried and true troupers in both solo and chorus numbers," the *Los Angeles Times* duly reported, and if it did not single out for special praise the precocious youngster who sang "I Can't Give You Anything But Love"—dressed, appropriately, as Cupid—the *Los Angeles Record* did. Echoing Ethel's own feelings, the reviewer wrote: "Once again we can complain only of the unprogrammed appearance. We have no names with which to lay tribute to. One small miss shook these well-known rafters with her songs à la Sophie Tucker."

In spite of the enthusiastic applause in the mighty Loew's State, Hollywood did not beckon. Ethel and Frank could only look on proudly as Baby was reduced to entertaining the Kiwanians back in Lancaster with her impersonation of Fanny Brice. Clearly, if they wanted to get ahead, the Gumms needed more than weekends in Los Angeles. Accordingly, on March 1, 1929, the *Ledger-Gazette* announced:

> Mrs. Frank Gumm and daughters leave next weekend for Los Angeles where they will reside indefinitely in order that the girls may pursue special studies. They will spend their weekends in Lancaster, Mrs. Gumm furnishing the music of the theater. Mr. Gumm will continue to reside at the family home on Cedar Avenue.

Anyone curious enough might have seen in this a sign that the Gumms' marriage was in serious difficulties.

Garland once said that the growing hostility between her parents was due to Frank's objections to having the girls pushed on the stage, but Virginia insisted that he was just as enthusiastic as Ethel about his daughters' careers. Garland liked to give the impression that she had been some sort of child-slave, but beyond the fact that she was prone to fall asleep in the classroom, the evidence is against her. She was a tomboy, who smoked surreptitiously and at the age of nine was the acknowledged leader of her group of friends. They loved dressing up in the Gumms' theatrical costumes, but she alone took this seriously. Frances enjoyed performing.

A youngster of her own age, Galen Reed, was paid a dollar for each time he partnered her on the stage of the theater, having been chosen as the only boy in town who could sing louder than she. On these occasions, the two of them would rehearse three or four nights a week on the front porch of the Gumms' house, where Ethel had a piano. Galen was Frances's first beau, sharing candy at the theater, and cigarettes in the back of the car which Virginia drove. But he only ever kissed her while they were playing "Spin the Bottle" or "Truth and Consequences." She spent other evenings at the theater with her friends Irma and Esther, watching movies.

Stardom was the natural goal for a child accustomed to receiving applause. In some form or other it turned up in most of the movies Frances watched in the Valley Theater—not necessarily movies about movies, but in countless rags-to-riches stories: store clerks who married into high society, stenographers who became fashion models, and a hundred other such tales, as acted by the likes of Colleen Moore, Billie Dove, Bebe Daniels, Alice Terry, Laura La Plante and Janet Gaynor. The precocious, seven-year-old Frances studied them, both as one professional looks at another and as a child identifying, wondering whether she would have done that gesture or that glance in quite the same way. That was the difference between her and her sisters: they sang, they danced, they posed, but she already knew how to "sell" a song.

There is no record, even when she spoke rancorously of her mother, of Garland complaining about the plans for the careers of "The Gumm Sisters," as they were now known. Opinions are sharply and evenly divided as to what extent Ethel was an ambitious, pushy "stage mother": her own friends were saddened and angered by Garland's later comments that her mother was "the real Wicked Witch of the West." Neighbors in Lancaster certainly considered Ethel a "stage mother," but a protective one. The only criticism they leveled at her was that she neglected her husband for the sake of her children.

Nothing that is known of Judy Garland suggests that she would have been content to remain in a small town and entertain as an amateur. One day she climbed onto a neighbor's knee and informed him that she was "going to be a movie star someday." This was to happen even sooner than she had predicted.

In the fall of 1928, Ethel enrolled the girls at the Ethel Meglin

Dance Studio, named after and run by a woman who had danced for Ziegfeld and Charles Dillingham in New York. Meglin and her fellow teachers specialized in training youngsters in all forms of dance, from ballet to tap, but they also taught the other skills which show-business children would need. The Studio was so well established with the dozens of vaudeville theaters (principally movie houses which booked vaudeville acts to supplement the main attraction) and the film companies, that it acted as an unofficial talent agency. On one occasion the girls had danced at the Biltmore Hotel, for fifty cents each, and, toward the end of December had appeared as three of the "100 Clever Children of the Twinkletoe KIDDIE REVUE" at Loew's State Theater. That was the trouble: they were in fact just three of *several hundred* children trying to crash show business.

In 1929, shortly after her seventh birthday, she appeared as one of the "One Hundred Meglin Wonder Kiddies . . . Kute . . . Klever and Kunning." Her screen debut was made with her sisters in *The Big Revue*, a Talkie short produced by Mayfair Pictures. It featured "Ethel Meglin's Famous Hollywood Wonder Kids," and the Gumms appeared both in the chorus and in a number of their own, "In the Sunny South," which Baby steals effortlessly from her sisters. Virginia appears self-conscious and Mary Jane performs as if her thoughts were elsewhere; but Baby, vivacious and with abundant natural talent, is totally assured. She appears to be competing with her sisters, even though they are putting up no opposition. The act, as a whole, is an uneasy compromise between the two older girls as a team and Baby as a solo performer.

As with *The Big Revue*, bookings were meager for this picture, and Mayfair discontinued its agreement. However, Ethel used the association with Meglin to get the girls additional stage bookings. At the nearby Bishop Theater, for example, they appeared on July 16 and 17 as an "Extra Added Attraction" to the main feature, which was *A Single Man*, an M-G-M comedy starring the popular team of Aileen Pringle and Lew Cody. "Harmony Songs, Tap and Acrobatic Dancing," promised the notice in the local newspaper, which duly published an enthusiastic review, concluding: "All do so well in their specialties that the discrimination of special mention is hardly just: but the remarkable work of Baby Frances particularly appeals to hearers because of her diminutive size and few years." The Gumm Sisters sang "In the Sunny South" once again, and Frances imitated Ted Lewis singing "Wear a Hat With a Silver Lining" and "Little Pal."

Back in Los Angeles, the girls had a chance to see some of the stars they had been impersonating from records and radio. In August, they supported the popular black comedian, Stepin Fetchit, in a Fanchon and Marco show at Loew's State for a week: but they were still just three among many, even though the troupe had now been reduced to "50 Meglin Kiddies." A numbed *Variety* reviewer mused: "How many mothers the management is struggling with isn't known, but the strain must be heavy . . . And always the same [show]—those gymnastics and roll-overs which come so easy to limber babies. Once in a while all right but not every week."

In spite of such appearances, Ethel decided to take the girls out of the Meglin Studio in August. The family was reunited in Lancaster while she decided upon her next move.

On November 8, the *Ledger-Gazette* announced with pride that the Valley Theater would soon be equipped to show Talkies, as indeed it had to, since most cinemas in the Los Angeles area had already been converted. This was to mean that Ethel would no longer be needed in the pit to accompany the picture shows, and the same report added that Frank Gumm's three daughters had returned to Los Angeles to rehearse with an organization called "The Hollywood Starlets." They were now billed as "The Hollywood Starlets Trio" on Big Brother Ken's radio show, becoming, said Virginia later, "the first children's trio ever."

The idea for the Starlets organization came from Gus Edwards, who if he is remembered at all today is as the original of the character played by Bing Crosby in the 1939 movie *The Starmaker*. The film's relation to the truth is somewhat fanciful, though it is true, as shown in the movie, that Edwards was a successful impresario specializing in "kiddie acts." It was Edwards who suggested that the Gumm Sisters should sing three-part harmony, rather than appear as a duet and solo act.

At this period, the Starlets were attached to Warner Bros. In 1927, Warners had introduced sound—in the form of some songs and lines of dialogue—in *The Jazz Singer*, but prior to that, they had been experimenting with a series of Vitaphone shorts—named after the manufacturers of the sound system. With the Talkie evolution an established fact, the demand for these shorts had grown.

In December 1929, First National (which Warners owned) released *Holiday in Storyland*, featuring the Hollywood Starlets, among whom were the Gumm Sisters, performing "Where the Butterflies Kiss the Buttercups" as a trio, and—in a solo spot—Baby singing "Blue

Butterfly." This film was followed by *The Wedding of Jack and Jill*, in which Baby sang—of all prophetic titles—"Hang on to a Rainbow." It was filmed in two-tone Technicolor, as was *Bubbles*, which also seems to have vanished without trace. Only a few prints were struck, because, like the Meglin films, the demand for the Hollywood Starlets was small. First National declined to use them again.

The Gumms stayed with the Starlets, and appeared in live engagements in 1930 in San Diego, Coronado and Los Angeles. As the Depression worsened, however, they reluctantly decided to leave Los Angeles and return to Lancaster, further disheartened because, although they had genuinely moved from the fringes of show business, they still had not managed to get to the heart of it. They continued to appear anywhere they could show off their skills, from local lodges to Walker's department store in Los Angeles, from the Jazz Café and Candy Store to the Pantages Theater on Hollywood Boulevard. The *Ledger-Gazette* continued to issue bulletins on the life and career of Baby Gumm: she had played Goldilocks in school, her eighth birthday had been celebrated by a swimming party and so on.

More than a year was to pass before there was any significant progress in the career of the Gumm Sisters. In July 1931, they featured in *Stars of Tomorrow*, a "juvenile extravaganza" which opened at the Wilshire-Ebell Theater on Wilshire Boulevard. The show was staged by Maurice L. Kusell, who ran the Kusell Dramatic Dance Studio, which had the reputation of being the most prestigious on the West Coast. He had also been dance director on several movies, but by this time the public was reeling from a surfeit of musicals. Ethel was engaged to play the piano in the show.

Stars of Tomorrow provided the Gumm Sisters with their most promising showcase so far. As "gardenettes," they appeared in a production number, "Garden of the Beautiful Flowers"; as "Harlem Crooners," they sang and danced to Irving Berlin's "Puttin' on the Ritz"; and in the grand finale, "Floatin' Down the Mississippi," Baby had a solo and a "plantation melody" duet with Miss Betty Jean Allen.

The encouraging consequence of the show was reported in the *Ledger-Gazette* on September 4, 1931. Under a photograph of "Miss Frances Gumm," looking plaintive, big-eyed and full-lipped, with a bow in her curls, was the news that:

This talented youngster . . . was signed for stage, screen, radio and television for five years by Frank and Dunlap, Inc., prominent Hollywood agents. The agency manages Peggy Shannon, George Bancroft, James Cagney and other stars. Frances is the first child they have ever put under contract . . . [They] are of the opinion that she will have a most successful future in stage and screen work. They have given her the name of Frances Gayne instead of Frances Gumm.

She will appear in person at the Valley Theater Sunday and Monday Sept. 6–7, in a group of clever song and dance specialties.

Kussell had introduced Ethel to George Frank of Frank and Dunlap at a party—at which the three girls had sung—after the *Stars of Tomorrow* show, and he had expressed interest in handling Frances. The deal was struck, but Frances's father decided that she was too young for a career—that if she became a star of any sort, it would split up the family. The two older girls adored their sister, but were sometimes resentful, after all their hard work, that she—to whom performing came naturally, without their sort of effort—was the one everyone talked about.

Frank had dreamed about being a vaudeville headliner, but now that the chance was available to his daughter, he balked, claiming that he would only consent if George Frank took on all three girls: he was resolutely opposed to offering up his baby on her own to the uncertainties of fame. Ethel was obliged to tell the agent that Frances was, after all, to have a normal childhood: she was not going to be the next Baby Peggy.

Ethel was, however, furious. She decided that it was time that the family was broken up. Frank could continue to run his movie house, while she would take the girls off for a career independent of him. For the moment, she bided her time, drawing comfort from the fact that Maurice Kusell continued to be interested in all three girls. He recruited the Gumm Sisters for a couple of recitals, and in the latter part of the year, Baby was allowed to appear solo in Coronado, Tehachapi, Bakersfield and Los Angeles. At Christmas, she participated in a "Kiddie Revue" at the Warner Bros. Theater in Los Angeles, and in January and March of the following year, she was featured in two "Star Night" shows at the Cocoanut Grove, where movie celebrities went to dance, dine and be seen.

Fanchon and Marco, who had produced the *Meglin Kiddie Revues* at Loew's State, also showed an interest. They booked the Gumm Sisters, as a trio, into twelve theaters in July and August 1932, culminating in a booking at the huge Paramount Theater in Los Angeles, where they supported *Devil and the Deep*, starring Gary Cooper and Tallulah Bankhead. The accompanying vaudeville was headed by the comic Fuzzy Knight, who had made a small name for himself providing light relief in Westerns, and the Gumms, billed as "Blue Harmony," were the third act to appear. On August 30, Judy Garland received her first review in *Variety*: "Gumm Sisters, harmony trio, socked with two numbers. Selling end of trio is the 10-year-old kid sister with a pip of a lowdown voice. Kid stopped the show, but wouldn't give more." There was no longer any point in Frank insisting that the Gumm Sisters could not be split up.

The Gumms had always wanted to play the Paramount and, that ambition satisfied, spent a comparatively quiet autumn. In December, Frances was booked into the Fox Arlington Theater in Santa Barbara for two days and into the Million Dollar Theater for a week over the New Year period. They would occasionally stay overnight in Los Angeles, but at other times drove all the way back to Lancaster. Frank remained unenthusiastic about his daughters' careers. "My father didn't want us to perform," Garland recalled, "and it certainly wasn't a financial necessity. He was doing very well with the theater. But whenever we worked any place, he'd come and watch."

It was not work to Frances. She loved performing. The two bookings in late 1932, coupled with memories of the summer, convinced Ethel once more that Lancaster was no place to be based. On December 31, 1932, the *Ledger-Gazette* announced: "After the first of the year, Mrs. Frank Gumm plans to spend the greater part of her time in Los Angeles where she will be associated with Maurice Kusell, producer." Kusell himself confirmed this in a message he sent to the Los Angeles papers: "An addition to the Kusell faculty is Ethel Gumm, personality and harmony jazz singing teacher. Mrs. Gumm trained the sensational juvenile singing trio, the Gumm Sisters, who have won acclaim as modern harmony singers."

What effect this unsettled period had on Frances is difficult to gauge. Garland later commented: "As I recall, my parents were separated and getting back together all the time. It was very hard for me to understand those things and, of course, I remember clearly the fear I had of those separations." She would rather have been with her father, but she was already on the treadmill which required her to sing for her supper. In spite of Garland's assertion that the Valley Theater was thriving, it had in fact felt the wind of the Depression and been obliged to lower its admission prices. She had begun to accept that she was marked out for a different destiny than that awaiting her schoolfellows. Neither she nor Ethel had really cared for

Lancaster: Los Angeles was much more exciting. Years later, Garland noted that John Wayne had also been raised in Lancaster: "He tells me, 'If you can live through Lancaster, Judy, you can live through anything.' He's right."

There were other reasons for Ethel wishing to distance herself from Lancaster. Once again, Frank's homosexuality was causing problems. Kusell recalled that everyone at his studio knew that Frank was homosexual, adding: "I hear he got into trouble along the way because of it." If he did, there is no report of it. The people of Lancaster liked him so much that they simply ignored the rumors. At the high school, however, Frank's sexuality was a byword among the boys, who joked about ways of getting free tickets at the Valley Theater. It may well be that the three girls were teased about this—an added incentive for Ethel to remove the two younger ones.

Mary Jane remained with her father so that she could graduate, though by the summer of 1933, she was reunited with her mother and sisters and appearing regularly on KFWB radio's *Junior Hi-Jinx Hour*. The reviewer of the *Los Angeles Examiner* reflected that, when the girls were singing, he imagined them

stomping and infusing their vigor into all spectators [*sic*]. They have radio personality so sadly lacking in most trios, "doubles" and "quartets" . . .

Those three juveniles from Lancaster are masquerading under false colors. They are not imitators. Nothing on the air at the moment is so original. Perhaps we should be abstemious in our praise of these youngsters for fear of curtailing their prospects of rising to full effulgence . . . Last week they "Shuffled Off to Buffalo" with a spirit and originality that must have moved every listener.

It was perhaps these notices which attracted the attention of Jack King and Bob Winkler, who booked the acts that performed between movies at RKO's theaters. They engaged the Gumm Sisters to play at the Hillstreet Theater, where the act included Frances singing "Rain, Rain, Go Away." It was here that they were seen by Ben Piazza, an M-G-M talent scout, but his enthusiasm for them failed to impress his studio.

For the moment, there was an even better engagement, at the Golden Gate Theater in San Francisco. Ethel took the girls by ship from San Pedro, and Frank drove up to join them in the act—one of the few times he did so professionally. *Variety* was a great deal less impressed with the act than it had been about the Paramount one the previous year. It described the seven acts on display as "a slap at whoever stated that 'vaude is coming back.' " Not even Frances dispelled the reviewer's gloom: "The Gumm Sisters, with Mama Gumm at the piano, and Papa Gumm in advance, deuced. Three girls of assorted sizes who sing in mediocre voice and style, with the majority of the burden falling on the youngest one, a mere tot, who lustily shouted three numbers, decidedly not of her type. And much too long."

The family played a further engagement at the Fox West Coast Theater in Long Beach, and rented a house at 2605 Ivanhoe Drive in the Silver Lake area of Los Angeles. Frank had disapproved of the small dwelling Ethel had previously taken: this one went to the opposite extreme. Probably chosen to impress friends, relatives and talent scouts, it was wonderful for the children, being circular and built on the side of a hill, with a bridge to the front door and the living room, beneath which was a gymnasium. Above were two further stories. Frank, however, returned to Lancaster to manage the theater and to find a smaller house for himself. When the children visited, they stayed with friends.

During the first week of September, the Gumms appeared at the Warner Bros. Theater in Hollywood. Billed second, as "Harmony Supreme," they garnered another unenthusiastic notice in *Variety*: "Two of the sisters are grownup, while third is a precocious juve whose mild attempts at comedy add nothing to the offering."

It was clear that further training was needed, and in the autumn of 1933, Frances and Virginia were enrolled at Mrs. Lawlor's School for Professional Children. Most of the pupils, such as Gloria De Haven and Marjorie Belcher (who later became one half of the dancing team, Marge and Gower Champion), came from show-business families. Many of them were already movie veterans: Frankie Darro, Bonita Granville, Dawn O'Day (who changed her name the following year, when she appeared in *Anne of Green Gables*, to Anne Shirley) and Joe Yule, Jr. As "Mickey McGuire," Yule (who was two years Frances's senior) had starred in some fifty short comedies based on a comic-strip character of that name, but by the time the series ended, he had already changed his name to Mickey Rooney. "I remember the day I met this girl," Rooney recalled. "Frances Gumm—how could I forget a name like that? I went home that day and told my mom, 'I met a girl today named Frances Gumm . . . she was kinda sticky!' The joke didn't go over so well then, either." He also remembered that "she had more bounce to the ounce than everyone else in the school put together"—perhaps not surprisingly. She had seen these kids on screen, and now she was in their company.

While awaiting film offers, she continued to perform live with her sisters. During April 1934, the Gumm Sisters had been one of seven acts on the bill of the Orpheum, Los Angeles, and they went from that directly to Seattle for a month's booking on the Paramount circuit, which concluded in San Francisco with week-long dates, but had five one-night stands between, in smaller towns. On their return to Los Angeles, Frances joined the Gilmore Circus as one of twenty-three personnel—most of them radio personalities—who entertained between the animal acts and the clowns. The circus played week-long engagements in San Diego, Long Beach and then at the Shrine Auditorium in L.A., where Frances was joined by her two sisters in her number. She sang "Why Darkies Are Born" and "Dinah," in what one Long Beach newspaper called "a singularly grownup little voice." A week later, the Gumms appeared as the "Trio Musicale" at the Gilmore Stadium, when the Screen Actors Guild sponsored *Movie Star Frolics*, starring Eddie Cantor, who led a cast of 500 amidst Gilmore's animals.

The *Ledger-Gazette* had already announced that the Gumms would head for Chicago and New York in the summer, but New York was not in fact a serious option, since Frances would not have been old enough to appear on a stage there. Chicago had been holding a "Century of Progress" exposition, which was now in its second year. Ethel and the girls decided to visit, and managed to get a four-week booking at the Old Mexico Café, one of several restaurants housed within the fairground. As the salary was only $35 a week, Frank argued that it was not worth going that far for so little reward. Ethel insisted that it would provide an opportunity for the girls to visit the World's Fair. Furthermore, Chicago might offer additional engagements, and there were no film offers to keep them in Hollywood.

A two-week booking in Denver would help to pay the way, but this caused further friction between Frank and Ethel. The second week was a nightclub engagement, and Frank thought Frances too young to appear in such a place. (The Cocoanut Grove was also a nightclub of course, but a famous one, and so respectable.) Ethel was determined to have her way and pointed out that they were fortunate in getting two dates, with differing clienteles, in one city. Frank knew that he would eventually have to capitulate, but when he did so, he presented Ethel with several hundred dollars in traveler's checks, just in case she decided to change her mind when she saw the nightclub.

It turned out to be even less suitable than Frank had imagined, for it was a gambling joint, and had been raided the night before the Gumm Sisters were scheduled to appear. Although officially closed to the public by the police, it remained open for the owner and a handful of cronies. When the Gumms performed for them, the owner was so impressed that he happily paid their week's fee, and arranged a further booking for them in Colorado Springs.

With three weeks' fees in her pocket, Ethel congratulated herself that the trip had begun so well. In Chicago, they stayed in a good hotel, the St. Lawrence; but the Old Mexico Café was badly situated in the exposition grounds—according to Virginia: "out on an island and it didn't draw flies." This was a pity, since Ethel had changed the act so that Baby Gumm was its undisputed star, drawing it to a dramatic close as she sat on the piano in the manner of Helen Morgan and sang the Jerome Kern–P.G. Wodehouse–Oscar Hammerstein II song "Bill," which Morgan had made her own in *Show Boat*. Jack Cathcart, who was playing trumpet in the band, told Frances that she was "phenomenal. You know, you just put your arms round that audience."

Cathcart was more interested in putting his arms round Mary Jane, now almost nineteen. Ethel was horrified. Musicians, she argued, made the worst possible husbands, with irregular hours, frequent absences from home and the proximity of showgirls all affording opportunities for infidelity. For the moment, Mary Jane was prepared to toe the line.

Because of poor attendances, Ethel asked for an advance and was given their first week's fee. When, at the end of the second week, no money was forthcoming, she was not entirely surprised, but she had no alternative than to accept assurances that business would pick up the following week, when she would be paid in full. In the middle of that week, they arrived to find the café boarded up. Ethel went to remonstrate with the manager, who told her that if she carried her complaint any further she might wind up at the bottom of Lake Michigan.

The Gumms moved out of the St. Lawrence Hotel into a small apartment. Ethel considered returning to Frank and admitting that his instincts about the trip had been only too right. However, some show-business friends advised them to present themselves at the

Belmont, which on Friday nights provided a showcase for new acts. There was usually someone from the William Morris Agency in the audience, but this particular Friday proved exceptional, as Ethel discovered when she called at the Agency the following morning.

Ethel had been determined not to cash any of the checks Frank had given her, but was eventually obliged to change her mind. Virginia recalled a morning not long after their appearance at the Belmont, when they discovered that they had nothing for breakfast. Ethel, who was laboriously washing the girls' sequin-studded costumes, suddenly started to laugh, and couldn't stop: "We thought there was something terribly wrong with her. She'd just been told she was going to be thrown into Lake Michigan, and here she was slaving over these damn costumes—and now all we had was one egg and a half a loaf of moldy bread . . ." The ability to laugh in adversity was one trait that Garland inherited from her mother.

It was, however, time to go home. As they were packing, Jack Cathcart called to say that he had found work for them at the Oriental Theater, where George Jessel was topping the bill. Another vocal trio had been scheduled for the show but suddenly had to be replaced and so a fill-in act was needed at short notice. Through friends in the orchestra, Cathcart had alerted the management to the Gumms' potential, and to the fact that they were troupers who could be relied upon in an emergency.

They were scheduled to go on after the first act and, since they were neither billed nor in the program, Jessel had to introduce them. Whether unwittingly or by design, he got an easy laugh by over-emphasizing "Gumm." At the third house, he introduced them as "The Garland Sisters." According to Gumm family tradition, he had borrowed the name from a friend to whom he had been speaking that day, Robert Garland, who was the drama critic of the *New York World-Telegram*. Other sources suggest that he chose the name after telling the three girls that they were as pretty "as a garland of flowers." The most likely explanation, however, is that the featured attraction at the Oriental was *Twentieth Century*, in which an actress (played by Carole Lombard) changes her name from Lily Plotka to Lily Garland.

Such was the Garland Sisters' success that they were moved up to take the spot immediately preceding Jessel, and this resulted in their signing a contract with the William Morris Agency. Jessel had advised them to revise the act to capitalize on Frances's magnificent, mature voice, which needed no microphone. In consequence, the bright and breezy introduction was followed by "Bill," which in *Show Boat* is performed by Julie La Verne, former star of the *Cotton Blossom*, who has fallen on hard times and is wornout and alcoholic. Alone on stage except for Ethel at the piano, Frances began the song hidden by a shawl: the gradual revelation that the song was in fact being performed by a child was designed to increase the audience's enthusiasm. Jessel was to say later that, even at the age of twelve, Judy Garland sang like "a woman with a heart that had been hurt."

3

Metro-Goldwyn-Mayer

LEGEND HAS PERSISTED that George Jessel introduced Judy and her sisters at the Oriental as "The Glumm Sisters," and it was under this name that they were billed the following week, by both the local papers and *Variety*, in an engagement Ethel secured for them at the Marboro Theater across town. By the time they reached Detroit, the first stop on the lap home to Los Angeles in September 1934, they were officially the Garland Sisters, though their contracts were signed with their real names. Real troupers at last, they also played Milwaukee, Kansas City, and St. Joseph. The William Morris Agency made these bookings, and the girls performed with ever increasing confidence. Garland later claimed mischievously that none of the sisters ever let their mother know how much they missed their father, although by now even Ethel had to admit that they were showing signs of homesickness. They had been away for more than four months, the longest the family had ever been apart.

A few days after their return to a tearful reunion with Frank, the girls appeared on their first really important radio program, singing sweet harmonies when the Vincent Lopez Orchestra broadcast from the Beverly-Wilshire Hotel. They temporarily reverted to a billing as the Gumm Sisters, as that was the name under which they had gained some reputation in the area. A week later, they were one of the acts in the "prologue" to *The Count of Monte Carlo* at Grauman's Chinese, the most prestigious theater in town. *Variety* reviewed them in its column, "New Acts," in November:

> Hardly a new act, this trio of youngsters has been kicking around the coast for two years, but has just found itself. As a trio, it means nothing, but with the youngest, Frances, 13 [she was in fact twelve], featured, it hops into class entertainment; for if such a thing is possible, the girl is a combination of Helen Morgan and Fuzzy Knight. Possessing a voice that, without a p.a. system, is audible throughout a house as large as the Chinese, she handles ballads like a veteran, and gets every note and word over with a personality that hits audiences. For comedy she effects a pan like Knight and delivers her stuff in the same manner as the comic. Nothing slow about her on hot stuff and to top it, she hoofs. Other two sisters merely form a background. Kid, with or without her sisters, is ready for the east. Caught on several previous shows, including the 5,000 seat Shrine Auditorium here, she never failed to stop the show, her current engagement being no exception.

It was now clear that all Baby Gumm needed to get into the movies was a break.

This break was provided through the Gumms' old friend Marc Rabwin. He was now married to Marcella Bannett, who had been secretary to David O. Selznick since his tenure at RKO. Selznick had told the indignant Marcella that he knew a nice young Jewish doctor she ought to marry. Two years later, Marcella met Rabwin independently, and was taken to meet the Gumms when Frank was in Los Angeles. Rabwin had joked that he could not marry without their approval.

Selznick was now at Metro-Goldwyn-Mayer, the studio run by his father-in-law, the legendary Louis B. Mayer, and Marcella was his assistant. By common consent, M-G-M was the leader of the industry. This position had been held by Paramount until 1922, when the distributor Marcus Loew merged two manufacturing companies under his control: his own Metro Pictures and the recently acquired Goldwyn Pictures, founded in 1916 by Samuel Goldfish and Edgar Selwyn. Goldfish changed his name to "Goldwyn," but had recently been forced out of the company. The purchase of Goldwyn Pictures brought Loew a vast studio in Culver City and an impressive array of creative talent, but poor management had prevented him from realizing its potential. Together, the two companies would provide more and better pictures for the large circuit of theaters Loew had expensively assembled. To realize his plans, he needed a capable head of production, and so appointed Louis B. Mayer, whose own company became amalgamated with the other two.

Mayer had been born in Minsk in Russia, but in 1888, aged three, had emigrated to America with his parents, who settled in St. John, New Brunswick. He received little formal education and began his working life unhappily in his father's scrap-metal business. In 1904, he escaped the parental yoke to set himself up in scrap metal in Boston, and by 1907 he had earned enough money to buy a cinema. He gradually acquired other theaters and in 1914 started a film distribution company. He started his own production company in 1917 and arrived in Los Angeles the following year.

Mayer was one of the many Jewish immigrants attracted to the vital new film industry, which, like themselves, was struggling to find an image and an identity. More than any other studio, M-G-M was to create an image of America as a serene, patriotic, democratic and decent country, where values were centered upon church, school and a happy family life. These were qualities which attracted movie moguls, no matter how much their own personalities and endeavors failed to match the ideal. Mayer presented a pious figure, but those who knew and feared him recognized him as one of the most ruthless moguls of them all, a tyrannical egomaniac whose wrath was thought to be all but lethal.

His flair for business was undeniable, however, and this was complemented by Irving Thalberg, who displayed brilliant intuition as Chief Production Executive. Thalberg had started work in 1918 at Universal Studios, founded by Carl Laemmle, a family friend. He was only nineteen, but so impressed Laemmle that within a year he was put in charge of the whole studio operation. He resigned from Universal in 1923, after refusing to marry Laemmle's daughter, and so arrived at M-G-M.

Mayer and Thalberg cordially disliked each other, but the combination of their talents was a rewarding one for Loew and his stockholders. One of the first projects they worked on was the vastly expensive but unsatisfactory *Ben-Hur*, which they inherited from Goldwyn Pictures. They poured money into it to get it right, and its subsequent success at the box office led directly to a policy of spending as much as one third again as the other studios on production costs. Both men were ardent believers in the star-system, though only Thalberg understood what constituted star quality: he built the career of Norma Shearer, whom he married, and made a star of Myrna Loy, who until then had been a supporting player at other studios. Mayer, on the other hand, signed Greta Garbo by default; no one knew what to do with her until she blazed away in a vehicle Shearer had turned down. He considered Clark Gable a flash in the pan until the public told him otherwise. Fortunately for him, as at every other studio, luck played a large part in the discovery of stars.

M-G-M was seen as the grandest of the studios, boasting "more stars than there are in heaven." Not everyone agreed with this image: "a pompous studio run by a pompous man" was Barbara Stanwyck's dismissive comment. This grandeur brought financial rewards, as box-office returns confirmed, but Mayer was a sentimentalist as well as a businessman and wanted to present the studio as a happy family, with himself as benevolent paterfamilias. Publicists were put to work night and day to create this alternative image.

Whether or not this happy family had room for Baby Gumm was another matter. Neither Selznick nor Thalberg was making the sort of film in which the talents of a twelve-year-old could find a place— not even a twelve-year-old with a powerful singing voice. There was, however, another producer at the studio, Bernie Hyman, whose team included Joseph L. Mankiewicz, who at twenty-six was one of the youngest and most respected writers on the lot. Marc Rabwin had met Joe Mankiewicz in his bachelor days, while playing poker, and the two men had become very close friends. Mankiewicz had been best man at Rabwin's wedding, and he and his wife, Elizabeth, dined with Marc and Marcella at least once a week. The Rabwins now arranged for Mankiewicz to hear Frances sing at one of their parties. "She had been billed as 'the little girl with the leather lungs,' which will give you some idea of the mother," Mankiewicz later recalled. "[Her] voice was something incredible even then and you knew, as you sat there, that you were in the presence of something that wasn't going to come around again in a long time." He agreed with the Rabwins that Frances was a natural for the movies, and determined to approach Mayer himself. The route he chose to take was circuitous, because Mayer's taste in music lay almost exclusively in Viennese-style waltzes.

Like almost everyone else in the film industry, however, Mayer was mesmerized by the success of Shirley Temple. At the age of six, or seven (the studios usually subtracted a year), she sang, she danced, she acted and she did impersonations: Depression America—the whole world—was besotted with her smiling, innocent optimism. As a consequence, every studio was signing up juveniles in a way unknown since the heyday of Mary Pickford. At twelve, Frances hardly qualified for the "kiddie-stakes." Indeed, her age was against her, for she was no longer a cute little "Baby," but was entering adolescence, with all its attendant growing problems, which, in her case, included a tendency to puppy-fat. The famous gossip columnist Hedda Hopper accurately described her as "a roly poly girl with eyes like saucers." Furthermore, Mankiewicz had no faith in Mayer's ability to spot talent. He knew, however, that many of M-G-M's most successful stars had been brought there because of the enthusiasm of Ida Koverman, the studio's *éminence grise*. A cultured, imposing Scotswoman, Koverman had once been confidential secretary to Herbert Hoover. Now, all her considerable energies were concentrated upon M-G-M, where her official job was the head of Mayer's personal staff, a position which reflected the mogul's complete trust in her. It was also a position of power: pictures could be made or abandoned according to her sensibilities. She was generous in her sympathies, however, and close enough to the throne to become the conduit of ideas, schemes and projects. It was to this formidable woman that Mankiewicz brought word of Frances Gumm.

Koverman not only recognized that stars were of primary importance to M-G-M, but she also knew that Mankiewicz was not given to extravagant judgments. On the contrary, he was inclined to cynicism and caution in many movie matters. She agreed to check out the Gumm Sisters' act.

Meanwhile, the girls played their last engagement under that name in Long Beach in November 1934. A few days later, as the Garland Sisters, they began a week's booking at the Orpheum, Los Angeles, which had abandoned straight vaudeville for a program of films preceded by live performances. On December 7, the girls said farewell to Lancaster with a recital there, and the following evening were back in Los Angeles, supporting Fuzzy Knight in Irving Strauss's *Sunday Night Frolics* at the Wilshire-Ebell. It was the most important night of their career so far; sitting in the audience were Mankiewicz and Koverman. The latter was sufficiently impressed to go backstage to meet the Gumms. Although she was doubtful whether Mayer would take to Frances, whose galvanic way of singing was unlikely to be to his taste, she told Ethel that she would arrange an audition.

Inevitably, a dozen or so people have claimed credit for bringing Judy Garland to M-G-M, and it is impossible now to determine who auditioned her. There were in fact three auditions in all, one done *after* Garland had already signed a contract with the studio. For the first one, Ethel took Frances to the studio to sing for Koverman and at least one executive—most probably Benny Thau, who was in charge of the contract list, or Bill Grady, who was responsible for hiring talent. Frances sang, accompanied by her mother at the piano, but this was merely a formality. A screen test was arranged, at which Frances and Ethel were taken in hand by Mankiewicz, who introduced them to George Sidney, who was to direct it. Judy performed a version of the doggerel poem, "Casey at the Bat," and the test proved unpersuasive. Frances Marion, then a screenwriter at the studio, later claimed that Mayer told Koverman: "If you want her, sign her." This *sounds* authentic, for it meant nothing in M-G-M's scheme of things, with 5,000 people on the payroll, to have a youngster under contract at $150 a week. Furthermore, there would be no need to bother Central Casting if the studio needed a plump and rather plain little girl to play the younger sister in a family film. If the public taste for such movies evaporated, she could be dropped when the six-month option on her services expired. That Koverman did not sign Garland, however, suggests that Mayer himself listened to the child and, for once, was adamant against accepting Koverman's advice. Garland was frumpy, dumpy and had an intensity which he would have found unappealing. She was the wrong age to endear herself to a public that doted on Shirley Temple, and seemed unlikely to grow into a beauty.

Garland was in fact also auditioned by Temple's studio, 20th Century-Fox. The producer, Sol Wurtzel, was looking for someone to play an older friend or sister, or, more importantly, a rival to Jane Withers, the studio's threat to Shirley Temple, in order to keep the diminutive star's mother in line. This audition was also unsuccessful, with Wurtzel merely commenting: "She's got a big voice for so little a girl." That Garland possessed different appeals from those of her juvenile rivals can be gauged from a review of the latter's appearance in the *Vaudeville Frolics* at the Wilshire-Ebell in December 1934.

Not your smart, adult-aping prodigy is this girl, but a youngster who has the divine instinct to be herself on the stage, along with a talent for singing, a trick of rocking the spectator with rhythms and a capacity for putting emotion into her performance that suggests what Bernhardt must have been at her age. It isn't the cloying, heavy sentiment her elders so often strive for on the vaudeville stage, but simple, sincere feeling that reaches the heart.

Variety took up the cause when the Garland Sisters appeared at the Paramount Theater, Los Angeles, some weeks later: "Little Frances Garland seems to have been mysteriously overlooked by local talent scouts because this remarkable youngster has an amazing talent for both stage and pix shows." Mankiewicz told the Rabwins not to be disheartened by Frances's setback at M-G-M; he was sure that there would be a role for their protégée later.

Early in the New Year the Gumm Sisters' own fortunes in movies seemed to be brightening. With an aggressive mother behind her, Shirley Temple had already racked up more movie credits than her fellow Lawlor academy alumnae, the veteran juveniles Bonita Granville and Anne Shirley put together. In April, her rendition of a song in *Stand Up and Cheer* had made her a star overnight. The panacea for the Depression had been found. Consequently, every stage mother had been galvanized, and the studios were looking more fondly on the Lawlor pupils. The Gumm Sisters were signed by Universal for a film about the flamboyant Broadway impresario Florenz Ziegfeld. The title role would be played by William Powell, while Ziegfeld's widow, Billie Burke, would appear as herself. Since Ziegfeld employed such legendary figures as Will Rogers, Fanny Brice, Marilyn Miller, W.C. Fields and Helen Morgan, many of whom, like Burke, were expected to play themselves in the film, the Gumms would be in exalted company. Unfortunately, Universal was limping from one financial crisis to the next and decided it could not afford the high production costs necessary to make the film a worthy tribute to Ziegfeld. The project was sold to M-G-M, but the Gumm sisters were not.

However, in Lancaster, Frank Gumm's tenancy of the Valley Theater was drawing to a close with a great deal of bitterness on all sides. An open letter published in the *Ledger-Gazette* on January 3, 1935, complaining about those who sat through the programs twice or expected free admission, belied the smiling good nature with which he had always welcomed patrons. This ill humor was caused by financial problems. He had fallen badly behind in his payments to the theater's owner, Whitford Carter, who consequently refused to renew the lease. Marc Rabwin's brother, Harry, tried to negotiate, but only succeeded in getting the lease extended until the end of March. In his last notice in the paper, Frank said that if he could not renew, he would be "forced temporarily out of business," and in the same issue a news item about the theater changing hands noted that Frank had "not yet announced his future plans."

The bungalow in which he was living was little more than a shack and was in stark contrast to the comfort in which the rest of the family lived in Los Angeles, largely supported those days by the earnings of Frances. There must have been strong reasons for his remaining in Lancaster, one of which, according to Virginia, was that Ethel was seeking a divorce. She had distanced herself geographically from Frank for some time, but not from Will Gilmore, who had moved to Los Angeles in the early 1930s and continued his long-running affair with her. Whatever the case, with the loss of the Valley Theater, Frank was left penniless, and he went to Los Angeles to be reunited with his family. It may be that Ethel had not the heart to kick a man when he was down; she may also have thought that a divorce would fatally unsettle Frances, who seemed to be on the verge of a break-through in her career. Frances was certainly delighted to have her father back in the family home, even though that home was a far from happy one. The couple were reunited by changing their name to Garland—possibly because Frank needed a degree of disguise after one liaison too many, or one too indiscreet—but the rift between them was merely underlined when they lived under the same roof.

The family moved into a new house on Mariposa Avenue, near Griffith Park in central Los Angeles, and Frank got a job managing a movie theater in Lomita, a suburb some twenty miles away. There the Garland Sisters dutifully performed in June, two days before Frances's thirteenth birthday. They were, of course, far more accomplished than they had been when they had introduced themselves to Frank's patrons in Lancaster, but neither they nor their father were ever to become part of the Lomita community. Frank was a broken man, a forlorn figure whose ambitions had now left him. He sat by numbly as Ethel continued to pursue ways of furthering the girls' careers.

There were other changes of name to come: Mary Jane became Janey, then Susanne, finally settling on Suzy; while Virginia became first Jinny, then Jimmy. Not to be outdone, Frances searched around for a new name. She had been, variously, Baby Gumm, Frances Gumm, Gracie Gumm, Alice Gumm, Frances Gayne and Frances Garland—not to mention one of the "Little Lees." She became Judy after chancing upon the song of that name by Hoagy Carmichael.

With her mischievous sense of humor, she pounced on one (somewhat prophetic) line of the lyric: "If you think she's a saint and you find out she ain't, that's Judy." Within the family she was still called "Baby," but this so annoyed her that she now refused to respond unless addressed as "Judy."

The assumption of a new identity was a signal that Frances was about to become a separate entity: Judy Garland. It was as Judy Garland that she left Los Angeles to fulfill what Ethel called a "working vacation," a six-week engagement with her sisters at the Cal-Neva Lodge at Lake Tahoe. This venue was curiously situated, with the state line running through the middle of the dance floor. "If you sat on one side of the dining room you paid a sales tax," Garland recalled; "on the other side, you didn't. During our act Jimmy and I would wave to each other from different states." While this was going on, Suzy would be ogling the band's saxophone-player, Lee Cahn. Almost twenty, Suzy had decided that love and marriage were preferable to a life in show business. Ethel approved as little of Suzy's new love as she had of her involvement with Jack Cathcart, but the argument that marriage would split up the trio no longer counted for much: it had become clear that Judy was set to have a solo career. Suzy, too, wanted a different life: she knew that the end of the Garland Sisters would only mean the beginning for Judy. After a whirlwind courtship, Suzy and Cahn were married on August 15. Because Cahn also played lead violin and clarinet in the band, he could not be spared for a marriage back in Los Angeles among Suzy's friends. The Morris Agency had arranged for the Garland Sisters to appear in a film, due to be shot three days after the wedding.

The film was *La Fiesta de Santa Barbara*, a short designed to demonstrate to audiences the splendors of "three-strip Technicolor." The only producer to show a committed interest in the process since its invention in 1934 was Walt Disney, who used it for his Silly Symphony cartoons. The first feature in three-strip Technicolor, *Becky Sharp*, an adaptation of Thackeray's *Vanity Fair* produced by Pioneer, was being shown throughout the States when the Garland Sisters were engaged to appear in *La Fiesta*. They had been chosen for the project after Louis Lewyn had caught their act at the Paramount in May. Lewyn was an independent producer with a contract to provide M-G-M with novelty short subjects for the theaters controlled by Loew's, and *La Fiesta* was hardly a showcase for the Garlands' talents. The film consists mainly of song-and-dance on a set purporting to be the Santa Barbara mission at carnival time. The title-card names the stars as Warner Baxter and Ralph Forbes, but Buster Keaton has as much footage as they. Also appearing, as themselves, were a number of actors supposedly enjoying the festivities and no doubt curious to see how they photographed in color: Ida Lupino, Binnie Barnes, Leo Carillo, Shirley Ross, Harpo Marx, an unbilled Gary Cooper, and others. The Garlands are one of the specialty acts, singing "La Cucaracha" in appropriate costumes. Photographed throughout in profile, they seem rather stilted, with Judy appearing almost comically shorter than her sisters.

As the family were traveling from the Cal-Neva Lodge to keep this appointment, Suzy suddenly realized that she had left her hat-box behind. Suspecting that this was merely a ploy to bid yet another farewell to Cahn, Ethel was not inclined to turn round and drive back. A few minutes later, Suzy announced that she had also forgotten to pack their music. This, too, might have been a ruse, but, unlike hats, music could not easily be replaced. They turned back. Judy was sent to fetch the missing items, but was stopped by Bones Remer, manager and bouncer of the club. He said that he had some important visitors in the bar to whom he had been singing her praises. The visitors turned out to be the songwriters Harry Akst and Lew Brown (of the celebrated team, De Sylva, Brown and Henderson) and Al Rosen, an independent actors' agent. Actually, according to John Fricke's account, Akst and Rosen, having been bowled over by Judy at her last performance and, after the show, effected an introduction to her, asked her to sing Akst's famous song "Dinah" with himself, the composer, at the piano. A depressed Lew Brown, in the throes of a distressing divorce, had not been with them that evening and Garland's sudden and unexpected reappearance gave him the chance to hear her as well. That done, she dashed off and the family piled back into the car and set off once more for Los Angeles and *La Fiesta de Santa Barbara.*

The moment shooting on the film finished, Suzy flew back to Lake Tahoe for her wedding, and a few days later Lew Brown telephoned Ethel to tell her that he had arranged an audition for Judy at Columbia, where he and Akst were temporarily berthed, working on the musical arrangements for *The Music Goes 'Round,* a vehicle for Harry Richman. The composer of most of the film's songs was Victor Schertzinger, who also directed, so it is likely that he was one of several people there who heard Judy sing. None of them shared Brown's enthusiasm.

In spite of the encouraging press notices Judy had received, William Morris had only managed to negotiate a single, unimpressive movie offer. Brown thought that his friend Al Rosen could do better. Rosen was small-time, but he began working hard on his new client's behalf. During the spring and summer of 1935, Garland recalled:

> Al towed me all over southern California. I think I had an audition at every studio and everyone kept saying, "She isn't *any* age. She isn't a child wonder, and she isn't grown up" . . . A teenager was regarded as a menace to the industry and fit only to be stuffed into a barrel until she could be made into a glamour girl.

Whether or not her version of events was true, she was certainly going through a difficult period. Virtually overnight, she had become detached from the Garland Sisters and now had to stand or fall on her own merits. This was precisely the thing her father had hoped to avoid, and he seemed to have been right as she faced rejection after rejection. Worse still, Ethel and Rosen had taken an instant and enduring dislike to each other, and this resulted in a tug-of-war in which the agent attempted to prevent the mother being present at any of the auditions he set up.

Meanwhile, at M-G-M, Ida Koverman continued to root for Judy and kept in touch with the family. A second audition at the studio was arranged for September. Frances Marion claimed that Koverman had told Judy to learn to sing the Jewish lament "Eli Eli" in order to win Mayer over. Judy had indeed added the song to her repertoire, and it was certainly not one which fitted comfortably into the Garland Sisters' act. Although Rosen claimed credit for setting up the second audition, this seems unlikely, for he was of insufficient standing for any M-G-M executive to have taken his call or answered a letter. Any executive, that is, except Koverman, because of her particular interest in the child. She decided that the man to see was Sam Katz, a new arrival at the studio.

Katz had made his reputation building up a cinema chain, the Balaban and Katz circuit, so impressing Paramount that they made him president of one of their subsidiaries. In 1935, he had come to M-G-M as a production executive at the invitation of Nicholas Schenck, whom Marcus Loew had appointed head of both Loew's and M-G-M. With the departure of Selznick, Schenck had reorganized production at Culver City, under Mayer, with Thalberg responsible for a number of carefully selected films and Katz in charge of all other major productions.

In the autumn of 1935, M-G-M was previewing *Broadway Melody of 1936*, a film intended to demonstrate its faith in the dancer Eleanor Powell as a major star of the future. Koverman thought that the formula of such films, in which flimsy plots about putting on shows acted as showcases for assorted studio talents, might easily accommodate an unphotogenic but vocally gifted juvenile such as Judy Garland. Under the new regime, the next *Broadway Melody* film would be Katz's responsibility.

Without any warning, Judy was peremptorily summoned to the studio to see Katz. So urgent was this summons that she did not even have time to change, and arrived wearing slacks and sneakers, telling herself that she had been turned down so often that what she wore no longer mattered. She was accompanied by her father, since Ethel had been out at the time of the telephone call, playing the piano at a musical rehearsal for Joe Pasternak's new revue. Rosen was waiting for them at the studio gate.

Almost everyone except Ida Koverman has given an account of this audition, but one fact is certain: Frank, whom Garland remembered as being extremely nervous, played so badly that Koverman sent to the music department for Roger Edens, whom she had been instrumental in bringing to the studio. Edens was to become the greatest single influence on Judy Garland throughout her career. An elegant, handsome, bisexual Southerner, who spoke softly in a deep baritone voice, Edens was equally at home with Manhattan dilettantes and hard-nosed Hollywood professionals. Born Rollin Edens in Hillsboro, Texas, he had begun his career as an accompanist to some ballroom dancers. In 1930, at the age of twenty-five, he was in that legendary pit orchestra—whose other members included Red Nichols, Harry James, Tommy and Jimmy Dorsey, Gene Krupa, Jack Teagarden and Glenn Miller—for the Gershwins' *Girl Crazy*. The show's star, Ethel Merman, asked Edens to take over as her accompanist and vocal arranger when the previous incumbent had a heart attack. He wrote "Eadie Was a Lady" for her (which became one of her trademarked songs, and which he allowed to be credited to Richard Whiting because characteristically he had no interest in receiving credit) and, at her request, was hired by Sam Goldwyn to provide special material for her in the film *Kid Millions*.

While on the West Coast, Edens was engaged to provide arrangements for Rudy Vallee's weekly radio show. Among Vallee's guests was the Silent star Carmel Myers, who performed a dramatic recitative with musical accompaniment. Earlier in the year, Myers had told

Koverman, an old friend, that Edens could be a considerable asset at M-G-M. Koverman had passed on the recommendation to the studio's resident lyricist, Arthur Freed, who was to be another major figure in Judy Garland's life. After hearing some of Edens's arrangements, Freed realized that his own songs would sound better after this talented young man had been to work on them. He invited Edens to join the studio as Musical Supervisor.

At Judy's audition, Koverman realized that, with Frank's nervous accompaniment, the young singer was impressing no one. When Edens took over, things improved considerably. "Can you change key?" Judy asked him. "Can you?" he replied. She claimed that word was sent to Mayer, who arrived, listened to her sing, and said merely: "Very nice. Thank you very much." Frank, who thought this very offhand, complained: "This is ridiculous. My child is tired." After perfunctory goodbyes, they left the studio. "Daddy and I thought it was a great big nothing," Garland recalled.

It is possible that Judy had mistaken another executive for Mayer, and there certainly exist alternative versions of the story. In his account, Al Rosen maintained that he had arranged for Katz to see the girl at a time he knew Mayer would be absent from the studio. He also said that Katz and Jack Robbins, who was in charge of the studio's music publishing companies, were responsible for her being offered a contract. He insisted that Mayer was furious to find Garland on the payroll when he returned to the studio, but this is in keeping with the mythology: Mayer was an ogre, and Garland had to be sneaked in behind his back.

One fact is clear: the audition was on September 13, 1935, Garland signed the contract on September 27, and it was ratified by the Superior Court on October 13. Judy was very proud of herself and the family was delighted. It was the first time her father had been involved in any business arrangement on her behalf, and he made light of it when writing to friends in Lancaster, mentioning the triumph only in passing: "Babe got her seven year contract with M-G-M and it started October 1 at $100 a week . . . a very attractive deal. Of course, it's all six months' options and she has to make good or they have the privilege of letting her go . . ."

As a girl who had been accustomed to having audiences clapping and cheering for as long as she could remember, this caveat did not worry Garland. Her principal feeling was one of great excitement at being on the same lot as her screen idols. The studio covered 117 acres and had twenty-three soundstages, more than any other studio could boast. They may have looked like barns from the outside and may have reeked of sawdust, but inside was a magical, make-believe world of palaces, ballrooms, opera houses and temples. There was a station on the back lot, as well as a lake, a harbor, city street, farmhouses and Tarzan's jungle.

M-G-M canceled the forthcoming appearance in Pasadena Ethel had arranged for Judy, and lost little time in introducing her on the air as the studio's newest contract player. On October 26, she appeared on NBC's Saturday evening variety show, *The Shell Chateau Hour*, usually hosted by Al Jolson. During his absences, Wallace Beery, one of M-G-M's biggest stars, substituted. One of those in the audience was Jackie Cooper, his youthful co-star in several films, including *The Champ* (1931), a lachrymose boxing melodrama, and the 1934 version of R.L. Stevenson's *Treasure Island*. About the time of the earlier film, Beery had developed an image as a lovable rogue, but his off-screen behavior was closer to that of the vicious villain he had just played in *China Seas*. It suited the studio to showcase him with two of M-G-M's children, and photographs taken of the broadcast show Berry looking benevolent, Cooper (who knew of Beery's rogue moods) looking suspicious, and Garland looking starstruck.

Beery brought Garland on for the "opportunity spot," introducing her as "so doggone good I really can't believe it," and prophesying that she was "going to be the sensation of pictures." When he asked her what she wanted to be when she became "a great big girl," she replied: "I want to be a singer, Mr. Beery, and I'd like to act, too." She eventually launched into "Broadway Rhythm," a song written by Nacio Herb Brown and Arthur Freed for the spectacular finale of the *Broadway Melody* film then on release. Its performance on the show would help sell copies of the sheet music, which could only please its composers and the M-G-M subsidiary which published it. It was almost certainly chosen for Garland by Roger Edens, who had already been assigned to work with her for two hours each day, and knew that she was the perfect interpreter. Now best known from Gene Kelly's version in *Singin' in the Rain* (1952), it is a song, as Ethan Mordden recently wrote, "about the intoxicating power of American show biz." It ends with the exhortation "Everybody sing and dance," and Garland puts more joy into this line, and gets more joy from it, than any other singer, before or since.

Just listening to this one song, one understands why, thirty years later, Edens would say of Garland: "She was the biggest thing to happen to the M-G-M musical." Pupil and teacher took to each other at once. Edens knew that her voice was a wonderful instrument—"as clear as a gold trumpet," as Hedda Hopper described it; he also knew that, like Ethel Merman's, it was loud, and realized that she must learn to use it with discretion. He remembered her as:

Bright. Cheerful. So anxious to please. So eager to work. Couldn't read music, but she didn't have to. Her talent was inborn. She had the perfect anatomy for a singer, built round a super muscle of a diaphragm. She had a wonderful memory. What could I teach her? How to sing a lyric? How to get the meaning across?

Garland recognized that Edens's knowledge of music was infinitely wider than her mother's, and she trusted and listened to him from their first lesson. In their different ways, they adored each other.

Alongside her sessions with Edens, Garland was taking lessons in acting, dancing, voice projection and public deportment. Presenting some difficulties were her face, hair and figure. Her anatomy may have been perfect for a singer, but it did not look well on camera. At just under five feet, she was small, and she suffered curvature of the spine. Indeed, her spine was so short that, as she once put it, her legs appeared to begin at her shoulders. Her teeth were uneven and needed to be capped, and a little putty would give her a more photogenic nose. The first stills issued by M-G-M show a reasonably attractive child.

Meanwhile, the publicity department was conferring with Ethel and Judy herself as to how to describe her previous life and career for the fan magazines. It was here that many of the myths about Garland's background and childhood were first created.

The one thing she did not do at M-G-M was make movies. She was, however, invited back on the radio by the producers of *Shell Chateau* on November 16. She was to perform "Zing! Went the Strings of My Heart," and was told to sing especially nicely for Daddy since, earlier in the day, Frank had gone into the hospital. He had awoken at four in the morning to find that his old ear infection had returned. By noon, his condition had deteriorated so seriously that he was taken to the Cedars of Lebanon Hospital, where Marc Rabwin was now a consultant. Rabwin telephoned Judy at the studio to tell her that he had managed to install a radio at Frank's bedside.

The following day, when Judy awoke, Ethel was already at the hospital. Grandmother Milne took Judy and Jimmy to join her, where they learned from Rabwin that Frank's condition was serious. He had developed spinal meningitis, and died at three in the afternoon. He was forty-nine. It was Ethel's birthday and Frank had arranged a surprise party. To the family's horror, guests were arriving from as far away as Grand Rapids. Devastated by shock and grief, they hardly knew what to say to them.

"I think my father's death was the most horrible thing that ever happened in my life," Garland said in the 1960s.

> I can say that now, because I'm more secure than I was then. But the terrible thing about it was that I wasn't able to cry at my father's funeral. I was ashamed that I couldn't cry, so I feigned it. But I just couldn't cry for eight days, and then I locked myself in a bathroom and cried for fourteen hours. I wasn't close to my father, but I wanted to be all my life. He had a funny sense of humor, and he laughed all the time—good and loud, like I do.

What she undoubtedly meant was that she was not as close as she would like to have been. Work had kept them apart, and although she was always his "baby," she was not the son, the buddy he really wanted. On his way to the hospital, Frank had picked up a blanket belonging to Judy to protect his ear. This blanket became one of her most precious possessions and she never forgave her mother when Ethel disposed of it without telling her. The suddenness of Frank's death was a blow from which Judy took a long time to recover. It was as if she was being punished for the happiness of getting a studio contract. She knew that her parents were not happy together, but she was—as Frank had been until recently—an optimist, and had set much store on the resumption of family life.

Personal tragedy could not stand in the way of her career, however. Victor Young, the leader of the orchestra on *Shell Chateau*, realized that she was a natural for the recording studios and recommended her to officials at Decca. On November 27, ten days after her father's death, she cut two sides, "No Other One" and "All's Well"; but in the event, the company decided not to release them.

Frank's death was far less disruptive for a youngster reporting each day to a Hollywood studio than it might have been for a normal child. "It's hard to explain what it's like to have a film corporation for a parent," Garland said later, "but when my father died, Metro-Goldwyn-Mayer more or less adopted me." She went from working with her mother and her sisters to working with a new "family"—and there were two old friends also taking lessons in the studio schoolroom:

Donald O'Connor, who had come backstage to meet her when she was performing at the Golden Gate Theater in 1933, and Mickey Rooney. O'Connor would not stay there much longer, but Rooney was already a veteran of the studios. "Watching Mickey," she said, "I was able to get an idea of the life I had let myself in for."

For some time yet, that life would not include appearing before the motion-picture cameras, and her self-confidence would be badly battered over the next year. M-G-M was producing feature films at a rate of almost one a week, including many intended for the lower half of double-bills, but not one of the forty-seven released by Loew's Inc. in 1936 contained an appearance by Judy Garland. Within two months of signing her contract she was rather upset to learn in December that the studio signed another girl of the same age for a film about the life of the opera singer Ernestine Schumann-Heink. The singer would be playing herself, and the new girl, Edna Mae Durbin, would play her as a child. As a singer, Durbin had the same "defect" (as the industry saw it) as Garland: her voice was very mature for her age. (It was for this reason that she would lose the opportunity to provide the singing voice for Snow White in Disney's 1937 animated feature.) She, too, had been brought to M-G-M by her agent and had sung for an entire afternoon in front of an audience of executives, including Sam Katz, who was so taken with her that he had her sing over the telephone to Mayer, who was in New York.

At some point, early in 1936, the two girls were brought together to make a test, described by Garland as "sort of jazz versus opera." She played an American, with "an apple in my hand and a dirty face," while Durbin played a European Princess ("of Transylvania," Garland later claimed). Jack Chertok, who was in charge of M-G-M's short subjects, was struck by the rapport between the girls, as was Koverman.

According to Hollywood legend, all Koverman's efforts were in vain. It had been decided that M-G-M did not have room for two young singers, and when Mayer was shown the film, he said: "Drop the fat one." It was Durbin, however, who left the studio. Schumann-Heink fell ill, the film about her life was canceled, and Durbin's option was not renewed.

Pictures taken during Durbin's six months with the studio show her in the schoolroom (an institution required by law, but also one publicists were happy to exploit) and the commissary (or canteen), with Garland, Rooney, Peggy Ryan, Freddie Bartholomew and Jackie Cooper. Bartholomew and Cooper were stars already, and Rooney was constantly at work. Of the three girls, Durbin, with her radiant smile, seems to have offered the most obvious star material, but her name never featured in the list of contract players supplied to the fan magazines; nor did Ryan's. Garland's name joined those of the three boys in July. As an avid reader of such publications, she was very excited to be on the same page as Claudette Colbert, Carole Lombard, Marlene Dietrich, Bing Crosby, James Cagney, Bette Davis and Edward G. Robinson. Of M-G-M's outstanding lineup, no fewer than 89 stars were listed out of the 250 contractees. Admittedly, not all of these were of the first rank. The list was arranged alphabetically, and Judy Garland was positioned between Greta Garbo and Igor Gorin, who was then a star of the Metropolitan Opera. Other forgotten names include Jean Chatburn, Mamo Clark and John Buckler, but the majority of the eighty-nine were household names.

Once Durbin had gone, Garland felt more secure, for, six months earlier, Sam Katz had already chosen a specific picture to launch her career. The film was *This Time It's Love*, in which she would appear opposite the actor-dancer Buddy Ebsen. The film's stars were to be Jessie Matthews, imported from Britain, and Robert Montgomery. When Matthews proved unavailable (her employers, Gaumont-British, feared that she might be overwhelmed by a sturdy, American, all-star cast), the script was rewritten for Eleanor Powell. It gradually evolved into another *Broadway Melody* film—the exact format Koverman had envisaged for her protégée. It was then decided that the film should be called *Born to Dance* in order to highlight Powell's tapping skills; Montgomery was dropped. The score was being written by Cole Porter, his first original one for a movie since 1929, when he had composed three songs for Gertrude Lawrence in *The Battle of Paris*. On March 10, Porter wrote in his diary: "We discussed casting, and I heard to my great joy that the picture will be played by Allan Jones opposite Eleanor Powell, Sid Silvers opposite Una Merkel, Buddy Ebsen opposite Judy Garland, and Frances Langford to play the jilted society girl." This was not, however, the final casting, and while Porter admired Garland enough to invite her to sing at his parties, he was unable to save her role in the picture. The script was once more reconstructed: the society girl became a Broadway star who brought similar complications to the plot. Virginia Bruce played this role, and the ousted Frances Langford displaced Garland as Ebsen's partner.

Garland was almost certainly written out of the picture because Katz thought her hoydenish quality would contrast too strongly with the other talents on show, all of which were established ones. As compensation for this disappointment, Koverman sent Garland to New York for "a working birthday holiday," which included another recording session for Decca, which had finally made up its collective mind that it wanted her. On June 12, 1936, she recorded "Swing, Mr. Charlie" and "Stomping at the Savoy" with Bob Crosby's Orchestra. These were wise choices: they were not novelty songs, like those sung by Shirley Temple, nor optimistic ballads of the kind caroled by the boy soprano Bobby Breen, who had just made his movie debut at RKO. Garland had an adult voice and a different solution was needed. Her earlier impersonations demonstrated that she could have performed comic ditties, as Fanny Brice did, or torch songs, like Helen Morgan, but what Decca chose for her were two up-tempo swing numbers. She handled them with characteristic verve, sounding like someone who might be any age between fifteen and fifty. Unfortunately, this was before the age of big spending by teenagers and the record achieved only modest sales. It would be a year before she returned to the Decca studios.

Koverman also arranged for Garland to sing on WHN, the Manhattan radio station owned by M-G-M: she hoped that the studio's New York executives would prove more receptive than those in Hollywood. Jesse Martin, head of WHN's Artists' Bureau, was wildly enthusiastic and was convinced that Garland would become a big star. He played unofficial host to Ethel and Judy, taking them to Broadway shows and Coney Island. With Martin's praises ringing in her ears, Garland had every reason to hope that there would be a film role awaiting her when she returned to Los Angeles.

There was; Ida Koverman had come up with a scheme to initiate Judy's debut. She had successfully lobbied Jack Chertok to come up with a short, using the title *Every Sunday*, to which Mayer had taken a liking. She suggested that it should feature the two girls, and asked him to find a song for Garland that would win over Mayer. Chertok hired Con Conrad and Herb Magidson, who had written "The Continental" for Fred Astaire and Ginger Rogers in RKO's *The Gay Divorcee*. The song had won an Oscar in 1934 and the composers did not come cheap, but they came up with a number for Garland called "Americana." If her rendering of it would not appeal to Mayer, its subject matter surely would.

Chertok set his writers to work on a story about two friends who are so appalled by the poor attendances at recitals given by a band in the park every Sunday that they canvass the town to drum up an audience to attend the weekly concert. When no one turns up, they jump on the bandstand, where one (Durbin) sings "classical" and the other (Garland) sings "hot." The seats fill and the crowd cheers after the girls sing a duet in their respective styles.

At its one-reel length, *Every Sunday* is described on the credits as "A Tabloid Musical." The two youngsters seem relaxed, happy and exactly what Hollywood strove to persuade the public Hollywood children were: paragons of sweetness and light, niceness and talent. They are called simply "Edna" and "Judy." Prerecorded in the last days of June, shooting was completed in the first days of July; by then Durbin's option had been dropped and she had gone to Universal. So the credits give Durbin the name under which she became internationally famous. Deanna.

For months there had been a steady, if sporadic campaign in the press and industrial journals to get M-G-M to make something of Garland's evident talents. There had been several offers from other studios, but M-G-M remained adamant in keeping her to themselves. Ever since the previous November roles had been assigned to her, but these hadn't actually come to pass. By the time *Every Sunday* was completed they realized they had to get Garland before the great movie public. So when someone from 20th Century-Fox approached them, perhaps prompted by Roger Edens, who equally despaired of Garland's enforced idleness, and made an offer to feature her in a production, they readily agreed. The film was *Pigskin Parade*, one of a myriad of college comedies, an assembly-line product of medium budget designed to be paired with a similarly modest movie. Garland's role was created specially for her, and Sidney Mitchell and Lew Pollack, who had written the score, subsequently penned three songs tailored to her virtually unique "belting" style. "It's a triple treat of girls, music and laughter," ran the tag in the ads for *Pigskin Parade*. The featured players were listed as "Stuart Erwin, Johnny Downs, Arline Judge, Betty Grable, Patsy Kelly, Jack Haley, The Yacht Club Boys, Dixie Dunbar, Tony Martin and Judy Garland": in other words, Garland stood tenth in an unspectacular lineup. Erwin was the only one who might possibly be considered of star status at that time, and if there is a common element in these chiefly secondary players it is that most of them were under long-term contracts to one or the other of the studios, including 20th Century-Fox.

The film was made to a common formula for musicals in those days: heavily dependent on vaudeville, it was designed to accommodate specialty acts and spots for pretty girls. *Pigskin Parade* follows the fortunes of some kids from a hayseed college who get to play in a big game against Yale, and although amiable enough, it looks as though it were rapidly thrown together. Garland is first seen in braids, barefoot and wearing a shapeless gingham dress. "J'all stop for melons?," she asks in an absurdly strong hick accent. She looks like the Judy Garland of whom the M-G-M makeup department had despaired. When she gets to sing at the college hop, however, she has been smartened up, with puff sleeves and a flower in her hair. "The Balboa" is supposed to be a new dance craze, and given the attack with which Garland sings it, it is no wonder that the collegians whip into it with such frenzy. Thereafter, her role is irrelevant to the plot, and her two other songs—"The Texas Tornado" and "It's Love I'm After"—are blatant show stoppers making the most of her rousing vocal talents.

She was noticed favorably in the *New York Times* as "cute, not too pretty, but a pleasingly fetching personality, who certainly knows how to sell a pop." Critics found the film fun and several singled out Garland's performance. She recalled attending a preview with her mother: "I thought I'd look as beautiful as Garbo or Crawford—that makeup and photography would automatically make me glamorous. Then I saw myself on the screen. It was the most awful moment of my life. My freckles stood out. I was *fat*. And my acting was terrible." She told her mother that she would have to return to vaudeville.

In August, however, she made her only radio broadcast of 1936, once again on *The Shell Chateau Hour* with Wallace Beery. She sang "After You've Gone," one of the songs which would become inseparably associated with her. Otherwise, she merely languished at M-G-M. Her home may have been listed only just below those of Clark Gable and Greta Garbo in *Photoplay*'s "Addresses of the Stars," but she seemed to have done little to earn this accolade. At the end of the year, for the third year running, the list of stars voted by exhibitors as the top-ten box-office draws was headed by seven-year-old Shirley Temple. Even with being cast for a role in *Broadway Melody of 1937* and committed to several radio appearances, Judy Garland at fourteen had a lot of catching up to do.

4

···◈◈◈◈◈···

Dear Mr. Gable

In July 1936, M-G-M was determined to retain Garland exclusively for itself. Having just assigned Garland to Fox for her first supporting role in a feature film, an offer for her services came from Joe Pasternak, a producer at Universal. The film, *Three Smart Girls*, a story about parents on the brink of divorce who are reunited by their three enterprising daughters, was just about to go into production. This was a musical featuring reliable but second-string attractions from many sources. The film's producer, Pasternak, had seen the test film that Garland and Durbin had made before *Every Sunday* and, consequently, had the role of the youngest daughter fashioned for Garland. Accordingly, he made overtures to Metro only to be told that Garland was not available, but that Durbin was.

The company casting director at Universal was Rufus LeMaire, recently poached from M-G-M. He had borrowed the original Durbin-Garland test and showed it to Pasternak, insisting that Durbin was not only right for the role in *Three Smart Girls*, but that she possessed all the qualities to be the big star Universal urgently needed. Pasternak agreed, and instructed the director, Henry Koster, to get a more spirited performance from Durbin than her gentle personality promised. However, since her singing style was very different to that of Garland, a new set of songs would be required.

When *Three Smart Girls* was released in January 1937, Durbin was acclaimed by the press and greeted by the public in such a way as to guarantee stardom—a prospect which exacerbated Garland's frustration. She cried all night after seeing the film. It was one thing, when she and Durbin were colleagues and co-workers, to feel themselves to be privileged to be on the same lot as their idols, whom they might one day join as star attractions; it was another to find that Durbin was as important to Universal as Shearer or Garbo was to Metro. It was not even as if she had the training and experience in vaudeville that Garland had. It seemed to Garland that M-G-M denied her the applause of live audiences and gave her nothing in return.

The following morning, Ethel telephoned Ida Koverman who, she felt, was the only one who could comfort her daughter. When Judy arrived in Koverman's office, she began crying again. "I've been in show business ten years, and Deanna's starred in a picture and I'm nothing." Koverman hoped that if Mayer, who was known to use tears himself to get his own way, saw Judy crying, he might relent and order someone to find the child a role in a movie. He had more important matters on his mind, however, of which the most urgent was to discover how M-G-M had managed to let the brightest new star in town slip through its fingers. Durbin's voice and the type of songs she sang were exactly to Mayer's taste. He had heard her on the *Eddie Cantor Show*, which made her nationally famous, and had been annoyed at losing her. On screen Durbin was even more magical than on the radio. There had been an outside chance that Universal would have been prepared to sell her, since the studio's finances were still in a parlous state; but, as he knew instinctively, *Three Smart Girls* was almost certain to change that.

While audiences in the big cities were flocking to see Durbin, M-G-M was reveling in the box-office returns of *Born to Dance*, from which Garland had been so unceremoniously dropped. At 20th Century-Fox, a large percentage of the studio's advertising budget was being spent on *One in a Million*, a big musical starring the skater Sonja Henie, who could not sing a note. Fox was very happy to let *Pigskin Parade* skip along brightly, but that was not going to make Garland into a star. Despite her repugnance on seeing herself in this film, she felt confident that the makeup magicians at Metro could do what had not been achieved at Fox. Indeed, they had made her look as attractive as Durbin in *Every Sunday*. Earlier in the month, Judy had such a well-received appearance on *Jack Oakie's College*, the comic's new radio series on CBS, that she was booked to appear throughout the rest of the season. So it was not as if she was entirely a back number. She had been relieved when her option had been picked up at the end of September, but as far as she could see, M-G-M had no plans for her, despite the overwhelming evidence provided by Durbin that the public would flock to see a singing teenager. Koverman continued to badger Mayer on Garland's behalf, and, as Frances Marion put it: "When a clever woman plots against a clever man, her only hope is to attack through his weakness." She finally got him to listen to Garland singing "Eli Eli" and his response was just what she had hoped for: he promised Garland that she would never leave the studio—provided that she did exactly as she was told, which meant remaining on a strict diet. From the start, the studio executives had been advised that Garland simply did not have the shape for stardom. She undoubtedly had a voice, she had good eyes, and her face photographed pleasantly. When the chance finally came for Garland to appear before the movie cameras, however, she would have to be slim. Preparation for stardom meant, as she put it, being "half-starved all the time."

If M-G-M had not yet presented Judy to the vast movie-going public, it was doing its best to draw attention to her in every other way possible. It was now two years since Koverman had first decided that Garland had star quality, and fifteen months since she had arrived at the studio. However, the sequence of events which began to propel Judy Garland to stardom was about to begin.

One of Koverman's jobs was to keep or make the stars happy on behalf of Mayer, and this included organizing the parties which helped to maintain M-G-M's image as the most relaxed and luxurious of the studios. In effect, it needed only a memo to Howard Strickling, head of publicity, to ensure that his staff had photographers on hand for such occasions. A surprise party was being planned for Clark Gable, to take place on the set of *Parnell*, which he was currently making with Myrna Loy. It was to mark the star's thirty-sixth birthday on February 1—and several people were determined to turn the occasion to Garland's benefit. Koverman asked Arthur Freed to produce a musical entertainment, knowing he would turn to Roger Edens, on whose taste and intelligence he relied so often and to such good purpose. Freed and Edens decided that Garland should serenade Gable, after which Mickey Rooney would do an impersonation of him.

Garland herself favored "Drums in My Heart," which Edens had arranged for Ethel Merman's nightclub act. She knew she could sing it, and was not inclined to agree that it was unsuitable for a youngster of her age. Edens insisted that if she went on the set as a junior Merman—or Helen Morgan or Sophie Tucker—she might at best land herself a guest spot in a movie. He had worked with her long enough to know that she would be shown to better advantage playing herself. He wanted to reveal her as a yearning, day-dreaming adolescent of the sort likely to captivate Mayer, who had so admired Deanna Durbin's rendering of "Someone to Care for Me" in *Three Smart Girls*.

There was no difficulty in deciding what she should sing to Gable. In her spot on the Rudy Vallee show, Carmel Myers had recently performed a sketch about meeting Clark Gable—or, rather, dreaming that she did. "Let's Fall in Love," an old Harold Arlen song, was adapted for the show, with Myers providing new lyrics, to which Edens had set the music. At the party, Garland would sing the original song to a photograph of Gable, and deliver a monologue, written by Edens, portraying the singer as a besotted fan. And so "Dear Mr. Gable" came into being. The title was something of an in-joke, for almost everyone in the studio knew that Gable was then being subjected to a series of letters, which began with those innocent words, from a woman claiming that he was the father of her child.

Garland had no trouble with the song, for even with its original lyric it clearly expressed what so many of Gable's fans felt about him. As written, it is a ballad about someone who has fallen in love despite herself, but Garland made this confession into a torch song. Its poignancy is underlined by the monologue which follows, which also emphasized another of Garland's great qualities, her self-deprecating humor:

. . . Then one time I saw you in a picture with Joan Crawford, and I had to cry a little, 'cause you loved her *so* much and you couldn't have her—not till the end of the picture, anyway. And then one time I saw you in person—you were going to the Cocoanut Grove one night, and I was standing there, when you got out of your car, and you almost knocked me down. Oh, but it wasn't your fault—no—I was in the way, but you looked at me and you smiled—yeah, you smiled right at me, as if you meant it—and I cried all the way home. Just 'cause you smiled at me for being in your way . . .

The reception was everything Edens, Koverman and Garland had hoped for, with some tears, much applause and a big hug from Gable for the young girl. Rooney knew he could not top it, so he abandoned the plan to do his impersonation. Edens had provided Garland with her first step toward legend.

On February 23, Garland reprised the routine on Jack Oakie's radio show with such success that she was invited to become a regular—which she did until the end of May, singing solos, the occasional duet and chatting. This brought her to a wide audience and gave her the sort of exposure which delighted studio executives. She sang "Dear Mr. Gable" again in May at a convention of M-G-M exhibitors, an annual event promoting the studio's current and future attractions, hosted on the Culver City lot. Gable appeared at the end to thank her, and the guests enthusiastically cheered both the studio's biggest star and its newest one. The reception on these three occasions left no doubt that Garland would be an asset to the studio, but it was only then, after the exhibitors assured the studio that they wanted to see the youngster on screen, that a decision was taken about her future.

By then, Jack Cummings had been instructed to have her sing "Dear Mr. Gable" in *Broadway Melody of 1937* (soon to be retitled *Broadway Melody of 1938*), an ironic development, since he had earlier failed to use her in the series. She was also to have a speaking role and sing three other songs: but not much else, because the script was already written and the sets ready. Even if she had been slotted into the picture earlier on, it is quite evident that her role in the film is an afterthought. When the running time ran overlength, Cummings compensated the loss of half of the four planned-for songs by having her sing over the opening credits, a practice rare at this time, and all the more surprising since she is only eighth on the cast list. This gain was offset by the loss of the song she should have sung in the finale, which was cut—possibly because it was felt her vibrancy might over-shadow Eleanor Powell, the film's rather antiseptic star. Garland plays the daughter of Sophie Tucker, the landlady of a theatrical boarding-house—a stagestruck kid described by Tucker as "born in a dressing-room, raised in a wardrobe trunk." She sings "Dear Mr. Gable" to photographs of him in her room, but her only other solo is "Everybody Sing," which she performs at an audition in a producer's office. She exhorts those listening to join in, and this proves an irresistible invitation. It is a snappy, jazzy number, and it prompted the advertisements to describe Garland as "the sensational little hot-singing discovery!" In the bang-up finale, she dances a few steps with Buddy Ebsen, who, twice her age and dwarfing her in white tie and tails, makes her look a trifle absurd in her white organdy frills and ankle socks. It is as if, at the last moment, she had been allowed to stay up to entertain at a grown-up's party.

As was customary, the studio sneak-previewed the film. With executives and creative personnel in attendance, it was shown at a cinema in a Los Angeles suburb in order to gauge audience reaction. The audiences on these occasions were well aware of expectations and liable to roar approval during the credits or after the end titles. Even more important to the studio were the cards on which spectators commented on the film itself. Fortunately they ignored the organdy frills: they only remembered the girl singing wistfully to Clark Gable, and they didn't care what age she was.

Their feelings were echoed by the press. "A girl named Judy Garland . . . does a heart-rending song about her unrequited love for Clark Gable, which the audience seemed to like," wrote Marguerite Tazelaar in the *New York Herald Tribune*, while Bosley Crowther in the *New York Times* noted the "amazing precocity of Judy Garland, Metro's answer to Deanna Durbin . . . Miss Garland particularly has a long tour de force in which she addresses lyrical apostrophes to a picture of Clark Gable. The idea and words are almost painfully silly— yet Judy . . . puts it over—in fact with a bang." The review in the *Hollywood Reporter* seemed something of a rebuke to M-G-M executives: "The sensational work of young Judy Garland causes wonder as to why she has been kept under wraps these many months. She sings two numbers that are show stoppers, and does a dance with Buddy Ebsen. Hers is a distinctive personality well worth careful promotion." In Britain, the reaction was equally enthusiastic. "Judy Garland, youngest member of the cast, can best be described as a 'Tucker in her Teens,' her torch singing being unquestionably first-rate," commented *Film Weekly's* critic. "Even a rather silly song designed to boost Gable, takes on touching pathos when she puts it over. Obviously a 'find' of whom more is going to be heard." *Photoplay* listed her among its dozen best performances of the month.

While Garland must have been delighted by such accolades, she would also have noted that another performance singled out by *Photoplay* was Deanna Durbin's in *100 Men and a Girl*, her second picture and an even greater personal triumph than her first; while beaming from the cover of that particular issue of the magazine was Shirley Temple, by now something of a veteran. Garland had been on the cover of the August issue of *Modern Movies*, but that was not quite in the same class as *Photoplay*. Still, the rush was on: the disappointment she may have felt when *Pigskin Parade* had not made her a star was now firmly in the past. Other pictures of Garland had begun appearing in the fan magazines, most memorably one showing Gable presenting her with a charm bracelet on her birthday inscribed "To Judy Garland, my favorite actress, Sincerely, Clark Gable." His sincerity was confirmed by an apparent knowledge of her life which came as no surprise to the most avid and diligent of the studio's publicists: the charms included not only a theater trunk, but wedding rings with her sisters' names on them and replicas of the seals of Grand Rapids and Murfreesboro.

As well as studying at school and with Roger Edens, she was required to appear regularly for portrait sessions in the Gallery, where publicity stills were taken. The considerable all that M-G-M could do to create a star persona had finally been put into motion. She also received an invitation to return to Decca, which issued "Dear Mr. Gable" and "Everybody Sing," with success. On August 20, 1937, the *Hollywood Reporter* carried an advertisement thanking Sam Katz, Jack Cummings and Roger Edens on her behalf. At the end of the year, M-G-M reciprocated by placing an ad in *Variety*. Beneath an hour-glass is the boast: "It's a little early to predict but here's a prophecy for 1938!" Beneath, between the words "Judy Garland" and "Stardom!" in huge letters, Garland leans out from a star shape.

The studio needed some new stars. Only Gable, Robert Taylor and the singing team of Jeanette MacDonald and Nelson Eddy remained surefire box office. William Powell was in poor health and working irregularly. Myrna Loy's large following remained intact, but there were doubts that it could be sustained if she was not partnered with Gable or Powell. Jean Harlow had died suddenly in the summer, and the other three leading female stars were all commercially vulnerable: Joan Crawford had suddenly begun to slip at the box office; Norma Shearer was no longer comfortable at the studio since the tragic death from pneumonia at the age of thirty-seven of her husband, Irving Thalberg; even Garbo's popularity in the States was waning (although she remained a prime attraction in Europe). Such stars embodied *soi-disant* glamour, but now something else seemed to be needed. To continue to crest the wave, M-G-M had to move, as Aljean Harmetz put it, "from sophistication to sentimentality." It was trying to make up for lost time and lost chances. Everyone now agreed that Garland was going to be a star, but no one could think of a child star who had yet made the transition to adult roles. The studio was determined to earn as much from this one while it was still possible—as may be gauged by the frequency with which it announced projects in which Garland was meant to play a leading role.

Even as production was in full swing on *Broadway Melody of 1938* in the spring of 1937, the studio was publishing plans for forthcoming movies. One of these, typically, was *Mollie, Bless You!*, which was based on an apocryphal incident in the life of Marie Dressler, the aging vaudevillian who had been one of the studio's most unexpected stars. Dressler had died in 1934, and Mayer, who had been looking for a replacement ever since, saw a likely candidate in Sophie Tucker, who was scheduled to co-star with Dressler's most popular partner, Wallace Beery, in a script by Frances Marion. The original announcement of the project in the *Hollywood Reporter* on April 13, 1937, did not mention the extent of Garland's participation, but by the time M-G-M issued its trailer-ads at the end of the year, she had become its third star. The film was canceled, however, when it became clear that Tucker was a much less effective screen presence than Dressler.*

Then, on May 26, the *Reporter* announced Garland's participation in *The Ugly Duckling*, and on June 8, mentioned her in connection with *Thoroughbreds Don't Cry*; on August 2 the tentatively titled *Listen, Darling* was described as her first starring vehicle.

The studio's haste and Garland's new-won importance are evident from the fact that, while arguments were going on about its title, *The Ugly Duckling* went into production as "Judy Garland Story." The first film to start shooting, however, by a few days, was *Thoroughbreds Don't Cry*. In order to get Garland before the public again as soon as possible, the two films had been rescheduled. Shooting began on both in the first week of September and she worked on them simultaneously. *Thoroughbreds*, a racetrack story, had been bought as a co-starring vehicle for Mickey Rooney and Freddie Bartholomew. A role was hastily written in for Garland—so quickly that, once again, she had almost nothing to do; in the first script she read there was not even a song for her. Once more, the solution was to add a song under the credits, with its three young stars striding toward the camera as Garland sings "Got a Pair of New Shoes," a song which had been dropped from *Broadway Melody*. The trade-ads name one of the young players Ronnie St. Clair instead of the Ronald Sinclair he became, and list a star-player who is not in the finished film—clear

*It was later made, in 1945, by 20th Century-Fox, as *Molly and Me* with Gracie Fields and Monty Woolley, and Roddy McDowall in the role meant for Garland.

evidence of a rushed production schedule. Sinclair had been brought in to replace Bartholomew, removed from the film by his aunt, who acted as his manager. Rooney's star was in the ascendant, while Bartholomew's was fading, and in their last film together, *The Devil Is a Sissy*, Rooney had stolen all the scenes in which they appeared together. Sinclair was near enough a duplicate of Bartholomew to unnerve his Aunt Cissy, who thereafter became more cooperative.

Sinclair plays a somewhat prissy English boy who helps his grandfather (Sir C. Aubrey Smith) to train a racehorse; Rooney is the "swell-headed" jockey who rides it. Garland was billed as "The girl you loved in *Broadway Melody*," and the new role was largely a reprise of the earlier film, with Sophie Tucker as the proprietress of a boarding-house and Garland as her niece, rather than her daughter. Almost her first words are "I'm going to be a great singer, and I'm going to be a great actress!," and, just as she had in *Pigskin Parade*, she sings to attract attention—in a charming, cheerful and still somewhat modest manner with not a little sense of self-mockery. The qualities that were to make her so gifted a performer are already in place.

Although *The Ugly Duckling* had gone into production as "Judy Garland Story," she eventually got only third billing, after Allan Jones and Fanny Brice. Jones, who had most recently co-starred with Jeanette MacDonald, could demand top billing; he certainly had enough clout to have the script rewritten because he refused to play an organ-grinder (he is a chef instead). Garland was upped to second billing in the final credits, however; and in the advertising campaign—where it mattered most, since this would influence those who fixed the names on the marquees—she takes the top spot. The movie was one of the many films about crazy families which proliferated after the success of *My Man Godfrey*, Gregory La Cava's comedy about a rich man posing as a tramp becoming the butler to millionaires. Everybody in *Duckling*, including the Garland character's parents (Billie Burke and Reginald Owen), the maid (Brice) and her older sister's boyfriend (Jones) are either involved with, or besotted by, show business. Garland is expelled from school for turning Mendelssohn's "Spring Song" into "Swing, Mr. Mendelssohn," and in the course of the action she gets to give out with some more songs, including a rousing "Down on Melody Farm," a supposedly improvised song performed on a bus with others of the cast, and a comic duet with the formidable Brice.

Thoroughbreds Don't Cry opened in November 1937, by which time studio executives were again having doubts about the wisdom of calling Garland's next picture *The Ugly Duckling*. They may still have been hoping for a swan to emerge, but it was hardly advisable to remind audiences that their newest star was not a beauty in the conventional sense: exhibitors, clamoring for the next Durbin film, might feel that they were only getting second best. When Garland went to the preview with Mickey Rooney, it had been retitled twice from *The Ugly Duckling*, for a while it was called *Swing Fever*, but by now it was known as that with which it opened in January 1938, *Everybody Sing*, another reminder of Garland's triumph in *Broadway Melody of 1938*, where she had performed the song of this title to such effect.

Film Weekly judged Garland

an extremely clever little comedienne. She proves it in a delightful duet with Fanny Brice, and anyone who stands up to Miss Brice at her own comedy game is very good indeed. Also, Garland's is the number which lifts the picture into the "excellent" class. Her burlesque of "Swing Low, Sweet Chariot," complete with blacked face and "Uncle Tom's Cabin" curls, is as good as anything I have seen in my recent film going.

Elsewhere the press was only cautiously encouraging. Bosley Crowther in the *New York Times* thought that the trouble with the film was that the new title was only too apt and that it was possible to leave the cinema "with a positive hatred of the human larynx." He added, however, "It is only fair to admit that Judy Garland of the rhythm, writin' and 'rithmatic age is a superb vocal technician, despite her not exactly underemphasized immaturity."

During these hectic months, Garland's agent, Al Rosen, had tried to get her a pay raise, but M-G-M declined to negotiate with him. The studio did, however, agree to pay Ethel $200 a week. Ethel had been offended when Peg DeVine had suggested to her that she ought to take a percentage of Garland's salary, but when it was pointed out to her that she was her daughter's chaperone, her unpaid secretary and, in effect, her manager—by this time, a full-time job—she decided that she could do so with a clear conscience. Unofficially, Garland had been given the raise for which Rosen asked, while Ethel's fee was deducted from her salary—though Ethel did not know this.

Ethel was all too well aware of the studio's contempt for Rosen, and since she and the agent disliked each other intensely, she terminated their agreement when Harry Rabwin, who was acting as the Garlands' lawyer, told her that Abe Lastfogel of the William Morris Agency was interested in handling her daughter. According to Gerold Frank's work, another possibility was Jesse Martin, who had taken such good care of Ethel and Judy when they were in New York making the record for Decca. Martin had told Ethel that he was planning to leave New York to set himself up as an agent on the West Coast, and she invited him and his wife to stay with her while setting up shop. She had decided that if Martin's plans worked out, she would ask him to take on Judy as one of his first clients. He had told her that Judy could become one of New York's most highly paid performers, and in the interim—before M-G-M realized that the girl could make money for them—she had reasoned that if such a triumph could be arranged for Judy, they would have M-G-M eating out of their hands. Although she thought Martin impetuous, she decided that his high regard for Judy's talent made him the right person to represent her.

He was also well connected. He had once roomed with one of Mayer's right-hand men, Benny Thau, and Ethel fully appreciated that the network of Jewish executives operating in Hollywood's boardrooms was powerful when it came to promoting talent it liked. Rosen had clearly not been part of it. When Martin wrote to say that he was coming to California, she dismissed any thought of Lastfogel. In the summer of 1937, she appointed Martin Judy Garland's new agent.

True to his word, Martin announced that the time was ripe for Judy to sing before a live audience in New York. He told Ethel that he could get her daughter $5,000 a week at the Paramount, but, after negotiations, accepted $3,500—only to find, not surprisingly, that the M-G-M management had no intention of letting Garland sing in a theater owned by a rival. They insisted that, if she were to appear at all in New York, it must be at Loew's State—and not for $3,500, since she was already under contract. A clause in that contract provided for personal appearances, so they were not obliged to pay her anything— and certainly not the sort of money Martin was demanding. After all, her weekly salary was about to go up to $300 a week, which was big money for a fifteen-year-old girl. The studio magnanimously agreed to pay her $1,750, exactly half of the Paramount's offer, for each week that she toured to bolster the first runs of *Everybody Sing*, provided that she did not pick up her usual salary check.

As it was, the studio would have to send a small contingent of publicists with Judy and Ethel, as well as Roger Edens, who was to accompany Garland on the piano. It was a seven-week, seven-city tour, beginning in Miami Beach, and taking in New York, Chicago, Pittsburgh, Detroit and Columbus, Ohio, where Garland was named "Sweetheart of Sigma Chi," after the song. There was also a brief trip to Grand Rapids on their way home, because stars being welcomed back to their home towns always generated a good amount of press coverage. Garland was formally introduced to the students at the high school and to audiences at the Rialto cinema.

In the event, no M-G-M publicity officer was needed to bring the crowds out for Judy Garland. Edens recalled her opening at Loew's State, the most important live performance of her career so far:

There was this unknown fifteen-year-old girl alone for the first time on an enormous stage, nervous, and singing much too loudly. The audience was coughing and a baby started crying. People laughed at the baby and Judy stopped her song, laughed and started again. That one thing steadied her and she wrapped that audience up from then on . . . She has been able to handle an audience ever since.

Her first song was "Take Me Back to Manhattan"; she also sang "Dear Mr. Gable" and "Bei Mir Bist Du Schön"—to the delight of Saul Chaplin and Sammy Cahn, who had collaborated on the English lyric and were in the audience by chance. After the show, they went backstage to meet her.

In its inimitable style, *Variety* reported:

Youngster is a resounding wallop in her first vaude appearance (as Judy Garland). Comes to the house with a rep in films and after a single date on the Chase and Sanborn radio show. Apparent from outset that girl is no mere flash, but has both the personality and the skill to develop into a box-office wow in any line of show business. Applause was solid and she encored twice, finally begging off with an ingratiating and shrewd thank you speech.

When she returned to Hollywood she was another step nearer stardom.

The price eventually paid for that stardom was a terrible one. Whether this was her own fault or that of M-G-M can never be determined with certainty. She was the first to laugh at herself, and could be ruefully funny about the reversals in her career; but she never learned to blame herself for any mistakes which arose from a flaw—impetuosity, revealed as capriciousness at this stage—in her character. That said, a Hollywood studio was hardly a healthy environment for an insecure teenager. The real Hollywood—not the one depicted in the fan magazines—was a place of hard work and stress. Conversely, it created fantasies, and those inside the dream, particularly the immature and inexperienced, often tried to realize their own. The difficulties Garland had suffered already in her short life had conditioned her to search for another happy ending, and yet another, and another . . . The greater her success, the stronger became her appetite for more.

"My life was a combination of absolute chaos and absolute solitude," Garland said in 1960. "I'd be alone with my teacher for ten minutes, reciting my French lessons. Then some assistant director comes along and says 'C'mon, kid, you're wanted on the set.' " She became so busy that she could no longer spend the statutory three hours a day in the schoolroom with other young performers, and so a tutor, Mrs. Rose Carter, was engaged to teach her whenever she was not required in front of the cameras. Making two films at a time—as she did in 1937 and again in 1938—while studying with Edens and with Mrs. Carter would be taxing for even the most energetic fifteen-year-old.

The consequent loneliness, she said, she could bear—"some people are born lonely, I guess," she once reflected—but the strict diet she was obliged to follow took a heavy toll, as she came to recognize: "It was only when I had to *starve* myself that the real anxieties began." At the age of fifteen, she was naturally pudgy and inclined—as she was throughout most of her life—to put on as much as twenty pounds in a few days without even trying, which was especially easy if one is less than five feet tall. She was no longer a little girl, but as she later put it:

> a property in which millions of dollars were invested . . . It was to the studio's financial advantage to keep their investment neat and photogenic and, to some extent, happy. But my primary function was to work. As long as I worked, the studio's investment in the property known as Garland paid off. If I got fat, I couldn't work. So, I mustn't get fat.

It had, after all, been Garland's shape which had kept her out of an M-G-M feature for so long. The costume department had thought her hopeless, and consoled itself with the expectation that she would improve as she matured and complement her long, attractive legs. Now that she had become such an asset to the studio, the most accomplished designers were put at her disposal. Their greatest achievement was to disguise the fact that she had no waist.

Not surprisingly, once Garland became aware of the efforts being made to give her a movie-star figure, she developed a complex about her body which remained with her all her life. Until she was in films, she had never given a thought to the way she looked; but once she did, she knew she did not like it. Nor, she said, did Ethel, who was only too anxious to see to it that Judy remained svelte and childlike, insisting that her daughter should dress in short skirts, sailor-collars and other clothes in order to keep her looking young, a policy approved by the studio, where no one wanted to see her grow up, either.

In retrospect, Garland resented the regimen to which she was subjected, but at the time she was a cheerful spirit who was able to get what she wanted by pleading with waiters in the commissary to sneak her an ice cream or a sandwich. Frances Marion remembered her at this period:

> She had all the characteristics of a chipmunk: she hated to sit still a moment; her bright eyes were always on the alert for fun or the threat of danger; she resented being caged, and she was forever greedily searching for something tasty to eat. As the joy of eating was *verboten*, she, like the chipmunk, had secret hiding places where she could tuck away a cookie, a chocolate bar, or a gooey piece of cake.

The canteen staff had orders to bring her only clear soup and cottage cheese; any known infringements—when she sneaked out for a malted milk, for example—were reported to one or another of Mayer's executives, who called her in to remind her of her obligations. One of the extraordinary features of Hollywood at this time was the network of spies, some of them paid, who were relied upon to keep those in authority informed of every aspect of the lives of important personnel under contract—or anyone being considered for a contract. At M-G-M, the head of the network was Howard Strickling, who was responsible for the studio's "image." It was felt that his staff could make generous use of all the printable activities of all the stars. Whatever excuses were made—surveillance was supposedly for publicity purposes—this did not make for a happy atmosphere, and was especially damaging for anyone of a sensitive or nervous disposition.

It has to be remembered that all Garland's remarks about studio life were made long after the event; at the time she was working so hard and was so deeply engrossed in her own fantasies that it is unlikely she had the time or the inclination for introspection. She was on the verge of becoming one of the brightest of Louis B. Mayer's stars. Convinced at last that she could rival if not outshine Universal's Deanna Durbin, he had developed a paternal affection for her, atoning for his initial neglect. This affection was not always conveyed in the most tactful manner. She claimed that he used to refer to her as "the fat kid" and "my little hunchback." On one occasion, in her presence, he said to some visitors, "Do you see this little girl? Look what I've made her into. She used to be a hunchback . . . Isn't that true, Judy?" The visitors looked at Garland, who, after an astonished pause, replied, "Why yes, Mr. Mayer, I suppose it is."

The older she became, and the more intractable her difficulties, the more she blamed Mayer personally. Louis B. Mayer was an autocrat, in the words of screenwriter Noel Langley, "a shark that killed when it wasn't hungry." He was by nature a loquacious man, uninterested in other people's opinions, and anyone who stepped out of line might face one of his lengthy lectures, a barrage of cajolement and fury, as well as threats—many of them not too veiled. However, Myrna Loy claimed that, for all his faults, he knew what was best for his stars, and Katharine Hepburn liked him:

> He gave me a lot of freedom and I gave him a lot of respect . . . I thought Metro was like a wonderful school from which you never graduated. That's what it seemed like to me. I didn't feel it was a prison at all. It was so comfortable. We were underpaid, but we were very well protected. If you got into trouble, you called Howard Strickling . . . Your problems were taken care of. It was a wonderful sensation.

In time, Garland, who had neither Hepburn's resilience nor her figure, would think of Culver City as a prison. Her life might have been very different if Mayer had not decided that Ida Koverman was far too sympathetic to Garland's woes. According to Hedda Hopper, he believed that Koverman was in danger of putting her protégée's interests before those of the studio, so much so that he warned her off: "You've got too much to do to look after the Garland." There is no doubt that Garland desperately needed someone to whom she could look for guidance and advice, particularly since she no longer trusted her mother. Ever since her father's death, she had been looking for a replacement, and there were two obvious candidates: Edens and Koverman. Edens, who resembled Frank in several ways, adored her, but he was careful to restrict his advice to musical matters. Koverman would have been ideal, but after she had been ordered by Mayer to distance herself from Garland, a real estrangement ensued, brought about by her disapproval of one of Judy's romantic liaisons. Garland spoke of Koverman's "desertion" and eventually came to condemn her as just another of those who had overworked her.

More unsettling still, Garland began to believe that when Mayer declined to do something she had requested, he was often acting upon Ethel's wishes. She later insisted that Mayer and Ethel were in unholy alliance, set on keeping her in line, but it is doubtful whether they met privately on more than two or three occasions. Although Mayer's devotion to the *idea* of mothers was so extreme as to verge on the manic, in real life he avoided them—which, given the protective guard around him, was easy to do. Indeed, it would seem that it was on his personal instructions that Ethel was barred from the lot for a year because she caused trouble, berating anyone who would listen about the cruelty of getting a child up at five in the morning, a story which suggests that Ethel was not as black as her daughter painted her. It seems likely, however, that with Koverman out of the picture, Mayer and Ethel came to a tacit understanding. As Garland's importance to the studio increased, and while she was still a minor, Mayer could not afford to antagonize her mother; as she became more independent, even rebellious, he needed her mother as an ally.

Had there been someone who could have protected her, she might have avoided the increasingly unreasonable demands of the studio, as well as the disastrous consequences. "I starved my appetite. I starved my system. I began to suffer from malnutrition," she recalled. "I began for the first time in my life, to suffer from moods of absolute depression. I remembered how terribly happy I'd been in vaudeville. I had never known such stage fright."

These alarming symptoms may also have been a side effect of another regime to which the young star was being subjected. It seems that no one saw anything wrong in using pills to control her weight. At the time, very few people were aware that diet pills contained amphetamines, and every star in Hollywood who was inclined to overweight was taking them. Years later, Garland's sister Jimmy was to say: "There are times, at a place like Metro, when they don't give a damn about your talent—all they're worrying about is how you look and they make a big thing about it." She went on to say that Garland was taking Benzedrine and that the studio doctor prescribed Seconal, but "nobody thought it bad. My mother didn't think it was bad—if she had, she wouldn't have let Judy take it."

The pills Garland took killed the desire for food but increased her hyperactivity, with the result that she would be wide awake when she should have been going to bed. She would then be given pills to help her sleep; then, when she awoke, too drowsy even to react when she arrived in the makeup department at seven, she would be given a dose of something else. She had unwittingly stumbled into a topsy-turvy world, and the results would be devastating.

In her innocence, she believed that she found it difficult to sleep because she had grown accustomed to working until late in vaudeville;

she thought that she had difficulty waking because filming involved hard work and late hours. She was someone who wanted to cram a hundred minutes into every hour, and pills helped. With hindsight, it is easy to blame M-G-M or the studio doctor, who had prescribed for most of the stars on the lot. Very few others became addicted; but then Garland was only fifteen. "I do not blame Hollywood for what happened to Judy Garland," wrote columnist Louella Parsons much later, "but it can only have happened in Hollywood."

5

The Wizard of Oz

ON DECEMBER 21, 1937, the first full-length animated cartoon, *Snow White and the Seven Dwarfs*, had opened at Radio City Music Hall. Walt Disney had been virtually alone in believing that the Brothers Grimm's fairy tale could catch the imagination of the world. When reviewers and audiences proved him all too right, other filmmakers inevitably searched for something comparable. L. Frank Baum's "Oz" books seemed to provide the answer, and on February 18, 1938, the *New York Times* reported that in the wake of the film's success no fewer than five studios were bidding for the rights to *The Wizard of Oz*, which were then owned by Sam Goldwyn. The scramble to acquire the rights was short-lived, and there had seldom been any doubt that the property would wind up at M-G-M.

Baum's book had first been published in 1900 as *The Wonderful Wizard of Oz*. It lost its adjective three years later and acquired a series of sequels, which continued after Baum's death in 1919, when his widow authorized one Ruth Plumly Thompson to write them. In 1902, Baum had dramatized the book which, under the direction of

Julian Mitchell, became "a musical extravaganza," with vaudevillians David C. Montgomery and Fred E. Stone as the Tin Woodman and the Scarecrow, respectively. The Selig studio produced a one-reel film version in 1910, and Chadwick a feature in 1925, directed by Larry Semon, who also played the Scarecrow; his wife, Dorothy Dwan, played the young heroine, Dorothy, and (a pre-Laurel) Oliver Hardy was the Tin Man. In 1933, Goldwyn opened negotiations for the film rights of the book, which he intended as a vehicle for Eddie Cantor, who would play the Scarecrow. It was to be a musical and in the new "three-strip Technicolor." In 1937, M-G-M had considered turning the Oz books into animated shorts.

The man who had tried to sell the books to the cartoon department was Frank Orsatti, who represented Colonel Frank Joslyn Baum, the author's son. There were three Orsatti brothers: Ernie, Vince and Frank. Ernie played baseball and was liked; Vince, a well-known ladies' man, helped run the agency and was also popular; Frank, however, was a dubious and disreputable figure in Hollywood. His natural habitat was the Del Mar racetrack or the Clover Club, an illegal gambling joint on the Strip, at both of which he was often seen in the company of Louis B. Mayer. It was well known that he had been Mayer's bootlegger and a sometime gangster. He was also a pimp, and had privileged access to those starlets at M-G-M who were kept on salary for looks rather than talent. Hollywood saw nothing strange about Mayer having a gangster as one of his cronies, but it was considered odd that Mayer had encouraged Orsatti to set up as a talent agent, either by lending or giving him money to do so.

Orsatti knew that Goldwyn had lost interest in the Oz rights when Cantor had refused to renew his contract. He also knew that M-G-M was looking for a star vehicle for Judy Garland. She was already almost too old to play Dorothy, which may be why the negotiations were concluded so quickly. In February 1938—while Garland was on the *Everybody Sing* seven-city tour—it was announced that M-G-M had acquired the screen rights of *The Wizard of Oz* from Goldwyn and assigned Judy Garland to the role of Dorothy. Mervyn LeRoy would produce. Instructions to buy the property came directly from Mayer, who in the usual circumstances would not have been involved. They were conducted by the studio's general manager, Eddie Mannix, who paid $75,000, bringing Goldwyn a handy profit of $35,000 on his original purchase.

Arthur Freed always claimed credit for bringing *The Wizard of Oz* to M-G-M, but then he also tried to hijack the credit for discovering

Judy Garland. Freed, who was to produce the greatest musicals in Hollywood's history, was a vulgar, ambitious, sentimental, reactionary, ruthless, insensitive and ill-educated man. He and Nacio Herb Brown had been the studio's "house" composers since the first *Broadway Melody* movie in 1929, to which they had contributed the title song, as well as "You Were Meant for Me" and "The Wedding of the Painted Doll." In the years between they had written such hits as "Singin' in the Rain," "Pagan Love Song" and "Temptation." By 1937, Freed had decided to abandon the writing of lyrics in order to become a full-time producer, and had reputedly accepted a salary cut from $1,500 to $300 a week while learning the ropes. He had impressed Mayer with the regularity with which he turned up at the studio's previews, and with the acuity of his comments, which were not always the ones his colleagues wanted to hear. He was so assiduous in his attentions to Mayer that there was a studio saying: "If you want to lick Mayer's ass, you'll have to shave Freed first."

As a producer, he knew how to "push the right buttons," as Roger Edens's associate, Leonard Gershe, put it. But he had no innate taste and was heavily dependent on the advice and opinions of Edens. It was Edens who was the real force behind the Freed musicals, but, perhaps because he liked to tread carefully, he never wanted to take credit where it was due. Freed, on the other hand, was always anxious to grab it, especially in the case of this particular picture.

The producer, however, was to be Mervyn LeRoy. "I wanted to make a movie out of *The Wizard of Oz* from the time I was a kid," he said in 1977. "I'm getting sick of hearing about Arthur Freed and *The Wizard of Oz*. Arthur Freed's name isn't on the picture. Mine is. Mr. Mayer asked me to take Arthur as my assistant, and he helped me a lot with the music. I never took credit for anything that didn't belong to me. But *I* produced that picture." Whatever LeRoy's *post facto* declarations, according to John Fricke, M-G-M's files reveal that Freed was assiduous in acquiring the rights, specifically as a Garland film. LeRoy had started out as a contract director at Warner Bros. (he was Harry Warner's son-in-law), where he had directed such notable pictures as *Little Caesar*, *I Am a Fugitive from a Chain Gang*, *Gold Diggers of 1933* and *Oil for the Lamps of China*. On loan to M-G-M, he had directed one of the studio's biggest-ever successes, *Tugboat Annie* (1933), though this picture largely owed its popularity to the team of Wallace Beery and Marie Dressler. He had made two of Warners' finest movies of 1936, *Anthony Adverse*, based on a sprawling historical best-seller, and *Three Men on a Horse*, based on an intimate Broadway comedy. In 1937 he produced as well as directed two films, one of which, a racial drama set in the Deep South entitled *They Won't Forget*, had been much admired. His credentials were such that, late in 1937, Nicholas Schenck invited him to join M-G-M as a producer.

Schenck believed the studio had owed its preeminence to the judgment of Irving Thalberg, allied to sound commercial instinct. Until not long before he died, Thalberg had made virtually every artistic decision at M-G-M, but ill-health, a desire for independence, and his uneasy relationship with Mayer, had meant that Sam Katz and other producers had begun to take over from him. After Thalberg's death in 1936, an Executive Committee was formed, which met weekly and consisted of Mayer, as vice-president, and other stalwarts, notably Eddie Mannix, Benny Thau, Harry Rapf and Al Lichtman. Also on the committee were the studio's art director, Cedric Gibbons, and several producers, who were growing in number to cope with the production load needed to maintain the studio's position. Even so, Schenck and Mayer continued to search for another Thalberg. In the meantime, LeRoy's ability to handle a wide range of subjects would clearly make him a valuable acquisition. Schenck agreed to pay him the enormous sum of $6,000 a week, provided that it be kept secret, lest other producers demand commensurate raises. LeRoy wanted to direct as well as produce *The Wizard of Oz*, but Mayer knew immediately that it was going to be an expensive production, and he was not prepared to let a fledgling producer work on it without supervision.

The story concerns Dorothy, a young girl from Kansas, whose house is swept up by a tornado and transported to the land of Oz. Her house is deposited in Munchkinland, fortuitously crashing down upon the Wicked Witch of the East, much to the delight of the Munchkins. In order to get home again, Dorothy, along with her dog Toto, has to follow the Yellow Brick Road in search of the Emerald City, where she will find the Wizard of Oz. Along the way, she meets a Scarecrow in search of a brain, a Tin Woodman in search of a heart, and a Cowardly Lion in search of courage. After numerous adventures, and the evil intervention of the Wicked Witch of the West, they reach the city, expose the Wizard as a fraud, and achieve their goals. Dorothy is returned to Kansas.

On March 15, an item appeared in *Daily Variety*, headlined "Ray Bolger and an all-star cast." There was no mention of Garland, but it was announced that Bolger would play the Tin Woodman and Buddy Ebsen would play the Scarecrow. Bolger was angered by this, since he claimed that when he had signed his contract with the studio in April 1936, there had been "a verbal agreement" that he would play the Scarecrow if M-G-M ever made a film of *The Wizard of Oz*. He was being paid $3,000 a week, which was a considerable sum for someone not particularly photogenic and whose specialty—eccentric dancing—more or less limited him to guest appearances. Indeed, one of the reasons M-G-M had wanted to acquire Baum's book had been that it would provide excellent roles both for him and for Garland. He went to see Mayer, who decided that Bolger and Ebsen should exchange roles.

Freed's first memo on casting, on January 31, had proposed Frank Morgan as the Wizard, which would have kept another of the leading roles within the M-G-M "family." LeRoy favored Ed Wynn, but he turned down the role as being too small as it then existed. W.C. Fields was approached, but there was a conflict with his schedule at Universal. As filming continued to be postponed, he became free, but demanded more for his services than M-G-M was prepared to pay. Both Victor Moore and Hugh Herbert—like Morgan and Wynn, masters of the "dither"—were considered, but the role eventually went to Morgan.

The Cowardly Lion did not figure in the preliminary casting and first appears in an April script conference when Bert Lahr was immediately cast in the role. The diminutive inhabitants of Munchkinland were played by some 124 midgets, rounded up by a specialist agent and deposited in a studio hotel. M-G-M's own Edna May Oliver was considered for the role of the Wicked Witch, and Gale Sondergaard was tested several times, sometimes looking like herself and then with makeup to make her uglier. Even though LeRoy had directed Sondergaard to an Academy Award in *Anthony Adverse*, she didn't want to appear grotesque and declined the role—but at the last minute it went to a less prestigious actress, Margaret Hamilton. At about this time Billie Burke was announced as being cast as the Good Witch Glinda, although at different times both Fanny Brice and Bea Lillie were being considered.

Before the announced starting date of April 19—subsequently twice postponed to April 22 and then to May 9—doubts about cost and casting had been expressed in the New York office. Garland's role was not yet secure as long as Schenck continued to discuss the possibility of borrowing Shirley Temple, a guaranteed box-office draw and therefore more likely than Garland to ensure a profit on what was clearly going to be an expensive undertaking. Edens, much to his annoyance, was dispatched to 20th Century-Fox to "investigate," but returned more convinced than ever that there was only one person who could play the role. Schenck also considered Deanna Durbin, but agreed with Mayer (who was still suffering each time a Durbin film drew raves from the press and crowds to the box office) that M-G-M was not in the business of furthering the career of someone under contract to another studio. In any case, Darryl F. Zanuck, head of production at Fox, declined to loan Temple, and Metro would have been similarly rebuffed by Universal, for whom Durbin was their only proven star. It was therefore decided that Garland would, after all, take the role of Dorothy, as originally intended.

LeRoy left the musical aspect of the film entirely to Freed and Edens, who chose Harold Arlen and E.Y. Harburg to compose the music and lyrics, signing them for fourteen weeks for a flat fee of $25,000 in May. Arlen was one of the most sophisticated of composers, but, with *Snow White* as the only guideline for this project, it was decided he needed to keep his tunes simple and catchy. What was to give both the composer and the lyricist the greatest satisfaction was to provide songs which arose directly from the plot, and advanced rather than held up the action. This was a comparatively new idea at the time.

"Yip" Harburg had heard Garland sing at Loew's State during her 1938 tour, and so began work with enthusiasm. It had already been decided that this film needed Technicolor, expensive though it was, but the framing Kansas sequences were to be in monochrome. As Harburg worked with the screenwriter, Noel Langley, to integrate the songs into the script, he came up with the idea of "Over the Rainbow" for the sepia-toned section of the film. When Arlen first played him the melody, however, he observed: "That's for Nelson Eddy, not a little girl in Kansas." He changed his mind, however, and was later to say:

> Judy was an unusual child, with an ability to project a song and a voice that penetrated your insides. She sang not just to your ears, but to your tear ducts. Just like a great cantor, she combined the superb voice with an understanding of the music and lyrics and this ability to sing into your soul. She was the most unusual voice in the first half of this century. When she started, Judy was the greatest. As a child, she sang with all the naturalness and clarity of a child . . . Honesty, not phoniness, moves people. Judy Garland was to singing what Gershwin's music was to music. They brought a quality and vitality that was typically and uniquely American.

The continual delays—caused principally by tinkering with the script—did not mean that M-G-M's new prize property had been idle. Indeed, during her absence on the *Everybody Sing* promotional tour, a role had been written for her in the latest adventure of Judge Hardy and his family, and she began playing it only a few days after returning in April 1938.

The Hardy family was the invention of Aurania Rouverol for a play, *Skidding*, which became an M-G-M movie in 1937 under the title *A Family Affair*. It was originally planned as a vehicle to reunite most of the cast of Clarence Brown's film of Eugene O'Neill's *Ah, Wilderness!*, which had been mildly successful in 1935, but in the end the studio lost faith in the material, and it was decided to produce the movie on a lower budget. The cast was headed by the venerable character actor Lionel Barrymore as Judge Hardy, but he declined to repeat the role in the sequel Mayer insisted upon when the film enjoyed a success beyond its modest aims. Mickey Rooney, as his son Andy, had stolen the piece, and Barrymore was not keen to have this happen a second time. Lewis Stone replaced him, with Fay Holden as his wife and Ann Rutherford as Andy's sweetheart, Polly Benedict. Cecilia Parker was second-billed, after Stone, as the Hardys' daughter, Marion.

The films are set in the emblematic and idealized small town of Carvel, and Judge Hardy pontificates throughout the series on the pillars of American life: family, church, state, civic virtue. The films enshrine not only what Mayer, the immigrant Jew, felt was essential to every U.S. citizen, but also what Americans wanted to believe about themselves during the end of the Depression and the first rumblings of a war in Europe. In 1943, M-G-M would be awarded a special Oscar for the series, "for its achievement in representing the American way of life." Seen today, they are smug, unvaried, banal and—with three exceptions—only watchable for die-hard fans of Mickey Rooney. As Andy Hardy, he often gets into trouble but always wins through in the end. He is fiercely loyal to his friends and contemptuous of phonies; he is also excessively filial, often telling his parents that no one ever had such a "swell" mom and dad. He is also at the awkward age, discovering the joys of dressing in a tux, of dancing—and of kissing. Following his amorous adventures in *Judge Hardy's Children* (1938), he was to be put center stage, and for the first time a Hardy film was awarded an A-picture budget and running-time.

Rooney had become America's favorite son, and as he and the

Hardy series advanced in popularity together, the scripts of further episodes were kept in readiness. However, none of these provided a suitable role for Garland, who was now unexpectedly free, and instructions went out from the Executive Committee to find a starring vehicle for the youngsters, whom the public had liked together in *Thoroughbreds Don't Cry*—either a musical or an entirely new Hardy picture. "Oh, What a Tangled Web," a story about teenage romance which had appeared in *Cosmopolitan* in September 1936, could have provided the basis for a full-blown musical, but almost overnight it became a Hardy film—one which none the less contained three songs for Garland. No fewer than 176 titles for the projected film were considered, but with market research confirming the popularity of Rooney and the character he played, *Love Finds Andy Hardy* was selected. It was the fourth in the series, and the first of three to feature Judy Garland. She takes supporting billing, which is all that the format allows, since the films begin with a picture of "The Hardy Family" before the title card.

While she and Rooney were friends and had played well together in *Thoroughbreds*, the Hardy picture is in no sense a teaming. Andy is still in love with Polly, but cannot decide whether to take her or Cynthia (Lana Turner) to the Christmas dance. Judy plays Betsy Booth, who is staying with her grandmother in Carvel for Christmas, and to Andy she is just the kid next door. Pining for him, she constantly blames her lack of glamour for his lack of interest. She attempts to win him by singing and by giving him an unusual present, an elaborate radiator cap for his automobile. Polly and Cynthia will love it, he tells her. When he receives a telegram from Polly confirming that she expects him to take her to the dance, he exclaims: "Two girls! Two girls for the same dance!" Neither of them is Betsy, and she is not much consoled by his assurance that "You'd love Polly and I'm sure she'd like you. . . . She adores children."

For Polly's sake, Betsy gets rid of Cynthia, but when Polly changes her mind about their date, Andy laments that he has no one to take to the dance. "We couldn't have that, could we?" says Betsy, as if her heart was breaking. Andy explains that he can't take just any girl— "she has to be sensational." Since no one sensational is to be had, Andy does eventually take Betsy to the dance. When the bandleader recognizes her and asks her to sing, Andy is impressed—but only because he, as her escort, can be seen in a new light. He still finds her of no romantic interest.

In Betsy Booth we recognize the Judy Garland that Roger Edens had created. Most of the films were directed by George B. Seltz, including the three that Garland made, and he certainly never achieved such poignancy in any of the others. Edens composed a song for her to sing, which expresses Betsy's feeling that she lacks glamour. "In-Between" has a lyric modeled on the recitative of "Dear Mr. Gable": "I'm too old for toys, and I'm too young for boys . . . I'm allowed to picture shows, at least if nurse is feeling able / But we only go to Mickey Mouse, I'm not allowed Clark Gable."

The situation in the film may have charmed audiences, but it also served to highlight Garland's own feelings of personal inadequacy. It was at about this time that Chico Marx's daughter, Maxine, found her crying in the ladies' room. "I'm so ugly," she wailed. "Look at Annie [Rutherford] and Lana Turner." "But they have none of your talent," Maxine replied. "You're the one who has it all." Garland did not find this at all consoling: "Who cares?" she said. Her inferiority complex in regard to Turner would take her years to conquer, even though at this period Turner was not especially glamorous, and was not expected, either by herself or anyone else, to become a star of the magnitude already predicted for Garland.

Her feelings were confirmed by a review of *Love Finds Andy Hardy* in the *New York Herald Tribune*. Howard Barnes deplored the "ill-advised attempt" to introduce songs: "Judy Garland sings them and they are catchy enough pieces," he wrote, but added: "Miss Garland is the least effective of the young players who have a hand in the photoplay. Ann Rutherford and Lana Turner are far better . . . ." It is a curious judgment. If Rutherford's healthy beauty is the one abiding virtue of the whole series, Turner hardly registers, either as an actress or as a personality. The film turned up at the ninth position on the *Film Daily* poll of exhibitors, and it is the only Hardy film ever to appear in the top ten. This may simply reflect the exhibitors' delight at the crowds which turned up to see it, but the only films in the series with any quality are those which feature Garland. Her few scenes in *Love Finds Andy Hardy* are heart-rending, and at the time they persuaded those doubters at M-G-M—including the man who had most to lose if *Oz* flopped, Mervyn LeRoy—that she could carry a major film.

Filming on the Hardy film finished on June 25, and, in spite of a memo from Freed to LeRoy, dated May 20, which stated that "Judy Garland should be delivered to us immediately upon her completion of the 'Judge Hardy' picture. We would need all her time from then on for rehearsals, costumes, tests, etc.," the studio was determined to make the most of Garland's youthful appeal before the actual filming of *Oz* started. A previously abandoned project, *Listen, Darling*, was hastily reactivated—so hastily that there was no time to make it worthy of the star who was soon to carry the most costly M-G-M movie in quite a while. The film turned out to be similar in plot to Deanna Durbin's *Mad About Music* (1938), inasmuch as a teenage girl (Garland) brings romance to her mother (Mary Astor) in the shape of a *beau idéal* (Walter Pidgeon), rather than the stuffy banker (Gene Lockhart) she planned to marry. "It sounds pretty icky," Astor recalled, "and it was."

> But working with Judy was sheer joy. She was young and vital and got the giggles regularly. You just couldn't get annoyed, because she couldn't help it—it was no act. Something would strike her funny, and her face would get red and 'There goes Judy!' would be the cry. And we just had to wait till she got over it. She was a kid, a real kid. It didn't take long for her to get over that.

Although Garland is billed above the title, along with Freddie Bartholomew, who plays her friend, she has little to do, despite her character's scheming. She does, however, have three songs, "Zing! Went the Strings of My Heart," "Ten Pins in the Sky" and "On the Bumpy Road to Love," the first two of which she recorded for Decca. But, at seventy minutes, the picture was a programmer which did not cost much and which lit no bonfires when it was released in October. Critical comment was muted, although the *New York Times* noted, "Besides being a charming young miss, Judy Garland has a fresh young voice which she uses happily . . ."

Garland's workload during the summer of 1938 was extraordinary for one so young, and there was to be no respite. She recorded "Zing! Went the Strings of My Heart" for *Listen, Darling* on September 22 and started prerecording the songs for *Oz* eight days later. She had passed her sixteenth birthday in June, and the longer *Oz* was delayed, the less convincingly she could appear as a younger girl. Langley had thought that the much-revised script, which he handed in on June 4, would be the final one, but there were further changes, by Samuel Hofenstein and Herbert Fields among others. Credit on the final film was shared by Langley with Florence Ryerson and Edgar Allan Woolf, who had written *Everybody Sing*.

In the meantime, a director had been chosen: Norman Taurog, who had signed a contract with M-G-M in May. In 1931, he had won an Oscar for the direction of *Skippy*, a sentimental waif story starring his nephew, Jackie Cooper. Most recently he had directed Cooper and Deanna Durbin in *That Certain Age*, and several child actors in *The Adventures of Tom Sawyer*, so he seemed a logical choice for both *Oz* and *Boys' Town*, a film planned around Rooney, which was to precede it. But as *Oz* remained stalled, Taurog directed only some tests, in July and August. On September 7, *Daily Variety* reported that he had been replaced by Richard Thorpe, a change "made to permit Taurog to start preparations for *Huckleberry Finn*"—a story he had already filmed once, with Jackie Cooper, in 1931. This time it would be very much a vehicle for Rooney.

Thorpe was an odd choice, except in one respect: he worked quickly, and was known for getting what he wanted in the first take. After a decade spent directing routine movies, he had been engaged by Mayer in 1935 precisely for this reason. It transpired, however, that his reputation was misleading: he was not the perfectionist Mayer imagined, but rather a director who was reluctant to grant his actors the luxury of a second take.

It was announced that shooting would begin on September 15, but Garland was still hard at work on *Listen, Darling*. The starting date was postponed three times, and filming did not begin until October 12. After two weeks, during which his working methods caused growing concern, Thorpe was discharged, with a press statement to the effect that he was "seriously ill." This was something that could more truthfully be said about Buddy Ebsen, who had developed an incapacitating lung complaint after inhaling the makeup he was required to wear as the Tin Man. In the hiatus caused by Thorpe's departure, Jack Haley was borrowed from 20th Century-Fox to replace the ailing Ebsen, who was obliged to spend some time in an iron lung.

In his search for a satisfactory director, LeRoy next contacted George Cukor, who was on loan to David O. Selznick to direct *Gone With the Wind* but was currently available because the producer had not yet found the ideal Scarlett O'Hara. Cukor had been responsible for some of M-G-M's most prestigious films—such as *Dinner at Eight, David Copperfield, Romeo and Juliet* and *Camille*—but was reluctant to take on this particular task because he thought Baum had written "a minor book full of fourth-rate imagery." He viewed Thorpe's footage and was appalled:

Judy Garland looked artificial. She was too made-up, too pretty. She was also very young and inexperienced—although very gifted—and so she was too *cute*, too inclined to act in a fairy-tale way. The whole joke was that she was this little literal girl from Kansas among all the freaks. If she is real, it makes the whole picture funny.

He was being kind. In the existing stills and tests of the Thorpe version there is nothing of the wistful girl who had sung of her adoration for Mr. Gable, or of the peppy youngster who had called upon everybody to sing. Instead, there is a crazy precursor of the Barbie Doll, painfully grave, with a carefully curled blond mane spilling over her shoulders. Cukor removed Garland's wig, and most of her makeup; he put her hair into braids and chose a simpler dress. He told her that a little girl from Kansas should not act "in a fancy-schmancy way" and, having spent a week on the picture, returned to *Gone With the Wind.*

LeRoy's next choice was someone with a reputation as high as Cukor's, but it was a reputation made on films which were the antithesis of this: men's action pictures, comedies and melodramas with stars like Jean Harlow and Clark Gable, such as *Red Dust, Bombshell, Reckless* and, most recently, *Test Pilot.* However, Victor Fleming's credits also included two stories with children in the leading roles, *Treasure Island* and *Captains Courageous*, as well as a charming rural movie, *The Farmer Takes a Wife*, which augured well for the Kansas sequences.

Fleming's first act was to bring in a contract writer, John Lee Mahin, with whom he had worked profitably before. Mahin reconstructed the scenes set in Kansas, but the only change he made to the central Oz sequence was to find more funny business for the Cowardly Lion. Although the three ex-vaudevillians, Bolger, Lahr and Haley, did not require much direction, they needed discipline. They were buddies in private, but on set became highly competitive. Furthermore, they were all well aware that they were not movie naturals, but they also knew that, despite being disguised under layers of heavy makeup, this was the best movie chance they were ever likely to get. Consequently they were ambivalent about the little girl who was top-billed and who had the leading role. They liked her as a person, they admired her talent, and they understood that M-G-M had great hopes for her: but Bolger and Haley in particular were damned if she was going to take any scenes from them. (Lahr was not only a greater artist than the other two, but a more confident and generous one.) From Garland's point of view, it was a pity that her old dancing partner, Ebsen, was no longer there, for he was at once more modest and more anxious to get the job done than the others, and would have been much less likely to have tried to up-stage her.

Fleming knew that none of the antics of the Scarecrow, the Tin Man or the Cowardly Lion would detract attention from Garland's Dorothy, provided that she never lost the "wonder" of a young girl finding herself in the upended world of Oz; and she never did. This is all the more remarkable in that, at sixteen, she was wearing a figure-flattener designed (by someone she said was called "the Cellini of corsets") to make her look an unspecified number of years younger.

Margaret Hamilton claimed that, except for Edens and LeRoy's assistant, Barron Polan—who was to become one of Garland's closest friends—the young star was surrounded by hostility. She was never aware of this, however, and later recollections paint a happier picture. To Haley she was "as lighthearted a person as I ever met in my life. She always wanted to hear something funny so she could laugh." Noel Langley found her "absolutely enchanting. Her manners were perfect, far better than anyone else's there. She always called you Mister." It is possible that she was unaware of any ill-feeling because she was distracted by thoughts of Fleming, upon whom she had a crush. She attempted to flirt with him, but he tactfully pretended not to notice.

It was an arduous shoot and, at twenty-three weeks, the longest in Metro's history, apart from such troubled productions as *Ben-Hur* and *Trader Horn*. When Garland was felled by a cold for five days, the delay put $150,000 on the budget, but there were no other hitches, even when, three weeks before the completion of principal photography, there was another change of director. George Cukor had been fired from *Gone With the Wind*, and Selznick had asked King Vidor to take over. Vidor was unhappy at the prospect of doing so at such short notice, since he customarily spent at least four months preparing a film. He read the several scripts of that film over one weekend and procrastinated. He was somewhat relieved when he learned that Clark Gable, the biggest of the four names in the film, had asked for Victor Fleming. Since M-G-M was to distribute the film, a deal was done, and Vidor was asked by Mayer as a favor to Selznick to take on *The Wizard of Oz* instead. He did so, he said, from "a certain loyalty to M-G-M," with whom he had been associated since *The Big Parade* in 1925. In the years immediately following, he had given them prestige successes in *The Crowd* and *Hallelujah*, but did not work there regularly as he did not particularly care for the studio or Mayer, who had agreed to make such films only reluctantly.

Fleming refused to report to *Gone With the Wind* until he had familiarized himself with the material, and had finished shooting the Oz scenes for M-G-M. He remained long enough to oversee the special effects being prepared for the tornado which sweeps Dorothy from Kansas to Oz. In comparison, Vidor's work, which began in February 1939, was very simple, primarily restricted to those mono-chrome scenes in Kansas which open and close the picture. He later observed that he got "a tremendous kick" whenever he saw the film or heard Garland's record of "Over the Rainbow," because he had staged it in the same manner as the songs in *Hallelujah*. "Previously in most of the Sound musicals someone stood up in front of the camera and sang directly to it. In directing 'Over the Rainbow' I was able to keep the movement of Judy Garland flowing freely very much in the style of a Silent scene."

The film finished shooting in March, but process work and post-production took another four months, during which the final cost rose to $2,777,080. There is some mystery about the original budget, which is not listed anywhere among all the details of its components— probably because Mayer did not want it known. But with knowledge of the length of the shoot and how much Garland's absence cost for the loss of five days, and taking into account the special effects, we can arrive at an original estimate of around $1,800,000—which might be expected to turn a small profit. Schenck, who was not enthusiastic about the project in the first place, rushed out to California when the budget exceeded $2,000,000. He was furious and, determined to find out who was accountable, called a meeting of the Executive Committee, at which he demanded to know why costs were escalat-ing. He was alarmed that *The Wizard of Oz* had become the third costliest film in the studio's history. More expensive were *Ben-Hur* (1926) at $3,967,000 and *The Good Earth* (1937) at $2,816,000— neither of which had made a profit on their original release.

The first of several previews took place in the suburbs of Los Angeles, when the film was found to be too long. It was suggested that two songs should be dropped: "The Jitterbug" and "Over the Rainbow." According to Freed, he used his influence with Mayer to get the latter restored on three occasions, after further previews had again led to the decision to delete it. He did not, however, fight for "The Jitterbug," which serves the plot in the same way as some of the *Snow White* songs do in Disney's film, to picture the cast in merry mood despite a lingering menace—in this case, bugs in the trees which give them the jitters. The soundtrack remains, but the only surviving footage of it is a home-movie taken on the set by Harold Arlen. On this evidence, the dance is pretty enough, but the song is badly placed, holding up the action. LeRoy was wise to drop it. Curiously, it is the only other song from the film which Garland recorded commercially, and it was issued on the reverse side of "Over the Rainbow." The other melodies were recorded by the Ken Darby Singers with Victor Young and his Orchestra, and packaged by Decca with Garland's record in a boxed set. This odd state of affairs was not rectified until 1956, when M-G-M Records issued a soundtrack album which integrated the songs and dialogue throughout.

The first press previews of the film were held on August 9 in Los Angeles and New York. *Snow White* was invoked by almost every reviewer, though not to *Oz's* detriment: the *Los Angeles Examiner* declared it "just as much a screen classic as was *Snow White.* You can see it again and again and never tire of its magic." The *New York Times* called it "a delightful piece of wonder-working which had the youngsters" eyes shining and brought a quietly amused gleam to the wiser ones of the oldsters . . . Judy Garland's Dorothy is a pert and fresh-faced miss with the wonder-lit eyes of a believer in fairy tales." The *Hollywood Citizen-News* thought Garland "rosy-cheeked, starry-eyed, and more alluring than a glamour girl," while the *New York Daily News* considered her "as clever a little actress as she is a singer and her special style of vocalizing is ideally adapted to the music of the picture." Few singled her out for special praise, however, and much of what they said was little different from the praise they had heaped on Shirley Temple.

The most serious reservations about the film have always concerned the decor, in particular the Emerald City, a hideous art-deco monstrosity, and Munchkinland, a syrupy evocation of calendar-art otherworldliness. The Kansas sequence which opens the film has acquired a historical poignancy, for audiences now know what lay over the rainbow for the young girl who sang so wistfully. It acts as an excellent prologue, however, to the film's magic, which begins as Dorothy, in her famous red slippers, takes the Munchkins' advice to "Follow the Yellow Brick Road," and more potently as she, with her dog Toto, breaks into a merry dance, "We're Off to See the Wizard."

The film made for a considerable amount of red ink in M-G-M's

1939 ledgers. It did well in the big cities, but with children allowed in at half-price, it took in only $3,017,000—which, with the cost of prints and advertising, produced no profit. The outbreak of the Second World War meant that most European markets were closed to it. Britain, in any case, was not too interested. M-G-M had been attracted to the story precisely because it was a specifically American fantasy, and although Baum's book had been published abroad, it had not achieved any renown there. When the film opened in Britain, Graham Greene, in the *Spectator*, noted that "the morality seems a little crude and the fancy material . . . rattles like dry goods." He approved of Garland, "with her delectable long-legged stride," but his enthusiasm was not shared by Dilys Powell, in the *Sunday Times*, who judged Garland "flagrantly too old for her shoes." Both critics were impressed by the lavishness of the film, however, and both pointed out the absurdity of the British Board of Censors giving the film an A Certificate, which meant that it could only be seen by children accompanied by an adult. They also singled out Margaret Hamilton for praise, and indeed she was the only other member of the cast mentioned by Greene. The casting was another obstacle to success in Britain and other overseas territories: only Frank Morgan, Billie Burke and Garland were names of any sort, but even they were not considered star attractions. Nor did Garland have the advantage she had in America of being familiar from records or radio appearances.

To overcome this disadvantage, M-G-M had arranged for her to sing before the Royal family on October 18, 1939, at a Command Performance at Britain's biggest cinema, the Gaumont State in the London suburb of Kilburn. The occasion was designed to benefit the Cinematograph Trades Benevolent Fund, and the Hardy family was also due to appear, but the event was canceled after the declaration of the war in Europe on September 4. Instead, Metro's publicity office in London started a buildup, and the first issue of *Picturegoer* in the new year contained a rare full-page advertisement announcing: "You will remember 1940 as the year that brought you *The Wizard of Oz*." In the event, the film managed no more than a meager two weeks' run at the company's flagship, the Empire, Leicester Square, attracting only 22,556 customers in the first week and 16,946 in the second. This is a poor showing: a month later, *Ninotchka*, starring Greta Garbo, played to 65,074 patrons during the first of its five weeks at the same theater. Nor did Garland's recording of "Over the Rainbow" become the instant success in Britain that it had in the

U.S. As the war became more serious, however, causing nationwide separations, its lyric took on a new meaning—as it would do in the States when America entered the war. By that time, all other recordings of the song had been long forgotten: it belonged exclusively to Judy Garland.

Meanwhile, back in America, Garland was being partnered once again with Mickey Rooney in a new film, *Babes in Arms*. The Garland-Rooney partnership which began properly, on an equal footing, with this film, was to become a very successful one for M-G-M. To the studio, the teaming was the most natural thing in the world. The two youngsters blended well, were near enough in age to become a romantic team, and had certain optimistic, "peppy" qualities in common. *Love Finds Andy Hardy* had proved that Rooney could casually overlook Garland's yearning for him—at least until the last reel. Indeed, there seemed to be nothing that Rooney could not do—even singing and dancing, neither of which he had done before the camera since he became a big draw—and M-G-M rightly thought that extensive exposure opposite him could turn Garland into an important attraction in her own right.

Babes in Arms was waiting to be plucked from Broadway, and could provide Freed with a successful movie musical, the first one on which he would be credited as producer.* One of the hits of the 1936/37 season, the show had been written by Richard Rodgers and Lorenz Hart, who provided both the book and the score. Freed rejected the first screenplay, written by Florence Ryerson and Edgar Allan Woolf, who, on the evidence of *Everybody Sing*, were supposed to be suited to writing for Garland. He replaced them with Jack McGowan, a former Broadway writer who had contributed to several M-G-M musicals of the 1930s, but he shares credit on the final film with Kay Van Riper, who, responsible for most of the Andy Hardy films, was an acknowledged expert on providing dialogue for Rooney. In the finished film, Rooney is very much center stage, as intended; and an earlier song-and-dance routine, done for M-G-M in a film called *Broadway to Hollywood* when he was twelve, is included in a montage showing vaudeville in its dying days. The plot concerns a group of old-time vaudeville players who go off to tour while the youngsters put on a show, starring Garland, to prove that they have talent, too.

*Yet another reason for doubting that *The Wizard of Oz* was Freed's idea is that he never showed any ambition beyond acquiring tried and true Broadway musicals before he assembled the creative personnel which became "the Freed unit."

When a has-been child star (June Preisser) invests money in the show in the hope of making a comeback, she is given all Garland's numbers. This gives Garland, leaving on a bus, the opportunity to sing her plaintive lament to a picture of Rooney, "I Cried for You"—but, of course, she is back for the minstrel show and "I'm Just Wild About Harry." The film actually concludes with a patriotic chant, "God's Country," written by Harburg and Arlen, who may be forgiven for one line alone: "We've got no Duce—we've got no Führer / But we've got Garbo and Norma Shearer."

There are several interpolated songs, by Edens and by Freed and Nacio Herb Brown, including "You Are My Lucky Star," which is sung in the film by Betty Jaynes, whom the ever-hopeful Mayer imagined might turn into another Deanna Durbin. Indeed, it is sung in counterpoint to another song by Garland, to make a duet clearly modeled on the "classical" versus "hot" finale in *Every Sunday*. The only Rodgers and Hart numbers left from the original score are the title song, quickly dispatched, "Where or When," and a snatch of "The Lady Is a Tramp," used as background music for the pert, blond Preisser, who, in a (perhaps unwitting) send-up of Shirley Temple, proves an admirable foil for Garland.

Whatever the studio's hopes for the Rooney-Garland team, the film was planned primarily as a vehicle for Rooney in Andy Hardy guise as the enterprising small-town boy. Backstage musicals tended to be costly, but this one was to concentrate on rehearsals rather than spectacular numbers, which would keep down the budget. It may seem odd, then, that as director, Freed chose Busby Berkeley, whose choreography for extravagant early Warner Bros. musicals such as *42nd Street* and *Gold Diggers of 1933* had given him the reputation of being one of Hollywood's most celebrated exponents of the form. "Forget the dances, forget all the trick steps, and think *only* of the camera," was his creed, as his traveling camera panned across vast spaces packed with chorus girls. When Warners had promoted him to director, however, Berkeley was given very limited financial resources for the production numbers in such musicals as *Gold Diggers of 1935* and *Hollywood Hotel*, and he had been obliged to compensate by using his powers of invention. Freed had admired the results, and had persuaded himself that Berkeley was the right man for *Babes in Arms*.

"Buzz" Berkeley had arrived at M-G-M on contract in January 1939, taking a salary cut from $2,250 a week to $1,500, probably consoling himself with the thought that his new employers rewarded box-office success with increased fees. In fact, Berkeley was fortunate to find himself in work at all. His last films as a director at Warners were undistinguished programmers, while his choreography for *Gold Diggers in Paris* and, at M-G-M, *Broadway Serenade*, is kitsch at its grimmest. Furthermore, his private life hardly equipped him to be a member of Mayer's happy family, although he *was* devoted to his mother (so much so that he attempted suicide after her death). Back in 1934, he had been accused first of manslaughter and then second-degree murder after his automobile had crashed head-on into another near Santa Monica. He made his initial court appearance on a stretcher, and the first two trials were adjourned because the jurors could not agree. Although he was acquitted on the third, much doubt remained. The crash had taken place after a Warner Bros. party, and the question was whether Berkeley had been too drunk to know that he was driving with a flat tire, or whether it had blown after the crash. He had been divorced for the second time a month after the third trial, and in 1938 had been sued for $250,000 by the actor Irving Wheeler for alienating the affections of his wife, Carole Landis. By the time he arrived at M-G-M, at the age of forty-three, he was an alcoholic. The music director, Max Meth, who had known Berkeley in the late 1920s, commented: "The brilliant guy of those days was gone. And all due to liquor—and his mother."

Freed, who had had little to do on *The Wizard of Oz* once post-production was completed, spent the early months of 1939 working with Berkeley on the choreography and production design of *Babes in Arms*. As the shooting of *Oz* dragged on, the start of *Babes in Arms*, too, looked problematical since Garland might not be free. In theory, she was allowed two months rest between the two pictures, but instead, she and Ethel went on an extended personal appearance tour which also took in performing with André Kostelanetz and his orchestra. Shooting eventually began on May 12, with a schedule of thirty-four days; but it had followed six days of recording and another ten of rehearsals, which in turn had been preceded by makeup and costume tests. On her seventeenth birthday, M-G-M presented Garland with her first automobile, a scarlet Cadillac. Naturally, she was pleased, but, like the other studio juveniles, she knew that the executives used expensive gifts to assuage their guilt about working their young performers so hard.

Freed's selection of an alcoholic egoist to guide these youngsters—particularly Garland, who did not have Rooney's experience—was a major blunder. This is not to say that the two juveniles did not enjoy the experience of making *Babes in Arms*, particularly when out of range of the sound-microphone. Required to whisper sweet nothings, Rooney might say "Are you wearing a green garter belt today?," to which Garland would whisper back "I hear the doctor says you have the clap." Berkeley did at least respond sufficiently to their natural, comic interplay to get some of it on film, but he was not an easy man to work with. "Berkeley could be charming," wrote Mickey Rooney, "with his flashing eyes and huge expressive eyebrows, and a smile that warmed everyone around him, but he had the alcoholic's perfectionism. If you couldn't toe the line, make it just so for Buzz, he'd go crazy." He insisted on shooting the musical numbers in one take, which was exhausting to the two stars: but by now they were both seasoned troupers and did not complain. Garland was less certain about his screaming "Google! Open them wide. I want to see your eyes!": she suspected that he had been told that she was not really pretty enough for the camera. Apart from this, he gave her no direction, which worried her, for this was her first "adult" role. She was too disciplined—and too happy about the way her career was shaping up—to complain, but the experience was vaguely unsettling. Making the film was like a roller-coaster: too much work, too much fun on the set, too little sleep, and a feeling that the man in charge did not care if the young performers were alive or dead as long as he got his shots in the camera.

The film closed eleven days behind schedule, one of which was lost—at a cost of $8,563—when Garland was suddenly called for retakes on *Oz*. Arthur Freed told Garland and Rooney that he had never known anyone to work so hard. For doing so, Rooney was paid $23,400, including a bonus called for under a new contract negotiated the previous year; but Garland's total pay worked out at a mere $8,833.

M-G-M publicized the film as "the dance-packed, song-jammed version of the stage hit that Broadway cheered for months," ignoring the fact that hardly any of the songs jammed in were the original ones. The *New York Daily News* observed that it had "lost some of its original sophistication and the elastic snap with which it went over on the stage," but called Rooney and Garland an "irresistible team." The *New York Post* admired them both, for Rooney's "mugging and undeniable song and dance talents," and Garland's "simply swell sense of swing," while the *New York Times* praised Rooney's "precocious virtuosity" and Garland's "beautiful imitation of Mrs. Roosevelt's broadcasting manner."

At a cost of $748,000, the film had gone $82,000 over budget, but it grossed $3,335,000 on its initial release. As it was scheduled to be released just after *The Wizard of Oz*, M-G-M decided that a Mickey-and-Judy tour could be arranged to promote both films at the same time. So, missing the Hollywood premiere of *Oz* at Grauman's Chinese Theater, Rooney and Garland were sent East. Accompanied by their respective mothers, Roger Edens, and the studio publicists, they left Los Angeles on August 6. Three days later, the *Hollywood Reporter* told its readers:

> The personal appearance of Judy and Mick at the Loew's Palace in Washington, in conjunction with *The Wizard of Oz*, set Washington on its heels. It looked as if another King and Queen had arrived,* from the number of people who tried to get inside the theater all morning and afternoon. Mick and Judy went on stage for the first show at two to do twelve minutes, and were kept there for forty with the packed house still yelling for more, while six thousand people lined up outside trying to get in. Finally, the house manager mounted the stage and informed seat holders that Mick and Judy were finished for that show, and pleaded with the audience to vacate their seats so others could get in for the next performance.

By the time this report was published, Garland and Rooney were already in Connecticut for three more personal appearances, in Bridgeport, New Haven and Hartford. On August 17, they were in New York, where their opening-day performances broke the house record at the Capitol, with 37,000 spectators. According to the *Reporter*:

> The lines started to form at 5:30 in the morning and when the box office opened at eight there were 15,000 four abreast lined up around the corner almost to Eighth Avenue . . . So many people were turned away that the overflow filled almost all the other Broadway houses, jammed the restaurants, soft drink parlors and candy stores.

Many of the fans were children: "Were there one child in greater New York who wasn't either in the Capitol or trying to get in," the *New York Daily Mirror* speculated, "that youngster must have been quarantined with the measles . . . A juvenile tempest raged on Broadway."

The theater manager asked the two young stars to do an extra performance that evening, making seven instead of the scheduled six. They played seven again at weekends, to nine screenings of the film,

*A reference to the recent visit by George VI and his consort.

and five on weekdays (to seven screenings); each performance lasted some thirty minutes. With an orchestra conducted by George Stoll, sent from Culver City, Garland sang "The Lamp Is Low" and "Comes Love"; together they sang "Good Morning" and "God's Country," to plug *Babes in Arms*; and as a finale they dueted on "Oceans Apart." Rooney also did his impressions of Clark Gable and Lionel Barrymore and had a session on the drums.

It was not only children who were impressed. *Variety* noted that it had been four years since the Capitol bill included live appearances:

> There's a vast difference between the current biz at the Capitol with that of its last stage show. Latter held Lou Holtz, Belle Baker, Block and Sully, Moore and Revel, and Tip, Tap and Toe, but the public was apathetic. It was stronger on paper than is the current layout, but the names of Rooney and Garland are evidently magic, plus the benefits accruing from the dandy exploitation campaign on *Oz*.

After noting that the crowds could hardly be turning up for the film, since the reviews had not yet appeared, the reviewer went on to say that they were getting their money's worth: "It's grade-A showmanship by both kids . . . They're young, fresh and on the upbeat in the public's affection and imagination—a tousle-haired imp and a cute, clean-cut girl with a smash singing voice and style."

Louis B. Mayer was in town to witness the hysteria of the crowds and to read the rave reviews. After lunching with Schenck and J. Robert Rubin (the lawyer who had introduced him to Marcus Loew back in 1923), he cabled to LeRoy: "We had the best lunch ever. Had the crowds for dessert." Garland and Rooney were pleased that he was there to see their triumph, but otherwise it was an odd experience for them. Half the time, most of New York wanted to meet them or play host to them. For the other half, they were virtually imprisoned inside the theater, with food brought in from the Waldorf. At least the management had installed a special solarium and prepared a roof garden, so they were not entirely confined to their dressing-rooms. Garland had been disappointed not to be able to go to the World's Fair, but after their last show on Sunday, August 27, Mayor Fiorello La Guardia organized a visit for them and provided a police escort. Garland recalled: "We raced from one exhibit to the next. We saw everything. We rode everything. I still remember it as the most wonderful night of my life."

She also enjoyed appearing on Fred Waring's radio show. She had understood that she was to make a guest appearance, but discovered that the entire program was dedicated to her, with "Over the Rainbow" providing the theme-song for the evening. "I sang all the songs from *The Wizard of Oz* for him," she remembered, "and a good time was had by all—most especially by me!"

The excitement and the sheer hard work inevitably took its toll. During one performance at the Capitol, Garland collapsed backstage and Rooney had to fill in until she had recovered sufficiently to resume. "If I hadn't mentioned her collapse, no one in the audience would have known," he wrote years later. "That's the sort of trouper Judy was."

Business in New York was so good that a trip to Philadelphia was canceled, and rather than move the picture over to second-run houses at the end of the second week, as originally intended, Bert Lahr and Ray Bolger were brought in to substitute for Rooney, who had to return to Hollywood to begin shooting a new film. Garland rehearsed with them, and on Rooney's last night, between shows, they were escorted to the Harvest Moon Ball at Madison Square Garden as an added attraction. Others on the bill included Alice Faye, Tony Martin, Sonja Henie, Anna Neagle, George Raft and the Jimmy Dorsey Band, as well as Lahr, Bolger and Jack Haley, but the greatest ovation went to Garland and Rooney, who at first appeared to be overwhelmed by the welcome they received from the twenty-thousand-strong audience. The following morning, Rooney was among the spectators at the Capitol to offer a farewell bouquet of roses to Garland, but there was a stampede at his mere appearance, interrupting the show, and he had to beat a hasty retreat.

Edens used Rooney's departure as an opportunity to change Garland's material, retaining "Come Love" but adding "Franklin D. Roosevelt Jones" and "Blue Evening." Lahr sang "Song of the Woodman," which Arlen and Harburg had written specially for him for *The Show Is On*, while Bolger clowned and danced. To conclude, the three of them sang "The Jitterbug," after explaining that it had been cut from the film for reasons of length. *Variety* felt that the right decision had been made, and assured its readers that the song was "not up to the other portions of the film."

All three artists were paid $3,500 each a week, $15,000 less than Rooney. Even so, Garland's total sum of $10,500 was, ironically, more than she had received for nineteen weeks' work on the picture, for which she had been paid just over $9,649.

Back in Hollywood after recording the two songs from the film, she appeared with Rooney on *Screen Guild Theater*, which also featured

Ann Sothern and Cary Grant. She became a regular on Bob Hope's radio show, both vocalizing and making jokes at his expense. Helped by Rooney, she pressed her hands and feet into the cement outside Grauman's Chinese Theater when *Babes in Arms* was premiered there.

Meanwhile, the death of Will Gilmore's wife had left him free to propose to Garland's mother. Garland did not approve of Gilmore in the least, and Ethel did little to improve matters by telling her daughter that the reason she had become attached to Gilmore back in Lancaster was that Frank not only drank but was also homosexual. Garland did not find this "explanation" sympathetic. The fact that Ethel was blackening her dead husband's name to excuse her own behavior only served to increase Garland's antipathy toward her. The prospect of her beloved father being supplanted by the unprepossessing Gilmore horrified her, but there was nothing she could do about it. On November 17, the couple eloped to Yuma, Arizona, where they were married. It was Ethel's forty-sixth birthday. It was also the fourth anniversary of Frank's death. "That was the most awful thing that ever happened," Garland said. "My mother marrying that awful man the same day that my daddy died."

6

Mrs. David Rose

WHILE *THE WIZARD OF OZ* and *Babes in Arms* dominated Garland's professional life in 1939, her private life was preoccupied with her first serious love affair. Romance was an absolute essential in Hollywood, both on and off the screen, and it is surprising that someone as impressionable as Garland had not fallen so completely in love before. In the prevailing atmosphere of Hollywood, romance was a requisite, even for those only capable of calf-love, and Garland had to be seen keeping company with a beau. The obvious options were Mickey Rooney, Freddie Bartholomew and Jackie Cooper. Rooney and Garland both said that they were never romantically involved, but she did have a few dates with Bartholomew. Of the three, however, Cooper was the only serious contender and, when they were barely fourteen, with the approval of their mothers, he and Garland saw each other frequently for a while. "I was crazy about her," Cooper recalled, "madly in love with her. To me she was beautiful, fantastic, but what I remember most was her sense of humor." They walked along the sands at Malibu, drank milkshakes together at the soda-fountain, listened to Benny Goodman records, and held hands in the back row at the pictures. The two of them had much in common: neither had enjoyed a proper childhood and both were in the business; and they both understood what that meant. When they were not together, they spent hours on the telephone. "She had to feel needed and wanted," said Cooper, emphasizing that then, shortly after she had arrived at M-G-M, she felt anything but that. "Even then she seemed buffeted about, burdened with problems beyond her years, but with this enormous spirit."

In her relationship with Cooper, she was already showing signs of the emotional instability that was to dog her throughout her life. She told Cooper that she loved him, but then only a few weeks later she explained to him that girls grew up faster than boys; she missed, she said, the company of "older men." The "older man" she had in mind was Billy Halop, a sixteen-year-old actor who had arrived in Hollywood in 1937 to repeat his stage role as a Bowery boy in the screen version of Sidney Kingsley's account of life on Manhattan's East Side, *Dead End*. Halop played his juvenile roles with a suggestion of itchy pants: he was not entirely acting. He was perhaps the first of the misguided romantic choices Garland was to make over the years, and it is possible that the studio stepped in to prevent their virginal young star being carried off by a Dead End Kid.

The man who absorbed most of her off-screen thoughts in 1939, however, was the bandleader and clarinet-player Artie Shaw, whom Garland had originally met on her first visit to New York in 1936. She had been taken by Ethel to see him conduct his orchestra at the Hotel Lexington, and has been so impressed that she had impulsively hastened backstage to congratulate him. Shaw was known as a musician's musician, and he in turn was impressed that Garland, then only fourteen, understood that. She had not forgotten this encounter, and when Shaw opened in the largest dancehall in Los Angeles, the Palomar Ballroom, on February 10, 1939, she insisted on being present. Halfway through the concert, Shaw collapsed and was rushed to the hospital. He had proved to be allergic to a medicine prescribed to him for a recent illness, and he hovered near death for some weeks.

Much to Ethel's distress, Garland sent him flowers and insisted on visiting him. Ethel continued to distrust musicians—especially since Suzy had returned home after her marriage to Lee Cahn had failed. Shaw may have been a more distinguished musician than either Cahn or Bobby Sherwood, whom Jimmy had married in 1936, but Ethel did not want him as a son-in-law. He was twenty-eight, with two broken marriages behind him and a reputation as a ladies' man. This was one of the reasons that Judy, ten years younger, was attracted to him. Furthermore, he was not only virile and attractive but also intelligent. He was well read and could not only discuss music but recommend which books she should read: he seemed to be the father figure she had been looking for. Her relationship with Victor Fleming on the long shoot of *The Wizard of Oz* had only served to remind her how much she missed her father, and the extent to which she was dependent on her mother to guide her in an adults' world. As for Shaw, neither then nor later was he immune to the charms of Hollywood's young leading ladies, and although flattered by her attention, any serious liaison with Garland was out of the question, he did not discourage her visits.

Accustomed to having her own way, Garland refused to listen to her mother's strictures about Shaw, and, when Ethel refused to take her, she went to the hospital with Betty Asher. Five years older than Garland, Betty Asher was the daughter of Ephraim Asher, who had been producing B movies at Universal under the Laemmile regime. She was reputed to be the girlfriend of Eddie Mannix who, as manager of the M-G-M studio, had an interest in Garland's activities. She was the second important figure to enter Garland's life at this time. She had just been assigned to the young star by Howard Strickling, and it was her job to see that her charge was reasonably happy when on the company's business. At the same time, she was expected to report back any of Garland's activities which could be used by the publicity department. Later in the year, she would assume the same duties toward Lana Turner.

During Shaw's protracted recuperation, Garland had to contrive ways of seeing him without Ethel knowing, and this was not easy. A new house was being built for her and her mother and stepfather on Stone Canyon Drive, and it occurred to Garland to insist on having a separate entrance to her own wing. This would mean that her movements could be less easily monitored, and she could escape to go for drives with Shaw. She told Ethel that she needed the separate entrance in order to avoid her new stepfather, whom she loathed. Since she was paying for the house, Ethel had no choice but to accept.

That Garland could see Shaw secretly gave her great satisfaction, for it was an act of rebellion against Ethel, who only allowed her daughter to see Shaw in public, properly chaperoned. He came to the house several times with friends, including Jack Cathcart, who had helped the Gumms in Chicago, and was to marry Suzy later in the year. Shaw was also a guest at Judy's seventeenth birthday party in June, and brought with him someone else who was to become a friend, Phil Silvers. He and Silvers had written and recorded a burlesque sketch for the occasion. Ethel kept an eye on the youngsters and the older musicians. Her attitude toward Shaw hardened further when she learned that he had tried to date Ann Rutherford. Four and a half years older than Judy, Rutherford was working in a film with Shaw and Lana Turner, *Dancing Co-ed:* her mother refused Shaw on Ann's behalf.

At seventeen, Garland hated to be treated like a child, as if she were always going to be wide-eyed, innocent Dorothy. It was particularly demoralizing at work, where she was refused "the glamour treatment" that was being given to Lana Turner, who, only a year earlier, had studied alongside her in the M-G-M schoolhouse. As Turner advanced to a stellar position at Culver City, the studio began to issue "pin-up" stills of her and created an image to match. Turner had always been one to turn men's heads; and, almost desperately, Garland wanted it to be recognized that she was no longer "little Judy," studio mascot, who had repeatedly sung about her adolescent crushes.

The studio's speech and drama coach, Lillian Burns, still spent an hour a day with Garland and Turner—though clearly had more success with the former. One afternoon, she suggested that Garland should read the role of Emily in Thornton Wilder's *Our Town,* and was so struck by her interpretation that she told her that there was nothing that she could not do. Garland disagreed: "Except that when I sit down at a table opposite a man, all he can see is my head. I haven't any neck."

"She constantly put herself up against criteria she could not measure up to," Shaw remembered:

Therefore, she was constantly dissatisfied with herself. She was always looking at the long-stemmed American beauty, which was synonymous with stardom. In other words, if you put yourself up against a girl like Elizabeth Taylor, you can be damn good-looking and still look pretty ugly to yourself . . . It was in her marrow. "I'm ugly. I'm funny. I don't look good. I can't sing." It wasn't as much an inferiority complex as it was something that had been imposed upon her by the environment that she lived in.

"I knew she had a crush on me," he said later, "but it never went beyond that." He was fully aware of the danger of this "moonstruck little kid" if her name were to be linked with a twice-divorced rake:

her status as America's favorite kid sister would be compromised, and the wrath of the studio would be upon him. He declined to call on her at her house, even by the separate entrance, but they continued to meet alone. One day, she telephoned Jackie Cooper and asked him to do her a "favor." She told him that he was the only one she could tell, and so would he pick her up in his Lincoln Zephyr and drive her to Shaw's house? He collected her later that evening, and as he drove her home had to listen to a long monologue about how wonderful and how fascinating Shaw was. "You have to understand that, short of homicide, I would have done anything for Judy," he explained. But by this time he had begun a serious romance with Bonita Granville and was no longer at Judy's disposal. She then persuaded her sister Jimmy to provide an alibi. Ethel would be told that Judy was ostensibly spending the evening at Jimmy's house; should Ethel telephone, Jimmy would explain that Judy had just slipped out for something at the drugstore.

Unfortunately for Garland, she had rivals for the affections of Shaw. At some point in the summer, Shaw began seeing Betty Grable, who had just signed a contract with 20th Century-Fox. Grable's screen career to this point had not been glorious, and she was best known to the public as the girl who had married the former child star, Jackie Coogan. When the Coogans were rather noisily divorced, Grable appeared at the courtroom on Shaw's arm, and the following day he accompanied her to New York, where she was to appear in *Du Barry Was a Lady*.

Their plans were strictly matrimonial, but Grable's mother—who had been guiding her career since adolescence—was violently opposed to the match, about which there was much speculation in the press, much to Garland's distress. In February 1940, both she and Grable were astonished to learn that Shaw and Lana Turner had eloped to be married in Las Vegas.

While Shaw and Turner had worked on *Dancing Co-ed*, there had been little love between them. When he visited her on the set of *Two Girls on Broadway*, however, she made for him "like a bee making for the honey," according to Phil Silvers, who was there. It was her twentieth birthday, and he invited her to dinner, with Silvers tagging along. In the car going home they began to discuss what each wanted in a partner, and before Silvers could draw breath they had turned around to hire a plane to Las Vegas, leaving him to drive Shaw's car home.

When the news broke the following day, Garland was devastated:

her beau had picked the one girl in the whole world whom she really envied. Her distress was deepened by a confrontation with Ethel, to whom she had blurted out—to explain her tears—what she considered her "involvement" with Shaw. She also intended to yell at Silvers. It had not taken the press long to discover that he had been at dinner with the newlyweds, and, after speaking to the first few reporters, he decided to escape the rest by fleeing to the golf course. He had been there some time, when he was paged by a caddy, summoning him to the clubhouse. There he was confronted by a tear-stained Garland. "How *could* they?" she cried. "I confided in her." Silvers told her that she was "the luckiest girl in the world" and that her relationship with Shaw had simply been a bad case of hero-worship. He slapped her playfully, an action which immediately restored her movie-star hauteur: she gave him a severe dressing down.

Her equilibrium was not so easily reestablished, however. She thought she had found her shining knight, only to have him denied to her not by Mayer or her mother, but by a friend and rival, a girl of her own age who, moreover, had been encouraged by the studio to be "sexy." The following day she was in tears again when she turned up at the NBC studio to rehearse an appearance on *The Bob Hope Show*. It provoked memories of the occasions when Shaw had escorted her there.

Down the corridor, a musician called David Rose was working on his arrangements for *The Tony Martin Show*. He was a close friend of Shaw's, and knew that Garland would be distraught. Learning that she was threatening that she could not go on, he went to her dressing-room in an attempt to console her. He had more success than Silvers, and with his encouragement went a slice of chocolate cake, something absolutely forbidden Garland by her strict diet. That evening, she went out with him. Undoubtedly she was attracted to him precisely because he was a close friend of Shaw's, and although they began to date, many of her friends believed that it would take a long time for her to recover from Shaw's rejection, and the way it was done.

David Rose was born in London but had lived in the U.S. since he was four. He had studied music at the Chicago Conservatoire, and started in show business as a pianist on local radio stations. He had moved to the West Coast, where he established a reputation as a composer of merit and a fine arranger. He was twenty-nine. The combination of age and experience made him doubly appealing to Garland. Naturally, it was not long before she was consulting him about her recording sessions for Decca, one of the few aspects of her career not controlled by M-G-M.

The reaction of Ethel and Louis B. Mayer to this new relationship was entirely predictable. Not only was Rose another musician, he was also still married to (though separated from) Martha Raye, a popular comedienne with a big mouth and a loud voice. No one at M-G-M thought it wise for the girl-next-door to take up with the cast-off of a slapstick comic, however distinguished he himself might be. Garland was forbidden to see him again. It was likely that he would be forgotten as she fulfilled her heavy schedule at the studio.

When Shaw and Turner returned to Hollywood, they expected Garland to visit them, but she was not interested. When Shaw, who knew she liked Turner, asked why, she replied: "Artie, she's a nice girl, but it's like sitting in a room with a beautiful vase." As it happened, there were not to be many more opportunities for such visits: the marriage was over within four months.*

Garland's new interest in Rose did not keep her from being reminded how and why she had lost Shaw. She was to be haunted by Turner as she had been by Deanna Durbin. On April 27, she read in Louella Parsons's column: "If Lana Turner will behave herself and not go completely berserk she is headed for a top spot. She is the most glamorous actress since Jean Harlow." She remembered the many letters to the fan magazines praising Durbin at the expense of other, unnamed, juveniles who sang "jazzy" songs and punched their "pep" to the audience.

Garland insisted that she was insufficiently appreciated at M-G-M. Her record of "Over the Rainbow" and the success of *Babes in Arms* had further increased her value, but she was to complain that "even after *The Wizard of Oz* they treated me like a poor relative at the studio. They convinced me I wasn't very good. They kept telling me I wasn't any good as a performer. Neither Mickey nor I were exposed to the fact that we were important properties."

That she *was* important to the studio became obvious when she started to rebel against what she considered to be the studio's treatment of her. Luise Rainer had recently redefined the word "temperament" and so, despite two Oscars, the studio had dropped her in mid-contract when they discovered that the public was not overkeen

---

*One of Turner's witnesses at the divorce hearings was Betty Asher. Beforehand, she also, in Shaw's words, "paid me a little visit and stayed three days." His later Hollywood conquests would include Evelyn Keyes and, before that, Ava Gardner, who had been married to Mickey Rooney—who was later Turner's lover.

on her. This was clearly not going to happen to Garland, whose popularity had been ringingly confirmed by the *Oz/Babes* tour. M-G-M was prepared to put up with much from her because it was clear that she was going to be one of their biggest stars. She had not, however, forgotten the year of neglect, when no film roles were offered and Mayer dismissed her as "a hunchback." According to Jackie Cooper, it was because of such treatment that "she got tough." M-G-M's executives thought she should be grateful to them for taking an ordinary little girl and making her a star. They expected her to be docile. She thought otherwise. She began making demands about every aspect of her career, from the clothes she wore to the roles she played, demands which were considered unseemly in one relatively inexperienced. Nor had her relationships with two older men gone unnoticed: both contravened the public image which the studio was creating. Romance was what she craved and that was precisely what, in any real sense, Mayer would not agree to. And she was honest enough not to want the kind of which he approved. The studio could exploit her later, as Universal had exploited Deanna Durbin's transition from juvenile to romantic lead by publicizing her first screen kiss, but there was still mileage to be had from a teenage kid with a big singing voice.

The studio knew that Garland was not wistful Dorothy or timid Betsy Booth, but it was these roles that had made her a star—and she was stuck with them. The real Judy Garland was intense, headstrong, volatile and, after *Babes in Arms*, anxious to play grown-up roles, as she told anyone who would listen. In some respects, her demands, which were reasonably put, were at odds with her otherwise improvident attitude toward her career. Most stars who were career-motivated studied their next screenplays in detail and frequently consulted with their colleagues. Garland, on the other hand, only thought negatively about her next film, until it was due to start. Unlike Durbin, who struck a happy balance at Universal between making demands and taking orders, Garland simply fretted when she could not get her way about something. Durbin was luckier: she had parents to advise her. Garland had only Ethel, and she became increasingly unwilling to pay any attention to what her mother might say about her career.

In its determination to keep Garland immature, the studio was supported by California law, under which she was still a child. Her juvenile status was emphasized in February 1940 at the Academy Awards ceremony, where she was allowed to wear lipstick but appeared in an outfit more suited to a hick-town girl at the college hop than a movie star at Hollywood's biggest social event of the year. Following the precedents of Durbin and Rooney, Garland was awarded a special juvenile Oscar for *The Wizard of Oz* (and it says much about this great age of child stars—without taking away anything from these three—that this award was expected to be awarded annually). Fittingly, Rooney presented it to her. It was already known that "Over the Rainbow" had won an Oscar for the best song and, since it was already ineluctably associated with her, she had been asked to sing it after accepting her own statuette. She later recalled this, with some elaboration, as

the most sensational moment of my career . . . The lump in my throat was so big when I sang that I sounded more like Flip the Frog than the most excited girl in all Hollywood. And I'll never forget how Mickey came to my rescue, for I was so nervous I thought I'd faint. He practically held me up through the second chorus.

After the ceremony, the press took so many pictures of them together that Rooney complained that he spent the rest of the evening trying to wipe the lipstick off his face.

Further excitement, of a less welcome kind, occurred a week later, when a nineteen-year-old drifter from Buffalo, Robert Wilson, telephoned the police to say that Garland was about to be kidnapped. He and a local boy, Frank Foster, had planned to abduct her from her Bel Air home, but Wilson panicked. The two men were arrested at a hotel in Santa Monica, where Wilson admitted that he was the instigator. He was not interested in a ransom, but had intended to let the world know of his passion for Garland, his "dream girl." M-G-M would happily have given her round-the-clock guards, but she felt that her life was already sufficiently constrained by the studio.

M-G-M was still keen to reunite Garland with Rooney, who, even though nearing twenty, looked young enough to continue to be America's favorite adolescent for several more years. The studio had bought *The Youngest Profession*, the story of a meddling brat who is also an autograph hound (chasing famous people gives the piece its title): this provided a role for Garland, but there was no obvious part for Rooney. The film—at least as it appeared in 1943 with Virginia Weidler in the Garland role—seems to have been a medium-budget affair of the kind Garland had been doing prior to *The Wizard of Oz*. It was obvious that the public wanted to see Garland and Rooney together again, however, so Arthur Freed was asked to find a vehicle which could be sold to exhibitors as one of M-G-M's major productions.

In the meantime, Garland was rushed into her second film about the Hardy family, *Andy Hardy Meets Debutante*. Rooney remembers that the studio was so eager to get it out that he was forced to work into the early hours on the last day of shooting. Garland's role is even less substantial than the one in *Love Finds Andy Hardy*. When the Judge has to go to New York on business, Mrs. Hardy says: "Now Andy can have Betsy Booth as a playmate. She must be fifteen years old now." This served to remind Garland of her image, and her frustration is echoed when Betsy says of the debutante (played by Diana Lewis, who retired soon after, when she married William Powell): "Without her makeup on she hasn't any more glamor than I have." The film concludes with Andy putting up Betsy's picture alongside those of the debutante and Polly, his regular girlfriend, and this may have consoled Garland for her wisp of a role. The character Lana Turner played in the earlier film is mentioned several times, but by now Turner was too big a draw for an Andy Hardy movie. So was Garland, and she had only been given the role to please the Mickey-and-Judy fans.

Such was the tight schedule that Garland did not even have the customary consolation for such roles of having any new songs written for her to perform. Instead, she sings "Alone," a Brown-Freed song from *A Night at the Opera*, and "I'm Nobody's Baby," an old song from the 1920s—the first in a vain attempt to attract Rooney's attention, and the second as a lament because he has yet to notice her in the way she would like. The only good thing to emerge from the film was that the latter song, coupled with "Buds Don't Bud," became her second best-selling record.

It was clear that Garland needed a new agent. During the making of *The Wizard of Oz*, Ida Koverman had told Ethel that her daughter's interests would best be served if she were represented by the Orsatti Agency. Jesse Martin had been hardly more welcome at the studio than Al Rosen—whereas Frank Orsatti had Mayer's ear at all times. Koverman was as aware as anybody of Orsatti's unsavory reputation, but had felt that he was in a position to get Garland proper remuneration for the hard and important work she was no doing. Ethel had informed Martin of the impending change, at home. Garland had been listening from the top of the stairs, and fled to her room in tears. A difficult situation had not been helped when, a few days later,

Benny Thau told Martin that the studio was perfectly happy with the way he was handling her affairs. Nevertheless, Martin had sold his agreement with the Garlands to Orsatti, who immediately managed to get the combined fee for Ethel and Judy raised from $350 a week to $500. Garland had been permitted to keep the fees she earned from radio appearances, but these should have been hers by right and not by M-G-M's kind consent. The habit of "creaming off" Garland's salary, later to become endemic, may well have begun with Orsatti.

As far as Garland was concerned, Orsatti's closeness to Mayer was now a disadvantage, since he was as likely to support the studio boss as he was his client in any arguments about the way her career was (or, rather, was not) developing. As it happened, Leland Hayward, arguably the most powerful agent in Hollywood, was anxious to take her on. Barron Polan had left M-G-M to join Hayward's staff and, as Judy's friend, he urged her to let Hayward represent her. Hayward's faith in Garland was shown when he bought her services from Orsatti for $25,000. He immediately started negotiations for a new contract, since she was still getting only $500 a week, which was hardly commensurate with the position she had now reached. Mayer had held open house at his own mansion to celebrate her eighteenth birthday in June, which was proof of her importance to the studio. After some hesitation, he decided to agree to Hayward's terms.

When the original contract was signed in 1935, Garland had been a child star, M-G-M's possible answer to Shirley Temple. Earlier in 1940, Darryl F. Zanuck had announced that the twelve-year-old Temple was being dropped from the contract list, a brutal acknowledgment that her popularity had disappeared with her childhood. A final nail in the coffin had been the recent failure of *The Blue Bird*, adapted from the Maeterlinck play, which had been planned as 20th Century-Fox's riposte to *The Wizard of Oz*. Although Temple's lack of genuine talent was amply demonstrated by comparisons with Garland and Durbin, Mayer persisted in his belief that M-G-M had a magical ability to handle child stars and signed her up. At one point she was scheduled to appear in the next Rooney-Garland opus, but in the event made only one minor film for the studio. Garland, on the other hand, as *Babes in Arms* had shown, was going to make an easy transition to adult roles, and her contract had only two more years to run. When she reached the age of twenty-one, she would no longer be under Ethel's jurisdiction: she might be persuaded by her agent, or a husband, that she had been badly underpaid and should move to another studio. M-G-M confidently anticipated another seven years of Mickey-and-Judydom, and accordingly raised her salary to $2,000 a week for three years, $2,500 for the next three, and then $3,000 for the last two years. This did not compare too unfavorably with the sums paid to Rooney, demonstrably a bigger draw than Garland. His contract gave him now, in its third year, $1,500 a week; if the studio exercised its option in a few months' time he would reach $1,750 a week and only $3,000 a week in its seventh and last year. But he did get a bonus of $25,000 per film, with a guarantee that he would make at least two movies a year.

Ethel signed the new contract in September 1940 as "the mother of the artist," agreeing to a reduced weekly personal stipend of $125. There was a tacit agreement that the Stone Canyon house, which Garland had paid for, would become Ethel's. It was Garland's avowed intention to provide her mother with a home, and then be done with her. Her mind was set on another house, any house, which she could enter as a bride. Meanwhile, Freed had settled on the next Rooney-Garland picture. As with *Babes in Arms*, he decided that its source should be a Broadway show. He alighted on the 1924 hit *No No Nanette* just as Warner Bros. sold the rights to RKO as a vehicle for Anna Neagle. He then started negotiations to buy another Broadway musical of the same vintage, *Good News*, but the Executive Committee decided that, with the war in Europe, audiences might not be that enthralled with a plot involving the outcome of a collegiate football game. Mayer suggested another Broadway show from that time, the Gershwins' *Strike Up the Band*, because, he said, "it sounds so patriotic." It was, in fact, a satire on warmongers, and although this did not worry Freed, it was not what M-G-M wanted. After some readjustments, however, *Strike Up the Band* eventually emerged as something not too far removed from *Good News*, the 1930 version of De Sylva, Brown and Henderson's hit show. It was to be a jolly Mickey-and-Judy treat which tried and succeeded in being as much like *Babes in Arms* as was decently possible.

The screenplay was written by John Monks, Jr., and Fred Finklehoffe, the authors of *Brother Rat*, a very successful play about romantic antics at a military academy. Finklehoffe was a particular admirer of Garland—both as a person and an actress—and Freed was to use him again on several of the vehicles he prepared for her. The story is set in a school, where Rooney dreams of conducting its dance orchestra—and not, as his mother hopes, of becoming a distinguished doctor. When the bandleader, Paul Whiteman (playing himself), announces a competition for school orchestras, Rooney exclaims that winning it "would put Riverwood High School on the front page of every newspaper in the world." Garland plays the band's vocalist, his best pal: he thinks she will make someone a wonderful wife one day. She also provides the most taking moments, with a plaintive ballad by Roger Edens, "I Ain't Got Nobody (and Nobody's Got Me)," which, with "Our Love Affair,"* brings out some of her appeal—her poignancy and her gaiety. For the latter song, another of Freed's Broadway protégées, Vincente Minnelli, conceived a trick number involving animated fruit. In spite of Garland's good showing with these two songs, Busby Berkeley, as director, was willfully insensitive to her talent. In the big production numbers, "La Conga" and the title song (the only Gershwin song retained from the original), she is just another finger-snapping singer, and is dressed in hideous frocks.

The reviewers liked her, however. The film was "spanking good entertainment" said the *New York Times*, noting that Garland sang "with a good deal of animal spirits." *Newsweek* found her "undismayed in the face of such comprehensive competition" (i.e., Rooney), and doing "some monopolizing of her own with a score that includes a possible new hit ('Our Love Affair'), a parody, and a handful of dated favorites." The juvenile stars, said the *New York Herald Tribune*, "give the show all the punch of a sure-fire hit." While Rooney was "just as effective and just as hammy as he ever was," Garland "plays her part in the proceedings with considerably more integrity," and sings with "vitality." The film, which cost $838,661, grossed $3,494,000 after its release in September 1940.

Strike Up the Band may have been a success, but Judy Garland was still playing schoolgirls. This was to change, thanks to Freed and Edens, who were always alive to the possibilities of Garland's talent. While lunching with Broadway's legendary composer-star-lyricist-dramatist George M. Cohan, Freed impulsively took an option on *Little Nellie Kelly*, a dated Broadway hit of 1922. If this could be fashioned as a vehicle for Garland, it would at least prove Edens's contention that she had more to offer than being merely one-half of a juvenile partnership. The story concerned a young Irishwoman who emigrates to America with her new husband and her doting but cantankerous father, who so disapproves of the match that he will not speak to his son-in-law, a perfectly respectable young man who gets a job as a New York cop. Nellie dies in childbirth, and father and

*Written by Edens and Georgie Stoll, an M-G-M orchestra conductor, according to the records in the Academy of Motion Picture Arts and Sciences, but credited elsewhere—significantly— to Edens and Freed.

grandfather, still unreconciled, are left to bring up the baby. Little Nellie Kelly grows up to become a charmer, who nevertheless fails to bring her father and her work-shy grandfather together. During a St. Patrick's Day parade, she meets the son of a fellow-immigrant, who has done well and founded a construction business. Their blossoming affair is thwarted by her selfish grandfather, who eventually leaves the house when opposed. To everyone's surprise, he gets a job driving a buggy in Central Park, and the story ends happily, with everyone reconciled and Nellie on the brink of romance.

Garland would play a double-role, mother and daughter, and although Mayer protested that "You can't let that baby have a child!," the sentiment of the piece was much to his liking. Garland jumped at the chance of taking her first adult role, but was nervous playing her first romantic clinch, wanting, she said, to announce to the unit, "Unaccustomed as I am to public love-scenes . . ." Fortunately, she spends more time on screen as the American-born daughter, since (despite her claims about her father's ancestry), her Irish accent is distinctly uncertain, unlike those of George Murphy, as the cop, and Charles Winninger as "Grandpa." One of the highlights of the film is the St. Patrick's Day parade, with Garland leading a rousing rendition of "It's a Great Day for the Irish," written for her by Edens. As sung, thrillingly, by her, it becomes an anthem to the Old Country, but it was not destined to become part of her later repertoire of her movie songs. She came to prefer "A Pretty Girl Milking Her Cow," sung in the film twice: first (in the role of the mother) as a ballad, then (in the role of the daughter) in a jazzed-up version. She also sings a jazzed-up version of "Singin' in the Rain" at a dinner-dance.

Norman Taurog directed the film, which apart from her performance, is about as appetizing as yesterday's warmed-up Irish stew. The reviews were accordingly lukewarm. The *New York Daily News* described it as "oversentimental," noting that Garland did "her best, but even her beguiling exuberance and her sweet way with a ballad cannot entirely overcome the deficiencies of the story." George Murphy disagreed, later describing the film as one of his own favorite pictures.

I was playing a scene with Judy Garland which was in the hospital when she was about to die during the birth of her only child, and I assure one and all that this was one of the greatest dramatic scenes that I have ever witnessed. It took me longer to get over the scene than it took Judy. And you might be interested that when the scene was finished the complete set was empty, with the exception of Norman Taurog, the director, Judy and myself. The grips, electricians, carpenters and all these so-called hard-bitten workers were so emotionally affected that they all had to get off the set so that their sobs would not disturb or disrupt the sound track.

Murphy was a star of the second echelon and an actor with a certain charm, but his scenes with Garland in the first half are underplayed. Douglas MacPhail, as the young man who falls in love with Little Nellie, was an unsure juvenile with a good singing voice and a career going nowhere. It was Garland who carried the film to box-office success, grossing $2,046,000 on an investment of $655,300.

Garland's off-screen romantic life was still causing problems. Ethel had been persuaded that David Rose's visits to the Stone Canyon house were made in order to discuss musical arrangements. One night, however, Gerold Frank reported, she happened to be driving past Rose's house, and was disconcerted to see her daughter's scarlet roadster parked outside: Judy had told her that she was going to the movies with some girlfriends. Ethel went home immediately and telephoned Rose, saying that if Judy was not back within fifteen minutes she would have the law on him. Garland felt humiliated, both for herself and for Rose. On another occasion, when Ethel spied the roadster outside Rose's house again, mother and daughter had a screaming match on the telephone. Later, Rose had a long session with Ethel, hinting that marriage might solve all their problems. At eighteen, Garland was old enough to marry without Ethel's consent and, apart from being already married (though separated), Rose was more than eligible: he was genial, cultured and, except for his elaborate model train set and Garland, only interested in his career. Unlike the suitors and husbands of some highly paid stars, he earned enough money to be independent.

In her battle to prevent the continuing romance, Ethel tried to enlist the support of many people, among them her daughter's former agent, Jesse Martin. She hoped that he could persuade Garland to change her mind. In the past, Martin had listened patiently while Judy spoke of her dreams of leaving show business to live a normal life. He realized, however, that she had now become far more successful than he had ever dreamed, and he knew that she enjoyed the tinsel and wonder and plaudits too much ever to quit. At the same time, the chubby, cheerful girl he had known so well was showing distinct signs of strain. She was clearly lonely, and he thought her chances of happiness would be greater in a life shared with David Rose than in one dominated by her mother. He counseled Garland that if she truly loved Rose she should go ahead and marry him.

Ethel had a more willing ally in her daughter's current agent, Leland Hayward, who pointed out to Garland that Rose already had one failed marriage. Another, to America's new sweetheart, might well lead to America falling out of love with her. Hayward also suspected that she was not really in love with Rose and, in trying to test the strength of her emotions, suggested that she and Rose live together without getting married. This so upset her that she never forgave him, and thereafter insisted that her business affairs be handled by Barron Polan, who did not wield Hayward's singular power.

Most of her friends thought that she only wanted to marry in order to be independent of Ethel, something which was confirmed by Mickey Rooney, who knew that in the spring of 1941 "she was at last in love with someone who loved her." Who this person was remains a mystery, but it was not Rose, and it was not Jackie Cooper, either, whom she had met again at a party at Barron Polan's house. She was Polan's date, and Cooper was escorting Bonita Granville. Garland whispered to Cooper that she was bored, and asked him to get rid of Granville and take her home. "I couldn't resist her," he said, "although I knew what Judy was about and what her proposition meant." Dutifully, he took Granville home and returned for Garland. He took her home, too, and "had a rowdy old time that night. She was a big girl, and I was a big boy, and it was a great night. But I knew, and she made it clear, that this was all it was, and I didn't even try to call her again."

It is clear that her first marriage, like others which followed, would be one in which love was not the determining factor.

Meanwhile, one of Mayer's pet projects was being realized. When the studio made *The Great Ziegfeld* in 1936, they had purchased the rights to the Ziegfeld name and his style of shows. Since, in that film, Ziegfeld had died, no one was sure how to use the valuable Ziegfeld name in a title—until in May 1938 it was announced that William Anthony McGuire, writer of the earlier picture, was planning a screenplay to show what life was like backstage at the Ziegfeld Follies. It was to be called *Ziegfeld Girl*, and the stars were to be Joan Crawford, Margaret Sullavan, Eleanor Powell and Virginia Bruce. A year later, it had been recast and was to star Fred Astaire and Powell, but that idea was scotched when Astaire decided, after *Broadway*

Melody of 1940, that he and Powell were basically incompatible as dancers. Because Mayer liked musicals, the studio purchased a large number of them, and it was obvious that a title like *Ziegfeld Girl* could be made to fit any story with a backstage setting. For a while, Sullavan's name was once again attached to the project, then, in the fanciful belief that she was ready for a strong dramatic role, Lana Turner was brought in to replace her. She was joined by Hedy Lamarr, who was scarcely a better actress, but *was* very beautiful. Neither of them could sing or dance, but the idea was that if the director kept the action going on around them, audiences would fail to notice this.

Pandro S. Berman, newly arrived from RKO, where he had produced the Astaire-Rogers series and the studio's few other quality films, was announced as the producer. Neither star temperament nor a large budget could unsettle him, and he was given *Ziegfeld Girl* as his first project at M-G-M, with a lineup which now included Walter Pidgeon, George Murphy and Frank Morgan—who were subsequently replaced by James Stewart, Tony Martin and Charles Winninger.

For Stewart, the subsidiary role of a truck driver from Flatbush was a come-down after the title role in Frank Capra's *Mr. Smith Goes to Washington*, but with that, and the still to be seen *The Philadelphia Story*, he was acknowledged as one of the studio's leading stars. At the time, there was nothing else ready for him, and the studio rewarded him with top billing. There was one last change: Judy Garland replaced Eleanor Powell, who was not registering well with the American public.

The film follows the stories of three Ziegfeld hopefuls, played by Lamarr, Turner and Garland. Lamarr flirts with a singer (Martin), but finds that she prefers her refugee husband (Philip Dorn), a violinist in the pit. Turner rejects her boyfriend (Stewart) for the diamonds offered by an older playboy; whereupon Stewart turns to bootlegging and she takes to drink. This hearts-and-flowers stuff was punctuated by too few songs, but these did include "You Stepped Out of a Dream," sung by Martin as the beautiful showgirls parade in the Ziegfeld manner which, to those wartime audiences in Europe who saw it, was escapism of the old order. Garland sang a plangent, slow-tempo rendering of an old favorite, "I'm Always Chasing Rainbows" (which not only echoed the sentiments of her most famous song, but offered a chance of duplicating the success of "I'm Nobody's Baby") and in the last third also as a mulatto "Minnie from Trinidad," who "wasn't good and who wasn't bad," a song composed for her by Edens. At the end, for her final close-up, she is made up to resemble Virginia Bruce, in order to utilize the elaborate "Wedding-cake" footage from *The Great Ziegfeld*.

She was given her most glamorous wardrobe yet, designed by Adrian, but felt that once again she was being outshone by her more beautiful co-stars. In contrast to their lacquered looks, she seems more than usually appealing; but, while they were given proper love scenes, she had to be content with some teenage flirting with Jackie Cooper. Being billed above Turner and Lamarr was no consolation. She could not be reconciled to the fact that, whereas the appearance on set of Turner and Lamarr was greeted by the film's technicians with wolf-whistles, all she got was a friendly "Hi, Judy!" Her nerves were further strained by the fact that Turner, already separated from Artie Shaw, was conducting a none-too-private romance with Tony Martin, to whom Garland was also attracted.

"She wanted to be Lana Turner and it didn't occur to her that Lana Turner might have liked to be Judy Garland," said the producer Joseph Pasternak, who was to arrive at M-G-M from Universal the following year, after failing to agree with its bosses on the progress of Deanna Durbin's career. He was speaking much later, after nine years on the M-G-M lot, which included three films with Garland (his contract with Metro stipulated that he would make at least one film with her). He also said: "She didn't realize how much talent she had or that she had more to offer than Lana Turner or Joan Crawford or the other clever girls around the place. She never believed that she had the strength: I mean feminine strength. She felt she was a failure in her private life."

Unlike the previous year, 1941 had begun well for Garland. She had just been voted, unexpectedly, into the Top Ten, the box-office listing compiled by America's exhibitors. She was tenth, with Bette Davis as the only other female on the list. Rooney was at first place for the third year running, which assured M-G-M's stockholders that another profitable year could be expected if the two youngsters could be reunited.

While Freed's writers struggled on a sequel to *Strike Up the Band*, Garland and Rooney were rushed yet again into a hastily assembled Hardy picture, *Life Begins for Andy Hardy*, in which Garland repeats her role as Betsy Booth, who in this case acts as Andy's guardian angel when he tries to make a career in New York. She has virtually nothing to do beyond reacting to him, and as a result this is probably the least effective of all her screen work. She recorded four songs for the film, including "America," but none was used. This is curious, for by now audiences going to a Judy Garland film expected to find her singing. Without any songs, and confined to half-a-dozen flattish scenes, she is reduced to being just another ingenue.

Throughout this period the Byzantine maneuvering and dictatorial mentality that pervaded M-G-M extended as far as possible into the public and private affairs of their stars. After all, these represented vast investments in time, money and public relations and this had to be protected. Mayer was still concerned that, against his wishes and better judgment, Garland persisted in continuing her involvement with David Rose. The previous September, Mayer had summoned Rose to his office and asked him to wait twelve months before marrying Garland. Rose's divorce decree would not become final until May 1941, and, in view of Garland's age, it was not unreasonable to give her two or three more months to be sure that she was doing the right thing. Mayer wanted to ensure that he had made his point. He took a proprietorial interest in his stars, and in Garland's case, he declared, a paternal one: should Rose do anything to harm her, it was unlikely that any studio or radio station in town would employ him again.

Garland's paltry exposure in *Life Begins for Andy Hardy* did nothing to solve her problems, which, in spite of her Top Ten rating, centered on her inability to identify herself as one of the studio's great stars. What could a mere girl-singer offer to compete with the sophisticated allure of Shearer, Garbo, Loy or Crawford, all of whom were in fact now less bankable than she was. She had sung about the awkward age in *Love Finds Andy Hardy*, in Edens's "In-Between," but on the threshold of adulthood, the title still applied to her. She continued to demand "the glamour treatment," and the M-G-M makeup team got to work with a real vengeance. Her hair was lightened, and the pictures now issuing from the stills Gallery were only *sometimes* of the girl next door. This had the unfortunate effect of making Garland even more unsure of who or what she was. For publicity reasons, all stars were expected to be seen in nightclubs, preferably not with the same partner. Dutifully, in order not to have Rose as the only string to her bow, Garland went out on dates with other men. She was not seen, however, with the two men with whom (despite her relationship with Rose) she continued to be infatuated because both were married.

One was Johnny Mercer, whom she met at a party given by Bob Hope. She and Hope were supposed to sing "Friendship" from Cole Porter's *Du Barry Was a Lady*, but Hope suggested Mercer as her partner instead. Encouraged by Rose, they recorded it, successfully, for Decca, and the sympathy apparent between them was carried into life. Indeed, a year later, Mercer wrote the lyric to a song by Harold Arlen, "That Old Black Magic," which, he told her, was the way he felt about her. He was thirty-one, the right age to help Garland cope with her problems.

The other man was Oscar Levant, who was thirty-four and, like Mercer, Shaw and Rose, a musician. Since she constantly needed reassurance, it was inevitable that she sought it from people operating in her own field, which was the one area in which she felt at ease. At the same time, Mercer and Levant—but not Rose—flattered her by their attentions, for they were intellectuals as well as musicians. Both men also enjoyed Garland's wicked sense of humor and could respond in kind, whereas Rose was merely lighthearted and easygoing. At this time Levant was, in his own words, "the terror of radio," and his recollections of Judy in his two books of memoirs are mainly of the time, later, when he was working at M-G-M. But he does have a charming anecdote of introducing her to Christopher Isherwood in 1941, when the novelist was a screenwriter working at M-G-M: "She told him how wonderful his writings were, and what a genius he was. To which Christopher kindly replied, 'Need I say the obvious in return?' It was the nearly perfect answer."

With Mercer and Levant out of the running, however, it was back to square one, which meant David Rose. He encouraged her efforts to write poetry, and she had nine poems published privately, *Thoughts and Poems by Judy Garland*, which she presented to friends. One of them runs:

> Would that my pen were tipped with a magic wand
> That I could but tell of my love for you,
> That I could but write with the surge I feel
> When I gaze upon your sweet face;
> Would that my throat were blessed by the nightingale
> That I could sing of my heart's great love
> In some lovely tree flooded with silver,

> Sing till I burst my breast with such passion,
> Sing, then fall dead at your feet!

What Rose thought of this stuff is not recorded, but he was enthusiastic about a story she had written, "Love's New Sweet Song," and composed the music for a dramatization which was broadcast on CBS's *Silver Theater* on January 26, 1941. Garland played the lead, somewhat defiantly, for the subject was the love of a girl for an older man. A month later, Rose escorted her to the Academy Award ceremony at which, after a radio address by President Roosevelt, she sang "America." Rose was seated at the M-G-M table, not far from Mayer, who tried, without success, to look pleased during the speech of the president whom he, as a staunch Republican, loathed.

Rose and Garland were together so often that Ethel and Mayer eventually bowed to the inevitable. Indeed, Ethel had come to the point where she not only welcomed the marriage but was talking of managing Rose's finances. For his part, Mayer had noted that the Durbin nuptials in April had been covered immoderately by the world press, and hoped that whatever the consequences for Garland of marrying someone he thought wholly unsuitable, M-G-M might benefit from some free publicity. Garland had also noticed the attention her erstwhile rival had been receiving, and responded by throwing what was quaintly called "a tea and cocktail party" on June 15, five days after her nineteenth birthday, designed expressly to put Deanna's shindig in the shade. The guest list included Joan Crawford, Ann Sothern, Jackie Cooper, Bonita Granville, John Payne, Ann Shirley, James Stewart, Eleanor Powell, Lana Turner, Freddie Bartholomew, George Murphy, Jane Withers, Tony Martin and Robert Sterling. The invitation included an announcement of Garland's engagement to Rose, which Ethel had anticipated by leaking the news to the press a few days earlier. The wedding would be in September, after Garland had finished work on her new film, a sequel, of sorts, to *Babes in Arms*, to be called *Babes on Broadway*.

The film was merely an excuse for Rooney and Garland to display their talents in every which way, and they are extravagantly good at doing that with numbers worthy of them. The screenplay, by Elaine Ryan, from a story by Fred Finklehoffe, fills in the spaces well enough, as directed by Busby Berkeley. The stars play out-of-work actors who are eventually seen by an impresario who engages them for his next musical smash. Rooney and Garland have a superb "improvised" number, "How About You?," and lead a crowd of kids in a splendid thing called "Hoe Down," which they appear to be enjoying enormously. In the blackface finale, Garland belts out "Franklin D. Roosevelt Jones" and "Waiting for the Robert E. Lee." Over $107,000, out of a total budget of $940,000, was spent on this section of the film, which was planned by Roger Edens. The cast rehearsed it for nine days and took another nine to shoot it. The result is as stirring as any of the bang-up M-G-M musical finales of the pre-Mickey-and-Judy era.

In the middle of shooting the film, to Mayer's fury, Garland eloped with Rose. Accompanied by Ethel, Will Gilmore and Betty Asher, the happy couple arrived in Las Vegas on July 27, and were married at one o'clock the following morning. The press made much of the fact that Garland's mother and stepfather were along for the honeymoon. Garland had cabled Mayer and Freed: "I AM SO VERY HAPPY DAVE AND I WERE MARRIED THIS AM PLEASE GIVE ME A LITTLE TIME AND I WILL BE BACK AND FINISH THE PICTURE WITH ONE TAKE ON EACH SCENE LOVE JUDY." Mayer had envisaged a wedding that would eclipse Durbin's, that would become as famous in Hollywood annals as that of Norma Shearer to Irving Thalberg or that of Vilma Banky to Rod La Rocque, with himself giving the bride away, in a church. He had been denied it and M-G-M had been robbed of the chance to orchestrate the publicity. The Roses were informed that under no circumstances could shooting be held up. The bride was back in the studio within twenty-four hours.

7

❖❖❖❖❖❖❖

Judy at War

THE FILMING OF *Babes on Broadway* lasted three months, from July to October 1941. In order to publicize the movie, Rooney and Garland made two radio appearances: a re-creation of *Babes in Arms* for CBS's *Screen Guild Theater* on November 9, and an adaptation of *Merton of the Movies* on *Lux Radio Theater* on November 17. During the second of these, Garland sang "The Peanut Vendor" and afterwards, from the new film, "How About You."

As with *Babes in Arms*, Rooney took most of the notices for the new film: he "doesn't leave much room for anyone else," said the *New York Times*, but "Judy Garland manages to stand out in the musical sequences." *Time* magazine saw it differently: "Miss Garland, now nineteen and wise to her co-star's propensity for stealing scenes, neatly takes the picture away from him. Rooney cannot sing but Judy Garland can and proves it pleasantly with [some] sure-fire numbers." The movie was, said the *New York Herald Tribune*, "a fresh and engaging entertainment for any holiday season. Mickey Rooney and Judy Garland are getting a bit on in years to be designated as babes, but they have lost none of their shrewd showmanship in their passage through adolescence."

In Britain, James Agate filled his column in the *Tatler* with praise for Rooney, even teasing two other critics who had not been bowled over by him. "He sings enough to eke out Miss Judy Garland whenever the director mistakenly thinks that young lady need eking out," he wrote. He particularly disliked the message of affection and admiration for the British contained in the film. It does start embarrassingly, as British evacuees talk over the transatlantic telephone to their parents. Then Garland takes over with a song which begins, "From the dark cafés of Paris to the streets of Amsterdam . . . to the shores of Uncle Sam / Wherever freedom's hope is true / Each heart cries out to you" and goes on to urge "Don't give up, Tommy Atkins . . . There's a whole world behind you shouting 'Stout fella.' " Agate thought this "Hollywood patronage at its least bearable," but to many it was very moving, partly because it is sung so thrillingly.

The film was released on December 3, 1941, four days before the attack on Pearl Harbor, with the result that its sentiments struck a chord with American audiences. On the day of the attack itself, December 7, Garland flew to Ford Ord, near Monterey, to entertain the troops with a "live" broadcast for *The Chase and Sanborn Hour*, whose other guests included the ventriloquist Edgar Bergen. Although interrupted by news bulletins, she sang "Zing! Went the Strings of My Heart" and was sassed by Bergen's dummy, Charlie McCarthy. A week later, she sang, on air from the Biltmore Bowl, "Abe Lincoln Had Only One Country," which might have been one of Jerome Kern's more patriotic efforts but is not one of his better ones.

The war had galvanized Garland. There was nothing she wanted to do more than sing to the boys who would be fighting. She was the first Hollywood star to entertain the troops after America entered the hostilities, and she did so with the approval of the Hollywood Victory Committee, which was headed by Clark Gable and the agent Charles K. Feldman. With Rose to accompany her at the piano, she started on January 21, 1942, singing in five midwestern training installations—Fort Custer, Fort Knox, Jefferson Barracks, Camp Robinson and Camp Wolters—over a three-week period. The trip included a detour to Florida for a belated honeymoon. This was urgently needed, because the marriage of seven months was already disintegrating.

The Roses had taken a lease on a Los Angeles mansion which had once belonged to Jean Harlow. They had not cared to live in Rose's own home in the San Fernando Valley because it was too small, nor did they wish to turn the Gilmores out of Garland's mansion. The new house had been redecorated since Harlow's dramatic days—her husband had committed suicide there—but was still pure Metro-Goldwyn-Mayer, with gilt, brocades and satins *à la Trianon*. To a still immature Garland, it was exactly what a movie star's home should look like. What attracted Rose to it was that it could accommodate his model railway, which comprised 780 feet of track. Garland had given him a new junction as a wedding present. Only too soon, she realized that he was more interested in his hobby than he was in her.

Having been raised in Hollywood, Garland had little contact with the real world, and had lived largely in a world of fantasy. There was certainly a strain in trying to assume the roles of hostess and housekeeper, roles for which she was completely unfitted. Never having learned domestic skills from Ethel, she left the running of her new house to the servants, who did not take her seriously when, on an occasional whim, she decided to give them instructions. "I found myself in a big house," she said. "It was frightening. I didn't know anything about cooking or keeping house. My mother had always been the most wonderful housekeeper, she never asked me to do anything."

Ethel's attempts to "help" only made matters worse, especially as she could not understand why Rose seemed unable to control Judy as she claimed to have done. Ethel had always acted as her secretary, and Garland never acquired the discipline of keeping an engagement diary. She did not do so now, and in a household of two people with busy careers this often resulted in a chaotic social life. The orderly, organized Rose was not so much angry as bewildered.

Apart from her need to escape from Mayer and her mother, Garland could not imagine why she had married Rose. She called him "irritatingly fair-minded," and resented the fact that he tried to improve both her musical knowledge and her voice. It was advice which only increased her insecurity and sense of inadequacy, the sense that "I wasn't really good enough—ever." She had always been happy with Edens's advice, but felt that Rose's was superfluous. The situation was compounded by Ethel's renewed contempt for Rose, whom she referred to as "the old man."

Marriage was also a potential impediment in the progress of Garland's career. The wedding ring which she refused to remove during filming provided a minor headache; a studio craftsman could add a device to disguise it: but pregnancy was something else again. It is not quite clear how many people knew she was pregnant, but it would appear to be a considerable number, especially as she was not noted for her secrecy where her own problems were concerned. When Rose failed to show much enthusiasm, she told Ethel, who in turn conveyed the news to the studio. There was general agreement that a baby would disrupt her work and finish off her youthful image, so it was decided she would have an abortion. Faced with unanimity on the subject, Garland turned to Barron Polan, who was not only her agent but a friend. He knew and liked Rose, who, after all, had some rights in the matter—even though he did not care to exercise them. Polan was sympathetic but noncommittal. Abortion was illegal in the state of California but, under M-G-M's auspices, the operation could be performed secretly and in as much comfort as possible.

Conditioned to the demands of her career, Garland submitted, and had the termination toward the end of the year, but her sense of grievance was profound. She could not forgive Freed, who declined to delay the start of her next picture, although this would have been possible, since filming was not due to start until some months after finishing the current one; still less could she forgive Ethel. The episode had doomed her marriage, for she was deeply hurt that Rose refused to take a stand on her behalf.

Her next film was to have been *Very Warm for May*. The Kern-Hammerstein musical had failed on Broadway, but Freed bought it as a starring vehicle for Garland, Ray McDonald and Marta Eggerth. He then declared that the plot bore too many resemblances to *Babes in Arms* and Garland, now a young wife, did not want to remain an adolescent for ever. Instead, she was assigned to *For Me and My Gal*, a patriotic vaudeville story, which, according to Eleanor Powell, had originally been planned as a vehicle for her and Dan Dailey, a young dancer whom M-G-M was planning to make a star. Powell had not only been succeeded by Garland as M-G-M's leading star of musicals, but she seemed to have exhausted whatever box-office pull she ever had. She recalled that she and Dailey had been rehearsing for the film when they were informed that they had been replaced by Garland and Gene Kelly.

Gene Kelly, trained as a dancer, had come to prominence on Broadway as the hoofer in William Saroyan's play *The Time of Your Life*. He made a big success in the title role of Rodgers and Hart's *Pal Joey*, and had recently signed a contract with Selznick, with a view to playing the lead in *The Keys of the Kingdom*. The project was stalled—it was eventually sold to 20th Century-Fox, which made it with Gregory Peck—and since Selznick had no plans for Kelly, he was happy to loan him to M-G-M. The suggestion to use Kelly came from Fred

Finklehoffe, who was working on the script. Freed jumped at the chance, and in the event Metro took over Kelly's contract.

The studio wanted to get *For Me and My Gal* into cinemas quickly. Set during the years of the First World War, it is the story of a fight between two vaudeville players for the same woman, played by Garland. Her original partner is George Murphy, but she is lured away from him by Gene Kelly, who proposes marriage to her. When she discovers that Kelly is avoiding joining up for the sake of his career, she leaves him. (Her brother has been killed in action.) Inevitably, the story ends happily, with Kelly performing a deed of heroism and he and Garland enjoying a last-reel reunion for a grand concert finale at the Palace in New York. Now that America was at war, the story had become topical, while as a musical it offered the escapist entertainment audiences at the time were thought to want.

George Murphy claimed that the film had originally been planned as a vehicle to reunite him and Garland. He was "downhearted" he said, "because at the outset that script had been written for me to play the lead." This role, however, was a natural for Kelly after his *Pal Joey*, one of the all-time small-time heels. "I'm never going to win any medals for being a nice guy," is one of the first lines of dialogue. The film was originally called *The Big Time*, and that is what these vaudevillians aspire to. Because of the sheer size of her voice, Freed could not see Garland as anything but a vaudevillian—even in *Little Nelly Kelly*, she is to be found leading the St. Patrick's Day parade or a chorus at the police ball. *For Me and My Girl* was Garland's first real adult role, but the dialogue has a familiar ring. If they team up, says Kelly, they'll achieve "the goal every vaudeville artist has." "Oh, I've dreamed of playing the Palace," she says, rather in the "let's-put-on-a-show" manner of her films with Rooney.

Once again, despite her objections, Garland was directed by Busby Berkeley, whom she found unreasonable and devoid of feeling. When she collapsed in the course of filming a strenuous dance routine, Berkeley called the studio doctor rather than send her home because the set was to be dismantled that night. The doctor gave her some tablets and sent her to her dressing-room to lie down, confident that she would be "on top of the world" in ten minutes. However, she did not sleep that night and arrived to work the following day "feeling like a wreck." She was given more tablets, and later said that "from that age I've been on a sort of treadmill," which suggests that this was the real beginning of her addiction to pills. She turned twenty just two weeks after filming finished, but in close-ups even soft focus cannot disguise the lines beneath her eyes.

Kelly was equally unhappy with the autocratic Berkeley, who resented the fact that this newcomer had usurped Murphy's place. Garland liked both Kelly and Murphy, but sided with Kelly in his disputes with Berkeley. Kelly was to remember the way Garland helped him on his first film when, in later years, his co-star's own career was in difficulties. He was to more than repay the debt.

When the film was previewed, at Westwood Village, 85 percent of the audience thought the genial Murphy should have got the girl rather than the pushy Kelly. The Executive Committee decreed some retakes to make the Kelly character more attractive, because it was clear that Kelly was going to be a much bigger star than Murphy. Whatever the demands of the plot, it is clear from their scenes together that Kelly and Garland make a wonderful team. The title song, in which he urges her to join him, is a joyous number, while in "Balling the Jack" she seems to be as expert a dancer as he. She also does a marvelous rendering of "After You've Gone," with a superb bluesy reprise, arranged by Edens, utilizing Sophie Tucker cadences and showing for the first time a more sophisticated "New York" style than the Hollywood-vaudeville techniques she had used until then. The song was one of those she was to use frequently in her concert career. She really exudes warmth when singing to an audience in the picture, as if reciprocating its feeling for her.

Her acting is of the same high order. Given two or three tearful close-ups, she never lets the lips quiver more than tentatively. As when teamed with Rooney, her yearning for a guy who is not aware of her love is tenderly expressed, her eyes melting. The reviewers noted a new, more adult Garland, "already well graduated from a sort of female Mickey Rooney into one of the more reliable song pluggers in the business," as *Time* magazine put it. "She also begins to show symptoms of dramatic discipline, and talent." The *New York Daily News* thought she looked "thin and frail," but noted that she seemed "to have developed enormously as an actress since her last screen assignment. She projects the old melodies charmingly . . . and she also dances with grace." "Miss Garland is someone to reckon with," announced the *New York Herald Tribune*. "Of all the youngsters who have graduated into mature roles in recent years, she has the surest command of her form of make-believe . . . she turns in a warm, persuasive and moving portrayal of the diffident hoofer and singer who loves a heel."

The film, which cost $802,000, grossed $4,371,000, proving for the first time that Garland was a star attraction in her own right. Previously, Rooney had been given equal billing, his name preceding hers, but in this film Kelly and Murphy were billed in letters half the size of hers.

Garland and Kelly recorded the title song and "When You Wore a Tulip" (a snatch of which had been heard in the movie), and this became one of her most popular Decca recordings. Rose and his orchestra accompanied her, as they did for two numbers written by Burton Lane and Yip Harburg for Jack Cummings's production *Ship Ahoy*, "Poor You" and "The Last Call for Love," which was one of the few Garland records which did not leave the store shelves. She and Rose were much better served by Decca with the coupling "I Never Knew" and "Poor Little Rich Girl."

Apart from *For Me and My Gal*, Garland's chief war effort early in 1942 was a challenging tour of army bases, heading an alfresco bill of old vaudevillians and new performers, some of them from the units to which she played. David Rose was once again her accompanist. They traveled sometimes on milk trains, trying to fit in four performances a day. She sang twelve songs, and when asking for encores discovered that her audience most wanted to hear "Over the Rainbow" and "Dear Mr. Gable"—but more than that, they wanted to talk. It brought out the best in her—her empathy with audiences, with ordinary people.

She also appeared on *Command Performance*, which was beamed by shortwave to the overseas war zones. Although they received no payment for being on the show, artists were always keen to take part, and Garland was saved up for Christmas Eve. She was fast becoming the armed forces' Sweetheart—not a pin-up, like Betty Grable, but a representative of the girl back home who was waiting for the boys to return.

For her twentieth birthday, Garland received sables from David Rose, who shortly thereafter joined the army. His absence did not make her heart grow fonder, for when he returned to their home on his two weekends a month of leave, he would find his wife surrounded by a new set of friends, mostly gathered from the burgeoning Freed unit, drawn together socially because they shared the same sense of humor, a feeling of exclusivity, and a common interest in complicated word games. Garland had always felt most at ease with musicians and vaudevillians, but many of these people were New York intellectuals, among whom Rose felt himself an interloper. She was shattered, however, when Rose brought up the subject of divorce, and as a result she went into her first serious decline. Marc Rabwin, like her own doctor, was seriously worried about her. It was not as though she was sorry the marriage was over, because she was not: it was rather as if she was determined to be miserable over the situation and determined to go to extremes. Anita Loos, never really fond of her, later recalled:

Judy Garland, already a star at the age of twelve, was a compulsive weeper. There are some characters who simply cannot endure success. Judy was one of them. She loved to pace the alley, stopping all and sundry to whimper about some imagined affront. "Nobody loves me!" Judy would lament. She was persecuted by L.B. [Mayer]; her family neglected her; even her servants overlooked Judy. "When I come home from work exhausted and ask for a cup of tea, the maid forgets all about it and I have to make it myself." Judy was such a good actress that listeners were frequently impressed. Not Hoppy [screenwriter Bob Hopkins]. He called Judy's tears "a Hollywood bath." Judy's mental attitude may have been pathetic but it turned her into a great bore. And if my memories are few, it comes from lack of interest in a character ruled by petulance.

M-G-M had no difficulty in persuading Rose to assume responsibility for the failure of the marriage. They did not announce their separation until February 2, 1943, by which time their union had become, like so many others, another casualty of war.

The war could not be blamed, however, for the crumbling of other marriages within the Gumm family. Ethel decided to leave Will Gilmore, after long rumblings, partly because of his determination to handle Garland's financial affairs. Jimmy's marriage to Bobby Sherwood was headed in the same direction. Several members of the family were reunited when Jimmy, who was now working at M-G-M as a scriptgirl, and her daughter, Judalein, moved into a house on Ogden Drive in West Hollywood, along with Ethel and Grandma Milne. Judalein's curious name (a Germanic diminutive of Judy) was used in order to distinguish her from her aunt, after whom she had been named. Garland was extremely fond of her niece, and Ethel, who doted upon the child, was delighted to be living with her. The Stone Canyon house was sold and Garland moved from the Harlow house because it was much too big for just one person. She lived briefly in a small apartment but did not like to be alone at night—there was no room for a maid—and so took a lease on a house belonging to Mary Martin.

Meanwhile, she was doing more radio broadcasts. On Christmas Day 1942, she and Bob Hope shared a section of the Elgin Watch Company's *Christmas Day Canteen*, a two-hour salute to fighting servicemen, which was emceed by Don Ameche and also featured Bette Davis, Gracie Fields, Abbott and Costello and Cass Daley. Of more lasting interest are two radio adaptations of famous movies on *Lux Radio Theater* (with Cecil B. DeMille exhorting listeners between reels to use Lux Flakes for the sake of their hands). In *Morning Glory* and *A Star Is Born*, Garland took the roles played originally by Katharine Hepburn and Janet Gaynor, respectively. In the first she co-starred with Adolphe Menjou (who had been in the original) and John Payne, and in the second she was partnered by Walter Pidgeon. She was working with mature leading men at last.

Garland's choice of these two vehicles, in both of which she plays aspiring actresses, is another indication of her obsession with show business, and her inability to see herself (despite that Kansas schoolgirl) in any other roles: but the delicacy, and indeed the perfection, of both performances show that M-G-M executives should have taken her more seriously as an actress. Instead, she was being considered for another pairing with Mickey Rooney. This decision had been taken by Arthur Freed, who, thanks in part to the Mickey-and-Judy films, had become the studio's leading producer of musicals. It was recognized that Garland's future was linked to the Freed unit. She herself had quickly dismissed him as the father-substitute for whom she was always searching, but nevertheless liked him. He in turn recognized her talent and its potential earning power for stockholders. However, he thought he knew far better than she did what direction her career should take, and he had no understanding of her personality. His bulkiness and insensitivity led her to calling him "the bulk."

Freed had decided that her next film with Rooney would be the Gershwin musical *Girl Crazy*, but as yet no one had come up with a suitable script. The show had already been filmed once, by RKO, in 1932. In 1939, RKO sold it to M-G-M, who intended to rework it under Jack Cummings's guidance for Fred Astaire (who, ironically, had just left RKO) and Eleanor Powell, as a follow-up to *Broadway Melody of 1940*. Astaire was less than enthusiastic, however, and the property was shelved for a while. It was subsequently dusted off—almost certainly at Edens's suggestion, for who better at M-G-M knew the glories of that particular score? Garland had already recorded one of the songs, "Embraceable You," in 1939, and he was able to persuade her that the Gershwin songs would compensate her for having to act out yet another teenage romance.

This project would not concern Garland for a while yet, however. At the same time, the studio was having some minor trouble with *Presenting*

Lily Mars, a Booth Tarkington story which had been acquired as a vehicle for Lana Turner. The finished screenplay was considered too "light" for someone with an insufficiently definite screen presence, so the Executive Committee handed it over to Joe Pasternak, because of its similarities to the Deanna Durbin vehicles which he had produced at Universal. Indeed, Pasternak had laid plans to do a musical *Little Women*, with Garland as Jo and Durbin as Meg, but that did not get very far. His first film at M-G-M had been *Seven Sweethearts* (1942), a story "inspired" by Jane Austen's *Pride and Prejudice* and devised to prove that Kathryn Grayson was the studio's long-hoped-for answer to Durbin. Adding the right sort of songs to *Lily Mars* would make it suitable for either Grayson or Garland, who was doing retakes for *For Me and My Gal* and easily the more valuable of the two properties.

It is clear that neither Turner nor Grayson would have been one-tenth as good as Garland. Her comic skills are well showcased in her role as a kid so stagestruck that she will stop at nothing to attract a young impresario (Van Heflin), who is visiting his home town: tricking him to come to her house to see her Lady Macbeth, or doing a Victorian melodrama outside his window. He thinks she's a pest and a brat until he finds her, weak from hunger, in his theater in New York. By a series of plot convolutions she replaces his leading lady (Marta Eggerth) in the Russian-style operetta he is producing. The film could have been dreadful, but M-G-M embellished it with all the swank and pizazz for which the company was famous.

Originally, Garland had only four songs in the film. The first, "Tom, Tom the Piper's Son," is a jazzed-up version of the nursery rhyme, sung to guests in an attempt to prevent Heflin ejecting her from a party she has gate-crashed. "Every Little Movement" is sung and danced in a darkened theater with the cleaning lady (Connie Gilchrist), who sees in Lily Mars the stage hopeful she once was. Garland also sings one of Eggerth's numbers, first seriously and then doing an impersonation of the actress: both this and the Victorian melodrama demonstrate Garland's flair for burlesque.

When the film was previewed, the tame ending and the weak patriotic number accompanying it were not liked. The song was thrown out and a more impressive and sophisticated finale devised. It was at last felt that Garland could be allowed to grow up: her hair was put up for the first time and Irene was commissioned to design her costume. Charles Walters was called in to stage the new finale, in which he would also appear, partnering Garland.

Chuck Walters was a former Broadway dancer who had progressed to being the juvenile opposite Betty Grable in *Du Barry Was a Lady*, which Freed had been filming with Gene Kelly earlier that year. Kelly had been dissatisfied with Seymour Felix's choreography of "Do I Love You?" and asked for Robert Alton or, failing him, Walters. In the event, both men became members of the Freed unit.

The finale Walters was called in to stage for *Presenting Lily Mars* was a big Broadway number, featuring Tommy Dorsey and his band. It clearly had nothing to do with the rest of the film, but does provide a more positive happy ending than the clinch with Heflin. It was arranged by Edens, and contains not only "Broadway Rhythm" but "Three O'Clock in the Morning," with an introduction about old songs for Garland to sing. The number lasts several minutes, and consists of few setups and long takes—proving that in being fleet of foot in intricate steps Garland could hold her own with any of the screen's trained dancers. It was filmed during a hiatus in the shooting of *Girl Crazy*. Hence the coup of having the Dorsey band, which did not come cheap but was under contract for that movie.

Mayer had told Pasternak to spare no expense in shooting the sequence. Garland was as aware of this as he was and both were delighted at the decision to put the finale entirely into the expert hands of the Freed unit. But, nevertheless, Pasternak, having agreed to step aside for what was to be a vital factor in the film's popularity, felt aggrieved when she made no effort to thank him for it. It would never have occurred to her to do so.

When Mayer saw Walters's performance in *Presenting Lily Mars*, he suggested to Freed that the young man be put under contract as a dancer. Freed, however, thought Walters would prove more useful to his unit as a choreographer and hired him with the promise that one day he might become a director. By this time, Freed had come to realize just how much the talents he was taking on were contributing to his musicals, making them easily superior to those being made by Cummings and Pasternak. Although these two producers were able to borrow talent—especially arrangers and conductors—from Freed, the Freed unit was quite distinct. Its members had an almost incestuous admiration for each other, both as artists and people, and this had the admirable effect of inspiring even better work. They helped each other out, did not mind who got the screen credit and laughed a lot together. "We understood each other's temperaments and talents," said Gene Kelly, "so when we came to work together on a project, there was usually a most wonderful blending of ideas."

Off set, they stuck together, and were not always popular, particularly when gathered together in such public places as the commissary, as the bandleader and arranger, Johnny Green, recalled:

> We were so loud and raucous and behaved as if we owned the place that a lot of people couldn't stand us, or the private jokes we had at their expense. I hate to admit it, but the Freed boys and girls were not liked. Talent frightens people. It makes them insecure and there were many of our fellow workers who hated us. We were, in short, regarded as the snob, inconsiderable, self-centered pricks of the studio.

Characteristic of their jokes were the nicknames they gave people: "Prune Venison" for June Allyson and "Nervous Nellie" for Fred Astaire.

There was, however, another reason that the unit was distrusted. Although Freed himself, like every other Hollywood producer, was inclined to avail himself of any available starlet, most of his group were sexually more complicated. Even in your wildest imagination, Vincent Price once said, you could not conceive what Hollywood's inhabitants could get up to. Show people had always been careless about morals, and in a town, and industry, dedicated to peddling glamour and romance, it would be surprising if the passions enacted before the cameras did not sometimes carry over into real life. Youngsters pouring into Los Angeles, desperate for a movie career, were prepared to risk the perils of the casting couch, and under contract at every studio were myriad starlets who were more likely to be found in the bedrooms of visiting firemen than enshrined on the screen. As the columnist Sheilah Graham remarked: "Everyone poked everyone in Hollywood. I think actors will put it anywhere it will go."

The outside world, however, was unaware of the existence of such a hedonistic, promiscuous society. Hollywood marketed glamour and beauty, but, with equal fervor, it promoted itself as a community of hard-working folks who just happened to be more fortunate and better-looking than those back home. Deanna Durbin once said her parents never ceased to lecture her on the subject of morality, but in the studio the values were diametrically opposed, a situation which she found quite heady. She was not alone.

Social life within the film colony provided plenty of opportunity for affairs and liaisons. Although stars were expected to put in decorous public appearances at nightclubs and in restaurants in order to provide copy and photo opportunities for the journalists, most of them preferred to pursue their entertainment in private. Home was not only more comfortable and more relaxing, but with servants to prepare excellent meals and look after the house, why go out? Apart from nightclubs, there was nowhere to go. The theater-minded might take in the latest production at the Pasadena Playhouse, but it was only of provincial standard; concerts at the Hollywood Bowl were few and far between.

Consequently, Hollywood was a party town, offering dance parties, costume parties, theme parties, bridge parties, pajama parties, come-as-you-are parties, games parties, "come-as-your-favorite-character" parties. At all such events, inhibitions were freed by drink and by drugs, as Jackie Cooper remembered:

> There was a lot of booze around. There was some marijuana. Some of the boys and girls had dexedrine—we didn't yet call it speed—and if we were planning to be up all night, we loved those little green pills. Maybe we were wrong, but it seemed to us that they deterred premature ejaculation—in fact, we learnt, to our dismay, that two of them would make you impotent for the night. So we'd break one in half, take half early, the other half later, and, with booze, you'd get pretty stoned.

Favorite party games included "Sardines," a pastime to which the stars' large mansions were particularly suited and which gave two happy, healthy and attractive young people the opportunity to be alone in the dark until found. If they happened to be of the same sex, that was something easily accommodated, since bisexuality was a Hollywood tradition, one upheld with some style by such stars as Tallulah Bankhead and Marlene Dietrich.

The preponderance of homosexuals and bisexuals on Freed's team led to its being known as "the fairy unit." Apart from Roger Edens, there were Charles Walters and Robert Alton, who enjoyed a long-standing affair, and a brilliant, inventive revue artist who, with her husband, had recently joined the unit. The revue artist's marriage did not stand in the way of homosexual affairs any more than Edens's marriage had. Looking at it from another angle, Walters's relationship with Alton did not prevent him from discussing marriage with Garland, who was so much at home in this milieu that she had even considered accepting him. On the record, she once said: "I'm intensely feminine. I don't think there's any other way to be a woman. It's nice to be that way. You can be hurt, but you can have children and still love and make a man feel important. There are more advantages to being a woman. But if you're half-man and half-woman, you're nowhere." Although this statement contains some elements of truth, it is at the same time somewhat ingenuous. She certainly never considered any of her homosexual friends of either sex as being incomplete people, and always enjoyed the company of gay men such as Van

Johnson and, later, Rock Hudson. She never regarded them as a threat, and there were several whom she succeeded in seducing, partly because she had developed an insatiable curiosity about sex. She had long ago outgrown her on-screen image as the girl next door. Many years later, she admitted that in her teens she could not wait to lose her virginity. By now, she was thoroughly experienced in sexual techniques and not much interested in traditional sexual intercourse. She once said the real reason her marriage to David Rose broke up was because he told her that she was "despicable" when she suggested that he go down on her.

Another alternative for her was homosexuality, and throughout her life she was to have affairs with women. One of these was a musical stylist, and there were few on the M-G-M lot who did not know about it. Garland was also widely suspected of pursuing a lesbian relationship with Betty Asher after the break-up of her marriage to David Rose. The two women had been friends ever since Asher had become Garland's publicist, but more recently their friendship appeared to have become more intimate, and they were often seen together either giggly and romantic or solemn and intense. An unfortunate legacy of this relationship was that Asher encouraged Garland to drink, which until then she had done without enthusiasm. They remained friends after the relationship cooled, but Garland later came to denounce Asher as "just another M-G-M spy." Asher certainly worked for the studio in this capacity, as most people on the lot knew, but Garland was intensely romantic and did not want to listen to those who thought that Asher had an ulterior motive in pursuing the affair. It is impossible to say to what extent Asher—a troubled person who eventually committed suicide— was genuinely involved, but Garland certainly was.

An involvement that was undoubtedly serious—one also complicated by sexual ambiguity—was with the actor Tyrone Power, upon whom Garland had developed a crush after Rose had drifted out of her life. Power was equally enchanted, and an affair had begun when he was on furlough from the Marine Corps, which he joined toward the end of 1942. At twenty-eight, he was younger than the men with whom Garland had previously been obsessed, but he had in common with her the responsibility of being, while still young, a major movie star. Both came from show-business families, though his was more illustrious (his father, Tyrone Power, Sr., had been a Broadway star and a leading supporting actor in Silents), and both had been early Hollywood rejects. In Power's case he had been given small supporting roles in movies from around 1932, before making a name for himself five years later. Neither had any illusions about show business, and yet they both had complexes: she knew that she had great talent but was uneasy about her looks, while he was spectacularly handsome with serious doubts about his merits as an actor.

The affair broke up Power's marriage to the French star Annabella— a much-publicized "secret" romance, which had taken place in Rio in 1939. In spite of this romantic background, Power was in fact homosexual—and if Garland was unaware of this, she was the only person in Hollywood who was. Nevertheless, their affair was of such intensity that Power confided in Edie Goetz, who was ideally placed to plead on their behalf with their employers: not only was she Louis B. Mayer's elder daughter, but she was married to William Goetz, vice-president of 20th Century-Fox, to whom Power was under contract. She was also a woman whose life was devoted to intrigue. The Fox executive did not exactly disapprove of the romance, because both Garland and Power were stars of the first magnitude. As with Mary Pickford and Douglas Fairbanks, and more recently Barbara Stanwyck and Robert Taylor, the publicity potential of such courtships and unions was virtually limitless. The Stanwyck-Taylor marriage was obviously a precedent, since both were basically attracted to people of their own sex. So-called lavender marriages were as common as not in show business.

Whether or not the M-G-M Executive Committee delved into the psychologies behind these unions—to what extent they were marriages of convenience, or the result of an attraction based on a mutual intoxication with each other's fame—the studio was not happy at the prospect of Garland becoming a bride for the second time before she was twenty-one, especially since the inevitable wartime separation could tarnish her image by making her a two-times divorcee within a few years. In the event, the affair finished abruptly when Garland discovered that Power had been reading her letters aloud to his Marine buddies at Quantico, Virginia. There were many of these letters, in which her feelings were passionately expressed. She felt betrayed. One result of the affair was that Garland was obliged to have another abortion.

As a token of love, Power had given Garland *Forever*, a novel by Mildred Cram, the subject of which was undying love in the manner of George du Maurier's *Peter Ibbetson* (which had been filmed by Paramount in 1935). Power thought it would make a good co-starring vehicle for them both, and Garland, ever the romantic, agreed. Nothing came of this, however.

Garland was later to say that she was persuaded that she had fallen in love with "a magazine cover." Unquestionably, part of Power's appeal for her had been that he was better-looking than any of Lana Turner's beaux, and she was ruefully amused when he returned from the war to engage in a supposedly torrid affair with Turner. Despite two further marriages, he later surrendered to his appetite for indiscriminate homosexual encounters.

Charles Walters later commented: "Judy got around. She had the frustration of not being a Lana Turner or Elizabeth Taylor. She tried to make people fall in love with her and she was quite successful at it." He also remembered that she set out to seduce one man for the simple reason that he was notoriously faithful to his wife. Later Walters passed her in the corridor and she signaled to him "thumb's up" to let him know she had achieved her aim. Kay Thompson, who knew as much as anyone about Garland's conquests, implied that there had been a considerable number of them when she observed that after Garland had finished with a man, "she knew how to cut him off at the ankles."

Garland's biggest prize—perhaps the greatest of her entire life— was Joseph L. Mankiewicz, a man of formidable intelligence and looks to match. He had a reputation as a ladies' man, and was thought to have been Joan Crawford's lover during the time he was producing her films. He was too intelligent to take these films seriously, but cynical enough to realize that such money-spinners pleased the studios. His standing as a producer had reached a high level with far worthier projects, notably *The Philadelphia Story* (1940) and *Woman of the Year* (1942), both with Katharine Hepburn—high enough to weather *Reunion in France* (1942), a Joan Crawford vehicle with the distinction of being even sillier than those which preceded it.

"Everyone was in love with Joseph L. Mankiewicz," commented Lena Horne's daughter, Gail Lumet Buckley, writing about M-G-M at this time. He was married to the Austrian actress Rosa Stradner, whom Mayer had acquired on one of his trips to Europe scouting for talent. After using her in only one film, *The Last Gangster* in 1937, the studio did not know what to do with her; and since she was ambitious, she developed the nervous instability that would eventually take her to the Menninger Clinic in Topeka, Kansas, hoping for a cure.

The marriage had taken place in 1939, and Mankiewicz knew almost immediately that he had made a most terrible mistake. By the time he met Garland again, in 1942, he had not recovered from it. The child he had known back in 1934 had become a woman who was skittish, witty and full of fun. She was as much unlike Rosa as anyone could be, with a completely different attitude to life. At the same time, like Mankiewicz himself, she had been bruised; but they laughed together to compensate for the pain they had inflicted on themselves.

Mankiewicz, who was thirty-three, had entered the industry as a writer, following his older brother, Herman J. Mankiewicz, whose many screenplays included, most notably, *Citizen Kane*. After a spell as a writer at Paramount, he joined M-G-M in the same capacity, but was quickly promoted to producer. He told Mayer that he wanted to direct, but Mayer told him that he had to learn to crawl before he could walk. Apart from the pictures with Crawford, he produced such notable films as the highly acclaimed *Fury* (1936) with Spencer Tracy, and *The Three Comrades* (1938), adapted from the novel by Erich Maria Remarque, but he disliked many of the others in which he had been involved, and longed to return to writing.

He had always been part of the Katz unit, but this had been dissolved, with the result that Mankiewicz was able to write the screenplays, if he so wished, for the films which he planned to produce. The first of these was to be *The Pirate*, based on a play by S.N. Behrman, which the studio had purchased for $225,025. On Broadway it had starred Alfred Lunt and Lynn Fontanne, and almost every Hollywood actress of ambition wanted to play Fontanne's role on screen. As far as M-G-M was concerned, it was a natural for Hedy Lamarr or Myrna Loy; however, it occurred to Mankiewicz while writing it that it might serve as a vehicle for Judy Garland.

He was aware that she was capable of far more demanding roles than teenage romances with Rooney, while she regarded their relationship as a means of breaking away from Freed—to be done with coy boy-and-girl stuff and play more sophisticated roles. This was something that Uncle Louis was unlikely to countenance, because he mistrusted Mankiewicz and admired Freed, whom he regarded as his protégé. Furthermore, the studio was turning out more musicals than at any time in its history, in order to meet the wartime mood, and no female star in Hollywood was as effective in the form as Garland. However, as it turned out, the disagreement that developed was not a professional one.

"My blazing row with him was about Judy Garland," Mankiewicz recalled.

Judy was then twenty and we were very good friends. She was beginning to show those signs—not showing up on time and taking too much benzedrine, that sort of thing. She was incredibly beautiful, enchanting . . . In many ways I've never met anyone like Judy was at that time. I'm not talking about her talent. She was just the most remarkably bright, gay, happy, helpless and engaging girl I've ever met . . . Christ Almighty, the girl reacted to the slightest bit of kindness as if it were a drug . . . We think of Judy now as a really big star at this time, but she was pushed around. She was treated by most people, including her mother, as a *thing* not a human being.

He remembered that as a child prodigy she had been rather shy among adults, and—since he had been instrumental in her coming to M-G-M—what disturbed him was that the intervening years had brought her praise and success, but given her very little sense of her own worth. He believed that her dependence on pills was physically dangerous, and was caused not so much by her workload, as by her sense of inadequacy—a sense of inadequacy which could, on occasion, extend to the bedroom. To both of them, much of the appeal of their affair was that it conformed to M-G-M's standards of hypocrisy: that it existed like Louis B. Mayer's affairs, but could not be acknowledged; that it could be conducted with a certain disregard for secrecy, but was not allowed to sully the studio's reputation of being morally above reproach. Johnny Green remembered that they were "a *scandale* in this 'free-thinking' community," but because of the unhappy circumstances of Mankiewicz's marriage, Hollywood's gossip columnists never mentioned the relationship.

Garland told the Rabwins that she and Mankiewicz were going to get married, and they were obviously deeply in love. Garland's pet name for her lover was "Josephus," and she loved to serenade him with a song from *Cabin in the Sky*, "Happiness Is Just a Thing Called Joe." In spite of the couple's evident happiness, the Rabwins knew that a marriage could not work. Mankiewicz described Garland as "like a dry desert waiting for an intellectual storm, and that could do incredible things to a man's ego," but they were basically unsuited. He introduced her to the writings of Dorothy Parker and Edna St. Vincent Millay, both of whom she adored: but the Rabwins knew that emotionally she was scarcely more mature than when she had first arrived at Metro. They also recognized that Mankiewicz was attracted to her precisely because she was the opposite of Rosa. Marc Rabwin wrote to Mankiewicz about his apprehensions, "because she was mad about him, and I knew it wasn't going to come to anything. It had to terminate, and she was going to get hurt," but he never sent the letter.

Mankiewicz—though he did not perhaps quite realize this until later—was obsessively interested in the psychology of the female star: how it coped with fame and especially aging—the need for more makeup and the fearful certainty of being replaced by someone younger. Garland, Mankiewicz felt, was on the threshold of a brilliant career, but was already developing a temperament which might ruin it. Jimmy considered her sister's fantasies merely "elaborations," but remembered Mankiewicz telling Garland that she was a pathological liar and should see a psychiatrist. He thought Garland's hostility to her mother and to Mayer even more damaging, and when Karl Menninger was visiting in Beverly Hills, he persuaded her to see him. "Miss Garland, you have some problems," Menninger said, "and we might be able to work them out if you'll give us a year. If not with us, some other psychoanalyst."

Since it was not possible for Garland to stay in the clinic in Topeka, Menninger recommended a local man, Dr. Ernest Simmel. She saw him five days a week on her way to work, and since Jimmy also had to be at the studio she sometimes drove her there. Neither she nor Ethel thought the sessions would continue for long, because Garland had a short attention span and would probably end them when the novelty wore off. Also, Garland admitted to Jimmy that she made up stories for the sake of Dr. Simmel, which suggested that she was not taking analysis seriously. The experienced Dr. Simmel was fully aware of what she was up to, however, and telephoned Ethel to say that he would be unable to help his patient if she skipped visits and persisted in lying. Ethel and Jimmy decided that Judy was only attending to please Mankiewicz—and, as Jimmy put it: "You couldn't tell her what Joe said was wrong without getting your head chopped off."

Mankiewicz had also told Garland that she should no longer let her mother handle her finances, that a star of her eminence should have a business manager. Mankiewicz, in fact, had far more control over Garland than her mother did, and what little Ethel had was slipping away. In the course of analysis, patients may regard talking about their dreams as curious and talking about themselves as an ego trip, but once they start to examine their childhood, it is extraordinary how many unpleasant events and incidents are found buried in the psyche. Jimmy believed that the visits to Dr. Simmel were what finally turned Garland against her mother. Although Simmel was neutral in the matter, he helped Garland remember things about Ethel which she had buried in her subconscious.

Ethel also thought that the sessions were turning her daughter against her, and went to see Louis B. Mayer. Although Jimmy thought she was wrong to do so, Ethel was within her rights, since Garland's revised 1940 contract continued to hold her responsible for certain aspects of her daughter's behavior, and Garland had recently been the last to arrive on set or the first to leave. She had also taken to forgetting her lines. Mayer would surely agree that the last thing anyone wanted was for Judy Garland to be a law unto herself.

Mayer and Mankiewicz had already had one quarrel over Garland. Mankiewicz was returning on the train from Topeka to Los Angeles when he bumped into Howard Strikling, who was traveling with Mayer. Mankiewicz was summoned to Mayer's compartment where, accurately guessing the subject of the conversation, he told the mogul that Garland should be given more grown-up roles. Mayer told Mankiewicz not to concern himself with Garland or her private life, and they soon got into a furious argument. Mayer calmed down to point out, as he often did, that he had the welfare of all his players at heart. "I'm talking to you like an angry father," he said. "No, you're not," Mankiewicz retorted. "You're talking like a jealous man. None of this father shit for me!"—and stormed out of the compartment.

Since Mayer was a vengeful man and Mankiewicz a stubborn one, the matter was decidedly unfinished. Mankiewicz had a year or so to go on his contract, which could not be canceled, so Mayer could either sell it or leave him idle. Mankiewicz felt that Mayer should apologize for intruding into his and Garland's private life. Ethel's visit to Mayer reinforced the mogul's belief that Mankiewicz was not a good influence on Garland. Mayer did not understand the science of psychoanalysis and did not want to, since he did not wish to blame himself for the nervous disorders for which his own wife had been treated during the last ten years.

Mankiewicz was summoned to Mayer's office:

He was *choleric* as I walked in. Obviously the word "psychiatrist" was enough to set him off. And Mrs. Gumm was there screaming, and Eddie Mannix, the wonderful Irish manager, sitting in a corner. And Mayer yelled, how dare I interfere in the life of Judy—a mother's love was all she needed. And I said "A mother's love, my ass." The mother said, "I know what to do with my daughter"—and it got into one of those screaming fights. I was so aghast that I finally said, "Look, Mr. Mayer, the studio is obviously not big enough for both of us. One of us has to go." At that, Eddie Mannix fell off his chair and I was at Fox within a week.

Frances Gumm (at center with kitten) surrounded by her sisters Virginia and Mary Jane on the lawn of their Grand Rapids home. (British Film Institute)

Baby Gumm in her stage costume, 1928. (British Film Institute)

Early MGM publicity shots of Judy. The studio wasn't
quite sure what to do with the plump adolescent.
(Bill Chapman Collection)

"You Made Me Love You"— Judy singing to Clark Gable.
(Bill Chapman Collection)

With Deanna Durbin at Judy's fourteenth birthday party given by her mother. (Bill Chapman Collection)

Jackie Cooper (left) and Mickey Rooney kissing Judy beside Louis B. Mayer's swimming pool, 1939. (British Film Institute)

Rooney and Garland with members of the "Official Reception Committee" for the East Coast premiere run of *The Wizard of Oz* in August 1939. (Photofest)

Judy besieged by autograph hunters in New Orleans. (Culver)

Judy immortalizing her footprints at Grauman's Chinese Theatre at the premiere of *Babes in Arms*, 1939. (Culver)

Judy serving cake to her first serious love, heartbreaker Artie Shaw, late 1939.
(Bill Chapman Collection)

Judy's mother and Louis B.
Mayer at Judy's eighteenth
birthday party in 1940. (Culver)

Judy returning to Los Angeles
with her first husband David
Rose from their elopement
to Las Vegas, 1941.
(Bill Chapman Collection)

Judy at her new white house in
Westwood, 1940.
(Bill Chapman Collection)

The bisexual Tyrone Power, with whom Judy had an affair in 1942. (Photofest)

The Garland sisters in 1942. Left to right: Suzy (Mary Jane), Judy, and Jimmy (Virginia). (British Film Institute)

Judy with her mother.
(Bill Chapman Collection)

Judy with First Lady Eleanor
Roosevelt inspecting a minia-
ture air raid shelter at Greek
war relief headquarters in
New York. (Culver)

Mankiewicz's agent arranged the deal at 20th Century-Fox so quickly that Mayer would not be seen to have fired him. He also obtained a pay raise for him, as well as the right to write and direct as well as produce, if he felt so inclined. Eventually the deal was to result in such cinema milestones as *A Letter to Three Wives* and *All About Eve*. He continued to see Garland.

In spite of Mankiewicz's belief, which Garland shared, that she should be given more adult roles, Freed was determined to team her once again with Mickey Rooney. A further example of his tank-like insensitivity was that he once again assigned Busby Berkeley to direct. *Girl Crazy* would have been the director's fourth film with Garland and Rooney, but in the event he did not work for long on the actual filming, which started in January 1943. Freed had ignored the earlier friction between Garland and Berkeley, and he rejected his star's pleas for another director. She complained constantly to Edens, who found the director belligerent and not very well and was horrified when he saw what Berkeley had done to the "I Got Rhythm" sequence. Edens had planned this as a simple, rhythmic number. The director had different ideas: "Berkeley got his big ensembles and trick cameras into it again," Edens recalled, "plus a lot of girls in Western outfits, with fringed skirts and people cracking whips, firing guns . . . and cannons going off all over my arrangement and Judy's voice." After a quarrel over this, Edens appealed to Freed, who discovered that the number had added almost $60,000 to the budget. Freed had insisted on Berkeley in the first place because he believed him capable of firmly controlling the various elements essential to an important musical production, and so he now dismissed him. He later claimed that he did so because Berkeley had "some sort of personality clash" with Garland. This is the first official comment on her temperament.

Production stopped for a month, enabling a weak and seriously underweight Garland to recuperate before reshooting the revised finale for *Presenting Lily Mars*. Direction on *Girl Crazy* was resumed under Norman Taurog, who had directed her in *Little Nelly Kelly*. As written for the screen by Fred Finklehoffe, the plot bore no relationship to the original book of the musical by Guy Bolton and Jack McGowan. Rooney is a playboy who is sent to a college out West, where his cockiness makes him enemies. He is dissuaded from quitting, mainly because he is smitten with Garland, the granddaughter of the dean. When he does leave, it is only to return because of Judy, and when the college is threatened with closure, he decides to go to its aid. His plans—which include a rodeo and the crowning of a beauty queen—create so much publicity that there are hundreds of applications to join the school.

It was Rooney who suggested shooting his duet with Garland, "Could You Use Me?," on location. The number might have been shot on the back lot, as were many of the other exteriors, but Rooney fancied a few days in Palm Springs, where the nearby desert could stand in for Arizona. The sequence was staged in an auto ride, with the car driven by Garland over rough ground to prove to Rooney the toughness of Westerners. Rehearsals began on a Sunday afternoon, after the cast and crew arrived; they continued until noon the following day, but technical difficulties prevented any footage from being shot. On the third day, as equipment was being arranged in unbearable heat, a sandstorm blew up. When filming was ready to recommence it was discovered that Garland was missing. Without telling anyone she had left for an assignation in Los Angeles. The crew sat around for several days waiting for her to return.

Garland's appointment seems to have been with Joe Mankiewicz, and while her unscheduled absence may have been due to the impulsiveness of someone in love, it was inconsiderate and unprofessional. It was also an act of defiance toward the employer who had always "protected" her, and revenge for being called back from her honeymoon. She was now too important to M-G-M to be humiliated as she had been then. It may even have been done in a competitive feeling—perhaps unconscious—toward Rooney, whose wish to be in Palm Springs had separated her from her lover. It may have been prompted by a headiness caused from being away from the watchful eye of Strickling and his underlings. It was an immature attempt to get herself considered, despite or because of her inferiority complex, to be one of M-G-M's most important stars. Others were equally irresponsible: for instance, hours of shooting time had been lost on *The Women* because of the behavior of Norma Shearer and Joan Crawford in trying to upstage each other.

Girl Crazy was trade-shown early in August 1943, but not released until late November—and not shown in some key cities, including New York, until after Christmas, in order to get as much mileage as possible from the Rooney-Garland partnership, since she made clear her own unwillingness to continue it. It went on to gross over $3,770,000, which was fortunate, since it had cost $1,140,850, some $322,950 over budget—partly because few companies then were accustomed to shooting on location. The five-month (January-May) shooting schedule included the lay-off after Berkeley left, and the difficulties in Palm Springs.

This last co-starring vehicle for the two erstwhile teenagers redefines their functions: when Rooney is not clowning, Garland is singing. When they unite to show off both talents in "Could You Use Me?" the result is stunning, partly because it is one of the most sophisticated of comic songs, and because the wit Garland brings to the lyric is uniquely hers.

Even so, James Agee, writing in *The Nation*, could find little in the film to recommend, "unless you are curious to see what makes one of the biggest box-office successes of the year." However, he thought the film viewable "if, like me, you like Judy Garland. Miss Garland is a good strident vaudeville actor too [like Rooney]; and has an apparent straightness and sweetness with which I sympathize. Judging by her frequent 'emotional' moments I would very much like to see her in straight dramatic roles." This was a cry taken up by the uncredited critic of *Time* magazine, who found Garland "open, cheerful and warming. If she were not so profitably good at her own game, she could obviously be a dramatic actress with a profit to all." This may also have been written by Agee, chief reviewer for the magazine.

"Hold your hats folks!" the *New York Times* warned. "Mickey and Judy are back in town. And if at this late date there are a few diehards who deny that they are the most incorrigibly talented pair of youngsters in movies, then *Girl Crazy* should serve as final rebuttal." The critic went on to say that Rooney has

Judy, who sings and acts like an earthbound angel, to temper his brashness—well, they can do almost anything they wish, and we'll like it even in spite of ourselves . . . Miss Garland's songs, such as "Bidin' My Time," should soothe even the most savage breast; of all the child prodigies of Hollywood, Miss Garland has outgrown her adolescence most gracefully and still sings a song with an appealing sincerity which is downright irresistible.

There seemed to be a great deal of indecision about Garland's career in 1943. M-G-M announced her for *The Story of Gaby Delys*, but little more was heard of this, while *Babes in Hollywood*, a projected reunion with Rooney, was abandoned. Freed was searching for a vehicle to co-star her with Fred Astaire, whose talent was of a very different order than Rooney's. Then *Show Boat* seemed a distinct possibility at one time. The property had been bought by M-G-M in

1943 from Universal—who had filmed it twice, in 1929 and 1936. The studio had intended to use it for Jeannette MacDonald and Nelson Eddy, but had subsequently lost interest in that team, reputedly because MacDonald had gone behind Mayer's back to the front office in New York on the matter of the dubbing of her voice in the foreign version of her films. This, at any rate, was the reason MacDonald gave when her contract was not renewed.

Meanwhile, on July 1, Garland made a rare live appearance, in a concert at the Robin Hill Dell, a huge outdoor auditorium in Philadelphia, where she was accompanied by André Kostelanetz and the Philadelphia Orchestra. The manager of the Dell had schemed for two years to get Garland together with Kostelanetz (with whom she had made the CBS broadcast in 1939) for a live performance. Kostelanetz was regarded as the classiest of those who played popular music, and 36,000 people attended the concert, with an estimated 15,000 turned away. According to the report in *Time* magazine, Garland "was never so petrified in her whole life . . . except for her startling red-blonde hair, she looked like a girl who had arrived at her first formal party and was scared stiff nobody would dance with her." A Gershwin set—"Someone to Watch Over Me," "Do, Do, Do," "Embraceable You" and "The Man I Love"—showed "little of the typical Garland exuberance," but she began to relax with "Strike Up the Band," and after the intermission was more impressive with some of her film songs, including "Over the Rainbow," "For Me and My Gal," and "You Made Me Love You." She said: "I thought later that they were probably thinking what was I doing there, so I just sang louder." She wound up with "The Joint Is Really Jumpin' at Carnegie Hall," which was so joyously received that she was said to be contemplating a concert tour in the winter.

That particular song had been written by Roger Edens, Hugh Martin and Ralph Blane for her to sing in her guest appearance in *Thousands Cheer*, which was released shortly after the concert. It was to be her last screen performance for over a year, though it was actually shown before *Girl Crazy* was released. The "Thousands" were GIs, and what they were cheering were half of the stars on the M-G-M lot, at the end of a puerile but topical "army" story featuring Gene Kelly and Kathryn Grayson. The film had been put together with footage from the abandoned *Broadway Melody of 1943*—at least, Eleanor Powell's dance had been originally shot for that—and was an attempt to show that M-G-M's stars were just as patriotic as those at Paramount, which had put together a similar revue a year earlier, entitled *Star-Spangled Rhythm*. The film also "introduced" the classical pianist José Iturbi, whose glum presence was to feature in some of the studio's lesser musicals over the next few years. He accompanied Garland on this occasion, in a number fashioned by Edens to prove that Iturbi could play boogie-woogie. It is also one of the very few ordinary pieces he composed with Garland in mind—standard hepcat stuff of the period. She does the verse with a sense of mockery, and it is the highlight of the picture, but she looks nervy and jumpy.

This is hardly surprising, for there had been rumors of a separation from David Rose and that she had been seriously ill. Mankiewicz had been aware that her behavior, both on and off the set, was becoming increasingly erratic, which is why he had suggested she should see a psychiatrist. Her sessions with Dr. Simmel had brought all the complicated and antagonistic feelings about her mother to the surface, which led to Ethel's attempt to intervene with Mayer. This, in turn, had led to the banishment of Mankiewicz. For a second time, the studio had attempted to interfere in her private life. The results were to be disastrous, for it was from now on that Garland's professional behavior began to cause problems.

Whatever her personal difficulties at this period, the Robin Hill Dell concert seemed to show that she had recovered sufficiently to be getting on with her career. A few days later, she appeared with Kostelanetz on his radio show, *The Pause That Refreshes On the Air*—the title refers to the show's sponsor, Coca-Cola—and, four days after that, she began a two-week tour of military installations for the United Service Organization. A spokesman for the USO was enthusiastic: "She has such a bright, clean image. The soldiers adore her. The fact that she isn't necessarily a sexpot makes her even more desired. Judy is the girl soldiers want to marry."

She had not long been back in Los Angeles when the Hollywood Victory Committee invited her to be one of the participants in its Third War Drive, along with Mickey Rooney, Betty Hutton, Fred Astaire, James Cagney, Greer Garson, Lucille Ball, Harpo Marx, Dick Powell, José Iturbi and the bandleader Kay Kyser, who was also the emcee. Spectators had to pledge a minimum of $25 each for war bonds. In twenty-three days, during a sixteen-city tour, the stars raised in excess of a billion dollars.

8

Meet Me in St. Louis

NEITHER JUDY GARLAND nor M-G-M was keen to make *Meet Me in St. Louis*. Sally Benson's stories, "5135 Kensington Avenue," had originally appeared in the *New Yorker* in 1941. They were based on childhood reminiscences, "a sort of valentine on the back of your hand," as she described them. Her memories of St. Louis ended in 1910, when her family moved to New York, but she set the stories back to 1904, to conclude with the opening of the World's Fair. They were brought to Arthur Freed's notice by the screenwriter Fred Finklehoffe. At this period, Hollywood was in thrall to the simple, amusing, autobiographical stories which were being published in the country's most sophisticated magazine. Two previous series had become successful Broadway plays, *Life With Father*, based on Clarence Day's reminiscences, and *My Sister Eileen*, based on those of Ruth McKenny. M-G-M had been beaten to the purchase of the film rights of these stories, by Warner Bros. and Columbia, respectively. *My Sister Eileen* had already become a popular movie, while *Life With Father* would have to wait to be filmed until it had finished its Broadway run (which lasted eight years; at this time, it was roughly at the halfway point). Sally Benson's stories had not achieved the same renown, but Finklehoffe knew that Freed had been kicking himself for missing out on *Life With Father*.

Freed realized that Benson's stories combined the appeal of the Hardy films with that of Day's reminiscences. The obvious similarity between the Days and the Smiths of St. Louis lies in the fact that the father believes himself to be the head of the household, while it is the gentle mother who is really in command. The Smiths have five children: two adolescent girls and two younger ones, and a boy about to leave for college. M-G-M purchased the screen rights in March 1942 for $25,000, plus a $10,000 option on the characters, in case they wanted to use them again. One of the studio's lawyers, I.H. Prinzmetal, suggested that if any sequels followed they should be as much like the Hardy films as possible.

Benson worked on a treatment at M-G-M in the spring of 1942, while she adapted the stories into a novel which was published by Random House, under the title of the old song, "Meet Me in St. Louis." Freed decided to use this song in the film, as well as others of the period; apart from this, he was only certain that he wanted it to be filmed in Technicolor (already traditional for period musicals) and wanted Garland to play one of the adolescent daughters. Since no romance featured in the original, Benson added "the boy next door" to her script, but the role as she conceived it was unsuitable for Mickey Rooney, and the Executive Committee believed that without him the result would not rival the popularity of the Andy Hardy films. With Rooney literally out of the picture, the studio went cold on the project.

Two other writers worked on a screenplay and, finding no plot, concocted one in which the seventeen-year-old Esther Smith—the role Garland would play—was blackmailed. This was no better received than Benson's treatment, and Freed turned the project over to Finklehoffe. At the time, Finklehoffe was more interested in producing a Broadway revue, *Show Time*, and so he asked for Irving Brecher as co-writer. The focal point of the story now became Mr. Smith's promotion to the New York office, with the consequent disappointment of the family, who would therefore miss the Fair. In the end, Mr. Smith realizes that "East, West—Home's Best," which was precisely the message of *The Wizard of Oz*.

George Cukor agreed to direct, which pleased Freed, since Cukor was one of the few people in the studio who were still enthusiastic about the project. Freed also remembered Cukor's success in 1933 with *Little Women* and his small but paramount contribution to *The Wizard of Oz*. For a second time, however, Cukor was denied the opportunity of directing Garland—this time because he was con-scripted into the army. There were other directors on the M-G-M lot capable of handling what was at the time just another "family" movie, but Freed decided to take a chance on a less tried talent, Vincente Minnelli.

Minnelli was born in 1903 and, as he said, if Garland was born in a trunk, he was born in a tent: his father was half-owner of the Minnelli Brothers Tent Theater, for which his mother was leading lady. His birthplace was Chicago, where his mother rested during the winter layoff, and he first acted, with her, in *East Lynne*, in which he played Little Willie. Motion pictures killed off precarious ventures such as the Tent Theater, and, after a spell as an amateur actor, Minnelli took a job as a photographer's assistant, in Chicago. It was here that he joined the Balaban and Katz organization, designing costumes for the live shows which preceded the main movie. When Balaban and Katz amalgamated with the Paramount-Publix circuit, he was transferred to New York, still designing their shows, until 1931, when Earl Carroll gave him the chance to design the curtain for the latest edition of his "Vanities," shows rather like the Ziegfeld Follies, though not quite as lavish. Minnelli was responsible for both sets and costumes for the subsequent productions, and in 1933 was appointed chief costume designer for the newly opened Radio City Music Hall.

In 1935 he directed one of the Music Hall's weekly spectacles with such success that one of his friends, the well-connected Lee Gershwin (wife of Ira Gershwin), asked him whether he would like to direct a Broadway show. She arranged an introduction to Lee and Jake Shu-bert, the leading theatrical impresarios of the day, and the brothers put him in charge of *At Home Abroad*, a revue starring Beatrice Lillie and featuring Ethel Waters, Eleanor Powell and the comic Herb Williams. Minnelli designed the costumes as well, and as director or designer, or both, worked on several other important productions, including the 1936 *Ziegfeld Follies*, *The Show Is On*, with Lillie and Bert Lahr, *Hooray for What!* and *Very Warm for May*.

During this period, he was approached by several studios who wanted to bring him to Hollywood. He eventually signed with Para-mount, who had offered him a producer-director contract, at $2,500 a week: but he spent most of his eight months there trying to get out of it. He disagreed with Paramount's executives about what made an effective screen musical, and when an offer came from Lee Shubert to return to Broadway, he bought himself out of his contract.

One day in 1940, Yip Harburg brought Arthur Freed to his New York home to meet Minnelli. Freed invited the young man to come to M-G-M, urging him to forget his previous experience in Hollywood. He offered him a year with his unit, watching and learning, and the prospect of becoming a movie director. Minnelli arrived with preconceived views of the Hollywood musical, all of them negative: he did not like Busby Berkeley chorus lines and the emphasis on backstage stories, or the way studios treated Broadway shows. In effect, apart from *The Wizard of Oz*, the only aspect of film musicals of which he *did* approve was the dancing of Fred Astaire.

He was introduced to Judy Garland when Freed asked him for suggestions about staging a number in *Strike Up the Band*; he also made some contributions to *Babes on Broadway*. He did not know, when his probation period was up, whether Freed would ask him to stay. However, after failing to buy *Porgy and Bess* for the studio, Freed had purchased another all-black show, *Cabin in the Sky*, in the belief that it could be filmed imaginatively on a small budget, and he invited Minnelli to direct it. The result was a critical success, which convinced Freed that Minnelli was the best replacement for Cukor on *Meet Me in St. Louis*.

Although *Cabin in the Sky* had a couple of lavish production numbers, its strength had been in some charming songs performed on the verandah and the sidewalk. So Minnelli decided that there were to be no gleaming sets for dancers in the Smiths' St. Louis, not even a theater, and this made the film virtually unique among Hollywood musicals. Freed announced all but four of the old songs he had chosen for the film and commissioned new ones which would advance the plot. Roger Edens, credited on the film with "musical adaptation" was in fact responsible for the way in which the music was integrated into the story.

By this time, Finklehoffe had departed to work on *Show Time*, leaving the script unfinished. Irving Brecher was left to work on the screenplay with Minnelli, while Hugh Martin and Ralph Blane wrote three new songs. As members of Kay Thompson's Rhythm Boys, they had worked for Minnelli on *Hooray for What!*, stepping in to conclude the vocal arrangements when Thompson had been fired. Over the next few years they had arranged some scores for Rodgers and Hart, and, by coincidence, Martin had been pianist with his own octet, the

Martins, which had opened the act for Garland and Rooney at the Capitol in 1939, while Blane had been among the singers. The two men had collaborated on the score for a Broadway musical, *Best Foot Forward*, and had arrived at M-G-M when the studio had bought the property for Freed. A new song written by them was thought more likely to be a "hit" number than any of the old songs of the period— and a hit would be sorely needed, in the opinion of studio executives, who remained pessimistic about the film's box-office chances.

All of these executives, Minnelli recalled, had "a special fatherly feeling" for Garland, but their advice on past occasions had often conflicted. Now they were unanimous: "This will set your career back twenty years," she had been assured. She had graduated to playing adult roles with *Presenting Lily Mars*, but in the new film she would once again be playing an adolescent. She turned to Mankiewicz, who did not help matters by telling her that the best role in the picture was that of the youngest daughter, Tootie. In the Andy Hardy films, Garland had had a crush on the boy next door: in the new film her love would be requited, but she was still a singing adolescent, and the *younger* of the two older sisters. Mankiewicz felt that, because of her wit, she should be playing sophisticated comedy. She complained to Freed, who advised her to trust him and Minnelli.

When she first discussed the film with Minnelli, Garland had no doubt that he would see her point of view. He remembered that she said either "This is awful, isn't it?" or "This isn't very good, is it?"— and that she looked at him "as if we were planning an armed robbery against the American public." He failed to persuade her of the picture's potential merit, and she appealed to Louis B. Mayer, who told Freed that she did not have to do it. Others of the Freed unit recalled that Mayer had been the sole champion of the project in the boardroom, because the story reflected his belief in the sanctity of family life. Whatever the case, Garland was finally won over when, "in a last desperate move," Freed got Brecher to read the script to her. She was finally convinced that the role of Esther Smith was a very good one for her.

She was also appeased by several factors, starting with a promise that her next picture would give her a straight dramatic role. Furthermore, this one was beginning to look like an expensive item, with the added cost of shooting in Technicolor: this was doubly attractive because the studio still made only a handful a year in that process. Lemuel Ayers, who had just caused great excitement on Broadway with his sets for Rodgers and Hammerstein's *Oklahoma!*, was brought out to work with Jack Martin Smith on the design. The least expensive option, costing only $58,275, would have been to convert the Hardy family's street for the Smiths of St. Louis, but, in consultation with Minnelli, they agreed to construct a completely new street at a cost of $208,275—out of a total cost for the sets of $497,000. The second heaviest line item of the budget was $234,000 for the music; because of the extensive rewrites, the cost of story and continuity was also above average, at $132,250. Several snags, and Technicolor's busy schedule, led to a two-month delay in starting shooting and helped to push up the budget from its original $1,395,000 to over $1,500,000.

Freed had assembled a first-rate cast, including such dependable scene-stealers as Marjorie Main to play the family cook and Harry Davenport to play Grandpa; Leon Ames and Mary Astor were cast as Mr. and Mrs. Smith, and their eldest daughter was to be played by Lucille Bremer, an untried talent but a personal protégée of Freed. Tootie was to be played by Margaret O'Brien, who was fast becoming a box-office attraction, but Garland's stellar position would be emphasized by the fact that her name would be in bigger letters than that of the child star. Garland's friend, Van Johnson, had been cast as the boy next door, but he had achieved greater prominence within the last year and, rather than tamper with the script in order to make his role larger, he was replaced by Tom Drake, a gentle actor in the same mold.

One aspect of pre-production which pleased Garland was the make-up tests. These were supervised by Dottie Ponedel, who had been responsible for the Dietrich look while she was at Paramount. Ponedel immediately threw out the rubber discs which had been inserted to change the shape of Garland's nose along with the caps which covered her teeth. "You don't need all this junk," she said. "You're a pretty girl. Let's see what we could do." She raised Garland's eyebrows, gave her a fuller lower lip and, with tweezers, carefully altered her hairline. For as long as Garland remained at M-G-M, Dottie Ponedel remained her makeup artist, constantly making changes when her weight was fluctuating. Others responsible for Garland's physical appearance on screen did not always recall her with affection, but Ponedel continued to act as adviser after Garland left the studio, and they were to remain friends for many years.

One problem which arose in the music department was a line in the script which said: "The trolley starts and the crowd starts to sing." Blane and Martin felt it "corny" to write a song about a trolley, so they wrote about people singing *on* a trolley. And then they wrote another, for Freed kept turning them all down. The best, they said, was "Know Where You're Going, and You'll Get There," a "jubilant spiritual thing which Judy did better than anyone. Edens liked it, but Freed again rejected it. He insisted that he wanted a song *about* a trolley and in desperation Blane went to the Beverly Hills Public Library to see if he could find a picture of a St. Louis trolley of the period. He did, and underneath it was the caption: "Clang, Clang, Went the Trolley." With that as their inspiration, they wrote "The Trolley Song." They had no trouble with "The Boy Next Door" or "Have Yourself a Merry Little Christmas," although Garland requested changes to several lyrics of the latter. After singing the opening line, she was to continue "It may be your last / Next year we will all be living in the past." She insisted that the song was sad enough as it was, without this additional downbeat reflection, which would make audiences want to leave the theater. So a substitute was found: "Let your heart be light / Next year all our troubles will be out of sight"—which turned out to be singularly appropriate, for the film was released just before the last Christmas of the Second World War.

According to Blane and Martin, their contribution was a major factor in Garland agreeing to do the film, but, in fact, only the script was in place when she did so. It was Edens who assured her that the three songs were wonderfully right for her. Even so, she did not begin work with any confidence. Having achieved her goal of a leading role in a major musical without Rooney, she was unsure whether she could carry the film, or to what extent she could compete with M-G-M's more glamorous stars. She had not managed to bury her qualms about the script and especially about her own role, which she considered vapid, and she was still fretting about the Mankiewicz affair. The first expression of her unease was when she complained about the month's schedule that Minnelli had set aside for rehearsals and pre-recording. He managed to calm her, but she made no secret of her doubts about the whole project when filming began on December 7.

The first scene to be shot was one in which she and her elder sister are primping before a mirror. Although inexperienced, Bremer played her role with feeling—a quality Garland declined to bring to hers. According to Minnelli, she "was making fun of the script . . . her intelligence showed through, and she didn't come off as an impressionable young girl." The footage he got was unusable. Freed visited Garland in her dressing-room, where she told him that she didn't know what Minnelli wanted, and didn't feel she could act anymore.

Freed assured her that Minnelli knew what he was doing, and the scene was eventually completed satisfactorily.

Minnelli knew that the film, built as it was around a family, could only work if the players worked as an ensemble, so after a short shooting day he asked the cast to do a run-through of a sequence still to be shot. Garland did not intend to oblige, and left; he had to have her car intercepted at the studio gate. Mary Astor insisted that Minnelli knew what he was doing. "Just go along with it," she advised Garland, "because it means something."

When Garland did not feel like "going along with it," she would retire to her dressing-room, complaining of migraine. As the star of the film, she carried the major burden of responsibility, a burden for which she did not have sufficient confidence. There was also the physical strain imposed by shooting, for she had to wear tight-corseted costumes and endure the extras lighting required for Technicolor. Such factors contributed to her trying behavior. The daily production reports show that she was late more often than not, with days when she failed to show up at all. On January 13, for instance, she was due in wardrobe at 9:00 a.m. and on the set at 10:00: but the assistant director, Al Jennings, reported:

Judy Garland phoned A.D. [assistant director] that she was well enough for work, but unable to drive because her eyes were bothering her, and would he please send a car for her. At 9:10 car left—returned with Miss Garland at 9:45. At 9:50 Miss Garland . . . had lost her toothbridge, her dentist Dr. Pinkus had a spare set and to send a car for them. [Unit Manager] Friedman called Transportation for O.K. to send car. At 10:00 car was sent for bridge, returned at 10:40 with them. Miss Garland arrived on stage at 10:40—made up and hair dressed but in street clothes.

For an hour she rehearsed a scene with Tom Drake in which the two characters turn out the gas-lamps and first realize they are in love, and, after getting into costume, managed eleven takes between 12:16 and 1:30. After an hour for lunch, cast and crew reconvened to rehearse the next setup, but work was disrupted for ten minutes when Garland retired to be treated for a headache, then again for half an hour for an adjustment to her costume. Before they stopped at 6:15, Minnelli managed to get six takes, plus another when Garland demanded "a better one."

Garland's friend, Charles Walters, who choreographed "The Trolley Song," found her behavior incomprehensible. All the "kids" were on the trolley, ready and waiting, but she remained in her dressing-room, finally responding to his entreaties by emerging briefly to do one take, then retiring once more. The film, like many to come, had become a contest between her psyche and the M-G-M system.

Mary Astor thought Garland was being unprofessional and decided to visit her in her dressing-room to tell her so. Garland greeted her with "Hi, Mom!" but did not look around from the mirror. "Judy," Astor said, "what's happened to you? You were a trouper—once." Garland merely stared into the mirror, so she continued, "You have kept the entire company out there waiting for two hours. Waiting for you to favor us with your presence. You know we're stuck—there's nothing we can do without you." Garland's response was to giggle and to say that she had heard that from others. Incensed by this response, Astor replied: "Well, then, either get the hell on set or *I'm going home.*" Garland blamed her behavior on her inability to sleep, to which Astor retorted: "Well, get to bed earlier than—like we all have to do. You're not so damn special, baby!"

It was only later, Astor said, that she knew what Garland had been going through.

The fun was still there and she seemed to have great energy. But it was intense, driven, tremulous. Anxious. She was working way over the capacities of any human being. She was recording at night and playing in the picture in the day, and people got annoyed when she was late on the set, and when she got jittery and weepy with fatigue . . . She was a hot little flame, and I'm surprised she didn't burn out long ago. She had a great love for her work, but she didn't know how to say "No" to pressure. It was "Go, Judy, go!" all her short life.

This accords with Arthur Freed's later estimation of Garland: "Talent? The greatest. But it's a hysterical talent."

Margaret Hamilton, hearing reports of Garland's temper tantrums and fits of hysteria, became concerned that this was not the girl she had known on *The Wizard of Oz*, and went to visit her. "They are giving me pills of some kind to go to sleep," Garland told her, "and then others to give me energy when I'm awake. And I don't feel good on those pills."

In spite of these difficulties, Minnelli sensed that Garland was gradually coming to regard the Smiths of St. Louis as affectionately as he did. The dancer Don Loper, whom he had known in New York, decided that the shoot might proceed more equably if she got to know Minnelli off the set and so, with his girlfriend, Ruth Brady, he arranged a double date. It was a great success and was repeated several times. "Judy's wit went so well with Don's sardonic outlook," Minnelli said. "I laughed at the time, not wondering why Judy invariably turned the humor on herself." He merely found her self-deprecation "disarming, and the vulnerability she disguised with it all the more touching. Like everyone else at the studio, I wanted to protect and love her. And Judy was affectionate and loving right back."

One evening, when Loper was ill, Minnelli telephoned Garland to cancel their date. She laughed. "We don't have to go out with Don and Ruth every time, do we? We can go alone." And so they did, on several occasions. She confessed to him: "I always have to be my best in front of the camera. You expect it of me too. Well, sometimes I don't feel my best. It's a struggle to get through the day . . . I use these pills. They carry me through." "Well," he replied, "as long as you don't overdo it."

Garland also dated Tom Drake, confessing to him at the end of the evening that she could not face work in the morning because she was exhausted. He recalled:

I'd leave with this knowledge and yet I'd have to get to the studio at six-thirty and play absolutely dumb. After the set was all lit up, Judy would send word that she would be two hours late—and everyone would stall for a couple of hours. Then, finally, word would come in that she wouldn't be in at all.

Although the atmosphere on the set remained tense, Garland's growing relationship with Minnelli was one reason why it became happier; he had persuaded her that this would be one of her best pictures, delicate and touching. The film finished shooting in April 1944, and as Minnelli began cutting, he and Garland began to live together. In his unreliable autobiography, Minnelli claims to have been circumspect in his romantic approach: "It was presumptuous to latch onto her, as I'd seen so many fellows around town do the same with established stars, and I wasn't about to be accused of doing the same thing." He had noticed that she was absolutely pliable both on set and off, and he did not want her to confuse her respect for him with love. Effectively, she was still David Rose's wife, and Minnelli was uncertain whether he wanted to be married at all. He was also conscious that he was nineteen years older, and saw this as an obstacle to marriage. In Garland's eyes, of course, this was a positive advantage. He was able to reinforce the self-confidence which Mankiewicz had first given her. For the first time she began to look upon herself as Minnelli and Mankiewicz did: as a glamorous star and not an oversized child.

In his autobiography, Minnelli makes no mention of another obstacle to marriage: his homosexuality. He was distinctly effeminate and his sexual preferences were so well known that friends were astonished that he and Garland were enjoying *any* sort of romance. As they sat gazing into each other's eyes at parties given by the Gene Kellys, it seemed that they were sharing the same dream—for, like Garland, Minnelli lived in his own fantasy world. He was also highly strung, and some people thought that the couple were drawn together by their neuroses. Onlookers assumed that Garland's passion for Minnelli was yet another of her foolish whims, one which would pass, as they all did. They were wrapped up in each other, but the idea of them marrying was laughable.

The first previews of *Meet Me in St. Louis* were given in June 1944. Apart from a general feeling that the film was too long, the response was excellent. In order to shorten the film, one of the songs would have to go. Since the Blane-Martin songs had hit-parade potential, Minnelli looked at the others. These included an old ditty, "Skip to My Lou," and "You and I," a sentimental ballad for Mr. and Mrs. Smith, which Freed wrote with his old partner, Nacio Herb Brown. Freed had also bought a song by Rodgers and Hammerstein called "Boys and Girls Like You and Me," which had been dropped from *Oklahoma!* on its try-out tour. A place had been found for it in the mid-film sequence in which Garland and Drake visit the building site for the fair.

Minnelli fought for "Skip to My Lou" because it offered a chance to see Esther Smith with her friends, as well as giving little Margaret O'Brien an opportunity to participate in the family party. Against the advice of many influential people at the studio, he also insisted on keeping the long Halloween sequence, which was a tour de force for O'Brien. This left "The Boy Next Door" and "Boys and Girls Like You and Me," which were alike in tempo and even content. Minnelli chose to keep the former because it advanced the plot, while the other slowed it up.

"Boys and Girls Like You and Me" was certainly not a vintage melody: but if the film has a major fault, it is that it lacks a musical number in the final moments. Furthermore, one less Garland song made the film that much less a Garland vehicle; Minnelli's decision to retain two sequences devoted to her precocious co-star had made the film seem more of a vehicle for Margaret O'Brien. Garland knew that the studio considered O'Brien a potential star, one who might become as big as Shirley Temple, but she did not blame Freed, who had stayed very much in the background during the eight months in which Minnelli had been preparing the film. She could see why Minnelli was being considered the first director to understand the musical form since Lubitsch, but her ardor for him cooled. The relationship, after only a few weeks, was finished.

In his autobiography, Minnelli gives a different reason for the breakup. "She'd been seeing another man before we started going together," he said. "She simply gravitated back to him just as she had toward me at the start of our affair. I theorized that Judy must have been flattered by the attentions of such a brilliant man, and intrigued by the fact that he was in analysis. It didn't alleviate my pain." The other man was Joe Mankiewicz. When he had walked out of M-G-M, he had not walked out of Garland's life, but he had told her that she should try seeing other men. He thought her foolish, when she had so much to offer, to sit at home waiting for his telephone calls. The intensity of her devotion worried him. He was still married, and had no intention of deserting a wife who was undergoing intensive therapy. He also had two sons to consider and was not sure that Garland would make the best of stepmothers.

When, in May 1944, Garland missed her period, she went straight to Mankiewicz, whose immediate reaction was to take her to New York, away from the prying eyes of Hollywood. If she was pregnant by him—and not for an instant did he think there was a chance of Minnelli being the father—he was resolved that she would no longer be pregnant by the time she returned to Hollywood. They took the train, and to avoid reporters, left it at Harmon Croton, where it changed engines. A car was waiting, and they fled to the apartment of one of Mankiewicz's friends, the literary agent Mark Hannah. The following day, he took her to a doctor, who later reported that she was not after all pregnant.

Garland's recollection of these two days in New York were entirely romantic, so she clearly felt that Mankiewicz had behaved beautifully over the whole incident. He had decided not to bring up the subject of an abortion unless it was necessary, and made no mention of his suspicions that she had been trying to force him into leaving his wife. This suspicion was confirmed years later when Garland told her daughter Liza Minnelli: "I really wanted to marry Joe. I wanted him to leave his wife. I didn't like sharing him." On another occasion, she recalled: "He was probably the great love of my life. I almost had his child, except that I wasn't pregnant by him." Whatever her later feelings, however, this incident marked the end of the affair.

With the prospect of *Meet Me in St. Louis* becoming a major success for his unit, Freed had assigned Minnelli to what he and everyone else considered the studio's most spectacular musical since *The Great Ziegfeld*. *Ziegfeld Follies* would prove that Metro could continue to produce lavish shows in the Ziegfeld tradition. It would be a revue, with no linking story, but, as in *Thousands Cheer*, most of the stars on the lot would appear in sketches and production numbers, when and as they were free from other assignments. This would necessitate a long shooting schedule, beginning in April 1944, and it was clear from the outset that the many sets and dance sequences would require extensive planning. In the original plan for *Ziegfeld Follies*, various spots were suggested for Garland. She had been suggested to partner Fred Astaire in "The Babbitt and the Bromide," in which eventually Astaire was paired with Kelly. But there were numerous sketches and sequences, in one of which Garland and Rooney were to do a song called "I Love You More in Technicolor Than I Do in Black and White," that never found their way to the screen.

Meanwhile, she began a professional partnership with Bing Crosby which, while mainly on the radio, included a record pairing "Yah-Ta-Ta, Yah-Ta-Ta" and "You've Got Me Where You Want Me." Neither is among the great comic duets, but they do reveal how well the skills of Garland and Crosby matched, and the record became a best-seller. She appeared with him twice on the *Command Performance* in the summer of 1944, and with him and Jimmy Durante in another radio show for the troops, *Mail Call*, in a sketch entitled "The Groaner, the Canary and the Nose." She also sang on Frank Sinatra's radio show and another half-dozen programs.

In June, just before her twenty-second birthday, she received her provisional divorce decree from David Rose, having testified that after the first months "our careers began to conflict. His work kept him away from home a great deal." The divorce would become final twelve months later. Although her affair with Minnelli had petered out, it was customary in Hollywood for directors and stars to exchange gifts, and for her birthday, he sent her a silver mesh evening bag. She wrote to him with characteristically self-deprecating humor:

VINCENTE DEAR

Your beautiful birthday gift has changed my outlook on life. It used to be a difficult task for me to walk into a room full of people with any self-assurance. But not any more. Now I merely hold my handbag at the proper angle, descend upon the group and dazzle each individual.

Thank you for one of the loveliest gifts I've ever received.

Love, JUDY

By this time, *Ziegfeld Follies* was well into the planning stage. It was agreed that William Powell would repeat his role of Ziegfeld from the earlier film, looking down from heaven to observe "some wonderful people remaining and so many wonderful people coming up in the meantime." How wonderful these people really were is a matter of taste, for among them were not only such dubious comic talents as Red Skelton, but also Esther Williams, whose swimming-with-a-smile may have been popular with audiences, but was basically sheer kitsch, as well as Kathryn Grayson, who tended to be shrill, and the decidedly limited Lucille Bremer. Powell's Ziegfeld was on safer ground in proffering Fred Astaire, who would emcee as well as dance a couple of numbers. Gene Kelly was brought in to replace Garland as his partner in "The Babbitt and the Bromide"—the only occasion that Hollywood's two greatest male dancers were to perform together on screen.* Their styles and techniques were so different that filming even this simple song-and-dance was tough work, made even tougher by Astaire's usual worrying and by Kelly's deference to his idol.

One of the numbers planned for the film was inspired by the Warner Bros. wartime revue, *Thank Your Lucky Stars*, in which Bette Davis had added further to her luster by growling her way through a satirical song, "They're Either Too Young or Too Old." Since Greer Garson occupied a similarly eminent position at M-G-M, she was scheduled to have something much like it to do in *Follies*. It was decided that she should guy her image even more than Davis had, letting the public know that she was not as starchy as was generally perceived. Kay Thompson and Roger Edens came up with the idea of having the great lady, leading a male chorus, satirizing her role in *Madame Curie*—not inventing radium but the safety pin. The idea had begun as a private joke. Thompson and Edens shared a birthday, November 9, and every year each of them penned a tribute to the other which they performed with friends carefully picked from among

---

*Except when hosting *That's Entertainment Part Two*, the 1976 compilation of scenes from M-G-M musicals.

the M-G-M personnel. At the most recent birthday party, Edens had written for Thompson "The Passion According to Saint Kate."

Edens and Thompson performed the number—somewhat toned down and under the new title "Madame Crematante" or "A Great Lady Has 'An Interview' "—at Freed's house before an audience made up of Garson, her mother, and her new husband, Richard Ney. Minnelli, also in attendance, told Garson that the number would be "charming" for her, but it was received in silence. This was broken by Ney, who complimented Freed on his home. Both he and his mother-in-law thought the song would demean Garson and advised her against doing it.

Since Garland had been among those performing the send-up at the birthday party, she was invited to take on the new version for the film. She jumped at the chance. Freed's only comment on hearing her sing it on the set was: "I think Bing Crosby is going to win the Academy Award for *Going My Way* this year." He refused to let Charles Walters, who staged it, shoot it, and gave the job to Minnelli. Although Minnelli is the credited director of the finished film, other sequences—both used and unused—were shot by other members of the Freed unit.

Minnelli was understandably ambivalent about working again with Garland, but in the event they had great fun shooting the number. "Judy came off extremely well," he recalled. "Her singing was as vibrant as ever, and she revealed a satirical style which owed a great deal to her terrific version of Kay's performance." The number was in rehearsal for nine days, in the recording studio for one day, and it was shot in three.

Nine days later, on August 1, Garland reported to the studio to begin work on her new film, *The Clock*. It had been decided by the Executive Committee that, after the experience of *Meet Me in St. Louis*, her next leading role should be in a more modest picture in black and white, one that would make fewer demands on what was now being recognized as her "temperament." The film was to be based on an unpublished story by Paul and Pauline Gallico, which had been acquired by Freed for $50,000 in March 1943. It was about a girl and a soldier who meet and marry in the course of forty-eight hours in New York, and its title refers to the scene of their rendezvous: the clock at the city's Penn Station. The role of the bride would be an ideal one for Garland, while the gentle GI was planned for either Van Johnson or Robert Walker. Freed did not care for the first screenplay, by Margaret Green, and passed the story on to Joseph Schrank and Robert Nathan. It was evidently decided that Robert Walker would be Garland's co-star, and one of the studio's old reliables, Jack Conway, was appointed director. However, Conway collapsed, as John Fricke found out, while shooting process location scenes for the film *Dragon Seed*, based on Pearl Buck's Sino-Japanese propagandist novel, and so Fred Zinnemann was brought in to direct *The Clock*.

The Viennese-born Zinnemann had been at M-G-M since 1937, initially working on the studio's short subjects. One of these, *That Mothers May Live*, had won an Oscar in 1938, and in 1942 he was elevated to B pictures. He was promoted to first features in 1944 with *The Seventh Cross*, which not only contains one of Spencer Tracy's best performances, but is arguably the best picture Hollywood made on Europe under the Nazi regime. The film had not actually been released when Zinnemann was assigned to *The Clock*, but the word was out that is was first-rate. He seemed the ideal director for a low-powered romantic picture.

Unfortunately, he and Garland did not get along. There was tension from the start and the shoot began to look as if it was going to be as troubled as that of *Meet Me in St. Louis*. Once again, Garland was worried about her casting. She arrived unprepared on the first day, and nothing Zinnemann could say could convince her that she was capable of playing an ordinary, New York working girl. Soft-spoken and introverted, Zinnemann was unable to give Garland the reassurance she needed in tackling her first dramatic role. She needed constant love and admiration, but such was the director's reticence that she never felt that she was getting it. She wheedled, she cajoled, she sulked, she burst into floods of tears. She told Freed: "I don't know—he must be a good director, but I just get nothing. We have no compatibility." She demanded that he be removed from the picture, but not before Zinnemann himself had offered his resignation. Freed, typically, was not interested in their dispute; but he was not happy; those elements which make for a distinguished, as opposed to a factory-line, film were fudged. Zinnemann was to go on to make some of the best films in movie history and if he had had a track record at this time, Garland might have trusted him and he might have remained in charge of *The Clock*. He said later: "I thought her a great talent and looked forward to working with her, but she just didn't like me."

After twenty-four days, Garland, who, in her insecurity, could relate to no one beside herself, felt there was no rapport with Zinnemann, an intelligent but quiet and laconic man, the film was closed down by the Executive Committee. The decision had not been taken lightly, for almost $200,000 had already been spent, including $66,450 for a replica of Penn Station, because it was impossible to shoot on location there under wartime conditions. The cost of this set was not abnormally high, particularly when compared with the Smiths' street in St. Louis, but the latter was an investment, since it could be used again in other films.

At the end of August, Garland invited Minnelli to lunch and asked if he would consider taking over *The Clock*, implying—or so he believed at the time—that she had Freed's tacit approval to do so. The fact is that there had been difficulties on two, if not three, of Garland's recent pictures, not entirely of her making, and this new venture was so different from the others that the Executive Committee was prepared to postpone a decision on *The Clock*. The successful reception of the previews of *Meet Me in St. Louis* convinced Garland that Minnelli had drawn from her her best screen work yet. Ignoring the fact that she had walked out of their relationship, she calmly suggested that they work together again.

Minnelli agreed to read the script and look at the footage already shot. Each scene, he decided, looked as though it came from a different picture. Zinnemann readily agreed that Minnelli should take over—though he made it clear that it was Garland's behavior which had led to his resignation—and on September 1, three days after Garland's original proposal, the studio agreed to allow Minnelli to come in as director. Much faith was put in the fact that, during the later stages of *Meet Me in St. Louis*, Minnelli had been able to control Garland. It was hoped that he might do so again.

Minnelli was unhappy with the script, but because the Penn Station set was taking up a whole soundstage, shooting had to start as soon as possible. The script would have to be reworked as they went along. He later said that the only existing footage which he used was that shot by the second unit in New York; but almost everything else was changed—some of the cast, costumes, script bore no resemblance to Zinnemann's footage. He extracted a promise from Garland that she would do exactly as he told her, and she assured him that she was only too happy to agree. This did not mean that she was easy to handle: he had to accompany her to make-up each morning to reassure her that she was capable of tackling the day's shooting, and on the set he used his tact and even more considerable patience when she was nervous. "The actors delivered one hundred and ten percent," he said, paying particular tribute to Walker, who was "always cheerful and on time."

Walker in fact had every excuse to behave as badly as Garland, since he was also having problems which were eventually to destroy him. He had arrived in Hollywood in 1939 with his wife, Phyllis Isley, who was "discovered" by David O. Selznick and rechristened "Jennifer Jones." In 1944, Jones won an Academy Award for *The Song of Bernadette*, by which time Walker had become one of M-G-M's promising new stars. However, Selznick's obsession with Jones, which clouded his vision until he died, had already begun.* While Walker was making *The Clock*, the situation at home was so fraught that he was seeking solace in the bottle.

Garland was aware of this, and on one occasion, while she and Dottie Ponedel were supposed to be having a hen party, they actually spent an entire evening searching for Walker in the bars of West Hollywood. They finally found him, and dried him out in Ponedel's apartment so that he would be ready to go on set the following morning.

In spite of such problems, Garland was happy about the movie. After the picture was finished, she sent Minnelli a desk clock with the following note:

DARLING,
Whenever you look to see what time it is—I hope you'll remember "the clock." You knew how much the picture meant to me—and only *you* could give me the confidence I so badly needed. If the picture is a success (and I think it's a cinch) my darling Vincente is responsible for the whole god damned thing.
Thank you for everything, angel. If I could only say what is in my heart—but that's impossible. So I'll say God bless you and I love you!

JUDY

She gave up her rented house in Beverly Hills and moved in with him. "I was ecstatic when Judy told me she wanted to marry me as soon as her divorce was final," he recalled. "I let go of my emotions, feeling so needed for the first time in my life that there was no alternative. We would face all problems together."

---

*The Walkers were eventually divorced in 1945, after which Selznick ditched his wife—Louis B. Mayer's daughter—and married Jones.

9

❖❖❖❖❖❖❖

The Harvey Girls

IMMEDIATELY AFTER *The Clock* finished production on November 21, 1944, the studio sent Garland and Minnelli to St. Louis where, appropriately enough, the world premiere of *Meet Me in St. Louis* was to take place. Garland took a taxi to the real 5135 Kensington Avenue, remaining there some time but not leaving the cab. The following week, she and Minnelli went to New York to attend the film's premiere there. This trip also gave Garland the opportunity to introduce her fiancé to the press.

Meet Me in St. Louis was Minnelli's third picture as director, showing style and innovation in such a way that the studio was assured that he would become a celebrity in his own right. This progression to fame brought certain responsibilities in its wake. Picturegoers were insatiably curious about every aspect of their idols' lives, and the publicists had to cover for many quirks and foibles. Minnelli had what were then euphemistically termed "artistic" tastes: his accomplishments as a designer had tended to be exotic, even precious, while his knowledge of antiques, jewelry and painting rendered him suspect to some. His graceful, dance-like gestures and gait, and the way in which he expressed himself, could only deepen suspicions. As his success was assured, it was clear that he was unlikely to return to Broadway, but would remain in Hollywood and settle down—naturally, with a wife.

When Garland had left him to return to Joe Mankiewicz, Minnelli had tentatively selected Marion Herwood Keyes, the costume supervisor (under the aegis of Irene) on *The Clock*, as a prospective bride. She was unaware that he had resumed his relationship with Garland and astonished when she learned of the engagement. He never explained or apologized, which so annoyed her that she told anyone who would listen that she was "the unkissed fiancée" and that his embraces had been detached and asexual.

Garland's reasons for wanting to marry again were infinitely more complex. The most evident one was that, by marrying a homosexual, she could continue to have romantic flings with other men without feeling any guilt. Indeed, even before the marriage, while supposedly committed to Minnelli, she had an affair with Orson Welles. This took place after Welles's marriage to Rita Hayworth started to break up, and while Garland and Minnelli were maintaining separate residences. Welles habitually arrived at Garland's house with vast amounts of flowers. On one occasion, he forgot to hand them over and returned home with them in the car—where his secretary, Shifra Haran, saw and hid the card addressed to Garland, thus enabling Hayworth to believe that the bouquet had been meant for her.

Another reason for Garland wanting to be married was that she wanted to be needed; as she often said, she could live without money but not without love. Minnelli flattered her, and to the movie-going world it was a brilliant match. They would become the acknowledged leaders of their profession, as the Lunts were in the New York theater (where Lunt's effeminacy did not go unremarked).

In New York, Garland showed Minnelli off to the press and he showed her the areas of New York he had reconstructed at the studio for *The Clock*—an Italian restaurant and acres of Central Park. He took her to the Metropolitan Opera House and to *Oklahoma!*; and he introduced her to his friends Richard and Dorothy Rodgers. Rodgers played the piano for them, concentrating on the songs of his which he knew she had sung; and they went to the first night of *The Seven Lively Arts*, Billy Rose's revue at the Ziegfeld, reckoned to be the most lavish ever staged, with a ballet by Balanchine to music by Stravinsky. Among the stars were a friend of his, Beatrice Lillie, and one of hers, Bert Lahr.

This was Garland's first extensive experience of a New York that seemed the center of the world in those wartime years. The important people in the arts and society all lived in New York; important events happened in New York. It was an exhilarating place to be, and this visit affected Garland for the rest of her life. Childlike, she thought that by acquiring culture and smart friends she was moving farther away from Grand Rapids, Ethel and Mickey Rooney; but the experience was also genuinely heady. For as Artie Shaw, Mankiewicz and now Minnelli all discovered, she was capable of interest—at least for a few days—in things never discussed in the Gumm household. She returned to Los Angeles "an eager student," as Minnelli put it, of the sophistication New York represented, anxious to find out more about paintings and antiques. He knew that she was learning from him, and was happy to share his knowledge.

He was less happy, however, about those days when she was unable to cope, when everything seemed to go wrong and she would resort to pills to restore her equilibrium—when he would return home "to find her speech and gestures going double time." He made her promise to give up pills, to which she responded "You know I'll try." She was driven by emotion, afraid of boredom. The only discipline she knew had been forced on her by work, and when she was not working she did not know how to channel her energies into planning ahead or pursuing new interests. If not occupied at the studio, she moved between a playful exuberance and a despair born of a seething desire to rebel.

Accordingly, Ethel remained a problem. On one day, her mother might be essential to be consulted on some matter about which she herself had little experience, and the next she was an ogre in league with Mayer to keep her daughter on the treadmill which had forced her into making twenty feature films in nine years at the studio (or, more to the point, eight years, for she still chafed about the year of neglect). Ethel did not help matters by writing a long letter to Minnelli to express her disapproval that the couple were living together. He did not, she claimed, have her daughter's interests at heart—and, since he was so much older, he should not forget Judy's immaturity. Since his homosexuality was an open secret at the studio, she would certainly have heard about it from Jimmy: she may well have concluded that her daughter was making the same mistake that she had.

M-G-M had decided to open *Meet Me in St. Louis* for Thanksgiving partly because it seemed an ideal time for a family picture. It was planned to play through the Christmas season, because the film contained a Christmas sequence—and Hollywood has never been happy releasing movies with snow and carols except in midwinter.

Not everyone at the studio was enchanted with the film—Eddie Mannix still thought the Halloween sequence should be cut—but Garland was no longer among them. After the first preview, she said to Freed: "Arthur, remind me not to tell you what kind of pictures to make." The experts at Decca agreed that "The Trolley Song" had hit-parade potential. Garland's version of it—there was little serious competition—was at the top of the hit parade when the film opened, which did not hurt it at all. The film had cost $1,707,561, and on first release it grossed $7,566,000—which was (except for *Gone With the Wind*) a new record for an M-G-M picture.

The reviews certainly encouraged people to flock to see the film. James Agee described it as "a musical that even the deaf should enjoy . . . one of the year's prettiest pictures." "Miss Garland is full of gay exuberance as the second sister of the lot, and sings, as we said, with a rich voice that grows riper and more expressive in each new film," commented the *New York Times*. "Her chortling of 'The Trolley Song' puts fresh zip into that inescapable tune, and her romantic singing of a sweet one, 'The Boy Next Door,' is good for mooning folks . . . in the words of one of the gentlemen, it is a ginger-peachy show." Howard Barnes in the *New York Herald Tribune* noted, "M-G-M has never been at a loss to have the right performer for the right role . . . Judy Garland is on hand to sing several songs expertly and to give dramatic effects to the small crises of family life." The sentiments of the film chimed with wartime audiences, as Britain's ablest critic, Richard Winnington, pointed out: "that ache we all have for lost times, when the sun was warmer, the days and nights longer and everything was cosy and safe." Another British critic, Dilys Powell, wrote in the *Sunday Times* that the film was "gaily and beautifully played, in particular by Miss Garland, whose talents as an actress are, I believe, of a much higher order than is generally recognised."

In fact, Garland's talents *were* being recognized, as reviews of *The Clock* proved. James Agee commented that Minnelli had "brought the budding talents of his betrothed, Judy Garland, into unmistakable bloom." He elaborated this point in the *Nation*, when he claimed that Minnelli proved "for the first time beyond anybody's doubt that Judy

Garland can be a very sensitive actress. In this film Miss Garland can handle every emotion in sight, in any size and shape, and the audience along with it."

Today, both films stand high among any in Hollywood's past. *Meet Me in St. Louis*, although much imitated (notably by 20th Century-Fox, with *State Fair*, *Centennial Summer* and *Margie*) is the most enchanting of any of these exercises in nostalgia, with Garland's lament for the boy next door, who had not, until then, noticed her, providing the most touching of love songs. She appears somewhat frenzied singing "The Trolley Song," seemingly overreacting to Minnelli's desire to get some tension into the scene (she is wondering whether the boy next door will catch the trolley), but the delicacy and drama she brings to "Have Yourself a Merry Little Christmas" remains a marvel.

Very few American actresses have equaled her simplicity in *The Clock*, partly because Minnelli's direction of her is so true. Walker, as a GI falling in love, is eager but uncertain—which is as nothing to Garland's performance in the scene after their post-wedding meal, when panic and self-pity well up inside her because she does not feel married, because she cannot eat and cannot express herself. She is suspicious about love and yet infinitely caring about him, as in the wordless scene the morning after, when they breakfast together.

In spite of the excellent reviews she received for this performance, she was not even nominated for an Oscar. Indeed, the film won not a single Academy Award. Garland's performance is infinitely more honest than that of Joan Crawford in *Mildred Pierce*, which received the Oscar for best actress that year. There is little to be praised in the performances of the other nominated actresses: Ingrid Bergman in *The Bells of St. Mary's*, Greer Garson in *The Valley of Decision*, Jennifer Jones in *Love Letters* and Gene Tierney in *Leave Her to Heaven*. Since Bergman, Garson and Jones had already won Oscars, they were by definition "great actresses." Bergman and Crawford were great stars; and Bergman's contributions to some of the films she made were paramount, but only seldom (as in *Casablanca*) is she as good as Garland in *The Clock*. People had different perceptions then: watching Crawford and Garson posing throughout *While Ladies Meet* (1941) now is likely to set one's teeth on edge. Ann Sothern, for instance, in the humble Maisie series or in the musicals she made for Freed, playing in the vernacular (Brooklyn showgirl, musical comedy star) is always more alive and natural than most of M-G-M's "great" actresses.

It would not be the last time that Garland was denied an Award that many thought rightfully hers, but she was content with her notices, and with the film's box-office performance—an entirely satisfactory gross of $2,783,000 on a budget of $1,324,000, which was high for a modest black-and-white movie, but which does include Zinnemann's false start. The film's success also brought her greater happiness since it undoubtedly brought her even closer to Minnelli. Her personal feelings toward him were always affected by her professional relationship with him, and the critics' praises for both films were suggesting that he was good for her. Something of what she felt was reflected in an interview she gave to the respected journalist Adela Rogers St. John:

I made one mistake, I don't want to make another. I love my work. I know there are girls who can give up their work and get married and just live at home. I don't believe I could . . . So I have to have someone that understands about me and my work and thinks it's important and—we have to work together. Vincente is wonderful. He's the most interesting man I've ever known. I don't know yet—maybe it will be right for us. We both know that a marriage can either be the most wonderful thing on earth or it can gum up your whole life and spoil everything. We're thinking it over.

While thinking it over, in January 1945, Garland sang on the radio for a birthday tribute to the President, and the next month she played "Snowflake" in a *Command Performance* version of *Dick Tracy*, which featured Bing Crosby in the title role, along with Bob Hope, Dinah Shore, Frank Sinatra, Jimmy Durante and Jerry Colonna.

Arthur Freed maintained that Garland "didn't do any more straight dramatic parts after *The Clock* because the public wanted to hear her sing, and there are so few people who can do that, while a lot of people can play dramatic parts." He was determined to co-star her with Astaire, whose next film, *Yolanda and the Thief*, based on a comic fable by Ludwig Bemelmans, had been conceived by Minnelli as a starring vehicle for the great dancer. It seemed to Garland that this was an occasion for all their dreams to come true, but Freed's commitment to an Astaire-Garland partnership took second place to his personal commitment to Lucille Bremer, whom he wanted to make a star. Since playing Garland's elder sister in *Meet Me in St. Louis*, Bremer had performed two dances with Astaire in *Ziegfeld Follies*, and at the previews, they had been acknowledged as among the high points in an otherwise disastrous film.

Garland was due to begin work on a new film, *The Harvey Girls*, and it seemed obvious to her that she and Bremer could switch roles. However, Bremer was certainly not a big enough star to carry a film designed as a star vehicle for Garland. Furthermore, *The Harvey Girls* was to be directed by George Sidney, whose mother, Lillian Burns, was not only Garland's drama coach but one of Mayer's circle, along with her husband, who was also a vice-president of the company. Sidney had enjoyed successes with *Thousands Cheer* and *Bathing Beauty* (1944), a musical featuring Esther Williams and Red Skelton. *The Harvey Girls* was to be his first picture for the Freed unit, and Freed had no intention of annoying Mayer by taking Garland out of the film.

What little enthusiasm Garland retained for *The Harvey Girls* had much to do with the fact that it was a personal project of Roger Edens. He had seen *Oklahoma!* on its try-out in New Haven, and had immediately recognized that it would stand Broadway on its head. Everyone Garland knew realized that the Rodgers and Hammerstein show had revolutionized the American musical, and Edens had persuaded her that *The Harvey Girls* would be as important to movies as that had been to the theater. Furthermore, her role was more substantial than the female lead in *Yolanda and the Thief*.

The Harvey Girls is set in the 1890s and based upon real events, when some intrepid, virginal Eastern girls were recruited to travel West to work as waitresses in Fred Harvey's chain of restaurants along the railway line. The property had been bought in 1942 by producer Bernie Hyman as a vehicle for Lana Turner. When, shortly afterwards, Hyman died, M-G-M started negotiations to sell the property to another studio, but the Harvey family voiced its objections, claiming that only M-G-M could make the movie. Once Edens expressed an interest in the material, Freed commissioned a script. At least eight writers toiled on it, not including the three who had provided the source material. Six of them received screen credit, including Samson Raphaelson, who had written the stage version of *The Jazz Singer* and contributed to the scripts of some of Ernst Lubitsch's brilliant comedies. Among those writers not credited was Guy Bolton, librettist of many successful Broadway shows of the twenties and thirties. Nothing was too much trouble for a Judy Garland vehicle.

Indeed, such was her clout now, that she was asked to choose the costume designer. Because this was a period musical, Mayer wanted that job to go to Helen Rose, whom he had brought to the studio after admiring her work on *Coney Island* and *Hello Frisco, Hello* for 20th

Century-Fox. He thought this film should look as much like those as possible, but Edens favored Irene, as being more in tune with the Freed unit than Rose, who (apart from doing some uncredited work on *Ziegfeld Follies*) had been languishing at the studio. To break the deadlock, Freed sent the script to both designers, with the request that they come up with something. Garland, not knowing who had done what, chose Rose's costumes. Rose had not seen Garland since her days as Baby Gumm: "She was slim and talented but strung tight like a violin string—quite different from the happy little roly-poly who sang her heart out at Grauman's Chinese Theater."

The music and lyrics were written by Harry Warren and Johnny Mercer, responsible either separately or together for some of the most successful songs of the period. They had already written the score for *The Belle of New York*, with Garland in mind, for Freed, but this did not reach the screen until 1952, and was made without her. *The Harvey Girls* did yield a treasure that nearly repeated the instant popularity of "The Trolley Song," which could be said to have inspired it, and that was the magnificent "On the Atcheson, Topeka and the Santa Fe." Warren was on home ground, since he had written the two best movie songs based on railway rhythms, "Shuffle Off to Buffalo" and "Chattanooga Choo-Choo" and this time he contrived a real humdinger for Garland, one which eventually won an Oscar.

The film was Garland's second consecutive musical set in the American past, but there is nothing to remind us of the Smiths' St. Louis. Minnelli's musical had finally freed the Hollywood musical from its dependence on theater settings, and the effect was gloriously liberating. The principal influence of *Oklahoma!* is that the songs do not belong exclusively to the principals. In the vehicles of Deanna Durbin, Bing Crosby, Alice Faye and Fred Astaire (with or without Ginger Rogers), it was rare for anyone but the star to perform the songs, although Universal's earlier *Can't Help Singing* had given two numbers to a chorus of pioneers, keeping Durbin front and center for the rest. Other musicals brought in guest stars to do their specialties, and even the trail-blazing *St. Louis* gave all but one of the songs to Garland. In *The Harvey Girls*, however, she not only shares one number with Virginia O'Brien and (a dubbed) Cyd Charisse, but she is part of *le tout ensemble* for others. Charisse, O'Brien, Kenny Baker and Angela Lansbury also have songs which in some way advance the plot, as Edens had planned.

He begins with a typically wistful song for Garland, "In the Valley Where the Evening Sun Goes Down." She is a mail-order bride, and also on the train are those "winsome waitresses" as the preface calls them, "one of the first civilizing influences" in the Old West. This is a very special train: its far-off whistle is answered in the town by the ringing of a bell, as the townsfolk start to celebrate its arrival. The passengers join in, the whole screen a-bustle as they (and the audience) wait for the film's star to appear and take over the song.

After she has done so, she meets her mail-order husband, played by Chill Wills, and decides to become a waitress instead ("I'm an awful housekeeper," she tells him. "I'm a terrible cook."). As in *Cyrano de Bergerac*—or Longfellow's poem "The Courtship of Miles Standish," mentioned in the script—his letters have been written by another, John Hodiak. Hodiak and Preston Foster are the bad men, Angela Lansbury (as usual acting much older than her years, in a role originally meant for Ann Sothern) is the bad girl, a saloon queen. Competition between the saloon and Harvey's Restaurant is keen, but clearly the picture will end with the bad girls ousted and Garland in the arms of a reformed Hodiak.

Kay Thompson, assisted by Ralph Blane, did the vocal arrangements and Robert Alton did the choreography. Everyone concerned was delighted when the preview audience cheered at the end of "On the Atcheson, Topeka and the Santa Fe," but there is another number which is prime Garland, "It's a Great Big World," an entrancing minuet-like number which she shares with O'Brien and Charisse, all in their night attire.

In spite of all the trouble that had been taken over music, costumes and cast, making the film did not prove a happy experience for everyone. Filming started on January 12 and finished, perilously overschedule, on June 5. This was due, in part, to the fact that the cast was bedeviled with accidents. The studio could take comfort from the fact that the film went on to take a happy $5,200,000 on a budget of $2,500,000, but even so, the budget was higher than estimated. This, too, was somewhat Garland's fault, as the following inter-office memos indicate:

January 10 1945
    Judy Garland had an 11:00 ready call this a.m. to make wardrobe tests; she arrived in studio at 10:45. At 12 noon she called Griffin, assistant on the picture, to say she couldn't be ready till after lunch. We went to lunch at 12:30 and on return she still was not ready; she arrived on the stage at 3:07 p.m. all made up but not in wardrobe; she came on set dressed at 3:25. At 4:00 she left the stage without making a test, for a conference with LB [Mayer] and did not return to the stage again.

January 11

Judy Garland had a 10 a.m. makeup call to be ready on the set at 1 p.m. She arrived at the studio at 12:12 and came on the set at 1:48.

January 12

Last night Judy Garland was given a call for this morning, by the assistant, 8:00 in makeup, 10:10 ready on set. She told him she wouldn't be in until 8:30 as she didn't need more than an hour and a half for makeup. This morning she arrived at the studio at 9:25, onstage 10:50, went into her dressing room and didn't come on the set until 11:25.

Since the number of people involved in tests was not high, it was only they who were inconvenienced—or so she may have persuaded herself. But the matter was more serious after shooting had begun, when a hundred or so people were kept waiting.

January 26

Miss Garland called at 3:20 this morning to say that she was not feeling well and could not come to work today. We will try to shoot whatever we can without her . . .

It has to be said that 3:20 a.m. gives everyone fair warning, though whether assistant directors cared to be woken up in the middle of the night is another matter. The pattern continued for another month, without any hint of an apology from Garland. She behaved exactly as if nothing untoward had occurred, laughing and joking—being the adorable Judy Garland most of them had long known. So much depended on her, and it really did not make sense to expect her to work when she was not at her best.

February 9

At 4:30 p.m. yesterday, Thursday, the company called Miss Garland to give her Friday's shooting call. At this time Miss Garland advised the company that she could not work until possibly Monday due to having two teeth extracted and for which a bridge was being made.

At 12:45 p.m. today, Friday, I telephoned Miss Garland at her studio dressing room to enquire if the situation was the same and she advised it was.

Mr. Grady communicated with Miss Garland's dentist, Dr. Pinckus, and received the information that Miss Garland will receive the bridge on Saturday, wear it Saturday and Sunday and be in Dr. Pinckus's office on Monday morning for a check-up. Mr. Grady therefore advises Miss Garland should be ready at 1 p.m. on Monday for shooting purposes *if* the dentist reports the bridge satisfactory.

Under the present conditions it would not be wise for the company to plan a shooting day on Lot 3 on Monday, with a big crew and talent list, on the possibility of getting a couple of hours' work in the event Miss Garland is available.

Inasmuch as we have nothing to shoot at this time without Miss Garland we must also avoid a shooting call for Saturday. We therefore plan on rehearsing musical numbers Saturday and Monday.

The film reveals little evidence of these difficulties: only two scenes in which close-ups of John Hodiak suggest that he was re-acting to a model dressed in her clothes, and in which back-projection behind her indicates that her own close-ups were filmed later. There is a horse in one of the scenes, not too close to her, as she had a pathological fear of them, and this was one of the troubles on this film, although they do not feature greatly. When it became clear that it was impossible to shoot around her, Freed remonstrated and she promised to mend her ways. But a few days later it was clear that her promise meant nothing, as this memo to him from an assistant indicates:

March 2 1945

The company was informed by Evelyn Powers, Judy Garland's secretary, that as of this date use of her Webster phone number was to be discontinued and that a new address but no phone number would be supplied to us March 3rd. Our contact with Judy Garland from now on is to be through Evelyn Powers and a call bureau. This, of course, will be of inconvenience to the company and of greater inconvenience to Judy Garland should we ever wish to change a call to a later hour. She is aware of the latter possibilities.

The front office did not take kindly to the idea of being unable to contact one of its properties directly. She had behaved in a provocative manner—and perhaps any other star would have been reprimanded. Several front office "uncles" pointed out that she was behaving unprofessionally, adding that the film's budget was being considerably extended because of her. She behaved well for a while, but:

April 19

Miss Garland had a 10:15 call to do loops today . . . At 8:45 a.m. she telephoned that she was all bruised up due to fight scenes of yesterday [between the Harvey waitresses and the saloon girls, in which she has nothing strenuous to do] and didn't feel well enough to work today.

April 24

At approximately 7:25 a.m. today, Judy Garland telephoned George Rhein, assistant director on above company, saying that she didn't feel well and didn't know whether she'd be in or not. Rhein telephoned me about it and I in turn telephoned Miss Garland, telling her that we had a

crowd of people ordered for the day and would like to know definitely whether she would be in; she then said that she didn't feel well and would not be in today. Call on extras was then canceled and company had to go on layoff but utilized the day in rehearsing wedding scene, lining up shot for it and also rehearsed fight routine with stunt doubles in Harvey House.
May 15

At 2:30 this morning Judy Garland called Griffin, second assistant on the picture, and told him she hadn't slept all night so far because she was making Decca records [of "If I Had You"] until 11:45 p.m. last night. She said that after she came home she wasn't able to sleep and knew that she wouldn't look good the next day, and since the scene was an important one she felt she better stay home today . . . She called up as she knew we had people ordered and could cancel before it was too late.

People were canceled on quarter checks and company was forced to lay off for the day as there are no scenes we could do without her.
May 24

Miss Garland had a 1 p.m. call today . . . to do loops; at 12:45 she telephoned Ted Hoffman on stage 2A that she was hoarse and would not be able to make the loops today but that the hoarseness was breaking and she'd be able to do them tomorrow. The loops were then set for 10 a.m., tomorrow.
May 26

Judy Garland had a 10:30 a.m. call today . . . to do loops; at 10:15 she telephoned that she was feeling ill and would not be able to do the loops.

Garland herself said of the experience:

I was a nervous wreck, jumpy and irritable from sleeping too little. I couldn't take the tension at the studio.

Everything at M-G-M was competition. Every day I went to work with tears in my eyes. Work gave me no pleasure. The studio had become a haunted house for me. It was all I could do to keep from screaming every time the director looked at me.

Her insecurities had grown, not lessened, with the years. Yet she worked hard and was responsible for bringing much money into the M-G-M coffers. It was difficult for her to accept that she should be disciplined. In later years, when there were no film offers, she often reminded reporters that none of her films had lost money—adding that few others could claim the same. Her misunderstanding of the situation was compounded by a massive surprise party on her birthday at this time, when there were so many presents that she and Minnelli took turns opening them.

Anita Loos, who did not care for Garland, once said, of stars in general: "The main tenets of film-star psychology are to be mysterious, difficult, irrational, and suspicious, thus bringing about confusion and giving the star the whip hand." Minnelli believed that Garland's "instincts were to do the right thing, and she was capable of the most profound good behavior." This opinion was echoed by Mary Ann Nyberg, costume supervisor on *A Star Is Born*:

> She had charm such as I have never in my life been around. She had an insatiable desire to please, to make you laugh, feel comfortable, feel totally equal. *Until* she got tired of you. Then it reversed exactly. Then she got as mean as she had been charming, as determined to make you uncomfortable as she had tried to make you comfortable.

But that, some may think, is the prerogative of a star.

Garland's larger-than-life quality—that which had made the studio recognize her star potential—was also her downfall, for she could never do anything by halves. "All my life I've done everything to excess," she said once. The studio was hamstrung because she had been sold as Betsy Booth and Oz's Dorothy, and she had never been at all like either. She was personally helpless and inclined to put her complete trust in others: but she was also headstrong and fully aware that "she had them by the balls," in Mankiewicz's expression. She was all contradiction.

"To be a movie star and not approve of her private self; to feel that Hollywood does not, and the public could not, approve of her private self, makes for a deadly state of confusion," Louise Brooks once wrote of Joan Crawford. She went on to say that every young actress in pictures has her life influenced by her early roles. In Garland's case, she longed to be like her screen image, as the modesty and uncertainty of any of her interviews shows. She also wanted to enjoy the extraordinary life of a movie star, for which she was basically unfitted. Her talent had matured much more quickly than her mind: on the one hand, she wanted to enjoy affairs with both men and women; on the other, these led to further confusion, because she thought she ought to feel guilty about them, and that was not in her makeup. In effect, she managed to worry about not worrying.

Of this period, Minnelli has little to say. She was a Gemini, he observed, which conferred on her a "twin personality. She was left-handed and folklore had told me that this usually meant a hot temper. And she was an actress, plagued by the temperament and insecurity which affects every great one." Mother, Mayer and the burden of working so hard as a child were the elements Garland blamed for her inability to cope.

The previews of *The Harvey Girls* were held in July 1945 and were very encouraging. In spite of all the problems on the shoot, very little needed to be changed. Dropped for reasons of length were three of Garland's songs, "The March of the Doagies" (which was filmed), "Hayride" with Ray Bolger (which was not), and "My Intuition" (which was). The film was not premiered until the following January, however, partly because *Meet Me in St. Louis*, which continued to do good business well into the spring of 1945, followed by *The Clock*, effectively gave the public two opportunities to see Judy Garland that year. Another consideration was that M-G-M had another enormously popular musical to play the autumn dates, *Anchors Aweigh*, with Gene Kelly, Frank Sinatra and Kathryn Grayson. This was to be followed by two pictures already booked into Loew's choice houses, an all-star remake of *Grand Hotel*, called *Weekend at the Waldorf*, and Clark Gable's first film since leaving the army, *Adventure*, which teamed him with Greer Garson. When *Adventure* attracted disastrous notices and small audiences, *The Harvey Girls* and *Ziegfeld Follies* were rushed out to replace it.

Garland received single billing above the title, with the names of Hodiak, Bolger and Lansbury in smaller letters below. Hodiak is not considered one of Hollywood's glories, but he had just given a magnificent performance in one of 20th Century-Fox's most prestigious films, *A Bell for Adano*. Starring at Fox, however, did not give him the right to be billed alongside Judy Garland at M-G-M, and it could be argued that his role was small. All the same, few films at this time were sent out with only one star name; indeed, this is the only M-G-M movie of 1946 which can boast that distinction. Garland was not the studio's premier star, as far as the public (or even M-G-M) perceived it, but Greer Garson, who was, had as co-stars Walter Pidgeon, Gregory Peck and Clark Gable. Judy Garland did not need a co-star.

In a poll conducted by Gallup in the summer of 1945, she was Hollywood's third most popular female star, preceded only by Ingrid Bergman and Bette Davis. At the end of the year, in the official box-office ballot conducted by the publishers of the *Motion Picture Yearbook*, she was in eighth position. In first position was Bing Crosby, followed by Van Johnson, Greer Garson, Betty Grable, Spencer Tracy, Humphrey Bogart and Gary Cooper (at joint sixth), and Bob Hope.

In spite of such popularity, her reviews for *The Harvey Girls* were warm, but not quite fulsome—she "handles herself in pleasing fashion," said the *New York Times*—but in *Time* magazine, James Agee made a significant point: "Miss Garland doesn't seem as recklessly happy as she was in St. Louis but she still appears to be having a pretty fine time." She is actually rather serious, but she handles her comic scenes with magical finesse, as when, in the opening sequence, she gives her meager lunch to someone (a child) even hungrier than she, or when she raids the saloon, toting guns, to retrieve the food stolen from the Harvey restaurant. Her smile, when it comes, lights up the cinema; but though never mechanical for an instant, she does not seem to be enjoying herself as much as she did, say, in the films with Rooney.

She might have taken comfort, however, from the reception accorded *Yolanda and the Thief*. Most people thought many of the problems Garland experienced while working on *The Harvey Girls* had been caused by her being pushed into this film rather than *Yolanda*, which had been occupying Minnelli and Freed so mightily. Freed had even returned to lyric-writing for the occasion, as this was intended to be the *Gone With the Wind* among M-G-M musicals.

That it was not became clear at the sneak preview in Pomona, which Garland attended. The audience cheered when it saw the M-G-M lion and Fred Astaire's name, but did not respond to that of Lucille Bremer. Freed was excessively nervous: he desperately wanted Bremer to be a star, but he had never been sure whether he had been right in letting Minnelli talk him into the project. As the film unrolled, a number of people walked out, and an atmosphere of gloom descended in the auditorium. At the end, there were a few slow hand-claps. By this time Freed was in the foyer, nervously jiggling the coins in his pocket. As the M-G-M contingent filed out, no one knew what to say to him. It was clear that no amount of retakes or studio tinkering could save the picture. As Garland passed him, she remarked: "Never mind, Arthur, Pomona isn't Lucille's town."*

Yolanda and the Thief had been scheduled for Loew's prime theaters, but wherever it played it disappeared quickly. It had cost only a little less than *The Harvey Girls*, and it took in only $1,790,000 at the box office. Garland had the satisfaction of being, after all, in the

---

*Years later, when Garland was asked what happened to Lucille Bremer, she said: "Oh she married, had babies. She left M-G-M." Then, after a pause: "And no one minded."

more successful picture; but she never looked back at *The Harvey Girls* with affection.

It was not a bad idea to have *The Harvey Girls* and *Ziegfeld Follies* on show simultaneously, for the two films demonstrated the range of Garland's talent. In the first, she was the tender but tough heroine (at any rate, tough enough to tote—with some trepidation—a couple of guns); in the second, she appeared as a satirical comedienne, giving promise, as the *New York Times* put it, "of a talent approaching Beatrice Lillie or Gertrude Lawrence." *Newsweek* discerned "an unexpected flair for occupational satire," but not everyone was impressed. "The person who gets the worst flogging in the deal is Judy Garland," announced the *New York Herald Tribune*. "Wound up in a sketch called 'The Interview,' Miss Garland has some mighty unpleasant stuff to do."

"Judy loved doing sophisticated parts like 'The Interview' sequence," commented Freed. "Mind you, that particular number was not one of her biggest successes except with a certain group"—which is ingenuous, given the enthusiasm within his own unit for the number. Whatever people thought of the sketch, however, it demonstrated that Garland was not just another singing-and-acting machine.

Among those who felt Garland could handle dramatic roles was George Cukor, who was about to film Somerset Maugham's *The Razor's Edge* for 20th Century-Fox. He inquired whether M-G-M would permit Garland to play the cabaret-singer, Sophie, who becomes a drug addict. It was a strong dramatic role, but not the biggest in the picture, and M-G-M indignantly refused to loan Garland. Had she done the part, she would have appeared alongside her old love, Tyrone Power, who was cast in the lead role. The role of Sophie eventually went to Anne Baxter, who won an Oscar for it, and Cukor was replaced by Edmund Goulding after Fox rejected the screenplay which Maugham himself had written.

Garland's Decca recording of "On the Atcheson, Topeka and the Santa Fe" did not match the sales of "The Trolley Song," but Liza Minnelli once observed that it marked a change in her mother's singing style, to a more mature, full-throated one. At the time, the record was notable in playing a role in ending Garland's contract with the company. Decca had made a lot of money from "The Trolley Song," featured in an M-G-M film and sung by an M-G-M star. The pattern might be repeated with the new song, which she had recorded with the Merry Macs on July 5, 1945. It was issued with "If I Had You" on the reverse. This old song had been chosen by Freed to use in an instrumental version as the theme of *The Clock*. Because, of the six songs in *The Harvey Girls*, only three were solos for Garland, she and the other artists had recorded all of them for a 78 rpm three-record album on September 2, with the M-G-M orchestra under Lenny Hayton. The Disney musical transfers apart, this Decca recording was the closest movies had come to an original soundtrack album. Loew's Incorporated already owned several music-publishing companies and in 1943 had formed a subsidiary, M-G-M Records. The company did nothing while Garland was still contracted to Decca, but made plans to issue songs from M-G-M soundtracks, sung by M-G-M stars—of whom the most successful, by far, was Judy Garland. She thus became the leading star of M-G-M records, when the company was eventually launched in 1946, with songs from *Till the Clouds Roll By*.

Before that, in October 1945, she had recorded three unpublished Gershwin songs, which had been found among his effects and reworked by brother Ira and Kay Swift for the film *The Shocking Miss Pilgrim* (1946), in which they were sung by Betty Grable and Dick Haymes. Like Garland, Haymes was under contract to Decca, and it was arranged that they should sing the two duets together, "For You, For Me, Forevermore" and "Aren't You Kinda Glad We Did?" for the film's album. The other song, "Changing My Tune," was sung in the film by Grable, who, according to box-office listings, was even more popular than Garland. Her voice, however, was not considered her major asset, although in a later era her popularity alone would have ensured a recording contract. Decca continued to reissue Garland's most successful records long after her contract ran out, until long-playing albums changed the state of the market.

One of the reasons the release of *The Harvey Girls* had been delayed was that no other Garland vehicle was in the offing. Garland may have felt that she needed a rest, but Freed was not entirely happy about this. She had always come through for him where it mattered—at the box office. She was a critics' pet. *Show Boat* was still on the agenda for her, and Fred Astaire was anxious to work with her. After the failure of *Yolanda and the Thief*, he had been talking of retirement, but Freed still held his long-cherished aim of co-starring the two of them. He had been thinking about *The Belle of New York* since 1943 as just such a vehicle, and in April 1944 Astaire had been announced as Garland's co-star. The basic plot, taken from the old musical of the same name, concerned an unworldly girl who blossoms under the tutelage of a Manhattan playboy, a story line which would take care of the twenty-three-year gap in their ages. In 1945 Rouben Mamoulian was announced as the director, but when script problems kept the film grounded, Freed decided to team Garland and Astaire in a musical version of Noël Coward's *Private Lives*.

Nothing more was heard of this project. Astaire was asked to replace a New York dancer, Paul Draper, in *Blue Skies*, which starred Bing Crosby, with whom he had been teamed so felicitously in *Holiday Inn* (1942). Both films had scores by Irving Berlin and, as Astaire said, it would be a big one to go out on. He told Freed that he would come back if they ever got the script of *The Belle of New York* right.

10

❖❖❖❖❖❖❖

Mrs. Vincente Minnelli

ON JUNE 15, 1945—five days after her twenty-third birthday—Judy
Garland became Mrs. Vincente Minnelli. For Minnelli's sake and to
be free of Hollywood brouhaha, Garland wanted to be married quietly
in New York; but that was not the way M-G-M would have it. Almost
everyone had doubts about the marriage, but Louis B. Mayer was not
one of them. In his view, Minnelli's homosexuality was no obstacle.
When, out of sheer malice, Peter Lawford's mother had gone to him
to advise him of her son's homosexuality (chiefly imagined), Mayer
summoned Lawford and told him: "We have other young men at the
studio with your problem, Peter, and we've been giving them hor-
mone shots to help them . . . and we can fix you up with some
beautiful women." Like many others at the time, Mayer believed that
homosexuality was a self-induced condition adopted by the perverse.
It was the sort of thing a good marriage could straighten out. As far
as Garland was concerned, Mayer agreed with those who thought that
marriage would steady her. Like everyone else, he had noted the tact
and kindness with which Minnelli had treated Garland on set, thus

avoiding the sort of scenes which had so disrupted the filming of *The Harvey Girls*.

Another consideration was that the war in Europe had ended two months earlier and Mayer, unlike Garland, felt that the world was ready for some of the old Hollywood razzmatazz. Minnelli was not, physically, the sort of guy the returning GIs wanted to see lead one of their favorite stars up the aisle, but he *was* one of Metro's own, and Hollywood's most promising young director. Having been deprived of the honor the first time round, Mayer intended to give the bride away.

In spite of Mayer's grandiose plans, Garland and Minnelli insisted that the wedding be a small affair. The ceremony, conducted by the Reverend William E. Roberts of the Beverly Hills Community Presbyterian Church, took place on the lawn of Ethel's house. Apart from Mayer, the M-G-M contingent included Freed and Howard Strickling—but not Ida Koverman, who, as a result of her supposed "defection," was deliberately excluded. Ira Gershwin was the best man and Betty Asher the maid of honor. The bride wore a high-necked, long-sleeved dress of softly draped gray jersey and carried a large bunch of pink and white peonies. At the end of the ceremony the minister brought out a symbolic wooden staff, to be grasped in turn by Asher, Gershwin, Garland and Minnelli. Mayer, uninvited, joined in—"establishing his territorial rights," as Minnelli put it. They were now married, he observed, not only in the eyes of God but a man "who in many instilled far greater dread."

That evening, the newlyweds left on the Santa Fe Super Chief for an extended honeymoon in New York, where they had been so fêted the year before. They took an apartment on Sutton Place, the exclusive neighborhood on the East River. Garland found the casual and sometimes impromptu entertaining by her husband's friends more congenial than the predictable and formalized Hollywood round. Eleanor Lambert, Minnelli's friend and press representative, took Garland to fashion shows, offering expert guidance on something which had not previously interested her. She knew now that her husband expected her to dress like a star.

Also proffering worldly advice was Ira Gershwin's wife, Lee, who was staying at the Plaza. Lee had been familiar with movie stars for years, but even she was astonished by the way Garland was mobbed by fans. She had to agree with Garland, who had already argued the point, that they could not simply walk round the corner to the couturiere, Hattie Carnegie's—not, at least, in broad daylight—so they took the car, there and back. At the hotel, they decided to take tea in the ornate Palm Court lounge, which was almost empty when they entered. Within minutes it was packed, with Garland signing autographs and laughing with her admirers. Lee associated her friend with laughter, and would remember these happy occasions at a later period of Garland's life.

Lee and Eleanor Lambert introduced Minnelli's new wife to his other friends, some of whom were determined to be unimpressed by a movie star. Aware of this, Garland set out to charm them. She had the necessary armory—not only a strong personality, but warmth, a keen deprecatory wit and a genuine interest in other people, not to mention a touch of informed malice in discussing the theater and its personalities. She was also frank in her opinions of the movie industry, agreeing with these New York sophisticates that it was not the greatest of human endeavors.

No honeymoon could prevent the happy bride from accepting some radio engagements while she was in New York. She was Judy Garland: she sang. She now decided that New York was where she wanted to be; and on the stage, like Beatrice Lillie and Gertrude Lawrence, because the praise she garnered in movies was as nothing to the adulation they received from the New York critics. She announced:

> I'm not going to re-sign with the studio when my contract expires. Oh, they've been wonderful to me at M-G-M, but I want to go on the stage. I was in vaudeville so many years when I was Frances Gumm, and I miss the sound of applause. If I could get a play on the order of "Lady in the Dark" [which Lawrence had done], a drama or a comedy with music, I would be terribly happy.

This was little more than another fantasy.

Walking in the city in the evening, Garland was recognized and affectionately greeted, always as "Judy" and never "Miss Garland." She responded easily, which impressed Minnelli—and he was touched when she introduced him: "And this is my husband. His name is Vincente Minnelli and he's a very fine film director."

One hot evening, when they were in a nightclub with friends, their pet poodle, Gobo, jumped out of the window of the car parked outside and got lost. After two hours searching the city streets for him, they returned to their apartment where Garland telephoned the police, the city pound and anyone else she thought might be able to locate the dog. "This is Judy Garland," she announced, relishing the power of fame in so urgent a matter. Many of New York's Finest spent the wee hours looking for Gobo, who was found just before dawn.

The Minnellis entertained in the apartment, where they gave a lavish farewell dinner party for all their East Coast friends—who included Beatrice Lillie, S.N. Behrman, Oscar and Dorothy Hammerstein, the Harold Arlens, and Moss Hart and his wife, Kitty Carlisle. Garland took an interest in every detail, enjoying herself hugely and having "the great good sense," as Minnelli put it (somewhat prophetically) to leave everything to the catering staff once the guests had arrived. "I think I'll keep you," he told his wife contentedly, when they had gone. "My dear sir, you do me such honor," she replied.

The way she spoke reminded him of Lynn Fontanne's delivery in Berhman's play *The Pirate*, and he decided that a film version should be their next joint project. Many years later, asked whether he knew that Joe Mankiewicz had been working on just that project when he left M-G-M, he pleaded ignorance; but studio records confirm that a film version was already on Freed's agenda.

There were two other events of significance on the trip. Not long after their arrival, they were strolling on the promenade along the East River when Garland suddenly asked Minnelli to hold her hand; and then, rather dramatically, she threw a vial of pills into the water. Minnelli felt that this was "a silent promise." He was not a psychologically perceptive person and saw no reason why the promise should not be kept. If she was not in love with him, she was giving a very good performance of someone who was. In one of his films, she had proved herself the predominant star of musicals, her chosen field. In another, in which she did not sing, she had shown that she could "handle any emotion in sight." He had known many other entertainers who relied on amphetamines to get them over temporary difficulties in their demanding careers. As far as he was concerned, her feelings of inadequacy as a movie star, as a desirable woman (which every female movie star, *ipso facto*, expected to be) were stilled for ever.

Further intimations of stability were provided when, toward the end of the visit, they consulted a doctor on Park Avenue, who confirmed Garland's own suspicion that she was pregnant. She was due to start a new film and they decided to withhold the news from Freed—who was to produce the film—until they could tell him in person. Garland did, however, telephone her mother: "I'm going to have a baby, Mama. Do you mind?" If it was a boy, he would be called Vincente Jr.; if a girl—well, Garland woke Minnelli in a Boston hotel room (where they had gone to attend the premiere of *Ziegfeld Follies*), to suggest Liza, after the song of that name which Al Jolson used to sing. It had been written by the Gershwins and Gus Kahn, and the Minnellis decided that Ira would take it as a tribute. Minnelli suggested Liza May, in memory of his mother. To the surprise of both Minnellis, Freed was delighted with their news. Whatever she wanted to be, to Freed and millions of other Americans, Judy Garland was the girl next door—famous, but not given to grandstanding or putting on airs. True, the jolly little girl he had first known had developed a taste for self-dramatization, but that was natural, given the pressures that she had been under. For a girl like this, the usual happy ending was a happy marriage and motherhood. When the baby was born, Garland could return to M-G-M to sing in more M-G-M musicals, all of which would make Loew's stockholders even happier. She was unique. She was Judy Garland. M-G-M had many exciting plans for her.

First of all, she would lend her name and talent to the next Freed musical without any danger of her being overstressed. Hers was not the pivotal role in *Till the Clouds Roll By*, a blatantly fictionalized biography of Jerome Kern, who was to be played by Robert Walker. Such plot as there was merely acted as a link between a selection of Kern's songs, which were to be handled in an M-G-M approximation of the original stagings, and sung by such M-G-M stars as Frank Sinatra, June Allyson, Lena Horne and—for this film only—Dinah Shore. Kern had been working chiefly in Hollywood since 1936, but his later output belonged to other studios, so the film was to concentrate on the songs he composed for Broadway, and especially for Ziegfeld. Kern's greatest interpreter then had been Helen Morgan, most notably in *Show Boat*, when she had played Julie. Little Frances Gumm used to imitate Morgan's performance in this role back in the vaudeville days, but for this film the part was given to Lena Horne. Garland was cast as another Ziegfeld star, the dancer, Marilyn Miller—"the wistful, lovely, unforgettable Marilyn Miller," as the film calls her.

The film's principal director was Richard Whorf, until then better known as an actor, but following precedent—most recently *Ziegfeld Follies*—others were involved. Robert Alton was to shoot all the musical numbers except the finale, which was to be directed by George Sidney. In assigning Minnelli to handle Garland's songs and her two dramatic scenes, Freed had considered her difficulties on her recent films. He was also acknowledging her reluctance to think of herself as consummate a dancer as she was a singer.

Garland's pregnancy was a major consideration, and Freed was able to speed up production of the film. Even so, she was four months pregnant when she began her first number, "Look for the Silver Lining," which Minnelli staged in the way it had been done originally, with the singer washing up at a sink. It has been suggested that by photographing her from behind a pile of crockery, he wanted to disguise her condition, but he himself said that her pregnancy did not begin to show until shooting began on her third number, "Sunny." This was a circus sequence for which she had a double for her stunts and her horseback scenes. "D'ye Love Me?" was filmed, but later cut. In the existing footage, Garland finishes it on a wrong note, admittedly after Minnelli had yelled, "Cut," but with an expression clearly disapproving of both the song and her rendering of it. "Who?" was an elaborate song-and-dance number in which she was surrounded by no less than thirty chorus boys in white tie and tails. As in *Presenting Lily Mars*, Garland proved to be as adept as any female dancer in movie history, and remarkably so; because she was pregnant, she was terrified of stumbling. Her importance to the project is confirmed by the fact that her three numbers cost $467,305, representing almost 20 percent of the total budget of $2,841,000. The budget was high due to the fact that filming took place over seven and a half months, from October 8, 1945, to May 23, 1946, and involved several layoffs while waiting for players to become available. During one of these, Kern suddenly died, and although shooting was resumed two days later, the script was revised—not that it bore much resemblence to his life in the first place. The critics were quick to point this out, but almost all of them thought the songs and their staging compensated. The film grossed over $6,724,000, making it one of M-G-M's biggest successes of 1947.

When, in October 1945, Garland retired to have her baby, she enjoyed the longest spell of professional inactivity (apart from some radio work) since M-G-M discovered that she had star potential. In January 1946, she negotiated a leave of absence on terms which reflected the studio's faith in her: her salary was to be raised by $500 immediately, instead of when it was due, in the summer. This meant that she was now being paid $3,000 a week, double the average salary of leading stars at that time. There was to be an agreement between both parties as to what was a reasonable period in which to recuperate, with such time as she was absent to be added to the duration of her present contract, which was due to expire in August 1947. She was allowed to broadcast, but not more than once a week, for whatever fee her agent could arrange. In return, M-G-M was to be mentioned, or any M-G-M film "as we may designate."

In December, she was one of the several stars of *Till the Clouds Roll By* who broadcast a tribute to Kern, and in January she starred in a version of *The Clock* for *Lux Radio Theater*. After the birth of her baby, her radio appearances included another movie adaptation, *Holiday*, which had starred Katharine Hepburn in 1938, and an episode of *Suspense*, which was written and produced by her friend Bill Spier, Kay Thompson's husband.

Minnelli's pink stucco house on Evanview Drive, overlooking Beverly Hills, was large by the standards of the place, but not large enough for a Beverly Hills family—certainly not when the parents were among its most highly paid citizens. An architect was engaged to remodel it, adding a nursery and enlarging the kitchen and Garland's dressing-room, at a cost of almost $70,000. Minnelli himself designed the dressing-room, a spacious chamber walled with mid-nineteenth-century glass and filled with English and French furniture from the same period. His study was converted into a nursery because it was the sunniest room in the house.

During the refitting, the couple rented a house on Malibu Beach, which enabled Garland to oversee most of the work while Minnelli was busy at the studio directing *Undercurrent*, a thriller starring Katharine Hepburn and Robert Taylor. They had an agreement that he would not bring his work home; any problems not settled at the studio were to be solved in his sleep. "Only after we'd settled into this truly spoiled existence," Minnelli recalled, "did we attempt to mesh our markedly different personalities and present them to the world as a unified entity."

Whatever was best for Garland was best for them both, they decided, and that was the impression they gave to their friends. They were among Hollywood's more prominent couples, hosts of frequent parties at home and guests at others. Privately, however, they went their separate ways. He was orderly and she was disorganized. Indeed, Minnelli was as maddeningly methodical in his behavior as David Rose had been. He returned from work to have precisely one dry martini before dinner, after which he liked to be absorbed in his library of art books, and read until it was time to go to bed. Garland preferred to listen to the radio or to go out. Minnelli did not care for parties, while she loved them. Provided that the press was not to be in attendance, she would go to parties with an escort, usually one of the homosexual actors she knew. Van Johnson was a particular favorite until he married in 1947.

The interests Minnelli and Garland *did* share were in fact new to her: fashion, antique jewelry, fine furniture; but while he was capable of concentrating for long periods, her own span of attention was short. She took up needlepoint to calm what her friend Sylvia Sidney called "jagged nerves," but this did not interest her for long. Minnelli was encouraged when he saw that Garland had begun to read theatrical biographies instead of the fan magazines and true romances which, until then, had been her literary diet. "It was in her dressing-room and bath that Judy felt most comfortable playing lady of the manor," he said; "plopped on the fur-covered chaise, she would spend hours there primping and reading." Both rooms were in permanent chaos, with dressing tables and cabinets littered with perfume bottles, cosmetics and anything else she happened to put down.

After all the years of high spirits, hard work and constant activity, Garland was becoming lazy. It was understood that Minnelli would run the household as he always had, attending to such details as the food for their dinner parties. Such things were important to him, and while she was capable of ordering a menu, she would have been quite happy to exist on her three favorite foods: eggs in butter, stewed tomatoes and peanut-butter sandwiches. Every so often, she emerged from her lethargy to seize the reins of domesticity, rather as if taking on a new role. Her efforts in this direction were haphazard and short-lived, but typically obsessive. "What pleased me most about Judy's homemaking was not that she did it well, but that she bothered to do it at all," Minnelli fondly remembered. "Her desire for constant approval was pathological," he added, recalling her attempts at scrubbing and cleaning, while the servants looked on. The staff were always patient, even when their new mistress's efforts to make a cake left the kitchen looking like a battlefield.

The situation was somewhat tense. The cook, the nurse, the housekeeper and the chauffeur looked upon Garland as an intruder, a temporary diversion of Minnelli's, and she in turn did not know what to make of them. Her sporadic attempts at giving orders or maintaining discipline were regarded by them as petulance or temperament. After any discord with them, she sought ways to cast Minnelli as the villain, and this restored her equilibrium. It was because she quickly bounced back to her usual jolly self that the staff tolerated what they considered to be her interference.

Garland did not anticipate any difficulty as a mother, but her moods vacillated from day to day—from hour to hour. Dr. Marc Rabwin advised that, because of her narrow pelvis, her baby should be delivered by cesarean section—at least, that was the reason he gave, knowing that she was terrified of physical pain. Minnelli was surprised that she accepted the news so calmly. "There was no turning to barbiturates or amphetamines," he recalled, rather as if, in spite of her honeymoon promise, this was what he would have expected. Hedda Hopper wanted to throw a different kind of baby shower for Garland, in which all the other guests were men, but Garland declined with a note: "I'd have been a dull guest of honor, but it was a wonderful idea. Thanks for thinking of me. Forgive me, and after March I'll be rarin' to go. I'll be my old self again." She was in fact her old vivacious self a week before the baby was due, at a party at the Gershwins, where she sang while Harold Arlen played the piano. Lee thought that she had never looked more beautiful, that she had never sung better or been more lighthearted or funnier.

Liza May Minnelli was born on March 12, 1946, at 7:28 a.m., weighing 6 lbs 10 1/2 oz. Minnelli's flowers threatened to engulf the Cedars of Lebanon Hospital, and every day until Garland returned home, he gave or sent her a small bouquet of white blossoms. Kay Thompson and Bill Spier were to be godparents. Those Hollywood cynics who had joked about Garland's immaculate conception were confounded when they saw the baby, who unquestionably had Minnelli's large eyes and generous lips, as well as Garland's petite, up-turned nose. With a fine, healthy baby, it seemed that the future was set fair for Hollywood's happiest family.

Garland's determination to be a good mother was severely shaken when she was racked with post-natal depression. As she emerged from this, she found that she was no longer sexually interested in her husband. This state of affairs may not have surprised anyone else, but it began to make her aware how little she and Minnelli were really suited to each other.

She adored Liza—they both did: but all her life Garland had been the center of attention and she was not certain whether she wanted to cede that position to a mere baby. Only a few months earlier, she had told Lee Gershwin that she wanted a hundred kids; but now she felt unable to cope with one. Of course, it was all right to leave the changing of diapers to the nurse, but how could she combine the roles of perfect mother and Judy Garland, movie star and the life and soul of the party? More than anything, she wanted to be a better mother than, as she saw it, Ethel had been, and she was stricken with the knowledge that she was unable to manage this. She insisted that Liza was as dependent on her as she once had been on her own mother: if she failed her, Liza might grow up to feel about her as she felt about Ethel. She bought a baby book in which to record the details of Liza's first year, but at the end of that year had failed to keep it up. Shortly after Liza's first birthday, she was obliged to bring it up to date in one go. She tried to be a mother in much the same way as she had tried baking cakes—with resolution and intensity, but with no gift for it. Had she been a whit less intelligent, she might not, given her pampered existence, have cared. Instead, the feelings of inadequacy and insecurity which had always plagued her were reinforced.

She fretted and grew much thinner; and she vacillated about returning to work. In her unease, she decided to change her agent. In 1944, Leland Hayward had sold his company to the Music Corporation of America so that he could concentrate on backing Broadway shows. He had retained an interest—he was vice-president of MCA—but it was unlikely that he himself would renegotiate her contract when it expired in 1948. Nor, remembering his opposition to her marriage to Rose, was she sure that she wanted him to. She had established no rapport with anyone at MCA, and they, in turn, had not done much to defend her when M-G-M complained of her behavior on her recent films. MCA made only token attempts to hold on to her services when she informed them that she was moving to a decidedly second-rate agency, Berg-Allenberg Inc.

Her career needed revitalizing, and she remembered the time when it had leaped ahead, with similarly small-time representation. In signing with Berg-Allenberg, she acted impulsively, not considering the consequences, but she appeared to have made the right decision when the agency decided to celebrate its new acquisition by inquiring whether M-G-M was willing to negotiate a new contract. Once again, the studio gave ample proof of its faith in her. Her current contract was scrapped and a new five-year one offered. This suited Garland, who was not sure whether she wanted to remain at M-G-M for even five years. When it expired, she would still be a young woman, but would have been a star for almost two decades, at a time when a star's "life" was thought to be five years. Her present weekly salary of $3,000 would rise to $5,619.23 a week for the entire period, and she would only have to make two pictures a year, each of them star vehicles, and she was to receive top billing if co-starred. The contract gave the studio the right to cancel if she was ill for more than three weeks, or if she failed to notify them of being ill within twenty-four hours. Penalties of this kind were standard practice, designed to give the studios a tight hold over their employees; but, like the morals clause, they were seldom invoked with stars as big as Judy Garland.

The new contract was to take effect from November 21, 1946, the day she was due to start work on *The Pirate*. When the time came, however, Minnelli told Freed that she needed two more weeks to be on top form. He said that he could work around her during that time, and so she was generously given leave to remain absent until December 2 if she wished. She did. Being paid more that $1,000 a day brought with it a great deal of responsibility and she was not sure that she was up to it. She was afraid of the picture.

There had been other possibilities for her return to the screen. Freed had bought *Good News* for her and Mickey Rooney, but their partnership was now clearly a thing of the past; added to which, Rooney had slipped precipitously at the box office, and M-G-M had no intention of allowing him to take Garland down with him. In any case, in this post–*Meet Me in St. Louis* era, a musical about college kids putting on a show seemed old hat. In August 1946 the studio announced that it would be making *Forever* with Garland, based on the book which Tyrone Power had given her; it was described as "a romantic drama with two songs." Also under consideration was a musical remake of Edna Ferber's Oklahoma-set family saga, *Cimarron*, which had been a great success for RKO in 1930. With *Oklahoma!* still running on Broadway, and now touring the country, and with Irving Berlin writing the score for a musical about the life of Annie Oakley, it seemed as if postwar America wanted to celebrate its past in song. Moreover, Berlin was writing his score for the producing team of Rodgers and Hammerstein, who as composer-lyricists had re-set Molnar's *Liliom* in turn-of-the-century Maine to come up with *Carousel*, a second consecutive Broadway success for them. *Cimarron* would have been a custom-built role for Garland, as the managing pioneer wife, and her co-star would be Gene Kelly, ideally cast as the roving, cocksure husband.

Freed's desire to re-team Garland and Kelly was one reason he had agreed to *The Pirate*. Another was because it was a pet project for Minnelli, whose reputation still rode high despite the failure of *Yo-*

landa and the Thief. Furthermore, Kelly was very enthusiastic. When he left the navy, he had found, to his surprise and dismay, that M-G-M's only plan for him was another naval musical with Frank Sinatra, on the lines of *Anchors Aweigh,* though it was as yet only an idea in Joe Pasternak's head. Kelly called Freed and, though longing for something meatier, suggested a musical with a baseball background. This eventually reached the screen as *Take Me Out to the Ball Game,* but in the meantime Kelly seized the chance to play the title role in *The Pirate.* He decided to play the role as an affectionate burlesque of two boyhood heroes, John Barrymore and Douglas Fairbanks.

S.N. Behrman had written the play for the Lunts, and it was very much a romp in the tradition of some of their greatest successes. Although it had been neither popular nor much admired, M-G-M had spent $225,026 to acquire the rights in the fifteenth week of its run in 1942, a large sum to pay, especially as the play was taken off very shortly afterwards. The first person who suggested turning it into a musical was Lemuel Ayers, whom Minnelli had brought to Hollywood for *St. Louis.* He had designed the original production of *The Pirate,* and in October 1944, a year before Minnelli decided that it would be a suitable vehicle for Garland, he brought the property to Freed's attention, suggesting Cole Porter as composer. Porter liked working for films and, delighted at the prospect of writing for Garland and Kelly, accepted a fee of $100,000.

The screenplay that Joe Mankiewicz had left behind when he fled M-G-M was raked out and rejected. A new one was commissioned from Anita Loos and Joseph Than, but a read-through for the principals was disastrous: the Kelly character had been changed from an actor who impersonates a pirate to a pirate impersonating an actor, which was not the same thing at all. Loos and Than had worked on the assumption that any change to the material could only be an improvement, but M-G-M did not agree. The screenplay was assigned to Albert Hackett and Frances Goodrich, the husband-and-wife team who had been writing successful scripts for the studio since 1933, including some of the MacDonald-Eddy musicals.

By this time, Garland's initial enthusiasm for the project had disappeared. In an attempt to reassure her, Minnelli reminded her that she had been wrong about *Meet Me in St. Louis.* He expressed his confidence in her ability to step into the shoes of Lynn Fontanne, who was considered one of the first ladies of the American theater. The picture, he said, "would be mounted with such sophistication and wit that she would now be in the same league as Greer Garson and Katharine Hepburn, the great and grand fillies of the Metro stable of stars." He put his head and heart into his work, not unduly concerned about her worries. He could bring her through. She had only to trust him.

The setting of the film was Martinique in the 1830s, and this was to erupt on the screen in a blaze of Technicolor, re-created by Jack Martin Smith (who had served Minnelli so generously on both *St. Louis* and *Yolanda*), with the aid of his "collection of prints and drawings of the period." An old New York colleague, Karinska, who had worked with Diaghilev, was engaged to design the costumes—which, in the event, were credited to her protégé, Tom Keogh. Clearly, Garland was being supported by some of the finest talents in show business. How could she fail when wearing a replica of a Worth gown which cost $3,462.23? Or, indeed, "a white satin wedding dress, with handmade antique lace from France and embroidered with a thousand pearls," costing $3,313.12? All the embroidery was done by hand and each of Garland's costumes had five petticoats. It is small wonder, then, that the total cost of the wardrobe was $141,395.30.

The whole powerhouse of creative energy available to Hollywood's greatest studio was deployed to help Minnelli display his wife's gifts. Heading the supporting cast were such favorite players as Walter Slezak, Gladys Cooper, Reginald Owen and, best of all, the Nicholas Brothers, a black dance team whose terpsichorean feats stopped every show in which they were featured. Garland could also draw comfort from the fact that trusted friends from the Freed unit were there to guide her. Vocal arrangements were being supplied by Kay Thompson, Roger Edens and Robert Tucker; Lennie Hayton was the conductor and Conrad Salinger the orchestrator; and the choreography was being planned by Robert Alton and Kelly himself.

Garland was not, however, reassured. One of her concerns was that Kelly might overwhelm her, as his was by far the showier of the two leading roles. Whenever she expressed her doubts to Minnelli, his response was to immerse himself in the physical appearance of the film, reassuring her that she had never had a more "sophisticated" or "witty" showcase for her talent. The trouble was that no one really listened to her. She knew that it was the wrong film at the wrong time, but as far as everyone else was concerned, it was a new form of screen musical, a costume burlesque. Freed had always known what was best for her, and it seemed that her own husband was now treating her in the same way. Since her Baby Gumm days, she had danced and sung prettily for the public, without ever being considered as someone with a mind of her own. As ever, she was expected to be nice little Judy, grateful for what others were doing on her behalf.

She did not feel like being nice to anyone, so she wasn't. She was manifestly miserable during the costume fittings, at which yet more frills were added to disguise the fact that she was woefully thin. She looked depressed during camera tests, and the years of barbiturates had aged her unnaturally. It was partly because, at twenty-four, she no longer looked young enough to play an ingenue, in spite of the magic wrought in the makeup room, that Minnelli had been attracted to *The Pirate* as a vehicle for her. When Fontanne had played the role on Broadway, she had been in her mid-fifties.

Liza's first Christmas momentarily cheered her spirits, but on December 27, Hugh Fordin relates, when she pre-recorded her first song, "Love of My Life," she could not deliver the old Garland magic. "Mack the Black," which called for several changes of mood and rhythm, was equally a failure the following day: the number had been "arranged" to within an inch of its life, and she sang it shrilly, unresponsive to its mixture of dreamy nonchalance and excitement. Freed put pre-recording aside for the time being.

Garland's worst fear was realized during rehearsals, when it became clear that Kelly was going to take the film away from her. He saw the film as a chance to take on-screen dancing closer to ballet, and he was working like a demon in pursuit of this notion. Garland admired him as a talent and liked him as a person, but this merely heightened her insecurity, since no blame could be attached to him. She had only herself to blame: she had been flattered and wooed into doing the role. She was not, however, good at accepting blame, and if it was not her fault, then it must be Minnelli's. The old pattern began to reassert itself. "Judy had periods when she didn't show up on the set," Kelly recalled. "This was my first indication that something was wrong."

Something was indeed very seriously wrong. She was fast becoming paranoid, and was resentful of the time Minnelli spent with Kelly, who, in stark contrast to her own behavior, had enthusiastically involved himself with every aspect of the production. She felt that Kelly did not need Minnelli's attention as much as she did, and made no secret of the fact that she was jealous of the time they spent together— time devoted to making Kelly shine all the brighter. Her paranoia was such that she began to worry that her co-star was having an affair with her husband, even though Kelly was married.

These fears may have been the result of guilt since she had been unfaithful to Minnelli the previous autumn. Her lover had been Yul Brynner, who at that time had been touring in *Lute Song*, the musical starring Mary Martin which had brought him his first flush of fame. Garland had visited him backstage after the first night of the Los Angeles engagement. A brief affair was not difficult to manage, since both their spouses were out of town. Complications set in when a theater became unexpectedly available in Chicago and the tour of Brynner's show was extended. Garland had already started work on *The Pirate*, and M-G-M refused to rearrange her schedule. She used her considerable clout to get a screen test at the studio for Brynner, ostensibly for a film about Rudolf Valentino. Most stage actors had clauses in their contracts for such emergencies, and Brynner's understudy took over while M-G-M flew him to Los Angeles. During the week he was there, he and Garland decided that they should not compromise their marriages by continuing the relationship, which lasted in all some four months. They remained friends, as she did with most of her lovers. Like Orson Welles, Brynner was a strong man. He was also clever, but in a more dashing way than Minnelli. For Garland, both lovers could only underline her husband's inadequacies.

The Pirate eventually began shooting on February 17, 1947; before very long, Garland had to resort to pills. The studio agreed that she should return to psychoanalysis, and at the end of the shooting day, Minnelli would drive her to see Dr. Simmel for a session which lasted exactly fifty minutes. She would leave, he reported, her mood "unaltered." When Minnelli was not free, Dottie Ponedel drove her there, and to her Garland was much more communicative: "I lied again," she would confess. "Oh God, Dottie, I lied so much today I don't know any longer what is true and untrue." She liked and respected Dr. Simmel, who was more of a father substitute than Mayer had ever been, and she achieved a certain grisly satisfaction in complaining to him of her victimization from childhood onwards. Once she had hammered Ethel into the ground, she started in on Ida Koverman.

As often as not, she was absent from the studio. She came in to rehearse, but could only manage an hour or so; or she would put in an appearance in the morning, only to vanish moments later. When she was taking amphetamines, Minnelli found that he had no control over her at all, so he gave up trying. This did not mean that he did not care; indeed, he went to considerable lengths to protect her. She was so high on one occasion that she was unable to perform. Seeing Freed approach, Minnelli deliberately stumbled, to divert the producer's attention away from her. Garland was a thoroughgoing addict, and no amount of strictures, warnings or surveillance could prevent her from getting pills; they were even found sewn into the hem of newly bought clothes. Minnelli was particularly frustrated by his wife's reluctance to eat. In the past, the studio's chief problem had been preventing her from eating and putting on unflattering pounds. Now she was painfully thin and, despite all his efforts, only pecked at her food. It was obvious that a healthy diet was far better for her than a fistful of pills. Garland agreed without enthusiasm: she might not be able to perform after a hearty lunch, but benzedrine would see her through. In any case she did not want a hearty lunch: it only left her feeling nauseous.

Hedda Hopper visited her in her dressing-room one afternoon and "she was shaking like an aspen leaf. She went into a frenzy of hysteria. Everybody who had once loved her had turned against her, she said. She had no friends." Mostly she railed against Ethel, who, she claimed, was tapping her telephone calls: "She is doing everything in her power to destroy me," she insisted, ignoring Hopper's remonstrations. Koverman's name was also high on her hate list: she repudiated "all those who had helped her out of so much potential trouble." At the end of the day, Hopper saw Garland being carried out of the dressing-room and put into a limousine, still wearing makeup and costume.

Not before time, the studio decided that something drastic was required. Another psychoanalyst was hired, his fee paid by Mayer as a gesture to Garland, as if to assure her that he had been wrong to side with Ethel against analysis some years earlier. Dr. Frederick Hacker, a young Viennese-born psychiatrist, was paid to attend to Garland whenever she needed advice or consultation—and to advise her colleagues about any matters which distressed her. Psychoanalysis had become so widespread in Hollywood that psychiatrists were almost as common as physicians, but this may have been the first time a studio had used one as a go-between.

One of Dr. Hacker's tasks was to accompany Garland to the rushes, where she judged her day's work. She had always been objective about her work and self-critical, but this admirable quality proved a problem on *The Pirate*. In spite of the difficulties she was causing, Minnelli and Kelly were pleased with what they were achieving.

They, and Dr. Hacker, wanted to reassure her about her own work, but this was not always what she wanted. On one occasion, she appeared to be in a reasonably equable mood, until the film's cutter murmured that she was "marvelous" in the rushes. She got up and moved over to the water cooler, where she pulled a handful of Benzedrines out of her pocket and swallowed them with the water. "I'm leaving," she announced.

By the beginning of April, her conduct was demoralizing the entire company. "Judy's disregard for her obligations as a star was appalling," wrote Anita Loos.

> I recall a day at the studio when mild little Vincente Minnelli was waiting to direct Judy in a scene for *The Pirate*. She was late for work, as usual, and everybody, including a hundred or more extras, had been marking time since nine that morning. Finally at noon, Vincente was summoned to the phone to learn that Judy required him to get home at once and escort her to an ice-cream parlor for a soda.

Perhaps he was glad that she was at least eating something. It is hardly surprising that her behavior was putting an intolerable strain on her marriage. The fact that the hapless director was also the husband of his temperamental star made it difficult for anyone else to help. Roger Edens had managed to control her on occasion on *The Harvey Girls* by taking her into her dressing-room for a lecture, but he decided that if he intervened in this case the situation between the couple might be worsened. He either absented himself from the set or confined his comments to the music.

Minnelli found his patience stretched beyond endurance. He and Garland bickered on the set and fought at home. As director and husband, he was a two-time loser. In both roles he understood her difficulties, but she made it almost impossible for him to express his sympathy. Her imagined slights and constant complaints forced him into arguments with her. If she had been calm on set, they usually managed to pass a relaxed evening; but more often her behavior swung between that of tyrant and victim. The Gershwins had a sofa he slept on when things became too much, but usually when he threatened to spend the night there, according to Gerold Frank, Garland would scream: "*I'll* go. After all, this is your home." On one occasion, he telephoned Lee Gershwin to ask whether he could use the sofa, but it was Garland who arrived fifteen minutes later. Lee took her to the spare room, where Garland began to scream. This went on for hours, Garland only pausing occasionally to catch her breath, and once to speak, after Lee had softly asked her whether there was anything she could do for her. "Do you believe me?" Garland asked. When Lee assured her that she did, she began to scream again, and continued until she fell asleep in Lee's arms.

The bickering and the quarrels were kept from Liza, who had her own room with her nurse; and they were dropped whenever she was brought up to be petted. Garland usually went down to give her a final hug before tucking her in, and Liza remembered her father looking on fondly. The servants, however, were spared neither the rows nor Garland's rages. They accepted the marital disputes and the fact that their mistress was ill. She had always been unpredictable, but she had become capable of lashing into them with a viciousness which some of them found unforgivable.

Back at the studio, Garland managed to pre-record the "Voodoo" number, but failed to turn up on time to film it. When she arrived, she was already angry, and Hugh Fordin states that when she saw the fires lit for the scene, she went berserk. "I'm going to burn to death!" she yelled. "They want me to burn to death!" Minnelli very gently pointed out that this was unlikely, to say the least, but she did not listen: she no longer trusted him as she had on earlier films. She ran hysterically to the large group of waiting extras, demanding of each of them if they had any benzedrine. For the crew, many of whom had known her since childhood, this was a terrifying experience. They watched sadly as she was led away.

She managed to work the following day, but then began another series of no-shows. Kelly invented an infection for a week so that she could rest. When he returned, Arthur Freed spent two hours in her dressing-room trying to reason with her, but her behavior rapidly deteriorated. "I just wouldn't be good enough today," she would tell her dresser, "I know it in my bones." Minnelli would rap gently on the door, saying: "Just dress and make up, and come down and see how you feel. If you think you just aren't up to a job today, we'll change the schedule and shoot around you."

Without any feeling of confidence, she made a second attempt at pre-recording "Love of My Life." Cole Porter arrived not long after the session had started and, with considerable restraint, made only a polite comment on her interpretation. She knew, as she did through-out her life, when she was off-form, but while rehearsing "You Can Do No Wrong," she launched into an attack on Porter over the minor matter of the scanning of the word "caviar." Edens calmed her, but he and Minnelli knew that something was very seriously wrong for her to attack Porter, whom she adored.

In the film, this particular song is preceded by a scene in which the Garland character stages a temper tantrum, throwing everything in the room at the character played by Kelly. The whole scene was supposed to be played lightheartedly, but Garland hurled herself into it with a ferocity which astonished everyone, and which required her to rest after each take. They finally got enough takes to fit the sequence together in the cutting room, but it was a near thing. By early June, the film was only half finished and, at $2,725,516, seriously over budget. The cast and crew struggled on, but Garland made little effort: for the next four weeks, she appeared only sporadically.

A great deal depended on the song "Be a Clown," which Porter had written for a weak spot in the picture. It was filmed, as first intended, with the Nicholas Brothers, and the result was so sensational that it was decided that the number should be reprised at the end of the film, with Kelly and Garland. This would give Garland the chance to cast off the shade of Lynn Fontanne and to be herself, the Judy Garland who adored clowning and fooling around, who remembered all the knockabout acts she had seen in vaudeville. The pre-recording did not bode well, however: her sense of humor was not much in evidence, and Porter's lyric was not about to restore it. He was very upset when Garland complained that she loathed the song, but refused to accept her criticisms. What started as a disagreement soon became a slanging match of the sort to make their differences over "Love of My Life" look like a civilized exchange. In all this, it should be pointed out that *The Pirate* is one of Porter's least successful scores, without a single number in it that could be counted among his best. He must have been aware of this, and, after his row with Garland, he noted in his diary: "She pointed out that there were hardly any laughs where I had attempted an infinite number. It was very embarrassing to have it pointed out."

When they came to film the number, however, in which Garland and Kelly are hit over the head with Indian clubs, she began to enjoy herself. Her sense of humor returned, as if she were aware that a knock on the head was exactly what she deserved. Jack Martin Smith, who had designed the set, was watching, and he said: "She and Minnelli screamed and screamed with laughter—they'd look and look at each other and roll on the floor. It helped with the mood of the number, but it was a bit peculiar."

Garland's participation in the film concluded on July 10, 1947, and she and Minnelli gave a party for all those involved, including Freed, Mayer, Sam Katz and Benjamin Thau, as well as Irving Berlin, who was writing the score for the next Garland-Kelly-Minnelli opus. Still to be filmed was Kelly's "Pirate" ballet, and production was finally completed on August 14. It had taken a total of 135 days, for 99 of which Garland had been absent.

There was no question of her starting a new film, and Dr. Simmel suggested a complete rest. More than ever, her health was causing concern at the studio, for she herself seemed disinclined to seek a cure. Her symptoms—paranoia, irrational fears, moments of remorse followed by even more extreme erratic behavior—were those of the classic drug addict. The two Romantic writers, Thomas De Quincey and Samuel Taylor Coleridge, who were both addicts of long standing, had confessed to similar behavior. De Quincey was aware that his suffering was "more oppressive and tormenting from the sense of inadequacy . . . incident to the neglect and procrastination of each day's . . . labours, and from remorse." He also recorded suffering "deep-seated anxiety and funereal melancholy" and "suicidal despondency." Both writers' relations with their families and friends deteriorated in extended quarrels in which they deluded themselves into believing that those closest to them were conspirators plotting against their well-being. No professional person could ignore these symptoms as they manifested themselves in Garland, but with all the battery of modern science and psychology, they were as helpless as their forerunners had been 150 years before. Apart from anything else, Garland had made it quite clear that she had no intention of giving up her vast assortment of pills. Until she did so, she was a liability to the studio.

The situation suddenly took an even more drastic turn. Gerold Frank describes how Ethel was with Liza in the nursery when they heard Garland screaming in her room, after an argument with Minnelli. "I'm going to kill myself," she cried, rushing into her bathroom and bolting the door before Minnelli or Ethel could stop her. This was not the first time that Garland had threatened suicide and they attempted to force the door. They could hear her sobbing, then they heard the sound of breaking glass. "Goddamn it, you open this door!" yelled Ethel, her voice at full power—which may be why her daughter obeyed. She had broken a tumbler, and her wrist was cut. The wound was not deep and Ethel covered it with a Band-Aid.

Garland's mental condition was now regarded by the studio with the utmost gravity. Mayer turned to one of his doctors, Jessie Marmorston, a Russian-born endocrinologist who was regarded in Hollywood as his unofficial analyst. Mayer was as reluctant to believe in psychiatry as at the time of the row with Mankiewicz, but he totally trusted Marmorston in such matters. After consultations with Marc Rabwin and Dr. Simmel, it was felt imperative to remove Garland from whatever demons she thought beset her. That was one way of putting it, and the way it would be presented to the press should the news leak out.

Dr. Simmel reserved a room for her at Las Campanas, a sanitorium on the outskirts of Compton, California, and decided that he, and not Minnelli, should drive her there. "She'll be quieter this way," he told him. He would give her something to make her sleep as soon as she arrived.

Minnelli was relieved to see her go. His efforts to help her had been ineffectual, and he was so emotionally battered that he needed time to recover. Both he and Garland were worried as to what Liza should be told. She must not think that her mother had deserted her, but he was not certain that he could assure her with conviction that Garland would be back soon, although that was what he did do. Liza was protected by "a very capable nurse" during her formative years, said Minnelli. "Between the two of us, we shielded the unhappy truth from her until Liza was old enough to cope with it."

Garland was lonely and frightened. She was installed in a bungalow close enough to hear the noises coming from what she called the "violent ward"—or so she later dramatized it. She was, however, speaking the truth when she said that she was fearful of what was in store for her. Nor did she know how long she would be there. For the first time in her life, she was dependent on the kindness of strangers, and it was costing her a considerable sum. M-G-M, after reckoning that *The Pirate* was unlikely to show a profit because of her conduct, was disinclined to keep her on salary, and the clinic was costing $300 a day. The Internal Revenue authorities had placed a lien on her earnings for taxes which Ethel and Will Gilmore had failed to pay on her behalf when they were handling her financial affairs. The bills of the clinic were handed directly to Garland, who had hardly ever seen such a thing. The doctors knew this and looked on it as a way to lure her from her movie-star fantasy world and face up to reality. It was a well-considered ploy, but it only reinforced her view that what she most urgently needed was someone older and preferably male to protect her.

The priority of her doctors was to end her addiction to pills, as the initial step in curing both malnutrition and depression. She was encouraged to mingle with the other patients, some of whom hoped for a glimpse of her as they passed her bungalow. On the second day, she went out to meet them. She liked them, and later observed that "not one of them was demented in the common sense. Most of them were just too highly strung and too sensitive for reality." With the realization that they were all self-absorbed, like herself, her sense of humor began to reassert itself. Recalling her first night, she turned it into a joke against herself: "It was very dark . . . Well, maybe it wasn't, but I was so out of it, that I couldn't make out anything. These two burly attendants met us at the car. They walked with me across the grounds. Suddenly, I tripped. They picked me up. I couldn't seem to control my feet. I tried to walk, but I kept stumbling. They held me up the rest of the way. 'This has to be the end of me,' I thought." She was given a sedative and she felt reasonably relaxed when she woke the next day—to look out of the window to a smooth green lawn: "Then I saw why I kept stumbling. I'd been tripping over the croquet wickets!"

This was the first of the many stories of her stay in what she later called "the first of my nuthouses." Almost all the stories were at her own expense, including one about the nurses searching her room for pills, since her cunning in obtaining them was not expected to stop just because she was in the care of a sanitorium. She was not the first illustrious Hollywood patient at Las Campanas, and the staff had strict instructions never to speak to the press. Such precautions were in vain, since her difficulties were common knowledge in Hollywood, and Louella Parsons had decided to air them in her column two days after Garland had finished work on *The Pirate*:

Judy Garland is a very sick girl and has suffered a complete nervous collapse.

For weeks there have been rumors that all was not well with Judy and Minnelli . . .

Yesterday, Minnelli said, "Judy is a very sick girl, and the only thing that is important now is to get her well. She is under a doctor's care and in a highly nervous state."

One of the reasons that Minnelli visited his wife infrequently was that he was still involved in post-production work on *The Pirate*. Another was Garland's conviction—which she never managed to hide—that he was responsible for all her ills. If people attempted to refute this idea, she would complain that he had failed to provide emotional support when it was most needed. She *did* want to see Liza, however, and the doctors agreed that this would be beneficial. Minnelli brought her, allowing her to walk unannounced and unaided into the bungalow. She toddled in and into her mother's arms. "I just didn't know what to say to her," Garland recalled.

> I just held her, and she just kept kissing me and looking at me with those huge, helpless eyes of hers. I jabbered a little but mostly held her. But we laughed too.
>
> After a short while they took her away. I lay down on the bed and started to cry. There have been many blue moments in my life, but I never remember having such a feeling. I almost died of anguish.

It was an anguish born of self-pity and guilt. She was aware that there was much she had not yet done for her child. Her love for Liza was one reason her doctors decided to let her go home after two weeks, when she asked them whether she could. There could be no better therapy for a young mother, they thought, than to have an eighteen-month baby bouncing on her knee.

Dr. Simmel disagreed and advised her against leaving, but he had known Garland long enough to know that she would do exactly as she pleased. Much later in her life, she would ridicule him, saying that she could never understand a word he said; but at the time she was very fond of him, and was overwhelmed with grief when he died the following December. He was already suffering from the illness which was to kill him and, baffled by his failure to help her, he recommended Dr. Herbert Kupper to take over treatment, while still being available to her if she needed him. He himself had never done house calls, but Dr. Kupper was prepared, other commitments permitting, to go to Garland's aid whenever and wherever she was if she felt herself seized by an attack of panic.

Whether he sometimes felt that his journey was not really necessary, we shall never know; but he decided almost immediately that she needed a further spell in a sanitorium. Since clinics in California were filled with patients with backgrounds like her own and, consequently, similar problems, he thought that she should go East, where she would be among patients who were similarly privileged, but had a different perception of the realities of this world. Once again, Dr. Marmorston and Marc Rabwin were consulted, and they chose the Austen Riggs Center in Stockbridge, Massachusetts, an institution not unknown to Culver City. Louis B. Mayer's wife had been treated there for severe depression for several years before they separated in 1944. Not only did the Riggs Foundation have a fine reputation to recommend it, but Stockbridge itself was an old-American community as different as possible from any that Garland had known in California. During the summer, there was thriving artistic activity, centered round Tanglewood and the Berkshire Music Festival, with Koussevitsky conducting. All this might give Garland a perspective very different from Hollywood. The clinic had a little theater, where Garland could use her expertise to help other patients. Most importantly, Dr. Edward Knight was leaving the Menninger Clinic to take up an appointment at Riggs on August 8: Kupper believed that Knight was better qualified than himself to get to the root of Garland's troubles. She was due to arrive in Stockbridge on August 4, so Kupper agreed to accompany her in case she needed therapy while waiting for Knight to arrive.

The Riggs Foundation was housed on Main Street in a former mansion surrounded by lawns and ancient trees. On arrival, Garland chose to stay instead at the justly famous and luxurious Red Lion Inn, taking rooms for herself, Kupper and a maid. Her treatment with Knight was to begin on August 15. In the meantime, Kupper spent hours listening to her as she dug into her past and her psyche. When Knight arrived, it was clear to him at once that Garland had become dependent on Kupper. He told Kupper that he expected him to leave before she began treatment with him, and he told Garland that he expected her to move into the clinic.

Garland had no desire to relinquish either her own doctor or the Red Lion Inn, but Kupper decided that it would be in her best interests if he left, and so departed on August 14. Against his better judgment, Knight allowed Garland to remain at the hotel, but she had to report to him daily. It had been agreed that her sessions with him would be long and intensive. Exhausted by the time she returned to the Red Lion, she found herself tearful and unable to sleep—and once again resorted to barbiturates.

On August 19, Knight issued an ultimatum: unless she moved into the Foundation, he would no longer be available for consultations. She pointed out that she would lose the one freedom to pick up the telephone and call California whenever she felt inclined. Knight reminded her that her whole purpose in being at the Riggs Foundation was to distance herself from California. The following day Garland checked out of the hotel and returned home.

The trip was not quite the fiasco it might have been. Kupper and

Knight had achieved more in two weeks of intensive therapy than Simmel in several years of fifty-minute sessions, partly because Garland did not permit herself the luxury—and the amusement—of lying. Away from familiar rooms and familiar surroundings, she had made some attempt to get at the traumas which lay hidden. Most of these traumas concerned her relationship with her father, his homosexuality and his death. One of her telephone calls from the Red Lion had been to Carleton Alsop, who had recently married her friend Sylvia Sidney. She told him that she had "found such peace! I can eat and I want to eat! I can sleep and I never think of taking a sleeping pill! I feel like a new woman."

This was exactly what M-G-M wanted to hear, since, in its existing form, *The Pirate* could not be released.

11

❖❖❖❖❖❖❖❖❖

Easter Parade

FREED LOOKED LONG and hard at *The Pirate* and did not like what he saw. He especially did not care for what could be seen of Garland's contribution. She was particularly poor in the "Voodoo" number, but rather than arouse old demons by asking her to do it again, Freed had it replaced by a restaging of "Mack the Black." The Hacketts were asked to write several new scenes, and Kelly, Walter Slezak and Gladys Cooper were recalled to shoot them with Garland.

Garland first saw the film, in a rough cut, on August 29, a week after returning from Stockbridge. Also present were Freed, Minnelli, Cole Porter and Irving Berlin. Porter's reaction was cool, but Freed and Berlin assured him that it was a great picture. "We shall see," said Porter. Garland shared his doubts: the film might confirm that Minnelli was an artist, but whether it would prove to be a milestone in her career, as he maintained, would be for the critics and the public to decide. She was, however, encouraged by the fact that Berlin liked it, since he was well known for his down-to-earth tastes.

Finally convinced that the film was at least going to make money, and to all appearances fully recovered, she worked quickly and easily during the reshoots. Freed felt that the film needed a few embellishments, and, since Kelly, Garland and Minnelli were all working at the studio on their next film, *Easter Parade*, he ordered further retakes. The film was finally finished in December.

After the previews, Kelly recalled: "Vincente and I honestly believed we were being so dazzlingly brilliant and clever that everybody would fall at our feet and swoon clear away in delight and ecstasy." They did not. Cole Porter later described it as: "a $5,000,000 Hollywood picture that was unspeakably wretched, the worst that money could buy." James Agee perhaps put his finger on what was wrong with the film when he commented: "It seems to me to have the death's head, culture-cute, 'mirthful' grin of the average Shakespearian comic." He did, however, admire the ambition of all those involved:

> As an all-out try at artful movie-making, this is among the most interesting pictures of the year. Unluckily, most of the considerable artistry that has gone into this production collides head-on with artiness or is spoiled by simpler kinds of miscalculation. Miss Garland's tense, ardent straightforwardness is sometimes very striking.

Although Garland's performance was generally praised, few critics noted it as a change of pace for her. Almost all the New York critics invoked the magic of the Lunts, who were a famously overrated couple but were well suited to this material, which needs mannered overage players to make its form of parody acceptable. Garland came out of the comparison reasonably well. She understood the sort of acting the film required, and she merely *hints* that the only approach to such artificial stuff is to send it up, whereas Kelly signals this by flailing his arms in the air. Her performance is another example of her fine artistic judgment, and if Minnelli's approach had been as light as hers, *The Pirate* might have become the film he wanted it to be. Only in some of the musical numbers does he achieve the swirl of fantasy for which he was aiming. Still, in view of the production's horribly muddled history, he could have done no better. Much later, he told *Cahiers du Cinema* that he "was very pleased the way the film turned out." He blamed its failure at the box office on bad merchandising.

In fact, the picture got off to a good start at his old hunting ground, Radio City Music Hall, but business fell off sharply after the first week, and there was never any question of holding it over. In London, it ran for one week only at M-G-M's flagship, the Empire, taking less in that time than *The Harvey Girls* had in its second week. Arthur

Freed had remarked proudly that *The Pirate* was twenty years ahead of its time—a not unusual Hollywood defense when asked by the front office to explain the red ink in the ledger books. The eventual cost of the film had been $3,768,496, more than half a million dollars over budget. The receipts at the box office totaled $2,956,000. Taking into account the costs of prints and publicity, the total loss was estimated at $2,290,000.

The failure of *The Pirate* did little to help the Minnellis' marriage. They kept up the front of being a happy couple, but their relationship was clearly deteriorating. Their troubles were put into perspective, however, by disturbing developments in the film colony during the summer and autumn of 1947. A witch-hunt had started in Washington and, like a reptile, it slithered its way westward. As the world situation darkened, with the Soviet Union taking control of most of Eastern Europe, and with Communists fighting for control in other parts of the world, many Americans feared for democracy in the Western Hemisphere. In Washington, a congressman called J. Parnell Thomas was heading the House of Representatives Un-American Activities Committee—whose members included Richard Nixon—and it was finding reds under any number of American beds. Thomas liked publicity, and uncovering subversives in Hollywood made bigger headlines than doing so in Washington. In this, he was supported by Nixon, who represented California and was particularly anxious to root every red out of the Sunshine State. Investigators arrived in Los Angeles to interview members of the film industry, and they gradually produced a list of people who should not be working in it—especially if they refused to testify before HUAC.

In September, the Minnellis, dressed in the clown costumes from *The Pirate*, were at a masquerade party held by Groucho Marx. The party refused to come to life because all the guests were concerned about the names on the list—the "Unfriendly Ten," as they were called. Most of them were writers, and they stood accused of having tried to insert Communist propaganda into their movie dialogue. Among the films cited was *Tender Comrade*, a wartime effort about a group of women who room together and pool their financial resources (earned as welders in the Douglas Aircraft plant). It had been directed by Edward Dmytryk and written by Dalton Trumbo, two of the Unfriendly Ten, and it had starred Ginger Rogers, whose mother testified that her daughter had objected to many of the lines she had been obliged to say. No one at the Marx party could quite remember

Tender Comrade, but if it had preached the joys of the Communist way of life, perhaps they were all unwittingly guilty.

A groundswell began among Hollywood's Democrats, starting within the Screen Writers' Guild, whose founder and first president, John Howard Lawson, was one of the names on the list. He had since been subpoenaed to testify before the Committee in Washington, D.C. The principle at issue was the right to free speech and not whether the men were Communists—which they mostly were, said John Huston, adding: "They were, for the most part, well-intentioned boobs, men mostly from poor backgrounds, and out in Hollywood they sort of felt guilty at living the good life. Most of these men's social conscience was no more acute than the next fellow."

Huston, who was then vice-president of the Screen Directors' Guild, joined with the director William Wyler and screenwriter Philip Dunne to form a group called Hollywood Fights Back, which was renamed the Committee for the First Amendment. One of its first meetings was held in the Gershwins' home and among those present were the Minnellis, the Bogarts, Huston, Wyler, Dunne, Edward G. Robinson, Gene Kelly, Danny Kaye, Burt Lancaster, Billy Wilder and Harry Kurnitz. After some speeches, it was decided to send a formal petition to Washington, which was eventually signed by over five hundred leading figures in the industry. The petition read:

> We, the undersigned, as American citizens who believe in constitutional democratic government, are disgusted and outraged by the continuing attempt at the House Committee on Un-American Activities to smear the Motion Picture Industry.
>
> We hold that these hearings are morally wrong because:
>
> Any investigation into the political beliefs of the individual is contrary to the basic principles of our democracy;
>
> Any attempt to curb freedom of expression and to set arbitrary standards of Americanism is in itself disloyal to the spirit and the letter of our Constitution.

Several of those who signed later flew to Washington, in a plane donated by Howard Hughes, but the Minnellis were not among them. However, in what Lauren Bacall has euphemistically called "a difficult time in Hollywood," they had stood up to be counted.

When Garland said, as she often did, that she wanted "to swap show business for a shopping cart" she did not mean it, but the one thing she had learned from her sessions with Kupper and Knight was that someone as intelligent as she should be able to cope with both. Yet the effort seemed beyond her. On days when she was not needed at the studio, she begged Minnelli to stay at home with her, angry when he refused (though knowing full well that he had to go to the studio), and defensively turning her attention to Liza, planning a day in the park or a visit to Mia Farrow, the daughter of John Farrow and his actress wife, Maureen O'Sullivan. She was, he said, "trying to keep her head above water," and one way she tried to do so was to employ a succession of psychiatrists. She had realized that she had been wasting her own time and Simmel's when she agreed to be treated by Kupper and Knight, so she ran from this one to the next one.

Even so, neither these problems nor the troubled history of *The Pirate* appear to have cast a shadow over the prospect of her next collaboration with the same team of director and co-star. If Minnelli was unable to help his wife in what he described as "the reality of our often sweet, occasionally bitter, life," he was determined not to fail her in "the business of make-believe. *Easter Parade* would have to be a great triumph." Garland shared his confidence. She no longer resented the time he spent with Gene Kelly: "I know you two have something great going," she told him. In the new film, she would not be expected to challenge the great ladies of Broadway, but would again play the sort of show-business aspirant she had done in the films she made before *Meet Me in St. Louis*. Irving Berlin was the driving force behind the new project. He was one of a generation of astonishingly gifted popular songwriters. Most of them were smart businessmen, and Berlin was the brightest of them all. As Freed said: "It took longer to write one of Irving's contracts than it did the script, but after it was done, he forgot about the contract and gave you anything you wanted." In 1938, 20th Century-Fox had enjoyed a great success with *Alexander's Ragtime Band*, the story of which was built round Berlin's first great hit song. Since them, Paramount had produced *Holiday Inn* and *Blue Skies*, which had proved that the public adored Berlin's songs. The screenplays of all three films had been based on ideas by Berlin, and his name appeared before the title. In 1947, Freed negotiated to buy two Berlin properties for M-G-M, both to be filmed with Judy Garland.

The first, chronologically, was *Annie Get Your Gun*, which Berlin had written for Ethel Merman at the behest of Rodgers and Hammerstein, in their capacity as Broadway producers. After the highest advance booking in Broadway history, it had opened in May 1946 to glowing notices. Since it seemed set to run for years, Berlin was in no hurry to sell the movie rights. The score yielded no fewer than nine hit songs, all of which had been written specially for the show. This was unusual, since Berlin had a trunk full of unpublished songs into which he would delve when writing a new show. All but one of these numbers had been sung by Merman, alone or with others, and she had scored a personal success. For all her attack across the footlights, however, she was not really suited to the cinema, as some of her movie appearances in the 1930s had proved. Knowing that she was unlikely to be invited to repeat her performance on film, Freed approached Berlin with the suggestion that Garland could take the role. Berlin was attracted to the idea because his most recent film, *Blue Skies*, which had been released a couple of months after *Annie Get Your Gun* had started its Broadway run, had not received particularly good reviews. He reckoned that a film of his new show would revive his cinematic fortunes.

On June 13, 1947, after almost a year's negotiations, Berlin, along with his librettists, Herbert and Dorothy Fields, signed an agreement with M-G-M. The sum paid, $650,000, was the highest yet for a Broadway musical. Mayer paid so much because he was convinced that no other star of screen musicals could play Annie Oakley as well as Judy Garland. Berlin was only too happy to concur. The deal was especially attractive to Berlin, as the money was to be paid in five annual installments. It was to Freed's advantage that, because of his background, fellow songwriters such as Berlin found him sympathetic. He could also boast that in *Meet Me in St. Louis* he had produced the most successful musical in Hollywood history. All the same, had another studio improved on that $650,000, Berlin would almost certainly have sold it elsewhere, as his negotiations over *Easter Parade* prove.

Since any film of *Annie Get Your Gun* could not open until the show closed on Broadway, a prospect still some years away, another project was required. The publicity "line" on *Easter Parade* was that it came about because Berlin wanted to work with Judy Garland, but the true story was rather more complicated.

When 20th Century-Fox had produced *Alexander's Ragtime Band*, the company's chairman had been Joseph M. Schenck, brother to Loew's Nicholas Schenck. He had been a childhood friend of Berlin, who had testified on his behalf when he was tried for tax evasion. Schenck had been obliged to resign from the Fox board, but he still carried some weight at the studio. When he left prison after serving a four-month sentence, Berlin made him a present of *Easter Parade*, another show-business story built around old Berlin songs, along with a promise to compose eight new ones especially for the picture. It was a present for which Fox had to pay, of course, but with *Annie Get Your Gun* proving that the old master's touch was more in tune than ever, this was something that the board was happy to accept. Berlin's terms included a share in the profits—something so rare in Hollywood as to be almost non-existent. When RKO had approached Berlin to write songs for Fred Astaire and Ginger Rogers in *Top Hat*, Berlin had used the company's financial plight to obtain a percentage deal. When he asked for another on *Easter Parade*, he and Joseph Schenck shook hands on the deal.

The board at Fox did not like this arrangement, and tried offering a larger sum up front instead. Louis B. Mayer, hearing of the project, bettered this by bidding $500,000—a considerable sum, especially as Berlin might earn as much again from sales of the sheet music, which he published himself, and royalties from the records. Far from being pleased, however, Berlin sent back an angry cable: "Dear Louis— why should I ask one thing from Twentieth and do another for you?" Since Freed was anxious to find a less whimsical vehicle than *The Pirate* for Kelly and Garland, who were unarguably the two finest musical talents on the contract list, and since everyone agreed that a conventional backstage story would be ideal, Mayer gave in to Berlin's demands: a participation deal in addition to the half a million dollars. Berlin's other stipulation, which had also been agreed by Schenck, was that the movie should be in Technicolor. This presented no problem, as all major M-G-M musicals were now made in this process.

The script would be written by Frances Goodrich and Albert Hackett, who agreed with Freed that the plot should be simple and intimate. "The *writing* of the scenes and the way they are played will take it out of the conventional," Freed announced. Berlin settled in on the M-G-M lot, in an office called "The Berlin Room," and worked with the Hacketts on the book and the songs. The story was set in 1912, and as he was one of the few people still in show business who had been part of it at that time, he had several suggestions to make. He enjoyed writing for what he called "the younger generation," and offered nine new songs instead of the contracted eight. When Freed asked for a comedy duet on the lines of "Be a Clown," Berlin came up with a tenth, "Let's Take an Old-Fashioned Walk." Freed did not care for it, however, so an hour later Berlin handed over "A Couple of Swells," which was precisely the sort of thing Freed had in mind. It went on to become the best known of the "new" songs, though it was not in fact new at all. Berlin had fetched it from his famous trunk, but it made a good story: the song Berlin composed in an hour. As it happened, all seven "new" songs which made it to the final print came from Berlin's bottom drawer.

"In my opinion the one person responsible for the whole musical context of the picture was Roger Edens," said Berlin. "Listen, you can't say enough about Edens where I'm concerned." It was Edens who chose the old songs from Berlin's catalogue of over 800, even digging up the forgotten "Shaking the Blues Away" (originally written for *Ziegfeld Follies of 1917*) as a solo for Ann Miller, in the role of the dancing partner who deserts Kelly, thus obliging him to train another, played by Garland. Miller was a substitute for Cyd Charisse, who had strained a tendon and had to be replaced—not an easy job, since the character was unsympathetic, walking out on the man, then trying to get him back after Garland has fallen in love with him. It was a happy choice all round, for offscreen she was being dated by Louis B. Mayer; and her work in this film earned her a contract with the studio, where she was destined to make several more films for Freed. Berlin, who originally opposed the casting—Miller's career had been spent in B musicals at RKO and Columbia—was so pleased with her work in the film that he toyed with the idea of writing a Broadway show specially for her.

There were two other major changes on the film. Minnelli was on the point of casting the supporting roles when Freed called him into his office. He looked grim and uneasy. "Vincente," he began, "I don't know how to tell you this." Minnelli thought that the front office had decided to abandon production, but instead Freed informed him that Garland's psychiatrist, Dr. Kupper, thought it would be "better all round" if Minnelli did not direct the film: "He feels Judy doesn't really want you as the director," Freed explained, "that you symbolize all her troubles with the studio." Minnelli was stunned. He had no option but to agree, but he felt hurt and frustrated: "Why hadn't Judy told me directly? Why did it have to go through two other people? Weren't married couples supposed to openly discuss such things with each other?" And why hadn't Freed, who was not normally sensitive, insisted that Garland tell him herself?

Minnelli went home immediately, where he was greeted by his wife at the front door with a kiss. "Hello, sweetheart," he said. The matter was not discussed, but conversation during the evening meal was "unduly formal and stilted." After dinner, he read some scripts while Garland read a book.

Freed replaced Minnelli with Charles Walters, who had graduated to full-scale directing that year with a remake of *Good News*, starring June Allyson and Peter Lawford. When, after hearing of the assignment, Walters first approached Garland, she was rehearsing "A Couple of Swells" with Kelly. "Look sweetie," she greeted him, "I'm no June Allyson, you know. Don't get cute with me. None of that batting-the-eyelids bit, or the fluffing of the hair routine for me, buddy! I'm Judy Garland and just you watch it!" As he said: "Judy loved to growl, loved to *pretend*." Her attitude to Berlin was similar. Although she revered him as much as she did Cole Porter, she recognized that his style was much less sophisticated than Porter's, and she was happy with that. When, in rehearsal, he offered some advice on her interpretation of one of his songs, she backed him against a wall and waved a forefinger at him: "Listen, buster, you write 'em. *I* sing 'em." Berlin howled with laughter: Judy Garland was back on form.

Kelly had begun work on September 15, rehearsing his first number in the film, "Drum Crazy," with the choreographer, Robert Alton. Four weeks later he fell in his backyard while playing touch football and broke his ankle. With his leg likely to be in plaster for two months, the only possible solution seemed to be to postpone the picture. However, when he told the studio what had happened, he suggested that Fred Astaire could replace him. He was a young man in a hurry, and although *Easter Parade* was a plum project, he did not mind losing it if Garland, as seemed likely, was to start playing up again.

Since Garland was clearly in what Minnelli called "one of her up periods," Freed was reluctant to consider any postponement. His long-held dream of teaming Garland with Astaire now seemed possible, and Berlin, who had already worked with Astaire on five pictures, was enthusiastic. Astaire was contacted on his ranch in San Diego County by a vice-president of the company, L. K. Sidney, who asked him if he cared to come "home" again. Once on the set, Astaire was to describe Garland as "the greatest artist who ever lived and probably ever will live," but he refused to commit himself at this stage until he had spoken to Kelly. What he said to him was: "Why don't you wait until your ankle mends. I really don't want to take this away from you." This was less than honest. He was not happy in retirement and had tentatively returned to entertaining by doing some broadcasting, as Freed well knew. Astaire was aware that Kelly's voice had as narrow a range as his own, so he was not afraid of the songs; but he was not certain that the dances, choreographed to Kelly's more athletic style, would be suitable. When assured that they could be modified if necessary, he agreed to do the film. "But if you look very closely," said Walters of the result, "you'll see that the numbers don't really fit Fred." He made one exception: "How good he was with Judy in 'A Couple of Swells.' Garland and Astaire as a couple of deadbeats, for God's sake! All I had to do was stand back and let it happen."

Garland was in awe of Astaire, whom she knew to be a perfectionist. This might have worried her more had *Easter Parade* been a project like *The Pirate*, but as it was, she jumped at the chance of working with him. "With Fred," Walters said, "you always have to settle a little short. He's so self-conscious—can't stand the sound of his own voice, did you know that? Worry, worry, worry about everything. A real old maid. A charmer but a worrier." One of his worries was about working with Garland, news of whose foibles had even reached San Diego County. However, contrary to the press releases, he had not had easy relationships with any of his leading ladies, too many of whom had not been professionally trained as dancers. "It was a twenty-five-year war," said Hermes Pan, who had choreographed his films at RKO. Nevertheless, his numbers with Garland, Astaire wrote in his memoir: "remain with me as high spots of enjoyment in my career. Judy's uncanny knowledge of show business impressed me more than ever as I worked with her. She was, of course, wonderful in the picture."

Astaire's autobiography is too determinedly nice about everyone to be altogether reliable, but Minnelli recorded that Astaire was genuinely impressed by his co-star: "Judy's really got it. I go through all these very intricate dance steps. She asks me to go through them again. That's all the instruction she needs, she picks it all up so quickly."

Among those less happy about the new co-starring team was Sidney Sheldon, who had been brought in to lighten the screenplay, which Walters had thought was terrible. The Hacketts denied that much of Sheldon's material ended up in the finished film, for which he received equal credit, and observed defensively that they had had their work cut out trying to devise ways of fitting seventeen songs into the plot. Sheldon—who later became a best-selling novelist—had just won an Oscar for his original screenplay for *The Bachelor and the Bobby-Soxer* at RKO, and he was working for Freed on a musical adaptation of *Pride and Prejudice*. When he was told that Astaire had replaced Kelly, he couldn't imagine Astaire saying lines specifically written for Kelly. He was even more concerned that, at forty-eight, Astaire was old enough to be Garland's father: "Fred's so much older that you could never get an audience rooting for him." Freed refused to listen, and Sheldon later agreed that he was right.

It was a happy set, because Astaire and Garland struck sparks even when not before the camera. They joked a lot and shared reminiscences of their childhoods in show business, and when Garland's turned to her litany of complaints about her mother and Mayer, Astaire paid her a compliment or kidded her into a more relaxed, confident mood. Because of his nature and his love of hard work, he managed to ignore her occasional lateness, or make light of it. He even quelled her chief doubt about the enterprise—that, as of old, she has to be a shy wallflower whose charm and beauty is not recognized until the last reel. In one scene Astaire complains that she is not the sort to turn men's heads, a theory she puts to the test as they walk along a street, she a little ahead of him. She smiles winningly at the men she passes, but they ignore her. After a while, Astaire notices that the men are indeed paying attention, happily grinning at Garland: he cannot see (as the audience can) that the reason for this is that Garland is pulling faces.

To give her part a lift, Edens seized upon one song of Berlin's which would show her more sophisticated style. For "Mister Monotony," Garland was filmed wearing an outfit she was to make famous when she wore it again two years later, to sing "Get Happy" in *Summer Stock*. It emphasized her currently svelte figure, consisting of an evening jacket worn over a pair of black tights, with her hair scraped up under a fedora. The number was eventually cut, partly because it proved *too* sophisticated, consisting of some louche *double-entendres*. The footage still exists to prove that the number was unsuitable for the character she played but that she could handle a comic lyric with enormous panache.

Freed's dream was wonderfully realized, in large measure to Sheldon's complete rewrite of the script. The whole show is Garland and Astaire together, as Freed and Walters understood. She was the best girl who ever worked in screen musicals, he the best fellow who ever danced on the screen: two nonpareils. When his dancing partner, played by Ann Miller, leaves him, he says he will pick a girl from the chorus. He finds Garland dancing in an Italian restaurant, where she is getting only fifteen bucks a week. He leaves before hearing her sing "I Wish I Were Back in Michigan," a plaintive ballad which she was born to sing, as Edens knew when he plucked it from the Berlin trunk. Consequently, Astaire is unaware of her talent as he tries to make her over as a dancer. They make a disastrous debut, in which the feathers in her dress flutter off—a deliberate reference to the Astaire–Rogers "Cheek to Cheek" dance in *Top Hat*. When Astaire realizes that he was wrong to insist on Garland merely being a carbon copy of Miller, they move into a different style of performing. The resulting number, a montage of "I Love a Piano," "Snooky Ookums," "Ragtime Violin" and "When the Midnight Choochoo Leaves for Alabam" is an invigorating a sequence as was ever put on film. As Yip Harburg remarked: "When anybody [else] dances with Fred Astaire, you don't see anybody but Fred. But when Judy danced with him, you looked at her."

Astaire was a challenge to her, however, and in the film she seems confident only in the dance numbers, especially in "A Couple of Swells," in which each exuberantly defers to the other's comic gifts. When acting, her nervous intensity is only too apparent. She has a scene in a restaurant with Peter Lawford, in which she explains that she cannot return his love because she is in love with Astaire, and if you watch her hands you see a tense actress. The lips curl up in a beguiling smile, but there is no joy in her eyes.

According to Minnelli, Garland was plagued by illness during the making of the film: "Most of the time she delivered for the studio, but at immense personal toll." He noticed that her weight fluctuated, and concluded that she was taking tablets to keep it down. He hesitated to mention the matter, fearful that a furious outburst would result. But when the news was about that M-G-M had a hit on its hands, Garland relaxed and the differences in the Minnelli ménage seemed to have been patched up. She was enjoying Liza more than ever and the Minnellis socialized with other married couples such as Lauren Bacall and Humphrey Bogart, Bill Spier and Kay Thompson and Sylvia and Carleton Alsop. When Alsop once asked Garland what she wanted as a birthday present, she replied that she had never met Ronald Colman. Since Colman was equally keen to meet Garland, with his customary sense of humor, he agreed to a novel introduction. The Alsops carried him in, wrapped in cellophane tied with a ribbon and sporting a large "Happy Birthday" tag.

In spite of such good-humored larks, Garland was once again heading for trouble, and it was at this time she began to turn to Alsop for advice. As the husband of a wealthy star, Alsop had no need to earn his living, and appeared to be always available when Garland needed him. An urbane man, he could, nevertheless, swear like a truck driver, especially at Garland. He amused her and, unlike Minnelli, he could handle her; Alsop roared, cutting her down to size and reminding her of her obligations to the studio—much as Edens did, but with brutal bluntness, as opposed to Edens's whiplash sarcasm. Perhaps significantly, she called him "Pa," and he was at her beck and call as she began to doubt, after all, her fitness to begin work so quickly.

The studio had promised Garland a long rest after *Easter Parade* but changed its collective mind because everyone was excited by the follow-up project to pair Garland and Astaire again, and as soon as possible, in *The Barkleys of Broadway*. Freed had commissioned an original screenplay from Betty Comden and Adolph Green (co-authors of *On the Town*, produced on Broadway in 1944), whom he brought to the studio initially to write the screenplay of *Good News*. This crafty couple based their story on an incident in Astaire's own life when his partnership with Ginger Rogers ended because she wanted to concentrate on dramatic roles. Comden and Green, who had themselves been performers, resorted to their old skills when they read the script to all concerned. It was agreed that if Astaire and Garland were only half as good, they would romp home. The score was being written by Harry Warren and Garland's friend, Ira Gershwin, and included "My One and Only Highland Fling," a comic duet to rival "A Couple of Swells." As plans were proceeding, *Easter Parade* was previewed at Westwood Village Theatre to a reception which presaged another success for the Freed unit.

When pre-production work on *The Barkleys of Broadway* gained momentum, and Garland became increasingly involved, she was back on pills, initially to increase her weight, and then to reduce it. She and Minnelli were constantly getting on each other's nerves. And, however frequently they told themselves, and others, that they would stay together for Liza's sake, divorce began to seem increasingly inevitable. Added to their emotional embroilment, their financial affairs were in a mess. It was then that Garland called on Carleton Alsop to disentangle their complicated arrangements. In time he learned that the studio was withholding $100,000 of Garland's salary, half of which was compensation for her absences during the making of *The Pirate*, the rest for the already incurred pre-production expenses on *The Barkleys of Broadway* (though these were to show up on the books at only $27,077). Alsop put his own producing plans aside to argue her case with Mayer, and did so without charging any fee. Garland, as usual, did not offer to pay. Alsop told Mayer that the studio had no legal grounds for withholding the money, and that he intended to go to law to establish this. After some weeks Mayer's response was to say that if Alsop could get Garland to sing one song in *Words and Music*, he would happily pay her $50,000. This film, which was already in mid-production, was an attempt to do for Rodgers and Hart what *Till the Clouds Roll By* did for Jerome Kern: that is, to tell a totally fictitious biographical story (Rodgers and the Hart estate had script approval), studded with some of their most brilliant songs. Tom Drake had been cast as Richard Rodgers, despite the fact that his acting had become anodyne since his charming performance in *Meet Me in St. Louis*. Mickey Rooney was chosen to play Lorenz Hart on the grounds that both were short and ebullient by nature—but there, in that miracle of miscasting the resemblance ended. Rooney had sung "Manhattan" in the "plot" section of the film, and Betty Garret had sung "It Never Entered My Mind," which, alas, did not make it to the final print. In guest spots, singing other Rodgers and Hart numbers, were Lena Horne, June Allyson, Ann Sothern, Mel Tormé and Perry Como (who killed a chance of a film career by swearing at Mayer before the assembled cast and crew).

Mayer's offer was generous, but there was no doubt that Judy Garland's name on the marquee would increase the value of the picture. Rooney's box-office standing had decreased to the point of near liability, and he could not have carried *Words and Music* without the help of all the other starry names. His contract was amended at this time, and although technically still an M-G-M star, this was to be his last film for the company in that capacity. Nevertheless, Mayer knew that an on-screen reunion with Garland after a gap of five years smacked of the showmanship for which M-G-M was famous.

When Alsop told Garland of Mayer's offer she agreed to do it. "Get me up, Pa," she said. "And so," Alsop recalled, "we took the glucose needle out of that thin little girl."

The song that Edens chose for her and Rooney to sing was "I Wish I Were in Love Again," an acidly sarcastic ditty which Garland had recorded as a solo in her last session for Decca. It had been written for *Babes in Arms*, but had not made it to the film version, as it was decided that Garland and Rooney were too young then to be convincing in it. Garland had no difficulties with the pre-recording, but it took her two attempts at arriving on the set before she was able to perform and do a few modest dance steps. In her scene in the film she plays herself. The setting is a Hollywood party at which Rooney (as Hart) yells across to her: "Hiya Judy." "Hi, Larry," she responds, and he takes her hand as they mount the podium to sing "I Wish I Were in Love Again" with the orchestra. She was photographed with

Freed, his arm protectively around her, then returned to the Alsops' house in a state of collapse. A few days earlier, she had officially notified the studio that Alsop was now her agent.

Meanwhile, as the first days of rehearsal on *The Barkleys of Broadway*, in early June, were fast approaching, Howard Strickling, Metro's head of publicity, was getting alarmed over Garland's frequently erratic behavior. He remembered that Adela Rogers St. John had once worked for Harry J. Anslinger, head of the Federal Bureau of Narcotics. He asked her to make an informal approach to Anslinger, to see whether anyone on his staff could offer advice. Anslinger himself talked to Garland and learned that above and beyond the medication prescribed by her doctors, she was getting clandestine supplies of pills containing morphine. This became very much a matter for the Bureau, but, before he acted against the suppliers, he conferred with Strickling, whose prime concern was to keep Garland's name well away from any action Anslinger might take. Anslinger said that this did not present any difficulties, but he advised that Garland needed a year's rest in which to recover from her addiction. Strickling had other priorities. He explained that he had put the matter to Mayer who responded, "We have fourteen million dollars tied up in her."

Anslinger's advice was rejected and Garland began to work. She rehearsed on *The Barkleys of Broadway* for the first two weeks of June without showing any signs of fatigue or nerves, but missed one day after losing a night's sleep because of a migraine. She turned up on the following day for wardrobe fittings, and then failed to show on July 7, and the next day and the next. On July 12, Freed telephoned her doctor, who told him that he had given her medication to help her sleep. When he asked whether she was well enough to start work he was told that "it would be a risky procedure." Garland's doctor said that she possibly could work four or five days, always under medication, and possibly blow up for a period and then work again for a few days. He was of the opinion that if she didn't have to work for a while it might not be too difficult to make a complete cure, but that her knowledge of having to report every morning would cause such a mental disturbance within her that the results would be in jeopardy. Freed could not afford a repetition of *The Pirate*—as much for Garland's sake as the studio's. He decided to replace her.

The obvious choice was Ginger Rogers. Astaire, who had welcomed the break with her in 1939, could see the commercial sense of this. So could Rogers, who had recently been finding offers somewhat thin on the ground. Given the urgency of the situation, her agent was able to negotiate a salary of $12,500 a week, which was more than twice what Garland had been paid. There was no doubt, however, that a reunion of Astaire and Rogers would be a second consecutive success for him and the studio. (As indeed it was, despite Rogers's rather grand performance and the fact that four songs had to be dropped because she could not sing them.)

Easter Parade was released on July 16 and had a generally enthusiastic reception, although Kate Cameron of the *New York Daily News*, one of the few critics who noticed Garland's tenseness, commented: "Judy, wan and frail, needs a little more flesh on her bones to give her more verve and bring her up to her old standard as an entertainer." The film had come in under budget by $191,280—it had actually cost $2,503,654 and in its first release grossed over $6,803,000—helped by generally fine reviews, though James Agee thought that "Fred Astaire, Judy Garland, Ann Miller, and several of Irving Berlin's old songs ought to add up to something better than this." As Garland read such reviews and the reports in the trade papers she discovered, to her dismay, that she was, nevertheless dispensible. She neither liked nor understood this, particularly at a time when the world was discovering that she and Astaire were a potent partnership. She was being punished; she had been unceremoniously ditched, and she would have been less bitter had she been told in person rather than by telephone. Yet both Mayer and Freed had visited her at home, sympathetic to her pleas of ill-health but quite firm that there were to be no more last chances on this particular film.

On July 18, she had received, via her agent, a long letter from M-G-M officially suspending her. It reminded her of the terms of her contract and referred to her doctor's conversation with Freed (though Freed was not mentioned by name).

> You will understand that in these circumstances we would not be legally or morally justified in assuming the risks inherent in the situation . . . We hope you will take advantage of the opportunity thus afforded to restore your condition to the point which will enable you safely and with reasonable assurances of continuity to render your required services. In that connection we would appreciate being kept advised of your progress in order that we may make appropriate plans for you when you are returned to health . . .

This was not the kindest letter to send to someone who was ill, and it merely confirmed her belief that the studio thought of her as little more than a highly profitable workhorse.

When she first received the news that she was being dropped from the film, Minnelli stayed at home in a vain attempt to comfort her. After she had recovered from the initial shock, she began to rave, no longer bothering to maintain the façade of a happy marriage. She lashed out at whoever was nearest—always excepting Liza. She felt betrayed by all those avuncular M-G-M executives, whose concern, as she had long suspected, had only been a means of getting the most out of her. She planned revenge—vindictively, irrationally and completely immune to reason.

She spent most of her time in bed, but awoke one morning determined that, suspended or not, she would participate in *The Barkleys of Broadway*. She arrived on the set in full makeup and costume. No one from either of those departments had had the forethought to warn anyone on the set, and the cast and crew watched incredulously as Garland went up to Ginger Rogers and gave her a withering look obviously taking in the down on Rogers's cheeks. To make sure Rogers would not forget what she meant Garland sent her a shaving mug. According to Oscar Levant, who was playing the part of a friend of the principals in the film, Garland "was presenting herself and parading around the set having a gala ball. She was very friendly with the operating cameraman, but when she posed herself behind [Levant presumably meant before] the camera it was unnerving. Ginger, a woman not given to quarrels, became overwrought and retired to her dressing room."

The crew were delighted to see Garland and, because she was Judy Garland, no one dared to ask her to leave; but the longer she remained, the less could be accomplished that day. Finally, Charles Walters, as kindly as possible, asked her to go. She refused, so he took her by the arm and led her to the door. As they disappeared together, Garland was still shouting abuse about Rogers.

For some time, unable to cope with the pressures of the studio and a disintegrating marriage, Garland had resorted to staying with the Alsops, seeking comfort from Sylvia, who herself had known the pressures of stardom and who was therefore well able to offer advice about Garland's particular problems. As was Carleton, whom she asked to negotiate with the studio, since her agent, baffled and frustrated, had given up. Alsop was virtually the one rock which stood between her and insolvency—and probably insanity. She turned her anger inward and, as Minnelli put it, it was a rage that threatened to consume her.

She told Minnelli that she had grown to loathe the house that they shared, which was understandable, because she had often seemed an intruder. Her latest psychiatrist had advised her that she needed more space, so that they were not always under each other's feet, and she took a year's lease on another, much larger, house at 10,000 Sunset boulevard. she later claimed that she was alone throughout this period, except for the Alsops, but Minnelli came and went according to her whim. He was at a loss to know what to do, but was too kind to desert her. Ethel was told to keep away in no uncertain terms.

The studio had offered Minnelli no new assignment since *The Pirate*. M-G-M blamed him for the ruination of Garland, its gilt-edged asset. She was already difficult before their ill-advised marriage, and although, for a while, it seemed as though he could handle her, she was now at the point where she could hardly function at all. Freed nodded distantly to Minnelli when they met, unable to show enthusiasm for any of his projects. In an industry given to the success of the moment, the triumph of *Meet Me in St. Louis* was four years in the past, *The Clock* just a little less. Whatever the virtues of Minnelli's films since then, they had not left Loew's stockholders crying for more.

Minnelli did not force the issue. In an effort to maintain his emotional balance, he read through piles of scripts and accepted the chore of shooting any test going. As he listened to his wife's often incoherent ramblings or faced the full force of her temper, he tried to remember the Judy Garland he had first known. He felt that if he could restore her to what she had been, he was ready to sacrifice his career. But his own self-confidence was failing rapidly.

Garland did not miss a chance to tell anyone who would listen that her marriage was over, and that she had never loved Minnelli in the first place. Once too often, she asked Lee Gershwin why she had ever let her marry him. Lee always pointed out that it had been her own decision, without needing to add the obvious point that Garland rarely listened to advice and was in the habit of getting what she wanted. On this occasion, however, she pointed to Liza, who was playing on the lawn, and said: "If you hadn't married Vincente you wouldn't have had Liza."

By September, after consultations with her doctors, she informed M-G-M that she was ready to return to work. Her self-confidence had been restored due in no small measure to her contribution to *Words and Music* and that she was contracted to a couple of radio broadcasts with Al Jolson and Bing Crosby—acknowledged as the foremost interpreters of popular song in America.

Meanwhile the sneak previews of *Words and Music* confirmed

Mayer's acumen in reuniting Garland and Rooney. He seized upon Garland's announcement and, through Alsop, offered her another $50,000 to perform another song in the film. "You know it looks pretty silly with a star of Judy's magnitude to do a number as only she can and to go off to such applause—and refuse to do an encore," he said. "We have got to have her do an encore." (It would also give M-G-M Records the opportunity to issue a 78 rpm disc with Garland on both sides.) This was exactly what she needed to hear. Edens chose another song from *Babes in Arms*, "Johnny One-Note," which she renders somewhat frenetically, and which caused some continuity problems. Since the first song had been filmed she had (thanks to Sylvia's cooking) put on weight; consequently, she is wearing a slightly different dress, cut along similar lines, but without a belt.

Her intention to return to work was well timed, for the studio had a problem. *In the Good Old Summertime* was to be a remake of one of its classiest successes, *The Shop Around the Corner* (1940), and June Allyson, who was set to co-star with Van Johnson, had become pregnant. To have Garland replace her provided a happy solution for everyone, since Johnson was a friend, and the producer was Joe Pasternak. It was thought desirable to keep her away from the Freed unit, whose members still loved her, but who, from experience, were now as wary of her as she of them. The veteran Robert Z. Leonard was director, and the cast included Buster Keaton, Spring Byington and S.Z. "Cuddles" Sakall, who was a friend of Pasternak and a fellow Hungarian. The fact that the project gave Sakall an important supporting role was what had attracted Pasternak to it in the first place.

The original film had been directed by Ernst Lubitsch, the undisputed master of comedy, and had featured Margaret Sullavan and James Stewart as gauche, antipathetic colleagues in a Budapest gift store. Each is unaware that the other is the pen-pal with whom each has been communicating. For the new version, the setting had been transferred to a shop selling sheet music in Chicago at the turn of the century but, apart from the addition of songs and Technicolor, Pasternak was not inclined to make many changes. Although the Hacketts and Ivan Tors wrote the screenplay, the original one by Samson Raphaelson was also credited, indicating that they had made only cosmetic alterations. What did change, however, when Garland took over from Allyson, was the film's score. The music-shop setting would have given Allyson a chance to sing, but, unlike Garland, she was primarily considered a straight actress. A 78 rpm record of two songs by Allyson might be a nice little seller; a Judy Garland album of six songs might just be sensational. Consequently, in addition to the two numbers, "Meet Me Tonight in Dreamland" and "Put Your Arms Around Me, Honey," which had already been set for Allyson, she would sing four more, added by Pasternak in consultation with Roger Edens. These included the charming "Play That Barber Shop Chord" and "I Don't Care," which had always been identified with the Broadway star Eva Tanguay. Garland had sung the latter effectively on the radio two years earlier, and both songs are done arbitrarily as party-pieces at a dinner thrown by the shop's proprietor, played by Sakall. Robert Alton's staging is simple, but does not disguise the fact that they were inserted at a late stage.

A fifth song, "Merry Christmas," is one of the prettiest Garland ever sang. It turns up at the end, but the sixth, "Last Night When We Were Young," got lost along the way. Garland had discovered this song on an old Lawrence Tibbett record, while making *The Wizard of Oz*, and she had purchased it because it was written by Arlen and Harburg. She often described it as her favorite song and it had been scheduled for *In the Good Old Summertime* at her request. As far as movies were concerned, the song was dogged by ill luck. It was dropped from the Tibbett film *Metropolitan*, and it was dropped again from this. Sinatra heard Garland's studio recording of it, and insisted on singing it in *Take Me Out to the Ball Game*, but once again, it failed to make it to the final print.

Apart from producing *Thousands Cheer*, in which she sang one song, Pasternak had not worked with Garland since *Presenting Lily Mars*, and once again he was impressed by her ability to learn quickly. Most stars of musicals took weeks to perfect their routines, but Garland would watch a stand-in go through the number once or twice, then get up and do it herself. A second take was seldom necessary. Nor was it when she was acting: she was able to glance at a script and say the lines without fluffing. She was never completely satisfied when she saw the rushes, Pasternak said, because she was a perfectionist; but she was not the sort who insisted on a re-take.

Like *The Shop Around the Corner*, *In the Good Old Summertime* takes its tone from its heroine, as interest focuses on when or whether she will discover that her beloved pen-pal is the bumptious chief clerk. The role might have been made for her. It gives her a chance to be funny and then wistful, as she dreams of her pen-friend with all the plangency and heartache of which she is capable. It is the sort of true, honest performance expected of her, and she looks healthier and happier here than in either of the films she made on each side of it.

She was in fact comparatively well while making it, and filming finished five days ahead of schedule. "What did you do to Judy?" Mayer asked Pasternak, who replied: "We made her feel needed. We joked with her and kept her happy." He also said: "There was never a word uttered in recrimination when she was late, didn't show up or couldn't go on. Those of us who worked with her knew her magical genius and respected it." He noticed that during the week they spent pre-recording, she always wore the same skirt. When he finally plucked up courage to ask her whether she had any others at home, she replied that work on the first day had gone so well that the skirt was clearly a lucky one. The only thing about the film that worried her was that its budget was lower than those to which she had been accustomed, and she complained about this to Minnelli whenever they were together.

The film was booked into Radio City Music Hall, where it stayed for a happy four weeks, helped by notices such as this, in *The Hollywood Reporter*:

> Great troupers come seldom in a theatrical generation, but when one does arrive, there is no mistaking the special magnetism that is their art. If there ever existed doubts that Judy Garland is one of the great screen personalities of the present celluloid era, the opportunity to alter the impression is offered in *In the Good Old Summertime* . . . it is her show from start to finish as she turns in a performance whose acting elements are no less enchanting than the moments of high excitement she provides with her singing.

12

❖❖❖❖❖❖❖

Fired

AFTER A YEAR of inactivity, during which Freed had no assignment for him, Minnelli received a telephone call in late 1948 from Pandro S. Berman, asking him whether he would be interested in directing *Madame Bovary*. Gustave Flaubert's novel of adultery in provincial France was not exactly a natural subject for Hollywood treatment, but Minnelli was excited by the project, not only because he was well versed in nineteenth-century French literature, but because he thought that Emma Bovary's fantasies were not unlike Judy Garland's, and these were something with which he was still trying to come to terms. Like Emma Bovary, Garland was haunted by fantasies of romantic love which could never be fulfilled, was discontented, and at times suicidal. Minnelli therefore seized upon the idea, delighted at the opportunity of working with such people as Jennifer Jones, Van Heflin, Louis Jourdan and especially James Mason, who had turned down a leading role in order to play Flaubert in the prologue. Filming started at the turn of the year, but Garland took no pleasure in her husband's return to the studio. Her only reaction to his news was predictable: "Here you're working with these great talents. And what am I doing? Still playing the shopgirl on the corner." From that moment, Minnelli did not think it worth making any more efforts to save the marriage.

In the summer of 1948, he had issued a terse statement: "We are happier apart." This had seemed obvious to their friends almost from the very beginning, but for Liza's sake they made several attempts at reconciliation over the next two years. Each was determined not to carry his or her animosity to the studio, partly so as not to provide material for gossip, but chiefly to confound those who had predicted that the marriage would not last. For his part, Minnelli was only too aware that he was seen as the villain of the piece.

In February 1949, shortly before the Minnellis had another public separation, M-G-M observed its silver anniversary with a party to which it invited a thousand of its employees the world over and some fifty of its own stars, as well as any others who happened to be working there at the time. The stars were to pose for a group photograph, like the one taken in 1943 for *Life*, and subsequently published in half the world's other magazines. Garland, conspicuous by her absence on the previous occasion, was aware of the competition offered by the studio's beauties, and dressed simply in a black blouse and a pale, white-based skirt. Katharine Hepburn, dressed as usual in her tailored slacks, was not impressed: "I knew I'd be badly dressed," she commented, "and I knew you'd be badly dressed. The only difference is that you took the time."

In the earlier photograph, Garland would have been in the front row with Hepburn, but postwar M-G-M was more democratic and the stars were seated alphabetically, which put her next to Ava Gardner: and that, said Garland, "was enough to make any girl feel like Primo Carnera." Clark Gable was on the other side of Ava and he leaned across to say: "Goddamn brat. You've ruined every one of my birthdays. They bring you out of the wallpaper to sing that song, and it's a pain in the ass." "Do you know," Garland reflected, "I've only begun to like him today, now that he's leveled with me."

The M-G-M of Garland and Gable—of Mayer and Thalberg—was in fact about to disintegrate, and faster than anyone present could have imagined. The process had begun on June 1, 1948, when Dore Schary arrived to become the new vice-president in charge of production, replacing Mayer, who was said to be considering retirement. In fact, Nicholas Schenck, president of Loew's, was looking back to the heady Thalberg days, especially as the company's only really successful films at present were the musicals produced by Freed, Pasternak and Cummings. If the postwar public, looking for more thoughtful fare, tired of musicals, M-G-M was going to be in trouble. As it was, its profits were seriously down in comparison to the other leading studios.

Schary, who had once been a writer at M-G-M, had initiated some memorable social dramas on becoming head of production at RKO, just a year earlier. In particular, *Crossfire*, a thriller with an anti-racist theme, had been much admired. In the meantime, Howard Hughes had bought that studio, and his tastes were the opposite of Schary's. So Schary was happy to move, especially as Schenck had agreed to his request for a healthy $6,000 a week. Unfortunately, he was linked to some of the Hollywood Unfriendly Ten, including Adrian Scott and Edward Dmytryk, respectively the producer and director of *Crossfire*. It was important to him to be seen as a company man, as fond as anyone of the lavish, often frivolous, films for which M-G-M was famous. He took a particular interest in what Freed was doing, because he was the most successful producer on the lot.

He was less than enchanted with Judy Garland and was well aware of how difficult she could be. On their first meeting, she complained about everything, especially about how hard she was being worked. On another she said "I don't give a shit what they give me," which he thought less than ladylike. Equally unladylike was Garland's involvement with another M-G-M employee, Mario Lanza. Although Lanza had only made two films, neither of which was successful, the second of them had contained a ballad, "Be My Love," which had become a gigantic jukebox favorite. As a result of this, Lanza looked as if he would be the studio's next big star. However, he was not only temperamental, but also a heavy drinker. He had staggered out of his dressing-room one afternoon and encountered an equally intoxicated Garland. They looked at each other, liked what they saw, and left the building to find a chauffeur, who drove them up into the Hollywood Hills, where they enjoyed each other on the back seat of the car. Schary, though long accustomed to the vagaries of movie-star behavior, was not pleased when the incident was reported to him.

In spite of Garland's failed marriage and her unpopularity with Schary, 1949 should have been a triumph for her. *Annie Get Your Gun* had completed its Broadway run of 1,147 performances, and filming could at last begin. Irving Berlin celebrated by writing a plaintive new ballad for Garland, "Let's Go West Again," which, although not outside Merman's range, would have been alien to her temperament. In October 1948, Sidney Sheldon began work on the screenplay, and in December, the studio announced that Liza would be playing Annie's baby sister, an idea which was subsequently abandoned. The story, based somewhat fancifully on historical characters, concerns the relationship between two Wild West show sharpshooters, Annie Oakley and Frank Butler, who start out as rivals but eventually fall in love. The role of Butler was to be played by Howard Keel, a tall, good-looking American, who had impressed British audiences in *Oklahoma!*. He had made one fairly insignificant British film, *The Small Voice* (1948), in which he played a hoodlum, but was virtually an unknown quantity to American audiences, so M-G-M had had to test him for the role. It was clear that he would be a magnificent and masculine Frank Butler, though *Annie Get Your Gun* had always been a woman's show.

Freed had promised Charles Walters that he could direct, provided that he renewed his contract. However, when Walters started to negotiate, he discovered that he was expected to continue on the salary he had been getting when he was only a choreographer. He walked out of the studio, leaving it to his agent to sort matters out. As he observed, "intrigue positively thrived at M-G-M in those days," and by the time the dispute was settled he had heard, from Arthur Akst, Freed's brother-in-law, that Busby Berkeley had been assigned to the picture. Freed told him bluntly that he had lost the picture because he was greedy.

Berkeley was a spectacularly odd choice. After *The Gang's All Here*, which he had made for 20th Century-Fox in 1943, he had again been plagued by personal troubles. He had slashed his throat and wrists in the wake of his beloved mother's death, and had spent some time in the psychiatric ward of Los Angeles General Hospital. He had been absent from movies for five years when Freed hired him to direct *Take Me Out to the Ball Game* (1949), but it was recognized that its creative impetus was due to the staging of the numbers, for which Gene Kelly and Stanley Donen were responsible. Berkeley was the forgotten man of the Hollywood musical, but he nevertheless persuaded Freed that he was the only man on the Metro lot with the breadth of vision to bring Berlin's musical to the screen and be able to control the large number of performers needed to realize the circuses and rodeos. In fact, Robert Alton was to be responsible for the staging and filming of the production numbers, which made the choice of Berkeley even more puzzling, since he was not noted for his handling of actors.

The project was made even more parlous because of Garland herself: she was behaving as badly as she had been during *The Pirate* and the preliminaries to *The Barkleys of Broadway*.

The studio once again, and as a last resort, turned to the medical profession for help. Many discussions had taken place about dropping her, many memos had been sent debating whether she was worth all the trouble and torment. It was decided that there was no longer any point in pretending that she was not a drug addict, and Dr. Fred Pobirs was engaged to cure her dependency by giving her shock treatment in the hospital. This proved effective, but only for a short time. Pobirs had been recommended by Marc Rabwin, who was so worried by her mental state that he had insisted she should have a doctor who lived nearby and could get to her quickly should one of her suicide attempts prove serious.

Freed had difficulty in placating Garland when she heard that Berkeley had replaced Walters, claiming that he had few alternatives. She did not want to be directed by Minnelli. George Sidney, who had made *The Harvey Girls*, had been making mainly straight films ever since. Rouben Mamoulian, considered as innovative as Minnelli, had been responsible for *Summer Holiday* (1948), one of Freed's few flops and so could not be entrusted with this prize property. Garland remembered all too clearly that working with Berkeley meant utter exhaustion and a total dependence on medication just to keep going. She knew about his personal problems and told Freed that she didn't think she and the director were a good combination. Freed insisted that he knew what he was doing.

Most people at the studio thought he was crazy. They knew of Garland's antipathy toward Berkeley and her readiness to retaliate for any real or imagined slights. In recent years, *Easter Parade* and *In the Good Old Summertime* excepted, she had been unable to work well even with people she liked. Even so, most members of the unit preferred her to Berkeley. Shooting was planned in order to keep them as far apart, and for as long, as possible.

Another worry for Garland was Howard Keel. Although she found him affable and unassuming, she was concerned that he would steal the limelight. It was a dilemma not unlike that which faced her on *The Pirate*. She would be carrying the film, one with an almost unprecedented budget of $3,000,000, with a co-star who lacked her popularity but who might well take away the film from her. In this case, she was infinitely happier with the material, but it was broader and bigger than any given her before. She even worried about the songs, each of which had been a triumph for Merman. By the time she came to pre-record them, in the last week of March 1949, she was once again suffering from insomnia, and was taking pills to control both that and her fluctuating weight. Listening to her from the sound booth, Edens and his assistant agreed that her interpretation was "nice," fully realizing that that was not the word they had ever used before to describe Judy Garland's voice.

Her first day on the set was taken up with tests and a rehearsal. She was on time and able to work the whole day, but her attendance thereafter was erratic. Most of Freed's films began in an atmosphere of happy anticipation, but in this case everyone but he knew that it was only a matter of time before star and director clashed. Shooting started on April 4, but she was not required on the first two days. On the second day, however, Keel suffered a serious accident, caused, he said later, by "a madman called Busby Berkeley," who yelled so loudly that the horse Keel was riding stumbled. He fell off, and the horse rolled on him, breaking his ankle. The doctors thought it unlikely that he would be able to walk normally for three months, although in the event he was only absent from the film for six weeks. The consequent rescheduling brought Berkeley and Garland together much sooner than anticipated. Their first scene, inside a Pullman car, was too brief for differences, but their second was an elaborate one in front of a hotel, leading into the song, "Doin' What Comes Naturally." Berkeley's brusque, even brutal, way of giving orders had never sat well with Garland. This time she tolerated it for only minutes before stalking off the set, complaining that she was seriously ill.

It was apparent that she was telling the truth. Not only was she suffering from insomnia, migraine and nausea, but her hair was falling out in clumps. Each day in makeup they gave her a false hairline to disguise this fact. She had a phobia about guns as well as horses. Looking at the daily rushes, she knew the performance she was giving was dreadful, and the misery she consequently suffered she wrapped around her like a cloak. As anxiety and insecurity seized her again, much worse than hitherto, she turned once more to drink and drugs, reassuring herself that she could, with such stimulants, after all, perform. This was true, to some extent, for in the surviving footage of "Doin' What Comes Naturally," she is in sparkling form, singing well and clowning with the children in the scene. In contrast, however, her performance of "I'm an Indian Too" is pitiful. It had been scheduled early in the shoot, when it was thought she would be at her best, but even at this stage, the number proved too much for her. She was required to sing and be funny in the midst of a large chorus of dancers dressed as Red Indians. She appears to be in a trance: her singing is barely competent, and she completely lacks the *joie de vivre* the number demands. Rehearsing it with Alton, she could not stand up and had to be physically supported by his assistant, Alex Romero, who was fortunately appearing in the scene. It was perhaps this day-to-day fluctuation between high achievement and abject failure—characteristic of the behavior of an addict—which prevented anyone from calling a halt. She may be hopeless one day, but could deliver the next. Even so, only in Hollywood at this period would someone unable to stand unsupported be expected to continue working. She spent six grueling days on the number and the result was unusable.

On another occasion, Freed was present when it was obvious that Garland was either too drunk or drugged to perform. When she fell down, Freed lost control and shouted at her in front of the whole cast and crew, something he had never done before. She had finally forfeited his good will, which only served to increase her anxieties. For the first time in her life, she was unable to learn lines.

Her simpler numbers had been saved for later in the shoot, when it was thought she might tire quickly. As it was, she was exhausted already. Working mainly with Alton, she managed to be present, if not always punctual, for most of April. Working with Berkeley, however, led predictably to battles and screaming fits, all of which made her performance deteriorate further.

It was not merely a clash of personalities. She complained that Berkeley was treating the material in a dull theatrical manner, with characters making their entrances and exits as if on a stage. Freed called in Charles Walters to have his opinion about this confirmed. "It was horrible!" said Walters, "Judy had never been worse. She couldn't decide whether she was Mary Martin, Ethel Merman, Martha Raye or herself. She didn't know who the hell she was. 'She's a mess,' I said." Freed concurred, and asked Walters to take over the picture. Walters agreed to do so, adding that his first priority was to confer with Garland. She had already told him, after viewing the rushes: "I think it's too late. This monster [Berkeley] treats me the same as when I was fifteen." Walters spent several hours with her in his office, supposedly for a story conference, but in fact attempting to restore her confidence. "It's too late, Chuck," she sobbed. "I haven't got the energy or the *nerve* anymore." This was all too apparent. "A couple of weeks [actually five days] later she really came apart at the seams," Walters remembered. "It was so sad. She couldn't manage anything, poor thing."

One afternoon, when she was not needed at the studio, she went shopping with Lee Gershwin. She appeared to be in high spirits, joking with a traffic cop who had asked if she would like an escort. Gershwin asked her whether she had any plans for the evening, and Garland replied gaily: "Yeah, I think I'll slash my wrists." Gershwin had no reason to suppose that this was not another joke. The next morning she was alarmed to receive a telephone call from the studio to ask whether Garland was with her: she had not arrived at the studio; nor was she answering calls. A studio representative was dispatched to Garland's home, to find that she had been true to her word. But as on the earlier occasion, the injuries she had inflicted upon herself had not been serious, and she had made sure that she would be found quickly and easily by servants.

On Saturday, May 7, she arrived for work at the studio, but, after a few minutes on the set, retired to her dressing-room, where she sat systematically banging her head against the wall. On Monday she did not show at all. The following day, May 10, she arrived at the studio to find a letter from L. K. Sidney, vice-president of the studio, which began:

Dear Miss Garland:
You must be aware of the fact that your contract with us requires you to be prompt in complying with our instructions and to perform your services conscientiously and to the full extent of your ability and as instructed by us. We desire to call your attention to the fact that on a great many occasions since the commencement of your services in *Annie Get Your Gun*, you were either late in arriving on the set in the morning, late in arriving on the set after lunch, or were otherwise responsible for substantial delays or curtailed production, all without our consent.

The letter concluded with a reminder that the studio had "the right to remove you from *Annie Get Your Gun*, to cast someone else in the role of 'Annie' and to refuse to pay you compensation until the completion of the role by such other person."

Dottie Ponedel was with her when the letter arrived and told her, as kindly as she could, that the studio was within its rights. Garland replied that the studio would not fire her—"Not me!"—but Ponedel tried to persuade her that the best possible response was to report to the set, ready to work. Her efforts were in vain, nor did Garland respond to any other request that she should go back to work.

There are conflicting reports of what exactly happened that day. Walters remembered Garland arriving in his office in tears before receiving the letter. "Chuck," she began, "I'm happy you're on the picture, but I'm afraid it's too late. I don't think I can make it. Buzz [Berkeley] has sliced me to ribbons. I cannot do it." He invited her to lunch with him, but she said that she was going to her dressing-room, just across from his office, for a drink. Minutes later, she called out to him: "Get the ice out! I'll be right over. I'm going to have that fucking drink! You won't believe—" She burst into his office, laughing hysterically: "I'm fired from *Annie!*" She proceeded to get drunk, which, in the circumstances, Walters thought the best solution. "I don't believe it!" she cried. "After the money I made for the sons of bitches! Those bastards! Those lousy bastards! Goddamn them!"

Those lousy bastards included Dore Schary, who knew that the studio had so far spent a million dollars on the film and had only six minutes of worthwhile footage to show for it. He had tried to reason with her, as had Mayer and Freed. Eventually, he had telephoned Nicholas Schenck in New York. "This is a tough one," he said, "but our feeling is to take her out because otherwise you're going to be in a hole—and you won't have a movie." "Do what you have to do," Schenck answered.

Garland was certainly in the studio in the afternoon, in makeup and her Indian costume, when she received a second letter from L.K. Sidney:

Dear Miss Garland
You have refused to comply with our instructions to report on the set of *Annie Get Your Gun* after lunch today and you have already advised that you do not intend to render your services in said photoplay. This is to notify you that for good and sufficient cause . . .

According to Gerold Frank, Lester Peterson, the studio aide who delivered the letter, remembered Garland throwing herself on the floor in anguish, crying "No! No! No!," but another version of the story has her saying to him: "You can't do this to me. With this makeup on, I don't even know what tribe I belong to. What reservation do I go to?"

She later claimed that she tried to get dozens of executives on the telephone in order to discuss the situation, but not one of them was available. She called Carleton Alsop, who arrived with her still in her dressing-room to find "all hell had broken out." Flinging the letter at him, she screamed: "Pa, make those sons of bitches treat me like they do Greer Garson, for God's sake, instead of the little hunchback girl they got from Bones Remer." Sobbing, she went on: "I never lost anybody any money in my life!" Alsop managed to see Mayer, who said that it was out of his hands, pointing out that virtually every executive there had warned Garland of the possibility of this happening.

At some point, Garland decided to go to the set, preceded by Dottie Ponedel, who told the assistant director: "Get them all back. Judy is on her way." But it was too late: everybody had gone. Walter Strohm, the production manager, remembered receiving a message from Garland saying: "I shall never come back—now or ever."

An interoffice memo was circulated on May 11: "For your information, Judy Garland's contract has been suspended as of May 10, 1949. She is not to be called or requested to render services of any kind whatsoever unless the matter is cleared with Mr. Mannix or Mr. Schary." One result of Garland's suspension without salary was that Ethel finally discovered that it was not M-G-M, but Judy herself, who had been paying her fee as "studio consultant" over the years. "Being a proud woman, she must have been furious to discover what the studio felt was her true worth," Minnelli speculated.

Annie continued shooting for another ten days, then production was closed down. The obvious replacement for Garland from the contract list was Betty Garrett, an excellent comedienne and a singer adept at both ballads and comic songs, but her agent failed to come to an agreement with the studio. Eventually, after considering June Allyson, the studio decided to borrow Betty Hutton from Paramount at a cost of $150,000. The two studios agreed on a new starting date, September 30, allowing Hutton a rest after finishing *Let's Dance* with Fred Astaire. Freed advised Walters to take a vacation, and while he did so he read in Hedda Hopper's column that *Annie Get Your Gun* would be directed by George Sidney, whose father, L.K. Sidney, had clinched the deal for him. Another change was necessitated by the death of Frank Morgan, who was to have played Buffalo Bill: Louis Calhern took over the role.

In the event, the film was a triumph for all concerned, taking in over $8 million at the box office. M-G-M was so pleased that it bought another "circus" show, *Billy Rose's Jumbo* as a vehicle for Keel and Hutton, but Hutton effectively finished her movie career when she quarreled with Paramount a while later. Keel said that she was so anxious to make a success of the role of Annie that she had little consideration for her fellow players. The studio, he added, should have waited for Garland: "Letting her go was the only tacky thing I knew M-G-M to do."

Meanwhile, Garland lay sedated at 10,000 Sunset, wanting to be Baby Gumm again, without worries or responsibilities. She yearned for the reassurance of applause from a live audience, a new kind of stimulus. She spoke of making a stage career, but there was no question of her performing again until she was well. In effect, this meant that she had to be cured of her addiction, by finding out the causes behind it. Alsop took on the difficult task of trying to decide what was best for her, consulting with the people most qualified to advise. Among these were Marc Rabwin, Garland's current psychiatrist and L.B. Mayer. Mayer turned again to Dr. Jessie Marmorston, who recommended that the ailing star be sent to the Peter Bent Brigham Hospital in Boston, which was noted for its close association with Harvard Medical School.

There was one major obstacle to this plan: Garland did not have the money to pay for treatment. She always claimed that Ethel had invested her money unwisely, but she had in fact handled her daughter's affairs capably until Garland herself took them over. Garland never understood the value of money any more than she understood the value of time. She was obliged to petition Mayer to see whether the studio would pay her hospital bills, which it agreed to do, to the tune of $40,000. After she had left the studio, M-G-M made her a personal loan of $9,000, with the proviso that this should be repaid at such time as she returned to work. That time would be when her consultant, Dr. Augustus Rose, "reasonably believed" that she was fit to do so.

She arrived at the hospital on May 29, accompanied by Alsop, who told the press that she was exhausted and needed only "to get away from Hollywood for a while." He advised Rose that Garland had despaired of being cured by psychiatric means, so it would help her if he described himself as a neurologist. Alsop stayed at the Ritz-Carlton, and Garland was able to visit him there on her twenty-seventh birthday. There was a brief reunion with Liza for the day, accompanied by her governess. A week after her arrival, Garland was strong enough to give a press conference for local journalists.

The process of weaning Garland off drugs was an unpleasant one.

Alsop would visit her sometimes and find her screaming as she struggled with withdrawal symptoms. He responded with therapeutic callousness, realizing that unless she was cured, she would have no career and no income: "If you need pills, this hospital if full of them. But if you can get over it, fine. If you can't, I'm going out to buy Christmas carols. We'd better start rehearsing now." Dr. Rose proved less brutal when summoned in the middle of the night because the nurses could not stop his patient yelling. He managed to calm her by persuading her to tell him what had brought on the attack.

She explained that the hospital had refused her medication because she had already had too much: "These migraine headaches were from malnutrition, benzedrine and sleeping tablets, from trying to keep up a schedule that was impossible for me." She gradually responded to three good meals a day and a regime which meant that she was in bed by nine in the evening, although she still suffered from insomnia. She was visited by Mayer, Freed and Minnelli, while Frank Sinatra telephoned daily and was among the many people who sent gifts. She left the hospital to spend the July 4 holiday with Alsop's wife, Sylvia Sidney, who was appearing in summer stock on Cape Cod. Although Sidney did not mention it, she had come to believe that Garland was having an affair with her husband.

Garland also went with the Alsops to visit Hugh Martin, who was playing the piano for a small theater company in Provincetown. The cast was astonished to see her with him, and, after a meal of hot dogs in the garden, he asked whether she might like to sing to them, offering to accompany her. "Pa, do you think I've any voice left?" she asked. Alsop replied: "Judy, you'd have a voice left unless they buried you face down and then you'd scratch yourself out and belt the shit out of—." That was all she needed to hear. She sang for over an hour. "I hadn't sung in four months," she remembered, "and it was the first time in years that I really felt good." She discovered an even more powerful voice that night—and, she added: "I've had that voice ever since."

The Alsops also took her to visit friends they had in the Boston area, and eventually the hospital decided she could stay out on the Cape. She sent for Liza and they took a cabin on the coast. She swam and sunbathed, and enjoyed the experience. She liked the Cape, with its sand dunes, the clusters of small villages, the bracing Atlantic breezes and the vaulting sky. Once again, away from Hollywood, Judy Garland became a different person.

Her health continued to improve after she returned to the hospital, and Rose, realizing that she needed her confidence restored, agreed to her being moved to a hotel. Sightseeing in Boston, or even her daily visits to Rose, meant that fans were able to approach her, which pleased her. Throughout her life, she was always kind and grateful to her fans—far more so than to her close friends. One day, when a group of them gathered below Dr. Rose's window, she opened it and began to sing to them. Rose felt that this was a deliberate attempt to show off for his benefit, and he told her that if she confused admiration with help she was doing herself no good at all.

In spite of her apparent recovery, he was, in fact, gravely worried about her. He suspected that her troubles might be due to a tumor on the brain, and so he sent her for tests at the neighboring Children's Hospital, which had the necessary equipment. Many of the patients were retarded and in another part of the hospital were children with rheumatoid defects. When Alsop joined her, he suggested that she visit the wards, because there was a great deal of excitement about her presence on the premises. She agreed, unwillingly, not knowing what to expect, but she found herself overwhelmed by their greeting. She went from bed to bed, talking to each child, holding their hands and singing a little. She had never had a more appreciative audience, and she insisted on returning to the wards every day until she left. She was even prepared to miss her train on the last day when she found that the one child who had withheld any response had finally melted. "I guess it was one of the great moments in my life when that child finally spoke like that," she said. "I felt I had . . ."—she paused and continued: "I just didn't give a damn how many pictures I'd been fired from, or how much humiliation . . . I had done a human being some good! I felt right back on top of the world."

Since she loved to elaborate on the truth, this story may not be true in detail. However, while it is not necessary to believe that one reserved child waited until the last minute to open out to her, there is no doubt that sharing the problems of others was of more therapeutic value than any psychiatric sessions. Many people have testified to her kindness to those less fortunate than herself. She was certainly given to exaggerating her emotions, like most movie stars, but she spoke from the heart when she said: "I loved feeling I could help somebody else for a change." Over the next few years, she was often to throw her garden open for any cause to benefit deprived or sick children, generously offering hospitality and a song or two. A particular favorite was the Therapeutic Education and Child Health (TEACH) Foundation.

When she left the hospital, she lived once again with Minnelli, largely for the sake of Liza. She seemed determined to start afresh. When he had visited her in the hospital, Mayer had been moved to tears by her apologies for past transgressions and her assurances about her future conduct. He told her that he loved her "like a father," and told her that she could always turn to him when things went wrong. They soon did, as became clear when she took to calling him at four in the morning. Her nighttime pleas for help were to become a lifetime habit, but she quickly learned who would help and who would not. Mayer told her not to bother him, as did Roger Edens; but Marc Rabwin was always available for her, day or night, often leaving his bed in order to drive over and see that she was all right. This habit of Garland's was to become so ingrained that she picked up the telephone whenever she was lonely, and since she had no concept of time, it never occurred to her that those at the other end of the line might be asleep. Some of those she called remembered that she only wanted to laugh and joke, while others found that she wanted to whine and bask in self-pity, or attempt to elicit sympathy for her various problems.

In all, she had spent eleven weeks in Boston, but her doctors were sure that this was not enough. As far as they were concerned, her return to Los Angeles should be only temporary. Dore Schary had told her before she left that she could take a year off, if she needed to, but when Freed visited her, he found her so much like her old self that he told her that M-G-M had a picture for her. This was not, as she might have expected, the long-delayed *Show Boat*, on which little progress had been made. Although the choice of the other leads varied with each announcement, Garland was always scheduled to play Julie. It was not the biggest part in the film, but she would be singing two of the greatest torch songs ever written, "Bill," which she had sung all those years ago as Baby Gumm, and "Can't Help Lovin' Dat Man." However, Freed had no intention of starting the project until he was convinced that she was fully recovered. She still looked drawn, and a warning sign that she had not yet regained her equilibrium occurred when she visited the set of *Annie Get Your Gun* and responded to Betty Hutton's cheery greeting by calling her a "goddamn son of a bitch."

What Freed had in mind for her was *Summer Stock*, which would be produced by Joe Pasternak. Garland might have been allowed a longer rest had it not been for the extraordinary rivalry between the three producers of musicals at M-G-M. This arose less from personal animosity than from the tight-knit loyalty of personnel in each unit. The evident superiority of Freed's films did not make the situation any easier. As far as talent was concerned, his unit had the very best, and its plum was Judy Garland. Experience had shown, however, that she could be trouble. Pasternak had been delighted to have her for *In the Good Old Summertime*, one of his most successful films, which had grossed $3,400,000, more than twice its cost. He had told her: "If you're half-dead, you're still better than anyone else. Any time Arthur will let you go, I'll use you in anything, if you'll just work for us."

Pasternak was not noted for his originality. Indeed, he believed in giving audiences what they had liked in the past. After inviting Harry Warren to compose the score, he had come up with a screenplay for a film which would reunite Judy Garland with Mickey Rooney—and, once again they would be putting on a show.

Nothing had happened since his departure from the studio to restore Rooney to public favor, and no one at M-G-M, apart from Pasternak, was keen to have him back. The obvious co-star for Garland was Gene Kelly, but after the sensational success of *On the Town*, the last subject to interest him was a tale about putting on a show in a barn. He eventually agreed to do *Summer Stock*, however, as a personal favor to Garland, as did Charles Walters, who was to direct.

While at the clinic, Garland had learned to eat heartily once more and as a consequence had put on a lot of weight, as she discovered during costume tests. "We tried to make her look as thin as possible," said Walter Plunkett, who designed the costumes, "but we weren't miracle workers." Aware of this, Garland began to take pills to help her reduce and immediately began coming in late or not at all.

After shooting started, everyone realized that it had clearly been a mistake for Garland to return to work so soon, but Mayer insisted that she was only happy when she was working, and that everybody had to make the best of a bad job. Mayer himself telephoned Dr. Rose in Boston and told him that the studio would pay his fees and expenses if he would only help to get her through the picture. Rose replied that she should not be doing it in the first place, but Mayer, who was accustomed to getting his own way, talked the doctor into accepting his offer.

When Rose arrived in Los Angeles, he went to confer with Garland, and also spoke to Mayer, Benjamin Thau, Walters and Kelly. Kelly told him that he was only doing the film because Garland had helped him on his first picture and he thought that now he could help her. It was not long after shooting began in November, however, that he found himself unequal to the task. Garland often came in late, the result either of a sleepless night, or of too many barbiturates taken to help her sleep. Since no one would prescribe these pills, Garland had to get them by other means, some of them extremely elaborate and clandestine. When she had begged Lee Gershwin for just one Seconal to help her get off to sleep, Gershwin was so distressed by her friend's anguish that she obliged, thinking that just one could do no harm. The plan was that Gershwin would leave the pill in her own mailbox, from which it would be collected by Garland or some-one else on her behalf. It was only later that Gershwin realized that Garland had made the same arrangement with other friends. Ann Straus, who ran the studio Gallery, had some Dexamyl, which had been prescribed for her mother. Discovering this, Garland stole some of the pills from Straus's handbag. When Straus realized that Garland was that desperate, she took pity on her. She also began to receive frantic telephone calls, and she too never knew who picked up the tablets.

In order to accommodate Garland, the shooting of *Summer Stock* was rescheduled to start at one in the afternoon and finish at seven. There were times when she would not leave her dressing-room except to assure Kelly that she had only turned up in the first place out of gratitude to him for accepting a project which she knew did not interest him. He gave her every encouragement: "I'll do anything for this girl," he told Pasternak. "If I have to come here and wait for a year I'd do it for her. That's the way I feel about her." And wait he did. "She was paranoid about her inability to work," said Walter Plunkett, "and felt that she was letting down Gene and Chuck Walters terribly. And the more she tried to pull herself together, the more hysterical she became. It was heartbreaking to see. She developed a hatred for herself and the way she looked which was quite alarming." However, he did not repeat what he had confided to a colleague: that she would insist that he and he alone would have to bathe her. She had also begun hallucinating, at which times she imagined everyone on the picture standing before her pointing accusingly at her.

As shooting dragged on, with no one on the lot believing that the film would ever be finished, there were cast parties for those dancers about to leave for other commitments. Garland always managed to show up for these. "The same woman who the day before was incapable of uttering a sound, would sing her heart out," Kelly remembered.

Each time Judy was the star turn. She'd perform for hours and the kids just loved and adored her. Everybody did. As long as the cameras weren't turning, she was fine . . . The thing about Judy was that she only worked when she thought she was going to be good. If she felt that she wasn't up to giving her best, she didn't appear on the set. It was as simple as that. Marilyn Monroe was the same.

Walters also observed that, as on *Annie Get Your Gun*, Garland's behavior was alarmingly erratic:

God, she was a problem on that picture—her nerves were shot, there was the weight thing, everything. We never knew what time she'd come in—or whether she was prepared for anything when she did. She'd come storming in and say "Look, buddy, if you expect any acting out of me, forget it!" And I had to sort of josh her out of it, pretend that I didn't care whether she worked or not . . .

There's a number in that film, "Friendly Star," which I think is one of the best things she ever did. I remember, at one point, I was on a boom just above her head, and we were moving in for a giant close-up. Judy looked up with those great liquid eyes of hers and it was the most fantastic shot in the world. "Cut!" I yelled. "Will someone please hand me a towel. I've just come!" Now that might be thought indelicate, but Judy loved that sort of foolishness. It really turned her on. "C'mon, what's next?" she'd ask. You always had to keep her spirits high. Once you had her in the mood for work you had to keep her there. Not that it was always easy. What was that number on the tractor? Oh, "Howdy Neighbor!" The days we spent on that. I can see her on that damn thing now mumbling. "What am I doing here? Please send for Vincente to take me home."

Acting as both agent and friend, Carleton Alsop tried to take matters in hand, berating both M-G-M and its wayward star:

I used to call the studio and tell them that they were treating her like a Belgian dray horse and she was a delicate, fragile woman and too recently out of hospital and as a result of their treatment she would be unable to work. And she'd say "That's right, you really told those so-and-so's." And I said, "Just wait a minute, what I told them is one thing, but don't blame the studio. A great deal of it is your fault—these things you're doing to destroy yourself."

Pasternak was obliged to reconsider his original assertion that, even "half-dead," Garland was still better than anyone else in the business.

I'd had just as much as I could take. The picture was costing thousands of dollars in delays, and there was no point in carrying on. Naturally we all did our best to help Judy, but it was no use. I told Mayer to cut his losses and forget about *Summer Stock*. I thought he'd welcome the idea. But surprisingly he said no. "Judy Garland," he said, "had made this studio a fortune in the good days, and the least we can do is to give her one more chance. If you stop production now, it'll finish her." So we all sighed heavily and went back to work.

The film eventually took six months to make, but in spite of this, Pasternak never once heard "a cross word, a tart comment, a bitter crack . . . they all understood." There is no doubt that Garland simply could not have got through the picture without the constant support of cast and crew, a support that at times took physical form, as Walters recalled:

> Gene took her left arm and I took her right one, and between us, we literally tried to keep her on her feet. But it wasn't easy. Emotionally she was at her lowest ebb. Physically she was pretty unsure of herself as well. There were even times when we had to nail the scenery down and provide her with supports so she wouldn't fall over. Once, I remember, she had to walk a few steps, and she couldn't do it. So I had to cheat the shot, and shoot the scene from a different angle. The whole experience was a ghastly, hideous nightmare which, happily, has become a blur in my memory.

In spite of Garland's poor state, *Summer Stock* contains several excellent numbers. Although these were credited to Nick Castle, Kelly was really responsible. He devised a magical solo for himself, "You, Wonderful You," and challenged Garland by devising two intricate dances for the two of them, "The Portland Fancy" and "All for You." He felt that if she were up to performing them, she could do anything, and in the event thought that she did them "magnificently . . . far better than anything in *For Me and My Gal*." However, the big show which is the film's finale contained a comic duet, "Heavenly Music," in the manner of "Be a Clown" and "A Couple of Swells," which Kelly eventually performed with Phil Silvers instead of her, when it became clear that she was far from being up to it.

Even in the midst of her misery, Garland still knew what was right for her. Kelly, who had worked wonderfully with Phil Silvers and Rita Hayworth on one trail-blazing number, "Make Way for Tomorrow," in *Cover Girl* (1944), had choreographed something similar for himself, Silvers and Garland, to end the film. But although Silvers was an old friend of hers, she declined to do it with him. "As I came on the set, costumed and made up, everyone avoided my eye," he recalled. "When I walked over to Judy, she broke into tears. Gene called me aside. 'She's more upset than you will be when I tell you. Judy doesn't think you should be up front with us.' Always the star. I didn't blame her, really." The number, without Silvers, makes an attractive finish to the film, but everyone agreed that something more was needed.

By this time, Garland had departed for Santa Barbara, where hypnotism was being tried to calm her nerves and help her lose weight. She had been there some weeks, and there was little chance of Harry Warren returning to compose a new song. In the event, she did not want him to, for she chose Harold Arlen's half-forgotten "Get Happy," which she had recently heard Arlen sing at a party. Castle was not available to choreograph it, nor Edens to do the orchestration. This last job went to Saul Chaplin, and Edens later told him that what he had done with the simple piece was overelaborate, but it turned out to be one of the high points of Garland's career. "I got some boys together, staged in three days, got Judy back, she rehearsed it in a day, we shot it in two, and she was back in Santa Barbara by the week's end," Walters claimed. It was not in fact as simple as that. Garland arrived in a manic state, her breath reeking of paraldehyde, a new medication recommended by her doctors. When Walters called "Cut" not long after she began to perform, she retreated to her dressing-room in confusion and fury. Walters followed her, and explained that he had been worried that she looked a bit "wobbly." This amused her, and she returned to the set determined to make up for all the trouble she had caused everyone in the past.

She had chosen to wear the costume designed for "Mister Monotony": black tights, a black jacket and a fedora tipped over one eye. She had lost so much weight in Santa Barbara that rumors persisted for years that the number was an out-take from an earlier film.

Seeing the film today, with Garland performing her songs and delivering her comic lines with relish, it is hard to believe that the shoot had been so traumatic for all concerned. It can be summed up by two lines of dialogue given to Kelly: "We're trying to tell a story with music and charm and dance"; and: "You're wonderful—everything I always hoped for in a leading lady."

It was precisely because the result on screen so belied the atmosphere on set that Garland was called back to work only three weeks later, instead of the six months break the studio had promised her. This seems incredible, but Freed knew that she had slimmed down and he needed a replacement in *Royal Wedding* when June Allyson, once again, became pregnant. Allyson claimed that Garland could have been suspended without pay had she refused to accept the part, in spite of the fact that she had not had her stipulated rest between films. As it was, she was looking forward to working again with Astaire, who was to co-star, and Charles Walters, who was to direct. Walters was less enthusiastic. He told Freed that the mere thought of a repetition of his experiences on *Summer Stock* brought him close to a nervous breakdown; he could not go through it all again. He was replaced by Stanley Donen.

The screenplay had been written by Alan Jay Lerner, recruited from Broadway after two big successes, *Brigadoon* and *Paint Your Wagon*. His composer-partner, Frederick Loewe, had taken a sabbatical, so Lerner decided to take Freed's offer of a Hollywood movie. Freed had acquired some Technicolor footage of the 1947 wedding of Princess Elizabeth to Philip Mountbatten, and Lerner came up with a story about a brother-and-sister vaudeville act who arrive in Britain at the time of the wedding. The brother falls in love with a dancer and the sister with a minor member of the aristocracy. This contained elements of autobiography as far as Astaire was concerned, since his partnership with his sister, Adele, had finished when she married one of the sons of the Duke of Devonshire.

Lerner had written the score with Burton Lane, and they were so excited by the prospect of Garland replacing Allyson that they considered writing a new song for her. Freed was rather more cautious. He told Helen Rose, the costume designer, to have only a few of Garland's dresses made up by the seamstress. It was a portent, and an unusual sort of economy for a studio as extravagant as M-G-M.

Garland started work on May 23, 1950, and for the first few days of costume-fittings and rehearsals arrived on time. She then started to come in late, complaining of the usual migraines and nausea. She told Donen that she could not rehearse both morning and afternoon and then be ready to face the camera in a few days' time. As before, work was rescheduled to begin at one, but even so, all too often Garland failed to come in. Once again, she was warned, threatened and cajoled, to no effect. The studio, ever more desperate, hoped she could pull the stops out just once more. It was all *so* right for her. For instance, she had a comic routine with Astaire, "How Could You Believe Me When I Said I Loved You When You Know I've Been a Liar All My Life," which would make "A Couple of Swells" look like small beer.

Garland did not see the film in the same light. She was in turmoil both professionally and privately, no longer Dorothy, who had followed the yellow brick road, or Esther Smith, who had longed for a glance from the boy next door, or even Manuela of *The Pirate*. She was no longer the supreme singing actress of Hollywood musicals, but a prematurely aged workhorse. She had few hopes for *Summer Stock*, due out in the summer. While the shooting on that had dragged on, Minnelli had made a sprightly comedy, *Father of the Bride*, which had enhanced his reputation, and she had to face the fact that the husband she despised might be more valuable to M-G-M than she was. *Annie Get Your Gun* had just opened and been a personal a triumph for Betty Hutton. And what was Judy Garland doing? Replacing, for the second time, June Allyson, whom she liked as a person but did not much admire as an artist. She would be working with the great Astaire, but as his *sister*, in a screenplay which was—at best— ordinary. The great days seemed to be over and she did not feel that she could make the sort of contribution which would bring them back.

Freed now concurred, but he allowed the unhappy situation to continue until mid-June. Garland was slimming again, and with that remarkable ability suddenly to change physically, she began to look fit. Helen Rose observed that she looked happier and more attractive than she had at any time since *The Harvey Girls*. She arrived one day for a final fitting of the costume she would wear for the "Liar" song. A crowd had gathered to see the test, which was due to follow the fitting, and a wave of applause greeted her as she left her dressing-room. It was, said Rose, "just the boost she needed." As she posed for the crowd, Freed appeared, apparently preoccupied. "What are you made up for?" he asked, just loud enough for her to hear. She burst into tears, rushed into her dressing-room and, after throwing the costume on a chair, put on her coat and went home. The combination of tactlessness on his part and hysterical touchiness on hers had been familiar for years. But in this case it proved the last straw. She never returned.

At the end of the week, on Saturday, June 17, she awoke with a migraine and telephoned at 11:25 a.m. to say that they would have to manage without her. Donen remonstrated, reiterating that she was needed for rehearsals, since pre-recording was due to begin on the Monday. She was adamant; she would not come in, not even for Fred Astaire.

Astaire was not in fact involved. He did not need to be. He knew that Walters had refused to direct Garland, and he now learned that Donen had made the same decision. According to Donen, Freed told Garland: "Stanley says he can't go on with the picture; we've got to change you . . . not that you're not doing your job, Judy; but we've got to change you." Donen, however, stated that he did not know that she had been fired until she had been replaced by Jane Powell. To some extent neither Freed nor Donen was involved. The decision was taken by Schenck and Schary.

On the Saturday afternoon a telegram arrived from Loew's New York office:

THIS IS TO NOTIFY YOU THAT FOR GOOD AND SUFFICIENT CAUSE AND IN ACCORDANCE WITH THE RIGHTS GRANTED TO US UNDER PROVISIONS OF PARAGRAPH 12 OF YOUR CONTRACT OF EMPLOYMENT WITH US DATED NOVEMBER 12, 1946 AND WITHOUT LIMITING OR RESTRICTING OTHER RIGHTS OR REMEDIES WHICH WE MAY HAVE, WE SHALL REFUSE TO PAY YOU ANY COMPENSATION COMMENCING AS OF JUNE 17, 1950 AND CONTINUING UNTIL THE EXPIRATION OF THE TIME WHICH WOULD HAVE BEEN REASONABLY REQUIRED TO COMPLETE THE ROLE OF "ELLEN" IN THE PHOTOPLAY NOW ENTITLED "ROYAL WEDDING" OR (SHOULD AN-OTHER PERSON BE ENGAGED TO PLAY SUCH ROLE) UNTIL THE COMPLE-TION OF SUCH ROLE BY SUCH OTHER PERSON, ANY AND ALL OTHER RIGHTS AND REMEDIES WHICH WE MAY HAVE IN THE PREMISES ARE EXPRESSLY RESERVED BY US.

On Monday, Garland thought, Carleton Alsop would see Mayer and sort things out. For the first time, however, Mayer was unavailable. Alsop went to his office and was taken, instead, to see the company's attorney, who handed him confirmation of Garland's suspension. The attorney pointed out that her behavior had added as much as 20 percent to the budget of several of her recent films. Alsop argued that she had earned $36,000,000 for M-G-M since she had arrived there as a child. Without much conviction, in view of the money the studio had spent on doctors for Garland, he went on to claim that Mayer would spend more on a lame race-horse than he did on his client: "I want to find out," he said, before storming out, "if he will do as much for a human being as he does for a goddamned race-horse."

Mayer's personal concern for Garland was no longer a factor. He was nearing the end of his career at M-G-M, and the process of getting rid of him had already begun. Schenck, Schary and the other executives were unanimous: Judy Garland was a pain in the neck and no longer an asset to the studio. At the age of twenty-eight, her career at Metro-Goldwyn-Mayer was over.

It was the end of an era, an era in which the most talented singer-actress in Hollywood history performed for the delectation of movie audiences the world over. Those taking her place at M-G-M would lack her particular gifts: Jane Powell, June Allyson, Kathryn Grayson, Debbie Reynolds, Vera-Ellen and Leslie Caron. To a degree, depending on the script, they would all be modeled on the Judy Garland character—the loyal, patient, loving and sweet-natured girl. Freed still thought that Garland was the only person who could play Julie in *Show Boat*, but in the end he cast a non-singer, Ava Gardner, in the role, and had her songs dubbed.

Of Garland's going, Pasternak said: "Wish her well, return her love, all you who cherish talent and genius and a great heart. For myself, I am lucky to have had the privilege of working with her." Harry Warren put it another way, though perhaps we should note that Garland never used any of the songs he had written for her in her concerts or on her later recordings—not even "On the Atcheson, Topeka and Santa Fe": "She was just too much trouble and too costly. So Metro let her go. But she was treated better at M-G-M than she would have been treated at any other studio. If she had been at Warners, they would have dropped her years earlier."

13

❖❖❖❖❖❖❖

Humiliated and Unwanted

THE INCONCEIVABLE HAD HAPPENED: Judy Garland was no longer a star at Metro-Goldwyn-Mayer.

It was not the end of the world, exactly, because there were other options open to her—pictures at other studios, personal appearances, a Broadway show. Minnelli and her secretary, Myrtle Tully (the widow of the journalist James Tully, who specialized in show-business stories) were discussing these possibilities at the Evanview house on the evening of Monday, June 19, 1950, the day Carleton Alsop had received confirmation that Garland had indeed been fired. Her contract still had two years to run, but the fact had to be faced that M-G-M's executives were unlikely to give her a fourth chance. She had failed to meet the challenge of the all-important *Annie Get Your Gun* and two films with one of the studio's most glittering prizes, Fred Astaire. You did not reject the chance of partnering Astaire once, let alone twice.

Garland listened in a state of lassitude, eventually rising to go to the bathroom. As Minnelli and Tully (as Judy always called her) talked, they were startled to hear Garland scream. They rushed to the bathroom, but the door was locked. "Leave me alone! I want to die!" she yelled. Minnelli broke down the door at the second attempt and found his wife holding a broken glass in one hand. She had an ugly, but not serious, gash on her neck. Minnelli took the glass and Tully gathered Garland into her arms. A doctor was summoned by one of the servants and a call put through to Alsop, who came straight over from his own house.

Alsop arrived to find Minnelli sobbing uncontrollably: "They finally killed my beautiful wife." Cradled in Tully's arms, Garland was calm: "Take care of Vincente, Pa," she whispered. This was not one of Alsop's priorities. On the contrary, he slugged him hard on the jaw, though whether to bring him to his senses or in anger neither knew. And neither was quite sure later why it was decided to move Garland to the house on Sunset, where she was officially resident. At this point there are different accounts of the sequence of events. According to one, so as not to tie up the telephones, Alsop ran down the hill to call for an ambulance from the Mocambo nightclub. As he entered, he was greeted by a reporter, who said: "It's on every news desk in town that Judy tried to kill herself. Is it true?" One of the servants had taken revenge upon Garland for all her outbursts against them. Alsop denied any knowledge of this rumor, which, he decided, would be further fueled if an ambulance was summoned. When he returned to the house, however, the newsmen were already there. Garland was smuggled into a car, and when they arrived at 10,000 Sunset, Alsop arranged for dozens of bouquets to be sent to the Evanview House in the hope of keeping the reporters there. They were not deceived. But John Fricke is much more convincing when he says that, in the early hours of the next morning, Alsop was tracked down by a reporter who forced him to confirm the rumor running around the Los Angeles newsdesks. As a result, a special edition of the *Los Angeles Mirror* was rushed out. Under a banner headline: JUDY GARLAND FAILS IN SUICIDE ATTEMPT. Florabel Muir told the nationwide syndicated story:

Judy Garland, despondent over being suspended by her studio, attempted suicide last night by slashing her throat with the shattered edge of a waterglass in the bathroom of her pink alabaster mansion. The wound was superficial. No stitches required. The 29-year-old [*sic*] actress, hollow-eyed, highly nervous and suffering from physical and mental exhaustion, was resting under a doctor's care today.

A doctor had been waiting at Sunset for them, and although he dismissed the wound as "only a scratch," he warned Alsop and Minnelli that suicide attempts were cries for help. He told the waiting reporters that the wound was a minor one, the result of an impulsive and hysterical act.

"I felt humiliated and unwanted," Garland recalled, "and I was faced with the bitter knowledge that I'd come to that unhappy position by my own actions. All my newfound hope evaporated, and all I could see ahead was more confusion. I wanted to black out the future as well as the past. I didn't want to live anymore. I wanted to hurt myself and others." Her recollections of the exact sequence of events differ from Minnelli's: she claimed that, after cutting herself, she realized: "I couldn't solve anything by running away—and that's what killing yourself is. I let them in and tried to make them understand how sorry I was."

Marc Rabwin, who always attended Garland and never once sent a bill, thought it most significant that Garland began experiencing nausea the moment she drove through the studio gates. It tended to worsen as the day went on, and this was the principal reason she had been unable to function—and had become, finally, desperate. Rabwin now called in two allergists, George Piness and George Alleys, in an attempt to get to the root of the problem.

Another person to arrive at the house was a publicity man from the studio. Minnelli and Alsop had denied that there had been a suicide attempt, but when the publicist was asked by a reporter what had happened, he swept his hand across his neck in a cutting gesture. Alsop yanked him back into the house and shouted: "You stupid son-of-a-bitch! All that's done is put them on twenty-four-hour duty." The publicist left, determined to distance himself and the studio from a washed-up star who had tried to commit suicide. That was not the sort of thing which sat easily with the benign M-G-M image. It was not something M-G-M's lion could roar about.

There was another story to be told—that of the star as victim of the Hollywood system. The press was aware of this, but remained silent. When, twelve years later, Marilyn Monroe committed suicide, the unanimous response of the press was to blame Hollywood—partly because she, too, had a vulnerable image. But in 1950, it made better copy to portray Judy Garland as another pampered movie star, ungrateful for her fame and good fortune.

Minnelli valiantly continued to deny the reports of suicide, and suggested that "some progress has been made" toward Garland returning to continue filming *Royal Wedding*. A spokesman for the studio told reporters: "Miss Garland is now resting under her doctor's care. She is asleep. I saw her and she has a slight bandage on her neck. No stitches were required." As speculation continued, however, the studio had no choice but to issue a much longer statement, ensuring that no blame could be attached to anyone—or indeed anything— at M-G-M for what had happened:

> Following completion of *Summer Stock*, and after consultation with the doctors in Boston, the studio placed her on vacation status. After a rest of two months, Miss Garland reported that she was feeling fine, and physicians of her own choosing considered her all over her difficulties.
>
> Some time thereafter, we learned that June Allyson, who was to appear in *Royal Wedding*, was to have a baby. With assurances from Miss Garland that she was in top physical condition, we submitted the script for her and she appeared most eager in accepting the role, promising there would be no more difficulties.
>
> Within a matter of a few days, delays had already begun, and these delays increased as time went on during rehearsals. She was then told by the producer that a warning letter was to be sent to her, but that he would ask to have it stopped if she would promise to cooperate. But the delays continued.
>
> With the responsibility and in justice to other artists, the studio had only one recourse, which was to take Miss Garland out of the picture, assume whatever losses were involved, recast it and go ahead.
>
> The substitution of an artist in any picture is never made on an arbitrary basis, and certainly a person of Miss Garland's talent is not easily replaced.
>
> The replacement is not a hasty move, prompted by pique or irritation. It is the last resort, arrived at with great regret after all other means have failed.

A reporter from one of the wire services, who read this in the middle of the night, telephoned Alsop for his comments. Alsop said that he had not seen the statement and asked the man to read it to him over the phone. When pressed for a comment, he said that the reporter should study the document to see if it extended "any sympathy or concern for Miss Garland."

Someone who did show sympathy and concern was Ethel. Shaken

by the news, she returned to Los Angeles from Dallas, where she had been living with Jimmy and her second husband, John Thompson, Jr. She told reporters that she would be staying until her daughter recovered, but she did not know whether Garland would agree to see her. Garland refused, but when Ethel returned to Dallas, she told her new friends that "they" would not let her see her daughter. She told Jimmy the truth, and added that she would be returning to Los Angeles to be close to Judy. Later, she got a job as a clerk with the Douglas Aircraft plant in Santa Monica, and when news of this eventually leaked out, it became the story of a loving mother and an ungrateful daughter.

The press continued to stake out the house, and while Garland, lying in bed, tried to adjust to the situation, Minnelli ordered a bar and buffet to be set up in the drive for the besieging newsmen. She received literally hundreds of bouquets, and, while she was overwhelmed by the flowers and orthodox expressions of sympathy, the cable she liked best came from Fred Finklehoffe and his wife, the Broadway star Ella Logan. It read: DEAR JUDY. SO GLAD YOU CUT YOUR THROAT. ALL THE OTHER GIRL SINGERS NEEDED THIS KIND OF BREAK. "God, Pa," she said to Alsop, "isn't that sweet?"

The industry as a whole was not sympathetic. "Suicide was a slap in the face to Hollywood's image as the world Utopian paradise," as Leland Hayward put it.* "It was played up rather than hushed up, but never forgiven." The situation at M-G-M was one of complete confusion, with many people feeling responsible and just as many saying that she had brought it all on herself. Louis B. Mayer was baffled. Most of the other studios believed that talent could be channeled, but M-G-M believed that the Culver City lot provided a relaxed atmosphere where it could flourish. So what had happened to the studio's own little Judy, the Judy it had nurtured and watched grow, was particularly disturbing.

George Cukor had once said, "Mayer knew that the coin he dealt in was talent. He would husband it and be very patient and put up with a lot of nonsense if he really believed in it." At the time Garland had been fired from *Annie Get Your Gun*, Dore Schary had told her the studio was prepared to take care of her financially for a year so that she could get over her problems. She had refused; she said she knew that she needed help, but would manage. The studio had not

---

*In 1948, to Lilli Palmer, after the suicide of Carole Landis, who had been having an affair with her husband, Rex Harrison.

forced her to return for *Summer Stock*, but Mayer, who loathed his successor, implied that Schary should have been more understanding. "She has made us millions of dollars," he told Katharine Hepburn. "We should be able to help her. Do you feel that you could do anything?"

Hepburn was supposed to be both clever and capable. Unofficially, she had been living for years with Spencer Tracy, whose drinking bouts were of spectacular length. Mayer believed, a little naïvely, that anyone who could cope with Tracy's drinking would understand Garland's problems. Even though she hardly knew Garland at this period, Hepburn said she would try. When she reached the house, she strode past the journalists, her look warning them not to take pictures. "Don't you have anything better to do?" she asked contemptuously. "Why don't you go back to work?" Once she reached the bedroom, she brushed past Minnelli and began to lecture Garland: "Now listen. You're one of the three greatest talents in the world. And your ass has hit the gutter. There's no place to go but up. Now, goddamit. Do it!"

She spent several hours with Garland, talking about the vicissitudes of her own career, partly to help Garland get her own into perspective and partly to get her mind off her recent troubles. She left, eventually, by the back door, jumping over a fence to avoid the newsmen. She was recognized in the street by some of them, who followed her as she marched on determinedly, not looking back. Suddenly, she nipped into a side street and vaulted a wall into the garden of a friend, Greta Garbo, who was not there at the time. She remained there until she decided that the newshounds had gone.

"I think Judy was an enormously complicated creature," Hepburn said later. "By this time she had worked hard. She had lived a lifetime. She was spent. In a way, for tormented creatures, work is the easiest thing they can do."

Another visitor was Mayer himself, to whom Garland confided her financial troubles. Mayer told her that she was not to worry and that he would see her attorney, Lloyd Wright, in a few days time. He told Wright that he was reasonably certain that the studio would make her a loan. According to Garland, she was in Mayer's office when he telephoned Nicholas Schenck. His appeal proved unsuccessful. "Mr. Schenck suggests that you go to a charity hospital. We're not in the money-lending business," he said, putting down the receiver. "He just looked at me," Garland recalled. "I'll never forget what he said. 'You know, if they'll do this to you, they'll do it to me.' He said that he was so ashamed that, personally, he would pay whatever expenses I would have." Mayer's requests had once been law, and to have one refused was a humiliation. Schenck was already easing the old mogul out: within a year, he would be gone.

Garland later described Mayer's gift as "conscience money," it was certainly not enough to keep her in the style to which she was accustomed, but Frank Sinatra offered a solution. He was now part-owner of the Cal-Neva Lodge at Lake Tahoe, where Garland had been "discovered" years before. She could stay there, with all expenses paid, and make an unheralded return to performing live—if she so pleased. M-G-M agreed to release Roger Edens and Charles Walters to help her prepare a stage act. She stayed at the Lodge, accompanied by her old makeup artist, Dottie Ponedel, and her beloved Tully, relaxing in the sun—but not performing. The three of them took off suddenly for Sun Valley, Idaho, where she was photographed, looking tanned and healthy, while catching a trout; and then the party traveled to New York because, Garland said, she wanted to catch the World Series.

In fact, she wanted to test the reaction to *Summer Stock*. At the previews in Hollywood, the public had applauded wildly when her name appeared on the screen; recognized in the lobby, she was greeted by people telling her that they loved her. But that was Los Angeles, proud of its place as the home of the movies: the rest of the country might be more critical. M-G-M rushed the film into release, partly to capitalize on the fact that Garland was "news," and partly to see whether her recent troubles had alienated her public. She was to discover the answer in a startling way. On September 5, she sneaked into the Capitol Theater on Broadway, where the picture was playing, and was recognized as the lights went up. Those nearest to her began to call out messages of support and, as she made her way through the lobby and outside to where her car was waiting, the crowd became a mob, shouting "Judy! We love you, Judy!" She was frightened, overwhelmed, reassured and grateful, as the car drew away slowly to avoid the crush.

Like everyone else, the critics were well aware of what Garland (and the filmmakers) had been through in order to make the picture, and this was reflected in their reviews. "The great song and dance actress makes this movie a personal triumph," said *Life*, overlooking the fact that the great song and dance actress looked uncomfortably heavy. Its stablemate, *Time*, was less gallant, noting her weight and her troubles with the studio:

But none of its seems to have affected her ability as one of Hollywood's few triple-threat girls. Thanks to Actress Garland's singing, dancing and acting (and some imaginative dancing by Gene Kelly) the picture seems considerably better than it is . . . Though the show's only distinguished song is an old one, "Get Happy," her voice and showmanlike delivery do wonders for the whole score.

Another public testimonial came from Billy Rose, sometime show-man, sometime songwriter, husband to Fanny Brice and at this time a journalist with a syndicated column. In an article headlined "Love Letter to a National Asset," he declared:

I found your portrayal of a farm girl in *Summer Stock* as convincing as a twenty-dollar gold piece, and when you leveled on Harold Arlen's old song, "Get Happy"—well, it was Al Jolson in lace panties, Maurice Chevalier in opera pumps! . . . Naturally you're wondering why I'm taking heart in ballpoint and writing you this love-and-kudos letter right out in the open. Well, like everyone else, I read the front-page stories about you a couple of months back, and from the lines between the lines I sensed that you had been having a bout with the jim-jams yourself, and that you no longer cared whether school kept out or not . . .

This letter—and I know it's plenty presumptuous—is to point out, in case you haven't thought of it yourself, how important it is to millions of people in this country that school continues for Judy Garland . . . It gets down to this, Judy: in an oblique and daffy sort of way, you are as much a national asset as our coal reserves—both of you help warm up our insides.

Settled into the Carlyle Hotel, she was also cheered by a telephone call from Fred Finklehoffe, who was in the process of being divorced from his wife. He and Garland had known each other a long while and, making up for lost time, they became lovers. They arranged to go to Billy Reed's Little Club on East 55th Street, where they were approached by a man in a beige suit. "You know Miss Garland," said Finklehoffe discouragingly. "This is Sid Luft."

Luft was an old friend and asked to sit down, but Finklehoffe replied: "I don't want any traffic with you at all, Sid. Get lost." Garland protested that, of course, Luft must join them. "You've heard of this character, haven't you?" Finklehoffe asked Garland. "Oh yes, I have. A great deal," she replied, in such a way that Luft was unable to decide whether what she had heard was good or bad. He stayed for a few minutes, chatting idly.

Garland had met Luft years before, when he had been living with

Eleanor Powell. He had completely ignored her then, and she was determined that he would not do so again. The following evening, Finklehoffe telephoned Luft to say that Garland had suggested that he join them to hear Billy Daniels sing at Ben Marden's Riviera, a supper club in New Jersey. After the show, the three of them joined Daniels in his dressing-room. As they were returning at dawn, over the George Washington Bridge, Finklehoffe decided to announce his claim on Garland: "You and I are having a romance—nothing spectacular . . . And you love me, don't you, Judy?" "Yes, I do, of course I do, Freddie," she replied, in a voice that Luft said "could destroy you."

"Now, let me tell you about this fellow you just met last night," Finklehoffe went on, "and out of the goodness of your heart took along tonight. He is the dirtiest, low-down S.O.B. you'll ever meet. He's bad news, and I'm warning you—" Garland interrupted to protest, but Finklehoffe was in full flood: "Remember that Freddie Finklehoffe told you this. I'll go on record. He's done something right now and will continue to do it and he'll call you. I get the vibrations—he's on the move. You're a cooked pigeon, baby." Garland, sitting between them on the back seat, laughed merrily and put her arm round both. She was impressed by Luft's silence. "You'd better watch yourself, because he's going to nail you," Finklehoffe concluded gloomily. When they dropped Luft at the Ritz Tower, where he was staying, she asked him to call her.

He did so twice, but she was not in. Nor did she return the calls. They met again by chance at a party given by Jackie Gleason, then best known as Chester A. Riley in television's "The Life of Riley." Luft was squiring a young actress and Garland was escorted by Carleton Alsop. She approached him and ignored his comment that he had called her. Instead, she asked him to take her out for a drink. For the second time he told her that he was with a date, but she said, shortly: "What difference does that make?" He told her that his companion might wish to leave early, as she had a television show to do in the morning: if that was the case, he would return to the party and buy her that drink. He did leave, and Garland was waiting when he came back.

She took him to The Golden Key, where her old friend Johnny Mercer was entertaining after hours at the piano. When Mercer saw her, he began playing her songs instead of his own. She sang her heart out. It was again almost dawn when she and Luft parted. Luft had only a few hours to snatch some sleep before taking a business trip to Philadelphia. Garland asked him to call her when he got back: she wanted to take him somewhere special for dinner.

He telephoned at eight that evening, and again half an hour later. On both occasions, he was told that she was not in, so he arranged to take his television actress to dinner instead. After leaving her, he had several dry martinis and got into an argument with the waiter and the manager, who at this hour were unable to change a hundred-dollar bill for six dollars' worth of drink. The difficulty was in deciding who would trust whom until the following day, and it led to fisticuffs in the street. When a police car drew alongside, everyone went inside, where a phone call to the Ritz Tower established Luft's credit and confirmed that a bellboy would bring six dollars round in the morning.

Luft nursed his anger in another bar, reflecting that Garland was the indirect cause of his inglorious moment. He picked up the telephone and, although it was almost three in the morning, she answered as if she had been waiting—as indeed she had.

Fred Finklehoffe's warning had not gone completely unheeded. She had vacillated over her evening's date, until a combination of pride and curiosity got the better of her. Few men stood up Judy Garland. When she discovered that he had called twice, her honor was satisfied. She dressed to go out and sat by the telephone to wait for a third call. She did not seem to mind that it had taken him several hours to make it, and said that she would come right over. She confessed that she had been swayed by Finklehoffe's remark. Luft told her about the fight at the bar and disclosed that during the course of it, he had lost his Vacheron-Constantin watch. Together, they retraced his steps along Lexington Avenue until they found it among the debris in the gutter.

Luft telephoned a few days later to ask her whether she would care to go to Jamaica with him on Saturday. Garland sent Tully to Hattie Carnegie for some appropriate outfits for the change of climate. The bellboys were struggling with her many cases when Luft arrived to pick her up. There had been a serious misunderstanding: he had meant the Jamaica racetrack. She sat on one of her cases and howled with laughter.

In background, appearance and personality, Sid Luft could hardly have been more different to Vincente Minnelli. Indeed, about the only way in which Luft resembled Minnelli was that, at thirty-eight, he was somewhat older than Garland. "That Luft," as she affectionately began to refer to him, had been born into a middle-class Jewish family in New Rochelle, though his mother, an overbearing and snobbish woman, liked to give the impression that she had Russian Imperial blood. He had been brought up in Bronxville, New York, where being Jewish was not exactly an advantage. To compensate, he enrolled at the Charles Atlas correspondence school for body-building and developed a competitive mentality which his fellow-students found brash. At the age of nineteen, he was in Ottawa, where he got a job on the production staff of an Aquacade. This gave him a taste for show business and, after a stint with the Royal Canadian Air Force, he headed for Los Angeles, where he looked up an old pal from his Bronxville days, Eleanor Powell. Officially, he acted as her general factotum and secretary, managing the house and making her travel arrangements.

He got a job as a test pilot for Douglas, which led to his being hired as technical adviser on *Charter Pilot*, a 1940 B-movie at 20th Century-Fox. The film's star was Lynn Bari, a contract player with a precarious hold on stardom. She played the lead in minor movies, but was usually "the other woman" in more important ones. Luft married her in 1943, with the conviction—which she sometimes shared—that with the right vehicle she could become a big star. He managed her career after her contract ended in 1946, but over the next four years she made only three pictures, all of them undistinguished. He also produced a film, *Kilroy Was Here* (1947), starring the former boy wonders, Jackie Coogan and Jackie Cooper, but it was for Monogram, whose B-pictures were invariably greeted by audiences with groans.

At the time he met Garland, he was headed for an acrimonious divorce from Bari. He had been a friend of Finklehoffe during happier times, and as Finklehoffe, too, was about to get divorced, they had a common woe. Garland, of course, was in the same situation. Another problem which she and Luft shared was that they were both looking for jobs.

Garland's notices for *Summer Stock* should have ensured her plenty of offers, which she needed if she was to pay her bills. She was borrowing from friends and she told the manager of the Carlyle to send her bill for her stay there to Berg-Allenberg, who may not have known officially that Carleton Alsop had been representing her. Her professional association with him was coming to an end, however. He had once worked for the FBI in Washington, and now decided to return to the capital for a job with the CIA. Looking after Garland had been "all-absorbing," he readily admitted, but it was unpaid. With his marriage on the rocks, he had chosen to quit show business.

There was more to life than coping with a talented but fractious star; and he had in fact been *en route* for Washington when he had danced attendance on Garland—for the last time—in New York.

With Alsop gone, Marc Rabwin took a hand. He had kept regularly in touch with Garland over the past two months, and she seemed to have been her old self. She had relaxed in Lake Tahoe and Sun Valley; she had been delighted by New York and the reviews for *Summer Stock*. When she returned to Los Angeles, however, she was again a mass of raw nerves and was still suffering from bouts of nausea. Rabwin knew that she was penniless, but he also knew that the mere thought of returning to the studio terrified her. The studio had been making vague noises about wanting her back on a limited basis, but Rabwin decided that it should not in any case have the opportunity. Without telling Garland, he telephoned L.B. Mayer for an appointment and said that in his considered opinion Judy Garland would not recover as long as she was bound to M-G-M. Mayer replied that he was personally sorry to see Garland's tie to the studio severed, but if Dr. Rabwin thought that it was in her best interests, he had no choice but to agree. If the right role came up, she would be engaged—and Freed still hoped that she would return to play Julie in *Show Boat*. Officially, she still owed the studio half the $9,000 she had borrowed in Boston, but in the circumstances this would be written off.

On September 28, 1950, it was officially announced that Judy Garland and M-G-M had parted company. Rabwin advised her to find a new agent, and it became clear that she badly needed one when the announcement failed to bring her a single offer of work. Myrtle Tully was wise in the ways of Hollywood, and she advised Garland to move quickly. The two chief components of Berg-Allenberg had, in fact, separated and the company no longer existed. Phil Berg had taken his clients to the William Morris Agency, which was headed by Abe Lastfogel, who remained one of the most respected and experienced agents in the business. He was just what Garland needed, and in October she signed up with him. It was announced that she would be available for guest appearances on radio, but not for television work "for the time being."

Lastfogel had acted speedily, for in the October 11 issue of *Variety*, there was speculation that Garland might take over the lead in the Broadway production of *South Pacific* when Mary Martin left to play in London. There was also a report that Jerry Wald and Norman Krasna, who had recently formed an independent unit within RKO, had spoken to her about a musical version of *Alice Adams*, which, as a straight film, had been a success for Katharine Hepburn in 1935.

That same day, Judy returned to radio, courtesy of CBS and Chesterfield Cigarettes—but more specifically of their star Bing Crosby, who, as a shareholder in Decca Records, had benefited from Garland's talent over the years. Apart from the records they had cut together, she had been a guest on his show from time to time. To demonstrate his faith in her, he not only invited her to be on the first show of the season, but in the second too, and another later in the season:

> He called me up one morning. Bless him—he was cute. "Judy," he said, "I know how busy you are" (busy ME! That was a laugh!) "and I was wondering if I could get you for three shows . . ." He could get me for thirty shows, or three hundred. That moment I felt the whole world change. It was real friendship. I needed that job more than I needed money. I could always borrow money: you can't borrow a job, you can't borrow the chance to put faith back in yourself. Somebody else has to have faith in you first. Well, Bing had faith in me—and thank God, I didn't let him down.

Indeed, as a contemporary review put it: "If radio is to be saved such shows as this will turn the trick." To ensure that audiences did not abandon the show for the new enemy, television, and to make them aware that Judy Garland was still very much in business, Crosby added another powerhouse talent, Bob Hope. The three of them appeared in comedy skits on both shows, and in the first of them they parodied "Goodnight Irene." Crosby and Garland sang "Sam's Song" and "Tzena, Tzena, Tzena," while Garland's solos, "Get Happy" and "Friendly Star," were taken from her most recent film; she was not only plugging the film for M-G-M, but also proving to the industry, via *Summer Stock*, that she was still a ranking star.

Radio suited her that season, especially as her weight tended to fluctuate; and these shows were recorded in advance. In November, she appeared with Thomas Mitchell and Anne Shoemaker (as her parents) in a dramatization for NBC of *Alice Adams*, perhaps to familiarize herself with the Booth Tarkington story. Alice is a provincial girl who lives in a world of fantasy because her family does not have the social prestige she would like them to have; but she eventually comes to appreciate them for what they are. It was an ideal role for Garland's combination of vulnerability and nervous energy.

When Al Jolson died, Crosby decided to pay a tribute on his show of December 6. At Minnelli's suggestion, Garland sang "Rockabye Your Baby With a Dixie Melody"—which suited her so well that she kept it in her repertory ever after. She and Crosby also sang "Rudolph the Red-Nosed Reindeer"—perhaps forgivably, as Gene Autry's recording of it then looked like overtaking Crosby's "White Christmas" as the biggest seasonal seller of all time.

She also agreed to re-create Dorothy in a broadcast of *The Wizard of Oz* for *Lux Radio Theater*, at Christmas; and in the New Year was a guest on *The Bob Hope Show* and *The Big Show*, which was then making new fans for Tallulah Bankhead. For Lux she also did *Miss Cinderella*, a charming comedy by Jerome Lawrence and Robert E. Lee, about a writer whose career is hampered because her stories are all variations on the fairy tale. She leaves a store with only one shoe because she cannot afford the other one. A dream sequence has her playing Cinderella in verse, until she wakes up for a happy ending.

Garland let it be known that she would be interested in having her own radio series, but the only new shows in which sponsors were interested were for television, which was beginning to wean audiences away from the radio. She made her first appearance on television on February 27, 1951, for a show to benefit the Red Cross, along with Ed Sullivan, Hope and Crosby and Kate Smith, a popular stage and radio star of the period who was inclined to sing "God Bless America" at the drop of a hat.

Meanwhile, Garland talked of returning to vaudeville. Like the heroine of *For Me and My Gal*, she longed to play the Palace, vaudeville's traditional home in New York, but Lastfogel was chary of this. New York, which presented an awesome challenge at the best of times, has seldom been susceptible to the sort of talents that flourished in Hollywood. Furthermore, it was hardly a propitious time to expose her there: it would remind critics and audiences that Judy Garland was currently one of the movie capital's rejects. A far better idea would be to try out her new act somewhere farther away—like London.

14

·❖·❖·❖·❖·❖·❖·❖·

London

LONDONERS, STARVED OF American entertainers during the war, had taken them uncritically to their hearts ever since. Vaudeville—or Variety as the British called it—was slowly dying. In the States, it had not long survived the dual onslaught of the Talkies and radio, and in Britain television was about to deal it the death blow. The only place it survived was at the Casino Theatre, which put on shows featuring the sort of people British audiences would not otherwise see in the flesh, such as American film stars. This rather more glamorous form of Variety was taken up by the London Palladium, Britain's largest music-hall theater, which was able to offer better money and more prestige than the Casino. Danny Kaye and Betty Hutton were two artists whose American careers gained somewhat from having hugely successful seasons at the Palladium. Indeed, Hutton's two-week engagement had sold out on the morning her notices appeared, and had been extended by another week.

Garland's response to what was by no means the first offer from the Palladium was an unenthusiastic "Why not?" When no other requests for her services were forthcoming, Lastfogel began negotiations. She continued to procrastinate, even when the Palladium agreed to pay her $20,000 a week, $5,000 more than they had originally offered. There is no doubt that she needed the money. In spite of being sacked by M-G-M, it had not occurred to her to stop living the way she had done for several years. Hotels and Hattie Carnegie would not hold their bills forever.

Lastfogel eventually invited her to dinner with another of his clients, Fanny Brice, the comedienne who had been featured with Garland in *Everybody Sing*. Brice, who had been playing the British halls since 1913, spoke of the warmth and kindness of British audiences, of the rewards of working on the stage, and the ups and downs of her own career. This was a tactful way of reminding Garland that no other work was available. Lastfogel pointed out that regular appearances in radio would eventually dim Garland's luster, whereas a triumph at the Palladium would be something else.

Garland's private life remained as complicated as ever. She was still sharing part of it in Los Angeles with Minnelli, who had finally and reluctantly come to the decision that he had failed her. He also recognized that she was partly to blame: "Judy had failed me too. She would never be able, or willing, to create a home with me. Our future would always be marred by her indulgences and compulsions. I'd either humored them or fought them for almost six years." His spirit was finally broken when he heard her say that she had lied to all her sixteen psychiatrists: "So what? . . . There's more than one way to get even with people." In early December, Gerold Frank recounts, after drinking enough martinis to pluck up the courage to tell Minnelli that she was leaving for good, Garland moved to an apartment on Sweetzer Avenue, off Sunset Strip, which had once belonged to Marlene Dietrich. There she could introduce Sid Luft to her Hollywood friends.

She had been seen publicly with him on both coasts, but discreetly, in supper clubs and restaurants unlikely to attract reporters. For the sake of Liza, who, at five, was almost old enough to understand, she did not want the relationship to be talked about. Over the next few months she became increasingly reliant on Luft. Looking on, Minnelli was obliged to concede that Luft had "seemingly discovered the secret to keeping Judy sane and healthy." Luft was blunt, uncomplicated, unflappable, and confident that Garland could take her career to even greater heights. He had no objection to her being the center of attention—if that was what she really wanted, but he told her that she needed to harness her talent and show the world that she wasn't finished.

By the spring of 1951, with Luft smiling encouragement, she and Roger Edens had worked out her act for the Palladium. Although her marriage to Minnelli was over, she nevertheless asked him to check out her act, and gave a recital just for him. A few days later, on March 23, she went into court to divorce him, charging (as did most Hollywood stars at this time) mental cruelty. She said in testimony:

When we were first married, we were very happy. We had many interests in common, and many mutual friends. But sometime later, without any explanation, my husband withdrew himself and shut himself out of my life. I had to appear in public without him. It was very embarrassing. Finally I didn't go anywhere myself because it was too difficult to explain his absence. I was terribly lonely. I frequently became hysterical. I had to go under a doctor's care. I just couldn't understand his attitudes. He lacked interest in me, my career, my friends, everything.

No movie star ever went to court in a divorce suit to tell the truth. Garland may have been impossible, but Minnelli, who continued to be a practicing homosexual in spite of subsequent marriages, was hardly the ideal husband. Although he was clearly upset by the consequences of M-G-M firing Garland, he had done nothing practical to help in a dispute between his wife and his employers. He had merely looked the other way.

In an unusual settlement, Garland was granted legal custody of Liza, with the proviso that the child should spend six months a year with her father; but this was to be interpreted loosely so that Liza felt no sense of regimentation. Minnelli would pay $500 a week to support his daughter when she was with her mother, and would pay any medical fees. In exchange for $25,000, he gave up any claim to the Evanview house and the beach house they had owned at Malibu.

The grimness of the court appearance, with Garland speaking as if by rote, was not reflected in the public perception of her at this time. She was the jolly girl who traded quips with Crosby on his radio show. Having noted that Hollywood was still disinclined to hire her, Crosby had invited Garland to return for his program of February 7, and all of the four programs in March. He later recalled: "She laughed infectiously you know. The . . . weeks we did together on radio were the best I ever had." One can hear her making him laugh in the comedy sketches, as she ad-libbed along with him; and they did one of their best duets on the March 7 show, the clever counterpoint lyric and melody that Irving Berlin had written for *Call Me Madam*, "You're Just in Love." On the March 21 show, there was the first mention of her leaving M-G-M, which enabled them to sing together the song from *Royal Wedding* which she should have performed with Fred Astaire, "How Could You Believe Me When I Said I Loved You When You Know I've Been a Liar All My Life." That these were happy occasions for her may be gauged by the fact that for the first time in public she sang three songs which were later to be part of her repertoire, "Mean to Me," "When You're Smiling" and "Carolina in the Morning." The last Crosby show contains a medley of "Limehouse Blues" (then, almost the only British song to have been popular in America), "April in Paris" and "Isle of Capri," designed as a send-off for her trip to Europe. Crosby made it quite clear that he was in no doubt of the great success she would enjoy at the London Palladium.

The program was broadcast on Wednesday, March 28, and two days later she sailed to England on the *Ile de France*. She was accompanied by Myrtle Tully and Dottie Ponedel, and the pianist Buddy Pepper, whom she had known since her days at the Lawlor school. Pepper had not seen her for some years and had fond memories of always laughing with her. Garland would need an experienced, all-round musician to accompany her at the Palladium, and Pepper had originally been approached about the job by her former "dance-in" at M-G-M, Betty Jane Graham. Garland was not used to working live with an orchestra, so Pepper was to set the musical pace for her and the musicians.

Despite Garland's recent difficulties, Pepper found her unchanged from their earlier friendship, always eager to laugh and joke on the voyage. She was, however, understandably nervous, and Ponedel called Luft from the ship to say that Garland needed him, echoing Garland's own entreaties before leaving America. Ponedel called him at least twice from the Dorchester Hotel in London, but Luft insisted that if he were to come it would only be for a week, and it would have to be as a surprise.

When the *Ile de France* docked at Plymouth, the other ships in port saluted Garland with signals that spelled out her name. The one constant of her press coverage, both of her arrival, and of her first night, was that she was "plump"; even *Sight & Sound*, the highbrow monthly, mentioned it in an otherwise loving tribute to the particular quality of her stardom. Everyone spoke of her "recent troubles,"

The great love of Judy's life, director Joseph Mankiewicz. (British Film Institute)

Judy and Bing Crosby rehearsing during a wartime radio broadcast in 1944. (Photofest)

Judy marrying Vincente Minnelli on June 15, 1945. From left, best man Ira Gershwin, Vincente, Judy, Louis B. Mayer, who gave Judy away, and maid of honor Betty Asher. (Photofest)

Singing with Frank Sinatra on a CBS radio broadcast in 1945. (Bill Chapman Collection)

Director Minnelli adjusting Judy's costume on the set of *The Pirate* in 1947.
Gene Kelly is at left. (The Kobal Collection)

Judy singing to Irving
Berlin's accompaniment
with a smiling Louis B.
Mayer in 1948.
(Bill Chapman Collection)

Judy in 1948 with Arthur Freed, producer of some of MGM's finest musicals and head of the notorious "fairy unit." (Bill Chapman Collection)

Judy with Bill Spier and his wife, Judy's very good friend Kay Thompson. (Bill Chapman Collection)

Judy with baby Liza. (British Film Institute)

At the MGM 25th Anniversary Luncheon in 1949. From left: Ava Gardner, Clark Gable, Judy, Fred Astaire, Betty Garrett, Errol Flynn, and Greer Garson. (Archive Photos)

At the 1952 Tony Awards. From left to right: Oscar Hammerstein, Gertrude Lawrence, Richard Rodgers, Helen Hayes, Phil Silvers, Judy, and Yul Brynner, with whom Judy had an affair. (UPI/Bettmann)

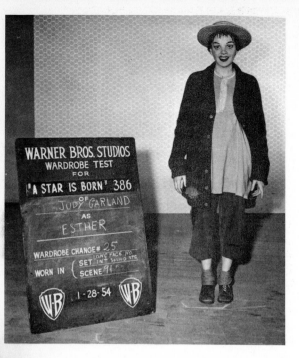

Wardrobe test for *A Star Is Born*, 1954.
(Bill Chapman Collection)

Judy being bussed by Joan Crawford
at Jack Warner's after-premiere party
for *A Star Is Born*. Cesar Romero is
pleased. (Bill Chapman Collection)

On the set of *A Star Is Born*. From left to right: producer Sid Luft, Judy, studio
mogul Jack Warner, and director George Cukor. (Culver)

With her pal Humphrey Bogart in Las Vegas in 1955. (Bill Chapman Collection)

From left, Faye Emerson, Sonja Henie, Edith Piaf, Judy, and Ginger Rogers in 1956.
(Bill Chapman Collection)

Judy with her mentor Roger Edens, Musical Supervisor at MGM, and her occasional date Van Johnson. (Bill Chapman Collection)

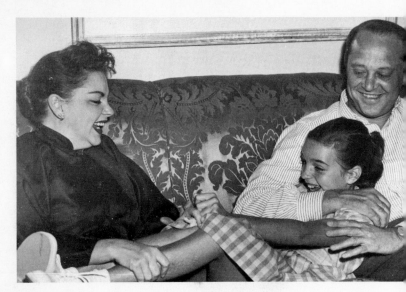

Judy and Sid Luft playing with ten-year-old Liza in 1956 in their suite at the Plaza Hotel in New York. (Bill Chapman Collection)

Judy, taking a break from her Palace gig, and Sid at the Stork Club's New Year's Eve party, 1956. (Archive Photos)

which had certainly been covered by the UK press, but in haphazard fashion, since in this age of postwar austerity, daily newspapers were still limited to four pages. In 1951 rationing was still in force, but the country was about to have a temporary lift, an escape from the severity of the times in the form of the Festival of Britain.

London's theaters were gearing up to several special events for the Festival, with attractions including Laurence Oliver and Vivien Leigh in the Cleopatra plays of Shakespeare and Bernard Shaw. Meanwhile, Cole Porter's *Kiss Me Kate* had opened at the Coliseum and Judy Garland was to star for four weeks at the Palladium. The impresario who ran the theater, Val Parnell, knew that he was taking a gamble. The only other star to head a four-week bill in the postwar period at the Palladium had been Danny Kaye. He was to begin an unprecedented eight weeks immediately Garland finished, but that was partly because it was expected that his run would be swelled by visitors to London for the Festival. Mickey Rooney, the Andrews Sisters, Martha Raye, Carmen Miranda and even Britain's own beloved Gracie Fields were only good for two. Parnell knew how ill Garland had been, and that she had a reputation for unreliability. He was also aware that she had not faced a live audience in eight years. A few years earlier, Gloria Jean, a second-rung Deanna Durbin at Universal, had been so overcome with nerves while performing at the Casino that she invariably fainted, bringing down the curtain every night. Gloria Jean was not Judy Garland; but at the salary Parnell was paying, he needed to sell every seat to make a profit, and could hardly afford canceled shows. However, to get a star of Garland's caliber was just the sort of coup for which the Palladium was noted.

There were to be two shows nightly, at 6:15 and 8:30, and Garland was due to sing for approximately thirty-five minutes. Luft surprised her, as planned, by turning up backstage during a rehearsal. He was with her in a box at the Palladium on the Saturday before her opening when, as was customary, she would be introduced to the theater's audience by the departing star, Hoagy Carmichael. Gerold Frank reports the accolade she received when he said: "Ladies and gentlemen, as you all know, a great little star from America who entertained you with her marvelous pictures is opening on Monday, and she hasn't been feeling too well—so be good to her: Miss Judy Garland." As he finished speaking, a spotlight picked out Garland and she stood to take a bow. It was equally customary, whatever the reaction toward the incoming star—and Garland's greeting was huge and engulfing—

for him or her not to do anything to take the limelight away from the preceding one. Garland sat down quickly, and Carmichael played and sang his song "Judy," the very one from which she had been named.

Also in town at that time was Kay Thompson, who was fulfilling an engagement at the Café de Paris. She had left the Freed unit after *The Pirate*, and had established herself as a chic cabaret entertainer in New York. She was an unknown quantity to Londoners, but the Café de Paris, which had not yet attained its later status, was willing to take a chance with her. Neither she nor Luft could persuade Garland that she was not headed for disaster; nor was Garland reassured by Thompson's promise to be in the wings for both performances on opening night, Monday, April 9. Garland's nerves were very bad. She said of the Sunday night before she opened: "I kept rushing to the bathroom to vomit. I couldn't eat, I couldn't sleep, I couldn't even sit down."

Anyone seeing this miserable creature would have been surprised to learn that she was taking her first step toward becoming one of the greatest stage performers of the century. An expectant audience sat through a bill consisting of The Palladium Girls, who toe-tapped; El Granadas & Peter, "a Mexican specialty"; Tony Fayne and David Evans, impressionists; and some acrobats. A young comedian, Max Bygraves, concluded the first half of the bill—except for some "modernistic dancers," who had been placed in this part of the program so that the inevitable rush to the bars did not interrupt Bygraves's act. After the intermission, an Australian aerialist performed; then the Palladium Girls tippy-tapped again while the stage was cleared and prepared for the star and her pianist. "I think I shall be all right," she had said before going on. "I've got the order of the songs. I know the words and so long as I don't fall down I shall be all right." A roar went up when the orchestra played her intro-music, which, predictably, was "Over the Rainbow." As, waiting in the wings, she heard the song strike up, she looked at Pepper, who was already standing at the piano, and muttered "Oh no!" He gave her a gentle shove as the curtain rose.

Another roar greeted her as she walked uncertainly toward the footlights. She stood, quietly acknowledging the applause. Marcella Rabwin recalled that in all the years she knew Garland, she never saw her well dressed, and on this occasion Garland was wearing a lemon dress with a flared organdy skirt to mid-calf, in the "New Look." *Summer Stock* had already been seen in Britain, but Garland knew that she looked older and stouter than her audience expected.

The fans obviously did not mind, and, as the cheers died, she began to sing a vigorous, rhythmic number composed by Edens for the occasion, a recitative explanation of why it had taken her so long to get to London, which began: "I thought it would never happen . . ." Danny Kaye had told her that she must play the Palladium, she went on, concluding that "it's a long, long way to Piccadilly . . . at long last here I am." The song had been designed for her to test the audience, to steal up on it, to make it wait for the numbers they associated with her. One of her strengths as a performer was her ability to make audiences believe every word that she was singing. The great star of Hollywood musicals was at last here in the flesh, and she was glad to be here. Her songs were greeted with such tidal waves of approval that, midway through the concert, Garland, astonished, retreated— and as she did so, fell over. The tumble was caused by a combination of an unwieldy skirt, high heels and excessive weight. The applause died at once, but she giggled as Pepper helped her to her feet: and she was applauded again. Even though she *had* fallen down, she would be all right. She made a joke of it, and continued to sing her way to what was widely regarded as a personal triumph.

Celebrities customarily attended the second house, which tended to be warmer than the first. However, since it did not usually finish until about 10:30, which was past the deadline for the following day's papers, the press usually came to the first house. One critic who saw both shows was John Barber of the *Daily Express*:

Judy Garland walked into the biggest welcome yet for a first-time-here Hollywood star . . . The audience opened eyes wider to drink all the big girl in.

Bigger still for wearing yellow, with spangles, and with diamond ice at ears, throat, waist and wrist—an ensemble that cheerfully upholds her reputation as the worst-dressed woman on the screen. I thought black would be better till I saw the black gown she chose for the second house. It is hard to recognise the blazing jazz kid in this jolly matron, as big now as is Deanna Durbin.

She sings her [varying] songs in the same pally manner. It hardly suits Cole Porter's 'Just One of Those Things'—nor needs all those mikes. Clutching them, she sways as she sings—mostly old numbers. Her voice is rangy, metallic, rhythmically lush. She bobs her bows, scraping back her hair—brown not auburn.

She melts even the flint-hearts who came to gloat over a star who once fell to earth all screaming nerves and hysteria. This endearing new Judy is the plump kid sister who got on—and wasn't spoiled. She jokes about her size. Backing out, she accidentally falls down and sits on the stage. "That's probably one of the most ungraceful exits ever made," she grins. No tap-dancing for her. And in the end she flops down on her accompanist's seat with a sigh—

"That's better."

This is irresistible. So no one laughs when she sings "Why can't I fly over the rainbow?" And when she admits "I'm nervous," they shout "Never mind. You're doing a great job." She may be a heavy-weight but she certainly hits her stuff home. What if the final cheers are for the *Wizard of Oz* child who trod the yellow brick road for us in the darkest days of the war? It was sincere, and only she had earned it.

I hope she took it as just London's thanks for that when screaming kerchiefed girls mobbed her in the drizzle as she fought her way into the theatre—kissing her, snatching at her hair, shoving placards in her face. For a strung-up artist, it must have been an unnerving ordeal.

The critic of the *Evening Standard*, Beverly Baxter, agreed about the sincerity of the audience's response:

The warmth of that welcome was genuine, kind and understanding—greater and deeper than ever would have been given her when she was the madcap princess of the movies. And genuiness was met by genuiness. This sturdy young woman bowed and smiled as the cheering went on, but there were no tears, no trembling of the lips or wobbling of the chin.

She was a trouper who had come to give a performance. That was what mattered to her.

Curiously enough there was nothing absurd about this Brunnhilde singing old favorites from the films. She possesses moments, and her face is expressive because she plays no tricks . . . The truth is that Miss Garland is now better than her material. This quality of vibrant sincerity opens up possibilities which probably she, herself, had failed to realise. She can command pathos without being maudlin. She is above the wailing nonsense of a crooner who could not sleep a wink last night and all that sort of drivel. In fact she is an artist.

We saw a brave woman on Monday, but more than that we saw a woman who has emerged from the shadows and finds that the public likes her as she is, even more than what she was.

Historically, these were the first of the many affectionate and astonishing appraisals that were to mark her career for the next eighteen years, and they are the first to raise the spectre, always to haunt her thereafter, of a great artist returning from the edge of doom. But she was not, then, a great stage artist. She aimed to please, and did so to the extent that she had the audience in the palm of her hand. She looked happy, recalling her younger days in song, and her few inter-

spersed comments were charmingly done. However, a pirated recording of one of her Palladium performances reveals her voice as
raucous. She belts out the numbers as if nervous that any pianissimo
notes would bore the audience. Yet if she was nervous, her first
allegiance was, as it had been and would always be, to the songs.

With the exceptions of "Limehouse Blues," "Love Is Sweeping the
Country," "Just One of Those Things" and "Rockabye Your Baby,"
all the numbers she sang were songs she had performed in her films—
which was giving the audience exactly what it wanted. But Edens's
intro to the medley of film songs she performed after the show's
opening number, was an even more potent ploy in the making of a
myth:

> For almost twenty years I've been a minstrel girl
> Singing for my supper in the throngs.
> And in that time my world has been a minstrel world
> And the history of my life is in my songs—
> Gay songs, sad songs,
> Good songs, bad songs,
> New songs, old songs,
> Shy songs and bold songs,
> Dusk songs, dawn songs
> Show-must-go-on songs,
> Ever-so-smart songs
> And oh, my broken heart songs.

It is a lyric which allows Judy Garland to do everything she did best:
to be plaintive, irreverent, assertive, playful and witty. Only a great
artist could get away with it, sending herself up slightly in the middle
section and finishing with a heartfelt, slow and "bluesy" vibrato—
which is capped by the modest, pleasing "Would you like to hear?,"
as if she did not expect the clapping which greeted the first few bars
of "You Made Me Love You."

The first-night notices led to the huge house being sold out for the
rest of the run within three days. During the four weeks, Garland
began to ease up and polish the act. On the first night she had made
small-talk with the audience, bantered with Pepper, taken a sip of
water; she had even taken off her shoes. She subsequently added a
few dance steps and gestures to emphasize points in the lyrics of her
songs. She was learning all over again to use the stage as her natural
habitat.

In the case of movie celebrities, it was not unusual for the Palladium to receive bookings from all parts of the country, but out-of-town ticket sales proved exceptionally high for this engagement. It seemed to Harry Foster, who represented William Morris in Great Britain, that he could capitalize on this demand by booking Garland for a provincial tour. Luft was encouraging, and Garland—being Garland—liked the idea of spreading herself around a bit, to show more of these Britishers what she could do. In spite of the evident success of the show, she had received no offers of engagements from America, but Lastfogel had been told that further experience in Britain would make her a safer bet for Broadway.

There was, however, the possibility of a movie in America. Crosby had again come to her assistance, and had persuaded Paramount to prepare a vehicle in which he would co-star with Garland. Paramount had agreed, it has to be said, without enthusiasm, partly because Garland's record proved she was unreliable, and partly because, with increasing age, Crosby was slipping from the pre-eminent place he had held at the box office. He was unlikely to regain the position with *Famous*, which cast him as a widowed songwriter-impresario-singer, whose teenage son falls in love with his leading lady—the role Garland was offered. The songs had been written by Harry Warren and Leo Robin, and it was to be filmed in Technicolor.

Garland was not enamored of the script which Crosby had sent, partly because her role was subsidiary to his. Luft was against her doing the film, because she would have to slim down for it, and this had led to difficulties in the past. She was currently in fine form physically and vocally. A short tour of the provinces would continue the process of restoring her self-confidence. Garland accepted Luft's advice, but only on condition that he cancel his flight home and accompany her. She offered to pay him $500 a week, which seemed to them both quite proper, because she was incapable of handling even the smallest practical arrangement, and needed a manager. Luft therefore did for Judy Garland what he had once done for Eleanor Powell.

Since the leading music halls—and Judy Garland could play no others—were already booked for May and June, Harry Foster needed to do a little juggling. He booked her into Glasgow, Manchester, Liverpool, Dublin and Birmingham for full weeks, and for one night into Blackpool. As there were some free weeks in between engagements, Luft suggested Edinburgh, which seemed a more attractive place to spend a week than the other cities, and would enable him to get in a few rounds of golf at St. Andrew's. Foster argued that Edinburgh was a duff venue for music hall, even for someone of Garland's stature, but Luft insisted. Foster reluctantly made the booking.

Meanwhile, at the Palladium, Judy Garland was the toast of the town, receiving celebrities in her dressing-room and holding court at the Dorchester. Even Winston Churchill came, and Britain's most distinguished actors, including Laurence Olivier and Vivien Leigh, who invited Garland and Luft to their country home, Notley Abbey, the *sine qua non* for a visiting show-business personality. One celebrity she did not see was Robert Donat, whom she had been longing to meet since childhood. She loved him far more even than Dear Mr. Gable. She was tremendously excited to receive a letter from him, handed to her in her dressing-room by his chauffeur; but instead of congratulating her on her performance he was recommending his psychiatrist. She could think of no answer to give the chauffeur, or Donat himself when he telephoned two days later to say that he was going out of town on location and could she hold on until he returned? She reflected that it was a bizarre way of not meeting the man of her dreams.

Although she was limp and exhausted after each performance, her extraordinary constitution enabled her to recover quickly. After her own first night, she had gone on to Kay Thompson's opening at the Café de Paris, where she had received a standing ovation. There were parties or celebratory dinners every night: London's nightclubs were there to be explored. But best of all, Garland was a success. As she said herself, she was reborn on that first night.

She had a fortnight's rest before beginning her tour, and had decided that she wanted to see Paris. Two days after she closed at the Palladium, she went there by train with Luft, Dottie Ponedel and Tully. Hollywood had always portrayed Paris as the most romantic of European cities, particularly the Paris it re-created on the back lot— as Minnelli had just done for *An American in Paris*. The differences between Minnelli and Luft were very apparent on this trip. Minnelli would have taken her to the Louvre: Luft took her to Longchamps. They did, however, go to Versailles and to the Paris Opera. She visited the salons of Balmain and Balanciaga, and she cheered herself up by buying two Balmain gowns.

She opened at the Empire, Glasgow, on Monday, May 21, but the house was not sold out. It seemed that provincial audiences were less likely to be impressed by a Hollywood star than those in London, but the people who came were equally enthusiastic. Further disappointment awaited her in Edinburgh, where only about 500 out of a possible 2,000 seats had been sold for the first house. The second house was packed, however. Even so, Garland needed to make all the money she could on this trip. After Edinburgh, she had a week before her next engagement in England, and in a move to economize, Dottie Ponedel returned to the US. The following day, Garland and Luft took a quick overnight trip to Paris. On her twenty-ninth birthday, Sunday, June 10, they traveled to Manchester, where she opened the following evening at the Palace, with the comedian Michael Bentine in support.

In the pictures published in the British press at this time, Sid Luft was identified as Judy Garland's business manager and a candidate for her next husband. Marriage had not been discussed, but she did ask him to take over her career, as Carleton Alsop had done, and manage her finances. She was still deeply in debt, and believed that Luft could cope with this, as he could cope with anything else, which was one reason she had been attracted to him in the first place.

They were a very odd couple, however, and no one seeing them together would imagine that they were happily in love, as Luft later claimed. It seems that there had even been another suicide attempt, since on the first night at the Palace, Garland went on stage with one wrist bandaged. Harry Rigg, the Northern press representative of EMI Records, decided to visit her in Manchester because EMI distributed Garland's M-G-M records in the UK. He discovered that Luft expected him to appear every night, and he did so. Each night, he reported, Garland left the stage like a limp rag, completely unable to cope with even the simplest task: but she was soon craving a drink and raring to go. After one show, Rigg took her to Manchester's only nightclub. Luft had been detained at the theater, and by the time he joined them, Garland had become so aggressive, flailing her arms about, that the manager asked Rigg to remove her. At this point Luft arrived, sized up the situation, and took her away.

In Rigg's opinion, she was drunk throughout the time he was with them in Manchester, but she was usually quiet, as if bewildered, as if she did not know where she was. He found her a pathetic figure, not helped by Luft, who appeared to treat her with complete contempt. Every night the two of them would stand in the wings as she waited to go on, and Luft would push her out, on one occasion saying: "Get out on stage, you drunken bitch." The combination of an antagonistic manager and deeply disturbed star was, Rigg thought, "explosive" and he was glad to see them go. Nor were the Manchester audiences as large as might have been expected.

On June 18 she began a week at the Empire, Liverpool, and on June 25 she was back at the Palladium, for a midnight matinee performance to honor the comedian Sid Field, who had died in January, leaving little money. The proceeds of the concert were to be put in a trust fund for his children. Field's reputation within the profession was such that it was a star-studded evening. Her old flame, Orson Welles, did conjuring tricks and Laurence Olivier, Vivien Leigh and Danny Kaye performed the comic ditty "Triplets." But to Noël Coward, who was in the audience, the "highest spot" was Judy Garland, who sang "Rockabye Your Baby With a Dixie Melody" and "Over the Rainbow." He hugged Judy in her dressing-room later and told her: "You're a very great artist, my darling." Kenneth Tynan recalled:

> She had made her comeback, plump as a peach, with that foxy little smile around her lips, and the voice as full of hope as ever. Is the vibrato a bit more pronounced than it was? Perhaps. Has she mislaid the frailty which was so winning when she sang: "They call us babes in arms—but we are babes in armour"? Again, perhaps. But she has only to open her throat, and send her voice pleading and appealing up to the roof, to leave no doubt that talent like hers is independent of age and appearance . . . The show had lasted three and a half hours before she came on, stood in a pale violet spot, and sang: "Rockabye Your Baby With a Dixie Melody." The house rose to her, in great crashing waves of applause, the kind for which the Palladium was built. If, as the story went, she had lost faith in herself, she had her answer that night.

After the benefit, she was free until she appeared at the Royal, Dublin, on Monday, July 2, and her tour concluded after a week at the Hippodrome, Birmingham, where she was joined by Liza, whom she had not seen for three months. It was with some apprehension that Minnelli had received Garland's request that their daughter join her in England. Liza was now five, with fond but intermittent memories of Garland as a mother. As a show-business parent, Garland had in fact behaved somewhat better than most, but Minnelli thought that Liza had too often seen her mother lying ill in bed, in the throes of self-doubt and rejection. Since Garland was wedded to the business, Minnelli thought this might be an opportunity for Liza to share in her mother's triumphs. He had decided that one week of watching her mother from the wings, with the prospect of an ocean voyage to follow, when she returned to the States with Garland, would prove beneficial to both mother and daughter. Accompanied by her governess, Liza had arrived on the *Queen Elizabeth*.

In Birmingham, Tully arranged for some fans to go backstage to meet Garland. She had not guaranteed a meeting, but said that they might ask at the stage door whether they had been lucky. They had, and one of them, Reg Needle, later recalled how impressed they had been by the way their idol had greeted them: "no pretension whatever, just very natural and ordinary. Judy said 'Hello, I've heard all about you, won't you come in and sit down please?' "—but there was nowhere to sit because the settee was piled high with toys and clothes for Liza. She told her visitors that she had noticed some sourpusses in the front row, pulling faces, and felt that she wanted to say to them: "Oh go away, go away. You don't want to see me, let those boys come from the back—they love me." She looked at them: "I was playing right to you, you know." As the fans left, telling her once again that she was "terrific," she returned to the subject: "You can work your heart out for some people and they never applaud."

One effect of Garland's addiction to pills was to magnify the importance of anyone who did not seem to be enjoying the show, but she did not have to worry about a few people in the front row. Unlike some of her British dates, the Birmingham engagement was a sell-out. As on some of the other last nights, the British audience did a very un-British thing by standing up and singing to her. The song chosen was "Auld Lang Syne."

15

✦✦✦✦✦✦✦

The Palace

"DON'T EVER STOP making pictures, Judy," one of the fans in Birmingham had said to her, and she had replied: "Don't worry, I won't." But the choice was not hers to make. *Famous* had gone ahead without her, partly because Paramount had cunningly suggested Jane Wyman in her place. Crosby and Wyman had teamed well recently in *Here Comes the Groom*, and since they had established an off-screen rapport, Crosby would find Wyman a welcome substitute.* For Garland, there were no more offers, and she lingered in Europe with Luft and Liza. She had been invited to sing at a charity benefit in Monte Carlo, and they decided to holiday at the Carlton Hotel in neighboring Cannes. Its exclusive beach enabled Garland and Liza to swim without being bothered by crowds. The three of them were not, however, a family, as became clear one evening at a party. Garland had gone off with Noël Coward's group, and Luft had gone with another which

---

*The film's title was changed to *Just for You*, and it was a damp squib when released in the summer of the following year.

included an available blonde. When he was awakened the next morning Garland was dismissive and told him to get himself ready for the luncheon date they had.

At the end of the holiday, Luft flew back to New York on his own. He disliked the enforced inactivity of a sea voyage and, more importantly, he wanted to be on the pier to welcome Garland when she arrived on the *Queen Elizabeth* on August 12. He was alone. After her reception in Britain, Garland had expected to be greeted by a crowd of waiting reporters. This was a terrible blow and something she and Luft decided not to discuss. *Variety* did send a number of its staff to interview her at the St. Regis Hotel, where she talked of a possible concert tour to conclude with a booking at Carnegie Hall. She also said that she was reading film scripts—"But look at me," she added. "I'm overdoing this 'pleasingly plump' business. But I don't care. I never felt better in my life." She also said that she was about to consult the William Morris Agency about her future plans, but Luft already knew that the only offer that Lastfogel had received for her services was for six radio shows at $1,500 each.

Gerold Frank, who after all had Luft's cooperation, is particularly good in relating how he arrived at a momentous decision: Luft was walking in Seventh Avenue, wondering how to let America know about Garland's triumphs in Britain, when he saw a girl he knew outside the Winter Garden Theater. She told him that she was playing the lead in the Winter Garden's current show. It was a theater particularly associated with Al Jolson, and if an unknown girl could stand in Jolson's spotlight, Judy Garland ought to be at the Palace, which in that same era had starred the greatest names of vaudeville: Sophie Tucker, Nora Bayes, Fanny Brice, Elsie Janis, Eva Tanguay, Jimmy Durante, the Dolly Sisters, Will Rogers, Lillian Russell and Eddie Cantor. That was long ago, however. The Palace had gone over to movies in 1933, in the middle of the Depression. In its checkered career since, it had functioned, briefly, as a radio studio, and it was currently playing dime movies—but at $1.25, because of the vaudeville show that augmented them: five assorted acts of a quality that attracted only people with nothing better to do. The theater was tattered and unkempt, its gilt and velvet obscured by layers of dust and years of tobacco smoke. Still, it was geographically at the very heart of New York's theaterland, and it was owned by RKO, whose several vice-presidents included an acquaintance of Luft's, Sol Schwartz.

Luft called RKO's office from a telephone booth near the Palace.

Schwartz suggested meeting in the theater lobby in a few minutes, and his greeting to him was: "Sid, are you thinking what I'm thinking?" He, at least, knew of Garland's transatlantic triumphs. He showed Luft over the theater, suggesting ideas for its refurbishments, and by the time they parted, Two-a-Day was scheduled to return to the old house under the title "Judy at the Palace."

Once back at the hotel, full of enthusiasm, he found a Garland miserably unhappy and uncomfortable—the air-conditioning in her suite had broken down. She received his news with excitement but no surprise, since by now she firmly believed that there was nothing he could not achieve for her. Lastfogel negotiated a contract with the Palace management which would give Garland a percentage of the gross, out of which she would pay the other performers on the bill. She expected to earn less than at the Palladium, which was almost twice the size, but the Palace was the Palace.

Despite their own excitement at the prospect of the Palace, the press was not very interested. She gave an impromptu, last-minute interview on the aptly named *Milkman's Matinee* early-morning radio program, for she said "The engagement is for four weeks with an option to go longer—if anybody comes to see it." As a local New York City program, *The Milkman's Matinee* did not have many listeners, but after she and Luft had flown to the West Coast, she netted a much larger fish—Louella Parsons, who was delighted to have Judy Garland on her show. Garland was equally pleased because chatting to Parsons on her widely syndicated Sunday evening gossip round-up was excellent exposure. As far as Parsons was concerned, Garland's return to Hollywood was news, as was her new career as a stage star, and she gushed as she discussed the success at the Palladium. She asked Judy whether she had been to M-G-M and was told:

M-G-M is still home for me, but I wasn't prepared for what they did when I asked if I could borrow some things for my act at the Palace. The gave me Chuck Walters, one of their best directors, and my favorite music man, Roger Edens, for the songs. We've been together for sixteen years. But what touched me most was that all the clothes that had been designed for me by Hattie Carnegie when I was supposed to be in *Royal Wedding* were put in a special box that nobody had even been allowed to open.

This last statement was touching, but totally untrue. Carnegie had not even designed any costumes for that ill-fated film, and only a couple of those designed for Garland by Helen Rose had been made up.

M-G-M may have loaned Garland Walters and Edens to advise her for the unfulfilled engagement at the Cal-Neva Lodge, but there was no guarantee that they would do so again, particularly since both men by now held high positions at the studio. In the event, Walters and Edens were happy to take leaves of absence. Edens had long wanted to see Garland before a live audience again, and would be arranging her songs and writing special material. He listened to the Palladium recording and became excited. The little girl who had once wanted to sing like the red hot mamas now courted comparison with no one. He had thwarted her attempts to be a junior Ethel Merman or Helen Morgan; now she was Judy Garland, whose voice could fill any theater. He planned her material accordingly. To emphasize the importance of the occasion, another old colleague, Hugh Martin, was delighted at the chance of accompanying her at the piano; again this was something less than his present standing in the industry warranted. M-G-M also gave Irene Sharaff permission to design some of Garland's costumes. She would also be wearing the Balmain dress she had bought in Paris.

It had been agreed almost immediately that the show was not to be just a repeat of her Palladium act, but would show off her skills as a dancer. Walters planned the choreography for Garland and her "Boyfriends," a chorus of eight young men. The show was also to be about twenty minutes longer, to capitalize on the excitement engendered in New York when it was first announced that vaudeville was returning to the Palace with a bill headed by Judy Garland.

Everything seemed to be going smoothly, when Garland discovered that she was pregnant. There was no way of pretending that Minnelli was the father. Her appearance at the Palace had priority over anything else, whatever trepidations she may have had. There was more to this New York commitment, for if, as they had every reason to believe, the success of the Palladium show were to be repeated there, then Los Angeles would follow and Hollywood would see just what Judy Garland could do. She and Luft agreed that she should have an abortion: her third.

While rehearsing with her Boyfriends, she worked harder than she had ever done before. This was partly because she was delighted with the plans that Edens and Walters had made, but hard work also acted as a diversion, for not all the publicity she was receiving at this time was good publicity.

This was the result of an accident which happened just after two in the morning of September 30, when Luft went through a red light at the intersection of La Cienega and Beverly Boulevard. He hit another car, got out and apologized, but was accused of being drunk by a witness. Luft was very polite, but those in the wrecked car were shouting at him. Garland joined in the altercation, at one point taking a swing at one of the witnesses, knocking off his spectacles, which broke as they hit the sidewalk. An independent witness claimed that Luft had punched him when he had arrived to offer assistance.

Luft tried to protect Garland by claiming that she had not been in the car, but had heard the crash either from the rehearsal hall or a neighboring bar. He also said that he was responsible for the broken spectacles. Fortunately for Garland, who, in the opinion of witnesses, was as drunk as Luft, the police asked only cursory questions when they recognized who she was. Luft was arrested for drunken driving and for carrying a gun without a license. The police had discovered this weapon in the car, and although Luft said it was his, it was found to be registered in the name of the director of security at the Douglas Aircraft factory.

For once, the fan magazines and the gossip columnists did not have to invent anything. Pictures of Luft graphically demonstrated his state—boozy and belligerent. When the case finally came to trial, Luft was fined $150 in lieu of thirty days in jail for drunken driving. The other charge was dismissed. The journalists were unanimous in declaring that he was the wrong man for a girl known to be hypersensitive and overemotional: hadn't she had enough trouble in her life?

Garland's friends concurred, but kept quiet, knowing that she never took any notice of unwelcome advice. She told anyone who would listen how much in love she was, and she enjoyed the idea of one of Hollywood's class acts tying herself up with one of its fly-by-nights— a man in complete contrast to Minnelli, Mankiewicz, and all the other men in her life. She loved the drama of the situation: this was another role for her to play, and was quite in keeping with the image of "helpless Judy." As many people at M-G-M have confirmed, in many ways she was not in the least helpless, but always in command, even at her most demented. Friends were also obliged to admit that she was patently happier, more at peace with herself, than she had been for years. As Buddy Pepper pointed out, she could never have tackled the British provincial tour without Luft, nor contemplated bringing vaudeville back to Broadway.

It was recognized that Luft was the prime operator in re-establishing her in the eye of the American public, and this was what the Palace engagement was meant to do. There were many who remained doubtful of Garland's abilities to breathe life back into vaudeville. These included a member of the Palace staff, who refused to paint her dressing-room until ordered to do so. He was equally reluctant to enlarge the orchestra pit. "We'd have to take out three five-dollar seats," he argued. "We'll need every cent we make. I don't expect this show to last long." Luft had the seats unbolted after the man had gone home.

In spite of the skeptics, advance bookings were heavy, with no seats available for the first week. The first-night house, on October 16, 1951, could have been sold out five times over. No one doubted the reason: a huge poster with her full-length portrait twelve feet high on the façade of the Palace. The unimpressive box of a lobby was hung with crystal chandeliers and part of the old Albee art collection, borrowed from other RKO theaters. The crowds surrounding the theater were so vast that by the time Garland arrived, she had to walk the last block, ducking in by the stage door. Among those waiting inside were Marlene Dietrich, Jimmy Durante, Irving Berlin, Sophie Tucker, Dorothy Lamour, Jack Benny, Gloria Swanson, Lauritz Melchior, Jane Froman, Moss Hart, Martha Raye, Sam Goldwyn, Lee Shubert, Blossom Seeley, Billy Rose—and, later in the week, General MacArthur.

The first half was not so different from the bill at the Palladium: an acrobat act, the Langs; Doodles and Spider, who mimed to popular records; a dancing European couple, Giselle and Francis Szony; Max Bygraves, making his American debut at Garland's request; and, for the sake of nostalgia, Smith and Dale, a cross-talk act who had played the Palace long years before. The second half opened with the Boyfriends dancing. They gathered together in a bunch, then gradually parted to reveal Garland advancing from behind them. At the mere sight of her, the audience erupted. The cheering went on for eight minutes, at the end of which, she knew that she could do no wrong. She shouted "Hello!" through the noise, which diminished as she and the Boyfriends launched into two pieces of special material by Edens, "Call the Papers" and "On the Town." She had great confidence in her first solo number, a tribute by Edens to the stars who had played the Palace in the past, followed by the songs associated with them: Nora Bayes's "Shine On, Harvest Moon"; Fanny Brice's "My Man" (which even Brice had never done so hauntingly); Sophie Tucker's "Some of These Days" (and it was years since Tucker's voice had soared so spectacularly on this one); and Eva Tanguay's "I Don't Care," which Garland tore into even more ecstatically than in *In the*

Good Old Summertime. After "Rockabye Your Baby With a Dixie Melody," Garland rhapsodized again—as at the Palladium—about her own role as a "minstrel girl," once more linking "You Made Me Love You," "For Me and My Gal," "The Boy Next Door" and "The Trolley Song." These were Judy's songs, reminders of her happy times. Later in the run, she rewarded her audiences with a special rendering of "A Pretty Girl Milking Her Cow" from *Little Nelly Kelly* as an encore. Otherwise the routines remained as they had been planned. The audience rose to her after each number, and again as she dashed into the wings to change. The Boyfriends danced while she did so, and she suddenly appeared among them once more, this time in her "Get Happy" costume—and she performed that number with just as much rhythmic confidence as she had done on screen.

The Boyfriends danced while she changed for another movie memory. "A Couple of Swells," which she performed with Max Bygraves—until he returned to England, after which she was partnered by one of the Boyfriends. But on this special first night, Walters chose to be her partner (particularly because he was not entirely happy with Bygraves's interpretation). Walters and Edens were jointly responsible for "the Garland legend," which was beginning to take shape this evening. A notable feature of the legend was when she sat at the footlights in her "Couple of Swells" clown makeup to sing the one song the audience always wanted to hear. "You've been wonderful to me tonight," she said, "and I'll never forget it. Now I want to do something special just for you—all of you . . ." And with a white spotlight on her face, she sang "Over the Rainbow." Everyone in the audience knew what she had been through over the years, and as she sang the last, wistful line, "Why then, oh why can't I?," the song no longer belonged to Dorothy: it belonged, forever, to Judy Garland.

The ushers brought bouquets up the aisles, as the diminutive figure stood there, nodding her head in humility and gratitude as the thunderous applause rolled on for ten minutes. "I just want to say I love you," she said. New friends and old tumbled into her dressing-room, while a crowd of several thousand waited on the sidewalk at the front of the theater. A Palace minion suggested that she could avoid them by leaving by the stage door, but an exultant Garland was not going to disappoint her fans.

In the event, it was she who was disappointed. As she and Walters made their way to the car, the crowd parted silently. Garland nodded and smiled, but there had been a sea-change in the public perception of her. In the car she complained to Walters: "Nobody said a fucking word! What's the matter with them?" He reassured her: they were in awe of her.

As they walked into the 21 Club she thought of the line Edens had written for her, and which she had sung so thrillingly: "Vaudeville's back at the Palace and I'm on the bill."

The press realized that what had happened that night was something out of the ordinary. *Life* reported that, by the end of the concert,

almost everyone in the theater was crying and for days afterwards people around Broadway talked of it as if they had beheld a miracle. What they had beheld was Judy Garland making her debut at the old Palace, which was having a comeback to straight two-a-day vaudeville.

But the real comeback was Judy's. The girl with the voice meant equally for lullabies, love songs and plain whooping and hollering deserved the most overworked word in her profession—great. And the long, unhappy years of illness, divorce and declining stardom were over.

Variety also recognized that it was not merely a question of Broadway sentiment:

Hers was a tour-de-force of no small caliber. The hep and sentimentally attuned firstnighters left the Palace in a burst of reflected stardust, for there is no disputing, at any time, that the ex-Metro songstress is simon pure stellar quality. Miss Garland is a singer's singer . . . with her you hear every word and phrase. She's a great natural singer . . . [who] combines a high-powered little girl quality with a mature, authoritative approach that is undeniable.

The enthusiasm of both audiences and the press proved infectious as New York went wild in its acclamation of Judy Garland. There were parties "from midnight to dawn," Max Bygraves remembered. "Anybody who was anybody wanted Judy at their party. All and sundry told her how great she was; you've got to start believing it if it's said as often as was said to her."

The first-night notices had made it abundantly clear that the run could be extended indefinitely, but by the end of the second week, Schwartz and Luft noticed that Garland's voice was beginning to sound hoarse.

In spite of her excellent notices, one newspaper had reported unkindly on her figure, and she began dieting again. This, combined with a party every night, would hardly be a sensible regime, even for a performer more disciplined than Garland. One Sunday matinee in November, while Luft was in Los Angeles dealing with legal matters (another dispute about alimony, and the drunk-driving charge), Garland complained that she felt sick. The house doctor could not be located, so another, a certain Dr. Salmon, who had been recommended by a friend, was brought in. Salmon gave her a sedative and told her not to go on. Garland insisted that she could not disappoint her audience. She believed that the sheer euphoria she experienced when confronting one would enable her body to rally: but that, alas, did not happen, and, realizing this, she did not even try to do the Palace medley, she lost her way in "Rockabye Your Baby With a Dixie Melody," for which she only too audibly blamed "that stupid man Al Jolson." Hearing scattered catcalls, she retreated, and Vivian Blaine (then playing Miss Adelaide in *Guys and Dolls*) valiantly stepped out of the audience to take over. She sang for twenty minutes, until relieved by the comedian Jan Miller, who finished the show. Garland's condition was diagnosed as nervous exhaustion, and she was forced to rest. Except for Mondays, when there was no matinee, she had done two shows every day (including Sundays) at 2:40 and 8:40. Luft decided to cut the Monday evening show and weekday matinees, reducing Garland's workload to eight shows a week. The Palace management had no complaints, as she had agreed to stay on and was playing to capacity at every performance. When she returned, five nights later, she received an ovation little short of the one on opening night.

Soon after his return from California Luft noticed that in the morning Garland's coordination was not too bright until she had breakfasted, and he suspected that she was taking some sort of drug. Most of those close to Garland tended to look the other way when she was popping pills—as long as she was able to perform. Gerold Frank states that when Luft heard her telephone Dr. Salmon, however, there was a row between them. She refused to allow Luft to remain in the room during the "consultation," telling him to "get the hell out." Luft knew that Garland would listen to any quack and decided that in Salmon he had discovered one. He told the doctor that he would kill him if he ever came back. Garland's mood immediately changed, and her response to Luft's behavior was docile: "I think you're right. I'll get in trouble with him."

In the first weeks of 1952, Clifton Fadiman, writing in *Holiday* magazine, was enraptured:

Where lay the magic? Why did we grow silent, self-forgetting, our faces lit as with so many candles, our eyes glittering with unregarded tears?

Why did we call her back again and again and again, not as if she had been giving a good performance, but as if she had been offering salvation.

Some of the effect may be traceable to the extraneous drama of Judy's personal life. After a period of too highly publicized grief and failure and misfortune, this was her comeback. Of *course* we wanted her to be wonderful, as if her triumphs could somehow help to wipe out our own sorrows and weaknesses. But there was more to it than that.

Much more. As we listened to her voice, with its unbelievable marriage of volume and control, as we watched her, in her tattered tramp costume, telling the most delicious jokes with arms, legs, head, and eyes, we forgot—and this is the acid test—who she was, and indeed who we were ourselves. As with all true clowns (for Judy Garland is as fine a clown as she is a singer) she seemed to be neither male nor female, young nor old, pretty nor plain. She had no "glamour," only magic. She was gaiety itself, yearning itself, fun itself. She expressed a few simple, common feelings so purely that they floated about in the dark theater, bodiless, as if detached from any specific personality. She wasn't being judged or enjoyed, not even watched or heard. She was only being felt, as one feels the quiet run of one's own blood, the shiver of the spine, Housman's prickle of the skin. And when, looking about eighteen inches high, sitting hunched over the stage apron with only a tiny spotlight pinpointing her elf face, she breathed the last phrases of "Over the Rainbow" and cried out its universal, unanswerable query, "Why can't I?" it was as though the bewildered hearts of all the people in the world had moved quietly together and become one, shaking in Judy's throat, and there breaking.

She missed other performances, and on occasion the show began as much as fifty minutes late, but the Palace appearances continued to be a success. Scalpers were getting as much as $30 each for orchestra seats, normally priced at $4.80. The comparative cheapness of the tickets was explained by Sol Schwartz: "We didn't know what we had in advance, and didn't want to raise prices after the main reviews." There were some changes to personnel. Max Meth, who conducted the orchestra for the intended two months, had to leave for another engagement and was succeeded, at Garland's request, by her brother-in-law Jack Cathcart, who arranged a rousing new overture for her entrance. When Bygraves had to take up another engagement in London, he was replaced by the ventriloquist Señor Wences, and Doodles and Spider were followed in their spot by the Nicholas Brothers, who had been in *The Pirate*.

In all, the show ran for nineteen weeks, finally closing on Sunday, February 24, 1952. As *Variety* noted: "It's generally conceded that

Miss Garland could have remained another nineteen weeks had she so desired." The run had

made show business history firstly by proving that two-a-day can be a top box office medium, and that the Palace name is still an important landmark. It needed a Judy Garland to prove that Vaudeville can still be sold at $4.80 and that a performer of Miss Garland's magnitude can run indefinitely on that basis.

The show had grossed some $750,000, $540,000 of this in the last week during which she gave eleven performances. It was a record figure for vaudeville.

The last night was almost as spectacular as the first, with over half the audience there for a return visit, having already seen the show earlier in its run, according to *Variety*. "The prevailing sentiment seemed to be lachrymose," and there were numerous encores. At the end of the show, Garland introduced the famous opera singer Lauritz Melchior as her successor on the bill the following week. He joined her on stage, for some jokes, and, as he returned to his seat, she said: "Well, I think I'd better go now." The audience would have none of that. "Speeches and three extra numbers didn't suffice." *Variety* reported. "The crowd just didn't move although most knew that she had done three numbers more than in her usual shows. There were requests from all over the house." Melchior suggested that the audience should sing to the star. "Sing me a song?" she said, "You want to sing me a song? All right. Come on, sing me a song. I'm tired of singing, come on." Melchior stood up, and after Hugh Martin had played the first few bars of "Auld Lang Syne" he led the audience in singing it to Garland. "It was one of the warmest tributes ever given a headliner in New York," observed *Variety*, which described the whole show as "one of the more memorable experiences in the history of the two-a-day."

Melchior did play the Palace but not for long. Over the weekend someone questioned the commercial validity of the booking, precisely because, as Marian Spitzer says in her history of the famous theater: "Judy Garland's sensational run had changed the habits of audiences and the history of the Palace. From that moment on, audiences would not be satisfied with anything less than a blockbuster." And she was proved right. The Garland formula was repeated when Betty Hutton opened three weeks later. *Variety* summed up what had taken place.

Miss Garland has set a pattern that will be hard for anyone to follow. At her opening, the public seemed to sense that she needed to make good on this assignment if her career was to continue. Theatergoers knew that she was a sick kid, and there was a collective feeling that they would give her the security that she needed. Her public may well have contributed considerably to her physical and mental comeback. Her professional status was never in doubt.

A few years later, there would unquestionably have been a commercial recording of the concert, but at the time albums of live performances were rare. Decca had exploited the show's success, however, by rushing out an album featuring some of the songs that she had been singing, along with others associated with her. They called it *Judy at the Palace*, and the sleeve carried a photograph of her onstage. It sold so well that Garland had no reason to go to a studio to record the same songs for any other company. Another result of the Palace engagement was that Garland was honored with a special Tony Award.

"New York had been a great stimulant," Garland announced. "I never knew I had so many friends. With such encouragement, I can do anything." She was adamant that this new confidence had come about as a result of Luft's faith in her. "He kept telling me that my career wasn't over, that it had just begun. He was so right. He took me through the dark times, and I'll never forget that." Luft had certainly discovered that he could no longer push her out on the stage, commanding her to perform. Once the initial euphoria of becoming a live performer had abated, however, she needed reassurance to appear. Since he could not always be with her, he had hired a "production assistant" during the Palace run. Vern Alves's real job, however, was to keep Garland in high spirits. A bachelor in his thirties, who had been General Mark Clark's adjutant during the war, Alves had more recently worked as Fred Finklehoffe's secretary. He was ideal for the job and Garland liked him on first sight.

Immediately after the Palace engagement ended, Luft and Garland went to Palm Beach for a vacation. This was at the suggestion of the Duke and Duchess of Windsor, with whom they hobnobbed on the golf course and in nightclubs. In March, they returned to Los Angeles, the obvious second stop of what was now called "The Judy Garland Show." Luft wanted her back in films, and more than ever he wanted Hollywood to see that not only was she reliable, but a powerhouse talent, who deserved to be back in front of the cameras. In November, at the height of her Palace triumph, Luft had arranged for Garland's film career to be handled by Charles K. Feldman, the outstanding agent of the day: but even Feldman was unable to get her any movie offers.*

She opened at the Los Angeles Civic Auditorium for a four-week run on April 21, 1952. On the first night, she stopped the cheering with a heartfelt announcement: "It's the happiest night of my life. I've missed you." Afterwards, the party at Romanoff's was attended by the industry's luminaries, most of whom had been at the concert: the Mayers, the Goldwyns, the Warners, the Cohns, the William Goetzes and Eddie Mannix. Joining them in a standing ovation as Garland entered, wearing scarlet velvet and an ermine wrap, were such stars as Humphrey Bogart and Lauren Bacall, Eleanor Parker, George Burns and Gracie Allen, Joan Crawford, the Jack Bennys, Jean Simmons, Claire Trevor, Danny Kaye, James Stewart, Jimmy McHugh, Louella Parsons, Esther Williams and June Allyson. Garland had a word for each of them, an embrace for some, and a kiss for Mayer.

The triumphant return to California brought problems in its wake, however. Before the engagement had opened, Luft was stopped in the foyer by a woman who introduced herself as Judy Garland's mother. Ethel asked whether Garland could help her with her life-insurance payments, which she was unable to meet from her salary. Luft told her not to worry, but to sign it over to Garland. Ethel said that she could not do that, because it was made out in the name of all three sisters. She also asked for the loan of $200. Luft said cheerfully that they would make her an allowance of $25 a week, but Ethel was too proud to accept this. Garland still refused to see her.

A month later, Ethel decided to make her woes public, and they made good copy. As a clerical worker with Douglas Aircraft, she earned $61 a week, while her ungrateful daughter was making thousands. On a percentage in New York, Garland had been earning about $15,000 a week, and in the much larger Civic Auditorium in Los Angeles, this became $25,000 weekly—though in each case she had to pay her company out of this sum.

In her column in *Daily Variety*, Sheilah Graham recorded Ethel's unflattering portrait of her famous daughter: "Judy has been selfish all her life. That's my fault. I made it too easy for her. She worked— that's all she ever wanted—to be an actress. She never said, 'I want to be kind or loved,' only 'I want to be famous.' " Graham also said:

*Garland was to remain with Feldman till 1960, when she made another comeback; but the agency destroyed its Garland file in 1966, depriving us of any record of what offers there were later in this period.

"Judy's mother tells me that she feels like a cross between Marjorie Main and Stella Dallas.* And added—'Judy and I never had a quarrel, she just brushed me off.' "

Encouraged by the sense of importance that these interviews gave her, Ethel decided to sue for maintenance. Garland faced the charge with equanimity. She pointed out that Ethel had enjoyed a successful career as a pianist, an accompanist, and a theater manager. She even managed to find papers to prove that she had paid Ethel handsomely at the time her mother had been her "manager." The case was dismissed.

Before going on to San Francisco, where she opened at the Curran on May 26 for a month's engagement, Garland recorded three more programs with Bing Crosby, to be broadcast on consecutive weeks from May 21. Crosby joked that, since she was the person who had brought back vaudeville, maybe she could do the same for radio. Many old stars had been revitalized by television, and some of the biggest names in the profession were making frequent appearances in the new medium: Bob Hope, Eddie Cantor, Jack Benny, Burns and Allen, Frank Sinatra, Perry Como, Groucho Marx, Ethel Waters, Dinah Shore—indeed, almost everyone from the "lighter" side of show business *except* Crosby, who was still holding out against it. He and Garland were as appealing together as they had ever been, joking and singing, but, without exception, Garland's songs were ones she had done before. The heart had gone out of radio.

In Palm Beach, on March 6, when her divorce decree from Minnelli became final, Garland told the press that she had no plans to marry Luft. But by March 21, when she and Luft arrived in Nassau for the Bahamas Country Club amateur gold cup tournament, she had changed her mind. Her divorce decree from Minnelli had finally come. She was pregnant again. She may have had Liza's welfare in mind; she could be more of a mother to her with Sid as stepfather. When she suggested it to Luft, he did not greet the idea with any enthusiasm. For one thing, he was aware that each had previously failed to make two marriages work, and that this did not bode well. His dilemma was that he did not really want to marry Garland, but

*Marjorie Main was one of the leading supporting actresses of the 1940s and 1950s and played comic rubes, including Ma Kettle. Stella Dallas is the eponymous heroine of Olive Higgins Prouty's novel: a Midwestern barman's daughter, she marries above herself and is unable to adapt to her husband's more refined ways, which eventually leads to a tragic falling out between herself and her grown-up daughter. It had been filmed with great success in 1925 and 1937.

he did not want to let her go. As long as he remained her manager and lover, it would be possible to extricate himself from the demands put upon him; as her husband, this would be much more difficult. As her husband, however, he would have a tighter control over someone capable of earning a great deal of money. On balance he was in favor of the marriage, but he made sure that she knew that he was very apprehensive. She realized that he was not entirely thrilled at the prospect when he began complaining that his former wife's lawyer would be at his throat, demanding more money for child support. (This did in fact happen.) It was one thing to let Garland have her own way, since that was the easiest way of handling her; it was quite another to allow her to believe that by doing so, it made everyone happier.

Once again, Garland had deluded herself that marriage would provide the happy ending she was always seeking. First of all she wanted to be married, to be someone's wife again. She and Luft got along, and so far he had proved more than capable in handling her career. That he had shown so little enthusiasm for marriage should have been a warning, even if the marriage was to last very much longer than her friends were predicting at the time.

It was decided that there should be no delay, and that the ceremony should be private. As usual, Luft, the miracle man, worked something out. He was creating a corporation to produce movies starring Garland, and one of its members was a racing partner, Ted Law, whose brother, Bob, owned a ranch ninety miles south of San Francisco. This turned out to be ideal: they could be married by a Justice of the Peace, she as Frances Gumm Minnelli, a name likely to go unnoticed in the hamlet of Hollister. Ted Law, who was to be best man, flew in for the ceremony with his wife; Tully was matron of honor. Bob Law and his wife were also present, as was Bob Heasley, the production manager of Garland's show. He had driven her party down from San Francisco on Sunday morning, June 8, two days before her thirtieth birthday. The ceremony was at six that evening, and they drove back the following day. Luft's former wife, Lynn Bari, from whom he had been divorced in 1950, was claiming that he had not kept up support payments for their son, John. As Luft's employer, Garland was subpoenaed to report on his financial affairs, but failed to appear at the hearing. When she did not appear on a second occasion, a warrant was issued for her arrest. She turned up late, claiming that such appearances created a "psychic trauma."

Louella Parsons had the story thirty-six hours later, under the heading: JUDY GARLAND'S SECRET MARRIAGE REVEALED. Liza, who was now six, learned about it from a television news bulletin. Some weeks earlier, Garland had asked Liza how she felt about her marrying Luft. Liza was unenthusiastic until her mother explained that if she did get married, Liza might have a little brother or a little sister. Liza was consoled for the impersonal way in which she received the news by Garland's assurance that she would have told her herself if Parsons had not been on to the story so quickly.

Another consolation for Liza was that she was going to live with her mother for the first time in a long while. The Lufts had taken a house from Joseph Fields, the writer, and his sister Dorothy, the lyricist, on Mapleton Drive, in Holmby Hills. It was a large dwelling of nineteen rooms, which was as well since it had to accommodate the newlyweds and their servants, Liza and Cozy (her governess), Tully, and Vern Alves, who had impressed Garland by his willingness to make her life as comfortable as possible. He was to continue to do so, both at home and on the film that Luft was planning. Also employed for that purpose and living in the house, though only temporarily, was a nurse with psychiatric training called Margaret Gundy. Later, the household was to be enlarged not only by the new baby but by John, Luft's six-year-old son by his marriage to Lynn Bari. It was an expensive establishment to maintain.

Luft also took an office on Camden Drive, about ten miles away, so that he could resume his career as a producer. His interest in racing had drawn him to a project called *Man o' War*, about the famous racehorse, and he was making plans for a film to star his wife.

On June 29, 1952, Garland was "roasted" by the Friars Club at the Biltmore Bowl in Los Angeles. The Friars was a Masonic organization involved in show-business charities, and the only other woman to have received this accolade was Sophie Tucker. It was a tribute to Garland from her peers of such warmth and admiration that she sat tearful-eyed and taken aback throughout the evening. Frank Sinatra sang "Dear Miss Garland, You Made Us Love You," and, according to the author, Homer Dickens, "the list of celebrities who honored Judy that night is long enough to fill the Beverly Hills phone book."

After the exertion of her concerts and the excitement of her marriage, Garland was resting, but she did just one job, as a favor to Bing Crosby, who returned on October 25 from a long stay with his French mistress in Europe to find that his wife was dying of cancer. Crosby's numerous infidelities were well known in Hollywood, but his public image had to be maintained. To this end, CBS was about to cancel the next three shows so that Crosby could be seen to be a caring husband, but Garland gladly stepped in when she was asked and substituted for the October 30 broadcast. Bill Morrow, Crosby's chief writer, provided her with some special material and later described her appearance on the show as "the most remarkable performance I've ever seen."

On Liza's first day in the Mapleton Drive house, Garland asked her to call Luft "Papa Sid," which she did quite easily, to everyone's satisfaction. Apart from a temporary paralysis of her arm, Garland had an easy pregnancy, and the baby was born on November 21, 1952, by cesarean section. The baby girl would be a half-sister for Liza and John, someone to draw them together while they were still having difficulty in adjusting to each other. She was named Lorna, after Lorna Moon, the strong-willed heroine of Clifford Odets's play *Golden Boy*, which Garland had admired; and Luft found the choice ideal since it was also a diminutive of his mother's name, Leonora. Garland made it clear that her own mother was not to see the baby; Ethel cried for three days on learning that she had been banned.

Garland was due to leave the hospital on the day Florence House, a horse which Luft had bought for her in Ireland, was scheduled to run at Bay Meadows track in San Francisco. Instead of keeping his appointment at the hospital, he flew up to watch the race, and was overjoyed to see it pay twenty-six to one. Garland was furious that she and the new baby had been obliged to make their own way home, but she was mollified when Luft pointed out that his winnings would cover the hospital fees.

Once again, as after the birth of Liza, Garland was prostrated by post-natal depression, and lay in bed weeping. Her chief physician was still Dr. Fred Pobirs, who had been recommended by Marc Rabwin at the time of her suspension from *Annie Get Your Gun*. Both of them cautioned Luft to watch her closely at all times. He did, and soon became aware that she was taking medication other than that prescribed by Dr. Pobirs. Luft had the house searched, and eventually Vern Alves confessed that he had been supplying Garland with Seconals and Dexedrine, a combination which could lead not only to hallucinations and shortness of breath, but to suicidal tendencies brought on by the patient's hatred of herself and others.

Luft found it easy to forgive Alves, since the situation was now an old one. For years, Rabwin had been warning each new doctor of Garland's dependence on drugs. Yet, like all those close to her, he seemed unable to make her realize what she was doing to herself. When Garland wanted something badly enough, she could be both charming and intimidating. Alves was only the latest in a long line of well-meaning people (such as Lee Gershwin and Ann Straus) whom she had persuaded into helping her "calm" her fears. Luft did not find it so easy to forgive Garland, however, and confronted her angrily. She denied taking any pills other than those prescribed. She seemed to be too drugged to listen to reason.

The butler, Taylor Hardin, had instructions to watch her when Luft was not there. On one occasion he telephoned Luft in his office to say that there was no answer from her room. He had been instructed to knock on her door every fifteen minutes or so, but she had told him to stop bothering her. Luft rushed home, when he broke down the door into his wife's suite, and then tried to break into her bathroom. In the third attempt, the lock broke. Garland lay on the floor in a pool of blood: this time she had taken a razor to her throat. Luft seized a towel and wrapped it round her neck, trying to staunch the blood as he carried her body to the bed. Dr. Pobirs arrived to stitch up the wound. "Judy, you keep this up and you're going to hurt yourself," he said.

Later, she asked what had happened. No one knew whether she was feigning or whether she had been so drugged-up that she was unaware of what she had done. Once again, it was plain that she could not have been *that* determined about suicide, for the following morning she had recovered quickly enough to summon Luft and Alves from their offices. Margaret Gundy had stayed by her during the night and was there when they entered the bedroom. "Sid, I just have to tell you this," she began gravely. "You must make the decision. It is either him or me." Luft began to laugh: he realized that she thought Alves had betrayed her by confessing to him that he had provided the pills. Infuriated by Luft's laughter, she screamed obscenities at him, until she herself was compelled to join in the general hilarity. The following day she telephoned Alves and asked him to drop by for lunch.

The incident did not make the papers, but rumors abounded in Hollywood. If they were confirmed, the Palladium, the Palace and all that had followed would have been in vain: Warner Bros. might even cancel the contract for *A Star Is Born*. Only eight days later, several influential guests were invited to a dinner party, given to squash the rumors. Garland wore a high-necked dress—and she sang. This must have been a physical as well as an emotional ordeal, but no one who heard her sing was aware of the hideous possibility of the stitches bursting open.

In January, she sang at another party. Jack L. Warner, who had signed an agreement to finance the film which Luft was planning, asked her to sing at a coming-out party he was giving for his daughter, Barbara, in New York. The occasion was meant to provide a congenial, friendly start to their business relationship, and Warner said the Lufts would be his guests in New York. The idea of a New Year's vacation in New York appealed to Garland, and she, Luft, Lorna and her nurse traveled to the city by rail. They celebrated Christmas on the train and were met at Grand Central Station by a Warner Bros. limousine, which whisked them to the Waldorf. They saw in the New Year at a private party at which the other guests included the Duke and Duchess of Windsor. She was in marvelous form at Barbara Warner's party, which was held at the St. Regis Roof and "hosted" by Elsa Maxwell.

That "inveterate party-giver," as the papers always called Maxwell, was to perform a similar function for a benefit at the Waldorf the following evening, at which Garland had promised to sing. Maxwell was devastated when informed by Luft during the day that was now unlikely, since he had received a telephone call from Harry Rabwin to say that Ethel had been found dead that morning. Her heart had failed as she had left her car at the Douglas Aircraft parking lot at about 7:30 in the morning, and she had been found four hours later, her body wedged between two cars.

As Luft suspected she would, Garland broke down when he told her; she rallied sufficiently to telephone her sisters, and agreed to return to Los Angeles at once by air. She had always been terrified of flying, and was sedated for the journey. Even so, Luft noticed, she was biting into a pillow to control her anguish.

At the house, she was reunited with her sisters, and they made the funeral arrangements together. There would be a private service at the Little Church of the Flowers at Forest Lawn Memorial Park. Before the funeral, accompanied by their husbands, the three sisters went to the funeral parlor to view their mother in her coffin. Sobbing, Garland threw herself on Jimmy's husband, Johnny, saying: "I didn't want her to die." He replied: "Judy, you better straighten up. I wouldn't want that on my conscience."

Garland's conscience was certainly something with which the press began to concern itself. Journalists contrasted the lives of the highly paid actress and singer with her humble mother, a clerk in a factory:

Judy Garland was ungrateful to the mother whose early efforts had helped to make her a star. Garland had her defenders among the press, those who believed her when she had told them that Ethel was responsible for the pressure on her and for investing her money unwisely. She eventually issued a statement to the effect that, although she had been estranged from her mother while she was recovering from her own troubles, she had been arranging for the purchase of some property for her at the time of her death. She was photographed at the funeral, wearing one of the pillbox hats she often favored, and the traditional dark glasses.

Garland never found it easy to blame herself for the things which went wrong in her life. Ethel had been a convenient scapegoat, and would remain one long after her death. How far Ethel was really to blame for her daughter's problems is not easy to determine. Psychiatrist after psychiatrist was told by Garland that she hated her mother, whom she was convinced was at the root of all her problems. There is no doubt that, even by the standards of "stage mothers," Ethel was extremely ambitious for her youngest daughter. This inevitably meant that she did not always act in Garland's best interests. This is not to say, however, that Garland was thrust unwillingly into her career: at her debut in Grand Rapids, at the age of three, it was more a case of dragging her off the stage than pushing her onto it, and Garland never lost that craving for the appreciative roar of an audience.

After a shaky start at M-G-M, when she felt unwanted and underemployed, Garland achieved remarkable success and a rapid rise to stardom. *The Wizard of Oz* put her into the front rank of M-G-M's stars, and the studio's enthusiasm for its youngest performer was trumpeted in countless articles and advertisements in the press. The films she made delighted audiences and made money, and it may be that the impressionable Garland came to believe in her own publicity—and believe that she could do no wrong. When things *did* go wrong, she blamed those nearest to her: her mother, Mayer and—later—Minnelli. Of these three, however, Ethel was always painted the blackest.

Whether or not she was right in apportioning blame to Ethel, Garland certainly got her revenge. It is hardly surprising that when Ethel died, she felt some guilt. The trouble between them did not end with Ethel's death. Garland continued to vilify her mother to the end of her life. She claimed that, before their estrangement, Ethel would telephone her at night to say: "Judy, you have something wrong with your brain, don't you know? You must be operated upon." She persisted in repeating that Ethel had locked her in cupboards in hotel rooms in faraway cities and pretended to leave her there alone. She eventually came to believe that what she said was true.

Unsurprisingly, Garland's temperament was not at its most tranquil in the wake of Ethel's death. Her marriage was going no better than expected, and on occasion Luft's face was black and blue after Garland had battered him with one of her high-heeled shoes. He was not so much bored or angered by her as exasperated, escaping from her demands as often as he could. Whether in work or out of it, she felt the pressures equally and the only way she could cope was to throw a tantrum. If someone said "night," she insisted it was "day." She knew no other way of going about the business of living. Luft stayed away as long as he could, always responding to her cheery telephone calls asking him sweetly to return. Then they retired to her bedroom, often for a couple of days, but perhaps less because of sex than the fact that they had both become fundamentally lazy. Garland had been a star for so long—almost a lifetime—that she sometimes felt she no longer had anything to prove to anyone. She had also come to realize that stardom brought with it problems she was unable to manage. She did not want to confront these difficulties, or indeed any manifestation of reality. Luft did not give a damn, either, except that one of them had to earn money to support their life-style: she had wanted a rose garden, so one was being planted; the house was being remodeled. It may also be that Garland's inertia and her lack of interest in work or life was a by-product of her post-natal depression.

One day in March 1953, Harry Rubin, one of the electricians who were re-wiring the house, arrived for work to find the black couple in charge of the kitchen in a panic because smoke was billowing from Garland's room. Rubin went into the room and found that the draperies were alight and that fierce flames were already attacking the ceiling. Garland was lying unconscious five feet away from the encroaching flames. Rubin grabbed her and brought her out of the room. As she came to, her first thought was of the children, who fortunately were on the other side of the house. Firemen, who arrived within minutes, found fire-fighting equipment—including a long hose—which had been installed in the hall cupboard by the producer, Hunt Stromberg, who had built the house, as a precaution against his habit of lighting his cigarettes and leaving live matches in the ashtray. In spite of having this useful additional equipment to hand, the firemen were unable to prevent an entire wing of the house being razed.

The press were informed that the fire had been caused by a mistake in the re-wiring of the house: in fact, it had been caused by Garland, who had gone to bed after leaving a glowing cigarette among the cushions of an armchair. She spent most of the day with her doctor, and when Luft returned the whole entourage moved temporarily into the Bel Air Hotel.

Harry Rubin was a twenty-six-year-old former hoodlum from Brooklyn, who had served time for some petty offenses. He was now highly respectable, and was in charge of the electricians. He and Luft hit it off immediately, and Luft offered him a job as general factotum. Rubin was as different from Vern Alves as it was possible to be, and Luft believed that he might be able to handle Garland when Alves's more gallant efforts failed. Garland was amused by Rubin's background and by his bluntness. He told her that if she treated him the way she treated Luft, she could stick the job up her ass.

16

❖❖❖❖❖❖❖

A Star Is Born

From his office on Camden Drive, Sid Luft set about producing Judy Garland's next film, which they both intended to be the comeback to dim all comebacks in movie history. In December 1942, she had performed in a radio broadcast of *A Star Is Born*, based on the 1937 movie produced by David O. Selznick and directed by William A. Wellman. That film had taken an older script—*What Price Hollywood?* (1932)—and added some further examples of Hollywood lore to provide the basic story of Esther Blodgett, a small-town girl (played by Janet Gaynor) who goes to Hollywood in search of stardom, with money given to her by her grandmother. Having failed to get work in films, she becomes a waitress. At a party, she meets an established star, Norman Maine (Fredric March). He marries her, is instrumental in getting her a contract and a new name, Vicki Lester, only to watch as her star rises and his fades, partly due to his alcoholism. So as not to ruin her career, he commits suicide by walking into the ocean. She decides to retire until her grandmother tells her that that is not what Norman would have wanted. At a premiere she introduces herself not as Vicki Lester, but with the quiet announcement: "This is Mrs. Norman Maine."

It is a sentimental gesture which would have seemed excessive anywhere but in Hollywood, and there was much speculation as to who had provided the models for the principal roles, as conceived by Dorothy Parker and her husband, Alan Campbell, who had written the screenplay with Robert Carson. There were numerous candidates. When Garland had taken part in the radio version, she identified only with Esther-Vicki, but now, in 1952, she also found aspects of herself in Norman, the drunken has-been.

She had suggested a remake of the film to Louis B. Mayer in the 1940s. Mayer saw it as an excellent vehicle for her, but Nicholas Schenck did not think a sad story, about a girl married to a drunk, was right for "our precious Judy." Luft claimed that he had thought of a remake while Judy was rehearsing for the Palace, when he read that the rights had been sold to Edward L. Alperson, a sometime producer and president of Film Classics, which intended to re-release the 1937 film. Since making *Gone With the Wind* in 1939, Selznick had curtailed production, but had survived financially by selling or leasing the properties he owned. He had sold *A Star Is Born*, and the re-acquired exhibition rights to thirteen foreign territories, so that although Alperson owned the negative, the story and the remake rights, a new version would infringe Selznick's copyright if shown in those countries.

A more considerable obstacle in Luft's plan had been that Alperson was not interested in a remake, especially one with Judy Garland. He had relented after seeing her at the Palace, however, and in November 1951 signed an agreement with Luft, which gave Alperson a 20 percent interest in the newly formed Transcona Enterprises (named after the town in which Luft had lived during his spell with the R.C.A.F.). As producer and star Luft and Garland owned 75 percent of the company, and the other five went to Ted Law, who had been their best man. The new company's only asset, apart from Judy Garland, was the rights to *A Star Is Born*.

Garland may have been an asset, but she was also something of a liability. She had been seen to crumble only too often on expensive pictures, and a greater risk was involved in allowing her to carry a full-length movie than in putting her on stage to sing for an hour. Furthermore, the popularity of television and rising seat-prices had led to a considerable decline in cinema attendances since her last film. Prepared to take the risk was Jack L. Warner, who admired

Garland professionally and personally. Having had under contract such stars as Bette Davis, James Cagney and Humphrey Bogart, he considered himself experienced in handling star temperament. He had also taken another M-G-M reject, Joan Crawford, and turned her once again into a box-office star.

Warner had an overriding ambition to see his studio overtake M-G-M as the industry's leader. Warner Bros. was run on more mundane lines, both more workmanlike and more of a factory. He played his hunches, which meant that among the punchy, demotic subjects produced there every year, there were a number of prestige productions: and it was with these that he hoped to overtake Metro. He was ready to ally himself with any ambitious independent unit which might enable him to do so.

The big studios had always considered independent filmmaking a threat to their monopoly, but many creative personnel had returned from the war determined to be rid of the studios' authority. The struggle, which at first had seemed to go against those seeking independence, had been won for them when, in 1940, the government decree was finally enforced divorcing exhibition from production and distribution. Since Warner Bros. had divested itself of its circuits for huge sums, it had money to invest. Warner himself was more ready than most to realize that the swing to independence would prevail. The 1951 film of Tennessee Williams's *A Streetcar Named Desire* had been made on the Warner lot, financed and distributed by Warners, but all artistic decisions had been made by its director, Elia Kazan, and its producer, Charles K. Feldman, to whom the rights would revert after seven years. In the meantime, it had generated much excitement and money, as well as four Oscars, which the public, at least, saw as awards to a Warner movie.

In August 1952, Warner made a nine-picture deal with Transcona, to include *A Star Is Born*, Luft's cherished horse-racing picture, *Man o' War*, which he expected to be the first to go into production, and *Snow Covered Wagons*, a property owned by Alperson about the disastrous Donner Party trek West through the Sierra Nevada in 1846–47. Warner announced the deal on September 8, saying that his company would finance and distribute three of Transcona's pictures, the first to be a musical remake of *A Star Is Born* with Judy Garland. By this time, Warner had in fact taken options on a further six movies, two of which were to star Garland.

Luft was given an office on the lot. As he showed him into it, Warner attempted to assert his authority by saying: "Hey buddy, we're running this show." Luft was a proud man and felt that, as instigator of the studio's most important picture of the year, he deserved more respect. He was not about to get it from Warner, who said of him: "He's one of the original guys who promised his parents he'd never work a day in his life and made good." Some aspects of the film, however, were to remain in Luft's hands. His first choice to compose the songs was Harold Arlen because he had given Garland "Over the Rainbow." Garland agreed, since she knew that Arlen was capable of writing more complex rhythms—and hence more exciting ones—than any of his peers.

For the screenplay, Garland wanted Moss Hart, who was delighted by the prospect of writing for her. He was chiefly known for a series of comedies, often in collaboration with George S. Kaufman, most of which had proved so successful that he had been able to deal with the film industry on his own terms. He was very much in demand, especially as his most recent screenplays—for *Gentlemen's Agreement* (1947), a drama about anti-Semitism directed by Elia Kazan, and *Hans Christian Andersen* (1952), a fairy tale about a teller of fairy tales, directed by Charles Vidor—had been much admired. Hart had also written the book for *Lady in the Dark*, the Kurt Weill musical with Gertrude Lawrence which Garland had so admired.* Her friend, Ira Gershwin, who had written the lyrics for the musical, agreed to collaborate on the songs for *A Star Is Born*.

The contract hammered out in December 1952 found Warners advancing the production costs of the three films: $500,000 for *Snow Covered Wagons*, $650,000 for *Man o'War* and $1,500,000 for *A Star Is Born*, of which $100,000 was to go to Garland. It stated that principal photography involving her should not exceed fifty-four days, and gave the studio the option of taking control if the budget was exceeded by 10 percent. Warners alone had the right to re-cut the film "with a view to giving it the highest box-office appeal to the general public." The studio had distribution rights for twelve years, with an option to re-purchase, and the company agreed to split the profits equally after a further agreement on expenses. Accompanying the contract was a memo listing the names of the directors and co-stars acceptable to both parties.

---

*Garland would perform in a broadcast of this musical on *Lux Radio Theater*, on February 17, 1953, as a way of thanking Hart. It turned out to be her last play for the radio, and provided her with an unusual role, that of a hard-boiled editor of a fashion magazine who turns to psychiatry to sort out her various romantic problems. She acted better than Hart's (abridged) script deserved, but did a charming version of "My Ship."

The list of directors was short but revealing: George Cukor, Daniel Mann, Charles Vidor, Michael Curtiz, Henry Koster and John Ford. Absent were the most admired names of that time: Joseph Mankiewicz, George Stevens, William Wyler, Billy Wilder and Elia Kazan—none of whom could be pushed around. This was also true of Curtiz and Ford, but they were happy to work within the studio system. The only newcomer was Mann, probably selected because he had just directed Shirley Booth to an Oscar in *Come Back Little Sheba*. Cukor was Garland's first choice. James Stewart, Ingrid Bergman, Ronald Colman, Shelley Winters and Judy Holliday had all won Oscars in films directed by him. He had also directed Garbo in *Camille* and Katharine Hepburn in some of her more memorable films. "I wanted George," she said at the time. "The picture had to be the greatest, it couldn't be merely good. I had too much at stake." Cukor was a fastidious, cultivated man, renowned not only for drawing superb performances from his players, but for making films with a certain elegance (he hated, with reason, being known as "a woman's director"). Garland had known him since childhood, and more recently he had become a regular guest at her home, along with Hepburn, Fanny Brice and Ethel Barrymore. "What do you suppose that we all have in common?" Garland asked one evening. "That's easy, my dear," said Barrymore. "We've been on the brink of disaster all our lives." In Cukor's case, this referred to his homosexuality, which, if publicly acknowledged, would have finished his career in Hollywood.

Cukor had wanted to direct Garland ever since hearing her sing "Happy Birthday" to Ethel Barrymore at a get-together in 1949, for she showed then "the emotional ability to be a great dramatic actress." The project also appealed to him because he was fascinated by the movie industry. The only reason he had turned down an offer to direct the earlier version of the film was that it had been a partial remake of *What Price Hollywood?*, which he had directed. In the years since, he had become even more clear-eyed about Hollywood and its mixture of talents, motives and ambitions. He believed that this view could be expressed in the film, and Luft began negotiations with M-G-M for his services.

In the meantime, Selznick, who had long been an admirer of Cukor's work, decided that the new film would be a blockbuster, and decided to put his early version into release in those territories for which he had the rights. He had the original negative in his possession, although he did not own it. With the complicated legal situation, he felt within his rights to hang on to it, which gave him an advantage when he told Warner that there might be thirteen countries in which his new film would find itself in competition with an older film of the same name. This led to a flurry of correspondence between the attorneys of both parties, which was finally resolved because Selznick wanted to return to production with a remake of *A Farewell to Arms*, as a vehicle for his wife, Jennifer Jones. Warners owned the rights, having already remade the film as *Force of Arms* in 1951, and so a deal was struck and the matter was settled.

The list of potential leading men was longer than that of potential directors, and began with Laurence Olivier, who was accustomed to turning down Hollywood offers. The second choice was Richard Burton, the hottest actor in town since the recent film version of Daphne du Maurier's *My Cousin Rachel*, but he was about to begin *The Robe* for 20th Century-Fox, to whom he was under contract. The original choice for his role in that film had been Tyrone Power, who was third on the list for *A Star Is Born*: but it was felt that if he could be relegated by his own studio, he was certainly not worth the price he was asking. Cary Grant, James Stewart, Glenn Ford, Stewart Granger, Robert Taylor, Gregory Peck, and Ray Milland were also on the list.

Of these, Grant was considered by Warner and Luft to be the most likely to perform satisfactorily on the set and at the box office. It might be thought that the few serious roles he had played bore out neither contention, but it would have been intriguing casting to have a star noted for his elegance playing a drunken has-been. He was aware that he needed an important film after a run of poor movies, but nevertheless asked $300,000 against 10 percent of the gross. Warner refused to give him a percentage, but offered a flat $450,000—a clear sign that he was prepared to increase the original budget.

With that consideration in mind, other names began to present themselves. Marlon Brando and Montgomery Clift were both less costly and better commercial propositions than Grant, but Garland's friend, Humphrey Bogart, was Warner's preferred choice. Luft, however, thought him too old for the role. Another friend, Frank Sinatra, put himself forward, but Warner considered him unsuitable. The trade press, following the casting with almost the same glee as it had watched the search for Scarlett O'Hara in *Gone With the Wind*, announced that Henry Fonda was about to be signed, but his long absence from films, while on Broadway, had reduced his box-office appeal.

The next actor to be considered for the role was Stewart Granger, whom Cukor invited to rehearse at his home, but Granger found the director so uncongenial (dismissing him in his memoirs as "an old woman"), that he declined to continue. Grant, who had been profitably directed by Cukor in the past, also went to the director's home to read, and in Cukor's view showed an unexpected range. At the same time, he knew that Grant would never expose himself emotionally in the same way before the camera. Grant could see elements of himself in the role, but it was not quite as simple as that. He would also have to risk being overshadowed by Garland, especially in those scenes in which he had little to do but listen to her sing. He decided to turn down the role. His wife, Betsy Drake, arrived unexpectedly at the Luft's house, just before midnight, still in tennis gear and in a highly emotional state, to break the news. On hearing it, Garland broke into tears.

A few days later, the role was offered to James Mason, who, like Garland, was represented by Feldman's Famous Artists. He had not yet fulfilled the promise of the British films which had established him as a romantic leading man, tough and aggressively masculine, and the country's top box-office draw. Transplanted to Hollywood, he had attempted to show a wider range, but even after such films as *Five Fingers* (1952) and *Julius Caesar* (1953), both directed by Joseph Mankiewicz, he was regarded as little more than a capable actor. He was looking for a role which would do something more for him. He had known Garland since he had worked with Minnelli on *Madame Bovary*, and "adored" her, both as a person and as an actress. He knew that Hart had written a fine script, and although he claimed that "in the end I grabbed it before it slipped away," his wife, Pamela, said that he was talked into doing it by herself and Ray Stark from the Feldman Office.

Mason knew that he was not the first choice for the role, and supposed that other actors had turned it down because no one would expect the combination of Judy Garland and *A Star Is Born* to be a "smooth and easy ride." "Judy will never make it," he was told, and later he learned from Garland herself that Arthur Freed had said of Garland and Luft, in the presence of mutual friends: "Those two alley-cats can't make a movie." Stark had shared these reservations, and did not believe Transcona's claim that the principal photography would be completed in fifty-four days. Consequently, although freelance stars were usually paid a single fee, he exacted a fee of $12,000 a week for his client when the contract was signed in May.

While the search had been going on for her leading man, Garland had returned to a recording studio. After examining several offers, Luft had done a deal with Mitch Miller of Columbia Records for a number of singles and, in a separate agreement, the soundtrack album of *A Star Is Born*. Miller, himself a conductor, was also an astute judge of talent, and at this time was working with such popular singers as Guy Mitchell, Doris Day, Rosemary Clooney, Frankie Laine, Johnny Ray and Jo Stafford—whose husband, Paul Weston, conducted the orchestra for Garland's session, which consisted of four sides: "Without a Memory," "Heartbroken," "Go Home, Joe" and "Send My Baby Back to Me." It took three hours and thirty renderings before Garland was satisfied, and her excited behavior during the playbacks indicated that she expected to follow Columbia's other artists into the Hit Parade. Miller had always insisted on Clooney recording songs she disliked, only to be consoled by their sales, but these two records of Garland's attracted few buyers. There were no requests for any others, and Luft did not care to renew the agreement when the soundtrack album and the singles extracted from it proved that Garland could be a potent force in the record shops.

By May, Moss Hart's outline had become a finished script. To celebrate, Hart presented Garland with a Chrysler, which she promptly gave to Harry Rubin. Luft marked the occasion by spending $75,000 on suits which he charged to the film, since they were supposedly for Mason. Warner noted, however, that Luft himself wore them, not Mason, and was not pleased. Hart had left the second half of the story much as it is in Selznick's version but he had made some major changes to the first half. Esther was no longer a starry-eyed provincial in Hollywood, but a girl who expected to spend her life singing with a band. Norman does not meet her at a party, but at a gala while he is on a drunken binge. She is performing, and there is something about her voice that makes him seek her out after sleeping off his drunk. As in the original, he gets her a screen test and then proceeds to fall in love with her. Even without the songs, it was going to be a lengthy shoot. Furthermore, the running time could not be settled until it was clear how the numbers were to be staged.

Gershwin and Arlen had completed two songs for the score, and were particularly pleased with one of them, "The Man That Got Away." When he learned that Arlen was to join the Lufts in Palm Springs to play golf, Gershwin forbade him to let Garland hear the song in any form. He wanted it to be a surprise they could spring on her together. Arlen promised, but found himself unable to resist whistling the main theme from the song while he was with the Lufts on the green. Hearing him, Garland asked him what the tune was.

Arlen feigned ignorance, but continued whistling. Suspecting that this haunting tune had something to do with the film, Garland eventually frogmarched the composer into the clubhouse, where there was a piano. With mock reluctance, Arlen sat down and played both "The Man That Got Away" and "Gotta Have Me Go With You," muttering that he did not know whether the Lufts would like the songs. They did, of course, and decided to visit Hart and try the song out on him. When he proved equally enthusiastic, a telephone call was made to Gershwin, who was so pleased by their reaction that he never referred to Arlen's broken promise.

Other substantial contributors to the film arrived at Cukor's behest. This was his first film in color, and he wanted it to look right—but more than that, because he believed that if the audience started to notice a film's appearance, the director had not done his job properly. Lemuel Ayers, who had returned to New York after *Meet Me in St. Louis*, was engaged as art director, but in the event fell sick and was replaced by his assistant, Malcolm Bert. The production design was to be handled by Gene Allen, a newcomer to Warners' art department, and as color consultant Cukor brought in the photographer George Hoyningen-Huene who, like Allen, was to be a collaborator on his future films. The original cinematographer was Harry Stradling, but as production was repeatedly delayed and he had a commitment to shoot the studio's spectacular *Helen of Troy* in Europe in the spring, he was replaced by Winton Hoch.

Ray Heindorf, head of the studio's music department, would be the conductor, and Hugh Martin was to do the vocal arrangements. Another old colleague of Garland's, Mary Ann Nyberg, was now a costume designer on *The Band Wagon*, which Minnelli had just filmed with Fred Astaire, and she was borrowed from M-G-M. A creative team was now in place, as distinguished as any that Freed had established.

There were only two supporting roles of any consequence, the considerate studio boss and his acid-tongued press agent. William Powell was offered the former part, but, although he was easing himself into supporting roles before retiring, he did not care to go beneath the title. In his place, Charles Bickford accepted an "also starring" credit below, as did Jack Carson, who had been above the title until comparatively recently, in the role of the agent.

The date for the start of principal photography was postponed from September 1 to September 16. Garland was pre-recording the songs, and Cukor bowed to her superior knowledge in deciding which takes to use. This unfortunately put him in an awkward position when Garland and her vocal coach, Hugh Martin, clashed over her interpretation of "The Man That Got Away." She wanted it "loud and brassy"; Martin, who had wanted it sweeter and in a lower key, walked off the set and flew back to New York. Since he was known to be an old friend, it seemed—to the industry, at least—that Garland was unchanged in her four years away from the set.

This was confirmed when she failed to show on the new starting date of October 3 for makeup or costume tests. She said she was dieting, and a new date was set for October 12. Jack Warner sent a gentle note to Luft, which concluded: "I am worried about all the delays and nervous tension, and we want to get this picture going." There came the day when nothing further could be done at the studio without Garland. When Luft telephoned her from the studio, she made it quite clear that she had no intention of coming in. She was terrified. Luft told Harry Rubin to get her to the studio by whatever means possible. Rubin packed her vodka, grapefruit juice and Canadian Club, in case she needed them in the car, and told her to get in, because her life depended on it. When they got to the studio, Luft and Warner were waiting at the entrance. Warner told Rubin (in Yiddish, so no one else could understand) that he was putting him on salary with the express purpose of getting Garland to the studio every day, on time.

Other delays had been caused by technical problems. The studio had been waiting for the arrival of its WarnerScope lenses, which were being manufactured by Zeiss in Germany. In Hollywood, 1953 was almost as momentous as 1927, the year that Talkies arrived. The wide screen came into being and, coincidentally, the end of the predominance of Technicolor with it. Eastmancolor's new system became "Warnercolor" at Warner Bros. and "Metrocolor" at M-G-M. It was also the year of 3-D, which had given Warner Bros. a big success in *House of Wax*. They made two further films in the process, *Hondo* with John Wayne and *Dial M for Murder*, directed by Alfred Hitchcock. M-G-M had even used it for a major musical, *Kiss Me Kate*, but in order to appreciate it, every customer had to be provided with a pair of special glasses. The industry's feeling, in general, was that it was a gimmick of which the public would soon tire.

The same was true of Cinerama, a wall-to-wall image from three projectors with two fuzzy breaks where the portions of film overlapped. More interest was centered on CinemaScope, a wide-screen process which gave spectators a panoramic picture, in color. This was something with which the small, monochrome television screen at home could not begin to compete. The patent was held by 20th Century-Fox, but they were prepared to share it with other studios for a fee of $25,000 per film, in order to persuade theater-owners to install the necessary equipment, which, with stereophonic sound and possible structural alterations, also cost in the region of $25,000. What was chicken feed to a movie mogul was a considerable investment to a theater owner and would only be worthwhile if a lot of films were made using this process. Fox was about to open its Biblical spectacle, *The Robe*, in CinemaScope, and to prove its faith in the system, a comedy, *How to Marry a Millionaire*, was already under way.

Cukor had rejected Warner's offer of 3-D, was unhappy with Warnercolor, and decided that WarnerScope's distortions were serious. As a consequence, when *A Star Is Born* began shooting on October 12, it was in Technicolor and in the normal screen ratio. This proved to be a costly error of judgment.

The Robe had opened at the Roxy in New York on September 16, and had attracted queues from the first day. It was a film of stultifying dullness, as the critics were the first to point out, but in those days the press had little effect on the box office, especially if the public really wanted to see a film. The talk everywhere was of CinemaScope. It began to be perceived as a box-office attraction in its own right, and every movie mogul in town was debating whether the immediate upcoming projects should be filmed in the new process. Clearly it was the only way to film Westerns, historical spectacles—and musicals. *Lucky Me*, starring Doris Day, went into production at once with the WarnerScope cameras and would be rushed out in April as "The First Musical in CinemaScope."

A Star Is Born would have a much longer shooting schedule, even if Garland were to behave herself, and furthermore it was a picture which could not be rushed. It was questionable whether, by the time it came out, the public would want to see *any* film in the old ratio, especially a musical—or at least it was questionable to Jack Warner as well as to his brothers, Albert and Harry, who were usually more cautious. Jack Warner visited Fox to view some CinemaScope footage, and could see immediately that it was superior to WarnerScope. It was agreed to shoot "The Man That Got Away," due to be filmed the following day, in both the old ratio and in CinemaScope. The song was ideal for the wide screen, with the performer in the center, as on a stage, to hold the audience's attention. The CinemaScope version was the more impressive and Warner, after discussion with Luft and

Cukor, decided to scrap the existing footage, at a cost of $300,000, and begin again in CinemaScope and Technicolor. Milton Krasner, who had been loaned by Fox for this shoot, was retained for the first few days, but as an expert on the system he was needed elsewhere. Winton Hoch was at home with Technicolor, but there were doubts whether he could light quickly enough for the demanding CinemaScope cameras, so he was replaced as cinematographer by Sam Leavitt. There were several advantages to hiring Leavitt: he had been camera operator on some of Garland's M-G-M pictures, and she liked him; furthermore, he had learned from his recent experience in television to work quickly.

The first thing he did was re-shoot "The Man That Got Away," because Garland had looked hideous in the original footage. Unfortunately it wasn't until the shooting was well under way that it turned out that Nyberg did not have the experience to disguise the defects of the star's figure, and so Jean Louis was hurriedly brought in from Columbia to devise a new outfit, then assigned to the rest of Garland's wardrobe. (In the event, both designers received screen credit.) Nobody liked the early staging. Cukor wanted a camera to move among the musicians, with Garland also moving, and Leavitt lit it with a stand-in. Even so, he made some mistakes, as Garland knew when she walked through it. She also knew that she had a great song; singing along with it, she did twenty-seven takes, either partial or complete, over the next three days. Each one left her emotionally drained, though this is not apparent from the six-minute take, without cuts, in the final film.

Since CinemaScope had the same shape as the stage, directors thought it should be treated in the same way and that if they used close-ups and cutting, audiences would grow restless. As a result, many early CinemaScope films were static, very often with actors walking into the frame and out of it. Cukor solved the perceived "problem" of CinemaScope by ignoring it. Those who saw the film when it came out were amazed by its visual vitality, especially after the torpidity of the Fox films in that process. He did, however, take a while to accustom himself to it and printed too many takes. This worried the producers, but when Luft expostulated, Cukor replied: "I must protect myself." Despite his friendship with Garland, Cukor had no more intention than Warner of regarding Luft as anything but the star's husband. This was unfair, since Luft had been the driving force behind the project. Cukor knew that Luft was inexperienced in productions of this size, however, and he was himself not only a veteran of some of the industry's biggest films but an autocrat and a perfectionist. When Luft realized that his advice was not going to be sought or taken, he went off to the racetrack.

Rather more worryingly, Garland also absented herself from the set because of illness, and by late November, when the crew broke for Thanksgiving, the film was nineteen days behind schedule. Almost $1,000,000 had been spent, producing one hour's worth of usable footage. Garland's problems might have been eased had she done a little less drinking.

In December, Luft snatched at the chance to escape to New York for his father's funeral. Garland used the occasion to say that she was unable to work. They shot around her. Mason was much admired for his willingness to work on unscheduled days when she was away and increasingly, if Warner was around, to participate in scenes which had no chance of appearing in the completed film. He regretted Garland's lack of discipline, but felt that Warner had only himself to blame for hiring her. In his memoir, thirty years later, Mason notes her reputation for "unreliability" and for taking

uppers and downers, nothing so bad as what the young stars inflict on themselves today . . . She was a party-goer, almost too eager, some may have thought, to join whoever was at the piano and sing along, while the hostess made sure that her medicine cabinet was safely locked . . . To get something as unique as Judy's talent, some patience and certain sacrifices were needed. If the film went over budget, only a small fraction of the overage was due to Judy's erratic timetable. When I think of it, my God they were well off! Judy was by no means a temperamental star. "Temperamental star" is usually a euphemism for selfish and bad-tempered, and a temperamental star of this sort can be a *real* time-waster. I have worked with some. And they are more rampant now than they used to be. And this was not Judy.

It is more than likely that this was the gallantry of a lover. Mason was exactly the calm, mature, cultured type which had always attracted Garland. Before shooting started, Alves was driving her to the studio when she said suddenly: "You know, of course, I'm going to fall in love with him. I always fall in love with my leading men." Although Mason was not divorced until 1964, his marriage had not been happy for many years. Harry Rubin certainly believed that they had an affair, and when Mason's wife was confronted by the rumors, she merely said: "If they are, she'll get thin and the film will be finished quicker." Jane Greer, who had acted with Mason in *The Prisoner of Zenda* said later: "If you saw them together on that set there was no doubt that

Judy had fallen in love with James. She had slimmed down, done everything to make her performance work and was just desperate to please him."

That said, it was not only Mason who defended Garland's on-set behavior. But it was unpredictable as Ronald Haver revealed in several anecdotes: Lucy Marlow, who played Mason's girlfriend in the film's opening sequence, had been warned about Garland: "There was talk that she was drinking heavily, that she was on drugs, and she was very, *very* difficult, so the best thing to do was to stay out of her way." This was not always possible, and one day, during a lunch break, she found herself "all alone with this monster." Far from treating Marlow with the customary hauteur of the star for a supporting player, however, Garland was the only person willing to unfasten Marlow's uncomfortable costume. As she did so, she observed that Cukor had said that Marlow was terrific. She went on: "Listen, honey, I've got money in this picture. If George says you're doing something to help the picture, I'm all for you—you're all right in my book." Marlow adored her thereafter. When Marlow tripped on a wet floor in a bathing suit (in a scene cut from the finished film), Garland knelt down and hugged her. Laughing, she said: "Honey, just lay there, and we'll sue the S.O.B."—a reference to Warner, with whom relations were never easy.

Even when she behaved badly, Garland was capable of making amends. When she was in makeup one morning, the assistant director, Earl Bellamy, greeted her cheerfully, and she "lit into" him. He left, slamming the door. Later on, on set, she said: "Hold it, everybody—hold it, quiet. I did something today to a fellow I like very much and I want to apologize to him." It was a rare moment, however; she seldom apologized. In general, her behavior on the film bore out the reputation she had earned at M-G-M. She either did not come in at all or left after an hour. The studio did everything possible to please her, but in the end she could not even be reached by telephone. By now, old friend or not, Cukor was losing patience with his star:

This is the behavior of someone unhinged, but there is an arrogance and a ruthless selfishness that eventually alienates one's sympathy. She's always saying that the trouble with her is that she's honest and direct, and that everyone lies to her. The fact is that when she's in this state the truth isn't in her, she's devious and untrustworthy. I found that not only had she no regard for anyone, but if you're forced by your work to be at the mercy of such erratic goings-on, you find yourself responding in an all-too-human way.

All too often, he had to coax her out of her dressing-room. Once, when he asked her whether anything was wrong, she snapped: "This is the story of my life. I'm about to shoot myself and I'm asked if anything's wrong."

Fortunately, Gavin Lambert wrote, Cukor also found her rewarding. Toward the end of the shoot, she had to film a scene after Norman's suicide, in which she is in utter despair. "You know what this is about. You really know this," Cukor said to her, and she nodded. She was required to scream, and when she did, it was "*absolutely* terrifying." Even so, Cukor needed further takes, and each time she managed a different and even more frightening scream. When at last, he was satisfied, he congratulated her. "Oh, that's nothing," she replied. "Come over to my house any afternoon. I do it every afternoon." She paused, then added: "But I only do it *once* at home."

Cukor described Garland as "a very original and resourceful actress . . . There was no prototype for Garland except Garland herself." This may have been true, but there were similarities with such actresses as Laurette Taylor, whose daughter and biographer came to watch Garland on set and said that if the biography was ever filmed, Garland would be the perfect choice for the lead role. "I had seen Laurette work," Cukor recalled, "and some of the things that I saw her do, some of the desperation, her vulnerability, had passed through me to Garland. I find that certain things that impress you somehow show up on the screen. It all becomes a pastiche of your experience." Another friend of Cukor's, Ina Claire, visited the set. She was not known for her generosity to other actresses, but she said of Garland: "That girl should work for two hours and take an ambulance home. How she gives herself!"

The problem, however, was to get Garland on to the set in the first place. When Harold Arlen was sent to try to persuade her to come in, she refused. He pointed out to her that over the past two years she had witnessed extraordinary proof of her popularity, of the love people had for her. He spoke encouragingly of "her" film, and its exciting possibilities. "With all that you have told me, Harold," she replied, according to Gerold Frank, "and in spite of what you have told me, if I had a barrel of Dexamyl, I would take it right now. I don't know where to turn or what to do."

By the time shooting officially finished, on February 26, 1954, she knew that she had alienated as many people at Warners as she had at M-G-M. Cukor was due to leave for Britain at the end of April to begin work on a film of John Masters's novel *Bhowani Junction*, and Mason was due at Disney a few days later to begin work on *20,000 Leagues Under the Sea*. Cukor was not interested in the necessary re-takes of the two musical numbers still to be filmed. One of these was "Lose That Long Face," which he thought superfluous, so he assigned it to the veteran dance director, Jack Donahue. When Donahue ordered a print after only one take, Garland was horrified. Russ Llewellyn, who had taken over from Earl Bellamy as assistant director, recalled to Ronald Haver: "That poor girl went out of her mind. You've never seen such tears; she shouted, she just went crazy. I never felt so sorry for anybody." When Cukor could not be found, Garland left. Harry Rubin handed her her vodka as she got into her limousine.

Haver also quotes Cukor, who was beside Donahue, nodding approval, when the number was attempted again. It should have taken a week to rehearse and three days to shoot, but after six weeks the dancers were paid off. Garland claimed that she needed a week's rest in order to complete it. In the end a double was used. Cukor suspected that there was "more drinking than resting," and was exasperated when he read in Louella Parson's column how "cute Judy was when she got up on the floor of the Mocambo last night and sang a couple of numbers."

On March 17, Warner arranged for all concerned to see the rough cut, after which he ordered not only the completion of "Lose That Long Face" (eliminating the double), but the re-shooting of five dramatic scenes with Garland, which he felt could be bettered.

She had one last chance, doing any necessary re-takes to disprove her reputation for unreliability. She confessed to Luft that she had been taking even more medication than he realized and that she needed his help. During the first two weeks of April, they went to Ojai, with its golf course, but not—in her case—to play golf. She was determined to cure herself and, with Luft's help, was willing endure "cold turkey." On the first evening, they stayed in their room, watching television and playing gin rummy. She began shaking and sweating at around midnight, and the next twelve hours were horrible, with Luft holding her down as she screamed into the pillow. At times she became unconscious, but she refused to let him call a doctor. At lunchtime on the second day she was ready to eat a hearty meal. And they spent the rest of the week happily in their fashion. This, at least, is the version of events as detailed in Gerold Frank's biography of Garland, a book on which Luft collaborated. It would certainly be uncharacteristic for Garland, with her horror of physical pain, to have submitted voluntarily to such an ordeal. Given that Garland had been an addict for many years, this "cure" seems little short of miraculous, and Harry Rubin does not believe it ever took place. He claims that she was never interested in any sort of cure that might have meant facing reality, and she was someone who never even picked up a newspaper in case it meant doing just that.

Whatever the truth of the matter, Garland felt sufficiently rested when she returned on April 14 to throw herself into her work. Cukor stood by as she resumed "Lose That Long Face," content to have it directed by Richard Barstow, who had done the choreography.

There remained one musical sequence to be shot, and it was a crucial one. Surprisingly, Cukor was not interested in handling it. He knew he lacked the assurance of Minnelli in staging musical numbers. The song is the means by which Vicki is catapulted to stardom. Since A Star Is Born was by now a very, very long film, it would have to play with an intermission. The planned number would end the first half, so both audiences, the real one and the one in the film, could file out to the lobby knowing exactly what made Vicki, and the actress playing her, so special.

Arlen and Gershwin had written three possible numbers, "Green Light Ahead," "I'm Off the Downbeat" and "Dancing Partner," but no one liked them. Luft took Roger Edens to lunch to ask whether he had any ideas. Edens had already contributed to the film, planning the form of "Someone at Last," which Vicki sings to Norman to cheer him up toward the end. Hart had suggested that it might be used to parody movie production numbers in various parts of the world. Edens chose France, China and Brazil. He and Garland made a twelve-minute record as they ad-libbed, and Hart used this in fashioning the dialogue for the sequence. Now, Edens turned to his assistant, Leonard Gershe, for an idea. Gershe had just one line and an upbeat melody. "I was born in a trunk in Tusacola, Idaho." (This later became Pocatello, Idaho.) Edens liked the idea: "Born in a Trunk" could be used for both a parody of show-business traditions and a tribute to the power of its glamour; and, like the "Minstrel Girl" introduction he wrote for Garland's stage concerts, it gave her a chance to show off her sense of self-mockery and her ability to throw a ballad up to the rafters. Gershe wrote the lyric and Edens the music, and together they chose the songs which, as in "Minstrel Girl," would tell this particular show-business story. Gershe choose "My Melancholy Baby," and Edens chose "Swanee," because he always loved the way

Garland sang it. From her Palace act, they borrowed the idea of Garland sitting at the footlights, pouring out her heart in song. Under the terms of his M-G-M contract, Edens could not take credit for the number, so this went to Gershe. They sold the song and the idea outright, getting $5,000 each. It was rare for Edens to receive payment for providing Garland with special material. In this instance, of course, Warners was paying, not Garland herself.

Cukor thought that the film was already very long, but since he would not be called upon to direct this additional sequence, he was not inclined to argue against it, especially when Warner considered that it might capture some of Garland's on-stage magic. The allocation of another $250,000 for just one number—albeit a long, splashy number—made the film dangerously expensive. Warner, however, was convinced that he already had a "winnah," and the film could carry this additional expenditure. His high opinion of the film was confirmed when he put on a special preview in May for such respected filmmakers as Billy Wilder, Elia Kazan, George Stevens, John Farrow, Raoul Walsh and Mervyn LeRoy. Although this version of the film lacked the "Born in a Trunk" sequence, some friends of Moss Hart, who were in the audience, wrote to him to praise the film, but complained of its length. Hart told Warner that he could suggest cuts, but Warner was happy with a completed running-time of 194 minutes. He said he might reconsider after the new number had been inserted.

At Cukor's request, Gene Allen and George Hoyningen-Huene remained as production designer and color consultant for the new sequence. Irene Sharaff was engaged to design the sets and costumes, but although she is credited with both, it was actually Allen who designed the sets, with her endorsement and Huene's approval. Garland began pre-recording on May 28 and rehearsals on June 7. Shooting began on June 30, as scheduled, and was completed on the appointed date, July 28, despite the fact that Garland lost one day because of illness. Richard Barstow, the choreographer, supervised the direction, with Luft much in evidence to keep Garland on her toes. Because she was not at her best in the morning, Luft persuaded Warner that the actual shooting should be done at night, in spite of the overtime fees involved.

Filming finished at 2:55 a.m. on July 29, after Garland had submitted to some re-takes for the "Peanut Vendor" section of the number. It had been the lengthiest Hollywood shoot, and resulted in the longest American film since *Gone With the Wind*. At a staggering cost of $5,019,770 it was not quite the most expensive film since Selznick's epic, but it was the most costly ever made by Warner Bros. It would have to generate the same sort of business as *Gone With the Wind* to make a profit. Warners, with perhaps pardonable exaggeration, decided to market the film with advertisment proclaiming "$6,000,000 and 2½ Years to Make It."

The studio's dubbing editors worked through a weekend to get a print ready for the first preview on August 2. This, and those that followed, were, said Cukor, extraordinary occasions: "Judy generates a kind of hysteria from an audience." *Variety* agreed with the director. In its issue of September 1, it carried the headline: "STAR" OUT-STANDING PRE-SOLD PIC OF RECENT TIMES DUE TO GARLAND AURA. The paper noted that the "actress is already a show business legend," and reported that, when the film was first announced, "WB ballyhooli-gans were swamped with requests for material" on her.

The interest in her "comeback" and rumor about the quality of the film were as manna to Warners' merchandising team, facing the mammoth task of getting the picture into the black, which meant that it had to earn twice its negative cost. They examined the precedents, to find that, according to *Variety*, only eight films had had the drawing power to gross $10 million or more: they were, in descending order, *Gone With the Wind* (1939), S33 million (including five reissues); *The Robe* (1953), $17 million; *The Greatest Show on Earth*, (1952) $12 million; *From Here to Eternity* (1953), $12 million; *Duel in the Sun* (1946), $11 million (including one reissue); *The Best Years of Our Lives* (1946), $11 million; *Samson and Delilah* (1950), $11 million; and *Quo Vadis?* (1961), $10 million. Rave reviews were anticipated for *A Star Is Born*, but these did not automatically turn into paying customers: of these top grossers, only *Gone With the Wind*, *From Here to Eternity* and *The Best Years of Our Lives* had been well received by the press.

The greatest obstacle to overcome was the film's inordinate length, which the "Born in a Trunk" sequence had increased dramatically. Although Cukor snipped away to get the running time down to 181 minutes, even this meant that most theaters could only show it three times a day. Benjamin Kalmenson, in charge of distribution, argued that the film needed further rigorous pruning, but Jack Warner pointed out that the summer reissue of *Gone With the Wind*, at 220 minutes, had done well, while the studio's own *The High and the Mighty* was then doing terrific business at 147 minutes. Whatever was decided, the picture would be a slow return on investment, since there were not enough theaters equipped for CinemaScope for it to be widely distributed. This could be turned to advantage, however, with exclusive first runs at higher prices.

Warner planned the most spectacular premiere in recent Hollywood history, with Garland in attendance there and at the premieres in New York, Chicago and Detroit. This plan was thwarted when his troublesome star announced that, although she was prepared to go to New York, she had no intention of speeding back and forth across the country for the sake of publicity. By this time, Warner had come to regard her as "a pain in the ass," and was not prepared to accept her refusal. In any case, as a Transcona shareholder, it was in her own interest to generate as much excitement about the film as possible. Warner had just received an enthusiastic cable from Sam Goldwyn, to tell him that, with proper handling, the picture could gross $25 million. In his foxy way, Warner offered the Lufts a European vacation if Garland would go to Chicago and Detroit. Anticipating their share in the $25 million, Luft asked for an advance instead. The vacation was still to go ahead, but Warner also signed a promissory note for $30,000.

In the meantime, preview audiences were still being shown the film. Garland saw the completed version for the first time with Harry Rubin, in Huntingdon, a suburb of Los Angeles. On the way there, she tried to reassure herself: "Of course it's a good picture. It's a great picture. Mason's great, the score is great, I'm great, the photography's great, it's a great picture . . . Isn't it?" She was so tense that she had to be taken to Dr. Pobirs on the way home; and what tension was left she got rid of by starting an affair with Rubin during the same journey.

The Lufts were divided about the prospective European trip. Garland longed to remain at home, resting with her family. She decided that what Warner intended was merely a disguised promotional trip. Luft, on the other hand, wanted to get away from the problems of the film—at this point Cukor was still re-cutting it—and he pointed out that they would not have to be in Warner's pocket the entire time. Garland acquiesced when he suggested quick trips to London and Paris.

She was soon to regret this. Warner had booked them a suite at the Hotel du Cap, the most luxurious hotel on the Riviera, which Garland did not mind at all. But it was just along the road from Warner's villa, where were gathered half the people she had hoped to leave behind in Hollywood as well as the jet-setters of the time, such as Prince Aly Khan, who invited Luft to Deauville to look over his stud farm. Garland would have preferred to go to London, and as a result she and Luft quarreled. Luft called Vern Alves, who was traveling with them, and when he arrived, Garland, who had been drinking, was completely out of control. A doctor was called, and he recommended a small psychiatric clinic, where the patient had to be strapped down. She later claimed that she had been beaten and refused even a glass of water. The following evening, Gerold Frank says, she telephoned Alves in a panic. When he and Luft went to fetch her, they found her in an even more hysterical state than the night before. She ignored Luft and went to Alves's suite, where she told him: "I don't know what happens now." She remained with him, since the small adjoining room had a bed she could use. Late in the night, drained emotionally and physically, she drifted off to sleep.

Sometimes she paid dearly for being Judy Garland but, being Judy Garland, she was fit and well the following day. She was, as she said, as strong as a panzer division, and she did get to visit London and Paris on the way home.

Warner had hustled, as only he knew how. Almost the entire Who's Who of Hollywood would be at the premiere at the Pantages Theater on September 29, 1954. One person who would not, however, was James Mason, who had no taste for Hollywood hoopla. Haver recounts that Warner wired his disapproval, saying that he had nevertheless had tickets left for Mason and his wife. "There's an old adage," he said. "One must put something back if they want to continue taking something out." Mason never made another picture at Warner Bros.

On the night, Garland was radiant. She wore a pillbox hat, and was accompanied by Luft and a grinning Jack Warner. Searchlights played in the sky and an estimated crowd of twenty thousand lined Hollywood Boulevard. Inside the lobby, NBC (for television) and ABC (for radio) were covering the occasion for nationwide audiences. In the theater, the audience roared its approval at the end of the film, and the guests at the party held afterwards at the Cocoanut Grove were euphoric.

This enthusiasm was echoed by the critics. *Variety* declared:

A *Star Is Born* is a socko candidate for anyone's must-see list, scoring on all counts as fine entertainment . . . It is among the top musicals that have come from the Hollywood studios . . . It is a big picture for big selling . . . and big box office should be the rule rather than the exception. The tremendous outlay of time and money . . . is fully justified . . . It is to the great credit of Jack Warner that he kept his mind and purse strings open and thus kept the project going despite the insurmountable stumbling blocks. For both Miss Garland and Warner the racking months that went into the making [of the film] will soon be forgotten in the joy of an artistic and box office smash.

The film opened in New York on October 11, at both the huge Paramount and the smaller Victoria Theater, with continuous performances starting at 8:30 a.m., to accommodate the expected crowds. Garland managed to appear at both theaters that evening. At the Paramount, there was a "formal premiere" which proved as glittering an event at the one at the Pantages.

The following day, Bosley Crowther wrote in the *New York Times*:

> The whole thing runs for three hours, and during this extraordinary time a remarkable range of entertainment is developed upon the screen . . . No one surpasses Mr. Cukor at handling this sort of thing, and he gets performances from Miss Garland and Mr. Mason that make the heart flutter and bleed. Such episodes as their meeting the night of a benefit show, their talking about marrying on a sound-stage under an eavesdropping microphone, their bitter-sweet reaching for each other in a million-dollar beach bungalow, their tormenting ordeal in a night court— these are wonderfully and genuinely played . . . Miss Garland is excellent in all things, but most winningly, perhaps, in the song "Here's What I'm Here For" [actually, "Someone at Last"], wherein she dances, sings and pantomimes the universal endeavors of the lady to capture the man . . . It is something to see, this *Star Is Born*.

Time magazine, outlining for its readers the film's troubled schedule, presented the film as a triumph over almost insurmountable odds:

> *Star* is a massive effort. The producers astonishing risks . . . The star, Judy Garland, was a 32-year-old has-been as infamous for temperament as she is famous for talent. What's more, all the producer's worst dreams came true. Day after day, while the high-priced help—including Judy's husband, Producer Sid Luft—stood around waiting for the shooting to start, Judy sulked in her dressing room. In the end *Star* took ten months to make, cost $6,000,000. But after Judy had done her worst in the dressing room, she did her best in front of the camera, with the result that she gives just about the greatest one-woman show in modern history . . . An expert vaudeville performance was to be expected from Judy; to find her a dramatic actress as well is the real surprise—although it should not be.

The review concluded that this was "a stunning comeback."

Judy Garland was back on top, but it was captious of *Time* to remind the world that she could be difficult.

17

❖❖ ❖❖❖❖❖❖

The Oscar Fiasco

AT THE NEW YORK PREMIERE of *A Star Is Born*, Ronald Haver reports that Albert Warner had announced: "I really can't recall a more wonderful occasion. It's a wonderful thrill because of the wonderful Judy Garland. It's the greatest thing we have done since we brought out the first talking picture." As business fell off drastically in the first month, however, the Warner brothers no long felt that Judy Garland was so wonderful.

Jack Warner had been ordered by his brother, Harry, to take approximately thirty minutes out of the film, and this new version was previewed at the 6:30 house at the Pantages in mid-October. Warners was encouraged by its reception, and announced on October 27 that it would play throughout the country in every house that was available, so that most audiences never saw the longer version.

Luft always maintained that only Hart, Cukor (who was then filming in India) or himself could have made the cuts intelligently. According to the Warner Bros. files, Barrie Richardson of the Sales Department decided upon the cuts, which were carried out by a studio editor,

Folmar Blangsted. Richardson recommended the deletion of only one song, "Lose That Long Face," a number Cukor had always thought unnecessary; for good measure Blangsted removed "Here's What I'm Here For" as well. Liza Minnelli remembered that her mother came home after hearing of the cuts and lay on the bed sobbing: "They don't care . . . They just don't care."

Evidence of that lack of care is all too apparent. Crucially lost was part of the story in which, after their first meeting, Norman and Esther lose touch. She thinks that he was just fooling around. She moves to cheaper digs, and he is unable to find her until he hears her voice on a television commercial. She has left the band, and the two separations underscore the transient nature of relationships in show business. The film cannot spare any of the dialogue between Norman and Esther, because it goes a long way to explaining their relationship. It is particularly true of the proposal scene, which poignantly follows the one revealing that marrying him will be bad for her, as well her complaint, "you drink too much," which, charmingly, she sings.

The film can spare this sequence much less than the song she sings in their honeymoon chalet, "It's a New World"; the loss of the other two songs, "Here's What I'm Here For" and "Lose That Long Face," meant that the second half is even more like the 1937 version, which may have been the intention. It becomes, however, an altogether less rich and less resonant film.

Cukor said later that Warner Bros. decision to cut the film was one of the "sad things of all time. Judy Garland and I felt like the English queen who had 'Calais' engraved on her heart. Neither of us could ever bear to see the final version." He had himself suggested three cuts: the proposal scene, "Lose That Long Face" and "Born in a Trunk." Mason agreed about the last:

> For one thing I thought that when they came to the great musical number, "Born in a Trunk," it was as if they had come to a great climatic point in the story and then the curtain had come down and the manager had come in front and said "And now our talented little star will entertain you with song and dance for a quarter of an hour," and it completely disrupted the continuity of the plot.

In fact, Mason preferred the 1937 film, "because it tells the story more simply and correctly, because the emphasis should be on the man rather than the girl." Most actors believe that their films should highlight them rather than their co-stars, but even so, Mason may be right. However, the earlier film does not have Judy Garland. Cukor's film was meant to showcase a great talent—to display her in all her moods, and it does this brilliantly. She is funny and warm and true. In the 1937 film, Janet Gaynor is a pretty face, charming and vulnerable, but she does not have the star quality that Norman Maine describes: "That little bell that rings inside your head, that little jolt of pleasure . . . that little extra something that Ellen Terry talked about." The earlier film also has a sentimental beginning, depicting Esther and her grandmother, while Cukor's opening, a gala Hollywood premiere, is dazzling, depicting a world of egomania, hysteria and vanity. It is a whirling bubble of a world, and the bubble is pricked when a drunken movie star, Norman Maine, does all he can to ruin the show.

If the first half of Cukor's film is Hollywood satire, the second is Hollywood tragedy. After the star is born, the movie swerves into romantic melodrama—and, since it is a show-business story, it has every right to wear its heart on its sleeve. The concern of Esther/Vicki and Norman for each other as their careers diverge is touchingly done, but by the time he arrives drunk at the Oscar ceremony, where Vicki is to receive an award, the film has become almost wholly melodramatic.

Mason serves the material more selflessly than Garland, who dominates it. She did the same at M-G-M, but never in this "hey, look at me, I'm Judy Garland" way. In *The Clock*, Minnelli had encouraged her to underplay, while here, Cukor seems to want her to respond to everything. She acts with a nervy edge.

It had appealed to Garland to appear in a movie about a star with an unhappy private life not of her own making, but in the end, the film only increased her inability to distinguish between her real self and her screen self. This feeling was further complicated by the fact that the whole saga of the film's production seemed like ending, comparatively, as tragically as its story. Garland had to face up to the possibility of failure.

The controversy over the cut version was hurting at the box office and alienating the critics. At that time they still had a choice, but most exhibitors booked the shorter version so that they could fit in more showings. In the *New York Times*, Bosley Crowther criticized Warner Bros. and called upon his fellow reviewers to "show displeasure for such post-release tampering." He expressed his doubt about now including the film in his Ten Best list. In the event he did not do so. The most ballyhooed movie of the year was excluded from the list of the most influential newspaper in the country. No one could console themselves, as in the past, that musicals did not appear in these prestigious lists, for Crowther did include both *The Glenn Miller Story* and *Seven Brides for Seven Brothers. Time* magazine's Ten Best list also included the latter.

The re-editing not only damaged the reputation of the film it also spoiled Garland's chances of having her performance recognized as the triumph that it was. The New York critics named Grace Kelly the year's best actress for *The Country Girl*, and while the National Board of Review listed *A Star Is Born* as one of the best films of the year, it also preferred Kelly, citing also her performance in *Rear Window* and *Dial M for Murder. Look* magazine may have named Garland actress of the year, but Hollywood foreign correspondents gave their Golden Globe award for best actress in the drama category to Kelly. Garland and Mason received awards in the comedy/musical category, but this was scant compensation, particularly since the award for best film went to another musical, *Carmen Jones.*

The Golden Globes did not, however, then have the importance that they have today. Everything depended on the Academy Award nominations, which were announced on February 12. The Oscar ceremony had been televised for the past two years, and its huge rating had proved that it had become a major draw. To capitalize on this, NBC decided to televise the announcement of the nominations from various Hollywood nightspots, including an NBC studio made to look like a nightclub, with Greer Garson as hostess. Many of the nominees were not present, but Garland was and was delighted to hear that she had received a Best Actress nomination. Apart from this, the occasion was not a happy one for her.

It was customary for studios to lobby or advertise on behalf of films they thought might win Oscars, but the Warner brothers had turned their collective back on *A Star Is Born*, and it was being roundly snubbed by the Academy. It did not appear on the list of those films nominated for Best Picture (*On the Waterfront, The Caine Mutiny, The Country Girl, Seven Brides for Seven Brothers* and *Three Coins in the Fountain*), and, astonishingly, both Cukor and Hart were overlooked in the Direction and Writing categories. The industry could hardly ignore the much-praised performances of Garland and Mason, but the only other nominations *Star* received were for Best Song ("The Man That Got Away"), Art Direction, Scoring and Costume Design.

Undeterred, Warners prepared to open the film in the cut version in Britain, and with some confidence, since Mason was a native and Garland's tour of 1951 was still fondly remembered. The ads, as in the States, featured a large picture of Garland with her hands cupped around her face, but Warners had dropped the tag about the film's cost to proclaim: "Sing Judy! Dance Judy! The world is waiting for your sunshine!" The BBC, which was usually very careful not to be involved in anything which looked like promotion, was in the foyer of the Warner Cinema, Leicester Square, for the premiere to broadcast live to its radio audience. Among those interviewed as they arrived were Britain's leading young actress, Dorothy Tutin; its most admired classical actress, Dame Edith Evans; its most popular movie star, Kenneth More; and the titanic figure who had turned down the role of Norman Maine, Sir Laurence Olivier, a man not given to attending movie premieres. Newsreel cameras were also on hand and these interviews, and scenes from the film, were shown on television the following week. The televising of such occasions, common enough today, was very rare at this period. Indeed, the event was considered so momentous by the *Evening News* that it made the front page.

> More than sixty stars of stage, screen, radio and television at a gala premiere at the Warner Theatre tomorrow evening will witness the greatest comeback I have known in 30 years of film criticism. Judy Garland is the star. *A Star Is Born* is the film. But in this case a star is re-born, because Hollywood had written off Judy. Yet she gives a performance in this 2½ hour film, which far outshines anything she did at the height of her triumphs.

The British had always loved Garland, and most of the critics penned copy that might have been written by Warners' publicity department. A review by Paul Dehn in the *News Chronicle*, appeared under the headline MISCAST, SHE'S MY JUDY STILL. Dehn suggested that Janet Gaynor was far more suited to the role, but declared:

> I find Judy, miscast, infinitely more memorable than Janet cast to perfection. This is partly because Warners have at least had the discernment to turn Janet's waitress into Judy's Hollywood nightclub singer. Her voice— with its thrilling *crescendo* that swells like the note of a mellifluously approaching tram in winter—is unaltered from the days when she riveted, with alto-hammer blows, our attention to the clang, clang, clang of the St. Louis trolley in spring.

Garland's troubles were no more a secret in Britain than they had been in the States, and most of the critics saw the film as a personal triumph, noting similarities between the lives of the star and the actress she portrayed. "There are things in this story that must have touched her deeply," wrote Campbell Dixon in the *Daily Telegraph*. "The little girl who wandered singing though the wonderland of Oz has known more setbacks than most, and this gives her performance an emotional depth rare in this kind of picture. *A Star Is Born* is a glorious comeback, a triumph of skill and sincerity where a glossier performer might have failed." C.A. Lejeune made a similar point in the *Observer*.

> Because Judy Garland has been through a good deal of life's rough and tumble, [the film] presents her as a heroine unabashedly rough and tumbled . . . But what the film has extra is the spring of feeling between the players, which makes the private life of these public characters extraordinarily human, and keeps their relations clear, moving and fresh.

The *Daily Mail* described Garland's performance as "a remarkable comeback appearance, not least because it has to compete with James Mason at the top of his form," while Penelope Houston in *Sight & Sound* wrote, "Her comeback picture proves the sort of triumph that helps to explain, and justify, the star system." "There has been a great deal of talk about Judy Garland's comeback," Dilys Powell commented in the *Sunday Times*.

> This prompts me to say that as far as I am concerned Miss Garland never went away. The other day we had the chance of seeing her in an early piece, *Meet Me in St Louis*; ravishing there, in the new film she displays an extraordinary maturing of her talents. It is not only that her singing has a new strength and edge; nobody can do better with a song such as, here, 'The Man That Got Away'; and in a satire, admirably staged by Richard Barstow, on what is known as a production number she shows a gift for parody which is brilliant. As an actress she has come a long way. Pathos she always had; but today the pathos has deepened, and her acting has a nervous tension which, when I saw the film, held the audience silent and tear-stained.

One senses that this extraordinary reaction was shared by the critics. "In this incandescent performance, the actress seems to be playing on her nerves; she cannot but strike ours," confessed Penelope Houston.

> Since Judy Garland temporarily deserted the screen . . . some of us have been grudging about even the best musicals. Whatever they had, they hadn't got Judy Garland, and although Hollywood may have found singers and dancers more expert, no one has been able to match the high-strung vitality, the tensely gay personality that made Miss Garland such a uniquely stimulating performer.

Virginia Graham, in the *Spectator* was equally overcome:

> In the end, however, it is for Judy Garland to withstand the full torrent of my admiration. She has lost a little in looks but gained enormously in talent. Warm, sensitive, touching she always was, but now her pathos has a poignancy and her singing a passion. After hearing her sing 'The Man That Got Away' and 'Born in a Trunk' I felt she had seized the torch I carry for her from my hand and scorched my soul with it!

While Coward found that "by the time we had endured montage after montage and repetition after repetition after repetition" in the "Born in a Trunk" sequence, "I found myself wishing dear enchanting Judy was at the bottom of the sea," William Whitebait of the *New Statesman* found this the highlight of the film: "It could go on forever in the splendid knowledge that it's got something: something as good as Astaire or Kelly at his best." Even C. A. Lejeune, who admitted "I still deplore some of the noises emitted by Miss Garland in the alleged process of her singing," conceded that: "for me she can sit on the edge of the stage, dangling her long legs into the orchestra pit for ever."

It is doubtful whether any actress in history ever got notices so filled not only with admiration but love. Warners might have taken out an ad in the trade papers to inform Academy members of these reviews, but their attitude seems to have been that no one was likely to care what a bunch of British critics thought. In Hollywood, however, the Best Actress stakes were regarded as a two-horse race: the also-rans were Dorothy Dandridge for *Carmen Jones*, Audrey Hepburn (who had won the previous year) for *Sabrina*, and Jane Wyman for *Magnificent Obsession*. James Bacon in his Associated Press release called it

> a class struggle. It's Judy Garland, born in a vaudeville trunk, versus Grace Kelly, born into a Philadelphia mansion. At this writing, the contest between Little Miss Showbusiness and the debutante actress looks like a draw. Hollywood, perhaps unconsciously, is taking sides strictly on the class basis. Performance-wise, both were superb. Sentiment, perhaps is on the side of Judy. One of the greatest of child actresses, she has led a heartbreak life—a has-been and a near suicide at 28, and Oscar favorite at 33. It's the kind of story Hollywood loves and one that needs an Academy Award for the happy ending.

Ironically, the score for *The Country Girl* had been written by Arlen and Gershwin after concluding their work on *A Star Is Born*. Furthermore, the plots of the two films were not dissimilar, since both concerned show-business alcoholics. Kelly played the wife of a washed-up actor-singer (played by Bing Crosby) attempting a comeback. *The Country Girl*'s third star was William Holden, and he and Kelly—rather than Crosby—were reckoned to be the key factors in its box-office success. Made modestly in black and white, it did not need any Oscars to help it balance its budget, whereas *Star*, which had almost exhausted its bookings, needed them badly if it were not to be awash forever in red ink in the Warners ledger.

An Oscar might also ensure Garland a new career in Hollywood by boosting the film's takings and endorsing her talent. With television covering the Awards ceremony, the nation as well as the industry might enjoy her triumph: this would not hurt *Star*, if Warners cared to release it. There was also a question of her own satisfaction: she had told James Bacon that she had never cared for herself in any of the movies she had made until this one. When asked about the challenge, however, she was decorously modest: "I feel great. But I really think Grace Kelly will win. Have you seen *County Girl*? Wasn't she just wonderful in it?"

Apart from the tension engendered by this contest, there was another anxiety: Garland was once again pregnant. She had discovered this in the South of France and she and Luft were delighted. Given her history, however, she had to see her doctors even more regularly than usual. Luft was also consulting a psychiatrist on his own behalf. Garland had ordered a maternity gown from the couturier Michael Woulfe for the Oscar ceremony, at which she was scheduled to sing "The Man That Got Away." Jean Negulesco, director of the show, thought her condition "inappropriate" for the job, however, and invited Rosemary Clooney to perform the song instead.

In the event, Garland did not attend the ceremony at all. Labor pains began prematurely, two weeks earlier than expected, on the evening of March 28, two days before the ceremony. She was rushed to the Cedars of Lebanon Hospital by her obstetrician, Dr. Morton, and her condition was sufficiently serious for her to be taken immediately to the operating theater. Frank Sinatra telephoned the Bogarts, asking them to accompany him to see Garland. Bogart declined because he had to work the following day, but Bacall went with Sinatra, who arranged for party food to be delivered to those waiting in the lobby when it was clear that the baby was on its way. He had brought along a cuddly toy, which he gave to Garland as she was wheeled from the recovery room, still dazed after the anesthetic. She was very touched. It was two in the morning, and she had given birth to a son—what she always wanted. It would be her last child: she had asked the doctor to tie her fallopian tubes after delivery.

Any celebrations of the birth were thought to be premature, however. Her doctors—including Marc Rabwin, now a senior consultant at the hospital—announced that the baby's left lung had failed to open, as sometimes happens during caesarean section, when birth is achieved without a struggle. He was in an incubator with only a 50 percent chance of survival. When Garland telephoned Liza, she said: "They tell me he's going to die, but he's not going to—and I won't let him." Liza, nine years old, did not know what to say, so Garland said: "I just wanted to call and tell you that. It won't happen."

The baby's lung did not open until the following afternoon, by which time his parents had decided on his name if he lived: Joseph Wiley, the second of these in honor of Jack Cathcart, whose middle name it was. NBC, meanwhile, had contacted Garland to ask whether they could install equipment in order to televise her reaction if she won the Best Actress Oscar. There was a precedent for this: Joan Crawford had been photographed in bed receiving her Oscar for *Mildred Pierce* after missing the ceremony because of a bad cold. In a couple of hours Garland's room was gradually transformed into a television studio. Technicians installed wiring and lighting, and a platform for the camera—"big enough to launch a rocket," according to Garland—was erected outside the window. She had sent out for a stunning bedjacket and there was even a dress rehearsal of her responding to the news of her victory. By the time she had been prepared—"My God, they're wiring me up like a radar," she commented—she was virtually immobile, and unable even to go to the bathroom for fear of disconnecting something. She liked to give the impression that she was surrounded by the crew, who were in fact outside the room, on the platform. Luft, Harry Rubin, nurse Gundy and John Royal, an old friend from NBC, were with her.

Since the ceremony, which was being held at the Pantages, with Bob Hope as master of ceremonies, was, as usual, interminable, Garland spent a long and uncomfortable evening. No comfort at all could be taken from the announcements, as *A Star Is Born* went unrewarded even in the minor awards for which it had been nominated. The musically complex and brilliantly written "The Man That Got Away" had seemed a shoo-in for Best Song, especially as three of the other four nominees were mediocre: "The High and the Mighty," "Hold My Hand" and Irving Berlin's "Count Your Blessings." The song that won, however, was less even than that: "Three Coins in the Fountain," by Jule Styne and Sammy Cahn, who were the first to admit that it was the most banal of their many collaborations.

In the event of Garland winning the Best Actress Oscar, the plan was for Lauren Bacall to accept the statuette on her behalf, and then Garland would be shown watching the ceremony on television and talking on camera to Hope and Bacall. When William Holden (last year's Best Actor) opened the envelope, however, he pronounced Grace Kelly the winner. "Okay, wrap it up," said one of the crew, Gerold Frank reported, detailing the entire episode, as they began to disconnect Garland and dismantle the rest of the equipment. She wanted to cry and was only prevented from doing so by astonishment, because the technicians were working so quickly, without the least regard for her except as something to be disentangled from the wires. She began to see the funny side of this, and joked: "Boys, don't short me!"

Luft, who had greeted the announcement by taking Garland in his arms and saying "Fuck the Academy Awards!" and launching into an incoherent tirade against "a fucking Jap who shot up Pearl Harbor" (a reference to *Gate of Hell*, a Japanese film which won the award for the Best Foreign Language Film), continued to curse. Garland had the consolation of her baby, however, and told him: "Forget it, darling. Open the champagne. I have my own Academy Award."

Luft did the only thing possible in the circumstances, he got as drunk as he could. Vern Alves turned up with more champagne, and Bacall arrived to help field the telephone calls which began to come in. Of over one thousand telegrams Garland received, the one from Groucho Marx has been the most quoted: DEAR JUDY: THIS IS THE BIGGEST ROBBERY SINCE BRINKS. As Bacall wrote:

> She carried it off beautifully, saying her son, Joey, was more important than any Oscar could be, but she was equally deeply disappointed—and hurt. It confirmed her belief that the industry was against her. She knew that it was then or never. Instinctively, all her friends knew the same. Judy wasn't like any other performer. There was so much emotion involved in her career—in her life—it was always all or nothing. And although she put on a hell of a front, this was one more slap in the face. She was bitter about it and, for that matter, all closest to her were.

With reason.

There was no question that Grace Kelly was the hottest star in Hollywood. She was under contract to M-G-M, but *The Country Girl* was made at Paramount. She had since returned to Paramount to make two more films. Basically, therefore, she had the support of the voting personnel at both studios, both of which mounted a campaign in the trade on her behalf. There was also a tradition that an Oscar went to any actress who could deglamorize herself, and everyone knew that Kelly was the daughter of one of Philadelphia's most prominent families. After looking chic in her previous two films, she had donned glasses and clothes from a bargain basement for *The Country Girl*. Seen today, the performance seems barely adequate.

Cukor believed that it was the butchery performed by Warner Bros. on *A Star Is Born* which cost Garland the Oscar, but this disregards the unanimous praise lavished on her performance in the rest of the world, which saw only the cut version. The fact remains that one of the most memorable films in Hollywood's history was simply shut out. There is no doubt of the excellence of *On the Waterfront*, which won the Best Film award, or of Marlon Brando and Elia Kazan, who were easy choices for Best Actor and Best Director. It was argued that Hollywood disliked films which washed its dirty linen in public, but four years earlier, Billy Wilder's *Sunset Boulevard* had received numerous nominations and carried off the award for Best Screenplay, despite denunciations by the moguls from Mayer downwards. The sad truth is that *A Star Is Born* was recognized as a failure, and Hollywood simply averted its gaze. The film ceased to exist.

The net result was that Garland had failed to re-establish herself in Hollywood. Warner Bros. had already announced before the Oscar ceremony that it would not be proceeding with any more pictures with Garland, in spite of the fact that such a statement might damage *A Star Is Born* in the foreign territories where it was still playing. The studio's decision seemed particularly odd in Britain, where, at the end of the year, *A Star Is Born* featured in the Ten Best list of virtually every critic, most of whom named Garland as the best actress of the year. When the readers of *Picturegoer* voted for 1955's Best Actress, Garland came first "by an astounding margin," with 30 percent more votes than her nearest competitor, Doris Day in *Love Me or Leave Me*. Grace Kelly came sixth. "Maybe Judy WON'T make another picture," commented the magazine. "But this is one triumph they can't take away from her."

Meanwhile, Jack Warner was fiddling the books, so that his business acumen in backing the film could not be questioned—not, at any rate, outside the studio. *A Star Is Born* came in at fourteenth on *Variety*'s list of the year's top-grossing movies. Warner managed this by claiming that it had taken $6,000,000, whereas the figure should have been $4,355,968—which meant, in effect, that it showed a loss on the cost of the negative of nearly $2 million.

For the present, the relationship between Warner and Luft was reduced to a series of recriminations. In his book *My First Hundred Years in Hollywood*, published in 1965, Warner accused Luft of borrowing $30,000 during the course of shooting *A Star Is Born*. He eventually sued for the recovery of this loan: "but trying to collect from Sid Luft was like finding a Popsicle in the desert," he complained. "I finally got a payment of $500 as full settlement."

He also accused Luft of "borrowing" the furniture for a cast party at Mapleton Drive, a reference to the fact that Luft had exercised a clause in their agreement permitting him to buy the set furnishings at 20 percent of the wholesale price. Since these included a Vlaminck and some expensive chinoiserie, as well as several Barcelona chairs, Luft got a bargain when he signed a check for $4,200. Luft admitted that pre-production costs on the film had been so high that he did not have the money to furnish the house properly. It was also costing about $100,000 a year to maintain.

These problems did not impinge on Garland, who, once again, was suffering from post-natal depression, compounded this time by concern for her weight, which, since Joey's birth, had still not gone down, and her disappointment over the Oscar. Luft realized that she had begun taking pills again, and set about scouring her suite. He found Seconal and Benzedrine secreted under carpets, behind books on the shelves, in the hems and seams of her dresses, in her slippers— indeed, virtually everywhere. Her only comment was that he had missed his vocation, he should have been a detective.

To get her out of the professional doldrums, he signed her to a contract with Capitol Records, which had been partly founded by her friend Johnny Mercer. Its most prominent stars were Nat "King" Cole, Gordon MacRae, Jo Stafford and, more recently, Frank Sinatra, whose first few albums had totally revitalized his recording career. In the wake of *A Star Is Born*, M-G-M Records had issued an album of Garland's soundtrack songs, and it was selling well: but there was no guarantee that the public would buy it in sufficient numbers to pay even for the booze bills. The contract with Capitol would last until 1961, after which it was renewed for another three years.

Garland had been wont to claim that she had more goddam talent than anyone else in town, to which Humphrey Bogart invariably replied: "Talent's no good in the living room, you've got to get out there and do it." There could be no argument against that. The whole point of A Star Is Born had been to provide Garland with a new film career, because she hated the burden of performing live. But there was no alternative.

Accordingly, Luft arranged a concert tour and on April 19, 1955, announced that "The Judy Garland Show" would tour California and the Pacific Northwest in July. Chuck Walters staged the production, which was to some extent a revival of the one at the Palace. The difference was that she appeared throughout the evening, between such acts as the Hi-Lo's, a popular recording team. The tour opened in San Diego, where Garland, in full and fine form, quipped: "Do you think figures like this will ever come back?" Not long after there was a benefit in Long Beach for retarded children, a cause dear to her heart since her experience at the hospital in Boston. Frank Sinatra organized an excursion by bus to Long Beach, bringing friends to cheer her on. No sooner were they seated than he got on stage with her to welcome the Bogarts, Debbie Reynolds and Eddie Fisher, Van Johnson, Sammy Davis Jr, Dean Martin, and June Allyson and Dick Powell.

There followed bookings in such cities as Portland, Spokane and Vancouver. "I took one look at all those people," she said, "laughing and applauding, and I fell hopelessly in love with audiences. I still love them, and it's been a serious romance." Nevertheless, it was a grueling experience, moving from town to town, day by day, and checking into a succession of hotels. Furthermore, she did not love audiences so much that she had no fear of facing them: she still suffered agonies of stage fright before going on. She was literally singing for her supper, sometimes in the same towns she had toured as a child. This realization disturbed her, and she missed one performance. But the audiences must have helped, because she agreed to a national tour in the autumn, taking in the Shrine Auditorium in Los Angeles, Orchestra Hall in Chicago, and concluding with a two-month stint in New York at the Winter Garden.

She remembered how much she had enjoyed traveling with the Hollywood Bond Cavalcade of Stars during the war—the camaraderie and the train journeys through the night. She loved the idea of a Judy Garland Cavalcade, sleeping and eating in the train, being greeted by town dignitaries, waving to fans from the look-out platform. She had read that Lucius Beebe, the dandified gossip columnist, was such an ardent train buff that he had a private Pullman car. She wondered whether this could be used to take the Garland troupe and its props and scenery across the country. Beebe agreed to rent it out, but given the thirty-or-so personnel involved and the cost of coupling Beebe's Pullman to the necessary trains, this would be an expensive undertaking.

In consultation with Jules Stein of MCA, who now handled her live performances (Feldman continued to represent her for films), Luft worked out that the tour could only turn a profit if the theaters would guarantee $10,000 per performance in the event of the customary 60 percent of the gross being any lower. Twenty theaters in twenty cities were prepared to book the show, but they were not exactly clamoring for it, and—in the wake of a disastrous tour by Dean Martin and Jerry Lewis—only seven of them were prepared to sign the guarantee. The previous year, Martin and Lewis had been rated the second biggest cinema box-office draw (after John Wayne), and if the public did not want to see *them* in the flesh, it was highly unlikely that it would want to pay to see yesterday's star, Judy Garland.

Luft was faced with a dilemma. He could not afford to put pressure on those theater managers who refused to sign, because if Garland ever failed to appear—which, as he and they knew, was not beyond the bounds of possibility—there would be all hell to pay. If he went ahead with the tour, he faced economic ruin; if he canceled it, the seven theater owners who had already signed contracts could sue—with the same result.

There was, however, a solution. The contract stated that the concerts could be canceled if offers were forthcoming from movies or television, provided forty-five days' notice was given. There seemed little chance of any offers from film studios, so Luft turned to Stein, who had been negotiating with television companies. In 1953, *The Ford 50th Anniversary Show* had made television history not only by being shown simultaneously on CBS and NBC, but by teaming the two acknowledged queens of the Broadway musical, Ethel Merman and Mary Martin. NBC had since had a great deal of success with "specials," and CBS was lagging behind in both prestige and the ratings. The Ford Motor Company proposed a monthly *Ford Star Jubilee* to start in September, and delighted CBS officials had begun to talk to MCA about Garland. When Garland had left M-G-M there had been less then five million households with a television set. By 1955, there was an estimated thirty-two million. Bing Crosby had finally joined the other major stars operating in the medium, many with their own weekly shows. Not only was Garland, because of her movies, a bigger name nationally than Merman or Martin, but she was one of the last hold-outs against television among the truly big names: to get her for the premiere show would be a true coup. To make the event even more special, it was to be the first CBS spectacular to be broadcast in color. At great expense, Ford had taken a Saturday evening spot—the best viewing night of the week. They were prepared to pay Garland $100,000, as well as a fee of $10,000 for Luft to produce.

There remained one major obstacle to overcome: Garland was terrified of television. Just after finishing *A Star Is Born*, she had turned down an offer of $50,000 to appear as a shy spinster, with James Mason as her tyrannical father, in an adaptation of Henry James's *The Heiress* on *Lux Video Theater*, the successor to *Lux Radio Theater*. Booked to appear on *The Ed Sullivan Show* to publicize *Star* by singing "It's a New World," with the composer at the piano, she backed out at the last minute, leaving Arlen to sing it himself. For the Ford show, she would have to play to a camera, but without the advantage, as in films, of a retake. In the event of her making a mistake, as when she fell at the London Palladium, she could not expect viewers at home to share the joke, especially as they would not necessarily be devoted fans, like those who had paid to see her on stage. On the contrary, she feared that they might be skeptical of her abilities in the first place.

The special was scheduled for September 24, 1955: it was now July, so she had to make up her mind quickly, before Ford went after someone else. The quicker she did, the longer she would have to rehearse. It was the only way she could avoid going on a loss-making concert tour. She had no choice.

The show was to last ninety minutes and follow the format of her stage shows, including the presence of a live audience, with her Boyfriends to help out while she changed into the four costumes designed by Irene Sharaff. Jack Cathcart was assigned to conduct the music, and David Wayne, a star in his own right, would emcee the show before joining Garland in "For Me and My Gal" and "A Couple of Swells." She would be performing fourteen numbers alone and unaided for the last part of the show.

CBS had put Harry Ackerman in charge of the show, and he had chosen Ralph Levy to direct. Awed and nervous at his first meeting with Garland, Levy made the mistake of saying that he was not impressed with one of her suggestions. She fired him on the spot. She was frantic enough about the whole venture without having to take orders from someone unimpressed by her. He was replaced.

The day before the transmission, she had laryngitis, which she ascribed to nerves. It would disappear once she started performing, she told the journalist, James Bacon, and: "If not, I'll just sing over it. I'm not going to worry about it. I'll just work my head off, get good and sick thirty minutes before airtime, and by Sunday morning we'll know whether or not I've laid an egg." That night she took an overdose of sleeping pills, probably accidentally. Her nerves had been taut-strung for days and she spent agonized hours awake. Luft was unable to rouse her at six. He carried her to the shower, where the cold water woke her, but she was unable to move. He walked her about until eight, when Dr. Pobirs arrived with a stimulant. Her throat doctor came at ten and prescribed Chinese food with soy sauce and as much iced tea as she could drink. The food was to absorb as much of the drug as possible, the soy would make her want to drink, and the tea would flush out the last traces.

By the time they arrived at the studio at one, she still could not speak without slurring her words. Luft explained that she was saving her voice. They were both frightened, he of handing CBS the most publicized no-show of all time, and she of doing or saying anything which might indicate to the CBS brass that she was not fit to perform. Executives of the company, of Ford, of Technicolor and the advertising agencies involved were not a little bewildered when it became clear that she intended only to walk through the dress rehearsal, which began at three. This lasted until five-thirty with breaks, during which Garland gulped more iced tea. The show was due to start at six-thirty local time, which was nine-thirty on the East Coast.

Garland's first number was "You Made Me Love You": she hoped that viewers might attribute the slurred words and the rather raucous timbre of her voice to nerves. Because she was to dance the next number, "Swanee," it had been pre-recorded, and from then on her will strengthened and her confidence began to return. By the time she finished "Over the Rainbow," she was back on form. It helped, perhaps, that she was wearing her tramp costume, which disguised her puffiness. And, it has to be said that in tights for "Get Happy," which was also pre-recorded, she didn't look too bad.

Variety was impressed:

When she was on camera, and particularly in the closing thirty minutes when it was her show, that ol' black magic and magnetism came through in all its treasured nuances . . . Finale was the inevitable and surefire "Over the Rainbow." What to the average viewer appeared to be an overstudied and over-emotional rendition was revealed later as genuine tears provoked by a case of laryngitis. (Some of the songs were pre-recorded.) Seemingly there were any number of less fortunate elements competing with Miss Garland and it's a tribute to the star that nothing else mattered when she was on and her vibrant personality took hold of things.

The reviewer liked little else, however, particularly not Wayne—except when he, Judy and a twelve-year-old Japanese singer, Mitsuko Sawamura (who also had a solo spot), teamed up to sing "It's De-Lovely": "In mood, pace, tempo, lighting, timing, and overall cohesion (and even color definition) the deficiencies reflected CBS's year behind [NBC] status."

One critic not too taken with Garland herself was Janet Kern of the *Chicago American*:

> There is something painfully pathetic in watching a talented star, still young and able, wallowing in reminiscence, never permitted to turn from wistful backward glances to hint that there is still a present and future in her horoscope. The material and treatment of this "Star Jubilee" would have been great . . . had the program been "This Is Your Life" with Sophie Tucker. But this was a Saturday night musical revue which called itself a "Jubilee" and the nostalgic star was thirty-three!

The format had worked for the Palace, however, and it had been used again for Judy's first Capitol recording, *Miss Show Business*, which was issued the following day. Cathcart conducted, and Edens and Gershe had written an introductory song, "This Is the Time of the Evening." It is sung gently by a chorus and concludes "and no one sings the old songs as romantically as Judy"—whereupon Garland comes in with a tender rendering of "While We're Young," which she had also sung on the television show. The album cover featured a black-and-white photograph of Garland, and on the reverse the photographs and the text reinforced the impression that this was purely an exercise in nostalgia. This appeared to be what the public wanted, for the record moved up to the fourth position among best-selling albums.

The format also appeared to have worked on television. CBS, noting the Nielsen rating of a happy 34.8 percent share of the audience, approached MCA to negotiate for further television appearances. In December, the company announced that it had signed Garland to an exclusive three-year contract for one color special a year, with almost $300,000. This would pay for the annual expenses of the house on

Mapleton Drive, and some more top-selling records might allow for other luxuries. Capitol was asking for another album, and Garland once again turned to Edens.

Because of his position at M-G-M, Edens could not receive credit for any of the advice he gave Garland during her years with Capitol, for whom she did some of her greatest work. Nor did Edens get paid. The composer and arranger Saul Chaplin observed that he, too, was always delighted to have the chance to work with Garland when she asked him, but that it never occurred to her or Luft to pay him. Nor did she ever express any gratitude. It simply was not in her nature.

On this occasion, Edens decided to be done with nostalgia: a new record, *Judy*, would feature standards with which she had never previously been identified, as a rare (unsigned) record review in the *New Yorker* indicates:

> Judy Garland is at the top of her form. In the past, for all her effectiveness on screen and at the Palace, she hasn't been too persuasive on records, but this time, thanks to some sure-footed orchestrations and a fine job of recording, she comes across triumphantly. The arrangements—by Nelson Riddle, whose knack for this sort of thing is also demonstrated on Frank Sinatra's recent records—are all apt, as well as flattering to Miss Garland's voice. What he has done with Harold Arlen's "Come Rain or Come Shine" is particularly striking. Always an engaging song, it becomes electrifying when Miss Garland, singing impulsively and altering the notes at will, is given a boost by her colleague's curiously driving instrumental support. In a sense, she and Mr. Riddle are pretty high-handed in the approach to the tune, but the results more than justify the liberties they have taken. Speaking of Arlen reminds me that Miss Garland, although she has otherwise shown little discrimination in her choice of material over the years, seems to have a penchant for his works ever since she introduced his memorable "Over the Rainbow." In addition to "Come Rain or Come Shine," he is also represented here by the attractive waltz "Last Night When We Were Young" and the loose-gaited "Any Place I Hang My Hat Is Home." These, as well as several nondescript pieces, "Dirty Hands, Dirty Face," "Life Is Just a Bowl of Cherries" and "April Showers" among them, are delivered by Miss Garland either exuberantly or tenderly, according to their mood, and one of the chief pleasures of the set is her change of pace when, right after the "Come Rain or Come Shine" pyrotechnics, she sings a couple of choruses of "Just Imagine" in a kind of simple wonderment.

Garland herself chose two of the songs, as is evident by the presence on the album of her father's favorite, "I Will Come Back," and, finally making it to the marketplace, her version of "Last Night When We Were Young."

Capitol's only problem was the pictures for the album's jacket, since a matronly, overweight Garland was not likely to appeal to any but her most diehard fans. The solution lay in using stills taken at the time of *A Star Is Born*. The cover was a treated frame blowup of her singing "My Melancholy Baby" in the film.

Early in 1956, CBS, conscious of Garland's special status, planned as the first of the shows under its new contract a thirty-minute program consisting of Judy Garland in concert, accompanied by Leonard Bernstein and the New York Philharmonic. Although negotiations with Bernstein broke down, all concerned continued to believe that the format should be a simple one, built around Garland and her songs. Most stars of her standing, whether in their weekly series or in specials, had guest visitors for jokes and duets, as on Crosby's radio program. However, Crosby, Perry Como and others were from time to time varying their formats by dispensing with guest stars and concentrating instead on displaying their own talents as singers and so it would be on this occasion.

Garland sensibly decided to use the songs on the new Capitol album as the basis of the show, emphasizing that she needed neither dancing boys nor nostalgia to be effective. Nelson Riddle replaced Bernstein as the conductor, with Leonard Pennario coming in as accompanist. His standing was reflected in his being given a solo. He proved amenable to playing only part of Ravel's *Bolero*, but when he learned that it was to be cut further, he protested and withdrew, on full pay. The esteemed jazz pianist Joe Bushkin replaced him.

Fred Finklehoffe wrote the spare linking material. Ralph Nelson was hired to direct, and Peter Gennaro from *The Perry Como Show* did the choreography. When Gennaro first met Garland, she was already in rehearsals, but had hurt her ankle, which was in a cast. She told him that she could learn the steps if he simply demonstrated them—and she did. "I couldn't believe it," he said, "but there it was. She was a wonderful musician and had such a great feeling for jazz, blues and all kinds of music. She could have been one of the greatest dancers ever."

The photographer Richard Avedon was engaged to provide the setting, which was not to intrude upon a great artist simply singing. *The Judy Garland Show* was to go out on April 8, in the Sunday evening spot usually occupied by *General Electric Theater*, whose host, Ronald Reagan, introduced her. She had managed to slim down a little, but she was not in good voice on either of the first two numbers, "I Feel a Song Coming On" and "I Will Come Back," on both of which she lip-synched. One reason her voice was rough and husky was that she had resorted to pills to calm her nerves. Somewhere along the way, someone had decided that mere singing would not be a good idea as long as Garland's voice was off form, and she did a rather silly dance to the second song, whirling a cane while a fan billowed out of her skirt.

She managed a touching version of "Last Night When We Were Young" and "Life Is Just a Bowl of Cherries" with only a couple of coarse notes, but lip-synching to "Dirty Hands, Dirty Face" while looking at a picture of Joey found her working "with misdirected intensity," wrote Coyne Steven Sanders in his book about the television series. "Rarely did Judy's instincts err in performing a song, but here she was overwrought and overemotional to an uncomfortable degree."

Nelson Riddle's stunning orchestral arrangement of "Come Rain or Come Shine" had prompted Gennaro to choreograph it with Garland in the center of a group of musicians (real or fancied). Unfortunately, the arrangement, with its darting rhythms, made him think Garland should do the same—moving playfully and excessively from one musician to the other. After that, the closing "April Showers" could only be an improvement but, again, it was over-produced, with the star performing the feat of walking backwards up a winding staircase still singing.

Whatever failings there were in the show were forgotten with old friends around her, such as Edens, Gershe and Kay Thompson. It was like old times, said Gershe, with laughter and jokes, and everyone happy—until they got back to Garland's house. The hostess went upstairs to freshen her makeup, and came down so drunk that the evening was ruined.

The strain of being Judy Garland remained a heavy burden, and the show was not rewarded by the good notices she had come to expect. Harriet Van Horne in the *New York World-Telegram* wrote that:

There was something amiss last night. [Garland's] usual control and discipline were lacking. The notes that tremble so gloriously in that rich throat trembled a little too long. There was too much anguish in the sad songs and there was too much wild glee—for my taste—in the production number that had Miss G. ruffling the hair of all the boys in the band. Every gesture, every emotion, was a little bigger than life.

Variety was marginally more kind:

Not even sheer determination and hard work of which she gave plenty, could bring this half-hour up to the standards of her full capacity. Possibly because she was doing some new songs, not very good ones either, her voice had a rough quality, especially in the higher registers. In one of her early numbers, her voice distinctly broke and her verve and showmanlike flair couldn't cover that up.

These flaws were thrown into relief by the album *Judy*, which was released the following week. Although it did not sell as well as *Miss Show Business*, it was superb by any standards. Judy Garland may no longer have been a star of the movies, but she was still in there pitching.

18

❖❖❖❖❖❖❖

Mrs. Sid Luft

RECORDS AND TELEVISION kept Judy Garland before the public eye, and at this time too she was seen at many social gatherings. This was largely due to her close friendship with the Bogarts. Not only was Bogart's fourth and last marriage, to Lauren Bacall, known to be happy, but he was one of the half-dozen most admired actors in Hollywood and a man with a reputation as a hellraiser. These were elements which made him newsworthy. He was the center of his crowd, most of whom liked a drink, and most of whom lived in Holmby Hills.

Much as he liked Garland, Bogart was not exactly impressed with Sid Luft. "You've got no fucking class, Sid, that's your problem," said Bogart when Luft bought a Rolls-Royce. "You can't buy it and you can't acquire it like a suntan. And I can tell you that you don't have it, my friend, and you never will. I know what I'm talking about because I was born with it. I've had it all my life—and I can also do without it." It was one of the principles of the Holmby Hills drinking set that they were not only frank with each other, but dangerously rude. They liked to hang out at Romanoff's restaurant, where Bogart referred to his friends as "The Free Loaders," a reference to their policy of always trying to get someone else to pay the bill.

The most prominent members of this set of friends, with whom Bogart liked to banter, argue and above all drink, were the Lufts, the David Nivens, the writer Nathaniel Benchley, Bogart's agent Irving "Swifty" Lazar, the composer Jimmy Van Heusen, Frank Sinatra and Mike Romanoff himself. They received a new name when Bacall surveyed them in Romanoff's upstairs room one evening and announced: "I see the rat pack is all here." Bogart seized upon the expression and, although the acknowledged leader of the group, he became merely "the rat in charge of public relations." Frank Sinatra was the pack master; Garland the first vice-president; Bacall the den mother; Luft the cage master; Lazar the recording secretary and treasurer; and Benchley the historian. Benchley designed the club's insignia, a rat chewing a human hand, with the motto: "Never rat on a rat."

At Bogart's insistence, John Huston and Noël Coward were honorary rats, and when the latter opened in Las Vegas in June 1955, Sinatra chartered a plane to take most of this group, along with Ernie Kovacs and Angie Dickinson, to see "The Master" in cabaret. The party had a fine time seeing the other shows and gambling, "only occasionally poking our noses outside to sniff the desert air and gauge the time of day," according to Niven. "After three days, Judy Garland slipped me something that she promised me would keep me going. It was the size of a horse-pill and inside were dozens of little multicolored 'energy' nuggets, timed to go off at intervals of forty minutes."

One agreement among the Rat Pack was that if an outside light was shining at a member's house, at any time, he or she was receiving. One afternoon Bogart tired of hearing of the Lufts' marital problems. According to Richard Burton, who was there, Bogart told them to get out, stay out, and never come back. "He added a few choice epithets and ended by admonishing Sid 'to take that dull wife with you.' " When Luft threatened to smash his face in, Bogart backed away, saying: "Sid, you won't lay a hand on me." "Why not?" Luft asked; to which Bogart replied gently: "Because you're my friend."

Bogart's remark was an example of brinkmanship, but not necessarily an inaccurate reflection of his own feelings. In general, however, Garland's friends liked Luft. He seemed a little awed by some of them, but he had charm and intelligence. It was recognized that he left her to earn most of the money, which he spent as freely as she, but also that she would not have been earning a cent without his help. Bacall said of Garland:

> She was a complicated woman of tremendous wit and intelligence who had survived a distorted childhood and distorted marriages which had left their mark. But she and I became good friends. She was fun and, when we'd sit quietly of an afternoon or evening, great company. It was hard for her to think beyond herself—it had been that way too long. But *A Star Is Born* was made in spite of the cynics' predictions, and it was Sid who helped her get through.

As to the marriage itself, it was always in a parlous state. It seems likely that Garland had persuaded herself that she was in love with Luft, because this is what happened in the movies. She was principally attracted to him because he took her career in hand and because he satisfied her sexually. The emotional charge between them had never been more than minimal, and even this was threatened when Garland's career faltered and financial difficulties recurred. Bogart once told Garland that Luft was going to ruin her, perhaps because of his gambling, and he recommended to them his own financial adviser, Morgan Maree. They were certainly in need of professional help: Internal Revenue had received little of its share of Garland's earnings since her season at the Palace back in 1951, and its officers were to spend the rest of the decade pursuing her for back taxes.

At the same time, the Lufts lived high on the hog: there were more pressing needs than paying back taxes—such as parties where a great deal of drink was consumed. The Lufts gave and went to a lot of these, at which Garland was usually seen at her best. Nobody who was at a party with her ever forgot it, because of her gaiety, her wit, her exuberance and the sheer joy she took in singing—not to prove anything, but simply to please her friends. Luft liked to watch admiringly from the sidelines, well aware that he would be ready to leave long before her. They would exchange a few words, he would shrug and make his goodbyes. She would leave in her own good time, often to return later because she had been locked out. "That was the way they played it," their friends agreed. Writing of the mid-1950s, Ned Wynn (the son of Keenan Wynn, who had been a contemporary of Garland's at M-G-M) noted "Judy's drinking is legendary now. She's out of control, a bad drunk." She sat on until the small hours, smoking, drinking and looking around for anyone still up and prepared to listen to her complaints about "the sonofabitch Sid." She would babble on with increasing incoherence until she had to be put to bed on a couch.

In the morning, the household tiptoed around her, fielding telephone calls from Luft, who was demanding to know when she would be home. And that evening she would be at the next party, sometimes early to help her hostess. "Royalty is forgiven everything," said Wynn. "If there is an error in my thinking, it is that people love Judy in spite of her excesses. I think they love her because of them."

Garland was a far from reliable commentator upon her marriage to Luft, partly because she was incapable of rational analysis and partly because most of her remarks were made for public consumption. In 1964, she was to tell *McCall's*:

> The birth of our daughter, Lorna, was the only bright spot in the first year of our marriage. From the beginning Sid and I weren't happy. I don't know why. I really don't. For me it was work, work, work and I didn't see much of Sid. He was always dashing off to places, lining up my appearances. I wasn't made any happier looking into mirrors, seeing myself balloon out of shape from liquids trapped in my body. The doctors said it was caused by metabolic imbalance, brought on by all those crash diets and nervous strain.

This was less than fair to Luft, heroically coping with a woman who always resorted to pills and alcohol, supposedly to maintain her equilibrium. In fact, they had the opposite effect. She was always able to separate the personal and professional side of their relationship: while Luft was producing her April television show, she had taken time off from rehearsal to sue for divorce. On February 4, 1956, she filed suit, charging him with "extreme cruelty." She asked the court to make an equitable division and to grant her custody of Lorna and Joey. The first Luft knew of this was when he returned home just before seven, to be contacted by a man from United Press. "This is baloney," he said. "She left no note or anything. I just got home and haven't even looked round to see if her clothes are gone. We didn't have any fight. This is a blow to me." He went on: "We had personal problems which I can't talk about, but every couple has those. Actresses often get emotionally upset and go to see lawyers."

He spent the night pondering the why and wherefores. He had never known her when she was not emotionally unstable, so he was not altogether surprised by her behavior. She came back in the morning, saying that she had changed her mind.

There was never any question of fidelity within the marriage. Garland enjoyed numerous extramarital liaisons, with both men and women, and she certainly wasn't referring to Luft the following year, in London, when she told reporters that one of the reasons she knew she had a successful show was because "I am in love for the first time." She could have been referring to Aly Khan, who spent a lot of time at the house, even when Luft was not there. She may have meant Frank Sinatra, with whom she had an intermittent affair for years, until he realized that she wanted to marry him. They remained friends, and he explained why: "Judy Garland can't relax any more than I can. It's just something inside of us, that's why we understand each other so well." Over the years, she always knew where to find him when she needed help, no matter where in the world he happened to be.

She may even have been referring to Harry Rubin, who stood in the wings to hand her a vodka and an ammonia capsule when she finished her act, limp as a rag and needing a pick-me-up. She once dragged him on stage and introduced him as "the man who holds my head up when I want to throw up." Kay Thompson thought Rubin deserved to be canonized for the pains he took with Garland. These pains included procuring tablets for her, something Garland found extremely useful. She may have seen herself as a great star, but she had no qualms about enjoying sex with an employee. Rubin never kowtowed to her because, as he said, she would have taken his balls and had them displayed on the mantelpiece. He also made her laugh. She liked him to tell her again and again of his sexual initiation as a boy by the woman next door, "Aunt Dolly." She used to roar with laughter about his stories of "Aunt Dolly with the cucumber up her cunt."

With characteristic inconsistency, she would tell some friends that sex was unimportant to her; but this belies the facts. She was fascinated by sex, and got a lot of it. Not that she always received satisfaction. Of one of her more famous lovers, she remarked: "All he wants are blow-jobs. Hell, you've got to fuck once in a while!" She did not limit herself to heterosexual men. She once tried to masturbate Harry Rubin while he was driving her in the car, but he was too tired. Undaunted, Garland got into the back of the car and went to work on one of her hairdressers, who was gay. She also boasted to Rubin that she had persuaded another of her homosexual employees to sodomize her. Anal and oral sex gave her more satisfaction than traditional intercourse. She particularly enjoyed encouraging relations between gay men, and there were always plenty of those about her. Rubin believed that she embarked on many of her own absurd liaisons because of her prurient interest in sex. She relished going to louche bars, though not alone, to sit and observe. This was not without its risks, for someone, male or female, might recognize her and suppose she was looking for a cheap pickup.

Garland's affair with Rubin lasted off and on for three years. She once sacked him because he absented himself on a public holiday to spend it with his wife. Luft told him to ignore the dismissal and hang around, which he did. Garland didn't complain. She also enjoyed setting him up with some of her famous friends: "She hasn't had it in a long, long time and she needs it badly. So you're going to take her to lunch at the best restaurant in town, give her a couple of strong martinis, and then you're going to be laid." When Rubin took up these suggestions, Garland would occasionally telephone to find out how matters were progressing. "What's taking you so long?" she would ask. Until he left her employ in 1959, Rubin was her court jester, as well as "her one island of safety," as one of her psychiatrists, Dr. Leonard Krauss, once told him.

In spite of such infidelities, and the ups and downs of their relationship, the Lufts remained together, united in panic and show-business exile. There were offers of films, from time to time; but they were all tentative efforts, tempered by her unreliability, professionally and physically, and conditional on barring Luft as a producer. CBS did not want another show until the next year, and her contract forbade her to work for the other networks. She knew that she could return to the Palladium and the Palace, but either booking might be just too soon to invoke the furor of the past. Luft did not want to get involved with the logistics of a tour, especially after his experiences the previous year, but money was short.

For a whole year, she had had only her income from television and records to sustain a costly household. However, there was excellent money to be made on the nightclub circuit. The offers were plentiful, but the job was not always easy, playing to drunken or disgruntled diners, many of whom might be regretting that they had forsaken the blackjack table or the roulette wheel. Nevertheless, Noël Coward had won unexpected acclaim (partly as a result of an album recorded at the time) from entertaining the punters of Las Vegas, and so Luft asked MCA to examine the offers and open negotiations for the most lucrative. This turned out to be an engagement at the New Frontier Hotel in Las Vegas for four weeks in late July, at $55,000 per week. This was above and beyond accommodating Garland and her entourage in the hotel—one suite for the children and another for herself and Luft. Edens and Walters had commitments which prevented them from advising, so Robert Alton and Kay Thompson stepped in.

"In an air of expectancy as electric as the opening of a promising new Broadway musical, one of the greatest modern-day singers caught fire last night in the first nitery engagement of her career," reported *Variety*. This was just as well, since the fee MCA had negotiated was the highest yet paid to an artist in cabaret. It appeared to be justified when 7,000 people were turned away during the first weekend, and the management hastily added a fifth week. "I imagine the greatest compliment ever paid the all-time-great Judy Garland," said Eddie Cantor, "came from a man who had just dropped several thousand dollars at a crap table in Las Vegas. He sat down in the nightclub adjoining the casino, heard Judy sing 'Over the Rainbow.' Then he turned to his companion and said, 'Brother, I'm even.' "

Unfortunately, the dry desert heat outside and the air-conditioning within were both causing Garland problems. She spoke little, drank as much liquid as possible and had her suite regularly moisturized, but nevertheless contracted laryngitis so badly during the second week that one night she was unable to perform. She appeared, however, with Jerry Lewis, who had recently split with Dean Martin and was desperately anxious to prove that he could make it as a solo performer. With her encouragement, he clowned while singing her songs.

It was while she was in Las Vegas that she received a movie offer from Nunnally Johnson, a writer-producer-director at 20th Century-Fox who had come to know her well through the Bogarts. It was a fascinating project. Two psychiatrists, Corbett H. Thigpen and Hervey M. Cleckley, had written a book, *The Three Faces of Eve*, based on their attempts to cure one of their patients, whom they called Eve White. An ordinary, suburban housewife, Eve was subject to headaches and fainting spells. After being treated, a different Eve emerged, promiscuous, irresponsible, hard-drinking and contemptuous of both her husband and the other Eve. After uncovering these opposing personalities, the doctors discovered a third, calmer, more mature and better integrated. Johnson wrote the screenplay, which he was also to produce and direct, with Garland in mind. He recognized that she had all these multiple qualities within herself, something confirmed by a psychiatrist who once treated her and remarked: "Split personality? For people like Miss Garland we need a new word. We need a word that means a personality that's split at least five ways." Johnson flew to Vegas with the script and some clandestine film the doctors had taken of Eve while she was changing from one personality to the other.

Garland was excited about the film and Johnson's wife, Dorris, sent her a bouquet of desert flowers to seal the agreement. This, however, was the last Johnson ever heard of the matter. "As so often happens with poor Judy, there were all kinds of complications," he recalled. He believed that she was unwilling to give up the sort of fees she could earn in Vegas, but in fact, the more she thought about the role, the more it terrified her. It was much too close to home, it would be a film without songs, she would have to slim for a screen appearance and was not sure whether she could. After studying the script, she eventually put it aside. The part was offered to Joanne Woodward, then new to films, and she was to win an Oscar for her performance.

There was also the possibility of another movie, for which, according to John Fricke, contracts and letters of agreement were about to be exchanged. In 1955, Howard Hughes sold RKO to General Teleradio Inc., a subsidiary of the General Tire and Rubber Company. Among its files, the new management came upon the plan to star Judy Garland in a remake of *Alice Adams*. The chief obstacle, however, in this case as well as *The Three Faces of Eve*, was the absolute refusal to allow Luft any participation in the projects. On top of that their insurers thought that she was too high a risk. They changed their minds.

As Garland broke records at Vegas, Luft asked MCA whether they could get her a New York booking. At first it was thought that she might play the Winter Garden, but in the end Sol Schwartz said that he would like her to return to the Palace. It was now five years since she had played there, and this really was long enough for an artist of her caliber to be absent. A season of two months was agreed on, starting on September 26, little more than three weeks after the Vegas engagement ended. Garland would once again be on a percentage, and was so confident of good houses that she took two separate apartments at the Park Lane Hotel, at a cost of $4,000 a week. She also insisted on having several items shipped from the Mapleton Drive house to make her feel at home.

Her optimism was entirely justified by the tremendous advance sale of tickets. Pandemonium reigned both inside and outside the theater on the first night, with police barricades erected to keep the crowds under control. The Palace recognized the significance of the event by laying out a red carpet for those attending. The first half of this "All Star Variety" consisted of the Amin Brothers, an acrobatic act; Bob Williams, a droll young man who was driven to despair when his dog refused to obey his commands; the Hungarian dance team of Kovach and Rabovsky; Garland's Boyfriends (now numbering twelve); and a brilliant young stand-up comic, Alan King. Luft, as he always did, had put together an excellent bill, but it was a thankless engagement for the support performers. They often played to half-empty houses, since many spectators were not interested in Variety, only in Judy Garland, and did not arrive until after the intermission. Alan King scored a personal success, however, not least by observing good-naturedly that he knew that they wanted him to get off so that Garland could get on.

The Vegas act would not have been suitable for New York, so Roger Edens and Charles Walters, with unfailing generosity, helped out again. Walters had devised a spectacular "entry" for Garland, prompted by her, since she had done something similar as a child. The auditorium and stage were in total darkness when the orchestra played the opening notes of "Over the Rainbow," exciting the audience to fever pitch. On the third note, a spotlight hit Garland's face and, as she moved forward to acknowledge the welcome, the spotlight opened out. It seemed that the applause would never stop, but when it did, she struck into "New York, New York, It's a Wonderful Town." She wore a black taffeta dress with numerous skirts, one of which became dislodged as she sang. "Something always happens to me," she said, and disappeared into the wings.

She sang "Rockabye Your Baby," "Swanee" and, after "Be a Clown," for which she was joined by her Boyfriends, the inevitable "Over the Rainbow," still in her clown makeup. Earlier, she had done some songs from her latest records, including "Come Rain or Come Shine," "Any Place I Hang My Hat Is Home" and "Happiness Is Just a Thing Called Joe," a song she once associated with Joe Mankiewicz but which she now dedicated to her son (who may, indeed, have been named after the *real* love of her life—a typical Garland touch). She sang, danced and clowned for sixty-five minutes. "I love you all!" she shouted out as she left the stage. "There may be those who insist that lightning won't strike twice at the same place," said one reviewer, "that history doesn't repeat itself. But you won't find them among those who attended Judy's return to the Palace."

"Nothing really important seems to have happened since Judy Garland was last here five years ago," wrote Brooks Atkinson in the *New*

York Times. "As on her previous visit, she takes over the second half of the program with the songs she sings as though she were composing them on the spot . . . A song has not really been sung until Judy pulls herself together and belts it through the theater."

The run was extended to January 8, making it just two weeks shorter than the 1951 engagement. It was not without mishap: she was on her best form for the original eight weeks, but the strain showed thereafter. She began to be plagued by laryngitis and worried that audiences would not be hearing the voice they knew from movies and records. One night, she knew that she could not manage the last two notes of "Over the Rainbow," but when she paused the audience knew it too, and broke into applause to encourage her. She croaked out the notes, and then ran offstage to sob in the arms of a stagehand before returning to take her bows.

To give herself longer between songs, she brought on the children, singing "Happiness Is Just a Thing Called Joe" to Joey and "Rockabye Your Baby" to Lorna. When Liza, then eleven, flew to New York to see her mother perform, she was called up on stage to dance while Garland sang "Swanee." Garland knew that Liza could perform—she had been showing them at home for years. For her part, Liza did not suspect that her purpose was to divert the audience from the difficulties her mother was having with the song. Bing Crosby was in the audience one night with Julie Andrews, with whom he was making a television special, and when Garland introduced them, the audience applauded so heartily that Crosby had to come up on stage and sing with her. After that she invited anyone she knew in the audience to join her for a song, and among those who accepted were Richard Rodgers and Harold Arlen. Eventually eight shows were canceled, and she checked into the Doctors Hospital to prepare herself for her return.

In November, her fans were reminded of the young Judy Garland, when *The Wizard of Oz* was broadcast for the first time on television. CBS, locked in its rating battle with NBC, had approached M-G-M with a view to leasing *Gone With the Wind*, but the company thought that the film still had reissue potential. M-G-M was willing to let CBS have *Oz*, however, for $225,000, with options for nine more showings. Although comparatively few homes had seen it in color, it had enjoyed great success.

She was still playing to capacity at the Palace, but she could not break the record she had set in 1951 because she was contracted to do her next television special for CBS, which had been announced for either February 25 or March 4. During her last week in concert, in January 1957, she examined the proposal for the new show from CBS, who already had Buick and L & M Filters lined up as co-sponsors. Looking at the two previous specials, CBS decided that the one which had gathered the most favorable response had been the one based on the Palace act. Since Garland had recently returned to the Palace, it made sense to return to that formula.

Garland disagreed. Guided by Roger Edens, she knew how to blend her familiar material with standard songs she had not sung publicly before. Since the "new" songs in the Palace act were those she had performed on television the previous year, and since much of the rest of it had been featured in the Ford special, she risked alienating television audiences—as well as perhaps deterring potential theater spectators, who might think her repertoire was dangerously small.

She did not want to do another variety show, which would be merely repetitious, and wanted to suit her television program to the medium: "I don't care for big production numbers, and I think it would be wise next time to try to use music in the most intimate way—because you are singing to people in their homes."

When Garland rejected the CBS proposal, Freddie Fields of MCA came up with an alternative of her singing to various accompaniments, including a symphony orchestra and a group of jazzmen. It was certainly one way of singing to people in their homes, but she was not prepared to do it for ninety whole minutes. To exacerbate the difficulties further, on January 10 an article appeared in the *New York Herald Tribune* by the paper's television writer, Marie Torre, in which she quoted one CBS executive as saying that Garland "is known for a highly developed inferiority complex" and that she did not "want to work because something is bothering her." As to what she could only guess, "but I wouldn't be surprised if it's because she thinks she's terribly fat."

This was not what the CBS legal department said. As far as the attorneys there were concerned, CBS had "sole discretion" on the format of Garland's shows, but it gave her "right of prior approval . . . which she shall not unreasonably withhold." Neither Garland nor her lawyers were prepared to accept that a script and a four-page outline were quite the same thing. A script as such would have come with the company's own suggestions for the major personnel, allowing Garland to counter with her own choices in case of disagreement.

Given that CBS had been happy to sell a star of Garland's magnitude to any sponsor, the fact that the contract was canceled six days later is telling. She was known for being temperamental and uncooperative, and CBS was going to teach her a lesson if she thought she could treat them the way she had treated M-G-M.

Further, the remarks by the unnamed executive indicate both dislike and distrust, almost certainly a result of her behavior during production on the last two specials. Even if CBS understood that her behavior had been caused by the medication she had taken to keep her weight down—something the company agreed was necessary—it might well have felt that it was hardly worth going through all that trouble again, especially for a second failure.

On March 15, Garland sued CBS, asking $1,000,000 for libel and $393,333 for breach of contract. Her suit disclosed that her agreement with CBS had in fact been for five years, not three, and that she was to be paid $83,333 for the first three programs, and subsequently $90,000 and then $95,000.

Marie Torre was not named in the suit, but in pre-trial hearings a year later she became the center of a *cause célèbre* when she refused to name her sources. Two CBS executives had sworn under oath that neither of them had made derogatory remarks about Garland, whose counsel, Lionel S. Popkin, argued that the identity of the executive was essential to the case. Torre argued that in her business, you simply didn't name your sources. The judge who was to try the case referred to her as the "Joan of Arc of her profession" and sentenced her to thirty days in prison; the following month, he reduced this to ten. She eventually served her term in November 1958, at which time the case was still in abeyance. It was to drag on for four years.

The public looked upon the dispute as one of those inevitable wranglings when parties fail to agree; but everyone in show business knew that it was another humiliation for Garland. The monies being asked were for loss of pride and in recompense for the probability that NBC would be unlikely to take on someone so summarily fired— which CBS had in fact considered before taking action.

Garland's sole professional joy at this juncture was a new Capitol album, appropriately titled *Alone*. She had always been associated with wistful songs such as "Over the Rainbow" or up-tempo ones such as "The Trolley Song," but here she took on the mantle of Helen Morgan with a selection of songs about losers and unhappy love affairs. Most of the numbers on the album were blues or torch songs, arranged and conducted by Gordon Jenkins, whose strings and slow tempi were almost as important to the company as Nelson Riddle's brass and brio. Jenkins had made his name with *Manhattan Tower*, a series of his own compositions which told a love story. As such he is the inventor of the "concept" album, in which the songs are linked—in this case, by mood and theme. None of those which she and Jenkins chose had previously been associated with her: they included "Little Girl Blue," "By Myself," "How About Me?" and Arlen's beautiful, intricate "I've Got a Right to Sing the Blues." There was yet another song associated with Jolson (one of his quieter ones), "Me and My Shadow," and two numbers contributed by Jenkins himself, "Blue Prelude" and "Happy New Year." Asked about the album, Garland said:

My style is really no style, because I try to sing each number differently. I've always believed that if style takes precedent over the words and music, the audience feels cheated. It's like when people see a fine play or movie. They imagine themselves in the leading role. I want them to imagine that they're singing—not just listening to someone else.

Interestingly, Sarah Vaughan claimed that she learned most about her craft by listening to Garland, and yet she is the supreme example of a singer who could, when she chose, overwhelm a song with style. Vaughan also disliked singing any song twice, because, once she had "explored" it, there was nothing new to discover, but Garland could sing the same song in many different ways. "The most exciting thing about her performance is that she is completely different every night," Jenkins commented.

There is never any fluctuation in quality or effort of presentation, but she seldom conquers a song in exactly the same way, and is constantly inserting little joyful bits of business that make every night seem new. I also keep getting the feeling that she gets better every performance, although I know this is probably a happy hallucination caused by constant exposure to this stage full of greatness.

The lyrics of the songs on *Alone* would have suggested to a lesser singer with the same range that the emotions should be belted out. Garland, however, sings as someone more bewildered than wounded by the vagaries of love. Only in "I've Got a Right to Sing the Blues" does she allow herself to crescendo, perhaps because the song had a special meaning for her. She was the first to confess that the songs she chose were those with lyrics with which she could identify.

In particular, Arlen's "The Man That Got Away," which she sang so effectively in *A Star Is Born*, and so often in concert thereafter, has lyrics which must have struck both Garland and her audiences as personally relevant. As its title suggests, the song is about an elusive, emblematic lover, and it is possible that Garland had Joe Mankiewicz in mind when she sang it. Once the specific references to the eponymous man are removed, however, the song has further resonances. Perhaps she was thinking of her own life, when she tackled such lines as: "The night is bitter, / The stars have lost their glitter, / The winds grow colder / Suddenly you're older . . ." Her post-M-G-M career had certainly shown that "The road gets rougher, it's lonelier and tougher . . . There's just no let up, the livelong night and day"; and her childhood fantasies of Hollywood stardom were long gone: "No more that old-time thrill, / For you've been through the mill— / The dreams you have dreamed have all gone astray . . ." Most poignantly of all, she must often have felt: "That great beginning / Has seen a final inning . . ." It was a song which she never sang the same way twice, because she was always exploring the lyric.

The cancellation of Garland's television contract meant that the family treasure chest needed replenishing, which meant that Luft needed to arrange further live appearances. She opened at the Flamingo, Las Vegas, on May 1, to an enthusiastic house which rose to its feet in the middle of "Over the Rainbow" and stood in silent tribute until she had finished it.

In the audience that night was Pearl Bailey, who had just completed her own engagement at Las Vegas. She usually left town immediately, but stayed on because she had never seen Garland perform in person. The celebrity-packed audience was cautious in its reaction to Garland's first two songs, but then she shook them by the shoulders as she sang Irving Berlin's "How About Me?": "It's over, all over, and soon somebody else will tell the world about you—but how about me?" "Hearing the way she sang that song made my heart drip tears," Bailey recalled. "She was confident, and at the same time afraid. I knew that she couldn't be afraid of her talent, but was probably more afraid of her life." The applause this time was thunderous, and as Garland acknowledged it, Bailey handed her a handkerchief to wipe away her nervous sweat. "You've spent thirty years up there," Bailey told her, "and I know they'll give you at least a minute to wipe your face." She had not expected anyone to notice, but the house had gone quiet on seeing one great artist speak to another. "Laughter came," said Bailey. "Wonderful laughter, warm and friendly. And the room became loose. Judy took that place by the corners and shook it, caressed it, and turned it upside down as she went through her program." As Garland took her bows, she turned to Bailey and gave her the red bandanna she had worn while performing "A Couple of Swells."

During the course of the four-week engagement, Liza performed "Swanee" and four-year-old Lorna was brought on to sing "Jingle Bells" in imitation of her mother's auspicious debut. Garland subsequently played a week at the Riviera, Detroit, and two at the Dallas State Fair, during which she was reunited with her sisters. It was here, one night during the run, that she declined to appear because M-G-M's dance director, her old friend, Robert Alton, had died. Gerold Frank quotes her: "I simply cannot entertain you tonight," she told the audience after just managing to get through four songs, and explaining why. "I do hope you will forgive me. Dear audience, just go to the box office and ask for your money back." As she was receiving 60 percent of the takings, this decision cost her $18,000.

She returned to Los Angeles to break records for two weeks at the huge, open-air Greek Theater, her first appearance in her "home town" for five years, but the profit on that engagement disappeared when MCA pocketed $37,000 in unpaid commissions. Disputes between them had rumbled on for some time. Garland was not an easy client: she simply preferred not to work, but would then be forced to by her financial problems, at which point MCA was expected to find her bookings quickly, and ones which paid top money.

It was now imperative to have some lined up at once, but only one interested her: the London Palladium. She remembered that it was there that her career had been resuscitated, and the British reception of *A Star Is Born* had made her eager to return. The previous Christmas, she had been to a party given by the theatrical impresario Gilbert Miller, where she had met the British actor Dirk Bogarde, who was in the States to discuss playing the male lead in *Gigi*, which Vincente Minnelli was to direct. Bogarde, who was an ardent fan of Garland's, had urged her to return to Britain and even offered to be her impresario if they could agree on the right theater. She had been flattered that he thought she could do a show without the support of the Boyfriends and the supporting acts, but would not consider it: "I couldn't do a whole show alone! For God's sake! What do you think

I am? Aimee Semple McPherson?" At the time, she had been enjoying her great success at the Palace, but she now needed a really good engagement. She was fed up with traipsing about America.

The Palladium was not available, but Luft found that the Dominion Theater in the Tottenham Court Road was free. Its owner, the Rank Organisation, signaled that they were willing to book Garland for four weeks. She refused to consider doing more than one show a night, and two matinees per week, however, and it was clear to Luft that even if she played to capacity on a 60 percent basis, the trip could not possibly show a profit. He estimated that the costs of transporting and housing her and an entourage of about twenty-five, including her Boyfriends, would be at least $25,000. When he pointed this out to her, she replied that she did not care. She was determined to play London and was confident that Luft would find enough money to pay the expenses so that she could. He calculated that the anticipated deficit on the trip might be offset if she were to fulfill two week-long engagements before leaving for London, where she was due to open on October 16. Garland reminded Luft that one of the main reasons she wanted to play in London was that she was sick of American cities. He replied that they could not afford to go to London unless she made some more money.

MCA managed to get her bookings at the Capitol Theater in Washington, starting September 16, and the Mastbaum in Philadelphia, starting September 26. She would do eight performances in each city, with three days between the engagements. Immediately the Washington booking was announced, the famous party-giver, Perle Mesta (upon whom Irving Berlin had based the central character of *Call Me Madam*), arranged a first-night reception, which was to contain the cream of Washington society. Beyond that, Luft gloomily expected trouble, which always turned up when Garland did anything against her will.

He was not disappointed. On the evening before her first concert, in their suite in the Sheraton, Garland announced that she was getting the flu. She looked fine, but since there was an incipient epidemic, Luft sent for the doctor. As usual, she refused to allow Luft to be present at the consultation, but when Luft accompanied the doctor back to the elevator, he warned him that any medication he had sent up should be innocuous. The doctor assured him that he was prescribing a mild sedative to help her sleep and something to drive out the bug. Three bottles were duly delivered, and Luft examined them without being any the wiser. When Garland woke the next morning with a hoarse voice, he knew at once that some of the pills had contained Seconal, which irritated the lining of her throat. He suspected that one of the other drugs contained Dexedrine, to counteract the effects of Seconal, but could not begin to guess what was in the third.

In spite of Garland's illness—if indeed it had existed—and this dangerous medication, she sang well on opening night, as she invariably did on first nights. As a perfectionist, she was unhappy when she knew that she was not at her best, and would tell herself that she would rather be anywhere than on stage. At the same time, she always recognized that her first allegiance was to her audiences. Her dilemma was to reconcile her need to give only of her best and her determination to go on regardless, for fear of ruining the evening of those who had paid to see her perform. She knew that the first-night audience in Washington would contain the press as well as her most idolatrous admirers, and she had learned how to disguise the fact when she knew that she was technically under par. When this failed, she knew she could appeal to her fans for sympathy. One critic, who recognized the special circumstances of Garland's relationship with her audience, described the evening for the readers of *Variety*:

> This is a different kind of theatrical engagement. It's a love affair between Judy Garland and the folks who are paying up to $6.60 top this week to hear her sing at the Capitol Theater here. Miss Garland makes a quick rapport with her audience, and you can feel the affection they have for her from the time she opens up with her big, deep voice . . . She was bothered Monday night by throat trouble. Once she apologized for failing to hit the high note at the end of a number. Explaining she had laryngitis, she cleared her throat on stage several times. From the audience came only sympathy and applause. This was their Judy and they were with her all the way.
>
> Actually, she socked home most of her numbers with no trouble, handsomely, with a big voice and the gestures that spell show business know-how.

However, she remained hoarse throughout the week and the doctor visited her daily. She was due to close on Sunday night, and when Luft woke her that morning for breakfast she went to the bathroom, still drugged from sleep. She reappeared a few minutes later, with blood pouring from her wrists. "Look what I did," she said, according to Gerold Frank. The cuts were deeper than in the past, and Luft had to use his neckties as tourniquets. To ask for an ambulance was to invite scandal; but the hotel doctor was not on duty. Luft reached him at home, and was told that the damage could be repaired there. It was a forty-five minute drive, but the chief difficulty was to get Garland through the Sheraton lobby, without drawing attention to her condition. Luft wrapped her up well, and Harry Rubin helped him half-carry her through the crowd. Their maid telephoned the theater to cancel the evening's performance and began to mop up the floor to get rid of the blood.

An hour later, the doctor gave Garland an injection and put ten stitches in each wrist. When she came to, ten minutes later, and asked what had happened, she showed neither contrition nor surprise. Luft found that she still had the ability to surprise him—though he did not believe that she had been conscious of what she was doing when she had taken the razor to her wrists. He thought, rather, that the medication prescribed had been so powerful that she had blacked out momentarily.

The cancellation of that evening's show was put down to a bout of Asian flu. Although the loss of takings had reduced the profits of the engagement to less than $2,000, Luft suggested canceling the Philadelphia booking. Garland refused to consider it, however, and kept the truth from the children by wearing flesh-colored bandages, long-sleeved outfits and bulky bracelets.

After the traumas of Washington, a twisted ankle in Philadelphia was a mere bagatelle. When Garland hobbled on stage in a plaster cast and her white toweling robe the crowd cheered plucky little Judy, who explained that she would have to do the show sitting down. She literally sang herself out, and was unable to go on for the last two performances.

Business for the first two days, which coincided with Yom Kippur, had been poor, and the house had been plentifully papered. Although it picked up at the weekend, the refund of $8,000 for the last two performances meant that the booking made a loss for both the theater and the Lufts. This meant that there was no money to pay the hotel bill in Philadelphia or the week's salaries, let alone a trip to London, with steamship tickets and a suite at the Savoy Hotel in London. They were due to leave the following day.

Luft wrote out checks to the value of $15,000, knowing that his bank would not honor them, and flew to New York in an attempt to raise some money. No one was lending any, not even friends and business associates. MCA told him it was not their problem; that old standby, Ted Law, was away from home. The situation seemed desperate until Fred Finklehoffe arrived in Luft's room at the Hotel

Pierre to remind him that one of his horses, which should have been running at Belmont that day, had broken a leg and had been scratched. Luft got on the telephone to its co-owner, Charles Whittingham, to discover that the animal had been destroyed. It had been insured for $30,000, and Whittingham was prepared to pay half of that amount into Luft's account.

Luft estimated that this sum would be only half the amount he needed. He then remembered that Ben Maksik, who ran the Town and Country Club in Brooklyn, had once inquired about the possibility of Garland fulfilling an engagement there. At the time, he had not even considered the proposal, but now he telephoned MCA to ask them to find out whether Maksik was still interested. The Town and Country seated almost two thousand diners and Maksik, who was clearly overjoyed at the prospect of introducing Judy Garland in person to Brooklyn, was prepared to offer her $25,000 a week for an engagement in the New Year. This was much less than the Las Vegas fees, and Brooklyn certainly did not have the same cachet, but there was no alternative. Maksik turned up at Garland's leaving party on board the *United States* the following day with a contract and the agreed advance of $15,000 in cash.

Meanwhile, in England, Capitol was preparing an extensive promotion of Garland's record albums. Not long before she joined them, the company had been bought by EMI, Britain's enormously rich gramophone company, which also owned another American company, Angel, as well as His Master's Voice, Columbia and Parlophone, which between them sold the lion's share of records in Britain. Garland's records had been selling well, and Capitol were to issue five tracks from them as singles, along with "It's Lovely to Be Back in London," which she planned to record as soon as she arrived in the city. Edens had written the song as an opening number for her show, and on the first night every member of the audience would be presented with a one-sided Capitol 45 rpm disc of it.

Equal enthusiasm was being shown by the Rank Organisation, which owned the 2,895-seated Dominion. For the last twenty-four years, it had been a cinema, latterly for second-run movies. Because of the competition from television, audiences were no longer filling it, so Rank had decided to find out how it might function once again as a theater. Louis Armstrong, Sophie Tucker and Bill Haley and his Comets had recently played short engagements there. Rank was so delighted to have Judy Garland, and as sole performer, that it spent

£60,000 (approximately $180,000 or about a million dollars by today's standards) on refurbishing the theater. These improvements included what was described as the most glamorous dressing-room seen in Britain since Marlene Dietrich filmed there.

The *United States* sailed on October 5, and by the time Garland arrived in Britain five days later (the ship had been delayed in Le Havre by fog), ticket sales at the Dominion had brought in some £30,000 (or $100,000). Had Luft contacted Rank or EMI, he would have found that London's interest in Garland's visit was both immense and intense, so who cared if the pictures in the newspapers showed a dumpy woman?

Garland did. London was plastered with posters and handbills for "The Judy Garland Show," but the two pictures used in them had been taken in her M-G-M days. The British had commented on her figure before and undoubtedly would again. She was very conscious that she was gross and hated looking in the mirror—which may have accounted for the incident at the Sheraton in Washington. She consoled herself that at least she would be back in the city which she had so much enjoyed in 1951, and she would have Lorna and Joey with her as well.

The advance bookings were more than gratifying, but she was scared. She often said that no matter how often she played to audiences she always suffered acute stage fright. During her last stint at the Palace, she had conquered it by persuading herself that audiences who had taken the trouble to leave their homes to see her wanted her to succeed: but her chronic insecurity refused to let her believe this for long. In London she declared herself "as nervous as a frightened cat," adding "but I would be insane not to be." She had a new reason for worrying about the opening: "I have to be better than I have ever been tonight. It's a debt I owe. London gave me back my faith in myself when I played here seven years ago."

On October 16, she lunched with Aly Khan, but barely pecked at her salmon. She tried to rest, but eventually left for the theater at five, three hours before the performance was due to start and more than four before she was due onstage. She even inspected the audience from the peephole in the curtain.

With the exception of Alan King, whom she had brought over from the States, the acts in the first half had been booked by the Rank Organisation. Edens provided the special material and, since Charles Walters had been unavailable, Richard Barstow had done the choreography. Gordon Jenkins, who had made such a large contribution to the *Alone* album, had been engaged to replace Jack Cathcart as conductor.

Peggy Lee once observed of Garland: "One thing she has that no one else ever had had—remember how they begin to applaud and shout *before* they can even see her? The mere announcement of her name, the news of her approach, fires them with enthusiasm, and she gets a welcome as no one else in our profession ever has." This was certainly the case at the Dominion, where there was a crash of applause like a giant wave hitting a rock, as Jenkins began the overture. This was Jenkins's own arrangement, which combined "The Trolley Song," an electrifying "The Man That Got Away," and "Over the Rainbow." Thereafter, Garland always used it as an introduction to her stage shows. Her ten Boyfriends (two had been mislaid) came out in bowler hats and pinstripes to dance and sing about "the greatest fall in history . . . when like a clumsy cow, she fell flat on the Palladium stage." When the curtain rose, Garland was revealed sitting on the floor—a further reminder of her accident-prone Palladium debut. This may have been fairly witless, but it worked. The house rose and, as the applause died, one man shouted "Welcome back, Judy!," to which she responded with an almost whispered "Oh *darling*!"

"It's Lovely to Be Back in London" had a self-mocking lyric—"Just to feel the thrill of London/I always come undone/I'm so glad I'm back"—which showed Edens at his least inspired. She did "I Feel a Song Coming On"; her "Minstrel Girl" medley; "Come Rain or Come Shine"; "The Man That Got Away"; "Rockabye Your Baby"; and—in an unflattering approximation of her "Get Happy" costume—"Lucky Day," in which she was joined by her Boyfriends. "This is slow," she said of "How About Me?"; "if you don't like it just stop me and we'll try to think of something else." She left the stage to change for the second time, as her Boyfriends wondered in song what she might do next: some card tricks or what? What she did do was an energetic "A Couple of Swells," partnered by Jimmy Brooks, one of the dancers. She paused when it was over: "And before we go any further, I would like to . . . *die*!" She finished "Over the Rainbow" to deafening applause, and because she did not leave the stage, the audience hoped for an encore. Cunningly, she chose "Me and My Shadow," which is not, as she plaintively sings it, an encore song. The audience still wanted more and titles of songs were being flung at her. "Sing anything," one man cried. She knew exactly how long to milk it—and then she caught one title and threw it back: "No, I won't. I'll do 'Swanee.' " They knew that she knew that she was incomparable in this—and she knew she would bow off with the audience still yelling for more.

She was very much the same Judy Garland who had appeared at the Palladium—plumper, perhaps, but also more assured. Her greatness lay in her ability to combine opposing qualities: she was serene, yet tense; edgy, but able to attack her songs with verve; she had both tenderness and aplomb; and in the stout matron, the wistful quality of the little girl who once longed to go over the rainbow was still discernible. In the audience were Donna Reed and Betty Garrett (contemporaries at M-G-M), Larry Parks, Richard Attenborough, Sheila Sim, Stanley Baker, Janet Blair, Rod Steiger, Tommy Steele and her old rival, Lana Turner. There were also a dozen British female singing "stars," each bearing a bouquet, who joined Garland on stage at the end, in a rare tribute to a star. With the exception of Vera Lynn and Petula Clark, they might have been expressly chosen to demonstrate the dismal inferiority of British talent.

In the *Observer*, Richard Finlater made a sly reference to this. He reported that Garland

turns the Dominion into a place of pilgrimage for all nostalgists who sigh for the splendours of the old-time music hall. Carefully rationed, atrociously dressed and brilliantly reinforced, she presents at first the melancholy sight of a star who has outgrown her myth. In the quick turn of her head, the upward glance of her eyes, one sees for a moment the little girl lost, trapped in someone else's body by time's practical joke. And then, as she warms up to the audience, one hears the sound of trumpets: the approach of the new Garland, lifting up her voice and making what Archie Rice calls "a great big beautiful noise" that cannonades around the theater.

Although "A Couple of Swells" has been fussed-up since she first danced it with Astaire on the screen, it is in the girl-tramp's patched and baggy trousers, with muck face and golliwog wig, that Miss Garland gets her freedom, and demonstrates that heart-warming strength and energy and exuberance in which our own songstresses are so sadly lacking, however tasteful their wardrobes, however slim their waists.

Finlater was not the only reviewer to comment on her appearance. According to Alan King, this was a period when she weighed 165 lbs and had "dresses lined with steel so she couldn't move." Matters were not much helped by her appalling dress sense, with white sequin skirts and the like. "Easy to see why she can't fly over the rainbow anymore," commented John Barber ungallantly in the *Daily Express*. He compared "square-faced, homely, bang-it-out Judy" with the heavyweight Sophie Tucker. Elsewhere she was described as "dumpy" and "a plump, heavy-moving, matronly version of the girl over the rainbow," but there was no doubt about the affection in which she was held, nor about the triumph of her return to London. "Our hearts went out to this 35-year-old from Minnesota whose life, both on and off the screen, has been so checkered," wrote Bill Boorne in the *Evening News*, speaking for many of those present. "She won us over before she had sung a note." "Judy Garland came back to London last night—and London loved her for it," wrote Clifford Davis in the *Daily Mirror*. "There will never be another like her." "All that is the essence of real star quality now holds the limelight at the Dominion Theatre," wrote Elizabeth Frank in the *News Chronicle*. "And it was a wonderful experience to feel a London audience of 3,000 give themselves in a flood of affection and warmth and, I like to think, a certain pride, to the miraculous, dumpy little waif, to whom they restored life and confidence six years ago." Barber astutely noted that: "It is hard, judging her, to tell where our loyalty ends and her art begins." Of that art, however, there was no question: there were references to her "perfect control," her "heartbreaking appeal" and "sheer artistry." "Judy is a great clown," Elizabeth Frank concluded. "That is why she can make you laugh and cry at the same time . . . the spotlight picked up the dirty little gamin's face, with its flyaway eyebrows, as she sang 'Over the Rainbow' squatting on the stage by the footlights, and we wondered at the strange guise in which genius can appear to us."

Variety proclaimed that: "While Judy Garland lives, Variety will never die," and she played to capacity houses for four and a half weeks, except for the mid-week matinee, when the management of the Dominion let it be known that anyone who presented an Equity card would be eligible for any available seats. On the final Wednesday, she was suffering from laryngitis so badly that, according to the *Stage*, "it looked as if the afternoon had been a disaster, but the section of the audience who had been admitted on their Equity cards, full of admiration for her tremendous courage and loyalty to the public, encouraged her to put up a performance that was nothing short of a triumph." "I feel terrible," she said that evening. "But you should have seen me this afternoon. I was worse." On another occasion she said: "I sound like Sophie Tucker's grandmother."

Her success was such that when she had to drop three of the big, belting numbers from the show, it made the newspapers. "Only she knows how great the strain has been," the *Daily Express* concluded.

She was certainly on wonderful form again for the last night, delighting audiences by repeating "A Couple of Swells."

The day before, she had attended a luncheon in her honor given by the Variety Club of Great Britain. Lord Attlee, the former prime minister, was among the other guests, who were otherwise mostly drawn from the upper echelons of show business. Garland, who was fifteen minutes late, was supposed to respond to the various encomiums, but she said simply: "It is wonderful to be here. I am no damn good at making speeches."

She also got to meet some of Britain's less elevated citizens. When she couldn't sleep, she used to invite Alan King to go for drives around the city. One night about two in the morning, in Curzon Street, she saw some prostitutes waiting around and insisted on inviting several of them back to the Savoy to tell her about their experiences. "Go on, what happened then?" she asked, longing for more details. And when they had finished, round about dawn, she made King pay them what they might have earned during that time. "I must be the only man," he said, "who has spent a whole night with a crowd of whores, and paid them, and not had sex with a single one of them."

Two nights after she closed, she returned to the London Palladium to sing to the Royal Family. The occasion was that odd, horribly formal annual event now called *The Royal Variety Show*, but then known as *The Royal Command Performance*. The evening was, and is, to benefit the Variety Artists' Benevolent Fund and, in theory, it is an honor to be invited to take part. That is why performers take the risk of playing to an audience which is usually difficult—if not impossible—to please, partly because of the huge sums they had paid for their seats. An additional incentive to performers would have been because, before the age of television, and the eventual televising of the show itself, it drew the greatest radio audience of the year, emptying cinemas, theaters and pubs all over the country. In practice, it was a showcase for a handful of genuine stars and many other artists whom the leading London impresarios wished to promote. At the time, it was considered a coup to have American performers on the bill, and apart from Garland there were also Count Basie and her former fling, Mario Lanza.

Gracie Fields would normally expect to top the bill, as she had always done, but Val Parnell, who organized the function, knew that "Our Gracie" would have difficulty following Judy Garland. He put her into the first half, but acknowledged her enormous popularity by bringing her on again at the finale to lead the company in "God Save the Queen." The top spot was awarded to Tommy Steele, a reasonably ingratiating performer, but not a gifted singer. His cocky confidence had made him a great favorite with the public, but he was poorly received by the press the following day, partly because he was obliged to follow Garland. Her special position in the business was recognized when she was permitted three songs, instead of the usual two, as well as some minutes to change costumes. She entered to what the *Daily Mail* described as "an overwhelming reception," which did nothing to calm an obvious attack of nerves. Dressed in a black frock with a glittering evening coat, she began "Rockabye Your Baby," with a quavering voice. Those in the stalls could see that her hands were shaking until well into the number. Her Boyfriends danced while she changed for "A Couple of Swells," performed with Jimmy Brooks, which she followed with "Over the Rainbow" sitting at the footlights. She had done the impossible: she had stopped the show. This had not happened at this event within memory. The applause thundered on for so long that she was tempted to an encore, but after looking into the wings for approval she grabbed a microphone from the orchestra and said: "I'm sorry. I'd like to sing some more—but bless you."

She was sobbing as she left the stage. It was altogether a tear-drenched night. At the line-up afterwards, when the artists were presented to the Royal Family, the Queen Mother told Garland that she had tears in her eyes during the star's rendition of "Over the Rainbow." "I have tears in my eyes now," Garland replied.

19

❖❖❖❖❖❖❖

Liza and Lorna

ALTHOUGH, ONCE AGAIN, an engagement in London had done wonders for Judy Garland's morale, it had done very little to ease her
financial problems. Indeed, after their return to the States, Luft reckoned that he only had $1,400 left, and that they had accumulated
debts over the past few months of $50,000. They parted company
with their financial adviser, Morgan Maree, because they owed him
commission. With no prospect of payment, Maree declined further
counsel, but he did offer one last piece of advice: that the Lufts file
for bankruptcy. This was not something Luft was prepared to consider. He had helped rebuild Garland's reputation, and declaring her
bankrupt would undo all his good work.

Their financial situation was due chiefly to their extravagance: Luft
was addicted to on-track betting and she refused, or was unable, to
live more modestly than in her M-G-M days, but this was not something she cared to have pointed out to her. The result was that she
had to return to work immediately: she was to be paid $40,000 a week
for a three-week return engagement at the Flamingo in Las Vegas,

starting December 26, 1957. Such, at any rate, had been the plan when they left for London back in October. After her overwhelming success at the Dominion, however, an engagement in Las Vegas seemed much less attractive, particularly since she would have less than two weeks in which to rest before taking it up. The management of the Flamingo refused to annul the contract, however, because it would be especially difficult to find a suitable replacement for the holiday period at short notice.

Bobby Van, who had briefly sung and danced in some M-G-M musicals, was to open the evening and join Garland in "A Couple of Swells." The engagement went badly from the start and turned out to be not so much a challenge as an endurance test. Most nightclub managements recognized the difficulty of performing to revelers and prohibited the serving of food or drink while their star was in the spotlight, but these rules tended to be stretched, if not broken, at holiday times. It did not help matters that Garland's voice was not at its best, and the combination of this and an inattentive and restive audience made performing hellish. On the third night, Gerold Frank relates, she stopped singing and brought on Liza, who had been watching from the wings. "Ladies and gentlemen, Liza Minnelli," she announced calmly, as if this was part of the act. "Take it," she said, leaving the child to sing a handful of songs which she knew only from hearing her mother sing them. The patrons apparently thought it was part of the act, but many of them made it clear that they did not want to listen to Liza Minnelli any more than they wanted to listen to Judy Garland.

Garland chose not to notice this: "You were terrific!" she told her daughter. She was often asked why she brought her children on stage while she was performing, and she replied that she was ambivalent about this:

I don't want to bring my children up as performers, I want to bring them up as human beings. But because I make a living in show business, I want them to know what it is I do, to understand completely that there are many other people involved, both backstage and in the audience . . . I think it would be a mistake to keep them from meeting the wonderful people I come in contact with. In addition, I want them to be unselfconscious in public, and to have a completely natural feeling about the fact that their mother is a public figure.

This is the sort of thing people like Judy Garland said in interviews, and hardly explains why an eleven-year-old child should be subjected to this particular baptism of fire. It was not like being on stage at the Palace, facing an audience of her mother's fans. This was a mob of disgruntled gamblers.

New Year's Eve was a fiasco. There was not even a pretense that food should not be served while Garland was performing, and, after struggling through five songs, she left the stage to complain. Luft was in Los Angeles, but Vern Alves was there to explain to her that the management had no choice in the matter. He advised her to cut the act short. When she returned to the stage, a woman shouted: "Get outta here. You're too overweight and we don't want to hear you anyway." Garland paused, affronted and uncertain whether the applause which followed was for her or for the heckler, and two other women took the opportunity to invade the stage, doing a drunken hula dance in an attempt to entertain in place of the evidently reluctant star. Garland once again left the stage. When she returned, she was greeted by boos. Sensibly, she had brought on Bobby Van and, even more sensibly, they launched into "Auld Lang Syne," after which she stormed off.

As far as she was concerned, the management had breached her contract by serving food. Luft had returned during the debacle, but nothing he said could persuade her otherwise. As he saw it, the incident was bound to result in hostile headlines, which would not make it any easier to get her subsequent bookings. He tried to calm her down and think the matter through. He suggested that the management could point out that she had tried to get out of the contract in the first place. She accused him of treachery, of siding with the Flamingo. New Year's Eve was New Year's Eve, he said: tomorrow would be different. The more he reasoned, the more furious she became. She had no intention of completing the engagement. He argued that she could not walk out: she had not been paid for the six days she had worked and they had no money at all. This was something she simply didn't understand: although she was in serious financial difficulties, principle was more important than money.

Luft solved the immediate problem by going to the cashier in the casino and getting $5,000 in chips, to be charged to the hotel. He played at the tables for a while, then redeemed the chips to the tune of $4,700, which he gave to Alves, who packed Garland's costumes and left the hotel. He was swiftly followed by his employers and Liza. Liza later claimed that she learned to leave hotels without paying the bill before she learned how to read or write, but this seems to be the first instance of the Lufts doing so.

This disagreement between Garland and the Flamingo remained unresolved. Both parties sued, and the matter eventually went to arbitration, in the course of which found in favor of Garland. She only received $22,000, however, most of which was eaten up by her legal fees.

The new year had begun disastrously; and so it was to continue. The row in her dressing-room at the Flamingo led to a complete breakdown of the Luft's relationship. Back home, Garland stayed in her room, refusing to see her husband. This was no surprise: Luft had long come to regard his wife's temperament as a price to be paid for her talent. Gordon Jenkins, with whom she worked often and well, thought it a price well worth paying:

> Judy, as all great stars, is inclined towards moodiness, which to me is as natural as rain. I believe that anyone who gives as much to the world as Judy does has a perfect right to be out of sorts if she feels like it. An artist without temperament is more likely to end up as a plumber than a star. It would be impossible for Judy to sustain the level of her performances throughout her daily life; it's much too high a pitch, too close to perfection for her not to be allowed an occasional imperfection afterwards. I have always believed that occasional discords in Judy's life were caused by only one thing—the people around her didn't love her enough to try to understand her. I think that all Judy ever wanted during those troubled days was to have a friendly arm around her . . .

Luft had done his best to understand, and throughout their troubled partnership he gave her an enormous amount of support. What most exasperated him, however, was her refusal to be sorry for anybody involved except herself. When he pointed this out to her, she replied: "You might as well get used to the fact that this is what you bargained for. This is what you're married to. I am what I am. I cannot change."

As she remained secluded, talking to friends by telephone both by day and by night, he had to find a way of paying for the household requirements. On the strength of her booking at the Town and Country, he secured a $25,000 loan from the bank. He eventually forced his way in to see her, but neither was in conciliatory mood. After an hour of shouting he walked out. "I've had it!" he yelled.

In March, she once again filed for divorce. This time she meant business: she employed Jerry Geisler, who handled all the high-profile Hollywood divorces. Geisler, however, told the press that no immediate legal action would be taken. To Luft he predicted: "It'll blow over." Garland also hired two armed guards, because she was afraid that Luft would forcibly try to remove Lorna and Joey. When Luft went to the house, he was stopped at the door: the guards refused to admit him. The battle for the children was to continue for years: it was one way for Garland to prove that she was the injured party. Her mistake was to hire the guards: her friends thought it was a sign either of paranoia or of her gut feeling that, of the two, Luft was the better parent.

Evidence of Garland's fitness as a parent is hard to come by, although people like Alan King insisted that she was devoted to her children: "I remember a performance at the Palace in '56 when Judy was almost about to crack, I walked on with Liza and she lit up at the sight of her—she was *such* a good mother, she loved those kids. Liza sang and Judy, given the respite and uplift, went on to do forty-five minutes in fine fettle." Whether or not this sort of behavior made Garland a good parent is a matter of opinion. Margaret Sullavan, an actress who, like Garland, combined an image of helpless vulnerability with a difficult temperament, described the perils of combining stardom and motherhood:

> Generally, by their very nature—that is, if they're at all dedicated— actors do not make good parents. They're altogether too egotistical and selfish. The better the actor—and I hate to say it, the bigger the star— why, the more that seems to hold true. Honestly, I don't think I've ever known one—not one!—star who was successfully able to combine a career and family life . . . I used to think acting was a kind of therapy, but now I think it creates psychological havoc. Actors become accustomed to be the center of attention, come to believe they're *special*, set apart from other people. That's dangerous and lonely. Actors *suffer*, look at all the instances of alcoholism, slit wrists, God knows what. As a result of which everyone around suffers too. Madness! And the built-in competition to be *special*, to be *different*, is deplorable.

Although she was speaking principally about herself, Sullavan may also have had Garland in mind.

Both Liza Minnelli and Lorna Luft remained ambivalent about their childhood. "I can't say that I was unhappy," said Liza. "With my mother I knew some intense joys and happy moments of which other people daren't dream"—but it was, she said, on another occasion, "a perilous kind of warmth." She explained once that it was no great tragedy being Judy Garland's daughter: "I had tremendously interesting childhood years—except that they had nothing to do with being a child." A family friend said: "I don't think she ever played with a doll again after her parents split. She was too busy holding together her mother's crumbling ego. She became mother to her mother." Liza recalled: "She'd put too much trust in somebody, then they'd do something slight, and she'd take it as a slap in the face. The thing I'd try to get through to her was that none of it really mattered. Of course people were going to let her down. They couldn't help it." Garland always treated Liza as an adult, for example confessing to her ten-year-old daughter how lonely she was: "Can you imagine being that vulnerable, confessing that kind of pain to a child?" Or, indeed, leaving it to a twelve-year-old to hire and fire servants because you were unable to do it yourself?

Lorna has been more reticent in talking about her mother than Liza, though she did say once:

> Now, in spite of all the evidence to the contrary, Mama was one of the happiest people I knew. Or let me put it another way: she had a happy disposition. Few people have had the sadness and tragedy she had in her life, but somehow, at a point when most people in her position would have thrown themselves out of the nearest window, she'd just look at me and say: "Well, honey, things *can't* get any worse!" and she'd have a darn good laugh.

In spite of such assertions, life with mother was not always merely amusing and exciting. On one occasion, while Liza and a schoolfriend were watching television, Garland left her room for the first time in days to announce that she was going to kill herself and ran into the bathroom. Outside the door Liza wailed, "Mama! Don't kill yourself!" The butler managed to break down the door, and they saw Garland pouring a bottle of aspirins into the toilet bowl. "All she wanted was attention," was Liza's later comment.

Liza's first husband, Peter Allen, painted a horrifying picture of two small girls attempting to cope with their unstable parent:

> As kids, Liza and Lorna had regular sessions emptying out Judy's sleeping capsules and refilling them with sugar. Liza was terrified her mother would take an accidental overdose. A doctor once warned her that more than a couple of sleeping pills a night might be fatal if Judy had been drinking. But Judy had this compulsive need to take more of everything.

Referring to Liza's reluctance to talk about her mother, he commented: "It's not surprising that [she] doesn't want to know about these things now." Equally unsurprising was the fact that the children were now in the care of the same psychiatrists who were trying to interpret their mother's acts, the more easily to understand her.

Psychological damage was not the only threat to the children's well-being. Once, when Luft had gone to the races, Garland telephoned Vern Alves: "I just wanted you to know that this is the end of it," she announced. "I've taken some medication." He could tell this from her voice—and worse was to come: "I've got Joey here and I may take him with me. I want you to pass the word along. Sid is not to have the children. Liza or Lorna are to be given to Dirk Bogarde or Capucine." Garland's friendship with Bogarde had strengthened while she was in London in 1957, and she may have met Capucine in Hollywood when her agent, Charles Feldman, was grooming this former model for stardom. They were certainly odd choices for step-parents: apart from anything else, both were unmarried—although stories about a romance between them were published in women's magazines at the period. Alves took her threat seriously and managed, not without difficulty, to fetch Luft from the races. He also called the police, in the belief that it was better to risk scandal rather than lose Garland, who, he discovered upon his arrival at the house, was firmly locked in her suite. Luft managed to get in, and found Garland and Joey asleep and unharmed. It took her a while to come to, and it took longer for the quarrel between Luft and Garland to subside.

Now they were heading for a divorce. Partly to pay her lawyer's fee of $5,000, Garland withdrew $9,000 from the bank's loan to Luft and, accompanied by her three children and their nurse, left by train to fulfill her engagement in Brooklyn, where the first night was scheduled for March 20. Bobby Van was again to open the act and partner her in "A Couple of Swells." Utterly at a loss as to how to manage her own affairs without Luft, she contacted Norman Weiss, who had signed the agreement on behalf of MCA. Weiss found Maksik so excited at the prospect of having Garland in his club that he installed her in a beach house he rented in Neponsit on Long Island, about twenty miles away. Luft followed by air, and telephoned Maksik to say that he could find him at the Warwick Hotel if need arose—as it did almost immediately.

New York State had placed a lien on Garland's forthcoming salary in order to reclaim over $8,000 in state taxes she had failed to pay during her 1951 engagement at the Palace. A warrant had been issued for her arrest, but she had refused to open the door to the sheriff. Maksik telephoned Luft, who saw her, for the first time since he had walked out, in the State Collector's Office. Maksik was with her, and a deal was worked out by which she would pay $3,000 weekly from her salary of $25,000 until the debt had been paid off. She and Luft behaved coolly toward each other.

Maksik's disenchantment with his new star set in when Garland refused to give two performances a night, as arranged. Weiss solved this problem by agreeing to a 50 percent reduction in her fee. On opening night, Maksik was relieved to find a full house, despite a blinding snowstorm which had made driving conditions virtually impossible. Although Garland was not enamored of the booking, she had worked hard on the act, adding several songs she had not sang on stage before: "I Guess I'll Have to Change My Plan," Arlen's "When the Sun Comes Out," "I Will Come Back" and, partnered by Bobby Van, "When You Wore a Tulip." There was no doubt of her drawing power, but on the second night she was below her best, and on the third even worse than that. Dissatisfied with herself, she began turning up late, then threatened not to appear at all unless Weiss sat with the younger children. By now, she was convinced that Maksik was in league with Luft to spirit them away.

Liza, who was just twelve, acted as her mother's nursemaid and dresser. After finding Garland crying, she learned that her mother was suffering from colitis, a painful and debilitating condition which went some way to explaining why she was going to pieces. Garland refused to explain matters to Maksik, who was tearing his hair out as her performance deteriorated nightly. He nevertheless threw a party to celebrate Joey's third birthday on Friday, March 29. Emboldened by this gesture of friendship, Garland telephoned Maksik the following day to ask for the rest of her fee, for the whole engagement, in a lump sum. When he refused, she told him that she had no intention of going on. He advised the customers of this sadly, but consoled himself with the thought that the nightmare of the past week appeared to be over.

Then Garland turned up, fifty minutes late, insisting that she would go on after all. Maksik told her that she was ill and he would not consider it. Weiss informed him that she was intent on fulfilling her contract. Luft, summoned by Garland, who had realized that she could not cope without him, was on his way to the club.

Garland did eventually appear on stage, but at the end of her second number—ironically "Life Is Just a Bowl of Cherries"—announced: "I have a bad case of laryngitis, I can't sing tonight." At this point, her microphone was switched off, so she walked to the front of the stage and said: "It doesn't matter anyway. I've been fired." She then ran off, crying: "It's wrong. It's wrong. I love you all." The whole situation was reminiscent of her behavior on *Annie Get Your Gun*.

When Luft arrived, he found Garland, Weiss and Maksik all yelling at each other in the lobby. According to Gerold Frank, Maksik shouted at him: "Get her out of here! She's crazy. Get her out!" The following day, he told the press: "She hit out at me, at everybody, her agent, her husband, she even went for me and tried to get me in the eyes." Garland announced that she would sue him for assault and battery because she had a bruised shoulder. The immediate issue was whether Maksik would release Garland's jewelry, which was locked up in his safe. Luft made it clear that the row would continue until it was handed over. No one was quite sure what the legal situation was, but they all knew that it could only be solved by lawyers, and Maksik handed over the jewelry rather than continue the argument. He eventually engaged Betty Hutton to replace Garland, but was not pleased when Hutton insisted on berating the unfortunate customers (who were not, after all, the same ones) for mistreating one of the greatest artists in show business.

Meanwhile, after checking into the Drake Hotel in New York with the children, the Lufts dined with Aly Khan, who promised to put his lawyers onto the matter of Garland's finances. No one seemed sure whether Maksik in fact owed Garland any money, or, if he did, whether it should be paid to her, to Luft, to the State, or to MCA, who were again demanding their commission. Of these, the most pressing was the State, which in the past few days had twice asked Garland to be declared in contempt of court for not responding to its charges. On April 3, she turned up at the General Court House in Queens to answer them. "Ever since I was three years old I've been working to support someone," she declared, with perhaps pardonable exaggeration. She agreed to leave her theatrical costumes and jewelry in lien until the dispute was settled. The tax she owed was eventually paid with the aid of loans from friends, including Aly Khan, who also helped with the household bills. She called off the divorce suit, and Luft looked for further bookings to pay off their debts. Although no one in the business was surprised that booking an artist of infamous temperament into a common-or-garden roadhouse had resulted in yet another disaster, no one wanted to take a chance on her in any other venue either. Judy Garland was "trouble."

Luft had to do something, however, since her only guaranteed income was her royalties from Capitol, where the producer, Voyle Gilmore, and Nelson Riddle, as arranger and conductor, were already planning her next record, *Judy in Love*. She and Riddle had agreed upon three prime songs by Cole Porter: "I Am Loved," "I Concentrate on You" and "Do I Love You?" and "This Is It" by Dorothy Fields and Arthur Schwartz. Capitol was so sure of the appeal of its singer that the name "Garland" does not appear on the album cover, which features a fanciful painting of her as she was when she made *A Star Is Born*. A publicity photograph taken for the movie adorns the back of the sleeve.

The notes were written by Jimmy McHugh, who composed "I Can't Give You Anything But Love," one of the songs on the album. He begins:

DEAR JUDY

The Star Studded Cinderella Girl—that's you, Judy Garland! with the wonderful magnetism, rich, varied talents, idolized by fans from the Kings and Queens to all audiences of the world. Yes, that's you Judy!

He wrote at length about her childhood; about her past—long past— movie triumphs (not, in spite of the pictures, mentioning *A Star Is Born*); about her breaking box-office records at the Palace; and he praises her interpretation of his own song. He concludes:

There is no doubt, Judy Garland, but that you are part of the best in the wonderful, extravagant, brilliant world of entertainment, along with the late Al Jolson and Will Rogers, Eddie Cantor, Jimmy Durante and Frank Sinatra. Seldom is a singer endowed with such stamina, virtuosity, and heart . . . in closing, Judy, may I say that your great big sentimental heart should never be sad when you think of the wonderful happiness you have given to millions. As long as there is a song, there will always be a Garland!

This may be sheer corn, but it encapsulates the mythology surrounding Judy Garland. She was show business's own and in spite of the publicity she had received for the problems which had beset her, both professionally and privately, underlying each sentiment is a message of cheer. Whatever disasters struck, it was the duty of those in "the wonderful extravagant, brilliant world of entertainment" to "Accentuate the Positive," as Bing Crosby put it in his famous 1945 song. Not for nothing did Garland wear the costume and makeup of a clown in her stage shows and later sing with such force Charles Chaplin's "Smile," with its prescription to: "Smile, though your heart is aching, / Smile, even though it's breaking . . ." The material Roger Edens wrote for her, which gently sent up, but at the same time celebrated, show-business sentiment, placed her firmly in this tradition. It is significant that the album's encomium was written by an old show-business hand, a man whose songs had been sung by the stars he mentioned, and who was a friend of Garland, someone who knew her well. For all its naked appeal, however, it was of no practical value.

Away from the fantasy world, which occasionally came true on stage but never off, Judy Garland was a mother of three, a singing machine, with myriad tax problems, no fixed income and a damaging track-record of quarrels with film and television studios, of broken contracts and canceled appearances. She was also painfully aware that she was unattractive, and all the happiness she had given to millions could not make up for that. Liza returned home from school one day crying because one of her fellow pupils—a film star's son—had said: "Your mother's a big fat pig!" Garland told her: "The next time that boy says your mother's fat, look him dead in the eye and say, 'My mother can get thin any time she wants to, but your father couldn't get talent if he took twenty years of private lessons from Sir Laurence Oliver.'"

Whatever Sid Luft's failings, there is no doubt that Garland could not have coped at all without him. Doris Day, who was also married to her manager, knew the Lufts well. She said that Garland had much less confidence in her manager-husband than she had in hers—which has to be one of the great ironies of show business, since after her husband died, Day discovered that he had cheated her out of her fortune. Garland and Day also had in common the fact that both had been in show business since an early age and had hardly known any other life. "My heart really went out to her," Day commented.

> She was one of the funniest, wittiest ladies I have ever known, a marvelous conversationalist who would set me laughing until I actually doubled over. I adored being around her. Unhappy as she was, there was something straight about Judy that I truly admired . . . I can't overemphasize the appeal of a person like that, especially in a place like Hollywood that is so shot through with phonies and pretenders . . .
>
> There was a scared little girl in Judy, afraid to come out. Maybe it was the childhood she never had. She kept so much of herself locked up, but what she did let out was beautiful.

Day also remembered Garland as "terribly confused," and noted that: "Sid's job was to keep Judy functioning and out of harm's way."

This was not always easy. Garland's only engagement since the Town and Country Club debacle had been in Minneapolis, in her home state, when she had sung to 20,000 people as part of the city's centennial celebrations in May. Luft did, however, manage to get her a two-week booking at the Cocoanut Grove, starting on July 23. She would not have the inconvenience of living in a hotel; she would have friends and fellow-professionals in the audience; and, given her reputation in Los Angeles, it was unlikely that she would cancel a single performance. Even so, the American Guild of Variety Artists, wary that on past record her behavior might throw members of the troupe out of work, insisted on a bond equivalent to two weeks of Garland's salary. They relented when it was decided that she would do a one-woman show. She was scheduled to do one show a night during the week, and two at weekends. Charles Walters staged the hour-long act and Roger Edens again wrote the special material, firstly for "When You're Smiling," with which she opened, walking through the tables. She also sang "Liza," and Liza herself came out to dance while her mother sang "Swanee." For almost the only time in her career, she sang a song which was currently popular, a novelty piece called "The Purple People Eater"—and because this was a new departure for her, the audience loved her for it even more. *Variety* reported:

> If Judy Garland had paused to clear her throat at her Cocoanut Grove opening (an all-time record for a Grove preem) the sell-out crowd would probably had demanded an encore. It was Miss Garland's first appearance since her truncated date at the Town & Country Club in Brooklyn four months ago, and there was the heightened excitement always present when an entertainer, specially one with Miss Garland's fanatic following, appears on her home ground after a period of some adversity. There was no doubt that the crowd was with her. It remained for Miss Garland to get ahead of the crowd and lead it, which she did: all the way . . .

Louella Parsons told her readers:

> In the years I've been covering this town I've never seen such a turnout of stars, nor have I felt under one roof such an outpouring of affection and love as greeted Judy, the home town girl, when she appeared at the top of the stairs in her cute "Lady Tuxedo" garb . . . What a show—what a night, with Judy giving back all that affection by singing her heart out. I think we all realized we were enjoying an event that has seldom been equaled and will hardly ever be topped.

Among those in the audience were Frank Sinatra, Lauren Bacall, Rock Hudson, Dean Martin, the Henry Fondas, the James Stewarts, the Don Murrays, the Pat Boones, Lana Turner and Jerry Lewis.

Capitol decided that it would try to capture some of the electricity and magic of a live Garland performance, but by the time they took in the recording apparatus, her voice was beginning to weaken. Capitol had also noticed that none of her subsequent records had sold as well as *Miss Show Business*, on which she had sung many of the songs associated with her. *Garland at the Grove* was accordingly an album attempting to cannibalize the familiar Garland material. The sleeve note claims that it was recorded on the first night, whereas it was, in fact, recorded on the last, and, because her voice is strained, the album is not one of her better efforts.

Her next album went to the other extreme. None of the songs on *The Letter* had ever been heard before. Gordon Jenkins had composed a suite, on the lines of his concept album, *Manhattan Tower*, in which she reflects on a broken love affair. The actor John Ireland played her lover in the dialogue passages, some of which gave her a chance to demonstrate her gift for comedy—as did one skittish song, "The Worst Kind of Man."

One of the curiosities of Garland's career with Capitol is that she never recorded any popular song of the moment, or even had a single issued which might have taken her into the Hit Parade. She had done so at Decca and so, at Capitol, did Frank Sinatra, Peggy Lee and Nat "King" Cole, the other three jewels of the company's crown. The Capitol management, however, did not like Judy Garland. She was conscientious when performing before a microphone, and she never minded how long she worked, but she was otherwise unreliable. Since she had no concept of time, she was capable of keeping the musicians waiting for hours. She turned up at one session armed with a large bottle of codeine, which she proceeded to empty between songs. She was only a little "hazy" toward the end, but this was unprofessional behavior. When Luft asked about singles, Capitol replied that her unique situation in show business could best be maintained if she made only albums. Besides, three singles had been issued during her British trip, but they had sold poorly compared with the albums from which they were taken. Garland did not in any case think of herself as a star of records, believing that the successful ones were due more to lucky circumstances than her singing.

Much less curious, given her weight, is that there were no movie offers. There has been some speculation—although nothing was said at the time in the trade press—that she was considered for the leads in the film versions of two Rodgers and Hammerstein musicals, *Carousel* and *South Pacific*. This may be true, for Rodgers and Hammerstein both liked and admired her: but, more than most musicians, they were canny businessmen. They had a heavy investment in *South Pacific* and, as it was to be shot mainly on location, would not have brooked the serious delays which seemed to occur whenever Judy Garland was filming. As far as *Carousel* was concerned, she was no longer any more suitable for it than she was for *Alice Adams*: both heroines were virginal, and although wonders had been achieved by make-up and camera on *A Star Is Born*, that was now well in the past.

Two other projects were much more suitable. A 1954 Broadway musical, *By the Beautiful Sea*, which had starred Shirley Booth and Wilbur Evans, was mentioned in the trade press as a co-starring vehicle for Garland and Bing Crosby. Set at the turn of the century in a Coney Island boardinghouse for vaudevillians, it would seem to have been ideal for both of them. The only movie project she herself discussed in interviews at this time was *Born in Wedlock*, set in the same period, in which she would play a singer with two children. She had been sufficiently interested in the possibilities of filming Margaret Echard's novel that she had taken an option on it, but no studio was willing to proceed with the project.

There was no alternative but to continue her career as a live performer. She played Orchestra Hall in Chicago in September for one week and the Sands in Las Vegas in October for two. The Flamingo in Las Vegas decided to take advantage of her presence there to claim an astonishing $7,500 for the long-distance calls she had made during her earlier aborted engagement, and there were more unpleasant headlines the following month when Lynn Bari declared that Garland's house was not a fit home for her son, who had spent some time with his father there.

In spite of all this, Garland returned home after the Vegas engagement in a relaxed mood, and on October 28 enjoyed a testimonial dinner in her honor thrown by the Masquers Club. George Jessel was master of ceremonies and Allan Jones sang the National Anthem. Janet Leigh, Tony Curtis, Jeff Chandler, Sammy Davis, Jr., and Louella Parsons paid tribute, while James Mason, Joe Pasternak, Arthur Freed and Roger Edens took bows. Garland concluded the evening by singing "When You're Smiling," "Rockabye Your Baby" and "Over the Rainbow."

It provided only a temporary fillip to her morale. As the weeks went by she became irritable and prone to behave irrationally and hysterically. "What kind of mood is Mama in?" was the first question Lorna and Liza asked when they returned from school.

The weeks preceding and succeeding the new year were occupied in preparing for the Gordon Jenkins record, "The Letter." The only engagement she could look forward to during a bleak 1958–59 winter season was for two weeks at the Fontainebleau Hotel in February. Otherwise, she mooned about the house, bored and dejected, becoming once again dangerously dependent on pills. She knew she looked dreadful: her face was puffy and her figure was bloated. Even so, there were bills to pay and she had to be put back to work. Luft hit upon the gimmick of booking her into the Metropolitan Opera House in New York, a place where large female singers were the norm. No performer of her kind had appeared at the Met since Harry Lauder in 1930, and, under the terms of the Met's franchise, she could only perform there for charity. Still, it would get her working again, and in the awesome setting of one of the world's most famous theaters.

Once the Miami show finished, Luft got things going and decided to mount the sort of show to do honor to the occasion and at the same time be the kind other large theaters would be happy to book. Gordon Jenkins would conduct an orchestra of fifty instead of the usual thirty; Alan King would do his act and partner Judy in "A Couple of Swells"; the costumes and choreography (by Richard Barstow) for the dancers would be more elaborate than usual—and they would also back the veteran black dancer John Bubbles, who would join Garland for "Me and My Shadow." With Walters and Edens again on hand, it would cost $150,000 to stage. Luft took a second mortgage on the house and borrowed from friends, knowing that Garland would only get $8,000 in expenses, and their bill at the Plaza for the week's stay would come to over $9,000. At up to $50 a ticket, the show would benefit the Children's Asthma Research Institute and Hospital in Denver.

It tried out for six performances, beginning May 5, at the Stanley Opera House in Baltimore, where its reception guaranteed success in New York. Every performance at the Met was sold out, and on the first night there were fourteen curtain calls. The show opened with Garland dressed as an operagoer, singing "What's Going on at the Opera . . . Did Mr. Bing make up with Maria Callas?" She did an abridged version of "The Letter" suite, introduced Edens's coupling of "Almost Like Being Love" and "This Can't Be Love," and sang Rodgers and Hammerstein's "A Wonderful Guy" and Cole Porter's "I Happen to Like New York."

The show was ecstatically received, with Kenneth Tynan leading the reviewers in the *New Yorker*: "The engagement, which is now over, was limited; the pleasure it gave was not. When the voice pours out, as rich and pleading as ever, we know where, and how moved, we are—in the presence of a star, and embarrassed by tears."

Garland needed such bolstering, for the week was marred by a legal wrangle with Ben Maksik, who was claiming $150,000 for the losses sustained when Garland walked out of his Town and Country Club. She had jeopardized his operation and had imperiled the jobs of three hundred people. According to him the Lufts had "been ducking responsibility for years"—they had not even responded to his requests for redress. As they were not residents of New York State, he could not sue them, but their presence in the city enabled him to request that her $8,000 fee for the Met engagement (but not the proceeds) be impounded. The Lufts' attorneys had no choice but to accept his writ, which became yet another of their debts. These were increased as there were two weeks' lay-offs before and after the next booking, a week at the Chicago Civic Opera, during which time the services of the supporting artists had to be retained, but no money was coming in. Chicago was followed by eleven days at the San Francisco Opera and one at the Los Angeles Shrine Auditorium.

The show was reviewed in the *Chicago Tribune* by Bently Stegner:

A little girl was born in a trunk stretched a rainbow from wall to wall of the cavernous Chicago Opera House Monday night. The personality of Judy Garland ranged from the tiara crowned operagoer she impersonated in her first number to the waif in tattered tramp's clothes in her last. But from the beginning to the end, from dowager to hobo, she carried the crowd over the rainbow on the strains of her soaring, throbbing voice . . .

She was weighted down with bouquets, but she set them aside for a go at "Chicago." The spectators sat in their seats and cheered until the asbestos curtain finally convinced them that Miss Show Business was really through for the night.

She did not merely have "a go" at Chicago. She gave the audience a stunning "Rockabye Your Baby" after "Over the Rainbow," knowing that she had something even more spectacular to do. Years ago Edens had arranged "After You've Gone," letting her sing it straight and then reprise it in a jazzy version making full use of her powers of crescendo. He did the same for "Chicago"—and for "San Francisco," for her to sing in that city. When she began his new verse for the latter, "I never will forget Jeanette MacDonald," the audience, already excited, roared—for not only was she about to sing a song which that narcissistic city loved, but she had a deliciously amusing verse recalling MacDonald's appearance in *San Francisco*, a famous M-G-M movie about the 1906 earthquake: "To think of her it gives my heart a pang / I never will forget / How that brave Jeanette / Stood there in the ruins and sang—a-a-a-a-a-and sang . . ."

Inactive again, apart from a stint at the Sahara in Las Vegas in October, she grew so obese that she waddled rather than walked, and had difficulty bending over. She decided to check in at a health farm in the San Fernando Valley run by Kay Mulvey, who had been in the publicity department of M-G-M when Garland had first arrived there. Luft went with her, for moral support, as did Liza: they both lost some weight, but in spite of a daily game of tennis Garland failed to take off even an inch.

Liza had made her television debut in April. At a party, she had joined Gene Kelly in singing "For Me and My Gal," and he arranged for them to reprise the song on his television special. It was only a start in show business, and a logical follow-on to appearing in her mother's acts, and she told Kelly how much she liked it. Judy merely reflected that Liza was in demand and she was not.

It was a black time for her:

I had so many fears, so many anxieties. I'd had them as a child and I guess they just grow worse as you get older and more self-centered. The fear of failure. The fear of ridicule. I hated the way I looked. I cried for no reason, laughed hysterically, made stupid decisions, couldn't tell a kind word from an insult. All the brain boilers gave me up. I staggered along in a nightmare, knowing something was vitally wrong, but what? It got to the point where I was a virtual automaton—with no memory! I played some very big dates in 1958 and 1959. I don't remember any of it. I didn't know what I was doing.

Luft was convinced that something was seriously wrong with her, but she refused to see a doctor. She only nibbled at her food and was drinking far too much. Luft persuaded two doctors, who were acquaintances, to come to the house in the guise of musicians. Knowing that she looked dreadful, she refused to see them, but curiosity got the better of her when she heard the sound of the piano. She came down and sat next to the pianist; during the course of the evening his friend managed to feel her shoulder as he reached over to turn over the music. He reported to Luft that she was waterlogged, which meant that either her liver or her kidneys—or both—were diseased.

The only hospital which Garland might agree to enter was the

Doctors Hospital in New York, because she had liked its luxurious accommodation when she was there before. If Luft could get her to New York, she might agree to consult his uncle, Dr. Israel Rappaport, whom she liked. As if on the spur of the moment, he told her that she was to be guest of honor at a party Elsa Maxwell was throwing for Aly Khan in Manhattan. It would, at least, relieve her boredom. She agreed to go but, depressed by her appearance, did not enjoy the party. In the morning, out of the blue, she told him that she was sick and wanted to go to a hospital. She agreed to see Dr. Rappaport, who reported that she was very ill indeed. Years of abusing her body with pills and alcohol had caused her liver to swell to four times its normal size, pouring poison into her body. Brushing this aside, she insisted on ordering a triple vodka before leaving for the Doctors Hospital, where her illness was diagnosed as acute hepatitis. The damage done to her liver could not be repaired, and the prognosis was not good: if she were to be cured, and there was some doubt, she could never touch hard liquor again; she would be a semi-invalid for the rest of her life. There was a chance that she would survive a while, provided she took good care of herself and never worked again.

20

❖•❖•❖•❖•❖•❖

Comeback

GARLAND WAS IN THE HOSPITAL for seven weeks, during which more than twenty quarts of liquid were drained from her body. Nevertheless, she was still heavy when she left, in a wheelchair, on January 5, 1960, to start a new life.

Believing rightly that the public was interested in every aspect of her life, she communicated some of the details of her illness to the press. Her doctors would only let her drink Blue Nun Liebfraumilch, on which she would, later, get drunk when she wanted to. The weeks in the hospital had put her on a reasonably even keel, but she was bored. To find something to occupy her time, and to get some much-needed cash, the indefatigable Luft persuaded Bennett Cerf of Random House to advance a first installment of $35,000 for her autobiography. "It's hilariously funny," she told a reporter, "as most of my life has been most of the time. Even at the worst times there has always been something hilarious happening to me." She talked to a ghost-writer for some time, until she decided that she had been pressured into signing the contract; she then refused to continue. Cerf eventually recovered some of his investment by selling the material to *McCall's*. She subsequently disowned it.

Hollywood showed some interest—not much, but enough. George Sidney, who had directed her in *The Harvey Girls*, had moved over to Columbia, partly because of his friendship with its boss, Harry Cohn. He arranged for Roger Edens to be seconded temporarily to help him on two projects, neither of which got off the ground. A third, however, was planned as a vehicle for the Mexican comedian Cantinflas, who had achieved a certain acclaim in 1956 with *Around the World in 80 Days*. As with that film, *Pepe* was to feature an all-star cast, including—as themselves—Bing Crosby, Maurice Chevalier, Frank Sinatra, Edward G. Robinson, Greer Garson and Jack Lemmon. The ads also promised "the voice of Judy Garland." André Previn and Dory Langdon (who was to become his wife) had written a ballad, "The Faraway Part of Town," for Garland to sing on the soundtrack, while Dan Dailey and Shirley Jones danced to it. The film was not a success. The recording of the song, in April, had given Garland no difficulty, and she returned to Capitol in June to record twelve songs for an album, *That's Entertainment*, with the Jack Marshall Orchestra.

This was her new life, and she did not like it. There was more to Judy Garland than making an occasional record. She fretted through four months of convalescence. "I was liked in California," she said, "but nobody needed me. The phone never rang, In Hollywood I was somebody who *had been* a movie star." She was recovering some of her old movie-star appearance: her weight remained a problem, but for the first time in fifteen years she could look in the mirror and see a face neither puffy nor prematurely aged. Her self-confidence returned and she began to pick up the threads of her social life. Through an old M-G-M colleague, Peter Lawford (with whom she had enjoyed a brief affair), she had got to know Senator John F. Kennedy, his brother-in-law, who was now starting his campaign for the presidency. This began in early July at the time of the Democratic Convention in Los Angeles and at the opening banquet, where she was guest of honor. "Judy was the belle of the party," the columnist Earl Wilson reported. She established a rapport with Kennedy, who took to telephoning her and asking her to sing "Over the Rainbow" for him. "Just the last eight bars," he would say, and after thanking her, he always told her that she had made his day. She kept a photograph of the two of them, taken that night, in her pocketbook until she died.

The day after the dinner, she flew to Europe. At one time, she used to shake whenever she was near an airport, but she had finally conquered her fear of flying, as well as her inability to do anything practical for herself. "I bought a ticket and got on a plane and went through Customs alone," she announced, "and I had never done any of these things before. They had always been done for me." She was carrying a copy of Willa Cather's novel, *A Lost Lady*.

Luft had been surprised by her decision to travel alone. It really proved that she was recovered. The only medication she was taking was Ritalin, a mild form of tranquilizer; and every day she was looking better. Part of her reason for going to Europe was that Liza had gone to France for the summer, with some fellow pupils, one of whose mothers was acting as chaperone. The plan was to make them better acquainted with the language, and they were staying at Annecy. Garland planned to visit Liza after spending two weeks in Rome, where Rossano Brazzi had lent her his house. Ethel Merman and Kay Thompson would be joining her and so, as she said, Rome would be "playing host to the three loudest singers in the world for a while." Another reason for leaving America was that she wanted work, but none was being offered in Hollywood. Capitol had just renewed her contract for another three years and had asked her, without much enthusiasm, to re-record some of her old hits in stereo sound. This was not a gilt-edged investment, and the company suggested that she do it in London, where costs were cheaper. She would be working with its parent company, EMI, whose executives might find her more sympathetic than they did.

She arrived in London on July 14, and gave a press conference, at which she announced: "I'm so damned calm these days, I guess I'm a pretty dull person. I go along the same old line all the time—no highs, no lows. I never lose my temper anymore and I never throw tantrums. When something happens to annoy me, I just walk away and forget it." She then went to stay with Dirk Bogarde at his house in the country. She returned to London for her recording sessions and began to look for a house, since she had decided to settle in England. As usual with Garland, a passing whim had suddenly become a major decision. She called another press conference to explain it all: "California is so expensive—we spent years building and getting together a beautiful house. But we were possessed by our possessions.

Well, I thought about it, and then I phoned my husband. I was worried about telling him at first—I didn't want to sound too much like a woman on the crest of a wave, riding on a sudden enthusiasm."

"California doesn't seem permanent anymore," she went on, warming to her theme:

It's like a film set waiting to be struck. The momentum of Hollywood has gone. I don't make a lot of pictures there anymore, and neither do they for that matter. It's like a ghost town. So many productions are being made in New York and London today. You know I'm thirty-eight—and thirty-six years of my life I've spent in California. It's a long time to be in one town. I want to see more of the world than the Sunset Strip. I think it's important for everyone to make changes, if they want to continue developing as a person. I love London—the tempo, the people, the way of life. I feel more relaxed here. New York is too fast and frenzied, California is too lethargic. I love rain and fog—in fact, I love the impermanent English weather, it's stimulating.

She added that she wanted security for her children, "emotionally and materially as well." She admitted that she had not made any investments when she was earning big money—for once, she was in too happy a mood to blame Ethel—and observed that journalists sometimes asked her why she was broke. "I'm not a millionaire," she explained. "I'm just like everybody else—comfortably off." This was not true: one of the attractions of England was that it was an ocean away from her creditors.

At that time, she could have lived in London like a millionaire on the $100,000 it took to run the house on Mapleton Drive. Luft was wary of her impulses, but he welcomed the idea of starting a new life. He was unable to join her, however, until he had sold the Vlaminck, which he eventually did for $11,000. To finance the preparations for the move, he borrowed $15,000 from Vern Alves, who in turn had borrowed this sum by putting up a property he owned as collateral. While Luft set about selling the house in Los Angeles, Garland settled into one she had rented from the film director Carol Reed in the King's Road, Chelsea. It was a three-story, Georgian town house, and its most unusual feature was the living room, which ran the whole length of the house, on two levels, and was lined with books and furnished with a piano and innumerable easy chairs and sofas. There was only a patch of garden in the front, but the French windows at the back looked out onto a lawn surrounded by flowers and trees. It was the least luxurious home she had lived in since becoming a star.

She had hardly used her singing voice for over a year, but now needed to practice for the forthcoming Capitol recording. Unable to sleep one night, she got up to take a shower, with the water turned on full both to drown out her singing and to provide steam as balm for her throat. She was so excited by the improvement in her voice, that she woke Luft with a list of thirty or so songs which she wanted to sing in a concert. When he asked whether the number was a bit excessive, she countered: "If I die we'll know it's too much." She said later:

If I had believed all the doctors I've met, I'd be a hopeless invalid. I said I'm just going to go out and do nothing but *sing*, by myself. Just get a good band and I'll sing for an hour, then ten minutes intermission, then another hour. Elaboration on a good theme isn't necessary. Perhaps it distracts an audience to see all the trappings, like chorus boys. Even though I'm working twice as hard as I did at the Palace, I get much more satisfaction, an *exultant* satisfaction out of this.

Luft moved swiftly, as did the impresario Harold Davison, who booked the London Palladium for "An Evening with Judy Garland" at less than three weeks notice, for Sunday, August 28, at 8 p.m. A news item on the concert was all that was needed. The house sold out within hours of the box-office opening. As a consequence Davison arranged "Another Evening with Judy Garland" for September 4.

In the meantime, she had made her recording for Capitol, under EMI's star conductor, Norrie Paramor, whom she called "Noilly Prat," affecting to be unable to pronounce his name. Paramor and the EMI staff were so in awe of her that they got only competent renditions of her most familiar songs, despite using the usual orchestrations. She needed the challenge of people like Roger Edens and Nelson Riddle to be at her best. Even after her career pushed off in exciting new directions, Capitol chose not to release the album. It eventually came out after her death, under the title, *Judy in London*. Paramor, however, had been delighted with what he had heard and had offered the services of himself and his orchestra for any concert she might give. He duly took the baton at the Palladium.

"Judy Garland, who has probably made more spectacular comebacks than a Cape Canaveral rocket, returned to the stage for the first time in a year last night," Peter Evans told readers of the *Daily Express*. From the very outset, it was clear that the evening would be a triumph. The applause during the overture was wholly spontaneous, owing everything to the way the members of the audience felt about her and what she meant in all their lives. There was an air of expectancy, but it was different from that in the Dominion, because everyone knew that she had had even more personal and professional difficulties since then and supposed, rightly, that this rare appearance was to share with them the fact that she knew that she was again in magnificent form.

She began with a song which few in the audience knew. "I Happen to Like This Town" was a Cole Porter number which she had sung on the 1959 tour, and it had been given a new lyric about London's suburbs by Roger Edens. She wore a black day dress with a short blue jacket lightly beaded with gold; in the second half she wore lounging pants and a diamanté jacket. For once, both outfits were cleverly chosen. The dress allowed the audience to see that her legs were as exquisite as ever, as gorgeously feminine. The pants emphasized a new adrogyny, the boyishness of her movements as she stood, like Kay Thompson (whose style she increasingly imitated), with legs apart.

She was palpably nervous, but she had developed a series of gestures to help her disguise this. She was, moreover, in superb voice. She sang Arlen's "Stormy Weather" publicly for the first time, taking it away from Lena Horne. With a jazz combo, she did two songs by Gershwin, "Who Cares?" and "How Long Has This Been Going On?" She said that she had not rehearsed "You'll Never Walk Alone," but wanted to sing it in tribute to Oscar Hammerstein, whose death had been announced five days earlier, and she called Bogarde from the audience and crooned "It Never Was You" to him. Above all, however, she built the evening, driving the audience into a frenzy with "San Francisco," "Chicago" and "Swanee." They began to call for other numbers, but she dismissed them: "Oh no, not that. I've been singing that for at least a hundred and eight years. Let's try a new one." Otherwise, she had little patter. She signaled rather than spoke her thanks.

The same could not be said of the audience. "Her reception . . . shook stagehands hardened by years of hysterical audience reaction," Dan Slater reported in the *Daily Herald*. He quoted the stage-doorkeeper as saying: "I haven't heard a reception like this since Nora Bayes, the American singer, was here in 1923." "At the conclusion of every number there was an outburst of applause of tornado-like dimensions," Isadore Green wrote in the *Record Mirror*, "at the end of an unforgettable performance, the reception was just as unforgettable. It was a standing ovation. People just went crazy with exhilaration. They stood up and clapped and cheered and shouted at the top of their voices."

Mollie Ellis in *The Stage* offered some good reasons for the acclaim:

> She could do no wrong. A forgotten line or two, improvised impishly or blatantly as the case may be, a dance movement or two, tender love songs, torrid torch songs, quiet songs, noisy songs, songs with a swing to them, songs with a sentimental strain to them, Judy gave us the lot . . . It seems incredible that we listened to thirty songs straight off, with only a short interval. And yet we did, and loved every moment. The mood changes very quickly, and very completely with Judy, and therein lies part of the secret. We never feel it is too much because of the constant change of voice, inflection, expression and mood.

The following Sunday, Garland faced the capacity house with an even more evident case of nerves, unsure whether lightning could strike twice in the same place. By the time she started the second half with "When You're Smiling," she was in full command. She surpassed her performance of the previous week, and when at the end the audience rose and began to rush to the footlights there was hysteria such as the Palladium, or any theater, had never before witnessed.

Her special place in show business was underscored when she received a round of applause when attending the first night of Noël Coward's *Waiting in the Wings*. She was enjoying the adulation and making new friends. She said she missed some of those back home, but "surprisingly few" there were close to her.

The children joined her in London, and although she contrived to give interviewers the impression that she was the perfect, truly domesticated mother, she did little more than walk them in Battersea Park or take them to school. A cook came with the house, and Garland shopped only for luxuries in Fortnum and Mason or Harrods. She was eager to work and, as a consequence, spent part of the autumn traveling.

Shortly after the concerts, she kept her promise to John F. Kennedy to tour the U.S. military installations in Germany, campaigning on his behalf in his bid for the presidency. She took no fee, and she was successful in her aim, as it turned out, though he was elected by one of the smallest majorities in history.

Passing through Paris, she inquired about a possible booking there. She was curious to know whether she could conquer that city. She spoke no French, but was aware that Petula Clark had carved out a new career for herself after singing, in English, at the Olympia Music Hall in the French capital. This was not a big theater, however, and Garland ambitiously chose to make her French debut at the Palais de Chaillot, which seated 2,700. It was certainly a gamble. The theater, which had once been the meeting place of the United Nations, was about as cozy as a football stadium. Furthermore, instead of the usual price for entertainers of the equivalent of two dollars a seat, the theater had decided to charge the equivalent of twenty for Garland. This was despite the fact that she was virtually an unknown quantity in France, where Hollywood musicals had never enjoyed much success. Indeed, when her early films were released there after the war, one magazine, *L'Ecran Français*, stated that Mickey Rooney and Judy Garland represented all that was most reprehensible in American youth. However, 1960 had seen the flowering of the *nouvelle vague* and the *auteur*-theory: Cukor and Minnelli were among the favored directors, and *Une Etoile est Née* and *Le Chant de Missouri* (*Meet Me in St. Louis*) had recently become staples at the myriad revival houses in Paris.

Two concerts, with Norrie Paramor and his orchestra, were arranged, for October 5 and 7. There was a packed, though, according to John Fricke, papered house to see the singer the press called "La Piaf Américaine" and "the volcano of Broadway." It included all the major stars of the French music hall, with Maurice Chevalier in the front row, as he had promised when he invited her to lunch. Ingrid Bergman, Anthony Perkins, Glenn Ford and Anatole Litvak were among the American contingent. The Duke and Duchess of Windsor were there, and ex-Queen Soraya of Persia, accompanied by the film director Terence Young.

Unlike the real Piaf, whose concerts took place in an awed hush, as if the audience were attending a religious ceremony, Garland turned her appearances into fiestas. "They even sang 'For Me and My Gal' with her," reported Philippe Labro in *France-Soir*, "and there aren't many artists who can with one word give a house packed with *le Tout Paris* the desire to sing with them." The French critics were as impressed as the audiences, even bracketing her with the great Charles Trenet. She took six curtain calls on the first night, and, as a result of her notices and the second sold-out capacity house, Bruno Coquatrix booked her into the Olympia, scene of some of Piaf's greatest triumphs, for a week beginning October 26. It was a risk for Coquatrix, since the Olympia was frequented by families and customers—the traditional "tired businessmen"—out for a jolly evening. He originally asked her to curtail the show, to follow the usual music-hall bill, but she prevailed upon him to let her do the whole evening. As *Variety* put it: "Musical pix and her disks are known mainly to specialists so her success was strictly on her boff talents which overcame lingo difficulties."

She had rediscovered herself as a live performer and was now keen to capitalize upon her success. Harold Davison arranged four Sunday bookings in Britain in between these French dates. Sometimes the largest auditoria to be found in cities were the Odeon cinemas, which, unlike the theaters, were accustomed to opening on Sunday, and easier to book into at short notice. She played the Leeds Odeon on October 16 and the one in Birmingham the following Sunday. After returning to Paris to fulfill her Olympia engagement, she played the De Montford Hall in Leicester on November 15.

She had been scheduled to play the Free Trade Hall in Manchester on November 5, but Lorna was felled by food poisoning. In order to avoid doing the concert, Garland told the management that it was she who was indisposed—and it was true that the whole family was affected to some degree. As it was Guy Fawkes Night, she sent the cook out to buy fireworks, which he was instructed to set off under Lorna's window. He managed to drop a lighted pinwheel into the box, however, and they exploded at once. "That's the way he cooks in the kitchen," Garland commented.

The Manchester concert was rescheduled for December 4, when Liza joined her mother on stage for "After You've Gone." Garland had learned how to change and vary the act, as in Birmingham, when she found it tough going to get the audience on her side in the first half. The second half went much better, and she tossed off "It's a Great Day for the Irish" as her finale, which brought members of the audience marching down the aisles.

A few days after the Manchester concert, she was in the Netherlands, which was easier ground to conquer than France. Much of the population spoke English, and Hollywood musicals were very popular, particularly among Amsterdam's large homosexual community. Garland had always had a large gay following and was to become a great favorite among professional female impersonators and amateur drag queens. The combination of her turbulent private life, her repertoire of songs about men who got away, and indeed her whole melodramatic persona had made her into something of a camp icon. Such was her following among "bachelors" that her most famous role was given new meaning in the slang term "a friend of Dorothy," still used as a camp synonym for "homosexual." This loyal audience turned out wherever she performed in the world, and it was said that on the night of December 10, there was no one in Amsterdam's numerous gay clubs who was *not* going to see Judy Garland. She had been booked into the city's largest theater, the splendid art-deco Tuschinski. Like the British Odeons, the Tuschinski also functioned as a cinema, but unlike them, it was a first-run house which attracted patrons from the neighboring towns, especially at weekends. This meant that the concert had to start after the film show (rather than replace it, as in Britain), so Garland appeared at midnight and sang until three in the morning. The concert was broadcast live, after the state radio service had been given a special dispensation to remain on the air after its usual closing time.

Reports of a revitalized Judy Garland had been circulating in American show-business circles since the Palladium concerts, and Arthur P. Jacobs signed an agreement for his company to handle her press relations. His chief assistant, John Springer, was a great admirer of Garland. After talking to her, Springer learned that MCA had just about given up on her, and that she was disenchanted with Luft as her manager. He had done a magnificent job in often grim circumstances, but he was, after all, an amateur. Inexplicably, she had just turned down the leading role in a big film musical, *Funny Girl*, a biopic of Fanny Brice which had been expressly fashioned for her. In the meantime, it had been remodeled as a Broadway show for Mary Martin. It was clear that Garland needed a new agent.

Springer contacted Freddie Fields, now a vice-president of MCA, whom he knew to be a Garland fan. He also knew that Fields was starting up on his own and looking for clients. He planned to handle only a select few, including his wife Polly Bergen, Phil Silvers, Ethel Merman and Peter Sellers. Fields flew to London in order to convince Garland that she was exactly the sort of talent he wanted to handle. Furthermore, he would be able to rid her of her mountain of debts. She liked both him and David Begelman, a former MCA associate who was on the point of becoming his partner. She was delighted by their compliments, their gentlemanly manners, their enthusiasm for her talent and their plans for her. She also liked the idea of being one of a small group of artists receiving special treatment: this included a contractual obligation for someone from the agency to accompany her when she toured.

She toured Europe at a leisurely pace. She was scheduled to give

Judy meets Queen Elizabeth in London after the Royal Variety Command
Performance at London's Palladium, 1957. (UPI/Bettmann)

Judy and four-year-old
Lorna performing in Las
Vegas in 1957. Liza and Joey
were in the audience.
(Bill Chapman Collection)

Liza, Jimmy McHugh, Judy, and redoubtable gossip columnist Louella Parsons at the Cocoanut Grove opening in 1958. (Bill Chapman Collection)

Eddie Fisher and his controversial bride, Elizabeth Taylor, visiting Judy backstage at the Metropolitan Opera House in New York, 1959. (Bill Chapman Collection)

Judy's beloved friends Marc and
Marcella Rabwin in 1959.
(Courtesy of Marcella Rabwin)

Stumping for her friend and admirer
JFK in Wiesbaden, Germany, in
October 1960. (UPI/Bettmann)

In concert in Paris,
October 1960.
(Photofest)

Arriving at Carnegie Hall in curlers, May 1961. (Bettmann Archive)

A slimmer Judy backstage after a performance in 1962. (Photofest)

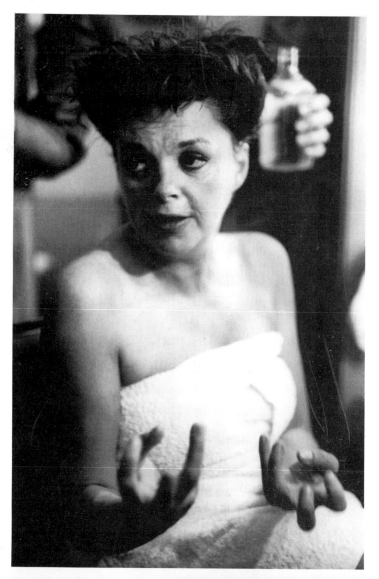

Liza, Joey, Judy, and Lorna at
Kennedy Airport, New York, 1964.
(Photofest)

Judy and Liza
at Liza's Broadway
debut, May 1965.
(Bettmann Archive)

With boyfriend Mark Herron,
June 1964. (Archive Photos)

Judy after a performance in 1967 with glitter in her hair. (Archive Photos)

Jacqueline Susann, author of *Valley of the Dolls*, and Judy announcing in 1967 that Judy will star in the film version of the bestseller. Susan Hayward finished the picture. (UPI/Bettmann)

After a court hearing, Judy is given the right to appear at The Talk of the Town, London, December 1968. (Photofest)

Judy celebrating with her fifth husband Mickey Deans (center) after their wedding on March 15, 1969. Singer Johnny Ray is at left. (Archive Photos)

With Mickey Deans at
Heathrow Airport en
route to New York, May
1969. (Archive Photos)

Kay Thompson, Lorna, Liza, and Peter Allen leaving Judy's funeral service at
Frank Campbell's in New York, June 27, 1969. (UPI/Bettmann)

three concerts in Copenhagen, one in Oslo and another in Paris in the new year, but these were canceled when she joined the new agency. On December 21 *Variety* disclosed that Fields had signed Garland to appear in London, in an unnamed show then playing on Broadway. The report also said that Fields was talking to the impresario David Merrick about a Broadway show, that he had acquired two film properties for Garland, and that she would be doing two television specials, in April and October, one of which would be for the British company Granada.

The unnamed show was *The Unsinkable Molly Brown*, based on the true story of a woman who survives the sinking of the *Titanic*, but the three-month London run that Fields had planned proved to be commercially unfeasible. With almost everything else happening in the States, Garland decided that it was time to go home.

21

❖❖❖❖❖❖❖

Carnegie Hall

The family spent Christmas in London and left on the last day of 1960 for New York, where they settled into the Carlyle Hotel. With Fields and Begelman on hand, Garland no longer needed Sid Luft. "During that awful blizzard of January 1961 I went for a walk in the snow one night," she recalled. "I thought *I* was the blizzard. Suddenly I realized that I didn't give a damn about him . . . for a few hours it was like being shot out of a cannon. It was really terrifying." She asked for a separation a few days later, and in view of this, he was not surprised when she told him that she had formed a production company in association with Fields and Begelman. She dubbed her new partners "Leopold and Loeb" (after the famous Chicago University "kill-for-thrill" murderers), on the grounds that they were so bright. The company was called Kingsrow Enterprises. "It's not like the usual artist-manager contract," she explained. "We're partners; they see that the lights work and the curtain goes up. They found schools for the children and they found this apartment"—though she might more accurately have said that this was done for them by Stevie Dumler,

Fields's personal assistant. The spacious, high-ceilinged apartment was in the Dakota Building, a turn-of-the-century pile on Central Park West, which had become fashionable after the war.

Fields and Begelman were ambivalent about Luft, both as Garland's husband and her business associate. Like many people in the entertainment industry, they regarded him as a leech who had attached himself to a tremendously gifted talent. A "real" producer would never have let *A Star Is Born* get out of hand, and its notorious financial losses only confirmed his reputation as an amateur. Now that Garland was being represented by a highly respected company, Freddie Fields Associates, as they were then, known to be committed to the professional welfare and reputation of its clients, she was unlikely to fall out of line, walk out of engagements or quarrel with the massively important CBS.

Between them, MCA and Luft had allowed the difference between the television company and the star to drag on for four years. She had seen no reason to drop her suit, since she had no desire to return to television. When Fields asked her to forget her quarrel, however, she agreed at once. CBS was happy to drop its countersuit, and on January 9, 1961, four years to the day after the falling-out, peace was formally announced, with CBS having an option on her services for the immediate future. She was prepared to try television again, for new developments in the industry meant that she would no longer have to perform in front of the cameras live.

Fields and Begelman wanted first to get her back into pictures, however. Among their new clients was Marlene Dietrich, who was to appear in a film about the trials of Nazi war criminals for the producer-director Stanley Kramer. Through Dietrich, Fields learned that there was one small but key role still be to be cast in *Judgment at Nuremberg*. When approached, Kramer thought that Judy Garland might be a welcome addition to the already starry cast; but he refused to commit himself. CMA asked when Kramer might need her, if he did, and began to book a tour which would leave those dates free.

Garland dreaded the idea of a tour, but there was absolutely no alternative. CMA had discovered that no Broadway producer would take a chance on her. It was an absurd situation: they were handling a star in better condition than she had been for a decade, and she was virtually unemployable. The best that Fields could do at short notice was a booking at the Concord Hotel in the Catskills, where New York's Jewish population traditionally took its summer vacation. Luft had kept Garland away from "the Borscht Circuit": it could pay good money, but it often headlined second-rate artists when the need occurred, and Luft had not wanted her devalued. Fields explained that the manager of the Concord was a friend, and that it did no harm to let people know that Judy Garland was back in business.

Her special position in that business was underlined when she went to Sammy Davis Jr's closing night at the Copacabana. Like several other artists, Davis was in the habit of introducing anyone famous in the audience and engaging them in an extended bantering match; it had become one of the most undisciplined rituals in the cabaret field. On this particular evening, Davis announced that he was dispensing with it because there were "two great ladies" in the audience. The first was his mother, who was mildly applauded. "The second great lady," he said, "has just returned from London, where she was recovering from a serious illness. Her name is Judy Garland." After an instant's silence, the audience burst into applause. As the spotlight picked her out, she walked across to Davis, nodding her thanks to the audience with tears in her eyes. One of the musicians played the first bars of "Over the Rainbow," and when the others joined in, Davis told her to sing it—for one thing, it would shut the audience up. At the end of the song, the audience went wild, but she refused to sing again, nodding her head in thanks eight times before resuming her seat. It was an agreeable, encouraging way to resume her career in the States.

The only way to prove that she was reliable, however, was for her to agree to tour. Furthermore, she needed the money. During January, she flew to Miami to fulfill an engagement she had been obliged to cancel when she was ill in the hospital; she was paid $10,000 for just one performance. The tour, to prove its purpose, had to be a fairly grueling one, but Fields and Begelman tried to arrange it to give Garland free time between engagements. They knew from their experiences at MCA that performing nightly took its toll and sometimes resulted in missed shows. Both of them would be traveling with her, along with Mort Lindsey, whom they had appointed as her conductor; his three musicians—a pianist, a lead trumpet and a drummer—were to be augmented by local players. Also accompanying them would be Stevie Dumler and Mr. Kenneth, Garland's hairdresser, though later in the tour she simplified matters by dispensing with his services in favor of a number of wigs he had designed for her.

In addition, at Garland's suggestion, Fields asked Vern Alves to be the "general production manager," which meant, as in the past, attending to her whims. Alves accepted, knowing that it would not be an easy ride. Even his knowledge of her shifting moods did not prepare him for her virulence when she made it clear that Luft was to have no part in her affairs.

It had been coming for a long time, but Luft, though more than willing to turn his wife's professional affairs over to others, did not feel that this was the best time to be shut out of her life altogether. Her engagements in Europe, while keeping them financially afloat, had done nothing to clear the pile of debts. He had been unable to sell the Mapleton Drive house, but was partly relieved about this, because it would now be a base for the family, however divided it became. He had taken out a third mortgage, but then found that the bank was going to foreclose because he could not find $10,000 for the first one. He consulted Fields, who told him that Garland would provide the money from the advances for her tour, but only if Luft would sign over the property (which they jointly owned) to her. Luft refused and borrowed the money from Ted Law.

The tour proper began on February 21, in Dallas, where she had a reunion with her sister Jimmy, and would continue for one night in Houston. Stanley Kramer was in the audience at Dallas. He had decided that he wanted to see her perform in person before making a decision on Fields' earlier recommendation about casting her in *Judgment at Nuremberg*. "I saw staid citizens acting like bobby-soxers at an Elvis Presley show," he said. "I was struck, too, by the tremendous emotional range of Judy's performance that night . . . The part was only an eighteen-minute one, but it was the first that anybody had offered her in years, and she nearly wept with joy." She would spend only eight days on the set, and Fields arranged a fee of $50,000. She was overweight, but this did not matter, since she would be playing a German *hausfrau*.

Judgment at Nuremberg had started out as a 1959 television play directed by George Roy Hill, starring Claude Rains, Paul Lukas and Maximilian Schell. The author, Abby Mann, was also responsible for the extended screenplay, which concentrates on one particular Nuremberg trial late in 1948. It is presided over by an American county judge, who is trying to assess the guilt of four German judges charged with submitting their legal duties to the demands of the Nazis. Schell, who had played the defending counsel on television, was repeating his role in the film, and Kramer had lined up a formidable supporting cast: Spencer Tracy in the Rains role of the American judge; Burt Lancaster, a last-minute replacement for Laurence Olivier, as one of the German judges; Marlene Dietrich as a widow who resented the fact all Germans were considered guilty; and Richard Widmark as the prosecuting counsel. Also appearing, in the part of a young baker's assistant who had been forcibly sterilized because he was considered "abnormal," was Montgomery Clift, who, like Garland, was a talent *maudit*, and was now alcoholic. Garland's role called for her to be a simple housewife appearing for the prosecution. She was charged with having a family friend, a Jew, who was condemned and executed because of the relationship.

The columnist Jim Henaghan was on the set in early March for Garland's first scene. He watched her walk through the crew, when

suddenly, as though on a subtle clue, everyone began to applaud, and the woman, blushing with embarrassment, but very pleased, walked toward Stanley Kramer, the director, and bowed her head in a theatrical nod, reporting for work. And then she sat in a chair Kramer indicated and smiled happily as the applause continued as though it would never stop.

That was Judy Garland's re-entry into movies after an absence of several years. The reception from her director, the cast and crew was spontaneous, as unrehearsed as a shed tear, a genuine tribute from the people of her own profession to a star who, despite dreadful publicity, a very undistinguished record in her final years in Hollywood at the box office, bereft now of almost all the attributes that had once made her the idol of millions, still held the number one position in the hearts of most of her peers in show business.

She was punctual and cooperative on set, grateful to be back in movies and relieved that, for the first time since childhood, she did not have to carry the entire film. Small as the part was, it was a new challenge and she had to be coaxed into it, suppressing any new ideas that she, or her advisers, had had overnight. She was being coached in her accent by a linguist expert recommended by the German-born actress Uta Hagen.

The first day, which began so promisingly, turned into something like the old M-G-M nightmare when she left the set during the sixth take of her first scene, in which she was supposed to burst into tears. "Damn it, Stanley," she exclaimed, "I can't do it. I've dried up. I'm too happy to cry." But she managed to do the scene after a ten-minute break. In spite of this hiatus, Kramer described her as "a great technician. There's nobody in the entertainment world today, actor or singer, who can run the complete range of emotions, from utter pathos to power . . . the way she can . . . She's like a piano. You touch any key, and a pure note of emotion comes out." The extent to which he directed her, however, is debatable, since he employed George Roy Hill as adviser on the set.

Garland said that she had not realized how much she missed the camaraderie of filming, and had forgotten how long the hours were:

Movie-making from dawn to dusk is quite a shock after years of concert dates, when you sing your heart out and then go home. People on the set are wonderful. But picture-making is never really satisfying to me because you are doing it in little bits and pieces. On the stage, at the end of a concert, the audience reaction is to your total effort for the evening—and it's a better and more exhilarating gauge as to how well you've done.

When her part was finished, she took a short vacation with her family, which on this occasion included Luft, since he and Garland had been reconciled since Joey's birthday on March 29.

On her last night before resuming the tour, she was at a party when Kramer telephoned her to say that he, Mann, Widmark and Tracy had been watching her performance for the first time in the rough-cut. When it was finished, they stood up to applaud. On hearing this, she said, she really cried for the first time since returning to Hollywood.

She recommenced the tour in Buffalo on April 6. Luft was with her again when she sang in Constitution Hall in Washington, D.C., on April 8, and the following day they went as husband and wife to a dinner party hosted by Robert and Ethel Kennedy at the White House. Kennedy lent her his car and gave her a copy of Irving Stone's novel about Michelangelo, *The Agony and the Ecstasy.* She said that she could not concentrate on reading, however: "On the day after a concert I'm mentally weary from remembering all the lyrics."

Luft left on business and she proceeded to Birmingham, Atlanta and Charlotte and Greensborough in North Carolina. After the Charlotte concert, she became dejected and then angry about being separated from the children: "Godammit," she shouted, wrote Gerold Frank, "I work my ass off, making money for everybody, can't even have my children with me!" Alves managed to calm her down, but later that night, he awoke to find her in anguish, pounding the wall and sobbing. (When traveling with her, he always slept in the next room and kept his door ajar.) Once again, he soothed her. As had happened before, she was cheerful and healthy by the morning, eating her normal truck driver's breakfast of orange juice, ham, eggs, hash-browns and toast.

The outburst was symptomatic of a psychological trouble as complex as any in the past. She was being flogged as hard as at any time since her days at Metro, and the better she became, the more she worried about being up to standard—just as Laurence Olivier, at the same stage in his career (after he became director of the National Theater), began to suffer from appalling stage fright. Garland returned to her habit of threatening not to go on. Begelman and Fields learned that the best way to calm her was to sing her songs to her in the dressing-room. Usually they would still be beside her in the wings, one each side, hollering to the overture: "The road gets rougher / It's lonelier and tougher." When it was over, they would egg her on, knowing that by this time, at last, she was as exhilarated by the prospect of the evening as the audience out front. The outcome always delighted her.

Except for her fear of failing, and she had been racked by nerves before every performance she had given since the Palladium in 1951, she *was* happy. She knew that she was always at her best when she was in love, and she was in love with David Begelman. Indeed, she knew that she had never sung better in her entire career.

"I have a tremendous desire to please," she told an interviewer.

I have a quite sincere love for people who pay for tickets, drive to theaters, park cars and sit in uncomfortable seats. I do wish people would feel everything I sing, hear the words and be affected by them. You must remember that over the years, multitudes of people have shown me a great deal of love and loyalty, a very, very deep love. The papers have often given me bad publicity. Some writers said I was through but, by God, the audiences came and bolstered me. What they were saying was, "We don't give a damn what the papers say, we love you." That's why I could never cheat on a performance, or coast through. My emotions are involved.

It was this emotional involvement, both with her audience and with her songs, that made Garland such an exciting stage performer. The stage director, Harold Clurman, caught this precisely five years earlier, when he wrote:

She is at bottom a sort of early twentieth-century country kid, but the marks of the big city wounds are upon her. Her poetry is not only in the things she survived, but in a violent need to pour them forth in vivid popular form, which makes her the very epitome of the theatrical personality. The tension between the unctuously bright slickness which is expected of her medium and environment and the fierceness of what her being wants to cry out produces something positively orgiastic in the final effect.

In his memoirs, Clurman's erstwhile colleague, Elia Kazan, tried to define "greatness" in a performer. He invoked Caruso and Callas, Raimu in *La Femme du Boulanger*, Garbo in *Camille* and "Judy Garland, at the end of her life, giving you flashes (by lightning, Hazlitt might have added, as he did of Kean) of her own life's pain when she sang the pop-blues."

The pre-eminent date of the tour was Carnegie Hall on April 23, and all available tickets had been bought within hours of going on sale. Many of those buying remembered that they had been unable to get tickets for Garland's week-long engagement at the much larger Metropolitan Opera House. There was a "buzz" in New York about the "new" Judy Garland. Outside the theater, touts were demanding $500 a ticket, and there were enough people to ask, as the doors remained closed until minutes before the curtain was due to rise. This led to the dreadful speculation that the star was not going to appear. She had in fact been in her dressing-room since five, petrified by fear and damned if she was going to go on. Fields and Begelman always took these threats seriously, but they had never seen her so adamant before. In the auditorium, the atmosphere was electric with anticipation; there was almost no time for the usual socializing in the very few minutes left before Mort Lindsey conducted the opening bars of the overture at 8:40.

Among those in the audience were Spencer Tracy, Julie Andrews, Lauren Bacall and Jason Robards (whom she married a few weeks later), Henry Fonda, Rock Hudson, Leonard Bernstein, Betty Comden and Adolph Green, Anthony Perkins, Eli Wallach and Anne Jackson, Hedda Hopper, Richard Burton, Carol Channing, Myrna Loy, Mike Nichols, Dore Schary, Merv Griffin, Henny Youngman (who was standing because he could not get a seat) and—especially gratifying to Garland—Kay Thompson, Roger Edens, Chuck Walters and Harold Arlen. Later, most of them were to go to a reception at Luchow's, the palatial German restaurant on 14th Street.

Only too aware of Garland's psyche at such times, Edens said:

It's right down deep inside: good, solid, raw talent creates excitement. That was the charm of the Carnegie Hall concert. I had never seen her on [a concert] stage before. I still don't believe anything like this could happen. She practically burnt the house down. She said "Let's do it," as though she had never done it before. It's there and when she touches it, it emerges. It's alchemy.

The Carnegie Hall concert has often been described as "the greatest night in show business history." The concert lasted over two and a half hours. *Variety* recorded that: "After her 24th number of the evening, she halted the tumultuous applause demanding still another encore with, 'We just don't have much more.' To which a voice from one of the boxes responded, 'Just stand there.' " In the event, she sang two more old favorites, "After You've Gone" and "Chicago." "Nothing in show business will ever top it," exclaimed Merv Griffin. "No Broadway opening, film premiere, nothing. Garland—performer and legend were one that night, and magic. All New York turned out to see her, and Judy left us standing on our chairs, weeping and cheering and totally drained."

Several critics noticed how well Garland looked: she had lost weight and was showing this off in a sheath dress and mandarin jacket. She appeared more confident and slender than in years. There was, however, an awkward moment during the second half when someone, who had clearly read of her problems with drink and weight, shouted out "Metracal" when Garland paused to take a glass of water. She froze, uncertain whether it was a joke posing as an insult or vice versa, and was so thrown off-balance that she introduced "If Love Were All" as "Bitter Sweet," which is the name of the show from which it came. She soon recovered, however, for she was among friends. She introduced Harold Arlen after singing his "Come Rain or Come Shine."

As the reviewers noted, Garland had conquered New York even more spectacularly than before. According to *Variety*, she had "pulled in a $20,100.62 gross" and a few days later, in a generous mood, told Luft that Kingsrow Enterprises were prepared to pay him $400 a week as associate producer for the tour. They went to P. J. Clarke's to celebrate, staying until four in the morning because Luft was discussing horses with the manager. Going home, she told him she wasn't interested in horses, but in her offer, which was made in gratitude for all that he had done for her. She wanted to know if he would accept it. Considering what he had done, $400 was not very much. It was also a mere "two-bit tip for a groom" compared to what she was now earning, and almost no help at all in paying off his considerable debts. Tempers rose; she slapped his face and he told her to "shove" the offer.

The second lap of the tour began in Philadelphia a week after the Carnegie Hall concert. After the performance, she became convinced that she was coming down with laryngitis, though it was probably just nerves. Begelman reminded her that she did not have another performance for several days, and at the hotel he tried to soothe her by reading her her reviews. Feeling miserable this was not what she wanted; she swore at him and ran from the room. Alves tried to comfort her after Begelman left. She told him that she did not want Lorna and Joey, asleep along the corridor, to know what had happened. He stayed until she fell asleep, but was awakened by her screams in the early hours. She was naked and trying to break everything in sight. He knew immediately that she had drugged herself to the point that she did not know what she was doing. At this period in her life, despite the frequent warnings from Dr. Marc about the danger of taking even an occasional Ritalin pill, she was now taking twenty a day. It was hardly surprising that she was subject to violent mood swings and that her behavior was erratic. Alves found her trying to open the lounge window, screaming that she wanted to throw herself out. It occurred to him that if she had been really serious about this, she could have done it without waking him first.

He managed to pull her over to the sofa and pin her down until she stopped shaking. Finally, white-faced, then, according to Gerold Frank, she said: "Let me go and clean up." She turned to him, "Oh shit, Vern . . . I guess—what the hell, it's no different now than it's been all my life. Why should I expect people to be considerate and understanding? They never were. So what the hell! Why am I killing myself over this?"

Back in New York that evening she asked Alves to stay with her because she was unwell. He wanted to go home to clean up because he had taken just one change of clothes to Philadelphia, but he remained until she fell asleep. When he returned the next morning, he found her quarreling with Luft, who had also arrived. She turned on Alves and told him that because of him she was now really sick, and to Luft she said: "You can get your ass out of here and take that little boyfriend with you." Alves returned to the West Coast. He had endured Garland's tantrums on and off for ten years. Enough was enough.

She soon forgave Begelman for his behavior in Philadelphia. She had added a new song to her repertoire, "Just in Time." And once, at a party, writes John Fricke, she came to the lines "No more doubt and fear / I've found my way," she always looked at him and Fields.

"You two are the luckiest thing that ever happened to me," she told them. "You're the best thing that ever happened to me," Field replied. "What a terrible thing!" she exclaimed. "What if I turned into a sentimental slob?"

She played engagements in Chicago, Dallas, Houston, Detroit and Cleveland, returning to Carnegie Hall for another sell-out concert and equally rapturous acclaim. She had just received a matrix from Capitol of the first show there, and she knew that it was sensational.

She had a free week in early June and flew to London, alone, to spend it with Dirk Bogarde and his companion, Anthony Forwood. On her last night they threw a party, from a guest list she had drawn up, which included Noël Coward, who was delighted to discover that since they had last sung together she had learned the lyrics of almost all his songs. She herself was delighted to receive a telephone call from Stanley Kramer offering her a role in a film about retarded children, *A Child Is Waiting*. She was also scheduled to appear in a picture called *The Lonely Stage*, which would be produced in England by Stuart Millar and Lawrence Turman, so it looked as though her film career was well and truly resuscitated. Begelman and Fields were discussing projects with M-G-M and the Mirisch brothers, who were among the classiest producers of the time. Her touring days would soon be over.

In spite of his celebrated difficulties with Marilyn Monroe on *Some Like It Hot* (1959), Billy Wilder was prepared to work with the by now famously uncooperative Garland. Indeed, he was so enthusiastic to cast her in *Irma La Douce*, which the Mirisch brothers were to produce, that he suggested altering the internationally successful play about a French hooker and a *flic* in order to incorporate more songs. Nothing came of this, however.

There is a story that one of the M-G-M projects was *Gypsy*, adapted from the Jule Styne–Stephen Sondheim musical about Gypsy Rose Lee and her formidable mother. A former member of the Freed unit later wrote to *American Film* magazine claiming that George Sidney had successfully negotiated for the rights of the show and had rung Dore Schary to give the good news, announcing: "I've got the film for Judy!" Schary was equally enthusiastic until he realized that Sidney was referring to Garland—who would certainly have suited the part of Mama Rose, the stage mother to end all stage mothers—rather than Judy Holliday. As a result of this, the deal was off. Sidney later dismissed this story as untrue.

Later, however, Freed seriously considered Garland for *Say It*

With Music, a musical built around an anthology of songs by Irving Berlin, to be directed by Minnelli. Other names associated with the project included Frank Sinatra, Sophia Loren and Julie Andrews, but it was eventually canceled during a change of management at Metro which sent Freed into retirement.

Meanwhile, back in New York, Garland sang to a capacity audience of 13,704 at the Forest Hills Tennis Club, on July 1, and two days later she took part in the "Music at Newport" jazz festival on Rhode Island. She found herself in the afternoon sun, on a small bandstand ten feet high, facing a vast sea of deck chairs, of which only 7,650 were occupied. She also found herself obliged to cope with the jazz aficionados who moved aimlessly among the seats, but the gross was $25,000.

At the suggestion of Robert Kennedy, she had taken a house at Hyannis Port for the summer. When Luft read in the paper that she had been hospitalized with a kidney complaint, which he knew from long experience was more likely to be an overdose, he called her doctor, who refused to discuss the matter over the telephone. When Garland found that he had spoken to her doctor, she called him to say that he was interfering. He said he wanted to see the children and she told him to speak to her lawyer. When he arrived in Hyannis Port, he was invited to the Kennedys, but Garland told him that because she was going he was not to accept. A few days later, she told him that she was once again filing for divorce.

22

I Could Go On Singing

JUDY AT CARNEGIE HALL was released in July 1961, in a two-record set. At the time the concert was recorded, *Variety* had predicted: "Even pruned to the limitations of an LP's running time, it should be a socko platter." It certainly was. Almost immediately it went to the Number One spot on the *Billboard* chart, where it remained for thirteen weeks. No other double-album—and certainly not one retailing at $10—had ever done remotely as well as that, and it remained in *Billboard*'s "Top Forty" for an astonishing seventy-three weeks. It also won five Grammy awards, including Album of the Year and Best Female Vocalist. It brought Garland a vast new army of admirers and made the industry regard her in a very different light. Sometimes she had been dismissed as merely the darling of the gay set, but anyone who could outsell Elvis Presley was a force to be reckoned with.

The record made Judy Garland the hottest attraction in show business, and Begelman and Fields lost no time in capitalizing on it. She had to interrupt her summer vacation to make a second appearance at Forest Hills on July 30, and again on August 4 to sing at Convention

Hall in Atlantic City. At the same time she made arrangements to rent a house in Scarsdale, a solid middle-class suburb of New York. She had no intention of returning to live in Los Angeles: "I hate the sun. For thirty-six years I looked out of the window and there it was, always the same. And I don't like swimming pools."

A week after the Atlantic City concert, she went to Boston with Kay Thompson and John Springer for the out-of-town opening of Noël Coward's *Sail Away*. As she walked down the aisle, she was greeted with applause, but during the intermission a woman said: "That's Judy Garland. She's so fat." Thompson hissed, "Shut up, you stupid bitch." "So what did I say?" the woman replied. "She *is* fat." Garland was destroyed. She wanted to leave, but Springer managed to persuade her that walking out of a Coward first night would be an insult to him and to everyone concerned. When the show was over, Thompson went to the first-night party, but Garland insisted upon returning to her hotel. She said nothing in the car, nor in her suite, and went to her bedroom while Springer watched television. After an hour, she reappeared, radiant, the incident forgotten. Springer took her to the party, where Coward greeted her by saying: "At last we can begin." He led her to a table where an aged couple were sitting. No one spoke, and after ten minutes Garland whispered to Springer: "I don't want to sit here with this dreary man and this dreary woman." Springer whispered back: "They're the Lunts." Without missing a beat, Garland cried: "Oh Miss Fontanne! Oh Mr. Lunt! I've always been such a great admirer of yours."

While still at Hyannis Port she had agreed to a busy schedule. The Atlantic City concert had been so successful that she had to follow it up with appearances nationwide; the autumn tour was to begin in San Francisco at the Civic Auditorium ten days later, followed by Denver a week after that and, in between, there was to be an appearance at the Hollywood Bowl. After the show there, Begelman and Fields promised to celebrate the event with a huge party. This boded well until, while still resting on Cape Cod, Garland found out that they had already given an elegant shindig in Hollywood without bothering to ask her. She was so annoyed that she decided to ask Roger Edens to host the Hollywood Bowl festivities instead. She rang Edens, but he was unavailable, so she then rang Leonard Gershe, who said that Edens was on location and could not be reached by telephone. When she complained about the way she had been treated, Gershe tried to point out that Begelman and Fields could hardly have supposed that she would have wanted to attend their party, seeing that she was on the opposite side of the country at the time. A few days later, she called again, furious because she had heard that Gershe was going around telling people that Begelman and Fields wanted to drop her. He tried to reason with her, but she refused to listen. Edens had told Gershe before he left that in no circumstances was he to let Garland have his telephone number. Now, Gershe too felt that Garland's tantrums were too much for anyone to handle. Her intemperance cost her dear: she lost Roger Edens.

It was to be a full week in Los Angeles. She had to do some retakes on *Judgment at Nuremberg*, and the thought of them sent her back into hysteria. She had to sing at the Hollywood Bowl that same evening, with over 18,600 seats sold, a sell-out capacity crowd. If she came down with laryngitis, that meant an awful lot of refunds to be made. The prospect terrified her. "I won't, I won't, I won't!" she was shouting at four in the morning, beating the floor with her fists. Fields alerted Stanley Kramer, who assured her that he could reschedule the filming. Chuck Walters and other old friends tried to calm her down. It took them four hours.

That night, just before she was about to go on stage it began to drizzle: some people had brought umbrellas, and others pulled their coats over their heads, but no one left. The audience went wild at the end, and Garland was so overcome by the response—almost twenty thousand sodden people on their feet, shouting their heads off, unwilling to leave—that after "Chicago" she was made to sing "San Francisco" for the second time.

There were other equally memorable concerts on the tour: in Denver she played to 7,500 people, in Pittsburgh to 12,500, and at the Boston Garden, again in a vast auditorium, to 13,909. At this last concert, the demand for tickets was such that the management printed them for seats not normally sold, behind the stage and with obstructed views. She also played dates in Newark, White Plains, Rochester and Haddonfield in New Jersey and Hartford, Connecticut. In each case she appeared in the largest auditorium available, sometimes an ice rink or a football stadium. The tour concluded at the Forum, Montreal, with two dates to follow in early December; at the newly opened O'Keefe Center, Toronto, for two nights; and the National Guard Armory in Washington for one—an astonishing record of forty-two concerts in ten months. This was a woman who, two years before, had been given five years to live at best and had been told that she could never work again.

* * *

In November, she had stayed in Los Angeles to record the soundtrack for an animated feature, *Gay Purr-ee*. The film was produced by UPA, a company which had managed, over the past few years, to usurp Disney's position as the most admired maker of short cartoons. *Gay Purr-ee* was the first major attempt to challenge Disney's supremacy in feature-length cartoons since the Fleischer brothers had failed in the early 1940s. Warner Bros. was to distribute and, most importantly from Garland's point of view, the songs had been composed by Harold Arlen and Yip Harburg, who had established another sort of supremacy in the field of movies for children with *The Wizard of Oz*.

Garland provided the voice of Mewsette, an amorous cat from Provence who, arrived in Paris, forgets her faithful swain, Jaune-Tom, as the dubious Mme Rubens-Chatte prepares her for a wealthy American bridegroom. Robert Goulet, then appearing in *Camelot*—and described by Judy as "an eight-by-ten glossy"—supplied the voice of Jaune-Tom, and the English comedienne Hermione Gingold that of the madame. "Judy was delightful and I adored her," said Gingold. "She had a fragile, nervous quality—one moment giggling and joking and the next seeming close to tears. Then she'd laugh again, and as soon as the recording tape started rolling, she'd concentrate with all the intensity of the professional she was, only to collapse again in giggles again when 'cut' was called."

Fields had negotiated for 10 percent of the gross, above and beyond a fee of $50,000 for the dubbing. As it turned out, the film contributed little to the Garland coffers (beyond her fee) or the Garland legend. She dutifully sang two songs—"Little Drops of Rain," "Paris Is a Lonely Town"—in concerts during 1962, but they were not among Arlen's best. Furthermore, the animation was a far cry from UPA's innovative work of a decade earlier. When the film was released in November 1962, *Newsweek* commented: "There seems to be an effort to reach a hitherto undiscovered audience—the fey four-year-old of recherché taste." Business on the U.S. bookings was so poor that Warners either did not open it at all overseas, or else sold it to television.

October also saw the first televising of *A Star Is Born*. Garland drove from Scarsdale to Manhattan to find Luft. Her chauffeur telephoned him from the lobby and he went down to find her sitting in the car with an ice bucket and a bottle of champagne. "You produced a great picture," she told him, wrote Gerold Frank. He replied: "Judy, it's your picture and you were great in it and it's great to see you again." They went to El Morocco to celebrate, and he returned to Scarsdale with her that night. They remained reunited, and it was he who in early December, paid by Creative Management Associates (as Freddie Fielding Associates was renamed), flew to Europe to escort her back when she was taken ill with pneumonia. She had gone there for two premieres of *Judgment at Nuremberg*, the first in West Berlin, at which Spencer Tracy, Montgomery Clift, Maximilian Schell and Richard Widmark were also present. She went on to Rome for a few days before going to the London premiere, which the Duke of Edinburgh was to attend, but she missed it because of her illness.

Bosley Crowther, writing in the *New York Times*, judged her performance "amazingly real" and, as she hoped, she was nominated for an Academy Award as Best Supporting Actress. She lost to Rita Moreno for *West Side Story*, who also took the Golden Globe, for which Garland had also been nominated. But at the latter ceremony, Garland was presented with the special award named after Cecil B. de Mille for services to the industry.

She knew she would need to lose weight and, in the first weeks of 1962 did manage it, if not as much as she would have liked. She was slimmer than she had been since *A Star Is Born* when she came to tape her television special in January. It was originally to be called *Miss Show Business*, but CBS decided that this was not entirely right for the mass television audience, and retitled it *The Judy Garland Show*.

Fields and Begelman spared no expense in assembling a creative team, which included the producer-director Norman Jewison, who had established a name in American television after leaving his native Canada. "I was loath to do it," he said, "as I had seen her at the Palladium in 1960 and wanted to remember her as she was then. She talked me into it, and I went out to some ice rink in [Haddonfield] New Jersey on a rainy night. She gave a performance to six thousand people and I couldn't stand it, everything was still there. Such charisma. I agreed to do the special." Kay Thompson was appointed creative consultant and Mort Lindsey was put in charge of the music. Garland herself chose her costumes, determined the lighting and directed herself for the camera. As she said: "If I didn't know how to do these things, I'd be pretty dumb after all these years. It's a protection for me to have technical knowledge."

For the guest appearances, ten names were submitted, from which Garland and Jewison had to choose two. They settled on Frank Sinatra and Dean Martin, but were worried that Sinatra might not be prepared to do it for the fee, which was much less than he was usually paid. In the event, he was happy to do it, even when asked whether he and Martin would mind rehearsing in the evenings, since Garland was at her best then. The tapings were also done at night.

Jewison had devised a simple formula: three singers singing, with virtually no chitchat. They sang fifteen songs in the hour (allowing for commercials), and Sinatra set the tone when he sang to Garland: "You're just too marvelous, too marvelous for words." The studio audience clearly agreed, applauding wildly in a deliberate attempt to invoke the hysteria of a Garland concert. Jewison knew his star—only someone of her caliber could get away with this as the images were beamed into ordinary homes. The final section of the show featured Garland alone: "The last seventeen minutes of that show was the most exciting TV I ever did," Jewison recalled.

The program went out on Sunday, February 25, and enough people deserted *Bonanza*, NBC's highly rated Western series, to take *The Judy Garland Show* into over twelve and a half million homes. She "held television in the palm of her hand last night," said Jack Gould in the *New York Times*. "In her first video appearance in six years the singer carried on the music hall tradition of Al Jolson and other greats; she sang her heart out with emotion, energy and magnetism . . . easily the most melodic hour of several TV seasons . . ."

She went on to work on *A Child Is Waiting*, the Kramer film in which she was to co-star with Burt Lancaster. The filming was a nightmare, though for once this was not of her making, alone. As with *Judgment at Nuremberg*, the screenplay had been adapted by Abby Mann from a television play he had written, originally shown in 1957. For the first time in almost a decade, Kramer was going to restrict himself to producing. As director, he had chosen Jack Clayton, but both Clayton and Ingrid Bergman, who had originally been cast in the Garland role, left the film when Lancaster was cast. With Lancaster's arrival, the budget increased considerably, which worried Kramer, since he knew that the film would appeal only to limited audiences. To replace Clayton, he chose John Cassavetes, a young actor-director who had enjoyed a *succés d'estime* in 1960 with his semi-amateur production, *Shadows*. The overall plot concerned a clash between a teacher (Garland), who responds to the pupils emotionally, and the school's principal (Lancaster), who works by the book. Appropriately enough, the Garland character is a failed musician in her thirties who thinks that she has at last found something useful to do with her life.

The Screen Actors Guild had given permission for genuinely retarded children to appear in the film rather than child actors, and this made it an emotional experience for Garland, to whom the cause of the mentally handicapped was dear. Cassavetes felt that the film's subject matter called for a raw, edgy quality to the film, but Kramer clashed with him over this, as did Lancaster, who at this stage of his career was not about to agree to anything which interfered with his idea of what the Burt Lancaster image should be. As the script has it, the Garland character eventually comes to realize that the Lancaster character's methods are the right ones, and a similar set of circumstances arose on the set. Lancaster, who had once tried to give Laurence Olivier acting lessons (with the result that Olivier walked out of a co-starring role with him in *Separate Tables*), insisted upon telling Garland how to play her role. He was considerate and encouraging— and also far too much of a force for her to resist. For the first time since her days with Mickey Rooney (cameo appearances aside), she was billed second, and she found herself caught in a trap, contending with the combined intransigence of Lancaster and Cassavetes. Although Kramer was more amenable, he too was a Hollywood professional, only too anxious to bow to the wishes of his leading star.

Cassavetes disowned the result:

Kramer had me replaced and the picture re-edited to suit himself. I didn't think his film—and that's what I consider it to be, *his* film—was so bad, just a lot more sentimental than mine. The philosophy of his film was that retarded children are separate and alone and therefore should be in institutions with others of their kind. My film said that retarded children should be anywhere, anytime, and that the problem is that we're a bunch of dopes, that it's our problem more than the kids'.

He went on to explain that by double-cutting on the close-ups Kramer had managed to sentimentalize the subject. He might have mentioned that at those moments which invite audiences to respond, a syrupy score by Ernest Gold has been coated on to ensure that they do. Lancaster is self-conscious, outshone by his co-star, who acts with warmth. She is still rather puffy, and many of her stances are the deliberately casual ones familiar from her concert appearances. There is spontaneous emotion in the one scene in which she sings, getting the children to join in a nursery rhyme. Her coal-black eyes seem always on the verge of tears, which is absolutely right for the character, and all the more touching because Cassavetes keeps her mannerisms to the minimum. "Garland and Lancaster radiate a warmth so genuine that one is certain that the children are responding to them, not merely following some vaguely comprehended script," wrote Arthur Knight in the *Saturday Review*.

Garland was due to begin another film almost immediately. *The Lonely Stage* had long been in preparation and had been postponed several times because of script troubles. Late in 1960 Stuart Millar and Laurence Turman had produced a film called *The Young Doctors*, a mildly successful hospital soap opera, and at that time they had commissioned Robert Dozier to write a screenplay for Garland, one that reflected to some extent her own life. Millar and Dozier had worked together in 1957 on *The Young Stranger*, an autobiographical piece based on Dozier's relationship with his father, who had once been production chief of RKO. *The Lonely Stage* also concerned a child's relationship with his parents, who in this case are divorced. His father, with whom the boy lives, is a Harley Street doctor, and his mother is an American singer. During an engagement at the London Palladium, the mother decides to ask for the boy back and, because the father refuses, she tries to win the child over with a rather tardy display of mother-love. The executives at United Artists, who had produced *The Young Doctors*, had little enthusiasm for the project, but, with Garland continuing to triumph in city after city on her concert tour, it could hardly be denied that the public wanted to see her.

She had first discussed the film with the press some weeks before the Carnegie Hall concert, when she said that her co-star would probably be Olivier. When he declined, however, she decided that it should be Dirk Bogarde, whom a year earlier she had announced as her partner in the long-delayed film based upon a novel called *Born in Wedlock*, which she and Luft had bought back in 1956. Bogarde had been popular in Britain for over a decade, but his four American-backed films had done little or nothing to establish him as a draw in the States. United Artists wanted an American actor in the role, or at least a bigger name, but Garland's will prevailed.

She was in the habit of telephoning Bogarde in what were the early hours of the morning, British time, and this was how he first heard that she wanted him to co-star in the film. She did not exactly sell the project to him: "It stinks," she said. Bogarde's response, not unnaturally, was to tell her that if this was the case, she should not be doing the film. She replied that she liked the *idea* of it: "This big, big star goes to London to do a concert and finds the man who got away . . . It's about me; I guess someone read my lyrics." The project was nothing like as promising a film as *Funny Girl*, which she had turned down, and her insistence upon playing the role in *The Lonely Stage* is another example of her penchant for living her life publicly.

Filming had to begin almost immediately, since Bogarde was due to start another film in July. This meant that Garland had only three weeks free between finishing *A Child Is Waiting* and starting work on the new movie. During that time she was hospitalized with a severe throat infection, and she filed for divorce yet again. One of the attractions of filming in Britain would be to get Lorna and Joey well away from Luft, but the practical arrangements proved beyond her. She was used to having things done for her and when the time came for her to leave for London in April, the children were found to be with their father. She called John Springer and Begelman in panic, and Begelman provided two strong-arm men who went to Luft's hotel suite and held him down while Garland removed the children. Liza, who had been visiting friends, joined them soon later, and they all set off for the airport. Lorna was entranced by the excitement of it all, but Joey was crying. Garland tried to comfort him by reminding him how much he liked *Oliver!*, which they would be able to see again in London, and she tried to get him to sing one of the songs from the show, "Food, Glorious Food." Luft arrived at the airport just as the plane took off, and he later took up the matter with the New York police. For the children's sake, however, he decided not to press charges.

Three days later, Garland told a press conference at the Savoy Hotel in London: "I don't know why Sid says I'm an unfit mother. The children love me. I hear he may be coming over to try to take them away from me. He will never do that. There is no chance of a reconciliation. My marriage is finished." David Begelman interrupted to say: "The studio will make sure that no unauthorized person— even Mr. Luft—will be allowed to see the children at this stage." They were, Garland said, "being guarded night and day in a hideout in Surrey" while lawyers in London arranged for them to be made wards of the court.

The "hideout" was the house the studio had rented for her next to the golf course in Sunningdale, in the mistaken belief that she liked to play a round. She quickly informed them that they were wrong, and although another was found, just off Hyde Park, the harm had been done. As far as she was concerned, the British executives of United Artists were bumbling amateurs.

It was not the most congenial time in her life to start on a movie, but matters seemed to be eased, as they often were, when she fell in love. At last, she told Dorris and Nunnally Johnson, it was "the real thing." She would not tell them who the man was, but the following day she informed Nunnally that it was Dirk Bogarde. When Johnson told his wife, they looked at each other in despair: once again, Garland had chosen the wrong man. The Johnsons could not be sure whether Bogarde would discourage her sufficiently, or whether she would take any notice if he did. She told one interviewer: "I have found some maturity now, and I think for myself, and out of everything that has happened I have love to return to people who offer it to me." When he asked her what she had learned for the future, she replied: "It is that everything passes. Friends go, and husbands and lovers and you can't stop it. You just have to rely on yourself. I think I can—now."

This was certainly true, and had been for years, but there were many things she chose not to do. So she turned to Bogarde and played up her role as "helpless Judy." Bogarde asked his agent, Dennis Van Thal, to assist her with her domestic problems, while he himself undertook to sort out the professional ones. The first of these was the script, now credited to one Mayo Simon, "from a story by" Dozier. The changes the studio had promised to make had not been carried out and Garland was not feeling co-operative. "It won't be the first contract I've broken," she told Bogarde. "I can't play this crap." Obligingly, but in desperation, he rewrote the first scene they were to do together. She was delighted.

The second problem was the British director, Ronald Neame, whose two most recent films with Alec Guinness, *The Horse's Mouth* and *Tunes of Glory*, had been much liked in the United States. His most recent film, *Escape From Zahrain*, was the first of the many he was to make for the American studios. Garland had approved him, partly because his reputation as a mild-mannered craftsman suggested that she could dominate him. This proved not to be the case. Like everyone else on the film, he had been looking forward to working with her. The first sign of trouble came when Begelman announced that he was returning to the States, three days before shooting was to begin. As Garland berated him for deserting her, he looked at Neame with pity, as if to say: "You see what you're in for?"

The first day was spent on location at the Palladium, which had to be cleared for the evening performance by 4:30 p.m. Garland was performing to a pre-recorded "Hello Bluebird" and did not think Neame was sufficiently appreciative. She told Bogarde: "Just tell Neame he'd better watch out for me. *I* get scared—he thinks he's the only one? I need help and trust. I don't trust him. I want him off the production."

"At times she could be unbearable," said Neame, "do and say terrible things. When I was her friend, I was 'Pussycat'; when I was her enemy I was 'The British Henry Hathaway.' She tried to destroy me on two separate occasions and yet there was this aura of magic that made working with her a wonderful experience. Nobody who wasn't on that set could have understood it." She was incapable of behaving the same way for more than a couple of hours at a time. When she was difficult, which was most of the time, it was not prompted by viciousness but by a consuming fear which prevented her from performing.

After one particularly trying day, she telephoned Neame from the local inn in which she was staying overnight. It was seven o'clock, and she was already in bed, with three bottles of Blue Nun on the table beside her. She was sick with a fever, and wanted a doctor. "Ronnie" would have to get one. He did so, with great difficulty, but Garland was not satisfied: she wanted another doctor. "How do I get a doctor who is going to do what you tell him to do?" Neame asked. He did eventually find another one, and he asked him to do all he could to see that she was on the set the following day. He apparently did, for she was and she gave no trouble.

Even so, she was unreliable. Neame decided that nothing he could say would prevent her from coming in late, or not at all. Bogarde, however, pointed out to her that if the delays continued he faced the prospect of losing the film he had signed to do in July. Garland told him to break the contract, but he had no intention of doing that. In that case, she replied, she would leave when he left, and there would be no *Lonely Stage*. He remonstrated, but she refused to listen. "Don't you tell me what I can't do! Everyone tells me what I can and can't do . . . I do what I want to do . . . and I don't want to shoot one bloody frame on this stinking mess after you have gone. When you leave for your oh-so-marvelous movie, I leave on the first flight to L.A. . . . don't you forget it!" In fact, she left the film so often that she became a familiar figure at London Airport. Because of her legal difficulties over the children, her passport had been impounded, a circumstance she was inclined to forget—or pretend that she had.

As in the past, filming was accompanied by further turmoil in her life. Luft had followed her to London, and she had readily agreed to let him see the children. Through lawyers, they fought for custody, with Garland claiming that she had been the sole breadwinner throughout the marriage and that, as her manager, he had made engagements for her without her consent. One deposition charged that he had not contributed "one penny piece" to the care of Lorna and Joey.

These wrangles clearly affected her ability to work, and to many she seemed to be living in her own world, expecting everyone else to be a part of it. Saul Chaplin, the musical supervisor, remembered one occasion during pre-recording when she turned up at seven in the evening for a rehearsal set up for eleven-thirty in the morning. She "didn't think anything was wrong," he said.

> Now, you'd expect some kind of apology—but no. Nothing. Her attitude was, "What's wrong with that?" She wasn't being temperamental or playing the star. It was just that she seemed to have no sense of time. When she got there, she'd be fine. She'd work till seven the next morning, if you asked her to—so you couldn't get mad at her.

Chaplin also noted that when he worked on numbers with most singers, the input was 40 percent his suggestions to 60 percent the performer's interpretation. In Garland's case, this became 10 percent and 90 percent, respectively.

When Garland had come to live in London in 1960, Dirk Bogarde had gone on record as saying: "Judy Garland is the only really enchanting woman in the world." By the end of filming, this enchantment had begun to wear off. There was an especially difficult moment during the one day's location filming at Canterbury. She refused to leave her caravan, and Bogarde went to placate her. It turned out that she was furious because he could not spend the night with her and the children in Folkestone, as she had planned. It was axiomatic: Judy Garland always got her way. When people attempted to steer a different course, she was not pleased, and she tried to stab Bogarde with her luncheon knife and then with her fork. As they struggled, she fell sobbing into his arms. She was ready to resume shooting almost immediately.

On his last week, at the end of June, she was in brilliant form. It was, he said, a week of "complete, unforgettable magic." Urged on by her, Bogarde had rewritten the scene in which the plot reaches a climax, before her character, Jenny Bowman, returns to the Palladium stage, with notions of mother-love forgotten. She was supposed to be drunk, from frustration, and she had been taken to the hospital with a sprained ankle. When her husband arrives, he tells her that he has come to take her to the theater.

"Oh no, you haven't [she replies]. I'm not going back there ever, ever, ever again."

"*They* are waiting."

"I don't care if *they're* fasting. Give them their money back and tell them to come back next fall."

"Jenny, it's a sellout."

"I'm always a sellout."

"You promised."

"The hell with them. I can't be spread so thin. I'm just one person. I don't want to be rolled out like pastry so that everyone has a nice big bite of me. I'm just me. I belong to me. I can do whatever I damn well please and no one can ask any questions."

"You know the last is not true."

". . . and that's final! It's just not worth all the deaths that I have to die."

"You have a show to do. You're going to do it and I'm going to see that you do."

"You think you can make me sing? You can get me there, but can you make me sing? I sing for myself. I sing what I want to, whenever I want to—just for me. I sing for my own pleasure. I'll do whatever I damn well want. You understand that?"

"I understand that. Just hang on to that."

"I've hung on to every bit of rubbish in life there is and thrown away the good bits. Can you tell me why I do that?"

This was the essence of Judy Garland—or the one who felt that there was a constant pressure on her. Even Neame thought she was improvising, and he sensed from the beginning of the scene that he could not strike this exposed raw nerve again. "I knew that I had to shoot it then," he explained, "because it would never happen again. We got in as close as we could and took it." Luck was on his side: normally he would have cut to change the lighting, but, with the crew moving the lights with the camera, he got an eight-minute take. Neame was not the only one to believe the scene was improvised. When the film was released, Penelope Gilliatt, reviewing it in the *Observer*, commented: "There is one single-take scene that should be in every drama-school library; it is obviously improvised, and done with wonderful skill and imaginative energy." Garland and Bogarde had been delighted by Neame's reaction: they had in fact rehearsed the scene for six hours.

Bogarde left that day. "You are walking away from me," Garland complained, "you are walking away, like they all do . . . walking away backwards, smiling." It was true. His loyalty was to his next film, and she resented that. Without his steadying presence, the situation deteriorated. Garland telephoned Neame at three in the morning to say that he would have to shoot around her: "Liza is more important to me than your fucking film. She has to be at the airport at eleven and I'm going with her." Neame asked her to come straight to the studio from Heathrow, but she told him that she might never come in again. At two the following afternoon, the assistant director learned that she was asleep and must not be disturbed. At three, she arrived in a foul temper, with curlers in her hair. When he asked for a retake on one scene, she refused to do it until he told her what was wrong with the first one; and as she started to move away, she said: "I'm not coming back till I'm treated like a lady." He followed her to her trailer, and pleaded with her: "Please let's stop fighting. We both want a good picture." "I'm not coming back till I feel like coming back," she replied.

Sometimes when she was absent, it was because of illness. One night, almost immediately after Bogarde's departure, she rushed to the London Clinic after supposedly cracking her head when she fell in the bathroom, but nobody connected with the film believed this. The tussle over custody of the children was still continuing, and her personal hairdresser, Al Paul, swore on deposition that she had had her stomach pumped at the Clinic. That was the end of his job. Luft, as he always did—even, as now, under great provocation—tried to protect her by not speaking of pills and medication, but by citing instead the fact that she had been treated by more than ten doctors during this trip. In spite of the legal quarrel, Garland asked her estranged husband to look after the children while she was in the Clinic, which he did. The couple were reconciled briefly after she left the hospital, when she thanked him for the roses he had had sent to her on her fortieth birthday. The battle was not over, however.

While she was away, Begelman and Fields came up with the ultimatum that she would not work a minute longer than the second week that was left in the filming schedule, despite the delays caused by her absences. The situation was not, however, in their hands. United

Artists never wavered in their support of Neame. Garland had again tried to have him fired after Bogarde left, and was warned once more that UA would close the picture down, and, with only a week to go, they intended to sue her for every penny expended so far. Privately, they asked Neame if the picture could be shown in its present state. He said that this would be possible only if Bogarde was brought back to do a voice-over to fill in for the missing scenes. Of these, the most important was the final sequence at the Palladium, and the theater had again been booked. Garland announced that she had not made up her mind whether or not she intended to appear. She did, eventually, at one in the afternoon, and shooting proceeded without mishap until five-thirty, when she finished for the day.

The British crew had long ago lost patience with the wayward star. They were astonished by her technical skill, but any liking they had for her had soon faded. At first, she was "Miss Garland," but by the end of the film, behind her back, they referred to her as "It." In fact, her behavior went beyond the pale; her trailer-dressing-room was without its contractual private toilet and rather than take the few steps to the ladies room she would march into the nearest private office, order the occupant out and make use of the wastepaper basket. Even with the prospect of seeing her go, morale remained at zero. John Shirley, who edited the film, found a moment or two not without a touch of the bizarre, as when he told her that due to a fault on the magnetic track her voice—in the hospital scene—had not come across. "I'm perfect," she said. "You fix it."

She finally walked off the set on July 13, yelling: "You'll miss me when I'm gone!" "We never saw her again," Neame recalled, "and, of course, we did miss her." It was curious, he found, that no matter how much she did to enrage and frustrate him or how much he railed against her, he still cared about her.

The pickup shots needed had to be done with a double. The film was unfinished. John Shirley in his editing had no "cover" material and had to use every inch of film shot to get a length of 100 minutes.

The Lufts both attended a hearing in the Law Courts just before she had to fly back to the States. She had asked permission for Lorna and Joey, as wards of the court, to go with her. Her wish was granted. A bewildered Luft told the press: "I'd naturally like everything to work out the best possible way for both of us—and the children. I shall be seeing them before they go. I have been able to see them here. It's all been very amicable—there haven't been any problems.

After all, we're civilized people." He did not mention that the children had spent much of their time being guarded by private detectives.

She flew home on August 12, deeply troubled by Marilyn Monroe's death on August 5. She said later: "I knew Marilyn Monroe and loved her dearly. She asked me for help. Me! I didn't know what to tell her. One night at a party at Clifton Webb's house, Marilyn followed me from room to room. 'I don't want to get too far away from you,' she said, 'I'm scared.' I told her, 'We're all scared. I'm scared, too.'" She clearly identified with the doomed star, and said of her death:

> I don't think Marilyn Monroe really meant to harm herself. It was partly because she had too many pills available, then she was deserted by her friends. You shouldn't be told you're completely irresponsible and be left alone with too much medication. It's too easy to forget. You take a couple of sleeping pills and you wake up in twenty minutes and you've forgotten you've taken them. So you take a couple more, and the next thing you know you've taken too many.

She might have been speaking of herself.

In California, Garland booked into a suite in the Beverly Hills Hotel. With the tour and television series in mind, she had, as usual, undergone a crash diet, surviving on tea alone, and was very edgy. Trouble, never far away, soon greeted her, this time from an unexpected source: her family. It was many years since she had taken any interest in any of her relatives on her father's or mother's side, but she had remained in touch with her sisters, if infrequently and uneasily, since Ethel's death. After Jack Cathcart had resigned as Garland's conductor, he had become musical director of the Riviera in Las Vegas. His marriage to Suzy deteriorated and she had taken refuge in alcohol and promiscuity. A divorce had been inevitable. When Cathcart's new wife announced that she was pregnant, Suzy had taken an overdose. Garland chartered a plane to be with her sister, and Jimmy arrived from Dallas. Once Suzy had recovered, there was a quarrel when Garland claimed that her sisters had not given a damn about her when she had been ill. Jimmy and Suzy retorted that they never knew when she was sick until they read it in the papers, but this failed to pacify her. The atmosphere was soured even further when there was an ill-considered reference to Ethel's funeral. Garland was cursing Luft over the phone, and Jimmy became incensed that she should use such language in front of the children. She wondered aloud why Judy was so sensitive about their mother's funeral, but not about the four-letter words she was throwing about. Garland began yelling at her, telling her repeatedly to "Get out!" They never saw each other again.

Although she had a nightclub engagement in Las Vegas, Garland went to Lake Tahoe in Nevada to sue for divorce again. On the morning of September 15, she was found unconscious in her room and was taken to the Carson-Tahoe Hospital, where Dr. Richard Grundy stated that she was suffering from acute pyelonephritis, an inflammation of the kidney. He denied reports that she had taken an accidental overdose of barbiturates.

Luft telephoned to inquire about her condition, which provoked, in Gerold Frank's words, a bitter exchange. "I'm doing awfully well," she told him. "For two years I've been working and supporting the children, and all these kind of things. *You* try to do as well. And in the meantime, don't bother my friends—or me."

"I'd like to see the children, by the way," Luft said.

"You can see them when the court says you can see them," Garland told him. "I just won't take any more of this nonsense from you anymore, ever. You've got two weeks to go—and then you're out of my life forever!" The argument continued for some time.

"Well, you'll get on your knees one day," Luft said.

"Oh, you won't find me on my knees unless I'm singing 'Mammy.' "

They continued to wrangle until she lost patience.

"Oh, get off the phone and stop bothering people here. Get lost. Just get lost. You can't win."

"I'm not trying to win anything," Luft reasoned. "I'm trying to do the decent thing, as I always have."

"Decent thing!" The concept of this sent her spinning. "You don't know the meaning of the word. Get lost!" She slammed the phone down.

For a long, long time she had not expected her life to be easy, and she knew what she had to do: get out on a stage and sing. Two days after leaving the hospital in Carson City, she opened at the Sahara Hotel in Las Vegas. The engagement was unusual in that she played the dinner shows only, with Ray Bolger taking the midnight house. Bolger had seen her from time to time since *The Harvey Girls*, and was aware of her troubles. He was nevertheless shocked by the state of her nerves: she shook with fright in the wings and was unable to steady herself until she was into the second or third song. He was saddened when she told him that, all her life, all she wanted to do was "eat and hide."

Even so, *Variety* thought her "more dramatically electric than ever, giving her stylized tones a virtual tour de force as she sobs, shouts and caresses." As the four weeks' booking, which had drawn capacity audiences every night, drew to a close, she was asked to stay on for two more weeks. She agreed to do so, but, since the earlier evening acts were booked, she had to start at 2:30 p.m. She still played to standing room only.

During the engagement, her lawyers filed once again for divorce, on the grounds of extreme mental cruelty. In Santa Monica, California, Luft countersued to have the petition dismissed on the grounds that she was not a resident of Nevada, where it had been issued. If it should proceed, he would claim that she was concealing $2,000,000 in "community property," by which he meant her percentages from *Gay Purr-ee, A Child Is Waiting* and *The Lonely Stage*. He demanded 50 percent of these, as well as custody of Lorna and Joey. The case was adjourned for the immediate future.

Gay Purr-ee opened in November, and Garland went to Chicago for the world premiere, because she was already booked for a concert at the huge Arie Crown Theater there two days earlier. She started with "Hello Bluebird," but a local condition called Chicago Throat caused her to pause. "The bluebird is in a little trouble," she said. Then she failed to find the final note of "Please Do It Again." "Oh damn it!" she exclaimed, going to the wings for a glass of water and a peppermint Life Saver. "Why don't you people just mill around for a while?" she said to the audience cheerfully as she tried to clear her throat. Then she tore into "Rockabye Your Baby" and had no further trouble even surpassing herself in "Swanee." Five thousand people gave her a standing ovation at the end, and an estimated three hundred of them raced to the footlights.

She told a reporter that on days when she was doing a concert she went into seclusion, "like Stalin lying in state," and described herself as being "halfway between a nun and an athlete." She also said "I think right now is possibly the best time of my life. I'm really starting to do my best work. I have three marvelous children, and I think I have a brand-new career opening up." She attributed this to her recovery from hepatitis three years earlier.

Also, I turned forty a few months ago, and when you hit that stage you feel that maybe now people won't think of you as a stupid backward child that you wind up and send out on a stage to sing . . . I'm not a half-child any more. Before, nobody ever let me do anything for myself. First my mother, then my husband. Oh, the early days at M-G-M were a lot of laughs. It was all right if you were young and frightened—and we stayed frightened. Look at us—Lana Turner, Elizabeth Taylor, Mickey Rooney and me—we all came out a little ticky and kooky. Now I'm getting too old to be towed around. I'm out of debt, and it's a nice feeling to have money in the bank. I have inner satisfaction and peace of mind for a change.

In the *Chicago Tribune*, Herb Lyon wrote of her press conference: "Chicago's press lads and lassies were overwhelmed by the magic transformation of Judy Garland . . . Judy again has the slender alive face she had during her teenage M-G-M movie days. Her vivacity, honesty and wit entranced the gathering."

The entire nation had the opportunity to sample these qualities on December 7, when she gave her first extended television interview on *The Jack Paar Show*. This was essentially to promote *Gay Purree*, and she sang two songs from it, and duetted with Robert Goulet on another. When Paar thanked her for being on the show, he said: "I don't even belong in the same building with you."

In the *New York Herald Tribune*, John Horn reported:

Judy Garland, seldom looking or sounding better, worked with a new team last night in most congenial surroundings. The upshot was a happy hour of spontaneous fun and joyous song . . . but the night and storytelling honors, thanks to the host's catalytic prompting, belong to Miss Garland. She revealed herself an engaging raconteur with an irrepressible urge to act out her stories, a gift for a telling phrase, and a large store of show business yarns. Her songs, new ones, sung with intensity and vibrance, were the kind of ballads she does best. In her performance, much of the child she was still glowed in the older woman.

Garland said that she liked herself for the first time on television. Acting on the principle that network executives felt similarly, Fields and Begelman began to promote her services in this field.

The struggle for supremacy between NBC and CBS continued, but ABC, tired of forever being Number Three, was beginning to throw checks around, and competition was keen. Television had cast up a host of stars of its own—that is, artists whose presence on television kept viewers at home—but none of these were as attractive as the stars of Hollywood. Gene Kelly had starred in a series *Going My Way* in 1962, and both Jerry Lewis and Danny Kaye had capitulated to offers to appear regularly in 1963. Fields and Begelman convinced

Garland that, by doing a weekly show, she could remain at home with her children, and that she could become very rich—rich enough to retire if she so chose. She was contracted to CBS for specials, and it was that network which won out for a weekly show, starting the following September. The deal was signed at the St. Regis Hotel in New York on December 28, 1962.

There had been one hideous hiccough in these negotiations when Begelman was approached by two Englishmen claiming that they had a photograph, taken in a London hospital, of Garland having her stomach pumped. They planned to sell it to a newspaper unless Garland paid for it. She was obliged to hand over $50,000. Begelman dealt with the matter for her. He considered going to the police, but if any hint of this blackmail was leaked to the press, CBS would ask questions. The company hardly needed reminding of Garland's emotional instability. She burned the picture and the negatives. Asked later by a reporter about a reported blackmail attempt, she said, unfazed: "There was a picture, a medical picture, pumping out my stomach. I think CBS bought it up before the TV series, but I had nothing to do with it."

Early in the new year, Garland, who was in Miami, telephoned Luft in Los Angeles and suggested that they meet at an equidistant point. They settled on New Orleans, and stayed at the same hotel, but in different rooms. They spent two days sightseeing before she suddenly checked out without warning. She did, however, leave an affectionate note. Luft failed to discover the point of the exercise, which was an attempt on Garland's part at a definitive reconciliation. She had endured too many scandalous headlines over the past years, and television viewers liked stars with whom they could identify— that is, happily married women.

She returned to New York almost immediately to tape a special for CBS, clumsily titled *Judy Garland and Her Guests Phil Silvers and Robert Goulet*, which (depending on which press release you read) was either a preview or a pilot for the forthcoming series. It promised songs, chatter and comedy, and was a bonanza for CMA, since they represented all three stars. Kingsrow had wanted Norman Jewison to direct, but he was otherwise engaged, and Charles S. Dubin was signed in his place. CBS and CMA wanted a bright, contemporary *comedy* show, to prove that Garland's series would not simply be trading on nostalgia, even though Garland and Silvers were to reminisce about their days in show business. So they contracted Burt Shevelove and Larry Gelbart, who had written the book of a current

Broadway success, *A Funny Thing Happened on the Way to the Forum*. It was agreed that Shevelove would produce and Gelbart would provide the dialogue for Garland and her guests. Mort Lindsey was to conduct the music, which was arranged by Saul Chaplin.

She opened and closed with two numbers from *The Lonely Stage*, respectively "Hello Bluebird" and "I Could Go on Singing," an old song (from 1926) and a new one, which Arlen and Harburg had written for her. Between these, she sang alone and with Goulet, and traded quips with Silvers in the first comedy routine she had done since her broadcasts with Bing Crosby. The trio also clowned, with quick costume changes. It took five nights to tape it, and Garland was exhausted by the end, falling asleep in her dressing-room before the final shots were complete.

A few days later, on Thursday, February 7, she honored a booking made some months earlier, by opening at Harrah's at Lake Tahoe. The performance on the following Monday was canceled, because she had the flu. She performed on Tuesday, but collapsed in her dressing-room on Wednesday as she prepared to go on stage. It was now announced that she did not have the flu after all, but was suffering from complete exhaustion. The following day she was taken to the hospital for tests. As a result of these, the management of Harrah's announced that she was too tired to continue and substituted Mickey Rooney for the remainder of the booking.

With CBS in mind, who were looking for sponsors for her very expensive show, she let it be known that she had suffered a simple bout of Asian flu, but to Louella Parsons she admitted that she was simply overworked. She added that she and Luft had been reconciled. She then went to New York for discussions with CBS, and flew on to Britain, alone, for the premiere of her film with Bogarde.

United Artists executives were so excited by *The Lonely Stage* that they had forgiven Garland her behavior during its making. They persuaded themselves that it was the best movie about show business since *The Jolson Story* of 1946, and would prove an even bigger hit. With that sort of potential, the film needed a title with a little more zing. It was retitled a month before the trade show where it was seen as *I Could Go on Singing*, after one of its songs. Now people would know it was a musical and that Judy Garland was singing on film again.

Their expectations seemed justified when Garland's arrival in London made the front page of every newspaper. This had only once before happened to a movie star, when Marilyn Monroe arrived to film in Britain in 1956. Garland's plane had been diverted to Manchester because of fog, so she arrived in London by train at St. Pancras Station, where she was met by the stationmaster in a top hat, by the film's producer, Stuart Millar, and hordes of photographers, alerted by the UA press office. She looked wonderful and journalists who remembered the legal battles with Luft which had so marred her previous visit, commented on her new happiness. Among the things making her happy was the money she expected to make from the film, since she was on a percentage, and it looked as though this would make her reasonably rich.

UA's management were further encouraged by the preview audiences, which had applauded when her name appeared on the credits, after each of her four songs, and at the conclusion of the film. This happened again at the premiere, which she attended with Bogarde on March 6. Huge crowds had gathered at the Plaza, Piccadilly Circus, simply to welcome her back and demonstrate their love.

The critics did the same: "A few great players are alchemists, who can turn corn golden; and Judy Garland is one of them," wrote Paul Dehn in the *Daily Herald*.

> The post-Oz personality, which she began to develop in *A Star Is Born*, flowers fully here, and only the plot's banality robs her performance of greatness. The spring of *Meet Me in St Louis* is a distant memory, but the autumn is still a long way off. She is in the August of her days and we are lucky who can be sunstruck for the price of a ticket.

In the *Observer*, Penelope Gilliatt described Garland as "a harrowingly good actress," and Felix Barker in the *Evening News* predicted that the film would "make every highbrow cinéaste grind his teeth and every box-office manager cheer." Few people were impressed with the film's plot, but everyone agreed about Garland's performance, which, as the *Monthly Film Bulletin* put it, proved "once again that a first-class talent can transcend the meanest material and even transmute it by some personal alchemy, at least for as long as one is in the theater, into pure gold." "Watching Judy Garland, I have a surge of affection," wrote Dilys Powell in the *Sunday Times*, reflecting the feelings of many cinemagoers. "Suddenly the intellectual stuff can go hang . . . Suddenly this dazzle of warmth on the screen is the real cinema. This, I say to myself, is it."

While Garland's co-star got his just deserts—"dear, loyal Dirk Bogarde . . . has never acted so self-effacingly well," reported the *New Statesman*'s William Whitebait—her director came in for criticism. David Robinson, in the *Financial Times*, found Garland "as superb as ever, as enchantingly vulnerable, as thrillingly strident. This is why one feels so angry with the director, Ronald Neame, at putting her through such foolish paces." Whatever anyone else had suffered during the making of the film, there was no doubt in the minds of Britain's critics: the movie belonged to Judy Garland.

Basking in this extraordinary adulation, she stayed on in Britain to appear on March 10 in what was then the country's top-rated television program, *Sunday Night at the Palladium*. She also received the highest fee ever paid by that show to an artist, said to be between £2,000 and £3,000 (almost $6,000 and $9,000), which she donated to Lady Hoare's Fund to Aid Thalidomide Children. It was a live show, which she did without a script, but with little in the way of chatter. After the medley of "Almost Like Being in Love" and "This Can't Be Love," she sang—publicly for the first time—Saul Chaplin's "Smile," a mediocre song which she transformed with her reading. She missed her cue on "Comes Once in a Lifetime," and said "Come on . . . Let's stop. We can even stop on television!," before making a successful second try. She finished with the title song of the film. (This was not one of Arlen's more successful songs, and Harburg's lyric was unfortunate. "I could go on singing till the cows come home . . ." was intended, like much of Roger Edens's work for Garland, as a slight send-up, but it did not come out that way. It was generally ridiculed, and did not help a film which, suddenly and unexpectedly, needed all the help it could get.)

There was hardly a person in Britain who did not know that Judy Garland's new film had just opened, but only a handful wanted to see it. Those who had worked on it were astonished. "It's as though there is a big sign outside the theater saying 'Smallpox inside,' " United Artists told Neame. In spite of the spectacular reviews, audiences stayed at home. "People just didn't want to see her on film," Neame recalled. "They would queue for hours to see her on stage, some of them just for the possibility that she would fall flat on her face or something like that. It was a terrible pity." Later, meeting Neame at a party in Hollywood, Garland said: "We did have a good film, didn't we, Pussycat?" He could not help feeling that she was in part to blame for its failure, if only because her behavior had prevented him from shooting the screenplay he had signed to direct. Because of the immense media coverage of her visit, United Artists opened it "wide"— that is, it went out on release immediately after the premiere. Those who did go were as enthusiastic about her performance as the British critics: but the poor regard for the film itself, and its close association with Garland's public persona deterred all but her most ardent admirers. CMA's carefully planned negotiations for Garland's triumphant return to the big screen had been a complete failure. *Gay Purr-ee*, scorned by Warners, was to have its British premiere on television, and United Artists, after the failure of *A Child Is Waiting* in the States, waited until 1966 to show it in Britain.

I Could Go on Singing opened to respectful notices in America in March, at the same time as the Garland-Silvers-Goulet special was broadcast. *Judy at Carnegie Hall* was still on the lists of best-selling records, but the film did as dismally in the States as it had in Britain. In both countries the advertising concentrated on the star: "It's JUDY!" This prompted Judith Crist to write: "Either you are or you aren't—a Judy Garland fan, that is. And if you aren't, forget about her new movie, *I Could Go on Singing*, and leave the discussion to us devotees"—which was not the sort of review to sell the film to a large audience. At least Crist praised Garland's performance; Bosley Crowther, in the *New York Times*, did not even do that: "Considering what Judy Garland has done in movies over the years and how many of her fans still love her, no matter what she does, it is sad to have to say that the little lady is not at the top of her form in her new film."

Crowther's influence was enough to ensure that there would be no Oscars. Few, if any, "failed" pictures ever show up among the nominations. As far as the film industry was concerned, Judy Garland once again proved to be just a name from the past.

23

❖❖❖❖❖❖❖

The Judy Garland
Show

THE DAY AFTER DOING *Sunday Night at the Palladium* Garland flew
to New York, and two days later, March 12, she threw a party to
celebrate Liza's seventeenth birthday. On March 14 she made another
attempt at suicide. The two events were not unrelated.

When Garland had taken a house in Scarsdale, Liza had attended
the local high school there. Her teachers had cast her as Anne Frank
in a school production of *The Diary of Anne Frank*, and after seeing
the performance, her mother had exclaimed, "My God, I've got an
annuity!" While Garland was in Britain making *I Could Go on Singing*,
the Scarsdale high school had obtained a grant enabling it to tour the
play in Israel, Greece and Italy. When the tour had ended, Liza
enrolled at the Sorbonne, but, after only a few days, she decided to
abandon an academic life for show business.

She had flown to New York to tell her father, who said: "Yes, I
think it's about time. You have so much energy you might as well
start using it." Liza had confided her doubts about her mother being
equally amenable. "Well, I'm all for it if that helps," said Minnelli.

"Just tell her as you told me." She flew to Las Vegas, where Garland was appearing at the Sahara. Garland's response had been rather less straightforward than Minnelli's:

All right you do as you please. I can't stop you. I won't try. But you're going to have to make it on your own. I know it's been bothering you for a long time. I hope you make it, baby, I really hope you do. But you might as well know something else now, so you won't expect it later. There will be no money from me. When you leave, you leave me and everything I have. It's got to be that way. You can't have me to fall back on every time you fail or you'll do nothing *but* fail, knowing I'm waiting. Do you understand what I mean?

Liza was not sure that she did; only vaguely did she understand that her mother's opinion of show business was that it was bound to lead to failure. In Liza's case, Garland thought it inevitable that she would go into the business, but she wanted to save her from the heartbreaking competition until she was old enough to handle it.

Although Garland was not prepared to help Liza financially, she was generous with advice, and Liza was grateful. She did not want to make it as "Judy Garland's daughter," but there was nothing she could do about that. In this respect she was helped by an actor she met at an audition: "He told me not to hesitate for a moment if being Judy Garland's daughter would get me in the door. But when you go on the stage, from the first moment they see you, let them know you're Liza Minnelli."

In the event, being Judy Garland's daughter got her her first break. A group of youngsters were planning an off-Broadway revival of the musical *Best Foot Forward*, and their director-choreographer, Danny Daniels, was aware that Liza was around town, either studying acting at the Herbert Berghof Studio in Greenwich Village or appearing in stock. At that time a name—of sorts—could prevent an off-Broadway show from instant oblivion, and there was additional publicity value in that the show's composer and lyricist, Hugh Martin and Ralph Blane, had provided Liza's mother with two of her biggest hits: "The Trolley Song" and "The Boy Next Door."

A friend of Daniels's glimpsed Liza on the corner of Broadway and 46th Street, and invited her to audition. "I thought he was kidding," she said later, "because nobody comes up to you on the street and says a thing like that. Except in a bad movie." It was, however, the way Liza wanted to start her career, backstairs, quietly learning, with her parents' approval. When Garland returned from Britain in March,

Liza was already rehearsing for the show, which was due to open April 2.

Garland had much to depress her on the evening of March 14: after the excitement of the London trip and Liza's party, she faced the prospect of being, eventually, the star's mother, as Ethel had been. She was apprehensive about her television series and disappointed by the failure of *A Child Is Waiting*. She was staying at the St. Regis Hotel, where Orval Paine, who had been her hairdresser since her engagement at the Sahara, was keeping her company. She went into another room to make a telephone call, and when Paine heard her weeping, he went to inquire what was the matter. She told him that she was lonely and then fell into a deep sleep from which he was unable to rouse her. Alarmed by this, he called for a doctor. The hotel staff had thought her agitated ever since she had arrived three days earlier. The doctor treated her in the hotel and Luft flew to her side.

CBS executives noted the incident just as they had noticed Garland's failure to complete her engagement at Harrah's the previous month. They had been reassured, however, by *Variety*'s favorable comments on the Garland-Silver-Goulet special:

> Taking her special last Tuesday as a sample of what may be in store when Judy Garland has her own weekly series on CBS-TV next fall, it's going to be welcome fare indeed . . . slimmed down to svelte proportions, she again has unlimited costuming possibilities that allow her the maximum range to show off a song . . . More important, her singing last Tuesday projected over the cathode tube almost as over the footlights, with an immediacy and an impact rarely achieved in video . . . The series will have a star who is steeped in the knowhow and who vocally is far from past her prime . . . Where CBS is concerned, the timing of the special couldn't have been better. If this performance doesn't bring in the final sponsor for next season's series, probably nothing will.

Fields and Begelman were not entirely considering her best interests in committing her to a weekly series. They had been her agents for two years and although they knew her to be physically strong, her behavior before many concerts showed her to be volatile and unstable. They attributed this to the rigors of touring rather than temperament; but most importantly, CMA was expanding, and they wanted it to be seen that they had done an exceptional deal for their most valued client. Also of course, they would be receiving 10 percent of the $140,000 per episode which CBS were paying Kingsrow Enterprises.

It *was* an exceptional deal—indeed, unique, for Garland had the right, as the network did not, to cancel after the first thirteen shows if she felt so inclined. CBS, preparing to inject perhaps $24,000,000 into *The Judy Garland Show* over a four-year period, defended the deal by claiming that she would almost certainly bow out quietly if she was not associated with what the trade called a "rating smash." From the fee of $140,000 Garland would net approximately $30,000 per week, with the remaining money going to production costs and salaries. Furthermore Kingsrow would own the shows outright, and would therefore be able to make almost limitless money from syndication and foreign sales. Fields reckoned that the tapes would be worth "at least three to four million."

> For once in her life, this little dynamo is going to be financially secure. And it's about time. Judy is forty-one. She's done everything there is to do in show business, from vaudeville to one-night stands. She's earned fortunes for other people, but she's been victimized over and over again. Before we made this deal with CBS, she was practically broke. But television is going to give her what it's given others much less talented than she—security. These shows are going to bring in money so that she doesn't have to sing her guts out in concerts night after night to support her kids.

CBS knew that she had lived on the edge of bankruptcy for some years and were gambling on the proposition that her hopes of a large annuity would ensure that she arrived at the studio on time and every day. As *Variety* bluntly informed its readers: "It's hardly betraying a secret that the multi-million dollar investment in Miss Garland represents a calculated risk—since there's no guarantee of a full-season lock-in on her services. Depending upon any number of reasons, Miss Garland, some feel, might suddenly decide to blow the whole thing." To cover for the possibility of her losing her voice or needing hospitalization, the show was to be videotaped in advance.

Accompanied by Luft and their children, Garland had a vacation in the Bahamas for two weeks, deliberately missing the opening night of *Best Foot Forward*, but pretending that she had muddled dates. Liza, who desperately wanted her mother's approval, was devastated, and it was only some time later that Garland explained that the reason she avoided the first night was that she feared her presence there might distract the audience.

On April 14, she was seen on television, when *The Ed Sullivan Show* broadcast scenes from the London premiere of *I Could Go on*

Singing, with Garland singing the song of that name and "Smile," excerpted from the London Palladium outing. CBS had intended this to whet the appetites of audiences for Garland's forthcoming series by stressing her special position in show business. She and Danny Kaye were the company's two big catches of the season, and care was being taken as to where to "place" their shows. Sunday night at nine was one of the prime spots, and the *Sullivan Show* gave it a strong lead-in: but in the ratings battle, NBC constantly took the hour with *Bonanza*, and Kaye absolutely refused to have his show broadcast in this slot. CBS, knowing that Garland had once trounced the popular Western series, scheduled her show against it, which meant that, with the Sullivan program, viewers watching CBS would be offered two solid hours of Variety-style entertainment every Sunday evening.

Mistakes were already being made, however. CBS was not a happy company. The chairman, William S. Paley, took credit for any success the company had, but the man really in charge was the president, James Aubrey, who was known as "The Smiling Cobra." CMA had been on the point of signing Garland to a deal with NBC when Aubrey decided not to let this prize catch slip away to the rival network. The man chiefly responsible for her coming to CBS was Hubbell Robinson, senior vice-president in charge of programming. Robinson believed that she would be such an asset to CBS that Aubrey should better NBC's offer. Robinson, who had returned to the network at Paley's request in 1962, found himself always at odds with Aubrey, who summarily fired him on March 11. Not only were mistakes being made, but *The Judy Garland Show* was losing friends.

Robinson had hired a veteran producer and director, Bill Hobin, for the show—but this was in New York. The head of programming on the West Coast was Mike Dann, and he was approached by George Schlatter, who found himself out of work when Dinah Shore decided not to continue her weekly series. Schlatter was a great admirer of talent and therefore a Garland fan: he longed for the chance to work with her and pursued Dann until he was given the job of producer. This meant that the show now had two people hired for the same position. The problem was settled by amending Hobin's contract so that he directed only.

There was further confusion as to whether the programs were to be shot on the West Coast or in New York. By the time the decision to film on the West Coast had been reached, Garland had bought a house on Rockingham Drive in Westwood, it was clear that taping could not begin until June; and that, for a September showing, left little leeway if the star's behavior should prove as erratic as every-one had predicted. The person in charge of operations on the West Coast was Hunt Stromberg, Jr., son of the producer who had been at M-G-M in Garland's early days there. Relations got off to a bad start when Schlatter crossed him over Garland's appearance at the May convention of CBS affiliates in New York, where they were to watch Danny Kaye in his one-man show at the Ziegfeld. They were also to attend "The CBS Parade of Stars" at the Waldorf-Astoria, which was to climax with Garland in concert, with Mort Lindsey conducting, as he would be for the series. Stromberg demanded that she also appear in the parade, but Schlatter refused: "The woman is an event," he argued, "you don't do it twice."

Her presence at the convention provided a current of tension. As Dwight Whitney put it, in an article called "The Great Garland Gamble" in *TV Guide*:

> The big question mark, and the one that set CBS nerves twanging like banjo strings, was Judy Garland, whose efforts to hoist herself over the rainbow to happiness have been headline news for 20 years. CBS knew, its affiliates knew, what almost everyone else knew about Miss Garland: that she was a woman in an almost constant state of emotional turmoil; that, as a result, her career as a movie superstar had been cut short because the studios deemed her undependable (which she denies); and that she had suffered several breakdowns.

Schlatter had established an immediate rapport with Garland when he introduced himself by announcing that although he was supposed to be difficult, there was no truth to the rumor. On the plane to New York, she had confided to him that she was terrified of trying to find words to reassure the convention of her goodwill. Together they began to sing the Cahn–Van Heusen song "Call Me Irresponsible," and Johnny Bradford, who was to write *The Judy Garland Show*, produced a special lyric, slightly altering Cahn's words. With her unerring instinct for effect, she knew that she had a superb opening and was not even thrown when her heel caught in a crack in the Waldorf ballroom floor. She took off both shoes, and began "Call me irrespon-sible / Call me unreliable / Call me unpredictable, too . . ." and she concluded: "But it's undeniably true / I'm irrevocably signed to you." The entire gathering went wild, standing to cheer. She had them all in the palm of her hand even before she began the concert proper.

As art director, Schlatter chose Gary Smith, who had designed the Garland-Sinatra-Martin special. He saw the *Show*, he said, as "a weekly series of specials." Edith Head, on her way to a record number of Oscars for costume design, was to be responsible for Garland's wardrobe. Ray Aghayan, who had worked with Schlatter on the Dinah Shore shows, was to design the costumes for Garland's guests.

To write special musical material for the show, Schlatter needed someone of the quality of Roger Edens or Nelson Riddle. Neither was available, so he made an unexpected and original choice, Mel Tormé, a respected singer in his own right and co-writer of the much-recorded "The Christmas Song." Tormé had a successful career of his own, but was flattered by Schlatter's persistence. He observed wryly that Garland was "not the most disciplined lady in show business," to which Schlatter replied: "We're gonna make this so much fun for her, she'll show up an hour early every day." He also told Tormé: "It won't hurt your image one bit to write for Judy. For any other singer, maybe, but not Judy." The matter was decided when Schlatter offered him two guest shots in the first thirteen shows. Tormé shared the view that by owning the show and consequently making a fortune out of it she would not repeat her past transgressions.

Garland was now looking forward to the show—at least, in public. She told an interviewer: "It was a big decision, but a wonderful decision. I don't think of it as so formidable. I'm going to be a female Perry Como. I'm going to take it easy, and have wonderful guests, and share the spotlight. I'm not going to try to carry the show every week by myself." On this, CBS and she were agreed. They did not want the Great Lady of Show Business, the Legend: they wanted to "humanize" her. They might have settled for the format used by Como or Bing Crosby, which depended on the songs chosen and the star's guests, but decided to give her "a television family," that is, supporting characters with whom viewers could identify. Then they changed their minds, and Schlatter was told to look for someone who could introduce the show and join its star in sketches or dances. Forced upon him was Dick Van Dyke's brother, Jerry Van Dyke, whom Stromberg—thought to be a judge of talent—insisted was bound for stardom.

None of the studios at CBS Television City equipped to have the scenery moved mechanically was large enough to hold an audience. This meant that all the scenery for the show would have to be moved manually, causing delays in shooting. Schlatter suggested hiring space elsewhere, but the idea did not appeal to CBS. Adjacent to the studio, CBS installed an air-conditioned trailer for the star, consisting of a bar, a kitchen, a makeup room and a lavishly appointed lounge. In spite of the company's decision to humanize Garland, the door of the trailer bore a sign which read "The Legend," and leading from it to the studio was a painted Yellow Brick Road. At a cost of $150,000 the trailer was a palace compared to the $75,000 spent on a penthouse suite for Danny Kaye, but some more established CBS attractions were resentful.

Relations between Garland and Mel Tormé would never be easy. She was very nervous and he vividly described in his book how she decided she needed to put Tormé in his place right from the beginning.

"Why would you take this job?" she asked him when they first met to discuss her songs. "Why this job? I don't get it." Tormé answered in the words put to him by Schlatter by telling her that she was "the only real superstar around these days." She persisted in testing him by declaring that Jack Jones was the best jazz singer in the world. In spite of his own reputation in this field, Tormé decided that it was politic to agree, and said that Jones was indeed a fine singer.

"No, but I mean, he's not just a fine singer," Garland replied. "There are a lot of fine singers. He's the best jazz singer in the world. Don't you think so?" Tormé, sizing up the situation, said that he preferred Ernest Tubbs, of whom she had never heard. An instant later she realized that he was putting her on.

"You'd better understand something right now," she said. "This is my show. My company produces it. You're working for me, and nobody puts me on. I'm gonna get respect around here. It's not going to be like the old Metro days. For once, *I'm* running things. You know how Mayer used to treat me in the old days? . . . Nothing you've heard could begin to tell the half of it. I had to take it then, but not any more." As Tormé recalled it, "she smiled a tight little mirthless smile." She went on, in full spate: "You want to know something? These days grown men are afraid of *me*. Even my lawyers, my managers. I really shake 'em up. They get out of line. I chew 'em up and spit 'em out! How about you, Melvin? You afraid of me?" By now, Tormé had the measure of her and said:

"We have to begin with a premise. The most appropriate one is that you are full of shit."

This was partially true but, in the main, she was riddled with insecurity, and neither Schlatter's jokes nor a best-selling record-set could buck that. She insisted that Tormé must bow to her will. He met the challenge without enjoying it: "Schlatter didn't just hire me to write special material for you. He wants me to pick tunes with you, to help you be comfortable with every aspect of the musical end of this show. Now, unless you intend to listen to my suggestions and ideas, then I am the wrong guy in the wrong job . . ."

"Are you finished?" she asked finally.

"I don't know, Judy, am I?"

She picked up one of the songs from her portfolio. "I like this tune," she said softly. "Let's try it."

"Jesus!" he said as she finished.

"We'll get along," she whispered as she left him. She later asked him to help her through her paces off-camera, as Edens or Chuck Walters would have done, and he agreed, while pointing out that this was not in his contract.

She knew exactly what she wanted to sing and not to sing. Among the latter was a send-up of "Over the Rainbow." "It's kind of . . . sacred," she said. "I don't want anybody *anywhere* to lose the thing they have about Dorothy or that song." CBS was dismayed, and even less pleased when she decided to substitute "I Will Come Back" as her bow-out number. Nor was it any more in favor of her decision to climax the first show with "Old Man River," a song seldom sung by a woman, as she well knew. She also knew that she could sing it magnificently. Among her other numbers was "Too Late Now" (which had originally been written for *Royal Wedding*), delivered in front of a large trunk, which was to provide her with a recollection each week.

Although she claimed she did not want to trade on nostalgia, her first guest was Mickey Rooney. She was rarely loyal or grateful to old friends and for years had avoided Rooney, and kept him away from her homes: "Don't let that asshole in here," she would tell Harry Rubin. But Rooney needed the money because he was about to file for bankruptcy and she knew that a reunion would draw attention to the show. Chiefly, she wanted him because she was nervous and hoped that he would help her to relax. The show's writers had been following her about to hear anecdotes about her past and catch the cadences of her speech. They came up with some reminiscences for Garland and Rooney about their days at M-G-M which were charming in themselves and went a long way to appeasing Rooney, who had been obliged to perform an unfunny sketch with Jerry Van Dyke.

The show was finally taped on June 24 between 8 and 9:30 p.m., without a hitch. It was followed by a party, held at Schlatter's insistence despite the company's objections. CBS was worried that Garland might not show and would therefore attract adverse publicity, but Schlatter had had no trouble at all with her. Among the guests were Lucille Ball, Natalie Wood, Jack Benny, Hedda Hopper and Louella Parsons (but not together) and Clint Eastwood, who had been present for the taping. Garland wore the simple, striped dress she had worn to most rehearsals instead of the Edith Head gowns. Schlatter disliked most of the Head costumes, finding them too somber, and, after Garland had expressed delight with some designs Ray Aghayan had done for other members of the cast, he asked Aghayan to design the star's costumes as well. He was to create a high-fashion image which she adored; such became her trust in him that sometimes she did not see the costumes until she tried them on.

The people who mattered—show-business journalists and CBS executives—were delighted with the show, which was just as well, as Judy's private life was again chaotic. Only two weeks after a party to celebrate their eleventh wedding anniversary and Garland's forty-first birthday, Luft moved out for what was to be the last time. At the time of their reconciliation in February, he had warned her that she should look more carefully at the huge sums pouring into CMA for her services, with particular regard to her immediate expenses. By now there was no love lost between Luft and CMA's Fields and Begelman. A press report had suggested that Garland might not re-sign with CMA, which might well have been because at that point she was siding with Luft.

The financial records from January 1961, when she first signed with CMA, had been examined by Luft's attorney, Guy Ward, who had turned them over to an accountant, Oscar Steinberg, for closer examination. As Garland began work on her second show, Luft showed her Steinberg's report, which listed "certain items requiring additional explanation." They all concerned Begelman.

David Begelman was not quite what he seemed. No one disputed that he was a zealous and indefatigable agent, but he did not have the qualifications—or the credentials—he claimed. He was in the insurance business when he met and married Esther Feldman, sister of the agent Charles Feldman. The best man at the wedding was Shep Fields, the bandleader, whose brother Freddie worked at MCA, which in due course hired Begelman.

According to Steinberg's report, thirteen checks, ranging from $500 to $6,000, drawn by Begelman on the Kingsrow account, had been cashed at the Dunes or Sahara hotels in Las Vegas between May and October 1962. The total amount came to $35,714, which appeared in Kingsrow's books as part of Garland's salary, labeled "Protection."

Another $10,000 had been drawn from Kingsrow's Chase Manhattan account to be paid into an account labeled "David Begelman in trust for Judy Garland," which was then transferred to a Begelman account with no other name attached. A further five checks of $490.33 each, signed by Begelman, went to CMA as "TV Production Supervisors" on the special with Goulet and Silvers, without any identification as to who these might be. Kingsrow had also paid CMA $750 commission as the agents' percentage for Garland's appearance on *The Jack Paar Show*, despite the fact that Paar's production company had itself paid the commission. The deal included a 1963 Cadillac convertible which, Luft said, Garland knew nothing about. She certainly had no car when beginning her CBS series. Luft later claimed that in 1965 he discovered that the car was registered in Begelman's name.

Even more damaging, part of the $50,000 Garland had paid to recover the photograph taken in the London Clinic had also found its way into Begelman's coffers. Garland had signed a letter of instruction to her bank for a transfer of the $50,000 with a proviso that $24,355 of that amount be deposited in Begelman's "Executive Producer Account, Special," noting that Begelman was "empowered to be the only signatory on the account." A further $3,245 was made payable to the account of "201 East 62nd Street Building Company, Inc."— at which address an apartment building was then being constructed. When the building was completed, Begelman and his wife moved in.

When Luft confronted Garland with Steinberg's report, she confounded him: "Look, suppose he did steal two hundred thousand dollars to three hundred thousand dollars. Sweep it under the rug now. I'm going to make twenty million on these television shows. What is three hundred thousand?"

Both Luft and Begelman's second wife, Lee Reynolds, believed that Begelman and Garland had an affair at one time. Later in the year, Garland herself told Jayne Meadows (when her husband, Steve Allen, was guesting on the show) that she still loved David but that he would not marry her because he was not in love with her. Unquestionably, one of Begelman's attractions toward Garland was that he had reestablished her reputation at a time when her career seemed to be over. A career which had earlier been endangered when Minnelli first came into her life, and later when she met Luft.

This may be the undisclosed reason she was willing to overlook the irregularities in the CMA accounts. She never had any idea how to handle money and had no intention of learning: but she now began to worry about it. There were still unpaid bills—one from a London hotel for over $3,000 worth of telephone calls had made its way into the papers. She knew that the television series was her last chance. If it failed, she would have to return to the rigors of touring. Once again, she had become dependent on pills.

It was clear to everyone that after a performance in which adrenaline ran that high, depression had to come in the hours that followed. Only on a few rare occasions did Garland not have the prospect of going home to an empty house. She knew that she had given more than value for money and she knew that she was Judy Garland, a unique and great entertainer. She was both fully alive and yet drained. She was just not the sort of woman who could simply go home, make herself a cup of cocoa and get into bed with a book.

George Schlatter became a member of what he called "the dawn patrol"—those whom she called in the early hours of the morning when she could not sleep and became jittery about the show. This had been a habit ever since she had suffered chronic insomnia, and she often asked friends to come over. Now, she could *command*. The show was not her only worry: she remained convinced that Luft would take Lorna and Joey away from her. "They're beautiful children," she once told Tormé. "They're the only good thing that bastard Sid ever did in his life." She was on the telephone to his office to inform him that she was "a bundle of nerves" and had therefore decided not to do a show that week. When Tormé told her not to apologize, she cut in sharply: "Who the hell is apologizing? I don't need to apologize for *anything* to *anyone*, bub! I own this whole frigging shebang, and if I decide not to work until 1971, that's my business!" Tormé says he calmed her down by telling her how much everyone liked the first show; a meeting was arranged before the third taping due in two weeks' time beginning July 6.

On the day of the recording, Bob Wynn, one of the assistants on the show, had been with her in the early hours, comforting her because Begelman had not kept his promise to come. She tried to take some pills but he grabbed them from her and they fought, Garland crying hysterically. After she had quietened down, she asked for a doctor because her back was causing her pain. Wynn decided that if a doctor gave her something to help her sleep, she would never be awake enough to do the show. He persuaded her to go to CBS with him; but while he telephoned Schlatter, she disappeared.

There was considerable consternation until, with her usual resilience, she turned up and was on form to tape the show. It began with her singing "I Hear Music" as the musicians of the Count Basie Band took their places on the darkened soundstage. Other songs included "The Sweetest Sounds" and "A Cottage for Sale." The other guests, apart from Basie, were Tormé and Judy Henske, a country-style singer, who did a sketch with Tormé and Van Dyke which was as dire as the one Van Dyke had done with Rooney. As a precaution, the dress rehearsal was also taped, as it was to be from then on, both to take the pressure off Garland and as a back-up in case everything was not all right on the final taping. CBS executives were uneasy about the show; they felt that the combination of Garland and Basie should have been more of an occasion.

On the third show, the guests were Liza Minnelli and Soupy Sales, a children's television comedian, and Garland clearly enjoyed herself. Lena Horne and Terry-Thomas were to be in the fourth show, and neither of them were too concerned when the star failed to show up on Tuesday, the first day of rehearsals. She did not come in on Wednesday, and on Thursday merely sat and watched the blocking from the back of the studio. She had greeted Horne warmly, but was content to watch her rehearse with her stand-in. She was not there when Horne's patience finally gave out. Without proper rehearsals, Horne had no idea whether she and Garland would sound good in the songs worked out for them, which included a medley in which each would sing numbers associated with the other. "It's the height of unprofessionalism," Horne fumed; but she was disarmed when Garland apologized. "She was a helluva singer who always pulled through," Horne said later. "But—oooh, honey, she could make you mad! But then you'd look at her, all smiley and cheery-eyed like nothing happened, and it was all right again." Garland's reluctance to rehearse, however, took its toll. In Coward's "Mad Dogs and Englishmen," a difficult number, she had to rely on Horne and Terry-Thomas to help her get through, and the result was below standard.

The comic on the next show was Dick Shawn, and the other guest was Tony Bennett, a singer in the same stellar class as Garland. She was reluctant to rehearse with him, although she had often cited him with Peggy Lee and Frank Sinatra as her three favorite singers. Their paths had never crossed before, but they worked together beautifully. Bennett said he learned much from watching her in action and was always to describe her as "the greatest singer this business has known." Another singer of the same caliber, Nat "King" Cole, began rehearsing in the first week of August, when that episode was suddenly canceled. Simultaneously Schlatter and the writers were fired.

"Everybody went," Garland said. "I thought I was going, too. They swept out a whole bunch of people and whoever got caught up in that whisk of the broom was out. I wish somebody would have warned me in advance—maybe I could have avoided anyone's being decapitated. I was stunned and bewildered, it came as such a shock."

There had in fact been one warning sign. CBS did not think Garland spoke enough; it did not think audiences could get to know her. As the one undoubted success in this direction had been her conversation on the Jack Paar show, it had been decided to give her a "Tea for Two" spot, where that particular song would introduce an impromptu chat spot with a friend or guest. This innovation had been introduced in great haste for the fourth show, in which the guest had been Terry-Thomas. Since he was *not* an old friend, he and Garland had chatted about London. Gene Kelly was scheduled for this spot in the show featuring Nat "King" Cole.

The sponsors had liked the shows, but none of them had yet been broadcast. CBS had done some random test screenings, with cards for members of the audience to fill in, as an electronic device to register their reaction. "Nobody judged the show," said someone who read the cards. "They judged what they read in the newspapers. On the cards, they commented on what they knew, not what they saw. They said things like 'I don't like her, she's nervous,' 'She seems unhappy' or 'She drinks.' They felt she was hiding her real self."

To replace the departed Schlatter, Garland chose Norman Jewison, who had already warned her not to take on a weekly series. He was available because he had just resigned from a Broadway show he was to direct—but only for two months, since he had a prior commitment to a Doris Day movie, *Send Me No Flowers*, in November. He liked Garland, but more than that, he knew how to handle her. He also understood that her financial future depended on these shows, and that she wanted to continue after the initial thirteen. His agent was also able to ask for a great deal of money—$12,500 a week (which would add up to $100,000 for eight shows). With payments for the redundancies, this raised the weekly cost from $160,000 to about $200,000. This deepened Garland's anxiety, but she knew that her 1962 special with Jewison and Kay Thompson had been her best work in television. Thompson was invited by Jewison to replace Tormé, but declined on the grounds that she could not top her work on that occasion. Tormé himself was told that CBS had intended a clean sweep but that Garland had interceded on his behalf.

A five-week hiatus was called, during which Garland had to confront the usual raft of problems. On July 21, Oscar Steinberg filed suit in Superior Court for $12,312 fees in respect of his work in examining the Kingsrow accounts. Three days later, it was announced that Judy Garland and Kingsrow had signed a new contract with CMA, who would represent her for another three years. With her future in television in serious doubt, she did not want to let CBS think there was any discord between her and Fields and Begelman, especially as she was simultaneously squabbling with Luft. She had posted guards around the house again to keep him out, and both she and her estranged husband were consulting lawyers over forthcoming custody battles.

On August 26, she entered the Cedars of Lebanon Hospital for what was described as her "annual checkup." She was there for only two days, but she certainly had not *anticipated* being there at all, since she had been obliged to cancel a brief trip to Paris and London, as well as another to Washington to participate in a Civil Rights march with other show-business names. The night she left the hospital, she had a long telephone conversation with Luft in which he cast doubts on the existence of the London clinic blackmail photograph. She insisted that she had seen it, however. That unhappy period in her life was recalled by a new rumor that the producers of *I Could Go on Singing* planned to write a book about the making of the film.

On September 6, the court granted Garland custody of Lorna, who was almost eleven, and Joey, who was eight. Luft was awarded visiting rights. The following evening, Luft was dining with the two children at the Rockingham house, when Garland unexpectedly appeared and offered him a drink. She mixed herself a vodka martini—a sure sign that she was not in a Blue Nun mood, or even a vodka-and-water one. She told Luft that she knew that he was in bad financial straits and would like to help. She wrote out a check for $10,000, saying, in Gerold Frank's account, "I owe you a great deal, I really do." After another quick martini, she said: "I'm so fucking mad at you—to think that we could be so good, so right together, but you're insisting on digging up all our past financial problems. I want to forget it, darling."

Since she had brought up the subject, he pointed out they owed back taxes as man and wife and could either settle jointly, or he would have to "disown" her as a wife. She asked him to settle the matter, but when he replied that it was too complex, she snarled: "You just do the goddam income tax. Do it, and I don't want to hear about it.

I'll do my shows, and don't interfere. Don't bother me or else I'll be upset and blow the whole thing." They began shouting at each other, and he tore the check up. Twice, when he tried to leave, he found that she had pressed the button in the kitchen which re-activated the gate. He stormed back and yelled at her: after that the gate remained open.

At four the following morning, she telephoned his hotel. She was hysterical: "There's a prowler about, come back here you son of a bitch, and guard your family." He told her to call the police and keep the gates closed; after she had phoned again, he told the switchboard not to put through any more calls. It would be some while before they met again.

During this period, Garland had an affair with the cabaret singer André Phillipe, whom she had met in a nightclub where he was performing. The relationship finished after a few months. At a reception Debbie Reynolds and her husband gave for the evangelist Billy Graham, she talked to Glenn Ford, whom she had briefly dated twenty years earlier, when he was a budding star at Columbia. He was currently a much bigger star at M-G-M, and in the interim had been married to and divorced from Eleanor Powell. He and Garland began seeing each other, holding hands like love-struck teenagers as they sat in his lounge listening to records. In adolescent mood, she picked up a lettering machine and made dozens of versions of "Glenn and Judy" and "Judy and Glenn," embossed on a plastic tape. Her behavior was partly appropriate, since Ford had a boyish nature and was capable of naïve behavior. He was certainly not the sort of father figure whom Garland had sought in the past, and his actor's ego meant that the relationship did not stand much of a chance. However, for the moment, the couple enjoyed each others' impulsive and uncomplicated romanticism. "I've needed someone like him for a long time," Garland told Mel Tormé. "Someone strong. Every woman needs that, even if she won't admit it." He replied that he had the impression that she did not like "strong-willed guys. Like Sid, for instance." Sid Luft, she replied was "something else again."

One result of the affair was that she changed doctors. Her own had been growing restive over calls for help in the middle of the night, so she started seeing Ford's physician, Lee Siegel, whose first duty, he decided, was to wean her off barbiturates. Since the only drug she trusted was Seconal, Siegel persuaded a pharmacist to fill Seconal capsules with a new drug, Valium. This worked, but the pharmacist refused to make the swap a second time on the grounds that the two tablets were manufactured by rival drug companies. Siegel reluctantly returned to Seconal, reducing the dosage, but the combination of these with uppers, and alcohol—she was now drinking vodka again regularly—meant that the old pattern resumed. The interaction of sedative, stimulant and spirits made each twice as strong. Siegel did what he could, treating her after her early-morning calls and reassuring himself that Garland's dismal record of drug abuse had never resulted in a really serious attempt to take her life.

She had reason enough, without pills, to be depressed, when CBS did not trouble to deny another rumor that arose. The *Hollywood Reporter* stated that the company was looking for a replacement "if a certain new live-on-tape hour show peters out." Throughout the series Garland gave a large number of good-humored interviews about the show which were not always exactly helpful. "I don't think I'd like to look at [it] every week," she claimed. "It's too enervating. I think it should be a bit easier for people to watch. We're in trouble unless we can calm it down a bit." This was of course impossible for her, as she explained: "I'm not the sort of performer who can relax and put her feet up and get paid all that money. It's not nerves. Maybe it's just a kind of exuberance which I've always had."

She was not helped on the first of the "new" shows by her chief guest, June Allyson, who had not recovered from the recent death of her husband, Dick Powell, and was terrified of appearing live after many years in films. A certain amount of Liebfraumilch seems to have been drunk, and the cutting of a cake, brought in to mark Tormé's birthday, was the cue for a custard-pie battle. Garland responded to the ensuing criticisms by saying: "I never in my life have had too much to drink—when I work or when I don't work. I really don't drink that much and neither does June." The custard-pie throwing she dismissed as "just silliness."

The show appeared to be descending into chaos. Garland was so dependent upon it for both her income and her future career that she simply did what she was asked. From an early age, she had been told what was right for her by her superiors, and although she often disagreed, she was obliged to rely upon the judgments of others. Throughout her career, she had mocked herself and allowed her image to be debunked, but this reached extraordinary proportions in the television shows. A critic in the *Saturday Evening Post* complained that "instead of the guests idolizing her, they say things on the air to denigrate her. The remarks are more painful than funny."

Chief of the remarks which infuriated friends and fans were those given to Van Dyke on such matters as Garland's former weight problems, her unreliability ("She'll never show up") and her age: "What have you done to yourself since Christmas, sweetie? . . . Let me ask you something. What's a nice little old lady like you doing on television?" and Jack Carter's comic monologue "This isn't the original, this is the twelfth Judy Garland. The original went over the rainbow years ago. There's a little farm in Pasadena that grows Judy Garlands." After Van Dyke and Donald O'Connor (in show seven) had mimed to Garland's *Carnegie Hall* recording of "The Man That Got Away," she entered and said: "If anyone sings this song, it's going to be this nice *little old lady*." This episode was taped when the series was in its third month of taping, but Norman Jewison had already decided that it should be the first to be broadcast.

"What should never happen to Judy Garland did last evening in the premiere of her weekly program over the Columbia Broadcasting System," wrote Jack Gould in the *New York Times*.

The busybodies got so in the way that the singer never had a chance to sing out as only she can. To call the hour a grievous disappointment would be to miss the point. It was an absolute mystery . . . Judy never looked more vivacious and sounded in fine voice. It was the network that rattled. The thinking of CBS executives apparently was to develop a "new" Judy, one who would indulge in light banter and make way for suitable guests to share the weekly tasks. By such tactics it was presumably thought that Miss Garland could be shielded from burning herself out musically. In only one number ("Fly Me to the Moon") was there the Judy who has filled theaters around the world. For the other 55 minutes, she was the prisoner of her own production . . . Those telephones on the 20th floor of CBS's home encampment should buzz this morning with but one directive to Hollywood. Free Judy!

On one matter, most reviewers were agreed: the contribution of Jerry Van Dyke. He, in turn, objected to the way his character had been changed from a sort of country bumpkin to someone much more aggressive. He would not have minded, he said, if his lines were funny. They were not, so he asked for and received his release after the first ten shows—or so it was reported. In fact, he was fired, which hardly surprised him, since Jewison had scarcely given him the time of day.

The next to go was Bill Hobin, who declined to remain after the agreed thirteen shows. His relationship with other members of the production team deteriorated after he had questioned the presence of the television actor George Maharis, as Garland's guest, adding that, although he was "hot," he was no singer. CBS clearly agreed, for the show he did was postponed at the last minute to be replaced by the most recently recorded one, with the twenty-one-year-old Barbra Streisand featured as co-guest with Ethel Merman joining Garland throughout. At this point in her career, Streisand had only had one hit record, a slowed-up version of "Happy Days Are Here Again." It was obvious that she should perform this song, and Garland, remembering that she had once done a slow-tempoed version of "Get Happy," decided that they should sing the two songs in counterpoint. This resulted in one of the most beguiling numbers in all the shows. Ethel Merman was taping *The Red Skelton Show* on an adjoining stage, and had agreed to appear provided that she could sing. At first, Garland demurred, since the conversation with Merman was supposed to be spontaneous, but she subsequently agreed that her guest could sing just a few bars of "You're Just in Love." Someone then suggested that since all three singers were famous for belting out songs, it would be a shame not to let them do so together—and Garland seized the chance to have herself and Streisand join Merman in a supposedly impromptu version of "There's No Business Like Show Business." The combination was electrifying.

Streisand was about to sign with CMA, who would help to make her a star with *Funny Girl*, in the role which Garland had turned down. Whether or not she knew that Garland had insisted on her being on the television show against the objections of CBS, Streisand referred to her then as "the greatest actress and the greatest singer" in the business. This did not prevent her from later appearing in a catastrophic remake of *A Star Is Born* and recording "Over the Rainbow" with a disastrous disregard for either lyric or melody. Gordon Jenkins, who described himself as "president for many years of the Hooray-for-Judy-Garland-Who-Are-All-Those-Other-People fan club" was once asked whether he would take two Barbra Streisands for one Judy Garland. "I wouldn't take two of anybody for Judy Garland," he replied.

The show with Merman and Streisand became a talking point as the trade press was again speculating on a cancellation—less because of anything that had appeared on screen than because of its troubled production history. Garland had become even further demoralized after the firing of Van Dyke and the defection of Hobin, whom she had asked to stay. Her tardiness in appearing at rehearsals increased, but was defended by Jewison. "Look," he said, "if you want somebody who's going to be right on time and attend every rehearsal, go work with Dinah Shore. I admit that Judy isn't known for arriving on time. She'll always be a little late. But I have never met anyone in my life who can pick up a routine so quickly." This was something on which many of those who had worked with her commented. "To work with her was indescribable," Saul Chaplin recalled. "Like a Xerox machine. You played something to her, and she sang it right back the way you did. She ate up music like a vacuum cleaner."

It was on precisely this skill that *The Judy Garland Show* foundered. One of her most admired virtues had become her greatest liability. Because she was a quick learner, she didn't feel the need to rehearse, and left her guests to lumber on, not knowing sometimes until the dress rehearsal how their talents would combine with hers. Cast, crew and guests often sat around marking time, and when the art director, Gary Smith, remonstrated with her she countered: "Let CBS pay for it . . . because they got me into this mess."

24

❖❖❖❖❖❖❖❖

The Final Taping

THE JUDY GARLAND SHOW was in deep trouble. Up to December 1963, CBS had been selling six minutes of advertising at $56,000 a minute, for a total of $336,000 an hour, which gave them a decent profit, but it was now clear that they would have to drop the price to around $20,000 per minute if there were going to be any more takers. Faced with this situation, they were searching for something—anything—to complain about. The best that they could find was that Garland touched her guest stars too much. Her impulsiveness and need to be liked were the reasons; she dismissed the criticism except to say that sometimes she touched her guests because they were nervous.

Although *The Danny Kaye Show* had also been suffering in the ratings battle, it began to show some improvement, while audiences for Garland's show continued to fall. These were the two most touted CBS shows of the season, which at the very least ought to have been prestige successes. Garland continued to commute to New York to discuss the show with CBS executives, and, after examining the terms of its contract with her, the network decided to go ahead with a further thirteen shows. There were, however, conditions. "We told her what we think, and she's listening," Mike Dann told the press. "She's far too insecure about TV to exercise her own judgment. She knows we know what's good for her."

As at M-G-M, she disagreed. She said that CBS wanted her to be "sort of the girl next door. But they couldn't find the right house, or the right door." Despite the renewal of the contract, speculation over the show's future continued. Garland herself was confused: she gave an interview to *Newsweek*, which printed it under the headline "Question Mark." She thought that the show should be:

> Like my own life, really. Full of interesting personalities. You just can't barge into people's living rooms and say "I'm a big star." I like them to get to know me. And I'm not that experienced with so much taping. You get the feeling that if you miss one word, you get shot. Maybe that's why I wanted so much to do the weekly series. For years, everyone's been saying I couldn't stand the pressure every week. Now it's kind of like sticking my tongue out and saying "See, I'm doing it." And I'm hoping to be very rich from this.

Basically, she was fighting for her own artistic integrity. Much of what she had learned from Edens she had passed on to Luft, so that, throughout her life, she had been surrounded by the best talents available. Her own instinct of what she herself could do was supreme. She had compromised with the grubby minds at CBS, but insufficiently for some of them, which is why they either despised her or despaired of her. Among the personalities she wanted in the show were Bing Crosby and Noël Coward: CBS was thinking more along the lines of Andy Griffith and Don Knotts. A compromise was again reached, but again with a bias toward her taste, with some classy singing acts, including Vic Damone (the only guest to appear three times), Ethel Merman and Peggy Lee.

The program with Lee, which was taped on November 8, 1963, concluded the first thirteen. There was a three-week break, during which some of the leading personnel again changed. Garland had not pursued her plan to have Schlatter reinstated, but, from a short list, picked Bill Colleran to be Jewison's replacement, doubtless at Begelman's request as Colleran (who was married to Lee Remick) was also a CMA client. Begelman told him: "She's a mess, she's impossible to work with, she's crazy. It's a helluva thing to ask you to do, but I think it would be good for your career and you'd be good for the show, with new, fresh ideas."

Colleran looked at all the shows that had been already taped, but liked none of them. He said that he was appalled to see that extraordinary talent being wasted in this way. He thought that CBS was deliberately trying to wreck the career of one of the greatest artists of the century. She had a very special place in the heart of the American public—chiefly for her singing. He was going to ensure that she sang and didn't share the show with third-rate talents.

He soon realized that Garland's situation at CBS was unusual. "What are you going to do with that fucking cunt?" Aubrey greeted him when he first discussed the show with him. Colleran knew: he was going to let her do what she did best, sing, either alone or with others of like quality. Bobby Darin, along with Bob Newhart, was to be her guest in the fourteenth show, due to be taped on November 30. They arrived in Hollywood on November 22, the day President Kennedy was assassinated in Dallas. The entire nation was traumatized, but the tragedy particularly affected Garland, since she knew and adored Kennedy. They had continued to speak to each other on a regular basis over the telephone, and he had been particularly supportive over her troubles with the television show. He had been full of praise for it and recently assured her: "We have changed our dinner hour at the White House so we can watch the show. Everyone at Hyannis Port listens, too. It is our favorite show. It is everybody's favorite show." He had followed its fortunes in the ratings, and consoled her by saying: "Fine art was never for the masses." If the show had not won America, it *had* won America's first family, and this really mattered to her.

It was part of Garland's nature to overreact, and for once she had a valid cause. On hearing the news from Dallas, she broke down completely, but rallied sufficiently to visit the late President's sister, Patricia, then married to her friend Peter Lawford. She expected CBS to cancel both the taping and the show, but was told that, although Sunday's immediate show (in which her guests were Jane Powell and Ray Bolger) would be postponed, the one she was about to tape would go ahead as planned, and would be aired the following week in its usual slot. By then, CBS said, the country would be returning to normal. Furthermore, if she canceled the show for any reason whatsoever, CBS would hold her responsible for any expenses incurred.

Given this ultimatum, she decided to devote the hour to patriotic songs, to pay homage to the President and as a way of re-affirming America's belief in itself. She did not intend to mention Kennedy or indeed to speak at all: the songs would carry the message. As always, her sense of what would work on such occasions was faultless. However, James Aubrey issued a decree that there would be no further tributes to the President when normal broadcasting resumed and, as far as he was concerned, this included Garland's planned hour of Americana. She threw herself heart and soul into the program and simply couldn't believe it when Gary Smith told her what Aubrey had dictated. After all, Kennedy held a very special place in her life. She told Smith to tell Aubrey to get lost.

Aubrey could not be budged, however, and Garland was obliged to go ahead and tape the show with Darin and Newhart, as originally planned. Normally, when thwarted she could make life difficult for a lot of people, but she buckled under, in the reasonable belief that her own troubles were as nothing compared to those of the nation. Aubrey's attitude to her played further havoc with her precarious equilibrium. Fortunately, she had taken to Bill Colleran, who was the right man in the right place at the right time. His admiration for her was, in her opinion, on the right side of idolatry and in his combination of humor, tact and discipline he displayed all the best qualities of Schlatter and Jewison.

The next show to be taped was the family Christmas, with all three children. Garland's relationship with Liza had been going through a difficult patch, so much so that in September she had ended up going to court over a contract with Begelman and Fields she had signed on her daughter's behalf. Garland had claimed in an interview that she was "very proud of" Liza, whose stage career was going "brilliantly." At the same time, she felt that, at seventeen, Liza was too young to look after her own earnings. The judge agreed and ruled that Liza could not touch them until she was twenty-one. Liza pleaded to be allowed to keep half of them, but it was decreed that she needed a court order to get anything—beyond the commission paid to CMA—unless Garland agreed.

As plans were being made for the Christmas show in September, Liza was still appearing in *Best Foot Forward* and had until then resisted her mother's pleas to join her on the West Coast. Garland decided to change her daughter's mind. Liza's current boyfriend, Tracy Everitt, who was dancing in the chorus of the Broadway production of *How to Succeed in Business Without Really Trying*, received an offer to join *The Judy Garland Show*. He flew to California, and Liza shortly quit her show in order to be with him—just as Garland had planned.

The Christmas show was Garland's own favorite of all the shows she had done until then, but there was a certain amount of backstage tension. She was going to open with "Have Yourself a Merry Little Christmas" and wanted to sing Mel Tormé's "The Christmas Song," with the composer at the piano. Tormé declined, since he felt that this would show him to be a less important guest than Jack Jones. Garland offered him a solo spot as well, and a duet with Jones in one of the medleys. Tormé finally agreed when she told him that this would count as an additional guest appearance to the three he was contracted for, and that she would emphasize his contribution in composing "The Christmas Song." He suspected, however, that her intention was to show that he was indeed a less important talent than Jones, which in terms of popularity was undeniable. Some withering looks passed between him and Garland when she made a couple of mistakes in the lyric of the song as they sang it together.

Tormé was perfectly well aware of the probable reason for her forgetting the lyrics of his song. In the early hours of that morning, she had telephoned him in panic. She told him there would be no show unless he came to see her at once. When he arrived, she was still frightened, but also drunk, and demanded to be taken to his house. When she got there, she swallowed a handful of pills, which terrified him. He called a doctor who, as it happened, had once been Garland's physician. The doctor assured Tormé that he should just let her sleep off the effect of the pills. Tormé went to the studio, instructing his wife to try and get in touch with Glenn Ford, who turned up to collect Garland. The rehearsal was due to begin at one, and as Colleran was despairing of having a Garland Christmas show—or indeed any show at all—his star bounced in, and cheerfully greeted her waiting children: "Hi, babies. Isn't this going to be fun? All of us together, singing on television, just like we do at home. Joey, did you learn your song?"

Garland's feelings toward CBS deteriorated even further when Aubrey announced that *The Danny Kaye Show* was to be renewed for the 1964–65 season. This was a public humiliation for her, since the announcement came many months before the networks usually announced plans for the following year. Anything might happen to Kaye's rating in the interim, and at 17.0 percent, it demonstrated that his show was by no means a success, especially as he had no significant opposition. Garland's own rating of 14.0 percent was in fact very healthy, given that she was pitched against *Bonanza*, which had held second position in the top-rated shows for almost two years. What stung the great minds at CBS was that *Bonanza* alone prevented CBS from having a clean sweep in the Top Ten week after week.

The next show was to feature Ethel Merman and Shelley Berman, and Garland told Colleran that she intended to close it by singing "The Battle Hymn of the Republic" as a tribute to JFK. She was delighted when he told her that he would back her to the hilt. Her first instinct had been to slip it in at the last minute, but it needed to be rehearsed; in any case, Aubrey could always order it to be cut, substituting another number from an earlier show. Aubrey and Stromberg were furious at the suggestion, but, backed by Colleran, Garland was in defiant mood. The show was doomed anyway, so from now on she was going to take fewer orders.

Her instincts were as sound as ever, and she sang with fire, spirit and feeling. When she taped the dress rehearsal, she introduced the song with a mention of Kennedy; but on the final taping she merely said: "You know, one of the greatest songs that was ever written is very seldom sung on television, and I would like to sing that song for you tonight." This was the version CBS decided to air. The simplicity of the introduction was touching, and as her audiences recognized the song, they knew why she was singing it, even though at the time of the telecast Kennedy had been dead seven weeks. She then bowed off, leaving the orchestra to play "I Will Come Back."

The song had received a standing ovation at the dress rehearsal, which did not surprise her, since she knew how right her voice was for it. Tears were streaming down her face as she sang, as they were down the faces of most of those watching, including Tormé, who recalled:

I could almost hear the collective heartbeats in the place, and when [the second] chorus was done, when I thought peak effectiveness had been attained, she planted her feet more firmly on the stage and sang yet a third chorus, one key higher, this time at a much slower, insistent tempo, each beat achieving a raw assertiveness of its own. When she eventually got to:

HIS—TRUTH—IS—
MARRRR-CHING-ONNNNNNNNNN!

she wrung out those final five words for every ounce of value they were worth.

The audience "rose in a body and gave her the most genuine standing ovation I have ever witnessed," Tormé concluded. Garland had spoken for every American, still haunted by the events in Dallas on November 22.

Emotional though the song was, the taping of the show was one of the happier, calmer moments of this period in her career. Colleran admitted that matters were in a bad way when he took over: "Judy didn't know what to do with the show. Everybody was a nervous wreck, afraid for their jobs, afraid of what Judy would or wouldn't do. They'd tiptoe around her. I think it was absolutely doomed by the time I walked in." He thought she was bored with the show, and only continued to do it for the money. Shelley Berman saw it rather differently. He knew that there were to be no more comebacks in her life. She was a mature artist with only so much to give. She knew that the show was in trouble, and it was traumatic for her. He noted Merman's patience and lack of complaint when Garland refused to appear—and although he expressed no surprise, he might have done so, since Merman's temper and tongue were probably the most vicious in the business. While Berman remembered Garland with the affection that most of her peers felt for her, he considered that she was chronically sick. Once again, as at M-G-M, she was unable to handle either her career or her private life.

He was right. She eventually realized that Fields and Begelman were foremost among the rats leaving a sinking ship, and talked of suing for misappropriation of her money. She telephoned Robert Kennedy, then Attorney General, but did not proceed with a suit. They continued to represent her. On January 30, 1964, Luft instituted a lawsuit against CMA, claiming that Fields and Begelman had defrauded Garland by charging in excess of 10 percent for her services, a figure which he estimated at $350,000. He further petitioned that she had given them an additional $100,000 since CMA had been handling her, so demanded $450,000 plus $1,000,000 in punitive and exemplary damages. The case was to drag on for some time.

Garland's personal life was not much happier. Her affair with Glenn Ford drew to an end, and she embarked upon another one with Gregson Bautzer, whom she had once retained to handle one of her divorce suits against Luft. Divorce was Bautzer's specialty, but he now convinced Garland that his firm, Bautzer, Irwin and Schwab, should handle her financial affairs.

Garland's romantic liaison with Bautzer did not last beyond the end of her television series, but she may have found it fulfilling in a complex way. He had a reputation not unlike that of Artie Shaw of having "squired" many of Hollywood's most famous stars: indeed, he had preceded Shaw in Lana Turner's life, and was publicly associated with Joan Crawford for several years.

Garland also endured another row with Liza, who was hospitalized with a kidney complaint in January. She had been offered the lead in a production of *Carnival*, which was booked for a four-week run on Long Island, but Garland did not think that she was well enough to work. The show's producers received a long cable from Garland's lawyers:

JUDY GARLAND MOTHER AND LEGAL GUARDIAN OF LIZA MINNELLI A MINOR HEREBY INFORMS YOU THAT BECAUSE OF CONCERN FOR HER DAUGHTER'S HEALTH SHE HAS NOT CONSENTED AND WILL NOT CONSENT TO MISS MINNELLI ENTERING INTO AN AGREEMENT WITH YOU FOR THE PERFORMANCES OF SERVICES BY MISS MINNELLI STOP IF YOU EMPLOY MISS MINNELLI YOU DO SO WITHOUT MISS GARLAND'S CONSENT AND AT YOUR OWN RISK STOP MISS GARLAND WILL TAKE ALL LEGAL STEPS NECESSARY IN CIRCUMSTANCES TO PROTECT HER DAUGHTERS HEALTH STOP

The management of the two theaters was prepared to give in, but Liza defied her mother and insisted on doing the show. It was only later, John Fricke says, that Judy told her that she had been infuriated, but couldn't help but admire her for it.

These problems were to some extent offset by a press campaign which got under way in January, as columnists began to pressure CBS to save her television show. Garland was cheered by this support, but it was too late. CBS merely hesitated before finally making up its mind after the taping of the nineteenth show. On January 22, a formal exchange of letters was issued, between Garland and Aubrey, in which she stated that she had reluctantly come to the decision that "the involvement that I must give to production and performing these shows to be incompatible with the time and attention that I must give to family matters"—and he, in return, on behalf of the network, was "genuinely sorry."

The notion that it had been Garland who had made the decision fooled no one, and CBS took a hammering from television critics. The network's own most popular star, Lucille Ball, spoke up for Garland: "I was furious when one of the biggest stars in America, Judy Garland, was given lines like 'I'm a little old lady,' and someone talking about 'the next Judy Garland.' I bet she's glad her series is over. She's the best. When you're working with a king or queen why talk about who will succeed you?"

The contract still had some time to run, however, and there were still shows to be made. Buoyed by the support of the critics and people like Ball, Garland and Colleran decided to change the format of the show. Colleran had already insisted on more songs and less chatter, and had teamed his star with two old friends, Martha Raye and Peter Lawford. Unfortunately, guest stars cost money, as did appropriate sets for them. The program had constantly gone over budget, and until it was repeated or sold for syndication, the only real money Garland would see was what she could save on the seven shows still to go. Colleran reasoned that if she could fill theaters the world over and have audiences yelling for more then *The Judy Garland Show* should consist almost wholly of Garland singing. Since Garland had come to the same conclusion, for the same reasons, she agreed immediately; but Colleran foresaw trouble with both Aubrey, who observed that her talent had gone, and Stromberg, who believed that she could not hold a show on her own. Informed by Colleran of their objections, she telephoned Aubrey and told him that unless he agreed to Colleran's format she would not turn up. Aubrey realized that this would make headlines, and that they would turn in her favor once she gave her reasons for refusing to do the show.

Aubrey's capitulation raised her spirits immediately, and she sought a sweet revenge for his refusal to sanction her projected program after Kennedy's death by singing some of the songs planned for that occasion: a medley of "Swing Low Sweet Chariot" and "He's Got the Whole World in His Hands" to begin, and "America the Beautiful" to conclude. Between the two, she had chosen several songs associated with her, and a medley of songs from the First World War. After "Make Someone Happy," she sang "Liza," "Happiness Is Just a Thing Called Joe," with Joey in attendance, and "Lorna" to her second daughter, to a theme tune composed by Mort Lindsey for the show with a lyric specially written by Johnny Mercer. No longer hampered by unworthy trappings, she was in magnificent form, as the trade press reported before the show was aired. *Variety* noted that she received a standing ovation from cast and crew at the end of the taping—and, as Mike Connolly wrote in the *Hollywood Reporter*: "One could hardly blaze out more gloriously than that."

The broadcast itself pleased the critics of such papers as the *New York Times*:

After five months of trial and error in which the show has been subjected to various and ill-fated formulas, CBS is going to let Miss Garland do what she does best—sing . . . Miss Garland did her solo performance of the season, singing songs with which she has been identified for years. Seemingly a simple format, the show still contained certain production techniques used to instill excitement for the audience. In the center of a huge stage was this little girl, everybody's Judy, singing her heart out for her public . . . The next day, many people who had known mostly disappointment in watching the Garland show were commenting about the delightful change. No wonder that CBS is going to put that same little girl back on that great big stage alone three Sunday evenings. It could be that the Garland show will register the highest rating of the season.

There were, in fact, six more shows, and they followed the same format, although in four of them the numbers were shared with, or performed solo, by other artists: Diahann Carroll, Mel Tormé, Vic Damone and the pianist Bobby Cole. The twenty-sixth and the very last show featured Judy Garland alone. She knew it was one of the best things she had ever done.

She had already met Cole on a trip to New York in a fashionable *boîte* called Jilly's, to which Peter Lawford had taken her; also present were Tony Bennett, Frank Sinatra and Jack Jones. As a result of the evening's caroling, Garland decided to invite Cole to Hollywood as her accompanist for $1,000 a week—and he left his wife to do so.

Garland had long been a believer in paying for the best available talent and, according to Jack Elliott, rehearsal pianist and dance arranger on the show, many of the songs Tormé chose were "tired." He did less work than required, he was indecisive, and he was also having trouble with his marriage. By replacing Tormé with Cole on the last three shows, Garland would also save herself $6,000, the difference between the two men's salaries.

Tormé's own account of working with Garland suggests nothing but quarrels, but, as she told him, he was a "smartass" with her, resolutely flippant, as if trying to cut her down to his own professional size. He criticized her after one of the "Born in a Trunk" sequences in which she spoke of being exploited by M-G-M. "I don't care whether you liked it or not," she replied. "I always swore I'd get even with Mayer, and goddammit, now I am." Anyone else might have left it there, since Garland was famous for her anecdotes, and this one was harmless enough, but Tormé asked her why she wanted to get even with a man who was in his grave, and he went on to advise her not to waste valuable air time.

He said at the time: "I've seen Judy behave erratically, but it's obvious she's a lot more disturbed than any of us ever realized. Now, you couple that troubled nature with brilliant talent, a great sense of humor and occasional glimpses of humanity, and you got the damnedest tiger-by-the-tail in the history of women." Many of those who worked on the show agreed with him, but given this analysis, it was unwise, ungallant and even cruel of him to attempt to make jokes in what was their final argument—even if he was irritated that Cole had reworked some of his arrangements of a Jeanette MacDonald–Nelson Eddy medley, which she then had difficulty in singing, and for which she blamed him. She had already had him fired twice, but he had decided to stay on, doing exactly what his contract required of him—and this did not include pacing Garland onstage.

Gary Smith was also fired, principally, he thought, because he was one of the few people who told Garland the truth. Both she and Colleran had been contemptuous of his suggestions for guests. He had also been against her "concert" shows, which had eventually proved the most successful of the series—an achievement against the odds since at the time she and Luft were in the midst of another custody battle. Luft's accusation that Garland had tried to commit suicide on no less than twenty occasions particularly and predictably upset her, especially as it made headlines across the country.

On March 10, three days before the final show was set to be taped, Tormé filed for breach of contract. He demanded $13,500 for his three canceled guest appearances, plus $9,000 for the last three weeks. Distraught and unfocused, but still meticulous about the way the numbers should be handled, for two weeks Garland stumbled through rehearsals and tapings, uncertain whether she was capable of performing to the best of her ability, but wanting the last show to be a great one to go out on. She vacillated about whether or not the fans and friends she had invited were to be herded in and out of the studio at both the dress rehearsal and the taping itself. Her only consolation was a Dietrich-style gold-lamé dress, which had been designed for the occasion by Aghayan—but knowing that she looked sensational was little comfort in the circumstances.

She had asked for the saviors of her career, Fields and Begelman, to be present to succour her, but a "personal emergency" had kept them away. This turned out to be the first night of *Funny Girl* on Broadway. Garland was incensed when she finally learned this, and was devastated to receive as a farewell present from Stromberg a potted orchid, with the message: "You were great. Thanks a lot. You're through. Hunt Stromberg, Jr."

She was in tears much of the time, and on set flubbed many of the lyrics, sometimes joking about this and at other times walking off stage. The final taping was due to begin at 9:30 p.m. but did not start until 12:30 a.m.—by which time the caterers had arrived for the "end-of-term" party. An endurance test for all concerned, the taping finished at 5:54 a.m.

That was the end of *The Judy Garland Show*.

Colleran had only thirty minutes of material, half what he needed, and was obliged to fill out the hour with songs shot for an earlier show. It did not, in the end, matter, as Terrence O'Flaherty observed in the *San Francisco Chronicle*:

The final Judy Garland show has come crackling over the air. It was the most crisp and stylish musical series of the season. In fact, I cannot recall any in television's history where the production was so polished or where the star burned with any brighter intensity. For Garland fans—as well as viewers who seek showmanship and sophistication—the demise is a disaster.

Tomorrow night her vacancy is filled by two half-hour game shows described by the CBS press department as "frivolous and fun-type" programs. I hope those who so bitterly attacked Miss Garland will be happy with the new series, as well as the critics who called her new series a flop, and particularly James Aubrey of CBS who gave her a false façade and mercilessly pitted her against "Bonanza," the greatest attraction on television . . .

Despite saying in her letter of resignation that she was quitting "to be able to give more attention to her children," Miss Garland was actually dropped. But she walked out of CBS a bigger star than when she came in . . .

I have little sympathy with the producers' woes. All those associated with the program were well aware that they were working with a highly charged superstar whose ups and downs are as well chronicled as the decline and fall of the Roman Empire . . .

The show wasn't a flop; it just happened to be up against the stiffest competition on TV. It is far easier to fly over the rainbow than to beat a good horse opera. The fact that Judy Garland attempted it provided some of the high spots of the season.

In retrospect, Bill Colleran felt the good times far exceeded the bad. There were many, many good times, problem free—or if there had been difficulties, they were certainly not difficulties of Garland's making. He grieved that she was now so unhappy with her life and her career that she had resorted to drugs and alcohol. But in the end her talent made up for everything. There had simply never been a performer of this quality.

Norman Jewison put it another way:

She turned my hair gray, but Judy was a great lady—probably one of the most exciting women I have ever known. She had emotional problems. There were times when you felt it was not worth going on with the show, and yet there would be, all of a sudden, a moment of pure brilliance which made you think it was all worth it. She was like quicksilver.

The quicksilver could not be recaptured. Sal Iannucci of NBC said that there had never been much chance of syndication or foreign sales because the show was recorded on tape rather than the more adaptable and durable film, and no one—meaning Fields and Begelman—had attempted to settle with the various musicians' unions in order to effect further sales. Danny Kaye knew better, and his advisers sold his show to the BBC in Britain, who used it to bolster the viewing figures for its recently launched second channel—without success. Garland, meanwhile, had to face the fact that, in spite of all she had been through, her show had not made her a penny richer.

25

⋄⋅⋄⋅⋄⋅⋄⋅⋄

"They Still Want Me!"

On February 8, 1964, as *The Judy Garland Show* struggled to its close, its star was rushed from the Sherry-Netherland Hotel to the Mount Sinai Hospital, after her maid had found her with cuts on her face. Dr. Kermit Osterman said that Garland was suffering from mild concussion; her attorney, Irving Erdheim, announced that she was "feeling great." She was hospitalized again in March with a "suspected appendicitis," which turned out to be "flu." On March 25 the Supreme Court found in favor of a New York hotel which had sued for an unpaid bill dating from 1959. On April 21 Lawrence W. Beilenson filed for $69,000 in legal fees in connection with work carried out on the Mapleton house between 1959 and 1962. Almost everybody concerned with the television show was suing Kingsrow. Garland decided to get away from it all. She went to Australia.

She did not go alone, but with a small-part actor, Mark Herron, whom she had met at a party given by Ray Aghayan, who had known him in college. Although he was thirty-one, Herron had not actually done much acting, but while living in Rome he had had a minor role in Federico Fellini's 8½. Garland was enchanted by him, and had decided to promote his career. She did not want to return to concerts, and movies and television seemed closed to her: so her thoughts had turned to the legitimate theater. She liked the idea of the two of them co-starring in a play, and suggested Tennessee Williams's *Sweet Bird of Youth*, the plot of which concerned the stormy relationship between an aging actress and a young gigolo. Herron pointed out that this was not entirely suitable, since it suggested, all too bluntly, their own relationship. She then hit upon another play of Williams's, *The Glass Menagerie*, in which she would play the Laurette Taylor part. Liza would play her daughter and Herron would be her son, Tom. Neither Herron nor CMA saw much chance of this becoming a reality and, anyway, for the immediate future CMA had already accepted an offer from Harry Miller of Pan Pacific Productions for Garland to appear in Australia in May. For only three concerts, two in Sydney and one in Melbourne, she was to be paid, according to *Variety*, "around $52 thousand." This was thought to be the highest fee ever paid to a performer Down Under; she was, in fact, getting $15,000 a concert plus expenses. Even so, she did not really want to go—even to evade her creditors. She was persuaded that this would be a working holiday, with a stopover in Honolulu on the way there and a slow return trip to Europe by way of Hong Kong, Tokyo and other cities—including Athens, Naples, Rome and Copenhagen—before arriving in her favorite one of all, London.

Garland had taken on a new manager, Karl Brent, to replace Luft, but he would have to return to the States after the concerts, so she invited Herron to share the trip. They spent a week together in Waikiki before being joined by the rest of her party, nine in all, for the flight to Sydney. When she arrived, panic set in when customs officers once again confiscated her supply of pills. A Chinese back-street abortionist was eventually found to replace them, but the ones he supplied were of different dosages to those to which she was accustomed. She was nevertheless in glowing form at her first press conference, laughing at the failure of her television series and responding to one journalist, who asked her how she planned to relax in Australia, by looking into his eyes and asking: "What have you got in mind?" Asked about comebacks, she said that she had had so many that when she returned from the bathroom it was regarded as a comeback.

The two Sydney concerts, on May 13 and 16, were held in the wrestling arena, where, on both occasions, she played to capacity audiences of 10,000. They were personal triumphs, despite the fact that she was forgetting words, stopping and starting and having impromptu conversations with Mort Lindsey, who was conducting. There was a nasty moment after the second concert, when she thought she had taken enough bows. One of the officials of the stadium told her to get back on stage, but she declined and he said, "Listen, only a jerk singer like you could produce such a response." Astonished by the implication that she was fifth-rate, however much the fans adored her, Garland asked the man to repeat the remark. He did so and she slapped him across the face. Anyone but Garland would hardly have cared what a house assistant thought or said, but this insult unnerved her and nagged at her. The consequences would be disastrous.

Harry Miller went some way to compensate for this incident by taking an ad in the press. In the form of a heart, he told her that he loved her because: "last Sat. night at the Sydney Stadium she was just unbelievably fantastic!"

The press had been invited to meet her on her arrival in Melbourne on Sunday, May 17, four days before the concert on the Wednesday. When she decided to make the journey from Sydney by car, the reception was postponed until Tuesday. However, she changed her mind again and eventually took the train, canceling the press conference altogether. It was an inauspicious start.

On Wednesday, May 20, 7,000 people gathered in the Festival Hall for the concert. The Sydney shows had been thirty minutes late in starting, said to be due to late arrivals, so the Melbourne audience sat patiently from 8:30 p.m., when she was scheduled to appear. Just after 9:00, some slow hand claps began, and at 9:20 a voice was heard on the loudspeaker, saying: "It's quite obvious Miss Garland has been delayed." There were cheers a few minutes later when the voice announced that she was "on her way." The orchestra finally began to assemble on stage and, seven minutes later, two hours late, Garland at last appeared, escorted by Herron.

She acknowledged the cheers, blowing kisses as she walked slowly across the stage. Then she stood, center-stage, with the microphone in her hand, as if undecided what to sing. She went to consult Mort Lindsey on his podium, slapping him lightly on the head as she did so, and then taking his baton as if to conduct the orchestra. A member of the bewildered audience called out, "You are late!" "I couldn't get out of my hotel," she replied, unperturbed. "Have another brandy!" someone else shouted. Still unfazed, and seeming totally at ease, she swung into "When You're Smiling," but stopped in mid-song to chat to a photographer who was flashing bulbs in the second row. She posed for him, and then decided to sing her next song sitting in a chair. She seemed far too relaxed, and by now the audience had become edgy.

As long as she sang, the evening might be saved, but just after launching into "San Francisco," she stopped to complain that the microphone squeaked. "Act your age!" someone called out. She looked out into the darkness and replied: "I'm younger than you are. I'm supposed to be temperamental and I'm *being* temperamental." She again seemed uncertain of what she wanted to sing, and bickered with the audience. She eventually got through "San Francisco," then left the stage.

After a prolonged intermission of twenty-five minutes, she returned. Customers had begun trickling out, while die-hard fans were still calling out that they loved her. She managed a dismal version of "Puttin' on the Ritz," interrupting herself constantly to grumble again about the microphone cord. The song over, she complained about the noise from the air-conditioning. Some slow hand claps had no effect. It was clear that she wanted to banter with the audience rather than sing. Lindsey forced her to sing by striking up the opening chords of "Rockabye Your Baby," and for a while she seemed her old self. She managed "A Foggy Day" and then, *Variety* reported, went into "By Myself"—to the surprise of the orchestra, which had not rehearsed it. Worse still, she had forgotten the words. The audience was by now restive, and Garland was crying. She broke off and said: "It's so lonely by myself—Good night," and rushed off. The orchestra ran through the opening bars of "Over the Rainbow" to the sound of booing then gave up. Most of the audience had already done so.

Those who asked for their money back were refused. Karl Brent said that Garland had given "an adequate performance," which he thought admirable since she was, he said, suffering from laryngitis. Asked for comment, Harry Miller could give no explanation, merely repeating that she had been "fabulous" in Sydney and that no artist had ever given him less trouble. Later, he admitted that the Melbourne concert had so upset him that he had left after the intermission, and added: "Even if she was desperate I would not touch a Garland show again." It was unlikely that anyone in Australia would. What many found unforgivable was that Garland had blamed the orchestra, turning on its members after messing up one song and saying: "What are we supposed to be doing—playing cards?" The jazz trumpeter Pete Candoli, who had been playing for her for years, said as he left: "From now on, as far as Miss Garland is concerned, that's it. No more for me." Nevertheless he later did return to her.

The newspapers had a field day. When she got to the airport and stopped for a moment to talk to a child, she suddenly became aware of a large crowd in which some were cheering her, but others were booing loudly. She was shattered.

She and Herron left for Hong Kong, where she gave a press conference at the Mandarin hotel, saying that she had been delayed on her way to the concert hall: "The press and photographers had the hotel covered and it took me an hour to penetrate their flashbulb barrier." Later she changed her story, saying that some medicine prescribed for her had affected her adversely and that she had asked for the concert to be postponed until the following evening. She did not know whether the request had been conveyed to Miller.

Almost immediately, Hong Kong was battered by a typhoon, which terrified her, and her mental state was not improved when she learned that the news of the Melbourne concert had spread and would not be forgotten. She read an article about it in *Time* magazine, which began: "At 41, Judy Garland may have gone over the rainbow for the last time." She took an overdose.

When Herron went to collect her for dinner, he found her door locked. Getting no response, he asked for a duplicate key. He found her in a coma and rushed her to Canossa Hospital. This time, it seemed that she had been serious about destroying herself. No one doubted the reason. One of her doctors, Fred Pobirs, once said that she had developed such a tolerance to Seconal that she was able to take doses which would have killed anyone else. Her stomach was pumped, but her condition was so serious that both Dr. Siegel and Karl Brent flew out from Los Angeles. She had come out of the coma by the time Siegel saw her. After consultation with her Hong Kong doctors, he warned her that she might never be able to sing again. She later claimed that she had been clinically dead for five hours. The dosage she had taken had so damaged her health that she was never to be altogether well again.

By a tragic coincidence, her sister Suzy had succeeded in taking her own life a few days earlier, on May 26 in Las Vegas. She had taken an overdose, though the press reported that she had died of cancer. Begelman wired Herron, asking him to tell Garland at his discretion.

Her condition made it necessary for Herron to talk to the press, which identified him as her "traveling companion." Soon after she left the hospital, he became her husband. Or, so they claimed, announcing the news during an evening at a nightclub. Legally, she was still married to Luft, so it was just as well that the details were vague. Herron denied that Garland was still married, claiming that she had secretly divorced Luft in Mexico. He said that he and Garland were in a taxi when they impulsively asked the driver whether he knew of a ship where they might be married. He replied that he did, that it was either Norwegian or Swedish, and he took them there.

Later, they discovered that it was illegal for a captain to conduct a wedding while his ship was in port. So they were married again in the Mandarin by a Buddhist priest on June 12. They produced a document to prove this, but unfortunately it was in Chinese. It had been signed by five people: Mark Herron, Judy Herron, John Mold, who was an American Express official, Snowda Wu, a nurse from the hospital who was to become Garland's maid for the next two years, and Kwong, a dressmaker.

"I had been fighting my fights uphill for so long. I couldn't fight it alone anymore," Garland explained. But her press agent, Guy MacElwaine, hastily issued a statement: "Judy has a great sense of humor. But she's too smart to get married when she still has to go to court to get a divorce from Sid Luft."

While Garland was in the hospital, Herron had been impressed with the Allen Brothers, an Australian act he had seen at the Hilton. When she recovered, she went to see them and was impressed too. In particular, she thought that Peter Allen had a promising future and said that she would do everything she could to help his career. He shortly found himself having to act as go-between when she started quarreling with Herron. When the Allen Brothers traveled to Tokyo, where they were to play the Hilton, Garland and Herron came along too. It was thought that the sea voyage would do Garland good. The couple then flew by stages to London. Garland had already telephoned Marcella Rabwin from Hong Kong.

In London, Garland had rented a large house in the Boltons. In the aftermath of Melbourne—and Hong Kong—CMA did not even try to get her any concert dates. She herself knew that her career needed a new turn and she had finally found a play for herself and Herron, *The Owl and the Pussycat*, a two-hander by Bill Manhoff which she planned to open in London and then take it to New York. A sexual comedy, it concerns the relationship between a hooker and a fellow lodger, which begins with them quarreling but ends with their falling in love. She was examining the possibilities of a London production, but it was about as suitable as most of the other projects she had in mind for herself and Herron, and nothing came of it.

Garland's London visit coincided with a semi-annual show in aid of various actors' charities, "Night of a Hundred Stars," held at midnight at the Palladium. Traditionally, the first half contained songs and sketches by such favorites as Dora Bryan and Frankie Howerd, together with stars doing unexpected things—Laurence Olivier and Kenneth More in a drag act, Burt Lancaster and Kirk Douglas singing and dancing, or, in this instance, the Beatles flying on wires as they sang "I'm Flying," from the musical version of *Peter Pan*. After the intermission, the stage was found to be prepared for a floorshow. In order to bring the number of stars up to the advertised one hundred, various star guests entered to applause, and bowed in acknowledgment before taking their seats at tables on the stage. They, and the Palladium audience, were then entertained by some of the biggest names in the business. When, ten years earlier, the event had started, the bill was topped by the likes of Marlene Dietrich or Noël Coward, whose continued patronage was one reason why the show was always a glittering occasion. Everyone involved in 1964 believed that Judy Garland would top the bill and that this was the reason she was in London.

A few days before the show, however, she went into the hospital again: "I was opening some trunks bound with steel," she explained. "I tried to open them with scissors and succeeded in cutting myself on the elbow and arms." She left the hospital on the same day as the show, expressly forbidden to sing, but she was allowed to appear as one of the guests at the floorshow. The instant the audience heard the announcer say "Miss Judy . . .," it went wild. As one, it rose to its feet, while she and Herron walked to the footlights to bow. They retired to their allotted table, but the crowd would have none of this. Still on its feet, the entire Palladium audience roared its welcome and then began chanting, "Sing, Judy! Sing, Judy!" for more than ten minutes. In the entire history of the theater, no show has ever been stopped so dramatically and so fervently. Garland bobbed up and down from time to time to acknowledge the greeting, until, when it was finally clear that she was *not* going to sing, the uproar subsided.

Topping the bill was Shirley Bassey, doing her usual unacknowledged amalgam, half–Eartha Kitt and half–Lena Horne. When she had finished her second song, "If Love Were All," she blew a kiss toward Garland, saying that she had sung it for her. It was the signal for pandemonium to break out again, but it subsided as Bassey began to sing "No Regrets." But this time, the crowd had the bit between its teeth. Applause for Bassey was drowned by a unified chant of "Sing, Judy!" After some minutes, the master of ceremonies, Richard Attenborough, walked over to Garland and led her center stage: it was the only thing for him to do. It was her evening, and the least she could do was to thank the audience, which was suddenly quite silent. A simple, whispered "It's nice to be home again," was the signal for the audience to make it crystal clear, if it had not done so already, that it felt the same way as she did. "All right," she asked, "what do you want to hear?" Again there was tumult, which she quietened by saying: "Well, you discuss it among yourselves, while I talk to the piano player." Actually, she consulted the orchestra leader, Billy Ternent: "Does anyone know what key I sing in?" Ternent tried a few bars of "Over the Rainbow," and Garland nodded. She could have beaten Bassey at her own game by singing every note fortissimo, but instead she chose to croon the number, gently, as wistfully as she had done before setting out on the Yellow Brick Road. Then, after joking with Ternent about the tempo for "Swanee," she tore into it. The audience was satisfied.

Garland herself was overwhelmed. She had expected a warm welcome, but nothing like this:

> Because these people were taking the trouble to show me that, to them, all the things that have happened in the past, all the things that have been said about me, didn't matter. They wanted me to know that they really cared, it was as if they were sending a great wave of love across to me. London has always been like home to me. Now it's more than ever like home. I don't know what happened there at the Palladium or why the people should have shown such emotion toward me. I guess it's something which just happened. And, believe me, it was the most exciting thing in the world.

She implied that London had saved her when her career was in ruins in 1951, and it had done so again when she found herself in the same situation after Melbourne. And that was why she ignored doctors' orders to sing.

The evening was reported in the *Listener*.

> Stars today have become devalued and it is tempting to dismiss them as merely a product of their publicity. So it is salutory to be reminded that a star is a star, with an inexplicable magic which more than justifies the fame and the ballyhoo . . . Tears were in many eyes at what appeared to

be a personal triumph over adversity, while Miss Garland's magnificent voice fully deserved the cheers which eclipsed any that had gone before in this genuinely starry show. This was an exceptional occasion which everyone present will remember for ever.

She flew to Rome with Herron, returning to London to record four songs from Lionel Bart's new show, *Maggie May*, for an extended-play 45 rpm disc. Bart had been a prominent member of the entourage of fans and friends with whom she surrounded herself in London, and they had been frequently photographed together. She had seldom attempted material of this poor caliber, and Capitol wisely decided against issuing the record in the States. In the wake of the *Carnegie Hall* album, Capitol had issued a single, "Sweet Danger" and "Comes Once in a Lifetime," but it did not sell well. Except for the album Capitol recorded at the Palladium later in the year, the *Maggie May* session ended Garland's association with the label, though the company was able to issue a couple of albums consisting of material already recorded.

Garland attended the first night of Bart's show in September and was admitted to the hospital the following day, once again with "suspected appendicitis." She talked to some of the television companies about doing a drama with Herron, but this was another plan which did not get beyond the discussion stage. She was very busy socially, attending many parties with Herron's homosexual friends, at some of which she was the only woman present. On September 16, for example, as guest of honor, she accompanied Herron to the opening of a new gay club. On this occasion, she explained that her voice was not at its best and instead of singing submitted to a question-and-answer session. Ten weeks later, she attended a meeting of her British fan club, reveling in five hours of undiluted admiration, and rewarding the members by singing two songs.

In October, her lawyers warned her that she could avoid what promised to be some more damaging publicity by staying well clear of the States. There was to be yet another custody battle, but it was not quite like any of the others. In the past, Luft had tried to protect Garland's image as much as he could and only reluctantly agreed with his attorneys that she should be declared an unfit mother. The gloves were now off. She was, he admitted, "suffering from mental illness as a result, in part, of her use of barbiturates to the degree that, in the absence of prolonged rest and hospitalization, she is unable to care for her minor children." Rhoda Chiolak, a one-time housekeeper, said that Garland was "intoxicated around the children many times"; she had only once seen Garland play with them, while Luft "showed love and affection" and taught them table manners. Albert Paul, the hairdresser she had sacked in London, testified that he was often required to bring her four quart-size bottles of wine in one bucket, and Vern Alves, described as her "manager," bore witness to her suicide attempt in Philadelphia. Luft informed the court that she had used the children in her act to benefit herself, and claimed that: "Lorna and Joe had attended at least eight different schools. Because they have been shunted from one place to another they are scholastically behind other children."

The only person who spoke up for Garland was Mrs. Hettie Chapman, Lorna's governess, who gallantly swore that she had never seen her employer take a drink. Garland's lawyers counterattacked: when Luft had the children, they claimed, he "has gone directly to his hotel and never taken them anywhere else. At the hotel he drinks intoxicating liquor in their presence. He takes their allowance from them and does not return it." Their attempt to blacken Luft was in vain: he was granted increased visiting days.

What Garland felt about Luft at this period may be gathered from some tapes she made as the first steps toward writing her autobiography. The likelihood of her ever actually putting pen to paper must have been remote, but talking aloud clearly served some therapeutic purpose. "Sid Luft is an animal," she announced to the machine. "I will tell the world whenever I can that he is a thief, a blackmailer, a sadist and a man who doesn't even care one bit one way or the other about any other living soul, let alone his nice children." This last remark might more justly be applied to Garland herself, who, on one tape lightly admits: "I don't really care about anybody but me." Her ramblings are as inconsistent as one might expect. She speaks at length about her children and the fate that has befallen them:

I respect them, I worship them. They give me the same respect, the same love in return. They're brave children. They have to be. Look who their father is . . . I want them with me, I gave birth to them, I supported them, I loved them, I still do, but for goodness' sake, for God's sake, what about the lawyers, what about the judges? They are being handed to a man—I hate that word in connection with Sid Luft—Michael Sidney Luft is not a man, he's not a father, he's not a worker, he's not a contributor, he's not anything. He's a pimp . . . The judges sit down—I don't know how he pays them off—and my children are stuck in Santa Monica. They didn't even get to visit me in school vacation. I am supposed to be an unfit mother.

In his deposition, Luft had described Mark Herron as "a person of questionable moral conduct . . . with no visible means of support . . . given to idleness, profligacy and dissipation." In court, he spoke of Garland squandering "family funds" on the young man, but by this time, Garland had put Herron to work. He was to be one of the producers of her next concert.

Liza had come on a visit to her mother in her Kensington home and Garland conceived the idea of them appearing together at the Palladium. There was little prospect of work for her in America. As for Liza, there had been some fleeting talk of starring her in a Broadway musical based on the film *Roman Holiday*, so identified with Audrey Hepburn that casting seems bizarre. There was equally no doubt, after the "Night of a Hundred Stars," that she could fill a theater on her own. She certainly needed the money, but she was not strong enough to sing for a whole evening. Her attitude toward Liza remained equivocal, but—perhaps in the light of the custody battle over her other two children—she wanted to show that she was genuinely proud of this talented young woman. What better way to do this than to share the stage of the Palladium with her?

The concert was arranged for a Sunday evening, November 8. As in 1960, it sold out so quickly that another was arranged a week later, but since the Palladium was already booked for that evening, the concert would have to start at midnight. Television cameras were in attendance for transmission over the Christmas period, and Capitol was also there to record it for another double album. Singly and together, mother and daughter sang a host of songs, some old, but many of them new to Garland's repertoire, and some of them arranged by the then unknown Marvin Hamlisch, who was a friend of Liza's. No one could ever forget Garland's heartfelt "Well, Hello Liza" to the tune of "Hello Dolly" as she introduced her daughter, but the concert as a whole was a question of *noli contendere*. At eighteen, Liza was gauche, gawky, eager—and up-staged at every turn by Garland, who constantly jerked her daughter's mike toward her mouth, as if she were not using it properly. Liza recalled:

It was like Mama suddenly realized I was good, that she didn't have to apologize for me. It was the strangest feeling. One minute I was on stage with my mother, the next moment I was on stage with Judy Garland. One minute she smiled at me, and the next minute she was like the lioness that owned the stage and suddenly found somebody invading her territory . . . the killer instinct of a performer had come out in her.

The recording Capitol made finds both mother and daughter shrill, but it is much less distorted than the abbreviated television version, which fails to convey the exhilaration they both felt at working together.

At the beginning of 1965, Garland crossed the Atlantic to fulfill a concert booking in Canada. While in New York, she consented to appear on a television variety show, *On Broadway Tonight*. When her forthcoming appearance was announced, the show's producer, Irving Mansfield, received 27,000 requests for tickets, for a studio which could seat only 1,000. The Allen Brothers were with her, and she kept her promise by inviting them to appear in her next few concerts. Liza had fallen in love with Peter Allen and they had become engaged. Garland encouraged the match, even though she knew that Allen was no more suitable for Liza than Herron was for her: he also was openly gay.

Herron was credited with supervising Garland's appearance at the O'Keefe Center, Toronto, on February 8. *Variety* noted the standing ovation, but said: "In truth, Miss Garland's voice was like sandpaper grinding, often missing the notes completely." Laryngitis kept her out of both shows one day and, although she was seldom on form throughout the one-week engagement, audiences did not seem to mind.

She fulfilled a one-week engagement at the Fontainebleau, Miami Beach, and then, unexpectedly, flew to Hollywood to start a film. A scurrilous biography of Jean Harlow had re-awakened interest in the famous star. The producer Joseph E. Levine was planning a film of her life starring Carroll Baker as Harlow, with Angela Lansbury in the plum role of her mother. The facts about Harlow were in the public domain, however, and another company planned to beat Levine to it. They could do this by making the movie on videotape, as for television, and then converting it for cinemas by transferring to a system they called "Electronovision." In this version, Carol Lynley was to play Harlow, and Garland had been cast as Mama Jean. It was, if not a get-rich-quick operation, an enterprise which was far below the standard to which Garland was accustomed. Just before the movie was due to start shooting on March 31, she had second thoughts, and was replaced by Eleanor Parker. Parker also thought better of it, and the role eventually went to Ginger Rogers. When the film finally appeared, it was little seen.

Garland was invited to Hollywood by Joe Pasternak, who was producing the Academy Awards ceremony. He asked her to sing a Cole Porter medley, arranged by Roger Edens, but it was soon clear to Edens and Johnny Green, who was conducting, that she was not up to it. She managed to get through a curtailed version, but if she looked better than she had, her voice was not up to it and didn't bring her any new admirers. It was Hollywood's great night and one of its legendary stars had proved that she was over the hill. She needed a vacation, and went with Lorna and Joey to Diamond Head in Hawaii. There, the house caught fire. Lorna discovered her mother trying to extinguish the flames with cans of water, and had to call the fire brigade.

Garland seemed much better when she appeared at the first night of *Flora, the Red Menace*, in which Liza made her Broadway debut in May. On May 20, she was at long last divorced from Luft, after testifying that "he struck me many times . . . did a lot of drinking . . . and used profane language before me and the children." The witnesses on her behalf were Karl Brent and her housekeeper, Mattie Oliver, who spoke of Garland's sleepless nights, which they both blamed on Luft. He was ordered to pay $150 a month maintenance each for Lorna and Joey.

Wretchedly ill, but needing the money, she accepted an engagement in Cincinnati in a boxing arena called Cincinnati Gardens. She managed seven songs in the first half, which lasted only twenty minutes. The intermission stretched to an hour. After which two local doctors and her own doctor, who had flown out from New York, were brought on to explain that she was suffering from "a virus infection." About a third of the audience of 4,500 disappointed spectators milled around outside her dressing-room, but she had already gone. The promoter, Dino J. Santangelo, told them that their tickets would be honored the following Sunday, but Karl Brent explained that it would cost her $8,000 in airfares and other costs just to return.

Her finances were, as usual, in chaos. She had taken to fleeing hotels in the middle of the night to avoid paying the bill, wearing as many clothes as she could under her coat. The children did the same. Three years later Hermione Gingold recalled catching a glimpse of Garland at this period:

I saw her . . . in New York standing outside a building on 57th Street. She was being turned out and having a row with a man who was holding her clothes and who was refusing to hand them over until she paid some back rent. I felt she might be embarrassed to think I'd seen this episode (I was in a taxi), but it still haunts me whether I should have stopped or not. I felt so sorry for her—she seemed completely alone.

When it was possible, she stayed in friends' houses, with photographs of her family propped up about her to give the impression to any potential interviewers that she was renting rather than borrowing.

Peter Lawford hosted a birthday party for her on June 10, and two days later she was taken to the UCLA Medical Center's Neuropsychiatric Institute for the treatment of "emotional upset" after an allergic reaction to a drug. She left the clinic for a two-week engagement at the Thunderbird in Las Vegas, which attracted capacity audiences. It went off without mishap, but her salary was sequestered by court order when an attorney, William Morse, filed for $4,000, including $3,000 for work on her divorce suit in 1962.

She attracted an audience of 10,000 when she returned to the Forest Hills Stadium in New York. Murray Schumach was on hand to report it for the *New York Times*:

> That fascinating phenomenon of modern show business, the long and widely publicized love affair between Judy Garland and her following, was on full display . . . [The audience] was extremely aware that Miss Garland's voice is just a memory; that she is often off pitch and that she frequently forgets lyrics. It was also quick to respond to that potent fervor that Miss Garland packs into her delivery, even when her voice quavers and cracks. This audience also appreciated her wondrous sense of showmanship, with calculated pause, imitation dance steps and hand gestures that were not merely the nervous mannerisms of many television performers.

Long after the concert was finished and the orchestra had left, she appeared on stage in her dressing gown to a huge crowd still yelling "We want Judy!" In her dressing-room, with tears streaming down her face, she kept repeating over and over: "They still want me!"

26

❖❖❖❖❖❖❖

Valley of the Dolls

AFTER A FIVE-PERFORMANCE ENGAGEMENT in San Carlos, California, at the end of August 1965, Garland returned to Los Angeles for a six-night booking starting on Monday, September 13, at the Greek Theater. She was guaranteed $35,000 and 65 percent of the gross above $65,000. On this engagement the house paid the supporting acts: the Young American Singers and ten dancers from the Los Angeles Ballet Company. She was fine on the first night, but after the performance, she fell over a pet dog and broke her arm. It was put into plaster and she insisted upon going on, although she was in considerable pain. She was late starting, and some show-business friends, Mickey Rooney, Martha Raye and Johnny Mathis, were brought on and rallied round her on stage, to enable her to get through the evening. Unfortunately, Garland's performance gave the impression that they had first joined her in her dressing-room for drinks.

The Wednesday and Thursday shows were canceled, and only the singers and dancers appeared on Friday, when the house paid out some $10,000 in refunds. Two extra shows had been scheduled for the Sunday, but these too were canceled. The total take for the week's engagement—which amounted to two performances—was $21,000. The total costs were much higher, as the management had had to pay the salary of the orchestra and make refunds of about $40,000. The matter went to litigation. "There's no arguing with a broken arm," as *Variety* put it, "but the long-term effects of the occurrence will, unfortunately, compound an impression that exists in the minds of some promoters and fans that Miss Garland cannot be relied upon to completely fulfill a commitment."

It was the beginning of the end. Friends, the industry at large, turned away. Los Angeles was, after all, her home town, and she hadn't even tried for them. It was not perhaps so much a conscious turning away as a feeling that if she couldn't help herself then no one could. She stumbled through the autumn, making several guest appearances on television, including *The Andy Williams Show*, which had been taped back in July, her comedy and pantomime effects were fine, as John Fricke wrote, but her vocal powers were subject to serious doubts. In an effort to minimize the recent damage to her career, she appeared live on *The Ed Sullivan Show* on October 3, and later in the month she accepted an invitation from ABC to play hostess at the *Hollywood Palace*, a weekly variety show whose guests on this occasion included Vic Damone. She sang "Some of These Days," and footage exists of the final rehearsal and the show itself to prove that she could rally at the last minute when required.

The show was televised on November 13, the day before she married Mark Herron in Las Vegas. The witnesses were her press agent, Guy McElwaine, and his wife, but Garland's children were not there. Liza was about to open at the Cocoanut Grove in Los Angeles; in any event, the middle of the night ceremony was an impromptu affair.

Those friends she still had were gradually alienated by her increasingly erratic behavior. A few days after the wedding she had been present at one of the smartest social occasions of the season, when Sharman Douglas was hostess of a party at the Bistro in Beverly Hills for Princess Margaret and her husband, Lord Snowdon. At some point, Douglas sent word to Garland that the guests of honor would like to hear her sing. She replied: "Go and tell that nasty, rude, little princess that we've known each other long enough and gabbed in enough ladies' rooms that she should skip the ho-hum royal routine and just pop on over here and ask me herself. Tell her I'll sing if she christens a ship first." But, sing she did and was the hit of the party.

At another party, given by Janet Leigh for Pat (Kennedy) Lawford, Garland asked the guest of honor: "Is it true that you've gone Republican?" She then poured her iced vodka down the back of Lawford's dress. She calmly went to the bathroom, where she remained so long that Leigh, fearing the worst, began to panic. When Garland finally emerged, she explained that she had found a copy of the magazine *Redbook*, which was serializing Ira Levin's novel, *Rosemary's Baby*.

At the end of November, she opened a two-week engagement at the Sahara in Las Vegas, for which she was paid $50,000 a week. Two days after it concluded, she appeared at the Astrodome in Houston for one night, supported by the popular Motown trio the Supremes. The arena was vast, seating 45,000, so an audience of only 15,000 was almost inconspicuous. She was paid $43,000 for the engagement, so the producer took a big loss, and this did not go unnoticed by the trade.

In February 1966, she played the Diplomat Hotel in Hollywood, Florida, and at the end of the engagement she visited the Children's Hospital in Miami. She did four guest appearances on television, once on *Hollywood Palace* again, once on NBC's *Kraft Music Hall*, and twice on Sammy Davis Jr's program.

On April 12, Herron opened in Noël Coward's *Private Lives* at the Ivar Theater in Hollywood, playing opposite Kathie Browne. Garland was accompanied by George Cukor at the first night, and she confessed herself very proud of her husband. They separated almost immediately afterwards.

This surprised no one. Peter Lawford once received an urgent call from Garland to say that Herron had attacked her with a razor. He dropped everything to get to her, and found that her face had been cut up badly in several places. While he was looking for some surgical spirit to cleanse the wounds, the maid told him that Garland had inflicted them on herself. He could find nothing suitable in the medicine cabinet, so used vodka instead.

Herron moved into a motel, to learn the lines of *Private Lives* undisturbed, as he put it, but Garland kept telephoning, saying that she needed him. When he learned that under California law he could be liable for half of her mountain of debts, he instigated divorce proceedings. His lawyer told him that she owed $400,000 in taxes and a lien might be placed on his salary for the rest of his life. They were not in fact divorced until April 1967, when the mud flew, most of it in his direction. Garland claimed that he did not decide to become an actor until after they were married, that he had had no intention of living as man and wife, and that the marriage had not been consummated. He drank two bottles of Scotch a day; he left her alone in the evening, perhaps returning at three or four in the morning. "He would kick me when I was down," she claimed. This was virtually the only one of her charges on which he passed comment, except to dismiss them as "ludicrous." If he did kick her, he explained, "it was all in self-defense." Garland managed to have three different agents during 1966, but, dogged by tax problems, she refused all offers of work. She had only two concert engagements during the entire year. The second was in August, at El Patio, a nightclub in Mexico City, where she was to have played for two weeks. The altitude affected her voice so badly that she could not continue and the booking was canceled after her second appearance.

In May 1966 she sang at the Americana in New York in a tribute to the brilliant comic actress Judy Holliday, who had died tragically young the year before. It was a gala to benefit the American Medical Center in Denver. Garland sang "When You're Smiling," "Rockabye Your Baby" and two songs written for Holliday, "Just in Time" and "The Party's Over," which drew such an onslaught of applause that she encored with her familiar medley of "You Made Me Love You," "For Me and My Gal," "The Trolley Song" and "Over the Rainbow."

In December, after several months of idleness, the *National Enquirer* ran a banner headline: JUDY GARLAND BROKE. "Once I was worth millions," she told Walter Benson, "but today I haven't got a dime. Once I had everybody at my feet. Today only the name counts—the money is gone." She said that she had earned $8,000,000 in her life, $400,000 of this before she was eighteen. She was currently three months in arrears with the monthly payments of $3,000 the courts had ordered her to make to Luft, until she had paid off a total of $150,000 for services rendered to her when he was still her manager. This was a role she now asked him to fill for her again.

It was not only her finances which were causing trouble. She had recently had an affair with a woman, and rumors of this were being spread around, probably by the woman in question. One of Garland's fans telephoned her to warn her about this, but found himself unable to put it in words. "I don't want to hurt you, Judy," he said. "I know it's not true." Garland knew what he wanted to say, and replied: "You can tell me." At this point, Lorna, who was fifteen, grabbed the telephone and said of the woman who was allegedly spreading the stories: "She's a dyke." Garland appeared to be highly amused and not remotely embarrassed.

In fact, the fan was really much more concerned about Garland's financial state. He suggested that he could talk to some of her other fans to see whether there was anything they could do to help her. Garland admitted: "I could need a buck. We're desperately in need of food and money." When he asked her whether she was offended by his suggestion, she said she thought "it's the most wonderful thing."

On more than one occasion there was so little food in the house that Marc Rabwin had to replenish the larder for the sake of the children. She was so short of funds that when Liza married Peter Allen in New York on March 3, 1967, she was unable to afford a present. She solved this problem by charging a tablecloth to her account at a Beverly Hills store, perfectly aware that the shop was unlikely ever to see the money. Liza herself paid for Lorna and Joey's airfares to New York; Garland's was paid for by 20th Century-Fox, for whom she was about to make a film. On the morning of the wedding, she telephoned Vincente Minnelli, to whom she hadn't spoken for years. "If you had any class, you'd escort me to our daughter's wedding," she told him, with the result that at the ceremony Judy Garland and Vincente Minnelli were seen together for the first time in sixteen years.

This family reunion was a happy occasion, but it did nothing to ease Garland's financial problems. She was running out of friends to borrow from, though there were a very few who gave her money whenever they were asked until the end of her life. On March 15, she filed suit against Begelman, Fields and CMA, claiming that they had withheld monies and mishandled her financial affairs, leaving her unable to pay her taxes.

It was because she was so desperate for money that she had accepted a role in what she later called "a dirty picture" being made by 20th Century-Fox. *Valley of the Dolls* was a show-business story based on Jacqueline Susann's best-selling, sensationalist novel. Susann was a friend of Begelman, and one of the characters in her novel is based loosely on him. Another character, the young pill-popping actress, who would be played in the film by Patty Duke, was based partly on Garland herself. Garland's own role was that of a composite character containing much of her old friend Ethel Merman, with whom Susann had once enjoyed a flagrantly public liaison.

Garland had no illusions about the project. She knew the background, though she had not read the book, and now, with the same distaste, declined to read the script. Hers was not the largest role, but it was an important one; and she would be being paid $75,000 for eight weeks' work.

Fox called a press conference in which Garland wittily diverted questions about herself to concentrate them on the author. When asked about the prevalence of drug addiction among show people she replied that it was equally common among journalists. Fox showed how pleased they were to have her by fitting up a luxurious new dressing-room, which contained a pool table, because this was her latest hobby. To protect her, the studio decreed that she was not to be approached for any publicity during filming. She was fine during the pre-recording of her one song, "I'll Plant My Own Tree," although she disliked it, and she was enthusiastic about the costumes, designed by Bill Travilla. (During the costume test she was asked to stand with her back against the wall. She retorted, "What? Without a cigarette and a blindfold?")

Once shooting began, however, it was the same old story. She arrived at, and departed from, the studio at the strangest hours, but could never be found when she was wanted on the set. She locked herself inside her dressing-room and refused to respond to anyone who tried to speak to her through the door. She cowered there, every day, "in abject terror" according to Patty Duke. On the third day, she managed to come on set, but the director, Mark Robson, got nothing from her that he could use.

One day, as she was wandering round the lot, she witnessed the filming of a torrid bedroom scene. "It's bawdily interesting, isn't it?" she commented. "It makes me feel like voyeurism could be fun!" She had no idea that the scene was being shot for inclusion in the *Valley of the Dolls*: when she discovered the truth, she was even more ambivalent about the project in which she had become involved.

She could not afford to be squeamish, however. One evening, Lorna telephoned Marc Rabwin to say that there was no food in the house, and that Garland needed medication to help her sleep. He managed to give her what she needed and he left some food. In the morning, he told the studio that she was unlikely to complete the film unless she had round-the-clock nursing and was given some money. Fox provided a nurse and $5,000, but to no avail. After a few more days, during which she refused to appear on set, she was fired by a Fox executive, Owen McLean, who told her: "We're tired of your foolishness. We're just not going to put up with it." Patty Duke heard a racket in Garland's dressing-room, and went to see what it was all about: "Finally she opened the door, looking like the wrath of God. She was not physically hurt, but the cloth on the room's antique pool table was broken, the light hanging over it was broken, there was glass everywhere."

The studio announced that Garland had resigned for personal reasons, but she immediately denied that: "I have not withdrawn. I was up at six this morning to go to work, it's a shocking thing. Why? That's what I want to know. Why?" Later, she claimed that Liza had persuaded her that the entire project was unworthy of her. What she really thought unworthy of her, however, was playing second fiddle to the much younger Duke, whose talents she did not in any case admire. It had very quickly become quite clear, according to contemporary reports contrary to Duke's account, that the two actresses cordially disliked one another. A further explanation for Garland's behavior was provided by Susann, who said she had advised Garland to behave in an irrational manner so that Fox would be forced to fire her, because if she quit voluntarily, she would forfeit her fee. In the event, Fox allowed Garland to keep half of it, $37,500, but Internal Revenue immediately seized $23,000. After her agents' commission had been deducted, she was left with approximately $10,000, and decided that she *did* want to make the film after all. Susann interceded with Zanuck on her behalf, but he told her that Garland had cost the film enough already.

On April 8, she was a guest at a dinner given by the *Beverly Hills Courier* to honor citizens who had benefited the community. The paper had just instituted an annual award, and the first two recipients were the mayor, Jake Stuchen, and Marcella Rabwin, who had done a great deal of work on behalf of various charities. James Stewart was the master of ceremonies, and Desi Arnaz and Rudy Vallee provided the entertainment. When the organizers heard that Garland had asked the Rabwins whether she could accompany them, a special spot was set aside for her at the end of the evening. She had brought along Lorna and Joey, and the Rabwins thought she seemed more herself than for a long time. Vallee went on for an hour. Garland soon grew bored, and disappeared to the ladies' room several times. Eventually, when the time came for her to sing, she was in no condition to do so. Uncertain what to do, the Rabwins allowed her to slur her way through two songs before stopping her. The room was silent as she resumed her seat next to Marcella. A man close to them said, quietly,

"Sing 'Over the Rainbow.' " Garland knew she had ruined Marcella's evening. With tears in her eyes, she looked to her friend as if asking permission, and Marcella, pitying her, nodded. Without accompaniment, Garland sang, as purely and as clearly as she had the first time she ever performed the song. The place broke into applause. "I know you hate me," she said softly to Marcella, who replied: "I could never hate you, Judy, but I may feel sorry for you."

Things were just picking up but not for long when she learned that the Internal Revenue intended to take possession of the house in Hollywood. She turned to her former co-star, George Murphy, who had left the movies and become a senator, and he managed to pull a few strings in order to delay the action. Luft eventually sold the house for $130,000, much less than it was worth, but this was only a fraction of what she owed in taxes.

In May she became engaged again. In October 1965, Guy McElwaine had introduced her to one of his colleagues, Tom Green, whom he thought could handle her publicity. The next summer, Green left McElwaine's company to work exclusively for Garland, as her manager for both personal and private affairs. He was from Lowell, Massachusetts, a Dartmouth graduate, some thirteen years younger than she. When the engagement was announced, the couple said they intended to marry in the chapel at Dartmouth. Green had taken his fiancée to Lowell for Christmas, and she said that it was the first time she had seen snow not manufactured by M-G-M. He firmly believed that she would never be well unless she could get away from show business but, even with loans from him and his family, she had to stay in business to pay her debts.

Any royalties to come from her record companies were already spoken for, either by government liens or in repaying advances already made to her. She asked Morgan Maree, who had cut free from the Lufts at the end of 1957, to return to manage her financial affairs; and she asked Luft to find her work.

Luft promptly contracted her services to a company called Group V. The five concerned, as she understood it, were herself, Luft and her three children. Characteristically, she did not read the contract before signing it, and it was not until later—too late—that she learned that the only member of her fragmented family who became part of Group V was Luft. The driving force behind Group V was a man called Raymond Filiberti, who had a police record.

Group V promised to find her work, but now owned her body and soul. She had read only the first page of the contract when Luft first presented it to her as they drove to her first engagement for Group V. Had she read further, she would have come across Clause 17 of this extraordinary document, which read:

> As used in this agreement, the term "incapacity" shall be deemed to refer to any of the following events occurring at any times during the term of this agreement: the material incapacity of Garland arising out of her illness or mental or physical disability or arising out of any accident involving personal injury to Garland; the disfigurement, impairment of voice or any material change in the physical appearance or voice of Garland; the death of Garland; and the prevention of Garland from rendering services by reason of any statute, law, ordinance, regulation, order, judgment or decree.
>
> Garland will give the Corporation written notice of her incapacity within twenty-four (24) hours after the commencement thereof, and if she fails to give such notice, any failure of Garland to report to the Corporation as and when instructed by the Corporation for the rendition of her required services hereunder may, at the option of the Corporation . . . be treated as Garland's default.

Whether she *ever* read the whole contract is doubtful, but she was persuaded at the time that its chief function was to protect her from the Internal Revenue. She was unwilling to accept offers to work because, John Fricke says, the more she did the deeper in debt she became. Filiberti was generously investing in a fading talent, and in return Group V were paying Luft $1,000 a week as her manager. She was to receive $1,500 for every appearance she made, plus a percentage of the box office; $100 would be deducted weekly from Luft's salary, and $300 from her fee whenever she worked, until their indebtedness to the U.S. Treasury was paid off.

She was in no condition to resume making concert tours, however. Luft wanted to get her back on television, but no company was interested. He suggested that she return to the Palace, which had become a legitimate theater since Garland last played there. It was to revert to vaudeville temporarily at the end of August, with Eddie Fisher and Buddy Hackett. In the meantime, *Sweet Charity* was nearing the end of its run there, but when the show's star, Gwen Verdon, had to go into the hospital, business fell away so rapidly that the Palace could more profitably go dark than prolong the run. Consequently, the management was only too happy to have Judy Garland back, for just four weeks. In the meantime, she did warm-up appearances at the Westbury Music Fair, New York, and the Camden Music Fair in New Jersey.

On July 31, 1967, "Judy Garland at Home at the Palace" opened under the auspices of Group V. Luft had brought Vern Alves back to help: Tom Green was on the payroll as Garland's publicity manager; Bobby Cole was in the pit. Lorna and Joey were part of the act, as again was John Bubbles, to dance "Me and My Shadow" with her. He also appeared in the first half, along with Jackie Vernon and Francis Brunn. Richard Barstow staged Garland's act, which began with her entering the theater from the back. Her clothes-sense had not much improved since her last appearance, and she wore the encrusted diamanté pants-suit made for *Valley of the Dolls*. Vincent Canby reported in the *New York Times*: "Judy Garland returned to the Palace last night like some raffish, sequin-suited female Lazarus. That magnificent talent is alive once more in New York, and so is one of the most remarkable personalities of the contemporary entertainment scene. That the voice—as of last night's performance, anyway—is now a memory seems almost beside the point." The screenwriter William Goldman was there the last night. "What do you think?" he heard someone say, "Is it theater?"—and the answer came: "Is it theater? You bet it's theater. It sure as hell ain't singing."

During the engagement, on August 4, Pathé Pictures joined the long list of people who sued Garland and Luft during the 1960s. Pathé's president, Barnett Glassman, had bought the rights to the twenty-six episodes of *The Judy Garland Show*, only to discover that he had bought a pig in a poke. Although Garland owned the tapes, syndication was impossible without the clearance, which she did not have, from participating guests and staff who were entitled to residual rights. Glassman estimated that Pathé had already spent $97,877 before discovering that they could not show the material, but was asking only the $154,000 which his company had paid for it. The case went into abeyance until 1976, by which time Glassman was seeking $2,500,000 damages against Luft. The judge dismissed the suit, but at the time he declined to rule on the ownership of the tapes.

Garland undertook another dozen engagements over the next few months, all over the country, mainly for one night, and then, when she tired, she left for a vacation in London with Ray Filiberti and his wife Sherwin. This was a mistake, since Garland and Mrs. Filiberti disliked each other. A certain amount of liquor was consumed, and in the course of the flight the women came to blows. Reporters, tipped off, were waiting at London Airport, when the plane touched down. A clearly disturbed Garland announced that she was returning at once to the States, rather than remain in London where the Filibertis were supposed to be staying with her. She "just couldn't take it," she said. Filiberti explained that Garland had developed a virus. She denied this, and when told that the Filibertis had also decided to return immediately to America, she snapped: "Not on my plane." She flew on Pam Am Flight 101; the Filibertis were on Flight 103 two hours later.

There was further trouble on December 4, when she was fulfilling a two-week engagement at Caesar's Palace in Las Vegas. She received news of Bert Lahr's death and refused to go on. An official of the hotel tore into her room, to find her quivering under the covers. "Christ, what a mess!" he bellowed at Green, who was with her. "Look at her, she can't even stand up. What the hell is she on, anyway, the hard stuff? The needle? Tell her she can have as much as she wants later, after the show, but to get her ass down there now and sing. Those people are paying good money to see a show and we're gonna lose 'em fast if something doesn't happen." He had to cancel the show, telling his customers that Garland might never appear at this venue again. He invited them to see Eartha Kitt in the lounge as his guests.

Negotiations continued throughout the following day, mainly because the management did not now want Garland to go on. She won, and appeared. At the end of the show, she dedicated "Over the Rainbow" to "my lovely Cowardly Lion," and many in the audience realized why she had been absent the previous night.

It still seemed that Garland's fans would forgive her anything. The Lebanese-born comic Danny Thomas was in the audience a few days later, and joined Garland on stage. He asked for the lights to be lowered, except a spot for the two of them, and sang "I'll See You in My Dreams" to her. When he came to the penultimate line, "They will light my way tonight," everyone in the audience struck a match, as he had asked them to do. Then he told her: "What you saw, all that light, is only an infinitesimal fraction of the brightness your loveliness has brought the world."

On Christmas Day, she opened for a week at Madison Square Garden, in its new auditorium, the Felt Forum. This was a vast arena with a flexible seating pattern, but at $12 for the best seats, the box-office receipts could amount to $40,000 a night. Garland's opening made $27,000 which *Variety* described as "nice." After noting a touch of laryngitis and some underrehearsal, the paper's reviewer said: "Here is the Garland myth and magic at work. Personal theater for many, vicarious nostalgia for the rest, there is a deep, or masochistic, sense of participation in almost every number: Will Our Judy Make It Over the Rainbow?"

The answer was negative. Garland found performing conditions horrendous and refused to go on again. She argued with Filiberti until the early hours, as he pointed out how much money Group V had poured into the show. When he promised to see to it that the lighting and the acoustics were improved, she relented and played for three more performances, but the final three were canceled; she had succumbed to laryngitis and bronchitis. The management sued, and she countersued for $251,000, claiming that conditions were not right for her. Since Garland had very little money, the outcome of most of these lawsuits was largely academic. Many litigants saw little point in pursuing the matter, since there was virtually no chance of remuneration and few of them wanted to be seen "persecuting" someone many regarded as a national asset. In consequence, a large number of suits were still outstanding at Garland's death.

Some time earlier in 1967, Luft talked to Sanford Dody, a writer, about ghosting Garland's autobiography. Dody quickly learned that, because she was Judy Garland, he could not expect his usual percentage. When he met her, however, he was enchanted by her, though somewhat surprised to hear her declare, quite seriously: "Isn't it remarkable that with all the horror, with all that I've been through, I never drifted into booze or pills?" Unsurprisingly, nothing more was heard of this project.

At the beginning of 1968, Garland developed a new obsession: she wanted to go "legit" on Broadway. Angela Lansbury was leaving the hit musical *Mame* to head the West Coast production, and Garland set her heart on taking over. She dressed up as "Auntie Mame," the show's eccentric heroine, complete with long cigarette-holder, and did a run-through of the songs for the composer, Jerry Herman, and others involved in the production. They were unanimous: if the curtain could go up for only one performance, it would be worthwhile. Her lawyers and doctors assured them that she would have difficulty doing even that. She was shattered. There were some in the business—like Saul Chaplin—who believed that it was because of these constant rejections that she had grown careless of her talent.

She was also growing careless of her friends. In April, she accused Tom Green of stealing two diamond rings worth $110,000, which she said he had taken from her room at the St. Moritz Hotel while she was once again in the hospital, to pawn for $1,000. It was unwise of her to press charges against her "former manager," who gallantly chose not to reveal that Garland was in the habit of getting him to pawn her jewelry to pay her debts or, as in this case, hospital bills. She denied that she had been engaged to him, dismissing him as "a former employee," and hinting that he had taken the rings because she had stopped paying his rent. His attorneys claimed, with much more accuracy, that he had "physically, emotionally and financially sustained her" for the past three years. The charge was dropped, but Garland lost one of the few people at this period of her life who genuinely wanted to help her.

The following month, it was reported that she had been locked out of the St. Moritz because she owed the hotel $1,800. It was not clear what the management planned to do with the three eight-week-old kittens that she had left in her room, but it certainly was not going to release her costumes. The resultant publicity affected the box office of the Back Bay Theater in Boston, where she was to appear a few days later for two performances. But Al Terban, manager of the Back Bay, had been encouraged by the press reception in Boston, where she sang "Over the Rainbow" to the inmates of the Chelsea Naval Hospital. The first performance, on Friday, May 25, when she appeared with Lorna and Joey, went on so long that, worried about overtime costs Terban asked her to curtail her act. She indulged in a slanging match with him from the stage. "Don't do anything or you'll have a lawsuit," she warned him. As far as time went, however, she gave value for money, and this meant that word-of-mouth was favorable. Business at the box office was good for the last night, but 2,000 people had to be turned away when the show was canceled without warning. A decision not of Garland's making, but of Group V's, which infuriated her. There were angry scenes in the lobby, and the police had to be called. Noting that the theater was about to close, Terban said: "I think she may have closed her career." Luft, pressed for comment, said he didn't know why she hadn't appeared, and that she had been perfectly well the last time he had seen her. This did nothing to placate her disgruntled fans.

Luft was in fact about to move out of Garland's life for the last time. On May 17, he and Filiberti sold her Group V contract as security for a loan of $18,750 to two businessmen, Howard Harper, who, like Filiberti, had a police record, and Leon Greenspan. For the payment of one dollar, they got the exclusive use of her services for the next year, the screenplay of the still unmade *Born in Wedlock*, and "certain coal deposits located in the counties of Grundy, Sequatchie, Bledsoe, and Cumberland in the State of Tennessee."

In June, she appeared at the Garden State Arts Center in Holmdel, New Jersey. "As long as I know I have love I can make it," she assured a cheering audience. And she did. Offstage, she was embroiled in more trouble, however. The owners of the Empress Motel accused her of defrauding them of $525. She moved to another, the Berkeley-Carteret, where the management almost immediately accused Luft of passing $3,600 in bad checks. Luft's attorney claimed that this was due to a misunderstanding: he had thought the Arts Center was going to pick up the bills.

Garland had just learned that Luft and Filiberti had assigned her contract exclusively to Harper and Greenspan. Furious, she demanded her nightly fee of $1,500, less $300 for back taxes, to be paid before she would leave the hotel for the Arts Center. She got through her act, though at least once she appeared to be asleep on stage. On the fifth, and last, night she was also very unsteady and off-key, and many people in the audience left before the end of the show, which came when she fell down a flight of stairs which formed part of the set. She left the theater in an ambulance.

On September 7, she signed a new contract with CMA, on the understanding that she would drop her suit against the company. This, coated with her acceptance of $8,000 in back royalties, was the only reason CMA agreed to the contract, for there was little prospect of them getting her work. They announced that she would be "enjoying life for the first time": there would be "fewer concerts, but more movies and some television." Luft was furious with her, though not surprised. He decided to pursue the suit against CMA on his own.

Judy Garland was now without a permanent home. She hoped that she could stay in the apartment owned by CMA, but she was told that this was for staff. She moved from pillar to post—at one stage, she spent three months sleeping on the floor of some friends of Liza's— cadging, or borrowing from friends. An entourage, predominantly gay, surrounded her, encouraging, enchanted and exasperated in turn. They put her up or went to stay with friends so that she could use their apartments. One acquaintance who loaned her his house for a month thoughtfully emptied the medicine chest of all pills before leaving. All that remained was one bottle of tablets for dog mange. When he came to visit her, he found that she had scoffed the lot.

The terminal decline in her own personal and professional fortunes was highlighted by the contrast with Liza, whose career was flourishing. She was living in relative comfort with Peter Allen, and was trying to forget her quarrels with her mother. Garland had also quarreled with Lorna, who was now sixteen. Lorna was accustomed to her mother's moods, but she rebelled against sheer pettiness—childish squabbles about making the beds and so on—and fled with Joey to the Allens. Garland now found herself in the same situation as her own mother had been: rejected.

She realized that she was unlikely to find employment again unless she was cured of her assorted addictions, so returned to Boston, where she rented an apartment and became a day-patient at the Peter Bent Brigham Hospital. This was little more than a gesture, for she made no serious attempt to give up either pills or vodka.

A new man came into her life at this time. Johnny Meyer was a young musician who had just written a song, "I'd Like to Hate Myself in the Morning." Garland liked the song and had decided to add it to her repertoire. Meyer was in awe of Garland's talent, and believed that he could help her. In the introduction to the book he wrote about his time with Garland, he said: "I had been chosen by some divine prankster because of my unique abilities—you needed humor, stamina and finally compassion . . . and it helped if you were musical. But I was to learn, what started as a divine prank ended in all too realistic tragedy, because these were the only resources I had . . . and they were not sufficient." He was prepared to take care of her, but her constant testing of him wore him down. "You keep upping the ante, raising the stakes, but honey, I'm gonna run out of chips, and that'll be that," he complained. "I won't have anything left for you to play with." Garland replied: "Well, thanks a lot. Thanks. It's my fault again. Everything is always *my* fault. All my fucking life. Always *my* fault. Mmm, maybe you're right. Mmm, maybe this is why I seem to have *alienated* everyone. My friends. My children."

Meyer decided to get Garland back to work, and to that end saw Begelman, who told him that no record company in town would touch her. However, Meyer himself was negotiating with a small firm which wanted to take her on. She could do no concerts until her orchestrations had been returned to her. These had been a subject of contention for some time, and were now being held by a man named Marelli. She had contracted to do a concert for him and had then canceled. He was happy for her to do the concert now, but his terms were a payment of $25,000 from her plus 2 percent of her earnings for the next year, and he wanted $5,000 in advance before he would hand over the orchestrations. Judy Garland did not have $5,000.

On November 17, she sang four Harold Arlen songs at a tribute to him, Vincent Youmans and Noël Coward, presented by ASCAP at Lincoln Center. She was warmly received, and in such good voice that both she and Meyer gave renewed thought to her career. A few days later, she telephoned Harold Davison to see whether he could get her any bookings in London, while Meyer spoke to several people in television who might be prepared to put her into a chat show or just let her sing in a guest spot. One of those he spoke to was Bob Shanks, producer of the popular, late-night *Merv Griffin Show*. Shanks booked her immediately, and agreed to book Meyer and Garland into the St. Regis Hotel when they arrived from Boston. He discovered, however, that Garland had been blacklisted by all the leading hotels in New York. According to Griffin, she was recognized by the night-manager of the Americana, who told her to leave before she was thrown out. Meyer gallantly claimed that the hotels they tried, although full, were helpful: they telephoned other hotels, only to learn that there were so many conventions in town that none of them had vacancies. Garland was indeed recognized at the Americana, and Meyer was asked for a deposit in cash. The hotel would not take a check. It was not simply that Garland and her entourage had left bills unpaid at hotels all over town; they had also had expensive items charged to the hotels. She and Meyer spend the night with his parents.

Griffin intervened in the morning to get her a room at the Hilton. Both he and Meyer agreed that Garland's reputation was such that any expenses she incurred would have to be severely limited, particularly as far as the bar was concerned. She nevertheless spent $160 on liquor.

She did two shows for Griffin, on one of which she deputized for him. When asked which guests she wanted to interview on camera, she made a long list, including James Mason and Burt Lancaster and, "of course," Liza. Griffin was astounded by the virulence with which she was turned down by people she considered friends. As for Liza, she "absolutely had to be out of town." The only guests they were able to get were the Wicked Witch of the West, Margaret Hamilton, Van Johnson and the black comedienne Moms Mabley.

Thanks to Meyer's efforts, Garland also appeared on *The Tonight Show* and *The Dick Cavett Show*; she was pathetically wraithlike and seemed not completely in control of herself, but could still banter with her natural wit and even managed some songs new to her. Through all the ups and downs of her life, her fans had rooted for her, but there was a grim inevitability about these last television appearances. It was as if she *wanted* to fail them.

Griffin invited her to his Christmas cast party at Arthur's, the fashionable discotheque owned by Richard Burton's former wife, Sybil. While there, Garland got into conversation with the night-manager, Mickey Deans, whom she had known for some time. They had first met when, through a mutual friend, Charlie Cochran, Deans had supplied her with some pills. He was younger than she, and had spent much of his life in nightclubs either as pianist or waiter. He understood nightclubs, the sort of people who went to them, and what their demands might be. It was while making his routine late-night telephone call to the club that Earl Wilson got the news that she and Deans were engaged to be married. Wilson asked the astonished Griffin to confirm. Griffin said: "I don't know, Earl, I just showed up and that's what they're saying."

Meyer was ill at the time, which may be the reason for Garland's impulsiveness. She thought he had no right to be ill when she needed his encouragement for her television appearances. He was astonished by the news. Garland had introduced him to Deans a few days earlier. "He was not unattractive, I have to admit," said Meyer. "He had a sharp, straight nose, and longish, unkempt hair. The word that came to my mind was 'raffish.' " On that occasion, Deans sat around in his jockey shorts, while Meyer and Cochran played the piano until Garland sent the latter away because, Meyer claimed, "she accused him of coming on to me."

In spite of the engagement, Meyer followed Garland to London, as intended, but it was now Deans and not he who shared her suite at the Ritz. Harold Davison had spoken to the impresario Bernard Delfont, who had promptly booked Garland into The Talk of the Town, a nightclub just off Leicester Square. The engagement was for five weeks, and Garland would be paid £2,500 a week. Delfont was the managing director of the company which owned the place, and her contract was with him, but the show preceding her appearance was staged by Robert Nesbitt. The Talk of the Town had been launched as a club in the late 1950s in the old Hippodrome, with prices and a policy to bring in the sort of people who usually did not go to nightclubs. Its luster had dimmed somewhat in recent years, and the Garland booking was meant to re-attract attention to the place. She would appear nightly at eleven, after the floor show, "Fine Feathers."

She arrived in London on December 28, and was scheduled to open two days later. Harper and Greenspan had taken out an injunction to prevent this, however. Their solicitor had been furnished with her original contract with Group V, and documents relating to its reassignment to them. Delfont and Nesbitt challenged the injunction in the courts. Garland maintained that she hadn't read the whole contract, and although she agreed that the actual concert fees of $1,500 and a percentage of the box office to which it had bound her were small for a performer of her stature, she had understood that the rest of what she earned was to have gone into trust funds for herself, Luft and their two children. After listening to both sides, Mr. Justice Magarry said: "This transaction is one to which I would not enjoin a dog. Certainly I would not enjoin Miss Garland." He gave Harper and Greenspan leave to appeal, but by awarding costs against them he made it clear that he did not approve of the contract. At the same time he said that his consent to Garland working applied to this engagement only.

As it turned out, the court case was the least of the troubles Garland caused Delfont and Nesbitt. Due to rehearse with Burt Rhodes and his orchestra on the day of her opening, she complained that she was not up to it. Furthermore, she had not brought all ten of her orchestrations, so Rhodes spent the day frantically listening to the record album of her Carnegie Hall concert. This enabled him to arrange the missing two songs. Her performance that night brought her her usual fond reviews from the British critics, although some complained that her voice was harsh or ragged, and some that she occasionally seemed more intent on chatter than actually singing. Even so, they all agreed that her star shone as brightly as ever.

Her unpredictable behavior soon became public, however. "Here's a toast to all of you for coming here tonight," she said to the audience one night, "—and here's to *me* for getting here tonight." The audience knew what she meant and laughed happily. Ticket-holders were less amused when she stopped singing to merely talk, or when she forgot the words. One evening, she was determined to sing "Chicago" when it was requested, but Rhodes explained to her that he had no orchestration for it. He offered to play "San Francisco" instead, but she was determined to perform "Chicago," with the result that she sang one song and the orchestra played another. She stopped mid-sentence to call out: "Chicago? San Francisco? Which town are we supposed to be in? Where are we?" The audience tried to laugh.

The management explained that Miss Garland's erratic conduct was due to a bout of flu. Delfont was never sure whether she would show up or if, when she did, she would be able to perform. Her tardiness did not affect attendances, but it did have an adverse effect on those who were there. One evening when she was more than an hour late, just after she appeared at last, a man grabbed the microphone and demanded an apology, adding: "If you can't turn up on time why turn up at all?" What annoyed many was that she coasted on. A particularly rowdy party began to heckle her and then took to bombarding her with bread sticks, cigarette butts and crumpled packets.

Garland rushed off the stage and for the next two nights was replaced by the singer Lonnie Donegan, who had been hired during the course of the engagement to keep the audience entertained during the protracted wait for Garland after the floorshow ended. With just over a week to go until the end of the run, Delfont delivered an ultimatum (conveyed to the press as a request): Garland was not to appear again until her doctor had given her permission to do so. She was more or less on time when she returned, but The Talk of the Town was not sorry when the engagement ended. Deans had arranged to have it recorded: In view of the quality of Garland's voice it is astonishing that a company was found to issue the album.

The whole of Britain had a chance to see Garland at her worst, when, during the run, Lena Horne was unable to appear on *Sunday Night at the Palladium*. Despite her fear of live television, Garland agreed to replace Horne after being assured that some musicians from The Talk of Town would be accompanying her. She did not arrive at the theater until ten minutes before she was due to appear in mid-show, and then had an argument in the wings while the orchestra played her overture. Burt Rhodes, who was conducting, had not even wanted to play it once, believing an overture unsuitable in the middle of a variety show. Rushing on late, she forgot the words of her first song and covered this with asides, but managed to finish properly. She chattered inanely in an attempt to disguise her failure and her three successive numbers, mistaken lyrics and all, won a resounding ovation from the audience even if viewers at home were bemused.

Garland had hoped to marry Deans on arriving in London, but Mark Herron had not sent the divorce papers that would enable her to do so. If Deans could not be her husband, he could at least be her manager—and he was able to do this, since he had been summarily fired from Arthur's. Time was running out, however. As a performer, Judy Garland had even less to offer than Edith Piaf at the end of her life.

She took a small mews house in Cadogan Lane, near Sloane Square, eating little but drinking heavily and listening to her old records— something she had rarely done when she was in peak condition. She was now wholly dependent on drugs. After leaving Dr. Pobirs she had found another doctor who, to Marc Rabwin's consternation, was prepared to prescribe anything she wanted. Her 3:00 a.m. telephone calls had become more incoherent than ever. Mike Billington, who hardly knew Garland but who had been romantically involved with Liza in 1967, then in Britain making her first film, was among those who received them. Billington simply listened, bewildered.

On March 15, 1969, she and Deans were married at Chelsea Registry office. Clinging desperately to him, she looked as frail as a bird. The reception was held in Quaglino's, and the guest list included Pat Peatfield, a thirty-two-year-old spastic who believed that she had learned to walk by listening to Garland's recording of "You'll Never Walk Alone." Seeing Peatfield at The Talk of the Town, Deans had arranged for her to go backstage and meet her idol, and a friendship had resulted.

Tricia and the bride were the only happy people at the wedding, which by all accounts was a dismal occasion. Deans and his best man, Johnny Ray, tried to put a good face on things, but without much success. Ray was the only show-business figure present, though many had been invited, at the last minute, including several American ones who were currently working in Britain. Among these were Bette Davis, Veronica Lake, Albert Finney, Ginger Rogers, John Gielgud, James Mason, Peter Finch, Laurence Harvey and Eva Gabor. None of them turned up because, it being early on a Saturday afternoon, most of them had previous working or social commitments and were unable and, indeed, unwilling to make other arrangements for such a quixotic event. The journalists who did were unable to make the occasion look well attended. Her friends—those who were left—had no intention of being seen to give their blessing to a marriage even more ill-advised than those to Minnelli and Herron.

The British press did its best for Deans, describing him variously as a "New York businessman" and a "discotheque owner." As a wedding present, he was reported to have given Garland a chain of 500 cinemas across the States, to be known as "The Judy Garland Theaters," the first of which was to open in twelve weeks' time. It had occurred to the enterprising groom that if Fred Astaire could lend his name to a franchise of dance studios, Garland might be able to do something similar, but this, like so much else, came to nothing.

At least David Rose and Minnelli had been men of substance, and Sid Luft became one, by virtue of his own strength of character and the position he occupied in his wife's career. The two other men she chose to marry were young drifters. In both cases, she thought that by involving them in her career she might elevate them, and Deans may have thought, as had, at one time, Luft, Green and Meyer, that she could still *have* a career. There was a strange, false bravado in the way she spoke of Deans, as if defying her friends. Those looking for an explanation for her last two marriages might have noted the lyrics of "Make Someone Happy," one of the songs in her repertory with which she clearly identified very strongly: "Fame, if you win it / Comes and goes in a minute / Where's the real stuff in life to cling to? / Love is the answer /Someone to love is the answer."

However much Garland and Deans smiled in public, they fought in private, and this may have been the reason why she insisted upon dragging him on stage and mawkishly introducing him. Her instincts as a performer had once been tremendous, but they were now as uncertain as her voice. The real Judy Garland would never have embarrassed an audience in this way. She might have opened up her heart to journalists in discussing the many troubles in her life, but on stage these were worth only the briefest quip. She did not seem to know where her private life ended and the public one began. This frail, spidery figure was a mere shadow of her former self, and many people who knew her suspected that she was now on hard drugs, a circumstance which would explain her rapid and dramatic physical deterioration.

Deans arranged a European tour for Garland and Johnny Ray, whose career had also gone into decline since his record hits of the early 1950s, and who was similarly in need of money. Once, he could command a Palladium audience; now, he was more likely to be found singing in the more *déclassé* sort of gay bars. His voice, too, had nearly gone, but, between them, he and Garland were able to attract audiences in places in which they had never before appeared—specifically, Stockholm and Malmö—but no one who saw them had any illusions about the quality of what they saw. Unless a miracle happened—as it had before, and did for a moment in Copenhagen—she was unlikely to work again. In order to bring in some money, Deans set up a film with the producer Arne Stivell, who ran a Swedish company, Music Artists of Europe. The idea was that Stivell's cameramen would eavesdrop on Garland during the tour, and the result—Judy Garland in public and private—would be offered to television stations worldwide. The result was not exactly a rousing success.

Some cuts were made after *A Day in the Life of Judy Garland* became the subject of litigation, and in the version that exists today, the scenes in Garland's dressing-room are chiefly of her making up. Throughout, she appears to have no idea where she is, or whether she is in public or not. John Fricke explains that because the voiceover was dubbed from a radio interview that she seems not to know whether she is speaking to a person or a camera as she constantly claims that she doesn't need to work, because she has a husband to look after her: "I know I'm married to a man who can give me protection and help me the way I want." "For once in my life *I have someone who needs me,*" she sings, looking for Deans, who is out of camera range. She just about manages half a dozen familiar songs and one new one, "Am I Blue?," which were taped at an after-concert party, but she starts it only after tremendous difficulty with both the words and the tune. By the time she has finished it, she is hysterical with laughter at having got through it at all. The renditions of "San Francisco," "The Man That Got Away" and "Over the Rainbow" are patently dubbed from the Copenhagen performance, but with versions so poor that it is hard to imagine that those she actually sang in Malmö and Stockholm could have been worse. These two concerts took place at the end of March. Another, scheduled in Göteborg, was canceled. So was another, to have taken place at the Olympia in Paris in May.

A Day in the Life of Judy Garland came before the courts when it was found to contain footage of Garland naked and obviously drugged. The film had been sent to London for processing, and the company concerned informed Garland's lawyer of the contents. He recommended Deans to seek an injunction. The court found against Deans, but a Swedish copyright law prevented the film being shown in that country. Fortunately, no other countries were interested.

In a further court case, Garland's name was bandied about when the East End gangster, Ronald Kray, who was on trial for murder, named her as an earlier drinking companion. There were few old friends left now, and many of the new ones were far from desirable.

* * *

In the second week of June, Garland decided that she wanted Deans to view *Meet Me in St. Louis*, which he had never seen. She telephoned Brian Baxter at the National Film Theater, but when Baxter asked M-G-M for a copy it turned out that no one on the present staff of the company had ever heard of Judy Garland. Instead, he got hold of a print of *The Awful Truth*, a sublime 1930s comedy about divorce, starring Irene Dunne and Cary Grant.

On Saturday, June 21, she and Deans had planned to go to the theater, but instead they stayed in with Philip Roberge, a twenty-nine-year-old American whom the *Daily Sketch* described as a "close friend" of Deans and someone who assisted him in his "recording and show business deals." They watched a documentary about the royal family on television, then Garland and Deans began another of their interminable quarrels, during which Garland ran screaming into the street, waking the neighbors. Deans left the house. When he returned, he thought Garland was sleeping. A transatlantic telephone call woke him. It was one of Garland's coterie, John Carlyle, who had been described as a friend of long-standing by the New York press at the time of her last Palace concert, when she was in fact engaged to Tom Green. When Deans went to find her, he found the bathroom door locked. He climbed through the bathroom window. She was sitting on the lavatory. Rigor mortis had already set in.

She had often said that when her number was up, she was going to ask for another one; but it had come up once too often.

"The greatest shock about her death was that there was no shock," wrote Vincent Canby in the *New York Times*. "One simply wondered how she survived for so long."

Epilogue

AT THE AGE OF FORTY-SEVEN, and $4 million in debt, Judy Garland was dead. Later that day, a Harley Street surgeon, Philip Lebon, called a press conference. "She had been living on borrowed time," he told journalists. "When I examined her about eight years ago she had cirrhosis of the liver. I thought that if she lasted five more years she would have done very well. She lived three years longer than I thought she would. She was always a fighter. She was under great stress, but for her it was always: 'The show must go on.'"

"Accidental death by an incautious dose of barbiturates," said the coroner, Gavin Thompson, at the inquest. "This is a clear picture of someone who had been habituated to barbiturates in the form of Seconal for a very long period of time . . . And who, on the night of June 21–22—perhaps in a state of confusion from a previous dose, although this is pure speculation—took more barbiturate then her body could tolerate." He added: "I think one should bring it out publicly there was no question of alcoholism."

Against this speculation by the coroner must be placed some information that did not come out at the inquest. Sonia Roy, wife of the dance band leader Harry Roy, later claimed that she was visited by Garland on the evening of June 21. Garland told the Roys that she intended to kill herself. The Roys tried to talk her out of it, and believed that they had succeeded.

Deans decided to fly the body to the States for burial and, after consultation with her children, it was agreed that the public could pay a last homage. It was the first time since the death of Rudolph Valentino that this had happened, and it provided a last encore as more than 21,000 people filed past the open casket in Campbells' Funeral Home in New York. James Mason delivered the eulogy at the funeral, during which he quoted Liza Minnelli: "It was her love of life which carried her through everything. The middle of the road was never for her. It bored her. She wanted the pinnacle of excitement. If she was happy, she wasn't just happy. She was ecstatic. And when she was sad she was sadder than anyone."

Among those attending the funeral were Mickey Rooney, Lauren Bacall, Ray Bolger, Freddie Bartholomew, Kay Thompson and Alan King, who observed to Liza that it was the first time her mother had ever been on time for a performance. Frank Sinatra generously offered to pay all the funeral expenses for which Liza was grateful, but she preferred to take the responsibility herself. Of her five husbands, only Mickey Deans and Sid Luft were present, while David Rose, Mark Herron and Vincente Minnelli sent floral tributes. Liza had telephoned Marc Rabwin, requesting that he attend, "because you were there in the beginning and I want you to be there at the end." Marcella Rabwin remembers the occasion as extraordinarily moving as the small congregation of only about forty people (as opposed to the thousands gathered outside the chapel) sang "The Battle Hymn of the Republic" while Garland's coffin was carried aloft by six hefty pallbearers.

Deans decided that she should be buried in Ferncliff Mausoleum in Hartsdale, Westchester County, on the odd grounds that it was not far from Scarsdale, where Garland had once briefly lived. The niche he selected cost $37,500, a sum he did not possess. Furthermore, the building he chose was still under construction. Learning of this hiatus, Liza paid the required sum and took over the arrangements for the burial, which eventually took place on November 4, 1970, over a year after Garland's death.

The vault is of flecked beige, polished marble, and the inscription reads simply: JUDY GARLAND 1922 1969.

Bibliography

Astaire, Fred. *Steps in Time*. New York: Harper & Row, 1959.

Astor, Mary. *A Life on Film*. New York: Delacorte Press, 1967.

Bacall, Lauren. *By Myself*. London: Jonathan Cape, 1979.

Beaton, Cecil and Kenneth Tynan. *Persona Grata*. London: Wingate, 1953.

Bergreen, Laurence. *As Thousands Cheer: The Life of Irving Berlin*. New York: Viking, 1990.

Bogarde, Dirk. *Snakes and Ladders*. London: Chatto & Windus, 1978.

Caspar, Joseph Andrew. *Stanley Donen*. Methuen, N.J.: The Scarecrow Press, 1983.

Coleman, Emily R. *The Complete Judy Garland*. New York: HarperCollins, 1990.

Coward, Noël (Graham Payn and Sheridan Morley, eds.). *The Noël Coward Diaries*. London: Weidenfeld and Nicolson, 1982.

Dahl, David and Barry Kehoe. *Young Judy*. New York: Mason/Charter, 1975.

Deans, Mickey and Ann Pinchot. *Weep No More My Lady*. New York: Hawthorn, 1972.

DiOrio, Al. *Little Girl Lost: The Life and Hard Times of Judy Garland*. London: Coronet, 1973.

Duke, Patty and Kenneth Turan. *Call Me Anna*. New York: Bantam, 1987.

Edwards, Anne. *Judy Garland: A Mortgaged Life*. New York: Simon and Schuster, 1975.

Eels, George. *The Life That Late He Led: A Biography of Cole Porter*. New York: Putnam, 1967.

Finch, Christopher. *Rainbow*. New York: Grosset & Dunlap, 1975.

Fordin, Hugh. *The World of Entertainment: Hollywood's Greatest Musicals*. Garden City, N.Y.: Doubleday, 1975.

Frank, Gerold. *Judy*. New York: Harper & Row, 1975.

Freedland, Michael. *Liza with a 'Z'*. London: W.H. Allen, 1988.

Fricke, John. *Judy Garland: World's Greatest Entertainer: A Pictorial History of Her Career*. New York: Henry Holt & Co., 1992.

Fricke, John, Jay Scarfone, and William Stillman. *The Wizard of Oz: The Official 50th Anniversary Pictorial History*. New York: Warner Books, 1989.

Gingold, Hermione. *Growing Old Disgracefully*. New York: St. Martin's Press, 1988.

Goldman, William. *The Season*. New York: Harcourt Brace and World, 1969.

Granger, Stewart. *Sparks Fly Upwards*. London: Granada, 1981.

Griffin, Merv, with Peter Barsocchini. *Merv*. New York: Simon and Schuster, 1980.

Harmetz, Aljean. *The Making of the Wizard of Oz*. New York: Knopf, 1977.

Harris, Radie. *Radie's World*. New York: Putnam, 1975.

Harvey, Stephen. *Directed by Vincente Minnelli*. New York: Museum of Modern Art/Harper & Row, 1989.

Haver, Ronald. *A Star Is Born: The Making of the 1954 Movie and Its 1983 Reconstruction*. New York: Knopf, 1988.

Hepburn, Katharine. *Me!* New York: Knopf, 1991.

Hirschhorn, Clive. *Gene Kelly*. London: W.H. Allen, revised edition 1984.

Hotchner, A.E. *Doris Day, Her Own Story*. New York: William Morrow, 1975.

Jablonski, Edward. *Happy with the Blues: A Life of Harold Arlen*. Garden City, N.Y.: Doubleday, 1961.

Johnson, Dorris and Ellen Leventhal (eds.). *The Letters of Nunnally Johnson*. New York: Knopf, 1981.

Lahr, John. *Notes on a Cowardly Lion*. New York: Knopf, 1969.

Loy, Myrna, with James Kotsilibas-Davis. *Being and Becoming*. New York: Knopf, 1987.

McClintlock, David. *Indecent Exposure*. New York: William Morrow, 1982.

Marion, Frances. *Off With Their Heads*. New York: Macmillan, 1972.

Mason, James. *Before I Forget*. London: Hamish Hamilton, 1981.

Meyer, John. *Heartbreaker*. Garden City, N.Y.: Doubleday, 1983.

Minnelli, Vincente, with Hector Arce. *I Remember It Well*. Garden City, N.Y.: Doubleday, 1974.

Morella, Joe and Edward Epstein. *Judy: The Films and Career of Judy Garland*. New York: The Citadel Press, 1969.

Niven, David. *The Moon's a Balloon*. London: Hamish Hamilton, 1971.

Rooney, Mickey. *Life is Too Short*. New York: Villard, 1991.

Sanders, Coyne Steven. *Rainbow's End: The Judy Garland Show*. New York: William Morrow, 1990.

Schatz, Thomas H. *The Genius of the System: Hollywood Filmmaking in the Studio Era*. New York: Simon and Schuster, 1988.

Smith, Lorna. *Judy With Love*. London: Robert Hale, 1975.

Spada, James. *Judy and Liza*. New York: Doubleday, 1983.

St. Johns, Adela Rogers. *Some are Born Great*. New York: Doubleday, 1974.

Tormé, Mel. *The Other Side of the Rainbow*. New York: William Morrow, 1970.

Warner, Jack L., with Dean Jennings. *My First Hundred Years in Hollywood*. New York: Random House, 1964.

Watson, Thomas J. and Bill Chapman. *Judy, Portrait of an American Legend*. New York: McGraw Hill, 1986.

Wiley, Mason and Damien Bona. *Inside Oscar: The Unofficial History of the Academy Awards*. New York: Ballantine, 1986.

Wynn, Ned. *We Will Always Live in Beverly Hills: Growing Up Crazy in Hollywood*. New York: William Morrow, 1990.

Zierold, Norman J. *The Child Stars*. New York: Coward McCann, 1965.

Index

Garland, Judy (*cont.*)
168–70, 200, 234, 317–18, 324, 351–53,
392, 408, 423, 448, 453, 464, 488–89,
492
romantic and sexual nature of, 138–40,
161–62, 169, 232, 317–18, 351–53, 453
schooling and professional training of, 23,
27, 29–30, 31, 32, 36–37, 54–55, 56,
57, 68, 74, 106
screen debut of, 30
self-assessment of, 61, 74, 87, 106, 120,
137, 180, 338, 358, 360, 393, 408,
431–32, 459, 480
self-deprecating mockery of, 65, 70, 73,
159, 162–63, 207, 472
self-hatred of, 247, 299, 389
self-pity and guilt of, 28, 200, 208, 221,
227, 240–41, 245, 257, 287, 301–3,
376, 407, 499
sleep problems of, 158, 159, 179, 209–10,
225, 237, 243, 247, 371, 449, 483, 490
social life of, 131, 136–38, 187–89, 193,
205, 213–14, 222, 301, 309, 348–49,
479, 486–87
solo debut of, 14–15
stage debut of, 1, 11, 12–13, 302, 362
stage fright of, 339, 367, 396, 397, 408,
416, 430
stamina of, 18, 279, 508
stardom as goal of, 29, 295
strong-willed determination of, 13, 14, 19
studio workload of, 74, 87–89, 97–101,
142, 158, 170
suicide threats and attempts of, 205, 236,
239, 256–59, 280, 300, 319, 364–65,
378–79, 411, 438, 468, 475, 480, 509
television appearances of, 268, 341–47,
418–19, 432–34, 440–71, 486, 487,
500–1, 503
temperamental and unreliable reputation
of, 273, 278, 317, 318, 320, 359, 444,
455, 457, 474, 486, 500
temper tantrums of, 26, 158, 201, 202–3,
205, 227, 228, 240–41, 303, 410
tomboy quality of, 28, 58–59, 396
Top Ten rating of, 120, 121
transition to adult roles by, 113, 115–17,
128–31, 134, 154
troops entertained by, 126, 131, 149, 397
unprofessional behavior of, 141–42, 144,
146, 149, 156–58, 159, 164–67, 176–80,
199–205, 227, 247–49, 251–53, 314,
317–19, 425, 450, 473–74, 490–91
vaudeville experience of, 12–15, 18–20,
27–28, 30–40, 63, 77, 129, 147, 204,
268, 288–96
vocal attributes of, 34, 36, 37, 39–40, 42,
44, 46, 55, 59, 60, 71, 84, 93, 171, 243,
281

vocal deterioration of, 290, 342, 346–47,
354, 357, 364, 374, 431, 479, 482, 483,
484, 486, 494, 496, 502
weeping of, 132, 165, 179, 205, 208, 209,
240, 249–50, 311, 320, 372, 380, 389,
440, 449
weight problems of, 45, 46, 57, 61, 64,
74–75, 77–78, 145, 155, 199, 201, 207,
222, 237, 246, 250, 261, 267, 284, 338,
358, 367–69, 375, 383, 389, 392, 415,
455
as wife and hostess, 127, 187–89, 192–94
wit and humor of, 26, 39, 49, 65, 70, 73,
88, 91, 102, 122, 140, 147, 154, 159,
204, 207, 336, 350, 383, 417, 468, 490
Garland, Robert, 39
Garland at the Grove, 385
Garland Sisters, 39, 41, 45, 47–51
Garrett, Betty, 224, 241, 369
Garson, Greer, 149, 163–64, 172, 181, 198,
241, 330, 392
Gate of Hell, 336
Gaumont-British, 58
Gay Divorcee, The, 59
Gaynor, Janet, 29, 133, 305, 329, 331
Gay Purr-ee, 417, 431, 432, 437
Geisler, Jerry, 376
Gelbart, Larry, 433–34
General Electric Theater, 346
General Teleradio Inc., 355
Gennaro, Peter, 345, 346
Gentlemen's Agreement, 308
George VI, King of England, 99n Gershe,
Leonard, 81, 321–22, 343, 415–16
Gershwin, George, 52, 84, 114, 133, 148,
184, 190, 396
Gershwin, Ira, 52, 114, 133, 148, 152, 184,
187, 190, 194, 202, 223, 308, 312–13,
321, 333
Gershwin, Lee, 152, 187–88, 194–95,
202–3, 228, 239, 247, 300
"Get Happy," 221, 250, 262, 267, 289, 342,
368, 456
Gibbons, Cedric, 82
Gigi, 362
Gilchrist, Connie, 134
Gilliatt, Penelope, 426–27, 435
Gilmore, Laura, 25, 102
Gilmore, Voyle, 381–82
Gilmore, Will, 25, 48, 102, 105, 124, 127,
132, 206
Gilmore Circus, 37
Gingold, Hermione, 417, 483–84
Girl Crazy (movie), 133, 135, 145–47, 148
Girl Crazy (Gershwin), 52, 133
Gish, Lillian, 20
Glassman, Barnett, 494
Glass Menagerie, The (Williams), 472
Gleason, Jackie, 263

Milne, Jack (uncle), 9, 21
Milne, John (grandfather), 5, 9, 21
Minnelli, Liza (daughter), xii-xiii, 472, 491,
    504
  birth of, 194, 299
  childhood and adolescence of, 199, 203,
    205, 206, 208, 215, 222, 223, 227, 228,
    235, 242, 243, 245, 270, 271, 281-83,
    298-99, 238, 335, 374-75, 377-79, 380,
    384, 386, 422, 438, 481-82
  education of, 392, 438
  on Garland, 377-78, 380, 481-82, 509
  Garland's performances with, 357,
    374-75, 377, 384, 389, 399, 450,
    481-82
  Garland's relationship with, 162, 194-95,
    203, 208, 215, 222, 243, 271, 281, 283,
    296, 357, 374-75, 377-79, 380, 393,
    427, 438-39, 441, 461, 465, 481-82,
    498-99, 500
  Peter Allen and, 378, 482, 489, 499
  show business career of, xiii, 438-41, 461,
    465, 481-82, 483, 486, 499
  television debut of, 389
  Vincente Minnelli and, xiii, 203, 271,
    281, 438-39
Minnelli, Vincente (second husband), 115,
    152-64, 264, 509
  character and personality of, 192-93, 227,
    271
  on Garland, 164, 180, 189, 192, 193, 218,
    270
  Garland on, 173, 271
  Garland's relationship with, 159-64,
    166-71, 173, 179-80, 186-94,
    197-208, 213, 215, 218-19, 222-23,
    227-28, 245, 255-60, 270-71, 296, 489,
    504, 505
  homosexuality of, xi, 160, 169, 170, 186,
    271
  Liza Minnelli and, xiii, 203, 271, 281,
    438-39
  theatrical background and career of,
    152-53, 168-69, 175, 182, 228, 232-33,
    252, 279, 311, 313, 321, 362, 398, 413
Minnelli Brothers Tent Theater, 152
"Minnie from Trinidad," 119-20
"Minstrel Girl," 277, 289, 321, 368
Miranda, Carmen, 273
Mirisch brothers, 412
Miss Cinderella, 268
Miss Show Business, 343, 347, 385
"Mister Monotony," 221, 250
Mitchell, Julian, 80
Mitchell, Sidney, 60
Mitchell, Thomas, 267
Modern Movies, 67-68
Modern Screen, 23
Mold, John, 476

Mollie, Bless You!, 69
Molly and Me, 69n
Molnar, Ferenc, 196
Monks, John, Jr., 114
Monogram Pictures, 265
Monroe, Marilyn, 248, 257-58, 412, 429,
    434
Montgomery, David, 80
Montgomery, Robert, 58
Monthly Film Bulletin, 435
Moore, Colleen, 29
Moore, Victor, 83
Mooren, Inga, 9
Mordden, Ethan, 54
More, Kenneth, 331, 477
Moreno, Rita, 418
Morgan, Frank, 83, 94, 119, 241
Morgan, Helen, 38, 42, 47, 59, 65, 190,
    286, 360
Morning Glory, 133
Morrow, Bill, 299
Morse, William, 484
motion picture industry, 16-18, 49-50,
    136-40
  advent of Talkies in, 30, 31, 314
  blacklisting in, 213-15
  child actors in, 18, 28, 31-32, 36-37,
    44-45, 46, 57-58, 89, 113
  early history of, 4-5
  Jewish immigrants attracted to, 43, 72, 85
Motion Picture Yearbook, 181
Motor Mad, 12
Movie Star Frolics, 37
Mrs. Lawlor's School for Professional
    Children, 36-37, 47, 272
Mr. Smith Goes to Washington, 119
Muir, Florabel, 256-57
Mulvey, Kay, 389
Murfreesboro, Tenn., xi, 1-3, 68
Murphy, George, 116-17, 119, 123,
    129-31, 492
Music Artists of Europe, 506
Music Corporation of America (MCA), 195,
    340, 343, 353-55, 358, 362, 363,
    365-66, 379, 381, 400, 403
Music Goes 'Round, The, 50
My Cousin Rachel, 310
Myers, Carmel, 20, 52-53, 65
My First Hundred Years in Hollywood
    (Warner), 338
"My Intuition," 181
"My Man," 288
My Man Godfrey, 70
"My Melancholy Baby," 321, 345
"My One and Only Highland Fling,"
    223
"My Ship," 308n
My Sister Eileen, 150
My Sister Eileen (McKenny), 150